REGULATION AND DEREGULATION

CASES AND MATERIALS

Second Edition

By

Jeffrey L. Harrison
Stephen C. O'Connell Professor of Law
The University of Florida College of Law

Thomas D. Morgan
Oppenheim Professor of Antitrust and Trade Regulation Law
The George Washington University Law School

Paul R. Verkuil
Professor of Law
Cardozo Law School
Yeshiva University

AMERICAN CASEBOOK SERIES®

Mat # 40242947

American Casebook Series and West Group are trademarks
registered in the U.S. Patent and Trademark Office.

COPYRIGHT © 1997 WEST PUBLISHING CO.

© 2004 West, a Thomson business
     610 Opperman Drive
     P.O. Box 64526
     St. Paul, MN 55164–0526
     1–800–328–9352

ISBN 0–314–15263–6

*TEXT IS PRINTED ON 10% POST
CONSUMER RECYCLED PAPER*

To Sarah

Jeffrey L. Harrison

To Kathryn

Thomas D. Morgan

To my brave new lawyers, Gibson and Alex

Paul R. Verkuil

*

Preface to the Second Edition

The regulatory landscape keeps changing. When we published the first edition of this book in 1997, we noted that what is described as "deregulation" is often simply regulation in another form.

That continues to be true. Deregulation of electricity and other forms of energy, for example, has led to the development of yet new rules. Likewise, even the deregulatory promises of the Telecommunications Act of 1996 have kept broadcasting and telephone service under substantial FCC control. And we cannot now fully appreciate how far corporate scandals in fields like energy and the investment banking/mutual fund industries might inspire yet new regulatory programs.

At the same time, innovative and market-based regulatory approaches have enjoyed a robust decade. We have expanded the chapter on cost-benefit analysis, self-regulation and privatization to reflect such developments. And we have given continued attention to the constitutional issues underpinning regulation, such as the Takings Clause, the First Amendment—and for the first time, the Twenty–First Amendment.

Still, in this field of law as in others, the more things change, the more they stay the same. The ability still to draw essential lessons from cases like *Charles River Bridge and Munn v. Illinois* which long ago defined the regulatory domain, remain for us a fascinating, challenging and ever rewarding reason to study this field.

The authors thank Rosario Chiarenza, Whitney W. Glaccum, and Sarah Harrison for their careful work in the editing process.

JEFFERY L. HARRISON
THOMAS D. MORGAN
PAUL R. VERKUIL

March 2004

*

Summary of Contents

Table of Contents

Table of Cases

The principal cases are in bold type. Cases cited or discussed in the text are roman type. References are to pages. Cases cited in principal cases and within other quoted materials are not included.

REGULATION AND DEREGULATION

CASES AND MATERIALS

Second Edition

*

Chapter 1

THE CONTEXT OF MODERN REGULATION

A. AN HISTORICAL REGULATORY FABLE

Imagine that you are a Massachusetts legislator in the year 1758. The State House has received a letter from several prominent Boston business executives complaining that the existing ferry across the Charles River is inconvenient and inadequate. They suggest that the public would benefit from the building of a bridge across the river. As a graduate of Harvard College, which owns the present ferry, you are concerned that a bridge would eliminate an important source of the College's income.[1]

A.   Putting aside your Harvard loyalties, would you as a legislator see any need for governmental action to encourage or discourage building of the bridge?

1.   Would you try to ascertain whether the existing service is "adequate"? How would you objectify the term "adequate" in this context?

2.   Would you try to determine whether the "benefits" from the new bridge would exceed its "costs"? What costs would you include in your calculation? Would Harvard College's lost revenue appropriately be considered such a cost?

3.   Would you simply let the market decide whether or not a bridge is necessary? Could you be confident that, if the builder of a bridge could make a profit, such a bridge would be built? Does that mean the government should have no role in determining whether and what kind of bridge should be built?

---

1.   This illustration is hypothetical but based on the facts set forth in Charles River Bridge v. Warren Bridge, 36 U.S. (11 Pet.) 420, 9 L.Ed. 773 (1837). Use of these facts to illustrate and challenge traditional justifications for regulation was made in two articles by Donald I. Baker, The Role of Competition in Regulated Industries, 11 Boston College Industrial & Commercial L. Rev. 571, 588–91 (1970), and Competition and Regulation: Charles River Bridge Recrossed, 60 Cornell L. Rev. 159, 165–77 (1975). We revisit the Bridge case in connection with the *Winstar* litigation in Ch. 4.

4. Suppose no firm would invest the capital necessary to build the first bridge without a 40–year guarantee that no competing bridge would be allowed within 20 miles? Would you vote to make that commitment?

5. If a second group of bridge builders later wanted to build a competing bridge, would you feel obliged to deny them that right in order to protect the builders of the first bridge?

B. If you thought government involvement in the bridge building decision was appropriate, what form would you have it take?

1. Would you have the state build the bridge and operate it as a state facility?

2. Would you provide grants or loans to the proposed builders?

3. Would you seek out other potential bridge builders and hold a competition to determine which promised to act most in the "public interest, convenience and necessity"?

4. Would you set standards of construction so as to increase safety, reduce impediments to navigation, and avoid unnecessary "visual pollution"?

5. Would you set limits on the tolls the builders or operators could charge? If so, when might you lift such limitations?

6. Suppose another bridge is built nearby by the Federal government—and out of your jurisdiction—as part of a pioneer interstate highway system. Would there be any reason to continue rate regulation?

C. What political considerations, if any, would influence your decision?

1. Would you be influenced by the potential gratitude that persons with a frequent need to cross the river would feel to those who voted to build the bridge? How about the potential for campaign contributions from barge owners eager not to lose a large portion of their business to wagons thus made more convenient?

2. Should compensation be provided to Harvard College for the loss of ferry business due to the new bridge? Would it be relevant that the Harvard ferry had been in existence since 1644 and that its revenues funded student scholarships? Would giving such compensation make you popular with all affected parties?

These questions, along with many others, almost certainly would occur to you or be brought to your attention by various persons and groups. This book is designed to give you some tools with which to approach these and similar issues. The answers will not be easy even after this course, but the questions should be less forbidding.

D. At the end of the day, the bridge was authorized in 1785 and Harvard did not get compensated initially. In 1792, however, the Massachusetts legislature extended Charles River Bridge's monopoly to 70 years on the condition that it pay Harvard £200 per year for 40 years. See Charles River Bridge v. Warren Bridge, 36 U.S. 420, 421–23 (1837).

In 1828 when the Charles River Bridge sought to enforce its franchise against a legislatively approved (and competing) Charles River bridge, the United States Supreme Court refused to find a violation by the State of the (impairment of) contracts clause, over a spirited dissent by Justice Story. To one historian the case presaged the modern era of transportation:

> The *Charles River Bridge* case had much more at stake than a relatively petty local dispute over a new, free bridge. The Warren Bridge was a symbol for the rapid technological developments competing for public acceptance against existing, privileged property forms. The destruction of vested interest in favor of beneficial change reflected a creative process vital to ongoing development and progress. Within its contemporary setting, and for its historical significance, the case assumes greater meaning if railroads and the development of a new and improved transportation infrastructure— or even the benefits the community could derive from all inventions and scientific knowledge—are substituted for bridges. The competing principles of the practices in the bridge case fundamentally involved the state's role and power of encouraging or implementing innovations for the advantage of the community . . .[2]

B. EVOLUTION OF THE REGULATION— DEREGULATION DEBATE

Obviously, the term "regulation" encompasses many situations. Far from describing a simple, straightforward phenomenon, "regulation" describes a complex set of activities that affect virtually every business and individual in some way. We mean for the term to be broadly descriptive, including within it laws and regulations of federal, state and local authorities.[3]

1. Regulation is both direct and indirect. The growth of the money supply affects each of us although we hardly realize the decisions being made. Import tariffs and other restrictions on international trade seek to protect domestic workers' jobs but tend to raise prices paid by domestic consumers for all goods wherever produced. Thus, while licensing authorities are said to have an almost life or death power over persons or entities subject to their jurisdiction, more subtle forms of regulation may be almost as significant.

---

2. Stanley I. Kutler, Privilege and Creative Destruction: The Charles River Bridge Case 11–13 (1971).

3. It is tempting to define "regulation" precisely, but we have kept the concept broad. Some regulation creates or restrains property rights—e.g., grants of broadcast licenses or patent rights—and thus is a form of "law" in its most general sense. Further, Chief Justice Marshall has observed "the word 'to regulate' implies full power over the thing to be regulated." Gib-

bons v. Ogden, 22 U.S. (9 Wheat.) 1, 205, 6 L.Ed. 23 (1824). The term "regulation" is also used in these materials to describe any other legal interference with parties' rights to act based on their independent decisions or private contracts. Considerations of politics, customs and mores can constrain or "regulate" behavior as well, but as we will use the term, "regulation" requires that there be legal force behind a given restraint on conduct.

2. Regulation is both pervasive and partial. Public utilities are regulated in almost all of their operations. Other firms are subject to product safety requirements and advertising restrictions, but few other limitations. To say that a business is "regulated," then, does not itself reveal how extensive the regulation is.

3. Regulation is imposed by both state and federal authorities. Largely for historic reasons, some activities have been reserved to the states for regulation, others to the federal government, and others are subject to joint regulation. Regulation, then, is not something imposed by a central planning agency for the whole country. Its strength—and its weakness—in part arise from the fragmented and divided responsibility for its imposition.

4. Regulation is not static or permanent. When is it time to deregulate previously regulated activities? Might some formerly unregulated phenomena now need regulation? When should activities go unregulated, i.e., just be left alone?

As you will see, these questions can rarely be answered in the abstract. Technological change—as well as increased public whim and wisdom—means the cycle of regulation and deregulation is destined to be a dynamic process.[4]

1. SOME HISTORICAL PERSPECTIVE ON MODERN REGULATION

Regulation is not a new phenomenon; neither is debate over the wisdom of its imposition. It is impossible to say when modern regulation began, but the following case provides both a sense of regulatory history and the legal context in which it can be analyzed.

MUNN v. ILLINOIS
Supreme Court of the United States, 1877.
94 U.S. (4 Otto) 113, 24 L.Ed. 77.

MR. CHIEF JUSTICE WAITE delivered the opinion of the court.

The question to be determined in this case is whether the general assembly of Illinois can, under the limitations upon the legislative power of the States imposed by the Constitution of the United States, fix by law the maximum of charges for the storage of grain in warehouses at Chicago and other places in the State having not less than one hundred thousand inhabitants, "in which grain is stored in bulk, and in which the grain of different owners is mixed together, or in which grain is stored in such a manner that the identity of different lots or parcels cannot be accurately preserved."

---

4. For a highly accessible introduction to some of the personalities and politics of this process, see the biographies of Charles Francis Adams, Louis Brandeis, James Landis, and Alfred Kahn in Thomas K. McCraw, Prophets of Regulation (1984). For an introduction to the regulation-deregulation debate in a number of other industrialized countries, see Kenneth Button & Dennis Swann, eds., The Age of Regulatory Reform (1989).

It is claimed that such a law is repugnant—

1.   To that part of sect. 8, art. 1, of the Constitution of the United States which confers upon Congress the power "to regulate commerce with foreign nations and among the several States;"

* * *

3.   To that part of amendment 14 which ordains that no State shall "deprive any person of life, liberty, or property, without due process of law, nor deny to any person within its jurisdiction the equal protection of the laws."

We will consider the last of these objections first.

Every statute is presumed to be constitutional. The courts ought not to declare one to be unconstitutional, unless it is clearly so. If there is doubt, the expressed will of the legislature should be sustained.

The Constitution contains no definition of the word "deprive," as used in the Fourteenth Amendment. To determine its signification, therefore, it is necessary to ascertain the effect which usage has given it, when employed in the same or a like connection.

While this provision of the amendment is new in the Constitution of the United States, as a limitation upon the powers of the States, it is old as a principle of civilized government. It is found in Magna Charta, and, in substance if not in form, in nearly or quite all the constitutions that have been from time to time adopted by the several States of the Union. By the Fifth Amendment, it was introduced into the Constitution of the United States as a limitation upon the powers of the national government, and by the Fourteenth, as a guaranty against any encroachment upon an acknowledged right of citizenship by the legislatures of the States.

When the people of the United Colonies separated from Great Britain, they changed the form, but not the substance, of their government. They retained for the purposes of government all the powers of the British Parliament, and through their State constitutions, or other forms of social compact, undertook to give practical effect to such as they deemed necessary for the common good and the security of life and property. All the powers which they retained they committed to their respective States, unless in express terms or by implication reserved to themselves. Subsequently, when it was found necessary to establish a national government for national purposes, a part of the powers of the States and of the people of the States was granted to the United States and the people of the United States. This grant operated as a further limitation upon the powers of the States, so that now the governments of the States possess all the powers of the Parliament of England, except such as have been delegated to the United States or reserved by the people. The reservations by the people are shown in the prohibitions of the constitutions.

When one becomes a member of society, he necessarily parts with some rights or privileges which, as an individual not affected by his relations to others, he might retain. "A body politic," as aptly defined in the preamble of the Constitution of Massachusetts, "is a social compact by which the whole people covenants with each citizen, and each citizen with the whole people, that all shall be governed by certain laws for the common good." This does not confer power upon the whole people to control rights which are purely and exclusively private, but it does authorize the establishment of laws requiring each citizen to so conduct himself, and so use his own property, as not unnecessarily to injure another. This is the very essence of government, and has found expression in the maxim *sic utere tuo ut alienum non laedas.* From this source come the police powers, which, as was said by Mr. Chief Justice Taney in the *License Cases,* 5 How. 583, "are nothing more or less than the powers of government inherent in every sovereignty, * * * that is to say, * * * the power to govern men and things." Under these powers the government regulates the conduct of its citizens one towards another, and the manner in which each shall use his own property, when such regulation becomes necessary for the public good. In their exercise it has been customary in England from time immemorial, and in this country from its first colonization, to regulate ferries, common carriers, hackmen, bakers, millers, wharfingers, innkeepers, & c., and in so doing to fix a maximum of charge to be made for services rendered, accommodations furnished, and articles sold. To this day, statutes are to be found in many of the States upon some or all these subjects; and we think it has never yet been successfully contended that such legislation came within any of the constitutional prohibitions against interference with private property. With the Fifth Amendment in force, Congress, in 1820, conferred power upon the city of Washington "to regulate * * * the rates of wharfage at private wharves, * * * the sweeping of chimneys, and to fix the rates of fees therefor, * * * and the weight and quality of bread," and, in 1848, "to make all necessary regulations respecting hackney carriages and the rates of fare of the same, and the rates of hauling by cartmen, wagoners, carmen, and draymen, and the rates of commission of auctioneers."

From this it is apparent that, down to the time of the adoption of the Fourteenth Amendment, it was not supposed that statutes regulating the use, or even the price of the use, of private property necessarily deprived an owner of his property without due process of law. Under some circumstances they may, but not under all. The amendment does not change the law in this particular: it simply prevents the States from doing that which will operate as such a deprivation.

This brings us to inquire as to the principles upon which this power of regulation rests, in order that we may determine what is within and what without its operative effect. Looking, then, to the common law, from whence came the right which the Constitution protects, we find that when private property is "affected with a public interest, it ceases to be *juris privati* only." This was said by Lord Chief Justice Hale more than two hundred years ago, in his treatise *De Portibus Maris,* and has been accepted without objection as an essential element in the law of property ever since. Property does become clothed with a public interest when used in a manner to make it of public consequence, and affect the community at large. When, therefore, one devotes his property to a use in which the public has an interest, he, in effect, grants to the public an interest in that use, and must submit to be controlled by the public for the common good, to the extent of the interest he has thus created. He may withdraw his grant by discontinuing the use; but, so long as he maintains the use, he must submit to the control.

* * *

From the same source comes the power to regulate the charges of common carriers, which was done in England as long ago as the third year of the reign of William and Mary, and continued until within a comparatively recent period. * * *

Common carriers exercise a sort of public office, and have duties to perform in which the public is interested. Their business is, therefore, "affected with a public interest," within the meaning of the doctrine which Lord Hale has so forcibly stated.

But we need not go further. Enough has already been said to show that, when private property is devoted to a public use, it is subject to public regulation. It remains only to ascertain whether the warehouses of these plaintiffs in error, and the business which is carried on there, come within the operation of this principle.

For this purpose we accept as true the statements of fact contained in the elaborate brief of one of the counsel of the plaintiffs in error. From these it appears that "the great producing region of the West and North-west sends its grain by water and rail to Chicago, where the greater part of it is shipped by vessel for transportation to the seaboard by the Great Lakes, and some of it is forwarded by railway to the Eastern ports. * * * The quantity [of grain] received in Chicago has made it the greatest grain market in the world. This business has created a demand for means by which the immense quantity of grain can be handled or stored, and these have been found in grain warehouses, which are commonly called elevators, because the grain is elevated from the boat or car, by machinery operated by steam, into the bins prepared for its reception, and elevated from the bins, by a like process, into the vessel or car which is to carry it on. * * * In this way the largest traffic between the citizens of the country north and west of Chicago and the citizens of the country lying on the Atlantic coast north of Washington is in grain which passes through the elevators of Chicago. In this way the trade in grain is carried on by the inhabitants of seven or eight of the great States of the West with four or five of the States lying on the seashore, and forms the largest part of inter-state commerce in these States. The grain warehouses or elevators in Chicago are immense structures, holding from 300,000 to 1,000,000 bushels at one time, according to size. They are divided into bins of large capacity and great strength. * * * They are located with the river harbor on one side and the railway tracks on the other; and the grain is run through them from car to vessel, or boat to car, as may be demanded in the course of business. It has been found impossible to preserve each owner's grain separate, and this has given rise to a system of inspection and grading, by which the grain of different owners is mixed, and receipts issued for the number of bushels which are negotiable, and redeemable in like kind, upon demand. This mode of conducting the business was inaugurated more than twenty years ago, and has grown to immense proportions. The railways have found it impracticable to own such elevators, and public policy forbids the transaction of such business by the carrier; the ownership has, therefore, been by private individuals, who have embarked their capital and devoted their industry to such business as a private pursuit."

In this connection it must also be borne in mind that, although in 1874 there were in Chicago fourteen warehouses adapted to this particular business, and owned by about thirty persons, nine business firms controlled them, and that the prices charged and received for storage were such "as have been from year to year agreed upon and established by the different elevators or warehouses in the city of Chicago, and which rates have been annually published in one or more newspapers printed in said city, in the month of January in each year, as the established rates for the year then next ensuing such publication." Thus it is apparent that all the elevating facilities through which these vast productions "of seven or eight great States of the West" must pass on the way "to four or five of the States on the seashore" may be a "virtual" monopoly.

Under such circumstances it is difficult to see why, if the common carrier, or the miller, or the ferryman, or the innkeeper, or the wharfinger, or the baker, or the cartman, or the hackney-coachman, pursues a public employment and exercises "a sort of public office," these plaintiffs in error do not. They stand, to use again the language of their counsel, in the very "gateway of commerce," and take toll from all who pass. Their business most certainly "tends to a common charge, and is become a thing of public interest and use." Every bushel of grain for its passage "pays a toll, which is a common charge," and, therefore, according to Lord Hale, every such warehouseman "ought to be under public regulation, viz., that he * * * take but reasonable toll." Certainly, if any business can be clothed "with a public interest, and cease to be *juris privati* only," this has been. It may not be made so by the operation of the Constitution of Illinois or this statute, but it is by the facts.

* * * For our purposes we must assume that, if a state of facts could exist that would justify such legislation, it actually did exist when the statute now under consideration was passed. For us the question is one of power, not of expediency. If no state of circumstances could exist to justify such a statute, then we may declare this one void, because in excess of the legislative power of the State. But if it could, we must presume it did. Of the propriety of legislative interference within the scope of legislative power the legislature is the exclusive judge.

Neither is it a matter of any moment that no precedent can be found for a statute precisely like this. It is conceded that the business is one of recent origin, that its growth has been rapid, and that it is already of great importance. And it must also be conceded that it is a business in which the whole public has a direct and positive interest. It presents, therefore, a case for the application of a long-known and well-established principle in social science, and this statute simply extends the law so as to meet this new development of commercial progress. There is no attempt to compel these owners to grant the public an interest in their property, but to declare their obligations, if they use it in this particular manner.

It matters not in this case that these plaintiffs in error had built their warehouses and established their business before the regulations complained of were adopted. What they did was from the beginning subject to the power of the body politic to require them to conform to such regulations as might be established by the proper authorities for the common good. They entered upon their business and provided themselves with the means to carry it on subject to this condition. If they did not wish to submit themselves to such interference, they should not have clothed the public with an interest in their concerns. The same principle applies to them that does to the proprietor of a hackney-carriage, and as to him it has never been supposed that he was exempt from regulating statutes or ordinances because he had purchased his horses and carriage and established his business before the statute or the ordinance was adopted.

It is insisted, however, that the owner of property is entitled to a reasonable compensation for its use, even though it be clothed with a public interest, and that what is reasonable is a judicial and not a legislative question.

As has already been shown, the practice has been otherwise. In countries where the common law prevails, it has been customary from time immemorial for the legislature to declare what shall be a reasonable compensation under such circumstances, or, perhaps more properly speaking, to fix a maximum beyond which any charge made would be unreasonable. Undoubtedly, in mere private contracts, relating to matters in which the public has no interest, what is reasonable must be ascertained judicially. But this is because the legislature has no control over such a contract. So, too, in matters which do affect the public interest, and as to which legislative control may be exercised, if there are no statutory regulations upon the subject, the courts must determine what is reasonable. The controlling fact is the power to regulate at all. If that exists, the right to establish the maximum of charge, as one of the means of regulation, is implied. In fact, the common-law rule, which requires the charge to be reasonable, is itself a regulation as to price. * * * To limit the rate of charge for services rendered in a public employment, or for the use of property in which the public has an interest, is only changing a regulation which existed before. It establishes no new principle in the law, but only gives a new effect to an old one.

We know that this is a power which may be abused; but that is no argument against its existence. For protection against abuses by legislatures the people must resort to the polls, not to the courts.

After what has already been said, it is unnecessary to refer at length to the effect of the other provision of the Fourteenth Amendment which is relied upon, viz., that no State shall "deny to any person within its jurisdiction the equal protection of the laws." Certainly, it cannot be claimed that this prevents the State from regulating the fares of hackmen or the charges of draymen in Chicago, unless it does the same thing in every other place within its jurisdiction. But, as has been seen, the power to regulate the business of warehouses depends upon the same principle as the power to regulate hackmen and draymen, and what cannot be done in the one case in this particular cannot be done in the other.

We come now to consider the effect upon this statute of the power of Congress to regulate commerce.

It was very properly said in the case of the State Tax on Railway Gross Receipts, 15 Wall. 293, that "it is not every thing that affects commerce that amounts to a regulation of it, within the meaning of the Constitution." The warehouses of these Plaintiffs in error are situated and their business carried on exclusively within the limits of the State of Illinois. They are used as instruments by those engaged in State as well as those engaged in inter-state commerce, but they are no more necessarily a part of commerce itself than the dray or the cart by which, but for them, grain would be transferred from one railroad station to another. Incidentally they may become connected with inter-state commerce, but not necessarily so. Their regulation is a thing of domestic concern, and, certainly, until Congress acts in reference to their inter-state relations, the State may exercise all the powers of government over them, even though in so doing it may indirectly operate upon commerce outside its immediate jurisdiction. We do not say that a case may not arise in which it will be found that a State, under the form of regulating its own affairs, has encroached upon the exclusive domain of Congress in respect to inter-state commerce. but we do say that, upon the facts as they are represented to us in this record, that has not been done.

* * *

Judgment affirmed.

MR. JUSTICE FIELD [joined by JUSTICE STRONG]. I am compelled to dissent from the decision of the court in this case, and from the reasons upon which that decision is founded. The principle upon which the opinion of the majority proceeds is, in my judgment, subversive of the rights of private property, heretofore believed to be protected by constitutional guaranties against legislative interference, and is in conflict with the authorities cited in its support.

* * *

The declaration of the Constitution of 1870, that private buildings used for private purposes shall be deemed public institutions, does not make them so. The receipt and storage of grain in a building erected by private means for that purpose does not constitute the building a public warehouse. There is no magic in the language, though used by a constitutional convention, which can change a private business into a public one, or alter the character of the building in which the business is transacted. A tailor's or a shoemaker's shop would still retain its private character, even though the assembled wisdom of the State should declare, by organic act or legislative ordinance, that such a place was a public workshop, and that the workmen were public tailors or public shoemakers. One might as well attempt to change the nature of colors, by giving them a new designation. The defendants were no more public warehousemen, as justly observed by, counsel, than the merchant who sells his merchandise to the public is a public merchant, or the blacksmith who shoes horses for the public is a public blacksmith; and it was a strange notion that by calling them so they would be brought under legislative control.

* * *

* * * [I]f there be no protection * * * in the prohibitions of the Constitution against such invasion of private rights, all property and all business in the State are held at the mercy of a majority of its legislature. The public has no greater interest in the use of buildings for the storage of grain than it has in the use of buildings for the residences of families, not, indeed, any thing like so great an interest; and according to the doctrine announced, the legislature may fix the rent of all tenements used for residences, without reference to the cost of their erection. If the owner does not like the rates prescribed, he may cease renting his houses. * * *

The doctrine of the State court, that no one is deprived of his property, within the meaning of the constitutional inhibition, so long as he retains its title and possession, and the doctrine of this court, that, whenever one's property is used in such a manner as to affect the community at large, it becomes by that fact clothed with a public interest, and ceases to be *juris privati* only, appear to me to destroy, for all useful purposes, the efficacy of the constitutional guaranty. All that is beneficial in property arises from its use, and the fruits of that use; and whatever deprives a person of them deprives him of all that is desirable or valuable in the title and possession. If the constitutional guaranty extends no further than to prevent a deprivation of title and possession, and allows a deprivation of use, and the fruits of that use, it does not merit the encomiums it has received.

* * *

There is nothing in the character of the business of the defendants as warehousemen which called for the interference complained of in this case. Their buildings are not nuisances; their occupation of receiving and storing grain infringes upon no rights of others, disturbs no neighborhood, infects not the air, and in no respect prevents others from using and enjoying their property as to them may seem best. The legislation in question is nothing less than a bold assertion of absolute power by the State to control at its discretion the property and business of the citizen, and fix the compensation he shall receive. The will of the legislature is made the condition upon which the owner shall receive the fruits of his property and the just reward of his labor, industry, and enterprise. "That government," says Story, "can scarcely be deemed to be free where the rights of property are left solely dependent upon the will of a legislative body without any restraint. The fundamental maxims of a free government seem to require that the rights of personal liberty and private property should be held sacred." Wilkeson v. Leland, 2 Pet. 657. The decision of the court in this case gives unrestrained license to legislative will.

* * *

Notes and Questions

1. It is often useful to analyze cases about regulation on three levels:

First, does the regulatory scheme make sense? Was it necessary when adopted?

Second, do any objections you may have to the scheme rise to legal or constitutional dimensions? That is, when is a statute so irrational and when does it so invade protected rights as to be unlawful?

Third, as part of the general electorate, a legislator or a member of a regulatory agency, what practical factors would have influenced your thinking about the regulation when it was proposed?

2. Asking yourself those questions with respect to Munn v. Illinois:

a. Would you ordinarily expect the rates charged by grain elevators to be an appropriate subject for regulation? Is the business one you would usually expect to be a natural monopoly? Is there any other reason competition would not produce the lowest price and best level of service in this industry?[5]

b. What was true about the grain elevator business in Chicago in the 1870s that might have made regulation seem necessary? If the Sherman Antitrust Law had been in effect (it was not passed until 1890) at the time of the regulation addressed in *Munn,* would you as a legislator have voted for the direct rate regulation employed here?

3. Even if you thought this regulation unwise or unnecessary, would you as a judge hold it unconstitutional?

---

5. Ask yourself this question again after you have looked at the traditional bases for regulation outlined in Part C of this Chapter, and in Chapters 3 & 4 of these materials.

a. What arguably protected constitutional right was invaded here? Precisely what interest of Munn and Scott's was "taken" by this regulation?

b. Does the term "affected with a public interest" provide a workable distinction between what is subject to regulation and what is not? What does the term mean to you? How broadly does the court seem to have meant it to apply?

c. Are Justices Field and Strong right that there is no business or profession *not* "affected with a public interest" as the court uses the phrase? Is that a powerful argument against the Court's decision or does it simply confirm the principle that regulatory decisions should be made by institutions more directly accountable to the public?

4. As a legislator what would have influenced your vote for or against this kind of regulation?

a. Would it be relevant to you that St. Louis, St.Paul, or some other rail hubs might prosper in the future if Chicago's grain elevator rates remained high? Put another way, would it be proper for you to factor in the benefits to other Chicago businesses if the grain elevators' rates were kept low? Should such "taxation" of one group for the broader good be unconstitutional? Is it instead the essence of appropriate legislative decisions about *both* taxation and regulation.[6]

b. Can legislators be expected to focus on the "public interest" apart from their personal interest? Are the two necessarily congruent? Will the rewards at the next election from persons grateful for lower grain elevator rates be proof that regulated rates were in the public interest?

c. Might the legal authority of legislators to impose rate limitations be used as a device to coerce campaign contributions from elevator owners who want to avoid such an imposition?[7] If so, are Justices Field and Strong right that the authority to regulate should be limited?

5. Munn v. Illinois is widely recognized as a landmark in the justification of regulation as we know it today. In a sense, however, that role is fortuitous. *Munn* was at one important level a constitutional decision construing the then-new Fourteenth Amendment which had been passed only nine years earlier. Arguably, it merely reflects a very cautious reading of the purpose of that Amendment. Just four years earlier in the Slaughter–House Cases, 83 U.S. (16 Wall.) 36, 21 L.Ed. 394 (1873), the Court had considered the claim of a meat renderer that a state law was unconstitutional because it limited the parts of a city in which he could operate his business. In upholding the regulation, the Court had said:

> * * * [In] the light of this recapitulation of events, almost too recent to be called history, but which are familiar to us all; and on the most casual examination of the language of these amendments, no one can fail to be impressed with the one pervading purpose found in them all, lying at the foundation of each, and without which none of them

6. Richard Posner provided an excellent analysis of the similarity between taxation and regulation in Taxation by Regulation, 2 Bell J. 22 (1971).

7. Professor Fred McChesney eloquently argues this position in several of his articles and books, e.g., Rent Extraction and Interest–Group Organization in a Coasian Model of Regulation, 20 J. Legal Studies 73 (1991).

would have been even suggested; we mean the freedom of the slave race, the security and firm establishment of that freedom, and the protection of the newly-made freeman and citizen from the oppressions of those who had formerly exercised unlimited dominion over him.

We do not say that no one else but the negro can share in this protection. Both the language and spirit of these articles are to have their fair and just weight in any question of construction. * * * But what we do say, and what we wish to be understood is, that in any fair and just construction of any section or phrase of these amendments, it is necessary to look to the purpose which we have said was the pervading spirit of them all, the evil which they were designed to remedy, and the process of continued addition to the Constitution, until that purpose was supposed to be accomplished, as far as constitutional law can accomplish it.

* * *

The argument has not been much pressed in these cases that the defendant's charter deprives the plaintiffs of their property without due process of law, or that it denies to them the equal protection of the law. The first of these paragraphs has been in the Constitution since the adoption of the fifth amendment, as a restraint upon the Federal power. It is also to be found in some form of expression in the constitutions of nearly all the States, as a restraint upon the power of the States. * * *

We are not without judicial interpretation, therefore, both State and National, of the meaning of this clause. And it is sufficient to say that under no construction of that provision that we have ever seen, or any that we deem admissible, can the restraint imposed by the State of Louisiana upon the exercise of their trade by the butchers of New Orleans be held to be a deprivation of property within the meaning of that provision.

"Nor shall any State deny to any person within its jurisdiction the equal protection of the laws."

In the light of the history of these amendments, and the pervading purpose of them, which we have already discussed, it is not difficult to give a meaning to this clause. The existence of laws in the States where the newly emancipated negroes resided, which discriminated with gross injustice and hardship against them as a class, was the evil to be remedied by this clause, and by it such laws are forbidden.

Munn v. Illinois was decided, then, by a Court which had expressed a narrow view of the scope of the Fourteenth Amendment. Indeed, it was not clear until nine years after *Munn* that a corporation was even a "person" entitled to the protection of the Fourteenth Amendment. See Santa Clara County v. Southern Pacific Railroad Co., 118 U.S. 394, 6 S.Ct. 1132, 30 L.Ed. 118 (1886).[8]

8. The openness to regulation seen in *Munn* was also reflected in the five "granger" cases that permitted state regulation of railroad rates. Chicago, Burlington & Quincy Railroad Co. v. Iowa, 94 U.S. (4 Otto) 155, 24 L.Ed. 94 (1877); Peik v. Chicago & North–Western Railway Co., 94 U.S. (4 Otto) 164, 24 L.Ed. 97 (1877); Chicago, Milwaukee & St. Paul Railroad Co. v. Ackley, 94 U.S. (4 Otto) 179, 24 L.Ed. 99

4. *Munn* was decided in 1877. The Interstate Commerce Commission was created in 1887, primarily to regulate the railroads, and the Sherman Act introduced antitrust regulation in 1890. But shortly thereafter, the judicial attitude toward regulation underwent a major change. In Chicago, Milwaukee & St. Paul Railway Co. v. Minnesota, 134 U.S. 418, 10 S.Ct. 462, 33 L.Ed. 970 (1890), for example, the Court held that due process required that the reasonableness of rates not be left to the legislature or to a commission (as in *Munn*) but instead be subject to judicial review. Five years later, the Court held in United States v. E.C. Knight Company, 156 U.S. 1, 15 S.Ct. 249, 39 L.Ed. 325 (1895), that sugar refining was not in interstate commerce and thus that a large merger in that industry could not be prosecuted under the Sherman Act. The next year, in Missouri Pacific Railway Co. v. Nebraska, 164 U.S. 403, 17 S.Ct. 130, 41 L.Ed. 489 (1896), the Court held that a state requirement that a railroad provide land for a grain elevator upon its right of way on the same terms it had permitted location of two other grain elevators there constituted a "taking" of the railroad's property for private use and was thus unconstitutional.

The period of active judicial review of state and federal regulatory programs that followed is well known. We need only recall some of the most important of the cases and the programs that they struck down. Lochner v. New York, 198 U.S. 45, 25 S.Ct. 539, 49 L.Ed. 937 (1905) (maximum hours of work for bakers); Adams v. Tanner, 244 U.S. 590, 37 S.Ct. 662, 61 L.Ed. 1336 (1917) (prohibition of private employment agency charging fees to workers); Adkins v. Children's Hospital, 261 U.S. 525, 43 S.Ct. 394, 67 L.Ed. 785 (1923) (minimum wages for women and children),[9] Charles Wolff Packing Co. v. Court of Industrial Relations, 262 U.S. 522, 43 S.Ct. 630, 67 L.Ed. 1103 (1923) (requirement of compulsory arbitration on food industry); Tyson & Brother v. Banton, 273 U.S. 418, 47 S.Ct. 426, 71 L.Ed. 718 (1927) (regulation of business of selling theater tickets).

2. THE MODERN ERA OF REGULATION

The wave of new regulation in the Depression years of the 1930s is well known, as is the decline of judicial resistance to it.[10] For almost 40

(1877); Winona & St. Peter Railroad Co. v. Blake, 94 U.S. (4 Otto) 180, 24 L.Ed. 99 (1877); Stone v. Wisconsin, 94 U.S. (4 Otto) 181, 24 L.Ed. 102 (1877).

Other cases sustained railroad regulation against a charge that it abrogated the railroads' corporate charters. Ruggles v. Illinois, 108 U.S. 526, 2 S.Ct. 832, 27 L.Ed. 812 (1883); Illinois Central Railroad Co. v. Illinois, 108 U.S. 541, 2 S.Ct. 839, 27 L.Ed. 818 (1883); Stone v. Farmers' Loan & Trust Co., 116 U.S. 307, 6 S.Ct. 334, 29 L.Ed. 636 (1886); Stone v. Illinois Central Railroad Co., 116 U.S. 347, 6 S.Ct. 348, 29 L.Ed. 650 (1886); Stone v. New Orleans & Northeastern Railroad Co., 116 U.S. 352, 6 S.Ct. 349 29 L.Ed. 651 (1886).

9. The Court had earlier sustained a law regulating the maximum hours women could work. Muller v. Oregon, 208 U.S. 412, 28 S.Ct. 324, 52 L.Ed. 551 (1908). Louis Brandeis had persuaded the Court with his famous "Brandeis brief" that tried to show more by facts and statistics than by traditional legal reasoning that women should be subject to different treatment than men and thus that *Lochner* did not control. How do you suppose an argument that "history discloses the fact that woman has always been dependent upon man" would fare today? Cf. United States v. Virginia, 518 U.S. 515, 116 S.Ct. 2264, 135 L.Ed.2d 735 (1996) ("gender-based developmental differences" do not justify failure to admit women to the Virginia Military Institute).

10. Compare, e.g., A.L.A. Schechter Poultry Corp. v. United States, 295 U.S. 495, 55 S.Ct. 837, 79 L.Ed. 1570 (1935), and Panama Refining Co. v. Ryan, 293 U.S. 388, 55 S.Ct. 241, 79 L.Ed. 446 (1935), finding

years thereafter, regulation was rarely reduced. Beginning in the late 1950s, civil rights concerns were at the center of new initiatives,[11] while in the early 1970s, environmental protection[12] and worker safety[13] were of special importance.

The last three decades, however, have also seen the rise of doubts—indeed, cynicism—about the necessity and effectiveness of regulation. Concerns seem first to have been raised in academic circles in the early 1960s by George Stigler, Ronald Coase, and others.[14] Also in the late 1960s, litigation initiated or joined by the Department of Justice began to test both the rationale and scope of several regulatory schemes.[15] About the same time, a series of studies conducted under the auspices of Ralph Nader served to get questions of administrative effectiveness before the public in a dramatic way.[16]

A search for causes of economic recession focused on criticism of regulatory ineffectiveness by the Ford Administration.[17] And when in 1974 the Justice Department filed an antitrust action against the American Telephone and Telegraph Company, the most basic issues of regulation were brought to the forefront of public attention.[18]

that Congress had exceeded its power to delegate regulatory authority, with NLRB v. Jones & Laughlin Steel Corp., 301 U.S. 1, 57 S.Ct. 615, 81 L.Ed. 893 (1937) and United States v. Carolene Products, 304 U.S. 144, 58 S.Ct. 778, 82 L.Ed. 1234 (1938), upholding federal regulation.

11. E.g., The Civil Rights Act of 1964, 78 Stat. 243, 42 U.S.C. § 2000a (requiring open access to places of public accommodation); 78 Stat. 253, 42 U.S.C. § 2000e (requiring equal employment opportunity); The Fair Housing Act of 1968, 82 Stat. 81, 42 U.S.C. § 3601, et seq. (prohibiting discrimination in sale, lease and financing of housing).

12. E.g., The National Environmental Policy Act, 83 Stat. 852, 42 U.S.C. § 4321 et seq. (1969); The Endangered Species Act, 87 Stat. 884, 16 U.S.C. § 1531, et seq. (1973).

13. E.g., The Occupational Safety and Health Act of 1970, 84 Stat. 1590, 29 U.S.C. § 651, et seq.

14. E.g., George Stigler and Claire Friedland, What Can Regulators Regulate? The Case of Electricity, 5 J.Law & Econ. 1 (1962); Ronald H. Coase, The Federal Communications Commission, 2 J.Law & Econ. 1 (1959). Later but equally important, was Harold Demsetz, Why Regulate Utilities, 11 J.Law & Econ. 55 (1968).

15. E.g., Carter v. AT & T, 250 F.Supp. 188 (N.D.Tex.1966), affirmed 365 F.2d 486 (5th Cir.1966), decided by FCC at 13 FCC 2d 420, 13 RR 2d 597 (FCC 1968); Microwave Communications, Inc., 18 FCC 2d 953,

16 RR 2d 1037 (FCC 1969); United States v. Interstate Commerce Commission, 396 U.S. 491, 90 S.Ct. 708, 24 L.Ed.2d 700 (1970).

16. E.g., Mark J. Green, ed., The Monopoly Makers: Ralph Nader's Study Group Report on Regulation and Competition (1973); Robert C. Fellmeth, The Interstate Commerce Omission: Ralph Nader's Study Group Report on the Interstate Commerce Commission & Transportation (1970); Edward Cox, et al., The Nader Report on the Federal Trade Commission (1969). Far less publicized, but at least as important in focusing official attention on the issues were the Report of the Task Force on Productivity and Competition (the Stigler Report), reprinted at 115 Cong.Rec. 15933–38 (1969), and Report of the Council of Economic Advisors in Economic Report of the President 90–117 (1970).

17. President Ford's address to a joint session of Congress initiated the official activity. 120 Cong.Rec. H 10120 (Daily Ed. Oct. 8, 1974). Then, in Congressional hearings in late 1974, Administration spokespersons expressed strong views on questions of regulatory reform. E.g., Hearings Before the Committee on Government Operations, U.S. Senate, on S. 704, et al. 93d Cong., 2d Sess. (Nov. 1974). See also, BNA Antitrust & Trade Reg.Rep., No. 683, p. E–1 (Oct. 8, 1974) (Speech of FTC Chairman Lewis Engman); Report of the Council of Economic Advisors in Economic Report of the President 147–59 (1975).

18. Civil Action 74–1698 (D.D.C.1974). See Chapters 3 & 6 of these materials.

Limiting regulation has not even been a controversial issue in Presidential campaigns since 1976; all major party candidates have pledged to control it. But change has come slowly. A breakthrough in substantive deregulation came as a result of the 1975 report by the Subcommittee on Administrative Practice & Procedure of the Senate Judiciary Committee, chaired by Senator Kennedy. That study was conducted by then-Professor Stephen Breyer of the Harvard Law School and clearly advocated competition in airline rates. The support of a powerful, liberal Senator for airline deregulation, coupled with President Carter's appointment of economist Alfred Kahn to chair the Civil Aeronautics Board, made possible passage of the Airline Deregulation Act of 1978.[19]

Two years earlier, a less dramatic but equally important development was the passage of the Railroad Revitalization and Regulatory Reform Act[20] that gave railroads substantially more pricing flexibility to meet or undercut truck rates so long as they priced above their variable costs. Trucking entry was also liberalized, much to the chagrin of the industry.[21] The Interstate Commerce Commission itself did not survive 1995. By that time its regulatory authority had dwindled since truck, rail and barge regulation had been largely eliminated during the 1970s and 1980s. Its few remaining functions have now been transferred to the Department of Transportation.[22]

"Self-regulation," long thought an oxymoron, has developed a new respectability as agencies try to become more effective in the use of the resources available to them.[23] Additional deregulatory steps have also been significant. Differences between banks and savings & loan associations were reduced by the Depository Institutions Deregulation and Monetary Control Act of 1980,[24] a deregulatory statute that arguably contributed to the rash of savings and loan failures in the 1980s.

The energy industry has undergone its own wave of deregulation with both natural gas and electric production and distribution being transformed in the process.[25]

Most dramatically, the settlement of the AT & T antitrust case in 1981 led to a substantial increase in firms providing discount long distance service and a broad range of facsimile, cellular and other communications services. The Telecommunications Act of 1996[26] was one more step in this process.

19. Pub.L. 95–504, 92 Stat. 1705 (1978).

20. Pub.L. 94–210, 90 Stat. 31 (1976). See also, Pub.L. 96–448, 94 Stat. 1895 (1980) (Staggers Rail Act of 1980).

21. Pub.L. 96–221, 90 Stat. 1337 (1980). See also Pub.L. 96–296 (1980) (Motor Carrier Act of 1980).

22. Pub.L. 104–113, 109 Stat. 803 (1995).

23. For materials on self-regulation see Chapter 4, infra.

24. Pub.L. 96–221, 94 Stat. 132 (1980). See also, Pub.L 97–320, 96 Stat. 1469 (1982) (Garn–St. Germain Depository Institutions Act of 1982).

25. See, e.g., the Energy Policy Act of 1992, Pub.L. 102–486, 106 Stat. 2776. See generally, Richard J. Pierce Jr., Reconstituting the Natural Gas Industry from Wellhead to Burnertip, 9 Energy L. J. 1 (1988).

26. Pub.L. 104–104, 110 Stat. 56 (Feb. 8, 1996).

Despite these impressive changes, however, deregulation has not been universally embraced. Securities regulation is, in some ways, increasing. Import restraints, whether "voluntary" or not, are seen as ways to preserve American jobs. Indeed, in his second term, President Reagan arguably slowed, not advanced, the deregulation process.[27] The first Bush Administration talked a deregulatory line, but legislative initiatives passed during his term, such as the Americans With Disabilities Act of 1990,[28] significantly increased the regulatory role in private decisions.

President Clinton entered office with plans for "reinventing government,"[29] but his efforts (and those of Vice President Gore) were devoted more to making governmental practices more "efficient" than to deregulating particular industries.[30] Even the "Contract with America," created as part of the Republican electoral initiatives in 1994, spoke more about reducing the burdens and costs of government than about deregulation.[31]

Although comprehensive regulatory reform legislation was not adopted during the Clinton Administration, in the 104th Congress the Republican majorities passed and President Clinton signed legislation mandating cost benefit analysis of rules expected to impose burdens of over $100 million on the affected parties,[32] and Congressional review and possible veto of new regulations.[33] In addition, calls for privatization have become the new theme in the "less intrusive government" movement, particularly at the state and local level.[34]

27. President Reagan was arguably more interested in a roll-back of regulation that he saw as a burden on business than he was in a reexamination of when regulation yielded net benefits to society and when it did not. See, e.g., George C. Eads & Michael Fix, Relief or Reform?: Reagan's Regulatory Dilemma (1984); Roger E. Meiners & Bruce Yandle, eds., Regulation and the Reagan Era: Politics, Bureaucracy and the Public Interest (1989).

28. Pub.L. 101–336, 104 Stat. 328, 42 U.S.C. § 12101 et seq. See generally, Richard Epstein, Forbidden Grounds—The Case Against Employment Discrimination Laws (1994).

29. Al Gore, The National Performance Review: Creating a Government that Works Better and Costs Less (1993); Jeffrey S. Lubbers, Better Regulations: The National Performance Review's Regulatory Reform Recommendations, 43 Duke L.J. 1165 (1994). Cf. Stephen Breyer, Breaking the Vicious Circle: Toward Effective Risk Regulation (1992); Paul R. Verkuil, Is Efficient Government an Oxymoron? 43 Duke L.J. 1221 (1994).

30. See, e.g., Richard H. Pildes & Cass R. Sunstein, Reinventing the Regulatory State, 62 U. Chicago L. Rev. 1 (1995) (ana-

lyzing President Clinton's Executive Order 12,866, including its emphasis on risk assessment).

31. Contract With America: The Bold Plan by Rep. Newt Gingrich, Rep. Dick Armey, and the House Republicans to Change the Nation (Ed Gillespie & Bob Schellhas, eds., 1994). For an account of some of the troubles experienced getting regulatory reform in the first session of the 104th Congress, see Cass R. Sunstein, Congress, Constitutional Moments, and the Cost–Benefit State, 48 Stanford L. Rev. 247 (1996).

32. The provisions were part of the Unfunded Mandates Reform Act of 1995, Pub.L. 104–4, 109 Stat. 48 (1995).

33. These provisions were part of the Small Business Regulatory Enforcement Fairness Act of 1996, Pub.L. 104–121, 110 Stat. 857 (1996).

34. See David E. Osborne & Ted C. Gaebler, Reinventing Government (1992). Cf. John Kay, Colin Mayer & David Thompson, Privatisation & Regulation—The UK Experience (1986); Paul R. Verkuil, Reverse Yardstick Competition: A New Deal for the Nineties, 45 Florida L. Rev. 1 (1993); Gillian E. Metzger, Privatization as Delegation, 103 Colum. L. Rev. 1367 (2003).

The George W. Bush Administration is supporting these trends toward increased private sector control, although the events of 9/11 and the Homeland Security Act have tended to restrain deregulatory impulses due to the perceived need for more extensive (federal) government control.[35] On the regulatory review front, President Bush kept President Clinton's Executive Order 12,866 in place, but his OIRA head, John Graham, has been more actively returning proposed rules to agencies for review. In Chapter 5, we address regulatory reform issues like privatization and self-regulation that would seem to reflect the deregulatory impulses of the current Administration.

In the materials that follow, keep in mind how narrow the distinction between regulation and deregulation can be. For example, when you think of deregulation, it is tempting to assume the government has stepped aside entirely and allowed competitive forces to take over. In fact, a great deal of what legislators call "deregulation" is not that at all. Sometimes, "deregulation" is used to describe situations in which the pervasiveness of regulation has been reduced. Other times, however, new regulation will be adopted to ease the industry toward competition. Thus, even with more "deregulation," our economy is likely to continue to be highly regulated. One should be as wary of taking deregulatory efforts at face value as of embracing regulatory proposals. In each case, identify the winners and the losers. Be sure to ask: Whose ox is being gored?

C. TOWARD UNDERSTANDING THE REGULATION—DEREGULATION DEBATE

Any process as rich, varied and subtle as the debate over deregulation—or for that matter, increased regulation—is hard to address systematically without simplifying the issues to the point of caricature. In these materials, we encourage you to address issues from three perspectives in order to help preserve the richness of the debate. We call these perspectives: (1) Public Interest, (2) Public Administration, and (3) Public Choice. The terms are in part our own but they mirror terms widely used in the academic and policy literature.[36]

Briefly, the "Public Interest" approach to regulation uses the perspective provided by economic analysis to suggest when regulation would increase citizen/consumer welfare and when it would not. The "Public

35. For example, the deregulatory policies of the Federal Communications Commission which favor the easing of internet rules have clashed with law enforcement desires to monitor communications on the internet. See Easing of Internet Rules Presents A Challenge to Surveillance Efforts, N.Y. Times, Jan. 22, 2004, at A1, C8.

36. Among the many works on analysis of regulation, see Roger G. Noll, ed., Regulatory Policy and the Social Sciences (1985) (applying insights from political science, anthropology and psychology as well as economics); Jack High, ed., Regulation: Economic Theory and History (1991). See also, Oliver E. Williamson, The Economic Institutions of Capitalism (1985) (a wide-ranging economic and social analysis).

Administration" perspective tends to assume that a regulatory program is directed at a legitimate problem but it asks how the regulatory process could be improved so as to be less intrusive, more effective or both. "Public Choice" theory, on the other hand, applies economic analysis to political deliberation. It suggests the possibility that interest groups may capture the regulatory process and cause regulation to do more harm than good.

All three approaches have been reflected in the notes and questions within each Chapter. This section further develops the ideas behind them.

1. THE PUBLIC INTEREST ANALYSIS OF REGULATION

As indicated, the Public Interest analysis of regulation uses economic theory to examine when and whether regulatory intervention is likely to improve the operation of a market economy.[37] To explore this approach, we first introduce microeconomic theory and illustrate how the market under ideal conditions would determine price, quantity produced, and general resource allocation. Later, we focus on ways in which markets may fail to address one or more societal interests.[38]

a. A Brief Introduction to Economic Theory

Economists like to talk about "efficiency." What they don't always tell you is that "efficiency" is a word with several possible meanings. Thus, the adjective that proceeds "efficiency" is important. For our purposes, two of the most important kinds of efficiency are "allocative efficiency" and "productive efficiency."[39] Productive efficiency is relatively easy to understand. It refers to the actual cost of producing a unit of output. The lower the cost per unit of production, the greater the productive efficiency. Allocative efficiency, on the other hand, refers to the use of society's resources in the production of the goods and services that are most highly valued. The explanation is a bit complex and requires an understanding of the concepts of demand and supply.

i. Demand

Demand is expressed as a *schedule* of prices and the amounts individuals would be willing and able to purchase at each price in a given

---

37. A well-known work on this approach to regulation is Alfred E. Kahn, The Economics of Regulation: Principles and Institutions (1988). See also, Daniel F. Spulber, Regulation and Markets (1989). For economic analysis more explicitly critical of regulatory programs, see Paul W. MacAvoy, Industry Regulation and the Performance of the American Economy (1992); Robert W. Poole, Jr., ed., Instead of Regulation: Alternatives to Federal Regulatory Agencies (1982).

38. The term "market failure" is often used in this analysis in one of two ways. The more technically correct of the two

refers to instances in which price, quantity, and quality are not determined in the context of a freely competitive market. In regulatory analysis, however, a more generic interpretation might be that there is "market failure" whenever the outcome of the market process is not regarded as socially desirable.

39. Yet another kind is "dynamic efficiency"—the condition most receptive to technological and other productive change. See, e.g., Thomas D. Morgan, Cases and Materials on Modern Antitrust Law and Its Origins 18–19 (2d ed. 2001).

market at a given time. One might determine the demand for a good or service by observing a number of people and seeing how many units of a particular item they buy at each of several prices. In effect, this would amount to deriving each individual's demand. In order to determine the *market* demand, the amounts each is willing and able to purchase at each price would be added together. As a practical substitute for such observations, each person in the class might be asked how many copies of John Rawls' *A Theory of Justice* (TJ) he or she would buy next week at a variety of prices. Summing the amounts at each price might lead to the schedule in Table 1.

TABLE 1

Price	Quantity Demanded
$35	1
$30	2
$25	3
$20	4
$15	5
$10	6
$ 5	7

As a technical matter, this entire schedule represents the "demand." The amount that would be purchased at each price is the "quantity demanded." The schedule illustrates the well-known inverse relationship between price and quantity. In other words, the quantity demanded increases as price decreases. Typically, demand is also illustrated using a graph. In Figure 1, the horizontal axis is labeled in terms of copies of TJ. The vertical axis is labeled in terms of prices. At each price, the quantity that would be purchased at that price has been plotted. As in the case of all but the most unusual demand curves, this demand curve slopes downward to the right.

Figure 1

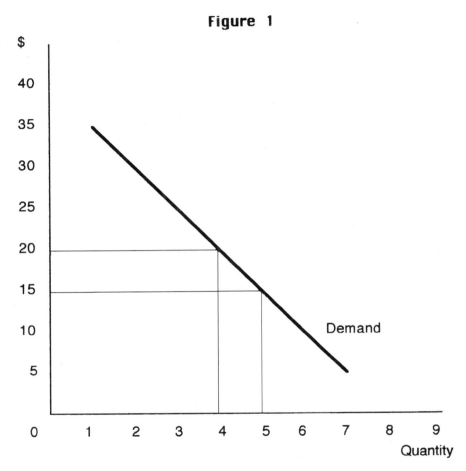

Typically, one thinks of demand as illustrating the quantity that individuals would be willing and able to purchase at each price. Thus, at a price of $15, classmates would be willing and able to purchase 5 copies of TJ. Another approach is to examine each quantity and ask what is the highest price that would be consistent with that quantity being purchased. For example, look at quantity 4. The highest price consistent with selling 4 copies of TJ would be $20.

For purposes of understanding the concept of "allocative efficiency," it is useful to focus on a change from one point on the demand curve to another. For example, at a price of $15, the quantity demanded is 5 and at a price of $10, the quantity demanded is 6. Thus, if one is asked "how much value was attributed to the sixth individual copy of TJ in this market?" the answer would be $10. At a higher price the sixth unit would not be demanded. If the cost of the resources used to produce the sixth unit exceed $10, economists would say it is not "allocatively efficient" to produce that unit. This will be clearer after a look at supply.

ii. Supply

Supply is also represented as a *schedule*—this time of prices and the quantities sellers would be willing and able to make available for sale at each price in a given market during a given time period. Like "demand," "supply" refers to the entire schedule, and the amount available at each price is the "quantity supplied." Like demand, supply could be determined by asking each potential seller how much they would be willing to sell at each price and then summing these amounts to get the total that would be available at each price.

For example, we might conduct a survey of possible producers and determine how many copies of TJ would be offered for sale at each price. The result could be as depicted in Table 2.

TABLE 2

Price	Quantity
$ 5	3
$10	4
$15	5
$20	6
$25	7
$30	8
$35	9

In Figure 2, the supply of TJ is illustrated graphically. As with demand, the vertical axis is in terms of dollars and the horizontal axis is in terms of quantity. Supply is usually viewed as sloping upwards, indicating that at higher prices, sellers will be willing to make more units available for sale.

Figure 2

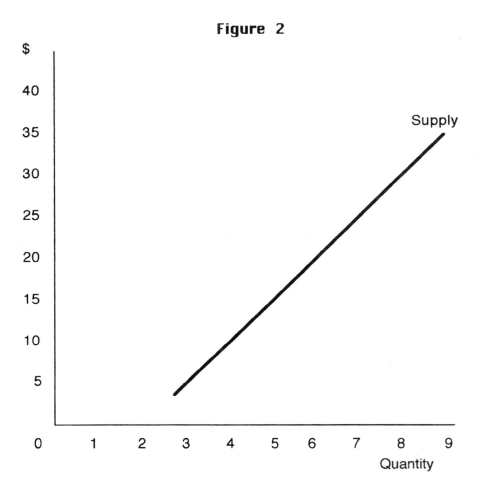

Using the supply schedule or curve, one can select a price and determine how many units will be available at that price. At least as important is the fact that the curve tells us the lowest price sellers will take for a specific level of output. Thus, in order for 6 units to be made available, the price must be no less than $20.

For purposes of understanding allocative efficiency, it is useful to focus on the change from output level 5 to level 6. As the schedule and curve indicate, 5 units would be made available at $15 and 6 would be made available at $20. You might ask yourself why the sixth unit is only available at a price of $20 and not at $15. The reason would have to be that the sixth unit is more costly to produce. In fact, the cost of the sixth unit must be $20 since this is the lowest price that would induce the producer to move to that level of output.

Economists use the term marginal cost to describe the cost of expanding output by one unit. Thus, the marginal cost of the sixth copy of TJ is $20. Using the same reasoning you can look at any level of output of TJ on the graph and determine the marginal cost of producing that unit. For example, since sellers will require a minimum price of $10 to produce 4 units and a price of $5 to produce 3 units, the marginal cost of the fourth unit must be $10. As it turns out, the supply curve is also the marginal cost curve. This tells us how many units would be available for sale at each price level *and* it tells us the extra cost of producing each additional unit.

It is useful to understand what gives rise to marginal cost. Presumably a potential producer goes into the market to buy inputs and finds that he or she must compete with other buyers who want those inputs for other uses. What each buyer is willing to pay for inputs is determined by the price for which he or she anticipates being able to sell the eventual output. Thus, when one buyer actually buys the input, the effect is to take away the opportunity that the input could be used to produce another type of good or service. And, the amount paid will be just enough to draw the input away from that competing use. Thus, in a very real sense, the marginal "cost" of producing one good or service represents the lost opportunity to produce some other good or service.

iii.   Market Equilibrium

In a market that is highly competitive, demand and supply will interact to determine the equilibrium market price and the quantity sold. By competitive, the economist means a market in which there is a large number of buyers and sellers who enjoy a free flow of information about prices and costs. The critical feature of a competitive market is that no one producer or group of producers can raise price above the competitive level for very long without losing sales to rivals.

Figure 3 includes the demand curve from Figure 1 and the supply curve from Figure 2. They intersect at a price of $15 and 5 units. This price and level of output are equilibrium levels, meaning that price will tend to move toward $15 and quantity toward 5. The reason is fairly obvious from the graph. Suppose price were higher than $15, say $25. The demand curve tells us that 3 units would be demanded at that price and 7 units would be available for sale. The quantity supplied would exceed the quantity demanded, creating a surplus. When there are surpluses in markets, prices tend to fall.

On the other hand, suppose price is $5. The quantity demanded would be 7 units and the quantity supplied would be 3 units. Since quantity demanded exceeds quantity supplied, there is a shortage in the market and prices will tend to rise. The only price at which there is not a tendency for the price to rise or fall is $15. This is due to the fact that the quantity demanded just equals the quantity supplied.

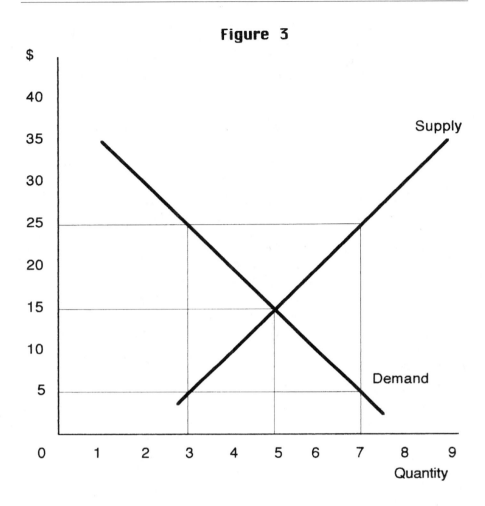

Figure 3

iv.   Allocative Efficiency

Aside from the determination of price and output, the free interaction of demand and supply results in "allocative efficiency." In other words, society's scarce resources are drawn into the production of goods and services that are most highly valued.

In order to understand what this means, it is useful to return to demand and supply. It will be recalled that the demand curve indicated the value attributed to each individual unit of output by potential buyers. Supply tells us the additional cost of producing each individual unit. More importantly, it can be viewed as indicating the "cost" in terms of opportunities lost to use those inputs in the production of other outputs.

Now take a specific level of output on Figure 3 like 3 copies of TJ. From the demand curve, we know that the value attributed to the third unit is $25. The value attributed to units 1 and 2 is even higher. The cost of producing unit 3, in terms of the value of the resources consumed, is $5. It is efficient to allocate resources to the production of unit 3. The same analysis applied to each unit out to unit 5. At that unit the value attributed to the output is just equal to the value of the resources consumed. Beyond unit 5, the additional cost of producing units (marginal cost) exceeds the value attributed to those units by buyers. It would be allocatively inefficient to produce these units.[40]

b. The Limits of Economic Theory—"Market Failure" and Pressures for Regulation

The above analysis suggests how the market should work. Pressures for regulation are the result of concerns about the possible market solution on two levels. First, markets rarely operate as perfectly as the theory suggests. Second, even if markets did act exactly as the model posits, it may be that "allocative efficiency" is not the only socially-desirable goal.

i. Market Power of Industry Participants

The most important purely economic concern about simply leaving markets alone in hopes of achieving allocative efficiency is that it may not happen. For example, the analysis so far has assumed that no single firm is important enough to the industry that it could raise prices above others and keep prices high. If it tried to do so, we have supposed it would quickly find it had lost all of its sales to eager competitors. As a factual matter, however, firms sometimes have what economists call "market power." This is the power to raise prices above competitive levels. The key is to differentiate one's product from others in the market or, by use of advertising, at least convince members of the public that the product or service is different. In extreme cases the firm may even become a monopolist—the single seller of a good or service for which there are no good substitutes.

The outcome of the existence of market power is illustrated in Figure 4. The Figure includes a demand and supply curve and an equilibrium price of P and equilibrium quantity of Q. It also includes a price, M, that might exist if a firm in the industry could raise prices above the competitive level of P.[41] There are a number of important consequences of pricing at level M. First, and obviously, the price is higher than it would be if the market were competitive. Second, the level of output of R is less than it would be if the market had remained competitive. Third, the level of output falls short of the allocatively efficient level. You can see this by comparing output level R with level Q. At output R and at all levels of output up to level Q, the demand curve

---

40. Students who want to read more about the theory might consult Robin Paul Malloy, Law & Economics, A Comparative Approach to Theory and Practice (1990); Mark Seidenfeld, Microeconomic Predicates to Law and Economics (1996). Further, much current economic theory is based, not on the static models used here, but on game theory. See, e.g., Ken Binmore, Fun and Games: A Text on Game Theory (1995).

41. The method by which a firm with market power determines the quantity it will sell and the price it charges is discussed in Chapter 3.

exceeds the supply or marginal cost curve. In other words, this space represents units of output that are more valuable to buyers than the resources that would be used in their production. But, unless the market is competitive, these units will not be produced.

Figure 4

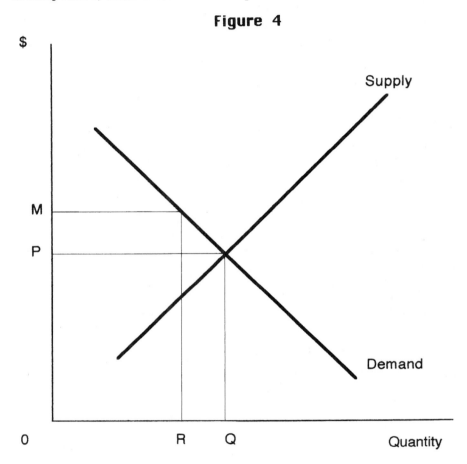

The antitrust laws, primarily the Sherman Act and the Clayton Act, are reactions to this type of market phenomenon.[42] The policy objective of these laws is to increase competition especially in markets in which firms have gained market power through agreements or by actions that exclude competitors without making buyers better off. A detailed analysis of government reactions to this type of market "imperfection" is left to a course in antitrust law.[43] Direct regulation addressed in this book is

---

42. See generally, E. Thomas Sullivan & Jeffrey L. Harrison, Understanding Antitrust and its Economic Implications (4th ed. 2003); Thomas D. Morgan, Cases and Materials on Modern Antitrust Law and its Origins (2d ed. 2001).

43. Such a course is the logical complement to a course focusing on regulation. The interplay between direct regulation and the antitrust laws, in turn, is the subject of Chapter 6 of these materials.

typically reserved for situations in which desired goals cannot be obtained simply by making an industry behave more competitively.

ii.   Competition Producing a Loss of Productive Efficiency

Much of the discussion so far has suggested that desirable outcomes flow from vigorous competition. Sometimes, however, the number of firms necessary to create a highly competitive market is inconsistent with achieving productive efficiency. Remember that productive efficiency simply means producing units of output at the lowest cost. Sometimes productive efficiency can be best achieved by having only one or a few firms producing the good or service in question. This can result when the industry is able to take advantage of "economies of scale," that is, reductions in the cost of production as output increases.

An extreme version of this phenomenon is a "natural monopoly," discussed in greater detail in Chapter Three. The problem is that an industry may be dominated by one or a few firms that are very efficient but do not feel competitive pressure to pass cost savings along to buyers in the form of lower prices. Antitrust enforcement is not an effective solution because trying to increase the number of firms in the industry for the sake of increased competition will lead to higher than necessary production costs and possibly even higher prices. In these instances, the solution may be to permit the existence of one firm but to regulate its price so that it approximates the price that would exist under more competitive conditions.[44]

Aside from the possibility of single-firm market power, there are a number of other reasons that markets may not behave as the simple competitive market suggests. Often firms act interdependently. For example, one firm may set a price depending on the price charged by a competitor. Their decisions can become "strategic" in the sense of taking into consideration a number of factors, some of which can only be assigned probabilities. These strategic considerations may mean the firms, rather than set competitive prices, actually set supracompetitive prices. A modern analysis of market behavior is not limited to competitive and monopolistic markets but must consider these dynamic interactions.[45]

iii.   The Arbitrary Nature of "Demand"

A further understanding of governmental intervention in the marketplace can be gleaned by looking more closely at demand. Demand is the expression of individuals in the market, but their expressions are only registered if the individuals are "willing and able" to back-up their desires with money. Under the basic theory a hungry person without

---

44. To some extent, this analysis still begs the issue: what is wrong with an unregulated monopolist? The answer will be developed in Chapter 3, but in general, people tend to be uncomfortable when a monopolist is able to sell at higher prices than would exist in markets with a number of producers.

45. See generally, Herbert Hovenkamp, Antitrust Policy After Chicago, 84 Mich. L. Rev. 213 (1985).

money does not "demand" food. In fact, since that person's desire for food does not manifest itself as "demand," in theory, it would be allocatively inefficient to give food to that person. (It would not be allocatively inefficient if some other person voluntarily purchased the food and gave it to the hungry person. Do you see why?)

Manifested demand may also be of limited usefulness in terms of allocative efficiency and other social goals when consumers have incomplete or inaccurate information. Some regulation is a response to discomfort with decisions made in the absence of good information and the failure of the market to produce that information. Requirements that food labels carry nutritional information, for example, and that credit terms be fully disclosed can be traced to the belief that resources are more efficiently allocated when consumers are well-informed.

Sometimes, even full information is not sufficient to result in market decisions that an objective observer would consider acceptable. In these instances, it is said that consumers are simply unable to understand what is in their welfare.[46] Age limitations on purchases of products such as alcohol, for example, can be connected to a distrust of "demand" as the only measure of what should be produced and sold.

iv. Transaction Costs

One of the characteristics of a highly competitive market in which resources are directed into their most valued uses is low transaction costs. Transaction costs are those costs associated with the actual exchange. It is important to note that the actual cost of an item is not a transaction cost. For example, the cost of a new car may be $20,000. This is not a transaction cost. The transaction cost would be the effort, time and money required to find the right car and negotiate a suitable price, to say nothing of the displeasure of simply having to interact with the sales person.

A great deal of regulation can be traced to the transaction cost problem. Indeed, a case can be made that the transaction cost problem is at the heart of most market breakdowns. The cost of information, for example, is a transaction cost. Disclosure requirements about credit terms and the fuel mileage expected from a new car are designed to lower such costs. Licensing and certification requirements allow buyers to save the transaction costs associated with finding everything from a competent barber to a physician with the right specialty.

Even this understates the pervasiveness of the transaction cost problem. For example, suppose you would like to build a fence between your yard and that of your neighbor. You value the fence enough to pay to build the whole fence. On the other hand, you would prefer that your neighbor spend his own money to build the fence. You might hold off on actually buying the fence and, if your neighbor adopts the same strategy,

---

46. See Jeffrey L. Harrison, Class, Personality, Contract and Unconscionability, 35 William & Mary L. Rev. 445 (1994); Cass Sunstein, Legal Interference with Preferences, 53 U. Chicago L. Rev. 1129 (1986).

no fence will be built even though you both sufficiently value it. In technical terms, the fence creates positive externalities and the stand-off that occurs is called the "chicken game."[47] That is, building the fence creates benefits that are not fully captured by the person responsible for its creation. The person who does not give in but benefits from the efforts of another is free riding. One consequence of free riding is that the good or service in question may be produced at inefficiently low levels. Regulation is sometimes employed to address the problem by requiring all others to pay the first to act—as in patent and copyright laws—and sometimes the option chosen is for the government to produce the good or service in question—as in police and fire protection.

The other side of this problem arises when the producer of a good is not required to bear all the costs of its production, e.g., its production may give rise to "negative externalities." For example, imagine a night club that features loud music may lower property values in the surrounding neighborhood. In an unregulated market, the damage to the neighborhood is not likely to be a factor in determining the club's cover charge or the price of a beer. In effect, the costs of production incurred by the club will be less than the actual costs its presence creates. Some regulations may be designed to force such firms to "internalize" all the costs of production so the supply/marginal cost curve will more accurately reflect the resources consumed in production.

But perhaps the most critical transaction cost problem is establishing a regime in which allocative efficiency can be approached. To be more precise, the challenge is to get from a state of nature to one in which property rights are sufficiently defined so that parties will have a clear sense of who is buying and who is selling. Thus, some of the most important government action relates to "rationalizing" the market by setting up basic definitions of such things as the length of a "foot" or the acceptable dimensions of a "two by four" piece of lumber.

v.   Ideas of Social Justice

So far the discussion has focused on various forms of efficiency. Very often, however, the allocation of resources that an economist might regard as efficient leads to a distribution of income, wealth, or access to goods and services that does not seem fair or equitable.[48] This sense of fairness may be related to the widely held belief that money is subject to diminishing marginal utility. In other words, as a person has more money, the utility he or she derives from one more dollar may decline. You can visualize this by thinking about how much extra enjoyment Ross Perot or Bill Gates might get from one more dollar and compare

---

47. Charles Goetz, Cases and Materials on Law and Economics 29–32 (1984); Jeffrey L. Harrison, Law and Economic: Cases, Materials and Behavioral Perspectives 67–69 (2001).

48. It is important to separate economics from the economist as a person. Economics as a discipline has little to say about "fairness." Economists have feelings about these issue that are likely to be no different than your own.

that to the enjoyment or utility it might bring to a homeless person.[49] If money is indeed subject to diminishing marginal utility, utility may be increased by redistributing money from the relatively well-off to the relatively deprived, and some regulation seems designed to do exactly that.

Regulations that reduce what is sometimes called "destructive competition," or that allocate inherently scarce resources like broadcast frequencies, also have important distributive consequences. In addition some decisions regulating prices seem to promote cross-subsidization. That is, charging some buyers higher prices may enable the regulated firm to charge lower prices to others.

Beyond distributive goals, it is clear that some regulations have higher moral objectives. For example, the regulations protecting endangered species suggest that at some level we, as a society, are unwilling to reduce all things to monetary terms. Put another way, future generations cannot participate in the current economic marketplace, and regulation may act as a surrogate for their interests.[50] Regulations governing things that may not be sold at all also suggest a discomfort with traditional market-based notions of value. Some examples are prohibitions on selling one's right to vote, organs of the body, or oneself into slavery.[51]

2. THE PUBLIC ADMINISTRATION APPROACH TO REGULATION

The Public Administration approach to regulation and regulatory reform acknowledges—indeed typically asserts—that regulation is needed to address societal problems. It has a more technical objective, that of making government work more effectively.[52]

In an important sense, this has been the challenge assumed by administrative lawyers for several generations. The Administrative Procedure Act, for example, adopted in 1946, has had among its purposes and most significant accomplishments the regularizing of agency processes and the balancing of agency flexibility with the requirements of due process.[53]

---

49. You should note that there is no guarantee that one more dollar is less "valuable" to a wealthy person than it is to a poor person. Indeed the rich person may feel poor because he or she may not ever be able to accumulate "enough" money and the poor person may attribute little value to material things. Still, most non-economists make the assumption that the marginal utility of an additional dollar is less for a wealthy person than a poor person.

50. See Lawrence Tribe, Ways not to Think About Plastic Trees: New Foundations for Environmental Law, 83 Yale L.J. 1321 (1974); Cass R. Sunstein, Incommensurability and Valuation in Law, 92 Michigan L. Rev. 779 (1994).

51. See, e.g., Guido Calabresi and A. Douglas Melamed, Property Rules, Liability Rules, and Inalienability: One View of the Cathedral, 85 Harvard L. Rev. 1089 (1972).

52. See, e.g., Ian Ayres & John Braithwaite, Responsive Regulation: Transcending the Deregulation Debate (1992); Marc Allen Eisner, Regulatory Politics in Transition (1993). Compare William F. Pederson, Contracting with the Regulated for Better Regulations, 53 Ad. L. Rev. 1067 (2001) (bringing environmental regulations into contact with the regulated).

53. See, e.g., Final Report of the Attorney General's Committee on Administrative Procedure (1941); Report of the President's

a. The Call for Better Management

The idea that most regulatory programs are sound in theory but have been poorly managed or diverted from their original objectives was the message of a series of reports by the Senate Committee on Governmental Affairs,[54] and internal studies by major agencies under fire.[55] The Government in the Sunshine Act[56] was yet another product of this view. It did not eliminate regulation but tried to "reform" the agencies' practices and procedures.

b. The Call for Greater Flexibility

Indeed, early in the process of regulatory reform in the 1970s, the American Bar Association Commission on Law and the Economy examined such issues as procedural flexibility and sunset legislation in a similar vein of adjusting processes to improve results.[57] Similarly, then-Professor Stephen Breyer of Harvard called attention to the "mismatch" he often saw between an economic problem and the type of regulatory process used to address it.[58] Breyer was concerned, for example, about the use of cost-based ratemaking in the pricing of natural gas and establishment of motor carrier rates,[59] and he urged the adoption of incentive-based ways to control pollution.[60]

Periodically, one hears calls for a restoration of "common sense" in regulation, often in the form of a call for less "red tape" and increased discretion for administrative officials.[61] The goal of flexibility has lead to proposals that permit greater individualized interaction between regulatory agencies and regulated firms. For example, the Environmental Protection Agency is in the early stages of Project X. What is envisioned is the "customization" of regulations in order to achieve specified environmental goals.[62] Similar flexibility is found in proposals for negoti-

---

Committee on Administrative Management (1937).

54. The reports criticized, *inter alia,* the appointments process, the lack of Congressional oversight, delay in the regulatory process, and alleged conflicts-of-interest of officials. Study of Federal Regulation, Committee on Governmental Affairs, United States Senate, 95th Cong., 1st Sess. (1977).

55. E.g., Report of the Civil Aeronautics Board Advisory Committee on Procedural Reform (1975); Blue Ribbon Staff Study Panel Report (Interstate Commerce Commission (1975)). The CAB also received a proposal for more sweeping reforms, C.A.B. Special Staff, Regulatory Reform (1975).

56. Pub.Law No. 94 409, 90 Stat. 1241 (Sept. 13, 1976). 5 U.S.C. 552b.

57. American Bar Association Commission on Law and the Economy, Federal Regulation: Roads to Reform (1978).

58. Stephen Breyer, Regulation and Its Reform (1982).

59. Id. at Chapters 12 & 13. These ratemaking issues are addressed in Chapter 5 of these materials.

60. Id. at Chapter 14. A more contemporary analysis of the variety of better approaches to take to regulation is provided in Cass R. Sunstein, Congress, Constitutional Moments, and the Cost–Benefit State, 48 Stanford L. Rev. 247 (1996). Both the Breyer and Sunstein Public Administration approaches are usually substantively consistent with the Public Interest analysis discussed earlier.

61. See, e.g., Philip K. Howard, The Death of Common Sense: How the Law is Suffocating America (1994).

62. See Stephen M. Johnson, "Economics v. Equity: Do Market–Based Environmental Reforms Exacerbate Environmental Injustice?", 56 Wash. & Lee L. Rev. 111 (1999).

ated regulation. Again the idea is that regulatory goals may be achieved more efficiently if the package of regulation is the product of give and take between regulators and those regulated.[63]

c. *The Call for Cost–Benefit Analysis*

But the most enduring proposals in this area have been those urging that regulatory programs undergo a regular cost-benefit analysis. Arguing that proponents of regulation have heretofore stressed only its benefits, defenders of this position have tried to identify and evaluate the associated costs.[64] The approach has been bi-partisan. President Ford initiated the Economic Impact Statement Program[65] in 1976 to require an assessment of the relative costs and benefits of major federal regulations. President Carter continued the effort.[66] Less than a month after taking office, President Reagan issued Executive Order 12,291 which required the Office of Management and Budget to do such a cost benefit analysis of all "major rules,"[67] and President Clinton's version of the program is contained in Executive Order 12,866.[68] However, in spite of apparent unanimity about the desirability of not producing regulations that do more harm than good, no clear consensus has emerged about how the analysis should be done.[69]

3. THE PUBLIC CHOICE ANALYSIS OF REGULATION

Finally, Public Choice analysts tend to accept the economic theory of Public Interest analysis and often the motives of Public Administration analysts. But they believe both are naive. They argue that it is misleading to think in terms of a simple transition from shortcomings in market performance to appropriate regulatory steps that further the public

63. See Phillip J. Harter, "Negotiated Regulation: A Cure for Malaise." 71 Geo. L. Rev. 1 (1982).

64. See, e.g., Domestic Council Review Group, The Challenge of Regulatory Reform (1977); Paul W. MacAvoy, ed., OSHA Safety Regulation: Report of the Presidential Task Force (1977); Report, Civil Aeronautics Board Practice and Procedures, Subcommittee on Administrative Practice & Procedure, United States Senate, 94th Cong., 1st Sess. (1975); Charles L. Schultze, The Public Use of Private Interest (1977).

65. The program was a follow-on to the Inflation Impact Statement Program begun in 1974. See Miller, Lessons of the Economic Impact Statement Program, 1 Regulation 14 (July/Aug. 1977).

66. Executive Order 12,044, issued March 23, 1978. Upon President Carter's leaving office, two of his former advisers even proposed establishment of a "regulatory budget" designed to precisely regulate the amount of new regulatory burden that could be imposed on the nation each year.

See Robert Litan and William Nordhaus, Reforming Federal Regulation (1983).

67. 46 Fed.Reg. 13193 (Feb. 17, 1981), 3 C.F.R. 172 (1982). See also Executive Order 12,498, issued January 4, 1985.

68. Executive Order 12,866, 3 C.F.R. 638 (1994). See also statutes cited in notes 29–39, *supra*.

69. See, e.g., Robert W. Hahn & John A. Hird, The Costs and Benefits of Regulation: Review and Synthesis, 8 Yale J. Regulation 233 (1991); Kenneth J. Arrow, et al., Benefit–Cost Analysis in Environmental, Health, and Safety Regulation (1996) (a "statement of principles" by a group of distinguished economists urging use of the analysis, but also urging use of consistent methodology and consideration of distributional effects and other costs that are hard to quantify); Stephen F. Williams. Squaring the Vicious Circle, 53 Ad. L. Rev. 257 (2001) (extolling the virtues of cost-benefit analyses). We will look closely at the costs and benefits of using cost-benefit analysis in Chapter 5 of these materials.

interest. They argue that it is one thing to spot instances of "regulatory failure" and quite another to make the problem better instead of worse.[70]

People see the world through the eyes of self-interest, Public Choice analysts argue. It will be hard enough for even people of good will to agree on what kind and degree of regulation is in the public interest. And even if we were able to reach consensus on what kind of regulation is warranted to achieve desired goals, implementation decisions will themselves always be political.

a. *Government as an Alternative Marketplace*

In political contexts, individuals are said to be as likely to be interested in maximizing self interest as they are in traditional markets. In other words, they tend to make those choices that make themselves better off. Thus, economists looking at the world with these assumptions analyze strategies that may be employed in various voting contexts, explain decisions of regulatory,[71] judicial[72] and legislative[73] institutions, and even ask why citizens decide to vote at all.[74]

One of the first efforts to connect political and traditional markets is found in the pioneering work of Nobel Prize winner James Buchanan and his longtime colleague Gordon Tullock:

> Both the economic relation and the political relation represent co-operation on the part of two or more individuals. * * * Men co-operate through exchange of goods and services in organized markets, and such co-operation implies mutual gain. The individual enters into an exchange relationship in which he furthers his own interest by providing some product or service that is of direct benefit to the individual on the other side of the transaction. At base, political collective action under the individualistic view of the state is much the same. Two or more individuals find it mutually advantageous to join forces to accomplish certain common purposes. In a very real sense, they "exchange" inputs in the securing of the commonly shared output.[75]

Note the explanation by Buchanan and Tullock for the rise in the formation of "interest groups":

70. See, e.g., Barry M. Mitnick, The Political Economy of Regulation: Creating, Designing, and Removing Regulatory Forms (1980); Roger G. Noll & Bruce M. Owen, The Political Economy of Deregulation: Interest Groups in the Regulatory Process (1983); Robert J. Mackay, James C. Miller III & Bruce Yandle, Public Choice and Regulation: A View from Inside the Federal Trade Commission (1987).

71. See George Stigler, The Theory of Economic Regulation, 2 Bell J. Econ. & Management Sci. 3 (1971).

72. See, e.g., Frank Easterbrook, Ways of Criticizing the Court, 95 Harv. L. Rev. 802 (1982).

73. See, e.g., Robert D. Tollison, Public Choice and Legislation, 74 Va. L. Rev. 339 (1988).

74. The debate over the validity of this analysis can be intense. See, e.g., Geoffrey Brennan & James M. Buchanan, Is Public Choice Immoral? The Case for the "Nobel" Lie, 74 Va. L. Rev. 179 (1988); Mark Kelman, On Democracy–Bashing: A Skeptical Look at the Theoretical and "Empirical" Practice of the Public Choice Movement, 74 Va. L. Rev. 199 (1988).

75. James Buchanan & Gordon Tullock, The Calculus of Consent 19 (1962).

A hypothesis explaining the increasing importance of the pressure group over the last half of the century need not rest on the presumption of a decline in the public morality. A far simpler and much more acceptable hypothesis is that interest-group activity, measured in terms of organization costs, is a direct function of the "profits" expected from the political process by functional groups. In an era when the whole of government activity was sharply limited and when the activities that were collectivized exerted a general impact over substantially all individuals and groups, the relative absence of organized special interests is readily explainable. However, as the importance of the public sector has increased relative to the private sector, and as this expansion has taken the form of an increasingly differential or discriminatory impact in the separate and identifiable groups of the population, the increased investment of organization aimed at securing differential gains by political means is a predictable result.[76]

Richard Posner and William Landes put an even finer point on the matter:

In the economists' version of the interest-group theory of government, legislation is supplied to groups or coalitions that outbid rival seekers of favorable legislation. The price that the winning group bids is determined by both the value of the legislative protection to the group's members and the group's ability to overcome the free-rider problems that plague coalitions. Payments take the form of campaign contributions, votes, implicit promises of future favors, and sometimes outright bribes. In short, legislation is "sold" by the legislature and "bought" by the beneficiaries of the legislation.[77]

To some, this paints a fairly bleak picture of how the government makes decisions. To others it is simply the inevitable result of self-interested behavior. In any case, as one studies the failures of the market to produce the most desired outcome, it is important to understand that in our democratic system, even the definitions of what is a desired "outcome" and what the reaction to it should be are ultimately bound up in politics.

b. The Phenomenon of Regulatory Capture

Of course, one of the issues that arise when we view the regulatory official as just another rational maximizer is the danger of regulatory "capture." Capture occurs when the regulatory agency responds to the needs of the regulated industry as much or more than to the broad regulatory objectives that explain its creation. In its most extreme form, capture may allow firms in the industry to maximize their interests by use of regulation. Indeed, competing firms may be able to act as a cartel,

76. Id.

77. William Landes and Richard Posner, The Independent Judiciary in an Interest–

Group Perspective, 18 J. Law & Economics 875 (1975).

something both harmful to consumers and illegal but for the regulation that is adapted by the firms for their gain.

This is not to say that capture is always or even frequently the result of direct bribes.[78] Instead, industry officials may have disproportionate influence on the appointments to regulatory bodies. Furthermore, the agency may become dependent on the industry as a source of information and for cooperation in carrying out or observing the regulation. Finally, the industry may be in a better position to harness greater and more immediate pressure than scattered and poorly organized consumers. Indeed, one important area of research is that dealing with how the influences might be managed to lower the incidence and severity of capture.[79]

Groups with a particular incentive to use the political process to protect their interests are those affected by previous regulation. The regulatory process creates a very real "fly paper effect"; that is, the regulation of one activity creates a need to regulate all other kinds of activity whose inroads could upset the delicate regulatory structure. Thus, as we will see, the trucking industry has been regulated in large part to protect the railroads, and the cable television industry has been regulated largely to protect over-the-air broadcasters.[80]

c. *Problems Created by the Cost of Collective Action*

The idea that law-making and regulation can be approached in the same manner as market decisions extends much further than simply adopting the assumption of rational self-interest. The political market can be subject to many of the imperfections and misallocations that were discussed earlier in this chapter. For example, suppose ten large corporations are opposed to new regulations relating to work-place safety. Suppose also that several million people may be made better off by the regulation. The ten firms arguably will prevail. They will be able to bring all their pressure to bear on the regulatory body. For the several million to make their wishes known would require the dissemination of information and a costly organizational effort. Obviously, this is a problem of transaction costs.[81]

In fact, the market for political action may be even more susceptible to certain types of market failures. The problem is that there is a high

---

78. While the buying of legislators usually connotes campaign contributions and electoral support that is legal, on occasion the "buy" is direct. See Gamblers Bought off Louisiana Legislators, N.Y. Times, August 23, 1995 (Louisiana legislators charged in F.B.I. probe with selling video bingo franchises to local restaurants.)

79. See Ian Ayres & John Braithwaite, Responsive Regulation (1992).

80. George Stigler created a sophisticated theory of when firms will seek to be regulated and under what conditions they will be successful in The Theory of Econom-

ic Regulation, 2 Bell J. 3 (1971). Richard Posner critically developed this explanation in Theories of Economic Regulation, 5 Bell J. 335 (1974). See also, Shepherd, Entry as a Substitute for Regulation, 63 Am.Econ. Rev. (No. 2) 98 (1973). Sam Peltzman, Toward a More General Theory of Regulation, 19 J.L. & Econ. 211 (1976) and Gordon Tullock, The Transitional Gains Trap, 6 Bell J. 671 (1975).

81. One of the seminal works examining such problems is Mancur Olson, The Logic of Collective Action: Public Goods and the Theory of Groups (1965).

degree of interdependence in the political context. For example, one cannot simply spend his or her votes and get some amount of what is desired, like spending money for an ice cream sundae. Instead, a number of people typically will have to share the same preference in order for anything to happen at all. This necessity, though, raises severe problems of free-riding.

For example, you might favor a political candidate very heavily. Or the company you work for may oppose a regulation that would make it more costly to operate. In each case, it might make sense to take some action—perhaps just making a political contribution—to further the respective objectives. Of course, an even better outcome is to hope that others who are similarly situated will make sufficient contributions and that you or your firm will enjoy the result. As it turns out, the likelihood of free-riding probably increases with the number of interested parties. This is because free-riding can be compared to cheating and the likelihood of being caught is less as the number of parties increases. What this suggests is that moderately-funded small groups may be more politically influential than better funded larger groups.[82] But, the more important point is that the actual desire for the regulation may be understated.

One final, intriguing, and, perhaps, hopeful question to keep in mind when applying economic analysis to political decisions is whether people alter their preferences depending on the "market" involved. More specifically, do people become less self-interested or selfish when they make choices in political markets as opposed to traditional markets? For example, economist Kenneth Boulding has made the point that people vote consistently with general "values" but that their market transactions reflect more narrowly drawn "tastes."[83] Perhaps the same distinction can be made in the case of elected officials or members of regulatory agencies. Are these people primarily or exclusively driven by the desire to be reelected or reappointed, or can they make choices that benefit broader interests and even interests that jeopardize their position?

For your purposes, the importance of Public Choice analysis is to get you to focus on factors that might influence a regulatory decision. Ask yourself how you might vote on a specific issue and why? If you were a member of Congress, could you vote for a measure that is better for the country as a whole but that will damage your congressional district? If not, one might conclude that one variable in your utility function would be the desire to be reelected.

Also, as the member of a regulatory agency could you vote in a way that would be damaging to the firms in a particular industry—as well as

82. Kevin Grier, Michael Munger & Brian Roberts, PAC IT OR LEAVE IT: Concentration and Corporate Political Participation, Paper delivered at 1990 Meetings of the Public Choice Society.

83. Kenneth Boulding, Social Choice and Individual Values (1963). See also Ha-

rold Margolis, Selfishness, Altruism and Morality (1982); Jeffrey L. Harrison, Egoism, Altruism and Market Illusions: The Limits of Law and Economics, 33 UCLA L. Rev. 1309 (1986).

the attorneys and lobbyists for that industry whom you see every day and whose children play with your children at school—in hopes that your vote may benefit a broad impersonal public that is unlikely to even know your name?

As we go through the materials that follow, then, try to think about more than just the nature of the decision being made. Think of the process of coming to that decision and pressures that might have been brought to bear. How might these pressures affect a regulator's decision?[84]

D. TWO CONTEMPORARY ILLUSTRATIONS

As suggested already, regulation is pervasive (if not persuasive). In fact, by reading this book you have already identified yourself as someone who is likely to be directly affected by a special type of regulation. The next case and the materials that follow it are designed to introduce you to regulation in action and the variety of parties whose interests are at stake.

1. REGULATION AND YOUR FUTURE

AMENDMENTS TO RULES OF THE SUPREME COURT RELATING TO ADMISSIONS TO THE BAR

Supreme Court of Florida, 2003.
843 So.2d 245.

Lewis, J.

The Florida Board of Bar Examiners petitions this Court to consider amendments to the Rules of the Supreme Court Relating to Admissions to the Bar. We have jurisdiction. * * *

The Board has petitioned to amend or create these rules: * * * rule 4–26.2 * * *. [raising the passing score].

The proposed amendments were published in *The Florida Bar News* on January 15, 2000, with an invitation for comments. * * * For the reasons stated below, we * * * adopt the amendment to rule 4–26.2.

We have received comments and recommendations from many individuals and groups concerning the Board's suggested amendment to rule 4–26.2, including the deans of six Florida law schools; the Florida Chapter of the National Bar Association; the Florida State Conference of NAACP Branches; the George Edgecomb Bar Association; the Society of American Law Teachers; Testing For the Public; attorneys Kevin C. Frein, Harley Scott Herman, David W. Langham, Kimberly M. Reid, Henry T. Sorensen II, and Wilfred C. Varn; and Mr. Tom Swavely. Additionally, Board Member Noel G. Lawrence filed a "minority report."

---

84. For further reading, see Symposium Getting Past Cynicism: New Theories of the Regulatory State, 87 Cornell L. Rev. 267 (2002).

In the course of the life of any institution or professional organization with acknowledged mandatory evaluation for membership and minimum requirements for admission necessary to protect the citizens of Florida, the entity must pause and evaluate its participation prerequisites to ensure that the conditions operate to adequately protect the public and also work to fulfill the overall goals and aspirations of the organization or profession itself. Reexamination of this type is necessary and essential to avoid the possibility that apathy or passiveness take root and undermine the laudable goals of the organization by allowing unqualified applicants to be admitted, although posing unacceptable and unnecessary risks to society. Nowhere is this principle more important than in the process of examining the standards for admission to The Florida Bar and its testing and certification process.

The Florida Board of Bar Examiners, as the administrative arm of this Court charged with the task of establishing and maintaining responsible admissions requirements, *see* Fla. Bar Admiss. R. 1–14.2, has been delegated the important responsibility of safeguarding the interests of all Floridians. This serious responsibility stems from the recognized principle that an attorney licensed to practice law in this state is capable of both rendering tremendous good, but is also in a position to inflict harm if care and caution are not implemented. The members of The Florida Bar, by their very nature as attorneys, are licensed to become intimately involved in the lives and matters of clients, and anything less than exacting standards of admission exposes Floridians to unacceptable risks. Thus, before the Board can recommend to this Court that an applicant be admitted to the Bar, it must be confident that the person is qualified with regard to both character and fitness, and also possesses a certain minimum technical and educational competence. *See* Fla. Bar Admiss. R. 1–16.

In 1998, because it had been almost twenty years since the last inquiry toward any examination or adjustment of the pass/fail line had been considered or performed, the Board began to reevaluate the standards underlying the current pass/fail line of 131. The Board retained Dr. Stephen P. Klein, the preeminent national expert on the psychometric characteristics of bar examinations, to perform a comprehensive review of the bar examination pass/fail line. Based upon interaction with Dr. Klein, the Board conducted two independent studies to evaluate whether the bar examination score acceptable for admission should be increased, lowered, or remain the same.

In the first of two studies, Dr. Klein requested the actual graders of essay questions from the February and July 1999 Florida Bar examinations to assign passing scores to particular essay responses. These passing scores were then used to determine the acceptable passing level—the percentage of applicants attaining scores at or above the average of the graders' individual passing scores. When total bar exam scores for the February exam were scaled and placed along the spectrum of passing rates, Dr. Klein calculated that an average score of 133.5 would have been the proper passing rate. Application of the same criteria resulted in an average total scaled score of 141 for the July 1999 exam. These studies alerted the Board to and demonstrated problems with the current Florida standards.

The second study involved the implementation of six panels comprised of four to five members. Each panel included a Florida Circuit Judge, an associate dean or professor from a Florida law school, a Board of Bar Examiners member, and members of The Florida Bar engaged in the practice of law. After proper preparation, each panelist was given a set of forty exam answers and asked to place each answer in one of the following categories: clear fail, marginal fail, marginal pass, or clear pass. Upon analysis, the results of this grading and evaluation process resulted in the conclusion that average pass/fail lines of 139.5 for the July 1998 exam, and 135 for the February 1999 exam should be implemented. Indeed, the undoubtable final conclusion was that each of the panels clearly condemned the current pass/fail line. Clear evidence—in fact, *the only evidence* before this Court, persuasively reveals that the current 131 pass/fail line is unacceptable.

Based upon these studies, Dr. Klein reported to the Board that an averaging of each of the panels' standards resulted in a scaled score of 137. After months of study and following thorough discussion and consideration of the issue at its October 1999 meeting, the full Board voted twelve to two to recommend that this Court increase, through a two-stage process, the pass/fail line from the present 131 to 136. It is also interesting to note, however, that one of the Board members casting a vote against the proposed change from 131 to 136 did so because the member was of the opinion that 136 was not high enough to protect the public.

It is imperative to note multiple important facets of the process undertaken by the Board here. First, all of the institutions and actors in the current system of legal education and practice were represented in these studies. The interaction of these educators, judges, bar examiners, and attorneys produced a clear determination that the current standard does not reflect the level of competence which should be expected of a practicing attorney in Florida to adequately protect the public. Indeed, the studies produced an explicit call to elevate the standard for admission to the Bar in an attempt to protect the public from possible exposure to harm created by incompetent attorneys. Thus, the Board responded by urging this Court to increase the pass/fail line to a proper level, as demonstrated by the evaluations.

Second, the current pass/fail line of 131 does not have, and never has had, any empirical or justifiable relationship for its existence or to ensure minimum competence to practice law. Prior to 1961, an applicant was required to answer seventy percent of the questions correctly to achieve a passing score, and for the twenty years following the discontinuation of this method in 1961, the pass/fail line varied from one examination to the next because the pass/fail line was established by averaging the top ten scores on the exam and subtracting twenty points from this average score. In 1981, however, this Court changed the grading method to a scaled procedure, and adopted a pass/fail score of 133—a level not justified by any empirical studies or verifiable standards and without any qualitative foundation. * * * Then, without any explanation, this Court *sua sponte* reduced the pass/fail line from 133 to 131 in 1982. * * * Clearly, an examination of the lifeline of the Florida pass/fail score, as well as the studies commissioned by the Board highlight the utterly baseless nature of the current standard historically applied.[85] Additionally, each and every study underwritten by the Board reveals that the current Florida Bar admission standard does not adequately reflect the minimum skills required for the competent practice of law. This action does not encompass a debate over whether the current Florida bar exam format is the ideal tool for measuring attorney competence. Indeed, we are not opposed to considering additional testing methodologies and expanding the testing required for admission if such is advisable. In sum, we must accept for the purposes of today's decision that the bar exam format as it exists now is an accurate system of measuring competence, because we are not prepared to shift to a system of open admission without testing which would be the result of accepting the opposition's arguments. Criticism of the current testing method is inapposite and does not address the issue before us today. Therefore, there is absolutely no reason to grant admission to applicants who do not possess the body of knowledge necessary to adequately represent the citizens of Florida under the proper standards for the testing now administered. The bar exam is in place to protect Floridians from incompetent lawyers, and any disagreement over the actual composition of the test, which we are always open to consider, does not change the clear indication of Dr. Klein's studies: that the current pass/fail score for the examination must be raised.

The competent, verified empirical evidence compiled by Dr. Klein and the Board reveals that the current standard for admission has absolutely no relationship whatsoever to ensuring the minimum competency of those admitted to the Florida Bar. This Court acts today to rectify the situation. In essence, all of the credible data and conclusions presented to this Court by the Board illuminate that the present standard at this time is invalid and totally without foundation. It is nothing more than a number picked from the air. Because it is without validity, the people of Florida would be placed at risk if we fail to approve the higher standard. The situation presented to this Court is simple: While the studies performed by the Board working with experts and all segments of the Bar direct that we should raise the pass/fail line, there is

---

85. It is telling that under the current 131 pass/fail line, examinees only need to answer fifty-six percent of the total questions correctly to achieve a passing score. Indeed, increasing the standard to 136 would only require applicants to answer fifty-nine percent of questions correctly. Obviously, both of these standards fall far below the seventy percent correct answer rate required of applicants prior to 1961. Additionally, it is worth noting that thirty-three jurisdictions presently have higher pass/fail standards than Florida, and this state's 131 pass/fail line is even three points lower than the national average. [Court's fn. 3]

simply no rational, objective basis for leaving the admission score at its current low level.

It is certainly worth noting that the Board and Dr. Klein have thoroughly defended their studies against attack by opponents to the increase of the pass/fail standard, and repelled all criticism. Indeed, the law school deans, as opponents to the Board's pass/fail line recommendations, relied upon the critique of Dr. Klein's studies that Dr. Michael Kane provided to the Minnesota Board of Law Examiners in August 2000. However, it is more important to note that upon receiving Dr. Klein's response to his comments, Dr. Kane admitted and concluded that "the general approach taken in the 1997 study was appropriate. My objections are to the implementation." Thus, even an expert employed specifically to impeach Dr. Klein's methodology could not take issue with his techniques. Kane's only continuing objection to Dr. Klein's usual standard-setting method was to an asserted graders' lack of instruction on the proper setting of pass/fail standards, without a factual basis for such objection. Because the participants in Dr. Klein's Florida studies were in fact fully briefed and informed on the purposes and goals of the bar examination prior to their involvement, this complaint is of questionable validity at best. Indeed, in light of the final exchange between Drs. Klein and Kane, the points of criticism presented by Dr. Kane which caused Minnesota to delay the increase of its pass/fail standard are both entirely unpersuasive and not controlling here.

* * *

Hypothetical application of the proposed new passage score has made clear that increasing the pass/fail line would impact all applicants evenly, regardless of gender, race, or ethnicity. Indeed, despite many allegations of such, and our keen attention to the possibility of such, no data before this Court supports the contention that raising the pass/fail score will adversely impact minority applicants in a manner any different from other applicants. While it is acknowledged that certain current disparities between racial groups may remain, facts demonstrate to us that such are not a product of the examination or its scoring, and it must be clear to all that the key to diversity and equality in bar admissions is not to be accomplished by promoting unqualified persons to be certified competent contrary to evaluation—indeed, the hallmark of fairness and egalitarianism has always been a commitment to ensuring the recognition of all those who have proven their capabilities, regardless of ethnicity or background.

The record shows that the Board of Bar Examiners has continuously probed and evaluated the examination for testing bias, a practice that is to be commended and which must be continued in a manner forever vigilant. Indeed, we certainly acknowledge the concerns of those responding to our call for comments who urged this Court to examine the putative discriminatory effects of increasing the pass/fail line. We have exhaustively done so, and have found none. The contention that an increase in the pass/fail line will disproportionately adversely affect minority applicants is simply opinion contrary to present fact. The empirical studies contained in the record before this Court which project the impact of an increase in the admission standard have generated clear statistical data which refutes the claim that minorities will be disproportionately affected, and simply saying that minorities will be adversely affected does not serve to contradict this data in any cognizable fashion. The hypothetical application of the proposed new passing level to recent bar examinations presents facts to us which demonstrate beyond dispute that the only people disadvantaged by an increase in the pass/fail line would be those who are not qualified to become practicing members of The Florida Bar in the first place, which crosses all populations equally, and there is no evidence of disparate gender, racial, or ethnic impact.[86]

If the opponents to the Board's proposal could, in some fashion, factually demonstrate that the bar examination is a discriminatory tool, then this Court would certainly be required to address the problem and take corrective action. Indeed, the Court should give, and has given, serious consideration to the comments of the Board's opponents here, and must continue to determine whether future bar examination results, without regard to any particular passage line, reflect any possible bias or unfairness to any group. However, there is absolutely no evidence before this Court showing that the proposed bar examination scheme would discriminate in its purpose or application against any group. The only discrimination occurring here is that which should occur—differentiation between those candidates qualified to serve the public and those who do not possess the minimum competence to practice law, so that we may fulfill our obligations to the citizens of this state.

Based upon the foregoing, we conclude that the Board's justifications for the proposed amendments are sound and adopt them as reflected in the appendix to this opinion. As noted in the appendix, the amendments to rule 4–26.2 shall occur in the two-stage process advocated by the Board. The pass/fail line is increased to 133 effective July 1, 2003, and raised further to 136 on July 1, 2004. * * *

It is so ordered.

* * *

PARIENTE, J., concurring in part and dissenting in part.

I concur with much of the majority opinion, and echo its commendation of the Florida Board of Bar Examiners ("Board") for its ongoing efforts to ensure the competency of attorneys that we admit into The Florida Bar. I agree with the amendments to all of the proposed rules except for rule 4–26.2 regarding raising the passing score. I support the

---

86. Indeed, an examination of the predicted results reveals that an increase in the pass/fail line would result in a higher percentage of the black University of Miami law students passing the bar examination than their white classmates (133 pass/fail line: white—80% passage, black—89% passage; 136 pass/fail line: white—70% pas- sage; black—78% passage), and a higher percentage of the Hispanic graduates of Florida State University College of Law passing the bar examination than white FSU examinees (133 pass/fail line: white—84% passage, Hispanic—91% passage; 136 pass/fail line: white—80% passage; Hispanic—91% passage). [Court's fn. 4]

important work of the Board in ensuring that attorneys licensed in this State demonstrate competence upon their initial entry to practice, as well as the important work of The Florida Bar, which provides the continuing education and monitoring of *all* attorneys necessary to ensure the high quality of an increasingly diverse Bar.

I certainly agree with the majority that the Board has "the important responsibility of safeguarding the interests of all Floridians," and I am certain that the Board's intent is to improve the quality of those attorneys licensed in this State. When all is said and done, however, the buck stops with this Court. With all due respect for the views of my colleagues, I disagree with the majority's statement that without raising the pass/fail score of the Bar examination, "the people of the State of Florida would be placed at risk." Accordingly, I write separately to express my serious reservations about the necessity of raising the passing score from 131 to 136 at this time.

My concerns are threefold. First, there is no indication that increasing the score to 136 will lead to higher attorney performance or proficiency. Correspondingly, there is no indication that the current passing score is not an appropriate passing score to ensure minimum qualifications.

Second, I am concerned that we are placing too much reliance on the 1999 studies performed by Dr. Klein, the expert hired by the Board, as the justification for setting a new and significantly higher passing score. Commentators have observed that the Klein methodology has a "fundamental flaw that produces an arbitrary passing score" in that it confuses the percentage of passing essays with the percentage of passing test takers. *See* Deborah J. Merritt et al., Raising the Bar: A Social Science Critique of Recent Increases to Passing Scores on the Bar Exam, 69 U. Cin. L.Rev. 929, 931, 950–65 (2001). Recently, after the Minnesota Board of Law Examiners received a critique by another expert of a study done by Dr. Klein, the Minnesota Board withdrew its recommendation to the Minnesota Supreme Court to raise the passing score. Although I would not want to make this a battle of the experts, the fact that other experts have called into question aspects of the Klein study suggests to me an additional reason to proceed cautiously before raising the passing score.

Third, like many of those who filed comments opposing an increase in the pass rate, including Board Member Noel G. Lawrence, the Society of American Law Teachers, the Florida Chapter of the National Bar Association, the George Edgecomb Bar Association, and six Florida law school deans, I am very concerned about the potential adverse effect this change could have on minorities. Indeed, it is not clear what effect an increased passing score will have upon varying minority groups, nor is it clear how this will affect racial disparities in the passing scores. In this regard, I cannot agree that the majority's hypothetical application of the new standards to examination results by test-takers from only two of the state's law schools demonstrates that the increase will have no adverse racial impact. * * * Confining results to examinees from individual law schools creates an unreliably small sample size.

In fact, applying the new standards to statewide results from the February 2000 and July 2000 examinations would have increased the already existing disparity in the pass rates between minority first-time test takers and all first-time test takers generally. On the February 2000 examination, minority pass rates for first-time test takers would have declined by 10 percent at a score of 133 and by 16 percent at a score of 136, compared to declines of 5 and 13 percent for all first-time test-takers. On the July 2000 examination, minority pass rates for first-time test takers would have declined by 5 and 12 percent at the new passing scores, compared to 4 and 10 percent declines for all first-time test takers. Even at a passing score of 131, first-time minority test-takers passed these examinations at much lower percentages than all first-time test takers, 58 to 71 percent on the February 2000 examination and 68 to 79 percent on the July 2000 examination. Combined results for first-time test takers in the two examinations administered in 2001 reflect greater declines for black first-time test takers than for whites. The pass rate for blacks would have declined by 6 percent at a passing score of 133 and 14 percent at a passing score of 136, compared to a 4 percent decline at a score of 133 and a 11 percent decline at a score of 136 for white test-takers.

As stated in the law review article cited above,

[T]here is substantial reason to fear that raising bar passing scores will, in fact, have a disproportionate impact on minority members. In general, increased passing scores on the bar exam affect minority applicants more than white ones. In other words, the gap in passing rates between minority and white applicants is likely to grow as passing scores go up and passing rates fall. As Klein himself has recognized, "[t]he size of the difference in bar passage rates between whites and minority applicants depends on several factors," and one of these factors is "the relative stringency of the state's pass/fail standard." In particular, "[s]tates that have relatively high passing rates tend to have smaller differences among groups than other states (because all groups have high rates when standards are low)." As a general matter, therefore, raising the bar passing score (and decreasing the passing rate) is likely to *increase* the gap between whites' and minorities' success rates.

Merritt et al., *supra,* at 966–67 (footnotes omitted). The authors conclude that an increase in the passing score will extend existing discrepancies, a result which is contrary to public policy at a time when the profession has embraced the need for diversity. *Id.* at 967.

In sum:

The basic issue is the choice of an appropriate passing score. Raising the passing score is very likely to increase failure rates and to have some adverse impact on groups with relatively lower scores. *If the change is necessary in order to ensure that new lawyers are minimal-*

ly qualified, the change seems justified. If the change is not necessary, it does not seem justified.

Michael T. Kane, Review of the Standard-setting Study of the July 1997 Minnesota Bar Exam 25 (August 2000) (emphasis supplied). I see no indication that changing the passing score from 131 to 136 is necessary to ensure that new lawyers are minimally qualified. Thus, I dissent from the raising of the passing score at this time and urge that this matter be returned to the current Board for further review, including a determination as to whether the current Bar examination testing procedures in fact measure the skills necessary to competently and professionally represent the citizens of this State.

[Justice Pariente's dissent was joined by Justices Quince and Shaw.]

Notes and Questions

1. Entry regulation is one of the most traditional forms of regulation. How does regulating entry into the practice of law protect the citizens of Florida? What would happen if everyone who were so inclined could hold themselves out as "practicing law?" How might an economist explain these events?

2. Could consumers find out which people claiming to practice law actually know what they are doing and which ones do not? Might this happen through the use of private certification and rating services? For example, a person wishing to practice law might take an exam administered by a private business. If he or she earned a passing score, a certificate indicating that the applicant was "qualified" could be displayed. In addition, periodically a process something like that used by *Consumer Reports* could be employed to rank attorneys. Is the current system superior to such private rating? Might your answer depend on whether a given client is well-educated and experienced in using the private rating system?

3. If consumers are protected by knowing that you received at least a passing score on the bar examination, would the protection be even greater if you were required to disclose your actual bar exam score in any materials that draw attention to your services? Or how about your grades in law school?

4. The practice of law is an instance of "self-regulation" in which the persons already in the profession play a big role in determining who can join them. Do you see any problems this system might create?

5. The deans of the law school in Florida opposed raising the bar exam passing score to 136. Why might this be? Do you think they have an insight that a score of 131 is high enough to protect the citizens of Florida? Might requiring a higher score have an impact on law school applications? Do law school deans have an interest in keeping law school applications high?

6. Both opinions discuss the impact on identifiable groups of raising the passing score. Suppose it were determined that raising the passing score increased the median intellectual quality of lawyers. Should that result be balanced against the impact of the higher score on the admission of particular applicants or on the availability of services to particular groups of clients?

Even if you wanted to strike such a balance, how could you realistically do so?

7.   Usually when something goes wrong with a service that is purchased in the market, we rely on contract law and tort law for the remedy. For example, a person purporting to practice law or medicine who blunders could be held liable in a private action. And, many times they are. Why not eliminate entry regulation for the professions and allow tort and contract to be the exclusive regulatory tools?

8.   Alternatively why not leave the accrediting function to law schools alone (assuming they are accredited by the state bar associations)? Does raising the bar examination score indicate a lack of confidence in law schools?

Are law schools more susceptible to lobbying (i.e. readmission, grades, etc.) behavior than the bar examiners? See generally, Stewert E. Sterk, Information, Production and Rent Seeking in Law School Administration, 83 B.U. L. Rev. 1141 (2003).

2.   A CONTEMPORARY POLICY CHOICE

Our final introductory illustration concerns another form of transportation—taxicabs. Taxis are of course the modern successors to the "hacks" that Munn v. Illinois noted had been regulated since "time immemorial" in England. In the 1930s taxis in major cities became the subject of rate, entry and exit regulation. In the depression years few cities were impressed by the fact that taxis are a classic example of competitive entities (small units of supply, no significant economies of scale, and so forth).[88] But even though little can be said for continued regulation, few cities have been able to dislodge the regime.[89] The reason is instructive: the complex problems of reordering interests of the affected taxi medallion owners produces regulatory inertia.

In a competitive market, of course, the value of a medallion would be close to zero since it would make no sense to pay a premium to enter a market where all you can earn are your marginal costs (which include a reasonable profit). But consider the following description of the New York City medallion situation written in 1970:

> In New York City, for example, the municipal government regulates taxi rates and, in addition, requires that a medallion exist for each taxicab operating within the city limits. The medallion system originated in the 1930's when all persons then operating taxis within the city were offered medallions at the nominal price of $10. Despite a large number of requests for the issuance of new medallions, no additional medallions have been issued; and, in fact, 1,794 of the original 13,566 medallions which were turned in to the city during World War II by owners going into the service have not

88.   See Paul R. Verkuil, The Economic Regulation of Taxicabs, 24 Rutgers L. Rev. 672 (1970).

89.   For another account of regulation of taxicabs, see Edmund Kitch, Marc Isaacson & Daniel Kasper, The Regulation of Taxicabs, 14 J. L. & Econ. 285 (1971).

been reissued. The result has been that, despite the increased demand for taxi service that increasing population and affluence and the need for greater mobility have generated, the number of cabs available to provide taxi service is actually less than it was in 1937. The artificial restriction on output resulting from holding supply constant in the face of increased demand tends both to make the availability of taxi service unnecessarily scarce and to push rates to artificially high levels—the consequence of each being the underutilization of taxi potential. Medallions are transferable, and the prices at which they are traded provide an indication of the magnitude of the costs in terms of resource misallocation that are associated with the artificial rate structure and barriers to entry which the medallion system implements. Thus, there are presently 11,722 outstanding taxicab medallions, and hence taxicabs, in New York City. On the open market they are presently valued at approximately $22,000 each. The value of a medallion results from its power to permit entry into the taxicab business. If that business were competitive (i.e., if costs of operation, including a reasonable return on investment, were roughly equal to revenues that could be earned), such a right to enter would be worth little, if anything. The value of a medallion consequently depends on the extent to which the industry is noncompetitive—the extent to which the cost of the medallion can be recovered by monopoly profits earned after entry.

Accordingly, the aggregate value of medallions—currently in excess of a quarter of a billion dollars in New York City—represents the free market's estimation of the capitalized value of the annual monopoly profits of the taxi industry. If a 12 percent rate of return figure is used in capitalizing the value of annual monopoly profits, the New York City taxi industry as a whole earns over $40 million of monopoly profits a year.

The $40 million figure itself may substantially understate the costs to New York City of its taxicab medallion system. The $40 million represents the artificially high earnings of taxi companies and the artificially high payments by taxicab users. The extent to which the artificially high rates that such earnings and payments reflect involve an inefficient allocation of resources depends on the extent to which such high rates restrict taxicab use—that is, upon the price elasticity of taxi usage (although even in the absence of any restriction on output, the monopoly profits would be undesirable in themselves since without apparent justification they substantially redistribute wealth from taxi riders to taxi owners). No precise measurement can be made of the extent to which taxi usage is so restricted.[90]

Now fast-forward 35 years since that article was written. Medallions have increased in value to about $225,000 each. In fact, in the past 70 years the value of medallions has increased by an average of 13% per

90. Paul R. Verkuil, supra note 88, at 676–77.

year, this outpacing the Dow Jones Industrial Average.[91] If you think about it, this increase reflects far more than simply limiting the number of medallions. As an economic matter, when prices are high people search for substitutes. If passengers could substitute away from taxis, one would expect the value of medallions to level off or even fall. The steady increase in the value of medallions also indicates that the supply of livery car services, limousines and gypsy cabs has been effectively controlled.

Recently, the City proposed a plan to increase the number of medallions by 900 over a three year period. This was coupled with a fare increase to make the proposal more palatable to current medallion holders, although it remains to be seen what type of increase will be satisfactory to incumbents. The idea, obviously, is to "compensate" current medallion owners for any loss suffered as a result of the increase.[92] The first hurdle was an examination of the impact on traffic and air quality before the proposed increase passed. Next are public hearings.

This may all seem a bit strange to you. In an unregulated market one would expect an increase in supply to lead to lower prices. Here, the City of New York seems to want to couple an increase in supply with an increase in prices. In effect, passengers may be both better and worse off: better off because if the increased number of taxis and worse off because the prices will be higher. Put differently, the plan seems to be one that will generally benefit the more affluent passengers while perhaps pricing others out of the market. Does this result suggest to you that the plan does not amount to deregulation at all?

But if you think the current proposal is likely to be adopted smoothly without a significant fare increase, this short introduction to the taxi cab skirmishes of New York may change your mind.

91. "Medallion Reports Update on Chicago and New York City Taxi Auctions," PR Newswire, January 8, 2004.

92. Remember that in the *Charles River Bridge* case Harvard had been compensated for the loss of its ferry franchise when The Bridge Company devalued its monopoly. See Charles River Bridge v. Warren Bridge, 36 U.S. 420, and Section A, supra. See also United States v. Winstar Corporation in Chapter 4 of these materials. Compensation of those who stand to lose by a transition to a competitive economy is a technique that has worked in Latin America and Great Britain when those countries shifted from state-run to privately-controlled companies. By letting employees of the public enterprises share generously in the stock of the newly-created private firms, opposition to the transition was significantly reduced. See David R. Henderson, Privatization Logic: Divide the Spoils and Conquer the Opposition, Wall Street J., Sept. 13, 1996, at A–11. Could this approach be adapted to the taxicab situation?

METROPOLITAN TAXICAB BOARD OF TRADE, INC. v. CITY OF NEW YORK

First Judicial Department
Supreme Court, New York County
New York Law Journal,
July 6, 1998.

JUSTICE OMANSKY

Petitioners in these two Article 78 proceedings challenge a new rule, adopted as an emergency measure on May 14, 1998 by the New York City Taxi & Limousine Commission ("TLC") permitting vehicles other than licensed medallion taxicabs to pick up passengers in Manhattan on a "hail" basis, and service LaGuardia and Kennedy Airports, on the grounds that the emergency rule contravenes the laws of the City of New York, violates provisions of the State and City environmental laws, and violates the constitutional right of individual taxi drivers to petition government peacefully for a redress of their grievances and their constitutional rights of free speech. Petitioners in Index No. 108814/98 include a trade association of companies owning and/or operating yellow medallion taxicabs, an individual company owning or operating yellow medallion taxicabs, a driver of a medallion taxicab and a resident of Manhattan. Petitioner in Index No. 108902/98 is an unincorporated association of companies managing medallion taxicabs on behalf of the medallion owners. The two proceedings are consolidated for purposes of disposition.

This court granted a temporary restraining order staying the effect of the new rule. The stay was automatically vacated when the City respondents filed a notice of appeal, and was then reinstated by an Appellate Division Justice, with leave to the City to reinvoke the new rule provided the TLC made a finding, based on objective criteria, that a general and significant work stoppage by the medallion cab drivers is imminent. The amended finding of an emergency made by the TLC is not before this court. The new rule, the subject matter of these proceedings, is currently in effect.

FACTS

On or about April 30, 1998, the TLC announced a series of new proposed regulations and guidelines applicable to drivers and owners of taxicabs. The proposed new regulations included, among other things, tougher new driving standards, higher fines, a more stringent point system than required by State regulations, and higher levels of insurance.

On Wednesday, May 13, 1998 approximately 95 percent of all medallion taxicab drivers engaged in a peaceful work stoppage—they stayed home and did not drive their vehicles. As a result of that work stoppage, taxicabs were virtually unavailable within the City. The TLC received reports from the taxicab industry threatening additional work stoppages to protest the proposed new regulations which were expected to be considered at a meeting of the TLC Commissioners on May 28, 1998.

On May 13, 1998 the day of the work stoppage, five members of the TLC present for an emergency meeting, including Chairperson Diane

McGrath–McKechnie, voted 5–0 to authorize the Chair to take emergency action to address the need for service caused by the work stoppage by taxicab drivers. * * *

On May 14, 1998, counsel for the TLC, in consultation with the Office of the Corporation Counsel, drafted an emergency rule, deemed effective as of May 13, 1998, designated New Rule 14 "Alternative Modes of Service." New Rule 14 was premised on a "finding" of an emergency, a "threat to a necessary public service." The finding of an emergency made by Mayor Giuliani and Chairperson McKechnie and signed on May 14, 1998 stated:

> Open violations of the laws and regulations of the City of New York by owners and/or drivers of medallion taxicabs licensed by the Commission are creating an imminent threat to the delivery of a necessary service in the City of New York. This situation is most severe at Kennedy and LaGuardia Airports, where there are limited alternative modes of transportation available, and multitudes of passengers unfamiliar with the City and its transportation systems rely on the services of taxicab drivers to travel from the airport to their destination. The actions of the taxicab owners and/or drivers, and the consequent difficulty presented to passengers, create the potential for unsafe crowd conditions to develop at the airports. In addition, further disruption of services is threatened by the medallion taxicab industry.

In New Rule 14, Respondent McGrath–McKechnie authorized for-hire vehicles licensed by the TLC ("for hires"), commuter vans licensed by the TLC and minibus service vans operating pursuant to a grant of authority by the Franchise and Concession Review Committee (collectively "vans") to pick up and discharge passengers at LaGuardia and Kennedy Airports, without regard to pre-arrangement, for destinations in Manhattan, and to pick up passengers in the Borough of Manhattan for destinations anywhere within that Borough or to the two airports.

At the time the New Rule 14 was passed a comprehensive scheme regulating the activities of taxicabs and other vehicles for hire in New York City existed, as enacted by the City Council. The New York City Administrative Code ("Administrative Code") permitted only licensed yellow medallion taxicabs "to accept hails from passengers in the street" (Title 19, Admin. Code, Sec. 19–502[1]). Taxicabs are defined as TLC-licensed vehicles designed to carry a maximum of five passengers, Admin. Code Sec. 19–502(1). Each taxicab is issued a metal plate, known as a medallion, reflecting its licensure by TLC, Admin. Code Sec. 19–502(h). The number of extant medallions is limited, Admin. Code Sec. 19–504(I).

* * *

DISCUSSION

* * *

There are 12,187 yellow medallion taxicabs that cruise the streets picking up and discharging passengers. New Rule 14 will add 30,000 vehicles to this number, and the amount of additional air pollution caused by the 30,000 additional cruising vehicles is incalculable. In the past, the City Council considered that increasing the number of taxicabs required environmental impact review. Thus, in 1987 when Local Law 14 was adopted amending the Administrative Code to allow the TLC to issue an additional 1,800 taxicab medallions, the City Council required the TLC to prepare a draft environmental impact statement before it could issue any additional licenses. The City Council further provided in Sec. 19–504 of the Administrative Code that in conducting the environmental impact statement, the TLC must, among other issues, consider:

"(a) the need for the city to comply with the state implementation plan promulgated pursuant to the federal clean air act, taking into account the number of taxicab licenses currently authorized and such licenses as may be issued pursuant to this section" Id. Sec. 19–504(c).

In 1996, when Local Law No. 28 was enacted repealing Local Law 14, the EIS prepared pursuant to that law "determined that no more than four hundred medallions could be issued without adversely affecting the environment."

There is no evidence whatsoever that the TLC considered * * * or determined whether its adoption of New Rule 14 would require environmental review. This failure constitutes a clear violation of those laws and requires invalidation of the rule (see, E.F.S. Ventures Corp. v. Foster, 71 NY2d 359, 371 [1988]).

Respondents argue that temporary emergency measures, such as Rule 14, are exempt from environmental review under state and local law. The * * * regulations explicitly exempt from environmental review those actions which are "immediately necessary on a limited emergency basis for the preservation and protection of life, health, property or natural resources." 6 NYCRR 517, 2(o)(6); see also 43 RCNY Sec. 04(h). * * * Although we have not addressed the qualitative sufficiency of the original finding of an emergency because of the ruling by the Appellate Division Justice, it is fair to say that crowd conditions at airports do not require immediate emergency action in order to preserve and protect life, health, property or natural resources. Concerns about crowd conditions are not on the same level as emergencies created by prisoner overcrowding which the City sought to alleviate by housing prisoners on a barge, which action was exempt from SEQRA requirements (see, Silver v. Koch, 137 AD2d 467 [1st Dept. 1988]) or the State Thruway Authority's decision to detour traffic where traffic problems created by existing detours contributed to two fatal accidents (see, New York State Thruway Authority v. Dufel, 129 AD2d 44, 47 [3d Dept. 1987]). Accordingly, the TLC's action in adopting new Rule 14 was not exempt from environmental review because of an emergency situation.

On May 14, 1998, the day Respondents Giuliani and McGrath–McKechnie made their "finding" of an emergency, Respondent Giuliani was quoted in the press as saying that he "would allow vans and livery cars to pick up passengers off the street . . . unless yellow cab drivers cancel plans to hold another demonstration next week." As reported in the New York Times article of May 15, 1998:

> Mr. Giuliani said that even if the drivers call off their plans for a second job action on Thursday, he still planned to use the strike as an opening to try to break the yellow cabs' 61–year monopoly on "street hails"—the ability to pick up passengers at the curb in the five boroughs.

> "They are presenting us with opportunities that I'm more than happy to take advantage of, which the city has not been able to take advantage of for the last 20 to 30 years, to introduce a lot more competition into their industry," the Mayor said at a news conference in midtown Manhattan.

Respondents' answer did not deny that these statements were made.

It is clear that respondents enacted New Rule 14 to retaliate for the taxicab drivers' peaceful work stoppage and protest of May 13, 1998, and to deter them from engaging in further peaceful protest in violation of their constitutional rights (see, McQueen v. Druker, 438 F.2d 781, 785 [1st Cir. 1971]). In upholding the taxi drivers' First Amendment rights to protest by motorcade, Federal Judge Patterson held:

> "Plaintiffs' right to express their disagreement with a proposed amendment in the regulations governing cab drivers in the City of New York is a fundamental right in this country grounded in the First Amendment of the United States Constitution. Accordingly, any abridgement of that right does constitute irreparable harm to those whose rights are thus affected."

United Yellow Cab Drivers Ass'n, Inc. v. Safir, 98 Civ. 3670 at 4 (S.D.N.Y. May 27, 1998, aff'd Dkt. No. 98–7737 [2d Cir. May 27, 1998] [1998 WL 274295].

In this case, the drivers' right to protest by staying home was punished by the adoption of New Rule 14 which adversely affects their livelihood. If there were a compelling state interest in providing taxicab service at the airports, it could easily have been accomplished by narrowly drafting the rule to meet the so-called emergency * * * namely to permit for hires and vans to service the airports without pre-arrangement for each day of the work stoppage, as TLC Commissioners Arout and Torres thought they were authorizing. Instead, respondents used the occasion of the work stoppage to implement the Mayor's personal plan to "break the yellow cabs' 61–year monopoly on street hails."

If New Rule 14 were not being set aside on other grounds, injunctive relief would be appropriate to prevent existing or threatened injuries to the drivers' constitutional rights (see, United Yellow Cab Drivers Ass'n,

Inc. v. Safir, supra; Farmland Dairies v. McGuire, 789 F.Supp. 1243, 1250 (S.D.N.Y. [1992]).

Accordingly, the petitions are granted, and New Rule 14 is set aside and vacated.

Notes and Questions

1. Sometimes you may have the feeling that economic regulation is about stuffy people coldly talking about efficiency and other refined economic concepts. In fact this book is about things that affect everyday people in all facets of their lives. Look at Mayor Giuliani's comments. Is this closer to a board meeting or a white collar fist fight?

2. Consider very closely the political nature of regulation. Mayors want to be reelected. More taxis and lower fares would do a great deal to please voters. On the other hand, if the cab drivers walk off the job, who do you think may ultimately be blamed? Eventually voters may ask, "Where was the mayor? Why can't he get along with the cab drivers?"

3. Most of the time, efforts to deregulate will not spill into the streets as they almost did in the case. Still, as you go through these materials, do not underestimate the power of inertia. People who favor the status quo often have superior access to information and an understanding of how to frame the issues to their advantage. The process of regulating an unregulated business or of deregulating a regulated one is almost always an uphill battle.

4. One question raised by the taxi medallion fight is the property interest in the medallion itself. Could the taxi owners prevent the addition of new cabs or medallions by asserting their rights against devaluation of the extremely valuable medallions?[93] Remember both that Harvard College got compensated for devaluation of its ferry monopoly by Charles River Bridge and how it received that compensation.

5. Medallion Financial Corporation is a publically traded company in New York that specializes in loaning money to buyers of taxi licenses in New York and other cities (and also buys fleet medallions for its own account). It is the belief of Medallion Financials' CEO that the issuance of 900 new medallions over three years, coupled with a significant rate increase, will actually create new demand for medallions. They plan to bid on 500 medallions outright. See A Lender Hopes to Profit from the New Taxi Math, New York Times, Jan. 25, 2004, at B8. The optimism was fueled by the way medallion prices rebounded after the sale of 400 medallions in 1996 and 1997. Can you continue to count on the market absorbing new medallions without limit? At what point does opening up the market approximate the level of competitive demand?

6. If you were the taxi cab Czar how would you solve the problem in New York? Think about your answer now and revisit it when the course is over to see if it changes.

---

93. See United States v. Turoff, 701 F.Supp. 981, 990 (E.D.N.Y. 1988) (holding for purposes of the mail fraud statute that taxi medallions are property and citing Charles Reich, The New Property, 73 Yale L.J. 733 (1964) for support).

Chapter 2

EVOLVING CONSTITUTIONAL LIMITS ON REGULATION

The Constitution has been a potential check on regulation since the early days of the Republic. The *Charles River Bridge* case, which we examined at the beginning of Chapter 1, used the Contracts Clause of the Constitution to challenge state repudiation of private franchise monopolies. And a century later, we saw Munn v. Illinois evaluate the constitutionality of state regulation under both the commerce clause and the 14th Amendment.

Beginning in the mid–1930s, the Constitution imposed no significant practical limitations on the imposition of economic regulation by Congress, the administrative agencies, or the states. However, during the 1990s, we witnessed significant changes in the constitutional review of economic regulation.

This chapter begins with a case illustrating—indeed initiating—the relative permissiveness toward regulation that prevailed for over 50 years. Other cases then provide examples of limitations on regulation that seem once again to be emerging from various provisions of the Constitution.

A. SUBSTANTIVE DUE PROCESS AND STATE REGULATION

In the early years of the 20th Century, the "affected with a public interest" standard employed by Munn v. Illinois to determine when an industry or practice could constitutionally be the subject of regulation was severely tested.

In Lochner v. New York, 198 U.S. 45, 25 S.Ct. 539, 49 L.Ed. 937 (1905), for example, the Supreme Court reasoned that a 60–hour limit on the hours a baker could work each week unconstitutionally interfered with the baker's freedom of contract. "The employee may desire to earn the extra money which would arise from his working more than the prescribed time," the Court said, "but this statute forbids the employer from permitting the employee to earn it." In famous dissents, Justices Holmes and Harlan pointed out that regulation frequently impaired personal freedom and that striking the proper balance between freedom of contract and public health was one of the essential functions of government.

In Adkins v. Children's Hospital, 261 U.S. 525, 43 S.Ct. 394, 67 L.Ed. 785 (1923), the Court struck down regulation of minimum wages of women and children. And in Williams v. Standard Oil Co., 278 U.S. 235, 49 S.Ct. 115, 73 L.Ed. 287 (1929), the Court held that even the sale of gasoline was not sufficiently "affected with a public interest" to warrant price regulation. While gasoline was "necessary and indispensable" for drivers in Tennessee, the industry had not been "devoted to a public use" and thus rendered subject to regulatory control.

It was in the context of these decisions and many others like them, that our first case offered a dramatic counterpoint. [1]

NEBBIA v. NEW YORK

United States Supreme Court, 1934.
291 U.S. 502, 54 S.Ct. 505, 78 L.Ed. 940.

MR. JUSTICE ROBERTS delivered the opinion of the Court.

The Legislature of New York established by chapter 158 of the Laws of 1933, a Milk Control Board with power, among other things to 'fix minimum and maximum * * * retail prices to be charged by * * * stores to consumers for consumption off the premises where sold.' The board fixed nine cents as the price to be charged by a store for a quart of milk. Nebbia, the proprietor of a grocery store in Rochester, sold two quarts and a 5–cent loaf of bread for 18 cents; and was convicted for violating the board's order. * * *

The question for decision is whether the Federal Constitution prohibits a state from so fixing the selling price of milk. * * *

During 1932 the prices received by farmers for milk were much below the cost of production. The decline in prices during 1931 and 1932 was much greater than that of prices generally. * * *

Milk is an essential item of diet. It cannot long be stored. It is an excellent medium for growth of bacteria. These facts necessitate safeguards in its production and handling for human consumption which greatly increase the cost of the business. Failure of producers to receive a reasonable return for their labor and investment over an extended period threaten a relaxation of vigilance against contamination.

---

1. While *Nebbia* reversed the Court's inclination to read the "affected with a public interest" standard narrowly, it was not the famous "switch in time" case that Justice Roberts is known for. That case was West Coast Hotel Co. v. Parrish, 300 U.S. 379, 57 S.Ct. 578, 81 L.Ed. 703 (1937), which reversed *Adkins*. See Richard Friedman, Switching Time and Other Thought Experiments: The Hughes Court and Constitutional Transformation, 142 U. Pa. L. Rev. 1891 (1994).

The production and distribution of milk is a paramount industry of the state, and largely affects the health and prosperity of its people. * * *

The fluid milk industry is affected by factors of instability peculiar to itself which call for special methods of control. Under the best practicable adjustment of supply to demand the industry must carry a surplus of about 20 per cent., because milk, an essential food, must be available as demanded by consumers every day in the year, and demand and supply vary from day to day and according to the season; but milk is perishable and cannot be stored. Close adjustment of supply to demand is hindered by several factors difficult to control. Thus surplus milk presents a serious problem, as the prices which can be realized for it for other uses are much less than those obtainable for milk sold for consumption in fluid form or as cream. A satisfactory stabilization of prices for fluid milk requires that the burden of surplus milk be shared equally by all producers and all distributors in the milk shed. So long as the surplus burden is unequally distributed the pressure to market surplus milk in fluid form will be a serious disturbing factor. The fact that the larger distributors find it necessary to carry large quantities of surplus milk, while the smaller distributors do not, leads to price-cutting and other forms of destructive competition. Smaller distributors, who take no responsibility for the surplus, by purchasing their milk at the blended prices (i.e., an average between the price paid the producer for milk for sale as fluid milk, and the lower surplus milk price paid by the larger organizations) can undersell the larger distributors. Indulgence in this price-cutting often compels the larger dealer to cut the price to his own and the producer's detriment.

Various remedies were suggested, amongst them united action by producers, the fixing of minimum prices for milk and cream by state authority, and the imposition of certain graded taxes on milk dealers proportioned so as to equalize the cost of milk and cream to all dealers and so remove the cause of price-cutting.

The Legislature adopted chapter 158 as a method of correcting the evils, which the report of the committee showed could not be expected to right themselves through the ordinary play of the forces of supply and demand, owing to the peculiar and uncontrollable factors affecting the industry. * * *

Save the conduct of railroads, no business has been so thoroughly regimented and regulated by the State of New York as the milk industry. Legislation controlling it in the interest of the public health was adopted in 1862 and subsequent statutes, have been carried into the general codification known as the Agriculture and Markets Law. A perusal of these statutes discloses that the milk industry has been progressively subjected to a larger measure of control. * * *

[This] court from the early days affirmed that the power to promote the general welfare is inherent in government. * * *

The Fifth Amendment, in the field of federal activity, and the Fourteenth, as respects state action, do not prohibit governmental regulation for the public welfare. They merely condition the exertion of the admitted power, by securing that the end shall be accomplished by methods consistent with due process. And the guaranty of due process, as has often been held, demands only that the law shall not be unreasonable, arbitrary, or capricious, and that the means selected shall have a real and substantial relation to the object sought to be attained. It results that a regulation valid for one sort of business, or in given circumstances, may be invalid for another sort, or for the same business under other circumstances, because the reasonableness of each regulation depends upon the relevant facts.

* * *

The Constitution does not guarantee the unrestricted privilege to engage in a business or to conduct it as one pleases. Certain kinds of business may be prohibited; and the right to conduct a business, or to pursue a calling, may be conditioned. Regulation of a business to prevent waste of the state's resources may be justified. And statutes prescribing the terms upon which those conducting certain businesses may contract, or imposing terms if they do enter into agreements, are within the state's competency.

Legislation concerning sales of goods, and incidentally affecting prices, has repeatedly been held valid. In this class fall laws forbidding unfair competition by the charging of lower prices in one locality than those exacted in another, by giving trade inducements to purchasers, and by other forms of price discrimination. The public policy with respect to free competition has engendered state and federal statutes prohibiting monopolies, which have been upheld. On the other hand, where the policy of the state dictated that a monopoly should be granted, statutes having that effect have been held inoffensive to the constitutional guarantees. Moreover, the state or a municipality may itself enter into business in competition with private proprietors, and thus effectively although indirectly control the prices charged by them.

* * *

* * * The legislative investigation of 1932 was persuasive of the fact that * * * unrestricted competition aggravated existing evils and the normal law of supply and demand was insufficient to correct maladjustments detrimental to the community. The inquiry disclosed destructive and demoralizing competitive conditions and unfair trade practices which resulted in retail price cutting and reduced the income of the farmer below the cost of production. * * *

We may as well say at once that the dairy industry is not, in the accepted sense of the phrase, a public utility. We think the appellant is also right in asserting that there is in this case no suggestion of any monopoly or monopolistic practice. It goes without saying that those engaged in the business are in no way dependent upon public grants or franchises for the privilege of conducting their activities. But if, as must be conceded, the industry is subject to regulation in the public interest, what constitutional principle bars the state from correcting existing maladjustments by legislation touching prices? We think there is no such principle. The due process clause makes no mention of sales or of prices any more than it speaks of business or contracts or buildings or other incidents of property. The thought seems nevertheless to have persisted that there is something peculiarly sacrosanct about the price one may charge for what he makes or sells, and that, however able to regulate other elements of manufacture or trade, with incidental effect upon price, the state is incapable of directly controlling the price itself. This view was negatived many years ago. Munn v. Illinois. The appellant's claim is, however, that this court, in there sustaining a statutory prescription of charges for storage by the proprietors of a grain elevator, limited permissible legislation of that type to businesses affected with a public interest, and he says no business is so affected except it have one or more of the characteristics he enumerates. But this is a misconception. Munn and Scott held no franchise from the state. They owned the property upon which their elevator was situated and conducted their business as private citizens. No doubt they felt at liberty to deal with whom they pleased and on such terms as they might deem just to themselves. Their enterprise could not fairly be called a monopoly, although it was referred to in the decision as a "virtual monopoly." This meant only that their elevator was strategically situated and that a large portion of the public found it highly inconvenient to deal with others. This court concluded the circumstances justified the legislation as an exercise of the governmental right to control the business in the public interest; that is, as an exercise of the police power. * * *

The touchstone of public interest in any business, its practices and charges, clearly is not the enjoyment of any franchise from the state, Munn v. Illinois. Nor is it the enjoyment of a monopoly; for in Brass v. North Dakota, 153 U.S. 391 [(1894)], a similar control of prices of grain elevators was upheld in spite of overwhelming and uncontradicted proof that about six hundred grain elevators existed along the line of the Great Northern Railroad, in North Dakota; that at the very station where the defendant's elevator was located two others operated; and that the business was keenly competitive throughout the state.

　　　* * *

Many other decisions show that the private character of a business does not necessarily remove it from the realm of regulation of charges or prices. The usury laws fix the price which may be exacted for the use of money, although no business more essentially private in character can be imagined than that of loaning one's personal funds. Griffith v. Connecticut, 218 U.S. 563 [(1911)]. Insurance agents' compensation may be regulated, though their contracts are private, because the business of insurance is considered one properly subject to public control. O'Gorman & Young v. Hartford Ins. Co., 282 U.S. 251 [(1931)]. * * *

It is clear that there is no closed class or category of businesses affected with a public interest, and the function of courts in the application of the Fifth and Fourteenth Amendments is to determine in each case whether circumstances vindicate the challenged regulation as a reasonable exertion of governmental authority or condemn it as arbitrary or discriminatory. Wolff Packing Co. v. Court of Industrial Relations, 262 U.S. 522, 535 [(1923)]. The phrase "affected with a public interest" can, in the nature of things, mean no more than that an industry, for adequate reason, is subject to control for the public good. * * *

* * * The Constitution does not secure to any one liberty to conduct his business in such fashion as to inflict injury upon the public at large, or upon any substantial group of the people. Price control, like any other form of regulation, is unconstitutional only if arbitrary, discriminatory, or demonstrably irrelevant to the policy the Legislature is free to adopt, and hence an unnecessary and unwarranted interference with individual liberty.

Tested by these considerations we find no basis in the due process clause of the Fourteenth Amendment for condemning the provisions of the Agriculture and Markets Law here drawn into question.

The judgment is affirmed.

Separate opinion of Mr. Justice McReynolds.

* * *

Our question is whether the control act, as applied to appellant through the order of the board, No. 5, deprives him of rights guaranteed by the Fourteenth Amendment. He was convicted of a crime for selling his own property—wholesome milk—in the ordinary course of business at a price satisfactory to himself and the customer. We are not immediately concerned with any other provision of the act or later orders. Prices at which the producer may sell were not prescribed—he may accept any price—nor was production in any way limited. "To stimulate the production of a vital food product" was not the purpose of the statute. There was an oversupply of an excellent article. The affirmation is "that milk has been selling too cheaply * * * and has thus created a temporary emergency; this emergency is remedied by making the sale of milk at a low price a crime."

* * *

It is argued that the report of the Legislative Committee, dated April 10, 1933, disclosed the essential facts. May one be convicted of crime upon such findings? Are federal rights subject to extinction by reports of committees? Heretofore, they have not been.

[W]e are told [by the legislative findings that] the number of dairy cows had been increasing and that favorable prices for milk bring more cows. For two years notwithstanding low prices the per capita consumption had been falling. "The obvious cause is the reduced buying power of consumers." Notwithstanding the low prices, farmers continued to produce a large surplus of wholesome milk for which there was no market. They had yielded to "the human tendency to raise too many heifers" when prices were high and "not until seven or eight years" after 1930 could one reasonably expect a reverse trend. This failure of demand had nothing to do with the quality of the milk—that was excellent. Consumers lacked funds with which to buy. In consequence the farmers became impoverished and their lands depreciated in value. Naturally they became discontented. The exigency is of the kind which inevitably arises when one set of men continue to produce more than all others can buy. The distressing result to the producer followed his ill-advised but voluntary efforts. Similar situations occur in almost every business. If here we have an emergency sufficient to empower the Legislature to fix sales prices, then whenever there is too much or too little of an essential thing—whether of milk or grain or pork or coal or shoes or clothes—constitutional provisions may be declared inoperative. * * *

Of the assailed statute the Court of Appeals says: * * * "With the wisdom of the legislation we have naught to do. It may be vain to hope by laws to oppose the general course of trade." Maybe, because of this conclusion, it said nothing concerning the possibility of obtaining increase of prices to producers—the thing definitely aimed at—through the means adopted.

But plainly, I think, this Court must have regard to the wisdom of the enactment. At least, we must inquire concerning its purpose and decide whether the means proposed have reasonable relation to something within legislative power—whether the end is legitimate, and the means appropriate. If a statute to prevent conflagrations should require householders to pour oil on their roofs as a means of curbing the spread of fire when discovered in the neighborhood, we could hardly uphold it. Here, we find direct interference with guaranteed rights defended upon the ground that the purpose was to promote the public welfare by increasing milk prices at the farm. Unless we can affirm that the end proposed is proper and the means adopted have reasonable relation to it, this action is unjustifiable.

The court below has not definitely affirmed this necessary relation; it has not attempted to indicate how higher charges at stores to impoverished customers when the output is excessive and sale prices by producers are unrestrained, can possibly increase receipts at the farm. The Legislative Committee pointed out as the obvious cause of decreased consumption, notwithstanding low prices, the consumers' reduced buying power. Higher store prices will not enlarge this power; nor will they decrease production. Low prices will bring less cows only after several years. The prime causes of the difficulties will remain. Nothing indicates early decreased output. Demand at low prices being wholly insufficient, the proposed plan is to raise and fix higher minimum prices at stores and thereby aid the producer whose output and prices remain unrestrained! It is not true as stated that "the State seeks to protect the producer by fixing a minimum price for his milk." She carefully refrained from doing this; but did undertake to fix the price after the milk had passed to other owners. Assuming that the views and facts reported by the Legislative Committee are correct, it appears to me wholly unreasonable to expect this legislation to accomplish the proposed end—increase of prices at the farm. * * *

Not only does the statute interfere arbitrarily with the rights of the little grocer to conduct his business according to standards long accepted—complete destruction may follow; but it takes away the liberty of 12,000,000 consumers to buy a necessity of life in an open market. It imposes direct and arbitrary burdens upon those already seriously impoverished with the alleged immediate design of affording special benefits to others. To him with less than 9 cents it says: You cannot procure a quart of milk from the grocer although he is anxious to accept what you can pay and the demands of your household are urgent! A super abundance; but no child can purchase from a willing storekeeper below the figure appointed by three men at headquarters! And this is true although the storekeeper himself may have bought from a willing producer at half that rate and must sell quickly or lose his stock through deterioration. The fanciful scheme is to protect the farmer against undue exactions by prescribing the price at which milk disposed of by him at will may be resold!

* * *

The judgment of the court below should be reversed.

MR. JUSTICE VAN DEVANTER, MR. JUSTICE SUTHERLAND, and MR. JUSTICE BUTLER authorize me to say that they concur in this opinion.

Notes and Questions

1. *Nebbia* is a wonderful case for seeing the intended and unintended effects of regulation. Would you as a legislator have voted for the regulation upheld here?

a. The Court says that "the normal law of supply and demand was insufficient to correct maladjustments detrimental to the community." Is the Court saying that the law of supply and demand is a poor way to allocate resources, or is it saying that for some unusual reason it does not work in the milk industry?

b. Was milk production an industry in which a few large farmers had obtained the power to charge monopoly prices? Was it instead a classically competitive industry?

c. Was it an industry in which producing units were too small to be efficient? Was it instead an industry that was apparently extremely efficient at producing milk?

d. Was the problem that consumers had an irrational demand for milk that somehow had to be restrained by higher prices?

e. Was the problem the transaction costs that would have been associated with trying to negotiate equitable prices in the absence of legislative fiat?

f. What "community" did the Court believe the normal law of supply and demand did not protect? Who got the real benefit from this legislation?[2] Was it really farmers or was it instead the dairies to whom farmers sold and from whom Leo Nebbia bought? Are commercial dairies simply more deserving of regulatory protection than hungry consumers?

2. We begin with questions about the wisdom of the regulation to highlight the significance of the constitutional questions. It is hard to conclude that this regulatory scheme was any more than special interest legislation or that the method of setting prices would be defended by any good analyst taking what we have called a Public Administration perspective. But should the fact that a regulation is foolish mean it is unconstitutional?

a. The Court says, "Price control, like any other form of regulation, is unconstitutional only if arbitrary, discriminatory or demonstrably irrelevant to the policy the legislature is free to adopt." Should there be limits to the freedom of legislatures to adopt policies that redistribute wealth from consumers to producers? If so, should those limits primarily be grounded in economic considerations or in equitable value judgments?

b. What business, if any, would it be unconstitutional to regulate under the *Nebbia* test? To what extent does the Court's decision depend on its findings that "milk is an essential item of diet" and that "the production and distribution of milk is a paramount industry of the state, and largely affects the health and prosperity of its people"? Can the same be said for any agricultural product?

3. Once *Nebbia* had largely closed the door to constitutional review of regulation, a wave of new legislation was upheld.

In United States v. Carolene Products Co., 304 U.S. 144, 58 S.Ct. 778, 82 L.Ed. 1234 (1938), for example, the court upheld the so-called "Filled Milk Act" in which Congress had determined that it was "unhealthful" and thus illegal to sell a product in which vegetable oils had been substituted for the milk's natural, cholesterol-rich butterfat.

Pacific States Box & Basket Co. v. White, 296 U.S. 176, 56 S.Ct. 159, 80 L.Ed. 138 (1935), upheld a statute prescribing "official standards" for containers of raspberries and strawberries. The statute had been explicitly passed "in order to promote, protect, further and develop the horticultural interests" of the state.

Williamson v. Lee Optical, 348 U.S. 483, 75 S.Ct. 461, 99 L.Ed. 563 (1955), sustained a prohibition against an optician's fitting or duplicating eyeglass lenses without a prescription from a licensed ophthalmologist or optometrist. "The Oklahoma law may exact a needless, wasteful requirement in many cases," said the court. "But it is for the legislature, not the courts, to balance the advantages and disadvantages of the new requirement."

4. But complaints continued that regulation often arbitrarily imposed costs on one group of citizens for the benefit of others. Indeed, in some cases,

---

2. Cf. Ruben A. Kessel, Economic Effects of Federal Regulation of Milk Markets,   10 J.L. & Econ. 51 (1967).

regulation arguably so limited one citizen's use of property as to constitute a "taking" for which compensation was required.

In Pennsylvania Coal Co. v. Mahon, 260 U.S. 393, 43 S.Ct. 158, 67 L.Ed. 322 (1922), for example, Justice Holmes wrote for the Court that the state could not—without compensation—prohibit a coal company from mining so as to keep the land from subsiding and damaging neighboring improved property.[3]

In Euclid v. Ambler Realty Co., 272 U.S. 365, 47 S.Ct. 114, 71 L.Ed. 303 (1926), however, the Court upheld a comprehensive land use ordinance that rendered some land valuable because it could be used for commercial purposes and rendered land limited to residential use less valuable. And in Penn Central Transportation Co. v. New York, 438 U.S. 104, 98 S.Ct. 2646, 57 L.Ed.2d 631 (1978), the Court found no "taking" where the city's Landmarks Preservation Commission cited aesthetic concerns in refusing to grant a railroad the right to build an office building over Grand Central Station.[4]

Permanent physical occupation of private property authorized by legislation or regulation, however, still amounted to a taking. Thus, in Loretto v. Teleprompter Manhattan CATV Corp., 458 U.S. 419, 102 S.Ct. 3164, 73 L.Ed.2d 868 (1982), the Court found a statute that required landlords to permit cable television companies to install their cable on a landlord's property entitled the landlord to just compensation.

Nollan v. California Coastal Commission, 483 U.S. 825, 107 S.Ct. 3141, 97 L.Ed.2d 677 (1987), presented a harder case. The Commission conditioned its grant of a permit for the landowner to build a larger house on the transfer to the public of an easement over the owner's strip of beach. This was clearly a permanent physical occupation of the land, but the Court held it would not require compensation if the regulation were related to some problem created by the grant of the permit, i.e., some burden imposed on the community. The desire for an easement was found to be unrelated to the expansion of the house and thus the State would have to pay for any such easement.[5]

[handwritten margin note: essential nexus b/w burden (cost) and the interest served]

It was in this context that the Court took up the following case:

DOLAN v. CITY OF TIGARD

Supreme Court of the United States, 1994.
512 U.S. 374, 114 S.Ct. 2309, 129 L.Ed.2d 304.

3. But see Keystone Bituminous Coal Ass'n v. DeBenedictis, 480 U.S. 470, 107 S.Ct. 1232, 94 L.Ed.2d 472 (1987), upholding a requirement that 50% of the coal beneath existing homes and public buildings be left in place to provide surface support.

4. See also, e.g., Agins v. Tiburon, 447 U.S. 255, 100 S.Ct. 2138, 65 L.Ed.2d 106 (1980) (zoning limitation of five homes on each five acre lot); Pennell v. City of San Jose, 485 U.S. 1, 108 S.Ct. 849, 99 L.Ed.2d 1 (1988) (rent control).

5. Another important case in this series was Lucas v. South Carolina Coastal Council, 505 U.S. 1003, 112 S.Ct. 2886, 120 L.Ed.2d 798 (1992). Mr. Lucas had bought two lots on a barrier island intending to build homes. Later, the State forbade new permanent structures on such island lots, rendering his investment essentially worthless. The Court held that regulations that deny all "economically viable use" of land entitle the landowner to compensation unless the limitation could be said to inhere in the property right itself.

CHIEF JUSTICE REHNQUIST delivered the opinion of the Court.

Petitioner challenges the decision of the Oregon Supreme Court which held that the city of Tigard could condition the approval of her building permit on the dedication of a portion of her property for flood control and traffic improvements. We granted certiorari to resolve a question left open by our decision in Nollan v. California Coastal Comm'n, 483 U.S. 825 (1987), of what is the required degree of connection between the exactions imposed by the city and the projected impacts of the proposed development.

I

The State of Oregon enacted a comprehensive land use management program in 1973. The program required all Oregon cities and counties to adopt new comprehensive land use plans that were consistent with the statewide planning goals. The plans are implemented by land use regulations which are part of an integrated hierarchy of legally binding goals, plans, and regulations. Pursuant to the State's requirements, the city of Tigard, a community of some 30,000 residents on the southwest edge of Portland, developed a comprehensive plan and codified it in its Community Development Code (CDC). The CDC requires property owners in the area zoned Central Business District to comply with a 15% open space and landscaping requirement, which limits total site coverage, including all structures and paved parking, to 85% of the parcel. After the completion of a transportation study that identified congestion in the Central Business District as a particular problem, the city adopted a plan for a pedestrian/bicycle pathway intended to encourage alternatives to automobile transportation for short trips. The CDC requires that new development facilitate this plan by dedicating land for pedestrian pathways where provided for in the pedestrian/bicycle pathway plan.

The city also adopted a Master Drainage Plan (Drainage Plan). The Drainage Plan noted that flooding occurred in several areas along Fanno Creek, including areas near petitioner's property. The Drainage Plan also established that the increase in impervious surfaces associated with continued urbanization would exacerbate these flooding problems. To combat these risks, the Drainage Plan suggested a series of improvements to the Fanno Creek Basin, including channel excavation in the area next to petitioner's property. Other recommendations included ensuring that the floodplain remains free of structures and that it be preserved as greenways to minimize flood damage to structures. The Drainage Plan concluded that the cost of these improvements should be shared based on both direct and indirect benefits, with property owners along the waterways paying more due to the direct benefit that they would receive. * * *

Petitioner Florence Dolan owns a plumbing and electric supply store located on Main Street in the Central Business District of the city. The store covers approximately 9,700 square feet on the eastern side of a 1.67–acre parcel, which includes a gravel parking lot. Fanno Creek flows through the southwestern corner of the lot and along its western boundary. The year-round flow of the creek renders the area within the creek's 100–year floodplain virtually unusable for commercial development. The city's comprehensive plan includes the Fanno Creek floodplain as part of the city's greenway system.

Petitioner applied to the city for a permit to redevelop the site. Her proposed plans called for nearly doubling the size of the store to 17,600 square feet, and paving a 39–space parking lot. The existing store, located on the opposite side of the parcel, would be razed in sections as construction progressed on the new building. In the second phase of the project, petitioner proposed to build an additional structure on the northeast side of the site for complementary businesses, and to provide more parking. The proposed expansion and intensified use are consistent with the city's zoning scheme in the Central Business District.

The City Planning Commission granted petitioner's permit application subject to conditions imposed by the city's CDC. The CDC establishes the following standard for site development review approval:

"Where landfill and/or development is allowed within and adjacent to the 100–year floodplain, the city shall require the dedication of sufficient open land area for greenway adjoining and within the floodplain. This area shall include portions at a suitable elevation for the construction of a pedestrian/bicycle pathway within the floodplain in accordance with the adopted pedestrian/bicycle plan."

Thus, the Commission required that petitioner dedicate the portion of her property lying within the 100–year floodplain for improvement of a storm drainage system along Fanno Creek and that she dedicate an additional 15–foot strip of land adjacent to the floodplain as a pedestrian/bicycle pathway. The dedication required by that condition encompasses approximately 7,000 square feet, or roughly 10% of the property. In accordance with city practice, petitioner could rely on the dedicated property to meet the 15% open space and landscaping requirement mandated by the city's zoning scheme. The city would bear the cost of maintaining a landscaped buffer between the dedicated area and the new store.

Petitioner requested variances from the CDC standards. Variances are granted only where it can be shown that, owing to special circumstances related to a specific piece of the land, the literal interpretation of the applicable zoning provisions would cause "an undue or unnecessary hardship" unless the variance is granted. Rather than posing alternative mitigating measures to offset the expected impacts of her proposed development, as allowed under the CDC, petitioner simply argued that her proposed development would not conflict with the policies of the comprehensive plan. The Commission denied the request.

The Commission made a series of findings concerning the relationship between the dedicated conditions and the projected impacts of petitioner's project. First, the Commission noted that "it is reasonable to assume that customers and employees of the future uses of this site could utilize a pedestrian/bicycle pathway adjacent to this development for their transportation and recreational needs." The Commission noted that the site plan has provided for bicycle parking in a rack in front of the proposed building and "it is reasonable to expect that some of the users of the bicycle parking provided for by the site plan will use the pathway adjacent to Fanno Creek if it is constructed." In addition, the Commission found that creation of a convenient, safe pedestrian/bicycle pathway system as an alternative means of transportation "could offset some of the traffic demand on [nearby] streets and lessen the increase in traffic congestion."

The Commission went on to note that the required floodplain dedication would be reasonably related to petitioner's request to intensify the use of the site given the increase in the impervious surface. The Commission stated that the "anticipated increased storm water flow from the subject property to an already strained creek and drainage basin can only add to the public need to manage the stream channel and floodplain for drainage purposes." Based on this anticipated increased storm water flow, the Commission concluded that "the requirement of dedication of the floodplain area on the site is related to the applicant's plan to intensify development on the site." The Tigard City Council approved the Commission's final order * * *.

Petitioner appealed to the Land Use Board of Appeals (LUBA) on the ground that the city's dedication requirements were not related to the proposed development, and, therefore, those requirements constituted an uncompensated taking of their property under the Fifth Amendment. * * * Given the undisputed fact that the proposed larger building and paved parking area would increase the amount of impervious surfaces and the runoff into Fanno Creek, LUBA concluded that "there is a 'reasonable relationship' between the proposed development and the requirement to dedicate land along Fanno Creek for a greenway." With respect to the pedestrian/bicycle pathway, LUBA noted the Commission's finding that a significantly larger retail sales building and parking lot would attract larger numbers of customers and employees and their vehicles. It again found a "reasonable relationship" between alleviating the impacts of increased traffic from the development and facilitating the provision of a pedestrian/bicycle pathway as an alternative means of transportation.

The Oregon Court of Appeals affirmed, rejecting petitioner's contention that in Nollan v. California Coastal Comm'n we had abandoned the "reasonable relationship" test in favor of a stricter "essential nexus" test. The Oregon Supreme Court affirmed. * * *

II

The Takings Clause of the Fifth Amendment of the United States Constitution [is] made applicable to the States through the Fourteenth Amendment. * * * One of the principal purposes of the Takings Clause is "to bar Government from forcing some people alone to bear public burdens which, in all fairness and justice, should be borne by the public as a whole." Without question, had the city simply required petitioner to dedicate a strip of land along Fanno Creek for public use, rather than conditioning the grant of her permit to redevelop her property on such a dedication, a taking would have occurred. Such public access would deprive petitioner of the right to exclude others, "one of the most essential sticks in the bundle of rights that are commonly characterized as property." Kaiser Aetna v. United States, 444 U.S. 164 (1979).

On the other side of the ledger, the authority of state and local governments to engage in land use planning has been sustained against constitutional challenge as long ago as our decision in Euclid v. Ambler Realty Co., 272 U.S. 365 (1926). "Government hardly could go on if to some extent values incident to property could not be diminished without paying for every such change in the general law." Pennsylvania Coal Co. v. Mahon, 260 U.S. 393 (1922). A land use regulation does not effect a taking if it "substantially advances legitimate state interests" and does not "deny an owner economically viable use of his land." Agins v. Tiburon, 447 U.S. 255 (1980).[6]

The sort of land use regulations discussed in the cases just cited, however, differ in two relevant particulars from the present case. First, they involved essentially legislative determinations classifying entire areas of the city, whereas here the city made an adjudicative decision to condition petitioner's application for a building permit on an individual parcel. Second, the conditions imposed were not simply a limitation on the use petitioner might make of her own parcel, but a requirement that she deed portions of the property to the city. In *Nollan,* supra, we held that governmental authority to exact such a condition was circumscribed by the Fifth and Fourteenth Amendments. Under the well-settled doctrine of "unconstitutional conditions," the government may not require a person to give up a constitutional right—here the right to receive just compensation when property is taken for a public use—in exchange for a discretionary benefit conferred by the government where the property sought has little or no relationship to the benefit.

Petitioner contends that the city has forced her to choose between the building permit and her right under the Fifth Amendment to just compensation for the public easements. Petitioner does not quarrel with the city's authority to exact some forms of dedication as a condition for the grant of a building permit, but challenges the showing made by the city to justify these exactions. She argues that the city has identified "no special benefits" conferred on her, and has not identified any "special quantifiable burdens" created by her new store that would justify the

---

6. There can be no argument that the permit conditions would deprive petitioner "economically beneficial use" of her property as she currently operates a retail store on the lot. Petitioner assuredly is able to derive some economic use from her proper-

ty. See, e.g., Lucas v. South Carolina, 505 U.S. 1003 (1992); Kaiser Aetna v. United States, 444 U.S. 164 (1979); Penn Central Transportation Co. v. New York City, 438 U.S. 104 (1978). [Court's fn. 6]

particular dedications required from her which are not required from the public at large.

III

In evaluating petitioner's claim, we must first determine whether the "essential nexus" exists between the "legitimate state interest" and the permit condition exacted by the city. If we find that a nexus exists, we must then decide the required degree of connection between the exactions and the projected impact of the proposed development. We were not required to reach this question in *Nollan*, because we concluded that the connection did not meet even the loosest standard. Here, however, we must decide this question.

A

We addressed the essential nexus question in *Nollan*. The California Coastal Commission demanded a lateral public easement across the Nollan's beachfront lot in exchange for a permit to demolish an existing bungalow and replace it with a three-bedroom house. The public easement was designed to connect two public beaches that were separated by the Nollan's property. The Coastal Commission had asserted that the public easement condition was imposed to promote the legitimate state interest of diminishing the "blockage of the view of the ocean" caused by construction of the larger house.

We agreed that the Coastal Commission's concern with protecting visual access to the ocean constituted a legitimate public interest. We also agreed that the permit condition would have been constitutional "even if it consisted of the requirement that the Nollans provide a viewing spot on their property for passersbys with whose sighting of the ocean their new house would interfere." We resolved, however, that the Coastal Commission's regulatory authority was set completely adrift from its constitutional moorings when it claimed that a nexus existed between visual access to the ocean and a permit condition requiring lateral public access along the Nollan's beachfront lot. How enhancing the public's ability to "traverse to and along the shorefront" served the same governmental purpose of "visual access to the ocean" from the roadway was beyond our ability to countenance. The absence of a nexus left the Coastal Commission in the position of simply trying to obtain an easement through gimmickry, which converted a valid regulation of land use into "an out-and-out plan of extortion."

No such gimmicks are associated with the permit conditions imposed by the city in this case. Undoubtedly, the prevention of flooding along Fanno Creek and the reduction of traffic congestion in the Central Business District qualify as the type of legitimate public purposes we have upheld. It seems equally obvious that a nexus exists between preventing flooding along Fanno Creek and limiting development within the creek's 100–year floodplain. Petitioner proposes to double the size of her retail store and to pave her now-gravel parking lot, thereby expanding the impervious surface on the property and increasing the amount of stormwater run-off into Fanno Creek.

The same may be said for the city's attempt to reduce traffic congestion by providing for alternative means of transportation. In theory, a pedestrian/bicycle pathway provides a useful alternative means of transportation for workers and shoppers * * *.

B

The second part of our analysis requires us to determine whether the degree of the exactions demanded by the city's permit conditions bear the required relationship to the projected impact of petitioner's proposed development. Here the Oregon Supreme Court deferred to what it termed the "city's unchallenged factual findings" supporting the dedication conditions and found them to be reasonably related to the impact of the expansion of petitioner's business.

* * * The city relies on the Commission's rather tentative findings that increased stormwater flow from petitioner's property "can only add to the public need to manage the [floodplain] for drainage purposes" to support its conclusion that the "requirement of dedication of the flood-plain area on the site is related to the applicant's plan to intensify development on the site."

The city made the following specific findings relevant to the pedestrian/bicycle pathway:

"In addition, the proposed expanded use of this site is anticipated to generate additional vehicular traffic thereby increasing congestion on nearby collector and arterial streets. Creation of a convenient, safe pedestrian/bicycle pathway system as an alternative means of transportation could offset some of the traffic demand on these nearby streets and lessen the increase in traffic congestion."

The question for us is whether these findings are constitutionally sufficient to justify the conditions imposed by the city on petitioner's building permit. Since state courts have been dealing with this question a good deal longer than we have, we turn to representative decisions made by them.

In some States, very generalized statements as to the necessary connection between the required dedication and the proposed development seem to suffice. We think this standard is too lax to adequately protect petitioner's right to just compensation if her property is taken for a public purpose.

Other state courts require a very exacting correspondence, described as the "specific and uniquely attributable" test. * * * Under this standard, if the local government cannot demonstrate that its exaction is directly proportional to the specifically created need, the exaction becomes "a veiled exercise of the power of eminent domain and a confiscation of private property behind the defense of police regulations." We do not think the Federal Constitution requires such exacting scrutiny, given the nature of the interests involved.

A number of state courts have taken an intermediate position, requiring the municipality to show a "reasonable relationship" between the required dedication and the impact of the proposed development. * * * [A] city may not require a property owner to dedicate private property for some future public use as a condition of obtaining a building permit when such future use is not "occasioned by the construction sought to be permitted."

* * *

We think the "reasonable relationship" test adopted by a majority of the state courts is closer to the federal constitutional norm than either of those previously discussed. But we do not adopt it as such, partly because the term "reasonable relationship" seems confusingly similar to the term "rational basis" which describes the minimal level of scrutiny under the Equal Protection Clause of the Fourteenth Amendment. We think a term such as "rough proportionality" best encapsulates what we hold to be the requirement of the Fifth Amendment. No precise mathematical calculation is required, but the city must make some sort of individualized determination that the required dedication is related both in nature and extent to the impact of the proposed development.[7]

Justice Stevens' dissent relies upon a law review article for the proposition that the city's conditional demands for part of petitioner's property are "a species of business regulation that heretofore warranted a strong presumption of constitutional validity." But simply denominating a governmental measure as a "business regulation" does not immunize it from constitutional challenge on the grounds that it violates a provision of the Bill of Rights. * * *

It is axiomatic that increasing the amount of impervious surface will increase the quantity and rate of storm-water flow from petitioner's property. Therefore, keeping the floodplain open and free from development would likely confine the pressures on Fanno Creek created by petitioner's development. In fact, because petitioner's property lies within the Central Business District, the Community Development Code already required that petitioner leave 15% of it as open space and the undeveloped floodplain would have nearly satisfied that requirement. But the city demanded more—it not only wanted petitioner not to build in the floodplain, but it also wanted petitioner's property along Fanno Creek for its Greenway system. The city has never said why a public greenway, as opposed to a private one, was required in the interest of flood control.

7. Justice Stevens' dissent takes us to task for placing the burden on the city to justify the required dedication. He is correct in arguing that in evaluating most generally applicable zoning regulations, the burden properly rests on the party challenging the regulation to prove that it constitutes an arbitrary regulation of property rights. See, e.g., Euclid v. Ambler Realty Co. Here, by contrast, the city made an adjudicative decision to condition petitioner's application for a building permit on an individual parcel. In this situation, the burden properly rests on the city. * * * [Court's fn. 8]

The difference to petitioner, of course, is the loss of her ability to exclude others. As we have noted, this right to exclude others is "one of the most essential sticks in the bundle of rights that are commonly characterized as property." *Kaiser Aetna.* It is difficult to see why recreational visitors trampling along petitioner's floodplain easement are sufficiently related to the city's legitimate interest in reducing flooding problems along Fanno Creek, and the city has not attempted to make any individualized determination to support this part of its request.

* * *

If petitioner's proposed development had somehow encroached on existing greenway space in the city, it would have been reasonable to require petitioner to provide some alternative greenway space for the public either on her property or elsewhere. * * * But that is not the case here. We conclude that the findings upon which the city relies do not show the required reasonable relationship between the floodplain easement and the petitioner's proposed new building.

With respect to the pedestrian/bicycle pathway, we have no doubt that the city was correct in finding that the larger retail sales facility proposed by petitioner will increase traffic on the streets of the Central Business District. The city estimates that the proposed development would generate roughly 435 additional trips per day. Dedications for streets, sidewalks, and other public ways are generally reasonable exactions to avoid excessive congestion from a proposed property use. But on the record before us, the city has not met its burden of demonstrating that the additional number of vehicle and bicycle trips generated by the petitioner's development reasonably relate to the city's requirement for a dedication of the pedestrian/bicycle pathway easement. The city simply found that the creation of the pathway "could offset some of the traffic demand . . . and lessen the increase in traffic congestion."[8]

* * * No precise mathematical calculation is required, but the city must make some effort to quantify its findings in support of the dedication for the pedestrian/bicycle pathway beyond the conclusory statement that it could offset some of the traffic demand generated.

IV

Cities have long engaged in the commendable task of land use planning, made necessary by increasing urbanization particularly in metropolitan areas such as Portland. The city's goals of reducing flooding hazards and traffic congestion, and providing for public greenways, are laudable, but there are outer limits to how this may be done. "A strong public desire to improve the public condition [will not] warrant

---

8. In rejecting petitioner's request for a variance from the pathway dedication condition, the city stated that omitting the planned section of the pathway across petitioner's property would conflict with its adopted policy of providing a continuous pathway system. But the Takings Clause requires the city to implement its policy by condemnation unless the required relationship between the petitioner's development and added traffic is shown. [Court's fn. 10]

achieving the desire by a shorter cut than the constitutional way of paying for the change." Pennsylvania Coal v. Mahon.

The judgment of the Supreme Court of Oregon is reversed, and the case is remanded for further proceedings consistent with this opinion.

JUSTICE STEVENS, with whom JUSTICE BLACKMUN and JUSTICE GINSBURG join, dissenting.

* * *

The Court is correct in concluding that the city may not attach arbitrary conditions to a building permit or to a variance even when it can rightfully deny the application outright. I also agree that state court decisions dealing with ordinances that govern municipal development plans provide useful guidance in a case of this kind. Yet the Court's description of the doctrinal underpinnings of its decision, the phrasing of its fledgling test of "rough proportionality," and the application of that test to this case run contrary to the traditional treatment of these cases and break considerable and unpropitious new ground.

I

* * *

Not one of the state cases cited by the Court announces anything akin to a "rough proportionality" requirement. For the most part, moreover, those cases that invalidated municipal ordinances did so on state law or unspecified grounds roughly equivalent to Nollan's "essential nexus" requirement. * * *

In addition, the Court ignores the state courts' willingness to consider what the property owner gains from the exchange in question. The Supreme Court of Wisconsin, for example, found it significant that the village's approval of a proposed subdivision plat "enables the subdivider to profit financially by selling the subdivision lots as home-building sites and thus realizing a greater price than could have been obtained if he had sold his property as unplatted lands." Jordan v. Village of Menomonee Falls, 28 Wis.2d 608, 619–620, 137 N.W.2d 442, 448 (1965). The required dedication as a condition of that approval was permissible "in return for this benefit." * * *

The state court decisions also are enlightening in the extent to which they required that the entire parcel be given controlling importance. All but one of the cases involve challenges to provisions in municipal ordinances requiring developers to dedicate either a percentage of the entire parcel (usually 7 or 10 percent of the platted subdivision) or an equivalent value in cash (usually a certain dollar amount per lot) to help finance the construction of roads, utilities, schools, parks and playgrounds. In assessing the legality of the conditions, the courts gave no indication that the transfer of an interest in realty was any more objectionable than a cash payment. None of the decisions identified the surrender of the fee owner's "power to exclude" as having any special significance. Instead, the courts uniformly examined the character of the entire economic transaction.

II

* * *

The Court's narrow focus on one strand in the property owner's bundle of rights is particularly misguided in a case involving the development of commercial property. As Professor Johnston has noted:

> "The subdivider is a manufacturer, processer, and marketer of a product; land is but one of his raw materials. In subdivision control disputes, the developer is not defending hearth and home against the king's intrusion, but simply attempting to maximize his profits from the sale of a finished product. As applied to him, subdivision control exactions are actually business regulations." Johnston, Constitutionality of Subdivision Control Exactions: The Quest for A Rationale, 52 Cornell L.Q. 871, 923 (1967).

The exactions associated with the development of a retail business are likewise a species of business regulation that heretofore warranted a strong presumption of constitutional validity.

* * *

III

* * *

In her objections to the floodplain condition, Dolan made no effort to demonstrate that the dedication of that portion of her property would be any more onerous than a simple prohibition against any development on that portion of her property. Given the commercial character of both the existing and the proposed use of the property as a retail store, it seems likely that potential customers "trampling along petitioner's floodplain," are more valuable than a useless parcel of vacant land. Moreover, the duty to pay taxes and the responsibility for potential tort liability may well make ownership of the fee interest in useless land a liability rather than an asset. * * *

The Court's rejection of the bike path condition amounts to nothing more than a play on words. Everyone agrees that the bike path "could" offset some of the increased traffic flow that the larger store will generate, but the findings do not unequivocally state that it will do so, or tell us just how many cyclists will replace motorists. Predictions on such matters are inherently nothing more than estimates. Certainly the assumption that there will be an offsetting benefit here is entirely reasonable and should suffice whether it amounts to 100 percent, 35 percent, or only 5 percent of the increase in automobile traffic that would otherwise occur. If the Court proposes to have the federal judiciary micromanage state decisions of this kind, it is indeed extending its welcome mat to a significant new class of litigants. Although there is no reason to believe that state courts have failed to rise to the task, property owners have surely found a new friend today.

IV

The Court has made a serious error by abandoning the traditional presumption of constitutionality and imposing a novel burden of proof on a city implementing an admittedly valid comprehensive land use plan. Even more consequential than its incorrect disposition of this case, however, is the Court's resurrection of a species of substantive due process analysis that it firmly rejected decades ago.

* * *

In our changing world one thing is certain: uncertainty will characterize predictions about the impact of new urban developments on the risks of floods, earthquakes, traffic congestion, or environmental harms. When there is doubt concerning the magnitude of those impacts, the public interest in averting them must outweigh the private interest of the commercial entrepreneur. If the government can demonstrate that the conditions it has imposed in a land-use permit are rational, impartial and conducive to fulfilling the aims of a valid land-use plan, a strong presumption of validity should attach to those conditions. The burden of demonstrating that those conditions have unreasonably impaired the economic value of the proposed improvement belongs squarely on the shoulders of the party challenging the state action's constitutionality. That allocation of burdens has served us well in the past. The Court has stumbled badly today by reversing it.

I respectfully dissent.

JUSTICE SOUTER, dissenting.

* * *

I cannot agree that the application of *Nollan* is a sound one here, since it appears that the Court has placed the burden of producing evidence of relationship on the city * * *. Having thus assigned the burden, the Court concludes that the City loses based on one word ("could" instead of "would"), and despite the fact that this record shows the connection the Court looks for. Dolan has put forward no evidence that the burden of granting a dedication for the bicycle path is unrelated in kind to the anticipated increase in traffic congestion, nor, if there exists a requirement that the relationship be related in degree, has Dolan shown that the exaction fails any such test. The city, by contrast, calculated the increased traffic flow that would result from Dolan's proposed development to be 435 trips per day, and its Comprehensive Plan, applied here, relied on studies showing the link between alternative modes of transportation, including bicycle paths, and reduced street traffic congestion. *Nollan*, therefore, is satisfied, and on that assumption the city's conditions should not be held to fail a further rough proportionality test or any other that might be devised to give meaning to the constitutional limits. * * *

Notes and Questions

1.   Did the regulatory burdens imposed on Ms. Dolan in this case make sense? Were improvement of the storm drainage and bicycle pathway systems in the city apparently necessary? Did anyone suggest that more efficient ways of accomplishing the public purposes were available?

2.   Are those the real questions? Who received the benefits of the regulatory burdens imposed on Ms. Dolan? Were the benefits shared by all the community's citizens, or at least by all of the shoppers? One can understand why those beneficiaries would prefer not to purchase the benefits by paying higher taxes, but as a matter of sound policy, why should they not be required to do so?

3.   Does it follow that the regulations should be seen to raise constitutional problems? Do you agree with the dissenters that if there is an "essential nexus" between a public problem and the regulation imposed, that should be the end of the Constitutional inquiry?

a.   What has the majority added to the "essential nexus" requirement? Does the majority deny that such a nexus exists? Then what is added by saying that a "rough proportionality" between the problem and the solution also must be found?

b.   Is Justice Souter right that what the majority basically has done is reverse the burden of proof in takings cases? If the takings concept is to have any substance at all, doesn't the burden have to be on the city? Can you imagine a set of facts in which the regulated party could sustain a burden of showing no "nexus", much less no "reasonable relationship" between a problem and a regulatory solution?

c.   One reason the city had not put on more evidence here, of course, is that it did not know it had the burden of doing so until the Court told it that it did. Do you believe the burden of justifying the "rough proportionality" is likely to be difficult? The Court says it does not require mathematical precision in the showing, but does it say how much precision will be enough?

4.   Are you convinced or at least troubled by Justice Stevens' dissent suggesting that the majority has revived, via the Takings Clause, the doctrine of substantive due process? In effect, are these constitutional clauses alter egos of each other? How can the Court avoid the implications of substantive due process in this setting?

5.   The majority emphasizes the difference between legislative and adjudicative land use determination by states and subdivisions. This distinction is reminiscent of the one drawn in the well-known due process cases of Londoner v. Denver, 210 U.S. 373, 28 S.Ct. 708, 52 L.Ed. 1103 (1908), and Bi–Metallic Investment Co. v. State Board of Equalization, 239 U.S. 441, 36 S.Ct. 141, 60 L.Ed. 372 (1915). The holding of those cases is that when a government entity makes a legislative decision (on property taxation) it need not provide a hearing; however, when the decision is fact-based, due process will require a hearing. Eventually, the Court drew the distinction for due process purposes between rulemaking and adjudication. See Richard Pierce,

Sidney Shapiro & Paul R. Verkuil, Administrative Law and Process (4th ed. 2004), at § 6.3.2.

a. Here of course an individualized determination was made and procedures had to be accorded. But is the *Dolan* Court concerned about the quality or sufficiency of those procedures, especially as they relate to the factual burdens the city must bear? Even assuming planning commissions as informal bodies are procedurally deficient, aren't these deficiencies correctable by state reviewing courts? Are there conflicts of interest present in local decisions that make procedures more important in that setting?

b. And what about federalism? To what extent does *Dolan* involve "judicial micromanagement" of state land use planning decisions as Justice Stevens claims? Why does it matter that there be one federal rule on takings decisions by state courts? Shouldn't states be able to decide whether they want "tight" or "loose" regulatory standards?

c. Are there other local regulations that raise "takings" issues? At what point should the Court call a halt to its constitutional review function in this regard?[9] Compare the *Hope Natural Gas* case discussed in Chapter 4.

6. After the decision in *Dolan*, the plaintiffs were sent back to the Tigard City Council. The Council voted 5–0 to allow the bigger store to be built, on the condition that the Dolans grant easements for the bicycle path and flood plain rather than conveyance of the real estate to the city. The mayor of Tigard thought this amounted to "rough proportionality" while Dan Dolan saw it as "pure contempt of the U.S. Supreme Court." H. Bodine, Dolans Won't Buy Tigard's Latest OK For New Building, *Oregonian*, August 31, 1995, at E2.

7. The relationship of Takings jurisprudence to land use, as applied in *Dolan,* has a long history, commencing with the "just compensation" provision of the Fifth Amendment. When it comes to regulatory takings (such as zoning), the Court has engaged in "essentially ad hoc, factual inquiries." Penn Central Transportation Co. v. New York, 438 U.S. 104, 124, 98 S.Ct. 2646, 57 L.Ed.2d 631 (1978). Even though the test remains the same, it has obviously become more stringent after *Dolan*. For an argument that regulatory (or "policymaking") takings should not require compensation, see Susan Rose–Ackerman & Jim Rossi, Disentangling Deregulatory Takings, 86 Va. L. Rev. 1441 (2000).

B. COMMERCE CLAUSE LIMITS ON FEDERAL REGULATION

At one point in constitutional history, the Commerce Clause was the principal tool by which the Supreme Court limited federal intrusion into areas of state authority. The Commerce Clause served as a weapon to strike down federal regulation in a way similar to that in which state regulation was challenged under substantive due process theories.

Thus, in Hammer v. Dagenhart, 247 U.S. 251, 38 S.Ct. 529, 62 L.Ed. 1101 (1918), the Court struck down a statute prohibiting shipment in

---

9. See generally, Douglas W. Kmiec, At Last, The Supreme Court Solves the Takings Puzzle, 19 Harvard J.L. & Public Policy 147 (1995); John E. Fee, Unearthing the Denominator in Regulatory Taking Claims, 61 U. Chicago L. Rev. 1535 (1994).

interstate commerce of certain goods produced by child labor. There is no federal authority, the Court said, to regulate the local conditions under which goods are produced even if the goods are sold across state lines.

The Commerce Clause was an important basis for striking down early New Deal legislation as well,[10] but ultimately, the Court adopted a less restrictive approach. In United States v. Darby, 312 U.S. 100, 61 S.Ct. 451, 85 L.Ed. 609 (1941), for example, the Court overruled Hammer v. Dagenhart and upheld regulation of the wages and hours of labor involved in production of goods for interstate commerce. In Wickard v. Filburn, 317 U.S. 111, 63 S.Ct. 82, 87 L.Ed. 122 (1942), the Court held that Congress could impose a marketing quota on a farmer who produced grain only for personal consumption or local sale.

Later, Congress' power to regulate interstate commerce underlay much of the legislation regulating racial discrimination in public hotels and restaurants, even if they served largely a local clientele.[11] The Court also upheld against a Commerce Clause challenge, the statute that makes it a crime for a person convicted of a felony to possess a firearm that has at any time been transported in interstate commerce.[12] But things were about to change.

UNITED STATES v. LOPEZ

Supreme Court of the United States, 1995.
514 U.S. 549, 115 S.Ct. 1624, 131 L.Ed.2d 626.

CHIEF JUSTICE REHNQUIST delivered the opinion of the Court.

In the Gun–Free School Zones Act of 1990, Congress made it a federal offense "for any individual knowingly to possess a firearm at a place that the individual knows, or has reasonable cause to believe, is a school zone." 18 U.S.C. § 922. The Act neither regulates a commercial activity nor contains a requirement that the possession be connected in any way to interstate commerce. We hold that the Act exceeds the authority of Congress "to regulate Commerce ... among the several States...." U.S. Const., Art. I, § 8, cl. 3.

On March 10, 1992, respondent, who was then a 12th-grade student, arrived at Edison High School in San Antonio, Texas, carrying a concealed .38 caliber handgun and five bullets. Acting upon an anonymous tip, school authorities confronted respondent, who admitted that he was carrying the weapon. He was arrested and charged under Texas law with

---

10. E.g., A.L.A. Schechter Poultry Corp. v. United States, 295 U.S. 495, 55 S.Ct. 837, 79 L.Ed. 1570 (1935); United States v. Butler, 297 U.S. 1, 56 S.Ct. 312, 80 L.Ed. 477 (1936); Carter v. Carter Coal Co., 298 U.S. 238, 56 S.Ct. 855, 80 L.Ed. 1160 (1936).

11. E.g., Heart of Atlanta Motel v. United States, 379 U.S. 241, 85 S.Ct. 348, 13 L.Ed.2d 258 (1964); Katzenbach v.

McClung, 379 U.S. 294, 85 S.Ct. 377, 13 L.Ed.2d 290 (1964).

12. Gun Control Act of 1968, 18 U.S.C. § 921–28. See, e.g., Barrett v. United States, 423 U.S. 212, 96 S.Ct. 498, 46 L.Ed.2d 450 (1976); Scarborough v. United States, 431 U.S. 563, 97 S.Ct. 1963, 52 L.Ed.2d 582 (1977).

firearm possession on school premises. The next day, the state charges were dismissed after federal agents charged respondent by complaint with violating the Gun–Free School Zones Act of 1990.

* * * Respondent moved to dismiss his federal indictment on the ground that § 922(q) "is unconstitutional as it is beyond the power of Congress to legislate control over our public schools." The District Court denied the motion, concluding that § 922(q) "is a constitutional exercise of Congress' well-defined power to regulate activities in and affecting commerce, and the 'business' of elementary, middle and high schools ... affects interstate commerce." * * * The District Court conducted a bench trial, found him guilty of violating § 922(q), and sentenced him to six months' imprisonment and two years' supervised release.

* * * The Court of Appeals for the Fifth Circuit * * * reversed respondent's conviction. * * * Because of the importance of the issue, we granted certiorari, and we now affirm.

We start with first principles. The Constitution creates a Federal Government of enumerated powers. As James Madison wrote, "the powers delegated by the proposed Constitution to the federal government are few and defined. Those which are to remain in the State governments are numerous and indefinite." The Federalist No. 45. * * *

* * *

* * * [W]e have identified three broad categories of activity that Congress may regulate under its commerce power. First, Congress may regulate the use of the channels of interstate commerce. Second, Congress is empowered to regulate and protect the instrumentalities of interstate commerce, or persons or things in interstate commerce, even though the threat may come only from intrastate activities. Finally, Congress' commerce authority includes the power to regulate those activities having a substantial relation to interstate commerce, i.e., those activities that substantially affect interstate commerce.

* * *

* * * The first two categories of authority may be quickly disposed of: § 922(q) is not a regulation of the use of the channels of interstate commerce, nor is it an attempt to prohibit the interstate transportation of a commodity through the channels of commerce; nor can § 922(q) be justified as a regulation by which Congress has sought to protect an instrumentality of interstate commerce or a thing in interstate commerce. Thus, if § 922(q) is to be sustained, it must be under the third category as a regulation of an activity that substantially affects interstate commerce.

First, we have upheld a wide variety of congressional Acts regulating intrastate economic activity where we have concluded that the activity substantially affected interstate commerce. Examples include the regulation of intrastate coal mining, intrastate extortionate credit transactions, restaurants utilizing substantial interstate supplies, inns and hotels catering to interstate guests, and production and consumption of home-grown wheat. Wickard v. Filburn, 317 U.S. 111 (1942). These examples are by no means exhaustive, but the pattern is clear. Where economic activity substantially affects interstate commerce, legislation regulating that activity will be sustained.

Even *Wickard*, which is perhaps the most far reaching example of Commerce Clause authority over intrastate activity, involved economic activity in a way that possession of a gun in a school zone does not.

* * *

Section 922(q) is a criminal statute that by its terms has nothing to do with "commerce" or any sort of economic enterprise, however broadly one might define those terms. Section 922(q) is not an essential part of a larger regulation of economic activity, in which the regulatory scheme could be undercut unless the intrastate activity were regulated. It cannot, therefore, be sustained under our cases upholding regulations of activities that arise out of or are connected with a commercial transaction, which viewed in the aggregate, substantially affects interstate commerce.

Second, § 922(q) contains no jurisdictional element which would ensure, through case-by-case inquiry, that the firearm possession in question affects interstate commerce. * * *

Although as part of our independent evaluation of constitutionality under the Commerce Clause we of course consider legislative findings, and indeed even congressional committee findings, regarding effect on interstate commerce, the Government concedes that "neither the statute nor its legislative history contains express congressional findings regarding the effects upon interstate commerce of gun possession in a school zone." We agree with the Government that Congress normally is not required to make formal findings as to the substantial burdens that an activity has on interstate commerce. But to the extent that congressional findings would enable us to evaluate the legislative judgment that the activity in question substantially affected interstate commerce, even though no such substantial effect was visible to the naked eye, they are lacking here.

* * *

The Government's essential contention, *in fine*, is that we may determine here that § 922(q) is valid because possession of a firearm in a local school zone does indeed substantially affect interstate commerce. The Government argues that possession of a firearm in a school zone may result in violent crime and that violent crime can be expected to affect the functioning of the national economy in two ways. First, the costs of violent crime are substantial, and, through the mechanism of insurance, those costs are spread throughout the population. Second, violent crime reduces the willingness of individuals to travel to areas within the country that are perceived to be unsafe. The Government also argues that the presence of guns in schools poses a substantial threat to the educational process by threatening the learning environment. A handicapped educational process, in turn, will result in a less productive citizenry. That, in turn, would have an adverse effect on the Nation's economic well-being. As a result, the Government argues that Congress could rationally have concluded that § 922(q) substantially affects interstate commerce.

We pause to consider the implications of the Government's arguments. The Government admits, under its "costs of crime" reasoning, that Congress could regulate not only all violent crime, but all activities that might lead to violent crime, regardless of how tenuously they relate to interstate commerce. Similarly, under the Government's "national productivity" reasoning, Congress could regulate any activity that it found was related to the economic productivity of individual citizens: family law (including marriage, divorce, and child custody), for example. Under the theories that the Government presents in support of § 922(q), it is difficult to perceive any limitation on federal power, even in areas such as criminal law enforcement or education where States historically have been sovereign. Thus, if we were to accept the Government's arguments, we are hard-pressed to posit any activity by an individual that Congress is without power to regulate.

To uphold the Government's contentions here, we would have to pile inference upon inference in a manner that would bid fair to convert congressional authority under the Commerce Clause to a general police power of the sort retained by the States. Admittedly, some of our prior cases have taken long steps down that road, giving great deference to congressional action. The broad language in these opinions has suggested the possibility of additional expansion, but we decline here to proceed any further. To do so would require us to conclude that the Constitution's enumeration of powers does not presuppose something not enumerated, and that there never will be a distinction between what is truly national and what is truly local. This we are unwilling to do.

For the foregoing reasons the judgment of the Court of Appeals is

Affirmed.

[The concurring opinions of JUSTICE KENNEDY, JUSTICE O'CONNOR and JUSTICE THOMAS are omitted.]

[The dissenting opinions of JUSTICE STEVENS and SOUTER are omitted.]

* * *

JUSTICE BREYER, with whom JUSTICE STEVENS, JUSTICE SOUTER, and JUSTICE GINSBURG join, dissenting.

* * * In my view, the statute falls well within the scope of the commerce power as this Court has understood that power over the last half-century.

I

In reaching this conclusion, I apply three basic principles of Commerce Clause interpretation. First, the power to "regulate Commerce . . .

among the several States," encompasses the power to regulate local activities insofar as they significantly affect interstate commerce. * * *

Second, in determining whether a local activity will likely have a significant effect upon interstate commerce, a court must consider, not the effect of an individual act (a single instance of gun possession), but rather the cumulative effect of all similar instances (i.e., the effect of all guns possessed in or near schools). * * *

Third, the Constitution requires us to judge the connection between a regulated activity and interstate commerce, not directly, but at one remove. Courts must give Congress a degree of leeway in determining the existence of a significant factual connection between the regulated activity and interstate commerce—both because the Constitution delegates the commerce power directly to Congress and because the determination requires an empirical judgment of a kind that a legislature is more likely than a court to make with accuracy. The traditional words "rational basis" capture this leeway. Thus, the specific question before us, as the Court recognizes, is not whether the "regulated activity sufficiently affected interstate commerce," but, rather, whether Congress could have had "a rational basis" for so concluding.

I recognize that we must judge this matter independently. And, I also recognize that Congress did not write specific "interstate commerce" findings into the law under which Lopez was convicted. Nonetheless, * * * the absence of findings, at most, deprives a statute of the benefit of some extra leeway. * * *

* * *

II

Applying these principles to the case at hand, we must ask whether Congress could have had a rational basis for finding a significant (or substantial) connection between gun-related school violence and interstate commerce. * * * As long as one views the commerce connection, not as a "technical legal conception," but as "a practical one," the answer to this question must be yes. Numerous reports and studies—generated both inside and outside government—make clear that Congress could reasonably have found the empirical connection that its law, implicitly or explicitly, asserts. * * *

For one thing, reports, hearings, and other readily available literature make clear that the problem of guns in and around schools is widespread and extremely serious. These materials report, for example, that four percent of American high school students (and six percent of inner-city high school students) carry a gun to school at least occasionally; that 12 percent of urban high school students have had guns fired at them, that 20 percent of those students have been threatened with guns, and that, in any 6-month period, several hundred thousand schoolchildren are victims of violent crimes in or near their schools. And, they report that this widespread violence in schools throughout the Nation significantly interferes with the quality of education in those schools.

Based on reports such as these, Congress obviously could have thought that guns and learning are mutually exclusive. And, Congress could therefore have found a substantial educational problem—teachers unable to teach, students unable to learn—and concluded that guns near schools contribute substantially to the size and scope of that problem.

Having found that guns in schools significantly undermine the quality of education in our Nation's classrooms, Congress could also have found, given the effect of education upon interstate and foreign commerce, that gun-related violence in and around schools is a commercial, as well as a human, problem. Education, although far more than a matter of economics, has long been inextricably intertwined with the Nation's economy. When this Nation began, most workers received their education in the workplace, typically (like Benjamin Franklin) as apprentices. * * * Scholars estimate that nearly a quarter of America's economic growth in the early years of this century is traceable directly to increased schooling, that investment in "human capital" (through spending on education) exceeded investment in "physical capital" by a ratio of almost two to one, and that the economic returns to this investment in education exceeded the returns to conventional capital investment.

> * * *

Increasing global competition also has made primary and secondary education economically more important. * * *

Finally, there is evidence that, today more than ever, many firms base their location decisions upon the presence, or absence, of a work force with a basic education. * * *

The economic links I have just sketched seem fairly obvious. Why then is it not equally obvious, in light of those links, that a widespread, serious, and substantial physical threat to teaching and learning also substantially threatens the commerce to which that teaching and learning is inextricably tied? * * * At the very least, Congress could rationally have concluded that the links are "substantial."

> * * *

To hold this statute constitutional is not to "obliterate" the "distinction of what is national and what is local," nor is it to hold that the Commerce Clause permits the Federal Government to "regulate any activity that it found was related to the economic productivity of individual citizens," to regulate "marriage, divorce, and child custody," or to regulate any and all aspects of education. * * * [T]he immediacy of the connection between education and the national economic well-being is documented by scholars and accepted by society at large in a way and to a degree that may not hold true for other social institutions. It must surely be the rare case, then, that a statute strikes at conduct that (when considered in the abstract) seems so removed from commerce, but which (practically speaking) has so significant an impact upon commerce.

In sum, a holding that the particular statute before us falls within the commerce power would not expand the scope of that Clause. Rather, it simply would apply pre-existing law to changing economic circumstances. * * *

* * *

Notes and Questions

1. Think back to *Munn*, decided in 1877, and dealing with the allocation of regulatory authority between states and the federal government. Has the nation changed over the past 120 years? Has the Constitution? Does the Court sound as though it is coming full circle in its constitutional analysis of where fundamental regulatory authority resides?

2. Who most convinces you about the relationship between guns and commerce? Is Justice Breyer correct that both guns and education affect interstate commerce and thus should be subject to federal regulation? Is the majority correct that such an understanding of interstate commerce would leave nothing within exclusive state control?

3. The holding of *Lopez* is bounded by its facts, of course, and those facts do not bear much resemblance to the kinds of regulation we will discuss. However, the dicta are broad and potentially far reaching. How far do you believe *Lopez* should be extended? What existing or proposed regulations might raise questions under this case?

4. In the background to *Lopez* is the substantive due process debate commenced long ago with Lochner v. New York. In the era of substantive due process, the Court also employed the Commerce Clause as an alternative means of striking down state law so it is easy to see why the two approaches are equated in the principal case. Does the revival of judicially-imposed Commerce Clause limitations create an inevitable return to substantive due process? Can you draw a line between them?

5. For a court that often counsels deference to judgments of the political branch, *Lopez* seems a departure. Compare, Babbitt v. Sweet Home Chapter in Chapter 5. When no principled distinction can be drawn between intra- and inter-state commerce, is there any reason not to defer to where Congress has drawn the line? Can the states adequately protect their federalism interests through their representatives in Congress? Might some states be able to do so, but not all? Should it matter whether a federal statute based on the Commerce Clause was adopted unanimously or by a close vote?

C. COMMERCE CLAUSE LIMITATIONS ON STATE REGULATION

The Commerce Clause has implications for state regulation as well. Early in the nation's history, Chief Justice Marshall in Gibbons v. Ogden, 22 U.S. (9 Wheat.) 1, 6 L.Ed. 23 (1824), gave a broad reading to "commerce" that was subject to federal regulation but also acknowledged some concurrent state regulatory authority over matters as to which the federal government had not acted.

Later, the Court tried to distinguish between matters that were inherently local and those that required uniform national treatment. E.g., Cooley v. Board of Wardens, 53 U.S. (12 How.) 299, 13 L.Ed. 996 (1851) (upholding requirement for local pilot in port of Philadelphia).

But ultimately, state regulation has come to be tested in terms of whether the regulatory burden imposed by the state discriminates against interstate commerce and whether the state's interest in enforcing its regulation is sufficiently great to justify that impact.

In Southern Pacific Co. v. Arizona, 325 U.S. 761, 65 S.Ct. 1515, 89 L.Ed. 1915 (1945), state law prohibited trains to operate in the state with more than 14 passenger cars or 70 freight cars. The regulation increased costs for long-haul shippers as trains either had to be broken up for the trip across Arizona or shorter trains had to be run across many other states as well. The Court found evidence the state offered as to the increased safety of shorter trains was unpersuasive, and because the burden on interstate commerce was significant, the regulation was invalidated.[13]

Similarly, in Dean Milk Co. v. City of Madison, 340 U.S. 349, 71 S.Ct. 295, 95 L.Ed. 329 (1951), a city ordinance requiring that milk sold in Madison, Wisconsin, be processed and bottled within 5 miles of the city was struck down as a discrimination against milk bottled in Illinois.

In Wyoming v. Oklahoma, 502 U.S. 437, 112 S.Ct. 789, 117 L.Ed.2d 1 (1992), a law requiring that at least 10% of the coal used to generate electricity in the state be mined there was struck down; and C & A Carbone, Inc. v. Town of Clarkstown, 511 U.S. 383, 114 S.Ct. 1677, 128 L.Ed.2d 399 (1994), even voided a town's requirement that a city's waste be deposited at the city dump rather than being sold in interstate commerce.[14]

But does the Commerce Clause mean a state can do nothing to benefit its producers or protect them against economic ruin? It was such a question that the Court addressed in the following case.

---

13. See also, Raymond Motor Transportation, Inc. v. Rice, 434 U.S. 429, 98 S.Ct. 787, 54 L.Ed.2d 664 (1978) (striking down limits on the length of trucks passing through state); Kassel v. Consolidated Freightways Corp., 450 U.S. 662, 101 S.Ct. 1309, 67 L.Ed.2d 580 (1981) ("Iowa made a more serious effort to support the safety rationale of its law . . . but its effort was no more persuasive."). However, a regulation of truck size was explicitly upheld in South Carolina State Highway Department v. Barnwell Brothers, Inc., 303 U.S. 177, 58 S.Ct. 510, 82 L.Ed. 734 (1938).

14. See also, Oregon Waste Sys. Inc. v. Department of Environmental Quality, 511 U.S. 93, 114 S.Ct. 1345, 128 L.Ed.2d 13 (1994); Daniel J. Gifford, Federalism, Efficiency, the Commerce Clause, and the Sherman Act: Why We Should Follow a Consistent Free–Market Policy, 44 Emory L.J. 1227 (1995); Daniel A. Farber & Robert E. Hudec, Free Trade and the Regulatory State: A GATT's–Eye View of the Dormant Commerce Clause, 47 Vanderbilt L. Rev. 1401 (1994). A less sanguine view of these developments is taken in Earl M. Maltz, The Impact of the Constitutional Revolution of 1937 on the Dormant Commerce Clause—A Case Study in the Decline of State Autonomy, 19 Harvard J.L. & Pub. Policy 121 (1995).

WEST LYNN CREAMERY, INC. v. HEALY

Supreme Court of the United States, 1994.
512 U.S. 186, 114 S.Ct. 2205, 129 L.Ed.2d 157.

JUSTICE STEVENS delivered the opinion of the Court.

A Massachusetts pricing order imposes an assessment on all fluid milk sold by dealers to Massachusetts retailers. About two-thirds of that milk is produced out of State. The entire assessment, however, is distributed to Massachusetts dairy farmers. The question presented is whether the pricing order unconstitutionally discriminates against interstate commerce. We hold that it does.

I

Petitioner West Lynn Creamery, Inc., is a milk dealer licensed to do business in Massachusetts. It purchases raw milk, which it processes, packages, and sells to wholesalers, retailers, and other milk dealers. About 97% of the raw milk it purchases is produced by out-of-state farmers. Petitioner LeComte's Dairy, Inc., is also a licensed Massachusetts milk dealer. It purchases all of its milk from West Lynn and distributes it to retail outlets in Massachusetts.

Since 1937, the Agricultural Marketing Agreement Act, 7 U.S.C. § 601 et seq., has authorized the Secretary of Agriculture to regulate the minimum prices paid to producers of raw milk by issuing marketing orders for particular geographic areas.[15] While the Federal Government sets minimum prices based on local conditions, those prices have not been so high as to prevent substantial competition among producers in different States. In the 1980's and early 1990's, Massachusetts dairy farmers began to lose market share to lower cost producers in neighboring States. In response, the Governor of Massachusetts appointed a Special Commission to study the dairy industry. The Commission found that many producers had sold their dairy farms during the past decade and that if prices paid to farmers for their milk were not significantly increased, a majority of the remaining farmers in Massachusetts would be "forced out of business within the year." On January 28, 1992, relying on the Commission's Report, the Commissioner of the Massachusetts Department of Food and Agriculture (respondent) declared a State

15. The minimum price is a "blend price" that is determined, in part, by the ultimate use of the raw milk. See 7 CFR § 1001.1 et seq. (1993). Raw milk used to produce fluid milk products has the highest price and is characterized in the federal order as "Class I" milk. Milk used for other products, such as eggnog, sour cream, and hard cheese, bears a lower price and is characterized as "Class II" and "Class III" milk. Each dealer is required to file a monthly report of its raw milk purchases and the use to which that milk is put. In computing the monthly blend price, the Federal Market Administrator calculates the weighted average price of the various classes of milk. If Class I milk predominates in the dealer reports, the blend price is high; if other classes predominate, the blend price is lower. Although all of the farmers are paid the same minimum blend price regardless of the use to which their milk is put, dealers who sell more than an average amount of Class I products pay a higher per unit price than those with relatively lower Class I sales. * * * Like the federal order, the Massachusetts order requires dealers to make payments into a fund that is disbursed to farmers on a monthly basis. The assessments, however, are only on Class I sales and the distributions are only to Massachusetts farmers. [Court's fn. 1]

of Emergency. In his declaration he noted that the average federal blend price had declined from $14.67 per hundred pounds (cwt) of raw milk in 1990 to $12.64/cwt in 1991, while costs of production for Massachusetts farmers had risen to an estimated average of $15.50/cwt. He concluded:

> "Regionally, the industry is in serious trouble and ultimately, a federal solution will be required. In the meantime, we must act on the state level to preserve our local industry, maintain reasonable minimum prices for the dairy farmers, thereby ensure a continuous and adequate supply of fresh milk for our market, and protect the public health."

Promptly after his declaration of emergency, respondent issued the pricing order that is challenged in this proceeding.

The order requires every "dealer" in Massachusetts to make a monthly "premium payment" into the "Massachusetts Dairy Equalization Fund." The amount of those payments is computed in two steps. First, the monthly "order premium" is determined by subtracting the federal blend price for that month from $15 and dividing the difference by three; thus if the federal price is $12/cwt, the order premium is $1/cwt.[16] Second, the premium is multiplied by the amount (in pounds) of the dealer's Class I sales in Massachusetts. Each month the fund is distributed to Massachusetts producers. Each Massachusetts producer receives a share of the total fund equal to his proportionate contribution to the State's total production of raw milk.

Petitioners West Lynn and LeComte's complied with the pricing order for two months, paying almost $200,000 into the Massachusetts Dairy Equalization Fund. Starting in July 1992, however, petitioners refused to make the premium payments, and respondent commenced license revocation proceedings. Petitioners then filed an action in state court seeking an injunction against enforcement of the order on the ground that it violated the Commerce Clause of the Federal Constitution. The state court denied relief and respondent conditionally revoked their licenses.

The * * * Supreme Judicial Court of Massachusetts affirmed, because it concluded that "the pricing order does not discriminate on its face, is evenhanded in its application, and only incidentally burdens interstate commerce." The Court noted that the "pricing order was designed to aid only Massachusetts producers." It conceded that "[c]ommon sense" indicated that the plan has an "adverse impact on interstate commerce" and that "the fund distribution scheme does burden out-of-

---

16. The Commissioner appears to have set the order premium at only a third of the difference between the federal price and $15 because Massachusetts farmers produce only about one-third of the milk sold as fluid milk in the State. Since Massachusetts dairy farmers produce one-third of the milk, an assessment of one-third the difference between $15 and the federal minimum price generates enough revenue to give Massa- chusetts dairy farmers the entire difference between $15 and the federal minimum price without leaving any surplus. By paying Massachusetts dairy farmers the entire difference between $15 and the federal mini- mum price, the order premium allows Mas- sachusetts farmers whose cost of production is $15/cwt to sell their milk without loss at the federal minimum price. [Court's fn. 5]

State producers." Nevertheless, the Court asserted that "the burden is incidental given the purpose and design of the program." Because it found that the "local benefits" provided to the Commonwealth's dairy industry "outweigh any incidental burden on interstate commerce," it sustained the constitutionality of the pricing order. We granted certiorari, and now reverse.

II

The Commerce Clause vests Congress with ample power to enact legislation providing for the regulation of prices paid to farmers for their products. United States v. Darby, 312 U.S. 100 (1941); Wickard v. Filburn, 317 U.S. 111 (1942); Mandeville Island Farms, Inc. v. American Crystal Sugar Co., 334 U.S. 219 (1948). An affirmative exercise of that power led to the promulgation of the federal order setting minimum milk prices. The Commerce Clause also limits the power of the Commonwealth of Massachusetts to adopt regulations that discriminate against interstate commerce. "This 'negative' aspect of the Commerce Clause prohibits economic protectionism—that is, regulatory measures designed to benefit in-state economic interests by burdening out-of-state competitors. . . . Thus, state statutes that clearly discriminate against interstate commerce are routinely struck down . . . unless the discrimination is demonstrably justified by a valid factor unrelated to economic protectionism . . ." New Energy Co. of Indiana v. Limbach, 486 U.S. 269, 273–274 (1988).[17]

The paradigmatic example of a law discriminating against interstate commerce is the protective tariff or customs duty, which taxes goods imported from other States, but does not tax similar products produced in State. A tariff is an attractive measure because it simultaneously raises revenue and benefits local producers by burdening their out-of-state competitors. Nevertheless, it violates the principle of the unitary national market by handicapping out-of-state competitors, thus artificially encouraging in-state production even when the same goods could be produced at lower cost in other States.

Because of their distorting effects on the geography of production, tariffs have long been recognized as violative of the Commerce Clause. In fact, tariffs against the products of other States are so patently unconstitutional that our cases reveal not a single attempt by any State to enact one. Instead, the cases are filled with state laws that aspire to reap some of the benefits of tariffs by other means. In Baldwin v. G.A.F. Seelig, Inc., 294 U.S. 511 (1935), the State of New York attempted to protect its dairy farmers from the adverse effects of Vermont competition by establishing a single minimum price for all milk, whether produced in

---

17. The "negative" aspect of the Commerce Clause was considered the more important by the "father of the Constitution," James Madison. In one of his letters, Madison wrote that the Commerce Clause "grew out of the abuse of the power by the importing States in taxing the non-importing, and was intended as a negative and preventive provision against injustice among the States themselves, rather than as a power to be used for the positive purposes of the General Government." 3 M. Farrand, Records of the Federal Convention of 1787, p. 478 (1911). [Court's fn. 9]

New York or elsewhere. This Court did not hesitate, however, to strike it down. Writing for a unanimous Court, Justice Cardozo reasoned: "Neither the power to tax nor the police power may be used by the state of destination with the aim and effect of establishing an economic barrier against competition with the products of another state or the labor of its residents. Restrictions so contrived are an unreasonable clog upon the mobility of commerce. They set up what is equivalent to a rampart of customs duties designed to neutralize advantages belonging to the place of origin." Thus, because the minimum price regulation had the same effect as a tariff or customs duty—neutralizing the advantage possessed by lower cost out-of-state producers—it was held unconstitutional. * * * Other cases of this kind are legion.

Under these cases, Massachusetts' pricing order is clearly unconstitutional. Its avowed purpose and its undisputed effect are to enable higher cost Massachusetts dairy farmers to compete with lower cost dairy farmers in other States. The "premium payments" are effectively a tax which makes milk produced out of State more expensive. Although the tax also applies to milk produced in Massachusetts, its effect on Massachusetts producers is entirely (indeed more than) offset by the subsidy provided exclusively to Massachusetts dairy farmers. Like an ordinary tariff, the tax is thus effectively imposed only on out-of-state products. The pricing order thus allows Massachusetts dairy farmers who produce at higher cost to sell at or below the price charged by lower cost out-of-state producers.[18] If there were no federal minimum prices for milk, out-of-state producers might still be able to retain their market share by lowering their prices. Nevertheless, out-of-staters' ability to remain competitive by lowering their prices would not immunize a discriminatory measure. In this case, because the Federal Government sets minimum prices, out-of-state producers may not even have the option of reducing prices in order to retain market share. The Massachusetts pricing order thus will almost certainly "cause local goods to constitute a larger share, and goods with an out-of-state source to constitute a smaller share, of the total sales in the market." Exxon Corp. v. Governor of Maryland, 437 U.S. 117, 126, n. 16 (1978). In fact, this effect was the motive behind the promulgation of the pricing order. This

---

18. A numerical example may make this effect clearer. Suppose the federal minimum price is $12/cwt, that out-of-state producers can sell milk profitably at that price, but that in-state producers need a price of $15/cwt in order to break even. Under the pricing order, the tax or "order premium" will be $1/cwt (one-third the difference between the $15/cwt target price and the $12/cwt federal minimum price). Assuming the tax generates sufficient funds (which will be the case as long as two-thirds of milk is produced out of State, which appears to be the case), the Massachusetts farmers will receive a subsidy of $3/cwt. This subsidy will allow them to lower their prices from $15/cwt to $12/cwt while still breaking even. Selling at $12/cwt, Massachusetts dairy farmers will now be able to compete with out-of-state producers. The net effect of the tax and subsidy, like that of a tariff, is to raise the after-tax price paid by the dealers. If exactly two-thirds of the milk sold in Massachusetts is produced out of State, net prices will rise by $1/cwt. If out-of-state farmers produce more than two-thirds of the raw milk, the Dairy Equalization Fund will have a surplus, which will be refunded to the milk dealers. This refund will mitigate the price increase, although it will have no effect on the ability of the program to enable higher-cost Massachusetts dairy farmers to compete with lower-cost out-of-staters. [Court's fn. 10]

effect renders the program unconstitutional, because it, like a tariff, "neutralize[s] advantages belonging to the place of origin." *Baldwin*, 294 U.S., at 527, 55 S.Ct., at 502.

* * *

III

Respondent advances four arguments against the conclusion that its pricing order imposes an unconstitutional burden on interstate commerce * * *.

A

Respondent's principal argument is that, because "the milk order achieves its goals through lawful means," the order as a whole is constitutional. He argues that the payments to Massachusetts dairy farmers from the Dairy Equalization Fund are valid, because subsidies are constitutional exercises of state power, and that the order premium which provides money for the Fund is valid, because it is a nondiscriminatory tax. Therefore the pricing order is constitutional, because it is merely the combination of two independently lawful regulations. * * *

Even granting respondent's assertion that both components of the pricing order would be constitutional standing alone,[19] the pricing order nevertheless must fall. A pure subsidy funded out of general revenue ordinarily imposes no burden on interstate commerce, but merely assists local business. The pricing order in this case, however, is funded principally from taxes on the sale of milk produced in other States.[20] By so funding the subsidy, respondent not only assists local farmers, but burdens interstate commerce. * * *

More fundamentally, respondent errs in assuming that the constitutionality of the pricing order follows logically from the constitutionality of its component parts. By conjoining a tax and a subsidy, Massachusetts has created a program more dangerous to interstate commerce than either part alone. Nondiscriminatory measures, like the evenhanded tax at issue here, are generally upheld, in spite of any adverse effects on interstate commerce, in part because "[t]he existence of major in-state interests adversely affected ... is a powerful safeguard against legislative abuse." Minnesota v. Clover Leaf Creamery Co., 449 U.S. 456, 473,

19. We have never squarely confronted the constitutionality of subsidies, and we need not do so now. We have, however, noted that "[d]irect subsidization of domestic industry does not ordinarily run afoul" of the negative Commerce Clause. New Energy Co. of Indiana v. Limbach, 486 U.S., at 278. In addition, it is undisputed that States may try to attract business by creating an environment conducive to economic activity, as by maintaining good roads, sound public education, or low taxes. [Court's fn. 15]

20. It is undisputed that an overwhelming majority of the milk sold in Massachusetts is produced elsewhere. Thus, even though the tax is applied even-handedly to milk produced in State and out of State, most of the tax collected comes from taxes on milk from other States. In addition, the tax on in-state milk, unlike that imposed on out-of-state milk, does not impose any burden on in-state producers, because in-state dairy farmers can be confident that the taxes paid on their milk will be returned to them via the Dairy Stabilization Fund. [Court's fn. 16]

n. 17 (1981). * * *[21] However, when a nondiscriminatory tax is coupled with a subsidy to one of the groups hurt by the tax, a state's political processes can no longer be relied upon to prevent legislative abuse, because one of the in-state interests which would otherwise lobby against the tax has been mollified by the subsidy. So, in this case, one would ordinarily have expected at least three groups to lobby against the order premium, which, as a tax, raises the price (and hence lowers demand) for milk: dairy farmers, milk dealers, and consumers. But because the tax was coupled with a subsidy, one of the most powerful of these groups, Massachusetts dairy farmers, instead of exerting their influence against the tax, were in fact its primary supporters.[22]

* * *

B

Respondent also argues that since the Massachusetts milk dealers who pay the order premiums are not competitors of the Massachusetts farmers, the pricing order imposes no discriminatory burden on commerce. This argument cannot withstand scrutiny. Is it possible to doubt that if Massachusetts imposed a higher sales tax on milk produced in Maine than milk produced in Massachusetts that the tax would be struck down, in spite of the fact that the sales tax was imposed on consumers, and consumers do not compete with dairy farmers? For over 150 years, our cases have rightly concluded that the imposition of a differential burden on any part of the stream of commerce—from wholesaler to retailer to consumer—is invalid, because a burden placed at any point will result in a disadvantage to the out-of-state producer.

C

Respondent also argues that "the operation of the Order disproves any claim of protectionism," because "only in-state consumers feel the effect of any retail price increase . . . [and] [t]he dealers themselves . . . have a substantial in-state presence." This argument, if accepted, would undermine almost every discriminatory tax case. State taxes are ordinarily paid by in-state businesses and consumers, yet if they discriminate against out-of-state products, they are unconstitutional. The idea that a discriminatory tax does not interfere with interstate commerce "merely

21. The same principle is recognized in the conceptually similar field of intergovernmental taxation, where nondiscrimination also plays a central role in setting the boundary between the permissible and the impermissible. Washington v. United States, 460 U.S. 536, 545 (1983) ("A 'political check' is provided when a state tax falls on a significant group of state citizens who can be counted upon to use their votes to keep the State from raising the tax excessively, and thus placing an unfair burden on the Federal Government"). [Court's fn. 17]

22. As the Governor's Special Commission Relative to the Establishment of a Dairy Stabilization Fund realized, consumers would be unlikely to organize effectively to oppose the pricing order. The Commission's report remarked, "the estimated two cent increase per quart of milk would not be noticed by the consuming public," because the price of milk varies so often and for so many reasons that consumers would be unlikely to feel the price increases or to attribute them to the pricing order. [Court's fn. 18]

because the burden of the tax was borne by consumers" in the taxing State was thoroughly repudiated in Bacchus Imports, Ltd. v. Dias, 468 U.S. [263 (1984)]. The cost of a tariff is also borne primarily by local consumers, yet a tariff is the paradigmatic Commerce Clause violation.

More fundamentally, respondent ignores the fact that Massachusetts dairy farmers are part of an integrated interstate market. As noted above, the purpose and effect of the pricing order are to divert market share to Massachusetts dairy farmers. This diversion necessarily injures the dairy farmers in neighboring States. Furthermore, the Massachusetts order regulates a portion of the same interstate market in milk that is more broadly regulated by a federal milk marketing order which covers most of New England. The Massachusetts producers who deliver milk to dealers in that regulated market are participants in the same interstate milk market as the out-of-state producers who sell in the same market and are guaranteed the same minimum blend price by the federal order. The fact that the Massachusetts order imposes assessments only on Massachusetts sales and distributes them only to Massachusetts producers does not exclude either the assessments or the payments from the interstate market. To the extent that those assessments affect the relative volume of Class I milk products sold in the marketing area as compared to other classes of milk products, they necessarily affect the blend price payable even to out-of-state producers who sell only in non-Massachusetts markets. The obvious impact of the order on out-of-state production demonstrates that it is simply wrong to assume that the pricing order burdens only Massachusetts consumers and dealers.

D

Finally, respondent argues that any incidental burden on interstate commerce "is outweighed by the 'local benefits' of preserving the Massachusetts dairy industry."[23] In a closely related argument, respondent urges that "the purpose of the order, to save an industry from collapse, is not protectionist." If we were to accept these arguments, we would make a virtue of the vice that the rule against discrimination condemns. Preservation of local industry by protecting it from the rigors of inter-

---

23. Among the "local benefits" that respondent identifies is "protecting unique open space and related benefits." As the Massachusetts Supreme Judicial Court recognized by relegating the "open space" point to a single footnote, the argument that environmental benefits were central and the enhancement of the market share of Massachusetts dairy farmers merely "incidental" turns the pricing order on its head. In addition, even if environmental preservation were the central purpose of the pricing order, that would not be sufficient to uphold a discriminatory regulation. Finally, the suggestion that the collapse of the dairy industry endangers open space is not self-evident. Dairy farms are enclosed by fences, and the decline of farming may well lead to less rather than more intensive land use. As one scholar noted: "Many people assume that . . . land lost from agriculture is now in urban uses. It is true that some agricultural land has been urbanized, especially since World War II, but the major portion of the land moving out of agriculture over the years has been abandoned to natural forest growth." J. Foster & W. MacConnell, Agricultural Land Use Change in Massachusetts 1951–1971, p. 5 (Research Bulletin No. 640, Jan. 1977). [Court's fn. 20]

state competition is the hallmark of the economic protectionism that the Commerce Clause prohibits. * * * With his characteristic eloquence, Justice Cardozo responded to an argument that respondent echoes today:

> "The argument is pressed upon us, however, that the end to be served by the Milk Control Act is something more than the economic welfare of the farmers or of any other class or classes. The end to be served is the maintenance of a regular and adequate supply of pure and wholesome milk, the supply being put in jeopardy when the farmers of the state are unable to earn a living income. Nebbia v. New York. Let such an exception be admitted, and all that a state will have to do in times of stress and strain is to say that its farmers and merchants and workmen must be protected against competition from without, lest they go upon the poor relief lists or perish altogether. To give entrance to that excuse would be to invite a speedy end of our national solidarity. The Constitution was framed under the dominion of a political philosophy less parochial in range. It was framed upon the theory that the peoples of the several states must sink or swim together, and that in the long run prosperity and salvation are in union and not division". Baldwin v. G.A.F. Seelig, 294 U.S., at 522–523.

* * *

The judgment of the Supreme Judicial Court of Massachusetts is reversed.

JUSTICE SCALIA, with whom JUSTICE THOMAS joins, concurring in judgment.

In my view the challenged Massachusetts pricing order is invalid under our negative–Commerce–Clause jurisprudence, for the reasons explained in Part II below. I do not agree with the reasons assigned by the Court, which seem to me, as explained in Part I, a broad expansion of current law. Accordingly, I concur only in the judgment of the Court.

I

The purpose of the negative Commerce Clause, we have often said, is to create a national market. It does not follow from that, however, and we have never held, that every state law which obstructs a national market violates the Commerce Clause. Yet that is what the Court says today. It seems to have canvassed the entire corpus of negative–Commerce–Clause opinions, culled out every free-market snippet of reasoning, and melded them into the sweeping principle that the Constitution is violated by any state law or regulation that "artificially encourag[es] in-state production even when the same goods could be produced at lower cost in other States."

As the Court seems to appreciate by its eagerness expressly to reserve the question of the constitutionality of subsidies for in-state industry, this expansive view of the Commerce Clause calls into question a wide variety of state laws that have hitherto been thought permissible.

It seems to me that a State subsidy would clearly be invalid under any formulation of the Court's guiding principle identified above. The Court guardedly asserts that a "pure subsidy funded out of general revenue ordinarily imposes no burden on interstate commerce, but merely assists local business," but under its analysis that must be taken to be true only because most local businesses (e.g., the local hardware store) are not competing with businesses out of State. The Court notes that, in funding this subsidy, Massachusetts has taxed milk produced in other States, and thus "not only assists local farmers, but burdens interstate commerce." But the same could be said of almost all subsidies funded from general state revenues, which almost invariably include monies from use taxes on out-of-state products. And even where the funding does not come in any part from taxes on out-of-state goods, "merely assist[ing]" in-state businesses, unquestionably neutralizes advantages possessed by out-of-state enterprises. Such subsidies, particularly where they are in the form of cash or (what comes to the same thing) tax forgiveness, are often admitted to have as their purpose—indeed, are nationally advertised as having as their purpose—making it more profitable to conduct business in-state than elsewhere, i.e., distorting normal market incentives.

The Court's guiding principle also appears to call into question many garden-variety state laws heretofore permissible under the negative Commerce Clause. A state law, for example, which requires, contrary to the industry practice, the use of recyclable packaging materials, favors local non-exporting producers, who do not have to establish an additional, separate packaging operation for in-state sales. If the Court's analysis is to be believed, such a law would be unconstitutional without regard to whether disruption of the "national market" is the real purpose of the restriction, and without the need to "balance" the importance of the state interests thereby pursued. These results would greatly extend the negative Commerce Clause beyond its current scope. If the Court does not intend these consequences, and does not want to foster needless litigation concerning them, it should not have adopted its expansive rationale. Another basis for deciding the case is available, which I proceed to discuss.

II

"The historical record provides no grounds for reading the Commerce Clause to be other than what it says—an authorization for Congress to regulate commerce." Nonetheless, we formally adopted the doctrine of the negative Commerce Clause 121 years ago, see Case of the State Freight Tax, 15 Wall. 232 (1873), and since then have decided a vast number of negative–Commerce–Clause cases, engendering considerable reliance interests. As a result, I will, on stare decisis grounds, enforce a self-executing "negative" Commerce Clause in two situations: (1) against a state law that facially discriminates against interstate commerce, and (2) against a state law that is indistinguishable from a type of law previously held unconstitutional by this Court.

* * *

There are at least four possible devices that would enable a State to produce the economic effect that Massachusetts has produced here: (1) a discriminatory tax upon the industry, imposing a higher liability on out-of-state members than on their in-state competitors; (2) a tax upon the industry that is nondiscriminatory in its assessment, but that has an "exemption" or "credit" for in-state members; (3) a nondiscriminatory tax upon the industry, the revenues from which are placed into a segregated fund, which fund is disbursed as "rebates" or "subsidies" to in-state members of the industry (the situation at issue in this case); and (4) with or without nondiscriminatory taxation of the industry, a subsidy for the in-state members of the industry, funded from the State's general revenues. It is long settled that the first of these methodologies is unconstitutional under the negative Commerce Clause. The second of them, "exemption" from or "credit" against a "neutral" tax, is no different in principle from the first, and has likewise been held invalid. The fourth methodology, application of a state subsidy from general revenues, is so far removed from what we have hitherto held to be unconstitutional, that prohibiting it must be regarded as an extension of our negative–Commerce–Clause jurisprudence and therefore, to me, unacceptable. Indeed, in my view our negative–Commerce–Clause cases have already approved the use of such subsidies.

The issue before us in the present case is whether the third of these methodologies must fall. Although the question is close, I conclude it would not be a principled point at which to disembark from the negative–Commerce–Clause train. The only difference between methodology (2) (discriminatory "exemption" from nondiscriminatory tax) and methodology (3) (discriminatory refund of nondiscriminatory tax) is that the money is taken and returned rather than simply left with the favored in-state taxpayer in the first place. The difference between (3) and (4), on the other hand, is the difference between assisting in-state industry through discriminatory taxation, and assisting in-state industry by other means.

I would therefore allow a State to subsidize its domestic industry so long as it does so from nondiscriminatory taxes that go into the State's general revenue fund. Perhaps, as some commentators contend, that line comports with an important economic reality: a State is less likely to maintain a subsidy when its citizens perceive that the money (in the general fund) is available for any number of competing, non-protectionist, purposes. That is not, however, the basis for my position, for as The Chief Justice explains, "[a]nalysis of interest group participation in the political process may serve many useful purposes, but serving as a basis for interpreting the dormant Commerce Clause is not one of them." Instead, I draw the line where I do because it is a clear, rational line at the limits of our extant negative–Commerce–Clause jurisprudence.

CHIEF JUSTICE REHNQUIST, with whom JUSTICE BLACKMUN joins, dissenting.

The Court is less than just in its description of the reasons which lay behind the Massachusetts law which it strikes down. The law undoubtedly sought to aid struggling Massachusetts dairy farmers, beset by steady or declining prices and escalating costs. This situation is apparently not unique to Massachusetts; New Jersey has filed an amicus brief in support of respondent because New Jersey has enacted a similar law. Both States lie in the northeastern metropolitan corridor, which is the most urbanized area in the United States, and has every prospect of becoming more so. The value of agricultural land located near metropolitan areas is driven up by the demand for housing and similar urban uses; distressed farmers eventually sell out to developers. Not merely farm produce is lost, as is the milk production in this case, but, as the Massachusetts Special Commission whose report was the basis for the order in question here found: "Without the continued existence of dairy farmers, the Commonwealth will lose its supply of locally produced fresh milk, together with the open lands that are used as wildlife refuges, for recreation, hunting, fishing, tourism, and education."

Massachusetts has dealt with this problem by providing a subsidy to aid its beleaguered dairy farmers. In case after case, we have approved the validity under the Commerce Clause of such enactments. * * * But today the Court relegates these well-established principles to a footnote and, at the same time, gratuitously casts doubt on the validity of state subsidies, observing that "[w]e have never squarely confronted" their constitutionality.

        * * *

Consistent with precedent, the Court observes: "A pure subsidy funded out of general revenue ordinarily imposes no burden on interstate commerce, but merely assists local business." And the Court correctly recognizes that "[n]ondiscriminatory measures, like the evenhanded tax at issue here, are generally upheld" due to the deference normally accorded to a State's political process in passing legislation in light of various competing interest groups. But the Court strikes down this method of state subsidization because the non-discriminatory tax levied against all milk dealers is coupled with a subsidy to milk producers. The Court does this because of its view that the method of imposing the tax and subsidy distorts the State's political process: the dairy farmers, who would otherwise lobby against the tax, have been mollified by the subsidy. But as the Court itself points out, there are still at least two strong interest groups opposed to the milk order—consumers and milk dealers. More importantly, nothing in the dormant Commerce Clause suggests that the fate of state regulation should turn upon the particular lawful manner in which the state subsidy is enacted or promulgated. Analysis of interest group participation in the political process may serve many useful purposes, but serving as a basis for interpreting the dormant Commerce Clause is not one of them.

        * * *

More than half a century ago, Justice Brandeis said in his dissenting opinion in New State Ice Co. v. Liebmann, 285 U.S. 262, 311 (1932): "To stay experimentation in things social and economic is a grave responsibility. Denial of the right to experiment may be fraught with serious consequences to the Nation. It is one of the happy incidents of the federal system that a single courageous State may, if its citizens choose, serve as a laboratory; and try novel social and economic experiments without risk to the rest of the country." Justice Brandeis' statement has been cited more than once in subsequent majority opinions of the Court. His observation bears heeding today, as it did when he made it. The wisdom of a messianic insistence on a grim sink-or-swim policy of laissez-faire economics would be debatable had Congress chosen to enact it; but Congress has done nothing of the kind. It is the Court which has imposed the policy under the dormant Commerce Clause, a policy which bodes ill for the values of federalism which have long animated our constitutional jurisprudence.

Notes and Questions

1. What approach to analysis of regulation is most useful to understanding this regime? Is the subsidy program based on one of the market failures discussed in Chapter 1? Which one, if any, might you cite? Is the program one that efficiently delivers the benefits the regulatory program is designed to provide? Has the state minimized the number of government employees needed to achieve its purpose, for example?

2. Is this a program best understood as providing a benefit to one group of a state's citizens at the expense of others?

a. How could a legislator get away with imposing a burden on a majority of his or her constituents for the benefit of a relatively few? Was the Commission cited in the Court's fn. 18 likely correct that the farmers would realize and appreciate the benefits of the program while consumers would likely overlook the increased prices they were required to pay?

b. Had the legislators here found a way to impose many of the burdens on people who could not vote, i.e., the producers in other states? Is that analytically a form of "taxation" without representation?

3. The "burden on interstate commerce" idea is probably the most likely successful way to challenge the constitutionality of state regulation. Are you convinced it is entirely different from the kind of challenge condemned in *Nebbia*?

a. What state interests could validly be set off against a burden on interstate commerce? Cf. Morgan v. Virginia, 328 U.S. 373, 66 S.Ct. 1050, 90 L.Ed. 1317 (1946) (segregated bus seating held a burden on commerce).

b. Is the "burden on interstate commerce" analysis really different from substantive due process? Can one argue that both are labels used when federal courts seek to reach out to strike down state legislative judgments? Cf. Southern Pacific Co. v. Arizona, 325 U.S. 761, 65 S.Ct. 1515, 89 L.Ed. 1915 (1945) (dissents of Justices Black and Douglas take this view).

4.   Are these cases best seen as "discrimination" cases, i.e. was this a case where Massachusetts favored its own milk producers over citizens of other states? Do you agree that such discrimination should be corrected by the federal courts? Is there any other institution in a position to correct it? Cf. Hunt v. Washington State Apple Advertising Commission, 432 U.S. 333, 97 S.Ct. 2434, 53 L.Ed.2d 383 (1977) (state requires sale and shipment of apples in closed containers with only federal grade displayed, allegedly so as to conceal the tougher grades which made other states' apples more attractive to consumers).

5.   The Commerce Clause has been used in other cases as well to strike down "discriminatory" or "burdensome" state laws. Consider the following provisions. Would you have voted for them in the legislature? Should they be sustained against constitutional challenge?

a.   A city tries to regulate how many and which firms interstate railroads may contract with to carry passengers between one Chicago rail terminal and another. Railroad Transfer Service, Inc. v. City of Chicago, 386 U.S. 351, 87 S.Ct. 1095, 18 L.Ed.2d 143 (1967).

b.   A state prohibits importation of another state's milk unless the other state agrees to reciprocal inspection standards. Great Atlantic & Pacific Tea Co. v. Cottrell, 424 U.S. 366, 96 S.Ct. 923, 47 L.Ed.2d 55 (1976); Cf. Sporhase v. Nebraska, 458 U.S. 941, 102 S.Ct. 3456, 73 L.Ed.2d 1254 (1982) (attempt to apply reciprocity provision to export of water).

6.   Commerce Clause litigation has an international counterpart.

a.   NAFTA negotiations with Mexico and Canada raised the issue of longer trucks from those countries potentially being barred because of state laws restricting their use. Safety still remains a problem. Studies have shown that large trucks are disproportionately represented in the truck crashes that kill more than 4,000 people annually. See K.C. Campbell, Ten Years of Large Truck Research, DOT Symposium July 18, 1990.

b.   And in a decision of the World Trade Organization's dispute resolution panel, the United States was found to have violated the General Agreement on Tariffs and Trade in that the U.S. Environmental Protection Agency set different standards for domestically refined gasoline than it did for gasoline refined in Venezuela and other foreign nations. WTO Dispute Settlement—Reformulated Gasoline, Document No. 40169, Jan. 19, 1996.

HEALD v. ENGLER

United States Court of Appeals, Sixth Circuit, 2003.
342 F.3d 517.

Before GUY, BOGGS, and DAUGHTERY, CIRCUIT JUDGES

DAUGHTREY, CIRCUIT JUDGE.

In this civil rights action brought pursuant to 42 U.S.C. § 1983, the plaintiffs raise a constitutional challenge to Michigan's alcohol distribution system, contending that state provisions differentiating between in-state and out-of-state wineries violate the Commerce Clause. Those regulations prohibit the direct shipment of alcoholic beverages from out-of-state wineries, while allowing in-state wineries to ship directly to consumers, provided that the in-state wineries comply with certain minimal regulatory requirements. The plaintiffs, who include wine connoisseurs, wine journalists, and one small California winery that ships its wines to customers in other states, claim that this system is unconstitutional under the dormant Commerce Clause because it interferes with the free flow of interstate commerce by discriminating against out-of-state wineries. The defendants, who include Michigan officials (referred to collectively in this opinion as "the state") and the intervening trade association, argue in response that Michigan's regulatory scheme is constitutional under the Twenty-first Amendment to the federal constitution.

* * *

The parties filed cross-motions for summary judgment, and the district court granted the state's motion and denied the plaintiffs' motion. The plaintiffs then filed a motion to reconsider, arguing that the district court should have addressed cross-motions to strike various evidence submitted by the two sides prior to the summary judgment decision. The district court denied the motion to reconsider, noting that it had effectively denied the cross-motions to strike as moot, because it did not consider the challenged evidence in deciding the summary judgment motions.

The plaintiffs now appeal both the grant of summary judgment and the denial of their motion to reconsider. For the reasons set out below, we conclude that the regulations in question are discriminatory in their application to out-of-state wineries, in violation of the dormant Commerce Clause, and cannot be justified as advancing the traditional "core concerns" of the Twenty-first Amendment. We therefore reverse the district court's judgment and remand the case with directions to the district court to enter judgment in favor of the plaintiffs.

PROCEDURAL AND FACTUAL BACKGROUND

Michigan regulates alcohol sales under a "three-tier system": consumers must purchase alcoholic beverages from licensed retailers; retailers must purchase them from licensed wholesalers; and wholesalers must purchase them from licensed manufacturers. This system is similar to that used by most states. *See* Vijay Shankar, Alcohol Direct Shipment Laws, 85 Va. L.Rev. 353, 355 (1999).

The plaintiffs allege that Michigan's system discriminates against out-of-state wineries in favor of in-state wineries because it prevents out-of-state wineries from shipping wine directly to Michigan consumers, which in-state wineries are allowed to do. As the district court correctly noted, this distinction between in-state and out-of-state wineries can only be understood by reading a number of provisions in conjunction with each other:

> [The distinction] can be gleaned from various Michigan Liquor Control Commission regulations, which are codified within the

Michigan Administrative Code. R436.1057 states that "[a] person shall not deliver, ship, or transport into this state beer, wine, or spirits without a license authorizing such action...." The only applicable license, an "outstate seller of wine license," may according to R436.1705(2)(d) be obtained by a "manufacturer which is located outside of this state, but in the United States, and which produces and bottles its own wine." However, under R436.1719(4) the holder of such a license may ship wine "only to a licensed wholesaler at the address of the licensed premises except upon written order of the commission." In answers to interrogatories, a representative of the Michigan Liquor Control Commission indicates that "[a]t present, there is no procedure whereby an out-of-state retailer or winery can obtain a license or approval to deliver wine directly to Michigan residents...."

In contrast, the Michigan Liquor Control Commission indicates that the "ability to deliver wine to the consumer is available to winemakers licensed in Michigan, inasmuch as under the provisions of M.C.L. § 436.1113(9) these licensees are permitted to sell at retail the wines they manufacture.... A licensed Michigan winemaker may deliver their [sic] own products to customers without an SDM [specially designated merchant] license...."

The plaintiffs contend that this differential treatment of in-state and out-of-state wineries violates the dormant Commerce Clause because it gives in-state wineries a competitive advantage over out-of-state wineries. In-state wineries can, for example, bypass the price mark-ups of a wholesaler and retailer, making in-state wines relatively cheaper to the consumer and allowing them to realize more profit per bottle. In addition, the cost to an out-of-state winery of the license that enables it to sell to a Michigan wholesaler is $300, while a comparable Michigan winery must pay only a $25 license fee to qualify to ship wine directly to Michigan customers. Finally, for customers who desire home delivery, Michigan wineries have a competitive advantage over out-of-state wineries that cannot ship directly to customers. In response, the state argues that the regulations to which an in-state winery is subject "more than offset, both in costs and burden, any nominal commercial advantage given by the ability to deliver directly to customers" and characterizes the burden on out-of-state wineries as "de minimis."

In its order granting summary judgment to the state and denying summary judgment to the plaintiffs, the district court held that "Michigan's direct shipment law is a permitted exercise of state power under § 2 of the 21st Amendment" because it is not "mere economic protectionism." In reaching this conclusion, the court found that Michigan's statutory scheme was designed "to ensure the collection of taxes from out-of-state wine manufacturers and to reduce the risk of alcohol falling into the hands of minors."

DISCUSSION

In reviewing challenges brought under the Commerce Clause, the Supreme Court has long held that statutes that facially discriminate are "virtually *per se*" invalid, citing as a clear example "a law that overtly blocks the flow of interstate commerce at a State's borders." Philadelphia v. New Jersey, 437 U.S. 617, 624, 98 S.Ct. 2531, 57 L.Ed.2d 475 (1978). However, a lower level of scrutiny is applied when a statute does not discriminate on its face:

> Where the statute regulates evenhandedly to effectuate a legitimate local public interest, and its effects on interstate commerce are only incidental, it will be upheld unless the burden imposed on such commerce is clearly excessive in relation to the putative local benefits.... [T]he extent of the burden that will be tolerated will of course depend on the nature of the local interest involved, and on whether it could be promoted as well with a lesser impact on interstate activities.

Id., quoting Pike v. Bruce Church, Inc., 397 U.S. 137, 142, 90 S.Ct. 844, 25 L.Ed.2d 174 (1970).

* * *

Here, it is clear that the Michigan statutory and regulatory scheme treats out-of-state and in-state wineries differently, with the effect of benefitting the in-state wineries and burdening those from out of state. As discussed above, Michigan wineries enjoy both greater access to consumers who wish to have wine delivered to their homes, and greater profit through their exemption from the three-tier system. Out-of-state wineries, on the other hand, must participate in the costly three-tier system, to their economic detriment and, although this is not clear from the record, may be shut out of the Michigan market altogether if unable to obtain a wholesaler. The Fourth Circuit reached a similar conclusion in a case considering North Carolina's alcohol distribution system, which is nearly identical to Michigan's. In Beskind v. Easley, 325 F.3d 506 (4th Cir.2003), the court found that North Carolina's alcohol distribution laws, which discriminate against out-of-state wineries in favor of in-state wineries, are unconstitutional unless "the State can show that it advances a legitimate local purpose that cannot be adequately served by reasonable nondiscriminatory alternatives." *Id.* at 515 (internal quotations and citations omitted).

Having determined that the provision is facially discriminatory, we now turn to the question of whether the regulatory scheme is nevertheless constitutional because it "fall[s] within the core of the State's power under the Twenty-first Amendment," having been enacted "in the interest of promoting temperance, ensuring orderly market conditions, and raising revenue," North Dakota v. United States, 495 U.S. 423, 432, 110 S.Ct. 1986, 109 L.Ed.2d 420 (1990), and because these interests "cannot be adequately served by reasonable nondiscriminatory alternatives." New Energy Co. of Ind. v. Limbach, 486 U.S. 269, 278, 108 S.Ct. 1803, 100 L.Ed.2d 302 (1988) (citations omitted).

We conclude, based on the evidence in the record, that defendants have not shown that the Michigan scheme's discrimination between in-state and out-of-state wineries furthers any of the concerns listed above, much less that no reasonable non-discriminatory means exists to satisfy these concerns. This is so even if, taking the evidence in the light most favorable to defendants, we assume that all of the evidence they submitted was admissible. It is important to keep in mind that the relevant inquiry is not whether Michigan's three-tier system *as a whole* promotes the goals of "temperance, ensuring an orderly market, and raising revenue," but whether the discriminatory scheme challenged in this case—the direct-shipment ban for out-of-state wineries—does so. *See, e.g., Beskind,* 325 F.3d at 517 ("The question is not whether North Carolina can advance its regulatory purpose by imposing fewer burdens on in-state wineries than out-of-state wineries.... Rather, the question is whether *discriminating* in favor of in-state wineries ... serves a Twenty-first Amendment interest."). Obviously, the state bears the burden of justifying a discriminatory statute, and "the standards for such justification are high." New Energy Co., 486 U.S. at 278, 108 S.Ct. 1803; *see also* Cooper v. McBeath, 11 F.3d 547, 553 (5th Cir.1994) (describing the burden of proof faced by the state as "towering"); Hughes v. Oklahoma, 441 U.S. 322, 337, 99 S.Ct. 1727, 60 L.Ed.2d 250 (1979) ("[F]acial discrimination by itself may be a fatal defect.... [A]t a minimum [it] invokes the strictest scrutiny.").

* * *

The district court in this case was correct in finding that the Michigan alcohol distribution system discriminates between in-state and out-of-state interests to the extent that in-state wineries may obtain licenses to ship wine directly to consumers, but out-of-state wineries may not and are instead required to go through the more costly three-tier system. What the district court did not do was undertake the necessary analysis that follows from such a finding. Instead, it concluded that Michigan's system "cannot be characterized as 'mere economic protectionism,' " because the system furthers the "core concerns" of the Twenty-first Amendment. The district court's observation that "[t]he Michigan Legislature has chosen this path to ensure the collection of taxes from out-of-state wine manufacturers and to reduce the risk of alcohol falling into the hands of minors" and its conclusion that "the 21st Amendment gives it the power to do so," without more, do not constitute strict scrutiny, as required by Supreme Court precedent. It is not enough that the Michigan Legislature has chosen this particular regulatory scheme to further what are legitimate objectives. The proper inquiry, detailed above, is whether it "advances a legitimate local purpose that cannot be adequately served by reasonable nondiscriminatory alternatives." New Energy Co. of Ind. v. Limbach, 486 U.S. 269, 278, 108 S.Ct. 1803, 100 L.Ed.2d 302 (1988). We find no evidence on this record that it does.

CONCLUSION

For the reasons set out above, we REVERSE the judgment of the district court granting summary judgment to the defendants and REMAND the case for entry of judgment in favor of the plaintiffs.

Notes and Questions

1.   The above case is only one of many concerning state restrictions on the importation of wine. Federal courts in North Carolina, Texas and Virginia have set aside state laws based on arguments like those in *Heald*. But, in New York, the Second Circuit recently reversed a district court decision which held New York's wine regulatory scheme in violation of the Commerce clause notwithstanding the Twenty–First Amendment. See Swedenburg v. Kelly, 358 F.3d 223 (2d Cir.2004) (distinguishing other cases, including *Heald*, on the grounds, among others, that, in New York, out of state wineries could obtain a license to distribute and sell in the state). These conflicting Circuit Court decisions invite a resolution by the United States Supreme Court. How would you come out?

2.   The wine producing behemoth is of course California, with Washington, Oregon and New York major players also. In states like Michigan, state based wineries have also objected to importation of out of state wine. Whose interests are being protected in cases like *Heald*, the small wineries in Michigan or the major wholesalers? Does this matter in your constitutional calculations?

3.   Wine is an $18 billion industry in the United States, but direct sales to consumers account for only $200 million of that total. These are the sales sought to be enhanced by internet traffic and direct vineyard purchases. Since these sales by smaller wineries effectively avoid the wholesalers, they are a "threat" to the established distribution system. But that is not a viable state interest as the *Heald* court recognizes. But is taxation of wine sales a valid interest?

4.   The Twenty–first Amendment gives the states control of alcohol distribution and several states (e.g. Pennsylvania) still control retail distribution through state stores. Are these states in a different position than New York, where private stores distribute? Is this a social or economic distinction for Twenty–first Amendment purposes?

A NOTE ON FEDERAL PREEMPTION OF STATE REGULATION

Concurrent with Commerce Clause developments affecting state and federal regulation have been a series of cases examining when federal policy preempts state regulation of particular conduct. Each has acknowledged that the Supremacy Clause sometimes requires that state regulation—even state causes of action—be subordinated to federal law. However, the Court has consistently sought to keep preemption as narrow as possible and to give effect to concurrent regulatory schemes.

In Silkwood v. Kerr–McGee Corp., 464 U.S. 238, 104 S.Ct. 615, 78 L.Ed.2d 443 (1984), for example, an employee of a nuclear fuel manufacturer was contaminated by nuclear material. Her estate sued the employer for punitive damages. The employer's defense was that it had complied with all relevant safety standards established by the Nuclear Regulatory Commission. Thus, any state award that would imply higher standards were required should be preempted. But the Court refused to find such preemption. The statutory scheme for nuclear regulation imposed a cap on certain damages but in so doing it implied that state tort remedies were to remain open to injured persons.

Cipollone v. Liggett Group, Inc., 505 U.S. 504, 112 S.Ct. 2608, 120 L.Ed.2d 407 (1992), involved a smoker's state law claim that cigarettes had caused his lung cancer. The defendant argued that the required health warning on all cigarette packages constituted a federal determination of the only way smokers were to be protected and thus preempted any state claim. The Federal Cigarette Labelling and Advertising Act did have a "preemption" provision forbidding any labelling requirement other than the one the statute required, but the Court held it did not preempt tort actions such as this. Some tort actions based on a failure to warn were held preempted, but plaintiffs' express warranty and conspiracy claims, as well as some claims for fraudulent misrepresentation, were not.

CSX Transportation, Inc. v. Easterwood, 507 U.S. 658, 113 S.Ct. 1732, 123 L.Ed.2d 387 (1993), involved a fatal accident at a railroad crossing. The Secretary of Transportation had issued regulations both as to the maximum speed of trains and certain safety requirements at crossings. The Court found the plaintiff's claim for excessive speed preempted by the regulations, but arguments that additional warning devices should have been installed at the crossing were allowed to stand.

Freightliner Corporation v. Myrick, 514 U.S. 280, 115 S.Ct. 1483, 131 L.Ed.2d 385 (1995), similarly held the fact that federal safety regulations did not mandate antilock brakes on trucks did not preempt a state tort action asserting that the failure to have them was negligent, and Medtronic, Inc. v. Lora Lohr, 518 U.S. 470, 116 S.Ct. 2240, 135 L.Ed.2d 700 (1996), affirmed that while the fact the FDA approved a medical device for human use would preempt state attempts to keep it off the market, it did not preempt a tort action alleging the design of the device was defective and that it had been negligently manufactured. But see, Barnett Bank of Marion County v. Nelson, 517 U.S. 25, 116 S.Ct. 1103, 134 L.Ed.2d 237 (1996) (federal law permitting banks to sell insurance preempts state law forbidding it).

Geier v. American Honda Motor Co, 529 U.S. 861, 120 S.Ct. 1913, 146 L.Ed.2d 914 (2000), dealt with the preemptive effect of motor vehicle safety standards promulgated by the Department of Transportation (DOT). The plaintiff motorist sought in a tort action to show that failure to install airbags was a per se act of negligence. The Court, in an opinion authored by Justice Breyer, held that the DOT standards were not express preemption provisions but they were nonetheless impliedly preemptive, since the tort action actually conflicted with the standard that required airbags in some but not all vehicles. So called "conflict" preemption turns on actual conflict and not on an express statement of preemptive intent.

D. FIRST AMENDMENT LIMITATIONS ON REGULATION OF ADVERTISING

For many years, it was received constitutional wisdom that the Constitution did not not protect "purely commercial advertising" against regulation.[24] Capital Broadcasting Co. v. Mitchell,[25] for example, upheld the prohibition of cigarette advertising on radio and television.

However, all that changed in the 1970s. In Bigelow v. Virginia, 421 U.S. 809, 95 S.Ct. 2222, 44 L.Ed.2d 600 (1975), the Court struck down a ban on abortion advertising that would have made it more difficult for women to know who provided such services. Similarly, Virginia State Board of Pharmacy v. Virginia Citizens Consumer Council, Inc., 425 U.S. 748, 96 S.Ct. 1817, 48 L.Ed.2d 346 (1976), struck down a ban on advertising of prescription drug prices.

The series of cases striking down restrictions on lawyer advertising followed, beginning with Bates v. State Bar of Arizona, 433 U.S. 350, 97 S.Ct. 2691, 53 L.Ed.2d 810 (1977).[26] Then, Central Hudson Gas & Electric Corp. v. Public Service Commission, 447 U.S. 557, 100 S.Ct. 2343, 65 L.Ed.2d 341 (1980), articulated a test for regulation of commercial speech that only a few regulatory schemes survived.[27] It was in that setting that the Court addressed advertising regulation in our next case.

44 LIQUORMART, INC. v. RHODE ISLAND

Supreme Court of the United States, 1996.
517 U.S. 484, 116 S.Ct. 1495, 134 L.Ed.2d 711.

JUSTICE STEVENS announced the judgment of the Court.

* * *

I

In 1956, the Rhode Island Legislature enacted two separate prohibitions against advertising the retail price of alcoholic beverages. The first applies to vendors licensed in Rhode Island as well as to out-of-state manufacturers, wholesalers, and shippers. It prohibits them from "advertising in any manner whatsoever" the price of any alcoholic beverage

---

24. The source of this principle was Valentine v. Chrestensen, 316 U.S. 52, 62 S.Ct. 920, 86 L.Ed. 1262.

25. 333 F.Supp. 582 (D.D.C.1971), affirmed without opinion sub nom. Capital Broadcasting Co. v. Kleindienst, 405 U.S. 1000, 92 S.Ct. 1289, 31 L.Ed.2d 472 (1972).

26. E.g., In re R.M.J., 455 U.S. 191, 102 S.Ct. 929, 71 L.Ed.2d 64 (1982); Zauderer v. Office of Disciplinary Counsel, 471 U.S. 626, 105 S.Ct. 2265, 85 L.Ed.2d 652 (1985); Shapero v. Kentucky Bar Association, 486 U.S. 466, 108 S.Ct. 1916, 100 L.Ed.2d 475 (1988). The string of cases striking down lawyer advertising regulations came to an end in Florida Bar v. Went For It, Inc., 515 U.S. 618, 115 S.Ct. 2371, 132 L.Ed.2d 541 (1995) (regulation of contacting accident victims within 30 days of the incident).

27. E.g., Posadas de Puerto Rico Associates v. Tourism Company, 478 U.S. 328, 106 S.Ct. 2968, 92 L.Ed.2d 266 (1986) (regulation of advertising of gambling to residents but not tourists); United States v. Edge Broadcasting Co., 509 U.S. 418, 113 S.Ct. 2696, 125 L.Ed.2d 345 (1993) (federal statute limiting broadcasting lottery results into states that prohibit lotteries).

offered for sale in the State; the only exception is for price tags or signs displayed with the merchandise within licensed premises and not visible from the street. The second statute applies to the Rhode Island news media. It contains a categorical prohibition against the publication or broadcast of any advertisements—even those referring to sales in other States—that "make reference to the price of any alcoholic beverages."

In two cases decided in 1985, the Rhode Island Supreme Court reviewed the constitutionality of these two statutes. * * * It concluded that the statute served the substantial state interest in " 'the promotion of temperance.' " Because the plaintiff failed to prove that the statute did not serve that interest, the court held that he had not carried his burden of establishing a violation of the First Amendment. In response to the dissent's argument that the court had placed the burden on the wrong party, the majority reasoned that the Twenty-first Amendment gave the statute " 'an added presumption [of] validity.' " * * *

II

* * * Petitioner 44 Liquormart operates a store in Rhode Island and petitioner Peoples operates several stores in Massachusetts that are patronized by Rhode Island residents. Peoples uses alcohol price advertising extensively in Massachusetts, where such advertising is permitted, but Rhode Island newspapers and other media outlets have refused to accept such ads.

Complaints from competitors about an advertisement placed by 44 Liquormart in a Rhode Island newspaper in 1991 generated enforcement proceedings that in turn led to the initiation of this litigation. The advertisement did not state the price of any alcoholic beverages. Indeed, it noted that "State law prohibits advertising liquor prices." The ad did, however, state the low prices at which peanuts, potato chips, and Schweppes mixers were being offered, identify various brands of packaged liquor, and include the word "WOW" in large letters next to pictures of vodka and rum bottles. Based on the conclusion that the implied reference to bargain prices for liquor violated the statutory ban on price advertising, the Rhode Island Liquor Control Administrator assessed a $400 fine.

After paying the fine, 44 Liquormart, joined by Peoples, filed this action against the administrator in the Federal District Court seeking a declaratory judgment that the two statutes and the administrator's implementing regulations violate the First Amendment and other provisions of federal law. * * * The parties stipulated that the price advertising ban is vigorously enforced, that Rhode Island permits "all advertising of alcoholic beverages excepting references to price outside the licensed premises," and that petitioners' proposed ads do not concern an illegal activity and presumably would not be false or misleading. The parties disagreed, however, about the impact of the ban on the promotion of temperance in Rhode Island. On that question the District

Court heard conflicting expert testimony and reviewed a number of studies.

In his findings of fact, the District Judge first noted that there was a pronounced lack of unanimity among researchers who have studied the impact of advertising on the level of consumption of alcoholic beverages. He referred to a 1985 Federal Trade Commission study that found no evidence that alcohol advertising significantly affects alcohol abuse. Another study indicated that Rhode Island ranks in the upper 30% of States in per capita consumption of alcoholic beverages; alcohol consumption is lower in other States that allow price advertising. After summarizing the testimony of the expert witnesses for both parties, he found "as a fact that Rhode Island's off-premises liquor price advertising ban has no significant impact on levels of alcohol consumption in Rhode Island."

As a matter of law, he concluded that the price advertising ban was unconstitutional because it did not "directly advance" the State's interest in reducing alcohol consumption and was "more extensive than necessary to serve that interest." He reasoned that the party seeking to uphold a restriction on commercial speech carries the burden of justifying it and that the Twenty-first Amendment did not shift or diminish that burden. Acknowledging that it might have been reasonable for the state legislature to "assume a correlation between the price advertising ban and reduced consumption," he held that more than a rational basis was required to justify the speech restriction, and that the State had failed to demonstrate a reasonable "fit" between its policy objectives and its chosen means.

The Court of Appeals reversed. * * * [We granted certiorari.]

* * *

III

Advertising has been a part of our culture throughout our history. Even in colonial days, the public relied on "commercial speech" for vital information about the market. Early newspapers displayed advertisements for goods and services on their front pages, and town criers called out prices in public squares. Indeed, commercial messages played such a central role in public life prior to the Founding that Benjamin Franklin authored his early defense of a free press in support of his decision to print, of all things, an advertisement for voyages to Barbados. Franklin, An Apology for Printers, June 10, 1731, reprinted in 2 Writings of Benjamin Franklin 172 (1907).

In accord with the role that commercial messages have long played, the law has developed to ensure that advertising provides consumers with accurate information about the availability of goods and services. In the early years, the common law, and later, statutes, served the consumers' interest in the receipt of accurate information in the commercial market by prohibiting fraudulent and misleading advertising. * * *

In addition, as the District Court noted, the State has not identified what price level would lead to a significant reduction in alcohol consumption, nor has it identified the amount that it believes prices would decrease without the ban. Thus, the State's own showing reveals that any connection between the ban and a significant change in alcohol consumption would be purely fortuitous.

* * *

As the State's own expert conceded, higher prices can be maintained either by direct regulation or by increased taxation. Per capita purchases could be limited as is the case with prescription drugs. Even educational campaigns focused on the problems of excessive, or even moderate, drinking might prove to be more effective.

As a result, even under the less than strict standard that generally applies in commercial speech cases, the State has failed to establish a "reasonable fit" between its abridgment of speech and its temperance goal. It necessarily follows that the price advertising ban cannot survive the more stringent constitutional review that *Central Hudson* itself concluded was appropriate for the complete suppression of truthful, nonmisleading commercial speech.

VI

The State responds by arguing that it merely exercised appropriate "legislative judgment" in determining that a price advertising ban would best promote temperance[, r]elying on the *Central Hudson* analysis set forth in Posadas de Puerto Rico Associates v. Tourism Co. of P. R., 478 U.S. 328, 106 S.Ct. 2968, 92 L.Ed.2d 266 (1986), and United States v. Edge Broadcasting Co., 509 U.S. 418, 113 S.Ct. 2696, 125 L.Ed.2d 345 (1993) * * *.

* * *

In *Edge*, we upheld a federal statute that permitted only those broadcasters located in States that had legalized lotteries to air lottery advertising. The statute was designed to regulate advertising about an activity that had been deemed illegal in the jurisdiction in which the broadcaster was located. Here, by contrast, the commercial speech ban targets information about entirely lawful behavior.

Posadas is more directly relevant. There, a five-Member majority held that, under the *Central Hudson* test, it was "up to the legislature" to choose to reduce gambling by suppressing in-state casino advertising rather than engaging in educational speech. Rhode Island argues that this logic demonstrates the constitutionality of its own decision to ban price advertising in lieu of raising taxes or employing some other less speech-restrictive means of promoting temperance.

The reasoning in *Posadas* does support the State's argument, but, on reflection, we are now persuaded that *Posadas* erroneously performed the First Amendment analysis. The casino advertising ban was designed to keep truthful, nonmisleading speech from members of the public for fear that they would be more likely to gamble if they received it. As a result, the advertising ban served to shield the State's antigambling policy from the public scrutiny that more direct, nonspeech regulation would draw.

Given our longstanding hostility to commercial speech regulation of this type, *Posadas* clearly erred in concluding that it was "up to the legislature" to choose suppression over a less speech-restrictive policy. The *Posadas* majority's conclusion on that point cannot be reconciled with the unbroken line of prior cases striking down similarly broad regulations on truthful, nonmisleading advertising when non-speech-related alternatives were available. See Kurland, Posadas de Puerto Rico v. Tourism Company: " 'Twas Strange, 'Twas Passing Strange; 'Twas Pitiful, 'Twas Wondrous Pitiful," 1986 S.Ct. Rev. 1, 12–15.

* * *

That the State has chosen to license its liquor retailers does not change the analysis. Even though government is under no obligation to provide a person, or the public, a particular benefit, it does not follow that conferral of the benefit may be conditioned on the surrender of a constitutional right. * * *

Thus, just as it is perfectly clear that Rhode Island could not ban all obscene liquor ads except those that advocated temperance, we think it equally clear that its power to ban the sale of liquor entirely does not include a power to censor all advertisements that contain accurate and nonmisleading information about the price of the product. As the entire Court apparently now agrees, the statements in the *Posadas* opinion on which Rhode Island relies are no longer persuasive.

Finally, we find unpersuasive the State's contention that, under *Posadas* and *Edge*, the price advertising ban should be upheld because it targets commercial speech that pertains to a "vice" activity. * * * The respondents misread our precedent. Our decision last Term striking down an alcohol-related advertising restriction effectively rejected the very contention respondents now make. See Rubin v. Coors Brewing Co., 514 U.S. 476, 115 S.Ct. 1585, 131 L.Ed. 2d 532(1995).

Moreover, the scope of any "vice" exception to the protection afforded by the First Amendment would be difficult, if not impossible, to define. Almost any product that poses some threat to public health or public morals might reasonably be characterized by a state legislature as relating to "vice activity". Such characterization, however, is anomalous when applied to products such as alcoholic beverages, lottery tickets, or playing cards, that may be lawfully purchased on the open market. The recognition of such an exception would also have the unfortunate conse-quence of either allowing state legislatures to justify censorship by the simple expedient of placing the "vice" label on selected lawful activities, or requiring the federal courts to establish a federal common law of vice. For these reasons, a "vice" label that is unaccompanied by a correspond-ing prohibition against the commercial behavior at issue fails to provide a principled justification for the regulation of commercial speech about that activity.

VII

* * * [T]he text of the Twenty-first Amendment supports the view that, while it grants the States authority over commerce that might otherwise be reserved to the Federal Government, it places no limit whatsoever on other constitutional provisions. Nevertheless, Rhode Island argues, and the Court of Appeals agreed, that in this case the Twenty-first Amendment tilts the First Amendment analysis in the State's favor.

In reaching its conclusion, the Court of Appeals relied on our decision in California v. LaRue, 409 U.S. 109, 93 S.Ct. 390, 34 L.Ed. 2d 342 (1972). In *LaRue*, five Members of the Court relied on the Twenty-first Amendment to buttress the conclusion that the First Amendment did not invalidate California's prohibition of certain grossly sexual exhibitions in premises licensed to serve alcoholic beverages. Specifically, the opinion stated that the Twenty-first Amendment required that the prohibition be given an added presumption in favor of its validity. We are now persuaded that the Court's analysis in *LaRue* would have led to precisely the same result if it had placed no reliance on the Twenty-first Amendment.

Entirely apart from the Twenty-first Amendment, the State has ample power to prohibit the sale of alcoholic beverages in inappropriate locations. Moreover, in subsequent cases the Court has recognized that the States' inherent police powers provide ample authority to restrict the kind of "bacchanalian revelries" described in the *LaRue* opinion regardless of whether alcoholic beverages are involved. * * *

Without questioning the holding in *LaRue*, we now disavow its reasoning insofar as it relied on the Twenty-first Amendment. * * * [W]e now hold that the Twenty-first Amendment does not qualify the constitutional prohibition against laws abridging the freedom of speech embodied in the First Amendment. The Twenty-first Amendment, therefore, cannot save Rhode Island's ban on liquor price advertising.

VIII

Because Rhode Island has failed to carry its heavy burden of justifying its complete ban on price advertising, we conclude that R.I. Gen. Laws §§ 3–8–7 and 3–8–8.1, as well as Regulation 32 of the Rhode Island Liquor Control Administration, abridge speech in violation of the First Amendment as made applicable to the States by the Due Process Clause of the Fourteenth Amendment. The judgment of the Court of Appeals is therefore reversed.

JUSTICE SCALIA, concurring in part and concurring in the judgment.

I share Justice Thomas's discomfort with the *Central Hudson* test, which seems to me to have nothing more than policy intuition to support it. I also share Justice Stevens' aversion towards paternalistic governmental policies that prevent men and women from hearing facts that might not be good for them. On the other hand, it would also be paternalism for us to prevent the people of the States from enacting laws that we consider paternalistic, unless we have good reason to believe that the Constitution itself forbids them. I will take my guidance as to what the Constitution forbids, with regard to a text as indeterminate as the First Amendment's preservation of "the freedom of speech," and where the core offense of suppressing particular political ideas is not at issue, from the long accepted practices of the American people.

* * *

JUSTICE THOMAS, concurring in Parts I, II, VI, and VII, and concurring in the judgment.

In cases such as this, in which the government's asserted interest is to keep legal users of a product or service ignorant in order to manipulate their choices in the marketplace, the balancing test adopted in Central Hudson Gas & Elec. Corp. v. Public Serv. Comm'n of N.Y. should not be applied, in my view. Rather, such an "interest" is per se illegitimate and can no more justify regulation of "commercial" speech than it can justify regulation of "noncommercial" speech.

* * *

* * * In my view, the *Central Hudson* test asks the courts to weigh incommensurables—the value of knowledge versus the value of ignorance—and to apply contradictory premises—that informed adults are the best judges of their own interests, and that they are not. Rather than continuing to apply a test that makes no sense to me when the asserted state interest is of the type involved here, I would return to the reasoning and holding of *Virginia Pharmacy Bd.* Under that decision, these restrictions fall.

JUSTICE O'CONNOR, with whom THE CHIEF JUSTICE, JUSTICE SOUTER, and JUSTICE BREYER join, concurring in the judgment.

Rhode Island prohibits advertisement of the retail price of alcoholic beverages, except at the place of sale. The State's only asserted justification for this ban is that it promotes temperance by increasing the cost of alcoholic beverages. I agree with the Court that Rhode Island's price-advertising ban is invalid. I would resolve this case more narrowly, however, by applying our established *Central Hudson* test to determine whether this commercial-speech regulation survives First Amendment scrutiny.

Under that test, we first determine whether the speech at issue concerns lawful activity and is not misleading, and whether the asserted governmental interest is substantial. If both these conditions are met, we must decide whether the regulation "directly advances the governmental interest asserted, and whether it is not more extensive than is necessary to serve that interest."

Given the means by which this regulation purportedly serves the State's interest, our conclusion is plain: Rhode Island's regulation fails First Amendment scrutiny.

Both parties agree that the first two prongs of the *Central Hudson* test are met. Even if we assume arguendo that Rhode Island's regulation also satisfies the requirement that it directly advance the governmental interest, Rhode Island's regulation fails the final prong; that is, its ban is more extensive than necessary to serve the State's interest.

As we have explained, in order for a speech restriction to pass muster under the final prong, there must be a fit between the legislature's goal and method, "a fit that is not necessarily perfect, but reasonable; that represents not necessarily the single best disposition but one whose scope is in proportion to the interest served." While the State need not employ the least restrictive means to accomplish its goal, the fit between means and ends must be "narrowly tailored." The scope of the restriction on speech must be reasonably, though it need not be perfectly, targeted to address the harm intended to be regulated. * * * The availability of less burdensome alternatives to reach the stated goal signals that the fit between the legislature's ends and the means chosen to accomplish those ends may be too imprecise to withstand First Amendment scrutiny. If alternative channels permit communication of the restricted speech, the regulation is more likely to be considered reasonable.

Rhode Island offers one, and only one, justification for its ban on price advertising. Rhode Island says that the ban is intended to keep alcohol prices high as a way to keep consumption low. By preventing sellers from informing customers of prices, the regulation prevents competition from driving prices down and requires consumers to spend more time to find the best price for alcohol. The higher cost of obtaining alcohol, Rhode Island argues, will lead to reduced consumption.

The fit between Rhode Island's method and this particular goal is not reasonable. If the target is simply higher prices generally to discourage consumption, the regulation imposes too great, and unnecessary, a prohibition on speech in order to achieve it. The State has other methods at its disposal—methods that would more directly accomplish this stated goal without intruding on sellers' ability to provide truthful, nonmisleading information to customers. Indeed, Rhode Island's own expert conceded that " 'the objective of lowering consumption of alcohol by banning price advertising could be accomplished by establishing minimum prices and/or by increasing sales taxes on alcoholic beverages.' " A tax, for example, is not normally very difficult to administer and would have a far more certain and direct effect on prices, without any restriction on speech. The principal opinion suggests further alternatives, such as limiting per capita purchases or conducting an educational campaign about the dangers of alcohol consumption. The ready availability of such alternatives—at least some of which would far more effectively achieve Rhode Island's only professed goal, at comparatively small additional administrative cost—demonstrates that the fit between ends and means is not narrowly tailored. Too, this regulation prevents sellers of alcohol from communicating price information anywhere but at the point of purchase. No channels exist at all to permit them to publicize the price of their products.

* * *

* * * The Twenty-first Amendment cannot save this otherwise invalid regulation. While I agree with the Court's finding that the regulation is invalid, I would decide that issue on narrower grounds. I therefore concur in the judgment.

Notes and Questions

1.　Would you have voted for the regulation of advertising at issue here? Was it designed to protect the public from liquor stores who had market power? Was this regulation designed to solve an economic problem or a social problem?

2.　Could the state have rendered criminal all sales of alcoholic beverages in Rhode Island? Does the Court concede that such action would be authorized by the Twenty-first Amendment? If that is true, what could be wrong with a state's stopping short of that and simply trying to raise the price of drinking? Does the case simply hold that a state must comply with *both* the First and Twenty–first Amendments? How does *Heald* fit in?

3.　Was the method of regulation well chosen? Might it be easier to regulate advertisers whose conduct is necessarily public than to shop at hundreds of stores to verify their compliance with some other limitations on liquor sales? Should ease of administration count for anything when evaluating the constitutionality of regulation?

4.　Who is the primary beneficiary of the commercial speech doctrine? Were the advertising restrictions here for the primary benefit of the public? Did they benefit the television stations and print media that carry advertising? Was the primary beneficiary the beverage industry that could use consumer ignorance to help keep prices high? Might that industry have been the one that asked for the regulation in the first place?

5.　Is constitutional litigation a good way to avoid the problems of regulatory capture, i.e., should First Amendment doctrine be invoked to protect unorganized consumers against an industry with good political connections? Is the commercial speech doctrine simply an illustration of the principle that the First Amendment should serve the interest of listeners even more than speakers?

6.　If it is unconstitutional to regulate advertising in *44 Liquormart* in an effort to reduce sales of alcohol, does it follow that it also would be unconstitutional to regulate advertising of cigarettes that is directed at children? Cf. Penn Advertising of Baltimore v. Mayor and City Council of Baltimore, 63 F.3d 1318 (4th Cir.1995) (upholding regulation of billboard advertising of cigarettes), vacated 518 U.S. 1030, 116 S.Ct. 2575, 135 L.Ed.2d 1090 (1996), in light of *44 Liquormart.*

7. In Lorillard Tobacco, Co. v. Reilly, 533 U.S. 525, 121 S.Ct. 2404, 150 L.Ed.2d 532 (2001) the Court ruled on the First Amendment challenges to the billboard and other state restrictions imposed under the state settlement of the tobacco cases. The Court held that various point of sale cigarette advertising regulations were preempted by the Federal Cigarette Labeling and Advertising Act (FCLAA). Also, under *Central Hudson* and *44 Liquormart*, billboard restrictions were held to violate the First Amendment. By prohibiting outdoor advertising within 1,000 feet of schools or playgrounds, the state regulation failed step four of *Central Hudson*, which "requires a reasonable fit between the means and ends of the regulatory scheme." Id. at 2425. Justices Kennedy, Scalia and Thomas, in their concurring opinions, continued to question whether *Central Hudson's* intermediate scrutiny test should be jettisoned in favor of traditional First Amendment strict scrutiny.

E. EQUAL PROTECTION LIMITS ON STATE REGULATION

Equal protection has been yet another Constitutional provision long largely unavailable to companies complaining about state or federal regulation. Subjecting economic regulations to a "rational basis" test, rather than to either "strict scrutiny" or "intermediate" review, allowed the Court to find a justified rationale for many regulatory distinctions.

In Railway Express Agency v. New York, 336 U.S. 106, 69 S.Ct. 463, 93 L.Ed. 533 (1949), for example, the Court upheld a prohibition of advertising on the sides of delivery vehicles other than for the owner's own business. Minnesota v. Clover Leaf Creamery Co., 449 U.S. 456, 101 S.Ct. 715, 66 L.Ed.2d 659 (1981), upheld a statute prohibiting the sale of milk in non-returnable plastic containers. But see Morey v. Doud, 354 U.S. 457, 77 S.Ct. 1344, 1 L.Ed.2d 1485 (1957), which was overruled in the next case.

CITY OF NEW ORLEANS v. DUKES

Supreme Court of the United States, 1976.
427 U.S. 297, 96 S.Ct. 2513, 49 L.Ed.2d 511.

Per Curiam.

The question presented by this case is whether the provision of a New Orleans ordinance, as amended in 1972, that excepts from the ordinance's prohibition against vendors' selling of foodstuffs from pushcarts in the Vieux Carre, or French Quarter, "vendors who have continuously operated the same business within the Vieux Carre ... for eight or more years prior to January 1, 1972 ..." denied appellee vendor equal protection of the laws in violation of the Fourteenth Amendment.

Appellee operates a vending business from pushcarts throughout New Orleans but had carried on that business in the Vieux Carre for only two years when the ordinance was amended in 1972 and barred her from continuing operations there. She had previously filed an action in the District Court for the Eastern District of Louisiana attacking the validity of the former version of the ordinance, and amended her complaint to challenge the application of the ordinance's "grandfather clause" the eight-years-or-more provision as a denial of equal protection. She prayed for an injunction and declaratory judgment. On cross-motions for summary judgment, the District Court, without opinion, granted appellant city's motion. The Court of Appeals for the Fifth Circuit reversed. * * * We * * * reverse the judgment of the Court of Appeals.

The Vieux Carre of the city of New Orleans is the heart of that city's considerable tourist industry and an integral component of the city's economy. The sector plays a special role in the city's life, and pursuant to the Louisiana State Constitution, c. 8 of Art. V of the city's Home Rule Charter grants the New Orleans City Council power to enact ordinances designed to preserve its distinctive charm, character, and economic vitality.

Chapter 46 of the Code of the City of New Orleans sets up a comprehensive scheme of permits for the conduct of various businesses in the city. In 1972, the Code was amended to restrict the validity of many of these permits to points outside the Vieux Carre. However, even as to those occupations including all pushcart food vendors which were to be banned from the Vieux Carre during seasons other than Mardi Gras, the City Council made the "grandfather provision" exception. Two pushcart food vendors one engaged in the sale of hot dogs and the other an ice cream vendor had operated in the Vieux Carre for 20 or more years and therefore qualified under the "grandfather clause" and continued to operate there. The Court of Appeals recognized the "City Council's legitimate authority generally to regulate business conducted on the public streets and sidewalks of the Vieux Carre in order to preserve the appearance and custom valued by the Quarter's residents and attractive to tourists," but nevertheless found that the Council's justification for the "grandfather" exception was "insufficient to support the discrimination imposed" and thus deprived appellee of equal protection. Stating expressly that this Court's decision in Morey v. Doud, 354 U.S. 457, 77 S.Ct. 1344, 1 L.Ed.2d 1485 (1957), was "our chief guide in resolving this case," the Court of Appeals focused on the "exclusionary character" of the ordinance and its concomitant "creation of a protected monopoly for the favored class member." The "pivotal defect" in the statutory scheme was perceived to be the fact that the favored class members need not "continue to operate in a manner more consistent with the traditions of the Quarter than would any other operator," and the fact that there was no reason to believe that length of operation "instills in the (favored) licensed vendors (or their likely transient operators) the kind of appreciation for the conservation of the Quarter's tradition" that would cause their operations to become or remain consistent with that tradition. Because these factors demonstrated the "insubstantiality of the relation between the nature of the discrimination and the legitimate governmental interest in conserving the traditional assets of the Vieux Carre," the ordinance was declared violative of equal protection as applied and the case was remanded for a determination of the severability of the "grand-father clause" from the remainder of the ordinance.

* * *

II

The record makes abundantly clear that the amended ordinance, including the "grandfather provision," is solely an economic regulation aimed at enhancing the vital role of the French Quarter's tourist-oriented charm in the economy of New Orleans.

When local economic regulation is challenged solely as violating the Equal Protection Clause, this Court consistently defers to legislative determinations as to the desirability of particular statutory discriminations. Unless a classification trammels fundamental personal rights or is drawn upon inherently suspect distinctions such as race, religion, or alienage, our decisions presume the constitutionality of the statutory discriminations and require only that the classification challenged be rationally related to a legitimate state interest. States are accorded wide latitude in the regulation of their local economies under their police powers, and rational distinctions may be made with substantially less than mathematical exactitude. Legislatures may implement their program step by step in such economic areas, adopting regulations that only partially ameliorate a perceived evil and deferring complete elimination of the evil to future regulations.

In short, the judiciary may not sit as a superlegislature to judge the wisdom or desirability of legislative policy determinations made in areas that neither affect fundamental rights nor proceed along suspect lines, * * * in the local economic sphere, it is only the invidious discrimination, the wholly arbitrary act, which cannot stand consistently with the Fourteenth Amendment.

* * *

It is suggested that the "grandfather provision," allowing the continued operation of some vendors was a totally arbitrary and irrational method of achieving the city's purpose. But rather than proceeding by the immediate and absolute abolition of all pushcart food vendors, the city could rationally choose initially to eliminate vendors of more recent vintage. This gradual approach to the problem is not constitutionally impermissible. The governing constitutional principle was stated in Katzenbach v. Morgan, supra, 384 U.S. [641], at 657, 86 S.Ct. [1717], at 1727:

> "(W)e are guided by the familiar principles that a 'statute is not invalid under the Constitution because it might have gone farther than it did,' that a legislature need not 'strike at all evils at the same time,' and that 'reform may take one step at a time, addressing itself to the phase of the problem which seems most acute to the legislative mind,' Williamson v. Lee Optical Co., 348 U.S. 483, 489, 75 S.Ct. 461, 465, 99 L.Ed. 563."

The city could reasonably decide that newer businesses were less likely to have built up substantial reliance interests in continued operation in the Vieux Carre and that the two vendors who qualified under the "grandfather clause" both of whom had operated in the area for over 20 years rather than only eight had themselves become part of the distinctive character and charm that distinguishes the Vieux Carre. We cannot say that these judgments so lack rationality that they constitute a constitutionally impermissible denial of equal protection.

Nevertheless, relying on Morey v. Doud as its "chief guide," the Court of Appeals held that even though the exemption of the two vendors was rationally related to legitimate city interests on the basis of facts extant when the ordinance was amended, the "grandfather clause" still could not stand because "the hypothesis that a present eight year veteran of the pushcart hot dog market in the Vieux Carre will continue to operate in a manner more consistent with the traditions of the Quarter than would any other operator is without foundation." Actually, the reliance on the statute's potential irrationality in Morey v. Doud, as the dissenters in that case correctly pointed out, was needlessly intrusive judicial infringement on the State's legislative powers, and we have concluded that the equal protection analysis employed in that opinion should no longer be followed. *Morey* was the only case in the last half century to invalidate a wholly economic regulation solely on equal protection grounds, and we are now satisfied that the decision was erroneous. * * * [T]he decision so far departs from proper equal protection analysis in cases of exclusively economic regulation that it should be, and it is, overruled.

The judgment of the Court of Appeals is reversed, and the case is remanded for further proceedings consistent with this opinion.

Notes and Questions

1.   New Orleans v. Dukes seems to close the door to Equal Protection challenges of purely economic regulation. Can you think of any situation in which the Court should open the door? How about cases raising the concerns expressed in the revived Takings cases such as *Dolan*?

2.   Is there anything particularly "rational" about choosing eight years as the cutoff for the grandfathering of French Quarter vendors? Would you like to know why that length of time was chosen and who it excluded? Suppose contributions to the New Orleans City Council (who created the regulation) were involved? You might want to take a look at Columbia v. Omni Outdoor Advertising that is discussed in Chapter 6.

3.   The interest in controlling vendors on city streets is not limited to New Orleans. In New York City, for example, the issue seems to have reached crisis proportions in the 42nd Street area, especially during the holiday season. A bill in the New York Senate would have required fingerprinting of disabled veteran vendors and forbidden vending in the areas around ground zero. Business organizations in Manhattan believe that disabled veterans "and hordes of so-called first amendment peddlers that

follow them drive off customers." See N.Y. Times, Albany Fails To Pass Bill To Regulate City's Vendors, Dec. 5, 2003 at Sec. B, p 1.

Do you believe that some classes of vendors, i.e., disabled veterans, should have priority in the effort to get sales permits? Should they have a right to sell their wares if they were to block vehicle or pedestrian traffic? Should the rights of such vendors trump the rights of those with long-standing permits? See Mitchell Duneier, Let New York's Veterans Vend, N.Y. Times, Jan. 4, 2004 (blaming large sidewalk planters, not veterans, for overcrowding on 33rd and 34th Streets). Planters, it appears are placed by business districts to combat street vendors. Should they be removed first?

A NOTE ON EQUAL PROTECTION ANALYSIS AND RACE–BASED REMEDIES

Suppose the vendors who were excluded by a given regulation were disproportionately women or members of minority groups? Would you expect the Court to reach the result it did in *Dukes*?

Equal Protection doctrine long has been central to preserving and extending the civil rights of citizens in a variety of settings. The most profound and far reaching use of the Equal Protection clause was unquestionably the Court's decision in Brown v. Board of Education, 347 U.S. 483, 74 S.Ct. 686, 98 L.Ed. 873 (1954). But regulatory bodies, too, have sought to affirm equal opportunity of all citizens and overcome the effects of past discrimination.

That history made the Supreme Court's decision in Adarand Constructors v. Pena, 515 U.S. 200, 115 S.Ct. 2097, 132 L.Ed.2d 158 (1995), surprising to many. A federal statute sought to give contractors on government projects a financial incentive to hire subcontractors controlled by "social and economically disadvantaged individuals." See Section 106 (c)(1) of the Surface Transportation and Uniform Relocation Assistance Act of 1987 (setting aside 10% of appropriated funds for this purpose). A contractor ineligible for such assistance argued that the provision violated the equal protection component of the Fifth Amendment's due process clause.

Justice O'Connor wrote for a majority of the Court and agreed that if this and related statutes were race neutral a "more lenient" standard of scrutiny should be applied. However, such a standard was not justified where a race-based classification was involved. The Court rejected use of even the intermediate scrutiny standard applied in Metro Broadcasting, Inc. v. FCC, 497 U.S. 547, 110 S.Ct. 2997, 111 L.Ed.2d 445 (1990) (upholding a "benign" racial classification designed to improve racial diversity in broadcasting). It instead required application of the strict scrutiny standard used in Richmond v. J.A. Croson, Co., 488 U.S. 469, 109 S.Ct. 706, 102 L.Ed.2d 854 (1989) (30% set aside for minority businesses).

On remand, the District Court found that the program could not survive strict scrutiny. The case was ultimately mooted, however, after the program itself was changed. See Adarand Constructors v. Mineta, 534 U.S. 103, 122 S.Ct. 511, 151 L.Ed.2d 489 (2001).

Notes and Questions

1. Can you think of any constitutional reason for the government to encourage contractors to hire minority subcontractors rather than non-minority subcontractors? Can you articulate the "compelling government interest" that would explain discriminating against lower-bidding non-minority subcontractors?

2. If a program is seen as remedial, i.e., to overcome the effects of past discrimination, how long should such a program continue? Long enough for the minority contractors to prove successful? Long enough to make up for contracts not obtained in the past?

3. Is offering an incentive to contractors in order to encourage them to hire minority subcontractors simply an effort to redistribute income and opportunities from the relatively affluent to those who are not so affluent? Is there anything that makes these programs superior to welfare programs involving direct payments? Would a system of direct payments be more or less likely to be found constitutional?

4. Is this opinion only significant with respect to racial classifications? If a state should adopt policies to give affirmative benefits to persons from Southeast Asia, for example, would that be condemned under this case? How about policies to benefit persons with AIDS?

5. The point is that Equal Protection could, in principle, be a basis for condemning almost any distinction drawn by a regulatory program if it could be described as having the effect of benefitting one group of citizens at the expense of another. If the principle were carried that far, would there be much regulation left to discuss?

6. Even if you agree with Justice O'Connor that race-based programs are a perverse idea, is it really only minority groups that need protection. Put another way, do majority contractors need constitutional protection against a minority taking advantage of them? Think about what Public Choice analysts would say. In their view, majority groups may be *less* able to take care of themselves politically than minorities might be because large groups are more costly to organize. Does such an argument persuade you?

7. Do you expect this opinion to be of far-reaching significance? Limited to its facts? See, e.g., Taxman v. Board of Education of Piscataway, 91 F.3d 1547 (3d Cir.1996) (en banc) (upholding damage award to white teacher laid off as part of effort to preserve racial diversity of teaching staff at time of personnel cutbacks). But see Grutter v. Bollinger, 539 U.S. 306, 123 S.Ct. 2325, 156 L.Ed.2d 304 (2003) (upholding law school admission program carefully tailored to achieve educational benefits of a diverse student body).

Chapter 3

EVOLVING RATIONALES FOR REGULATION AND DEREGULATION

As you remember from Chapter 1, the Public Interest analysis of regulation raises concerns about efficiency—both allocative and productive—and avoiding distributive results or market outcomes that are considered unacceptable. The Public Administration approach acknowledges these purposes for regulation but asks by what means the objectives can best be achieved. Public Choice analysis, on the other hand, argues that most or all regulation consists of efforts by powerful groups to be made better off at the expense of less well-posistioned groups.

The analysis of when deregulation is appropriate is very similar. For example, a particular regulation may be "inefficient" in that the expense and inconvenience may exceed its benefits. Or, a regulation may produce undesired effects as changes in technology or the market make formerly desirable regulations obsolete. And, of course, the process of deregulation can itself be disruptive and arguably unfair to those who have arranged their businesses on the supposition that regulation would continue.

This Chapter organizes efforts at regulation and deregulation around four headings, each a traditional Public Interest rationale for regulation. They are:

1. The Natural Monopoly Rationale
2. The Excessive Competition Rationale
3. Responding to Transaction Costs
4. Allocation of Inherently Scarce Resources

These labels describe market conditions that prevent the achievement of efficiency goals. The labels alone do not necessarily tell us very much. As you consider the regulatory schemes under each of these headings, ask yourself what the actual justification for the regulation is. Furthermore, although we take these rationales up one at a time, do not infer that they are unrelated. In reality, the underlying allocative and distributive goals of many of them are the same.

121

Remember again that the term "deregulation" is itself imprecise. At one extreme, it describes the legalization of conduct formerly treated as unlawful. On the other hand, news media sometimes use the term to describe the abolition of an independent agency even if many of the agency's functions are transferred elsewhere in the government. Other times, the term "deregulation" is used to say that the form of regulation has been changed. It is also imprecise to infer that competition means a lack of regulation. In fact, in some industries, the introduction of competition has required a great deal of regulation designed to establish the "ground rules" for competition. Watch for these differences as you consider the materials in this chapter.

A. THE NATURAL MONOPOLY RATIONALE

1. THE ECONOMIC PROBLEMS PRESENTED BY NATURAL MONOPOLY

IN THE MATTER OF A PETITION BY THE CITY OF ROCHESTER

Minnesota Court of Appeals, 1991.
478 N.W.2d 329.

AMUNDSON, JUDGE.

Relator City of Rochester filed a petition with the Minnesota Public Utilities Commission (Commission), requesting the city's municipal utility be allowed to extend electric service to street lights located within respondent People's Cooperative Power Association's (Association) assigned service area. The city argued it should be allowed to provide service to the street lights pursuant to a provision within the Public Utilities Act which allows a utility to serve its "own utility property and facilities." * * * The city also claimed a right to serve the street lights under a theory that such service is a proper municipal function. The Commission concluded the city should not be allowed to extend electric service to the street lights located within the Association's assigned service area. We agree and affirm.

FACTS

The Minnesota Public Utilities Act (Act) was adopted in 1974. * * *. The Act required the establishment of assigned service areas, within which utilities would be allowed to provide electric service to customers on an exclusive basis. Pursuant to the Act's requirements, the City of Rochester's municipal utility and People's Cooperative Power Association were assigned electric service areas in and around the city.

The city's municipal utility has provided and maintained street lights in the city since the late 1800's. In December 1990, the city filed a petition with the Commission, requesting authorization to provide electric service to a new street light project involving eighty-two street lights. Fifty-two of the new street lights were located in the Association's assigned service area.

Following a hearing on the city's petition, the Commission issued findings and a decision prohibiting the city from serving the street lights located in the Association's territory. The Commission based its decision upon the assigned service area requirements in the Public Utilities Act.

* * *

The city has obtained a writ of certiorari, seeking review of the Commission's decision.

Does the Public Utilities Act prohibit the city from extending electric service to street lights located in the Association's assigned service area?

The legislature granted electric utilities exclusive service rights within assigned service areas. Minn.Stat. § 216B.40 (1990). The legislature has, however, provided an exception to the assigned service area requirements:

> [A]ny electric utility may extend electric lines for electric service to its own utility property and facilities.

Minn.Stat. § 216B.42, subd. 2 (1990). The city argues that the street lights should be characterized as "its own utility property and facilities."

When construing statutory language, the court's primary goal is to ascertain and effectuate the legislature's intent. Minn.Stat. § 645.16 (1990). We will consider, and often defer to, an agency's interpretation of its governing statutes. *See* Minn.Stat. § 645.16(8) (1990). We have stated:

> When agency conclusions are based on legal rather than factual considerations * * *, the reviewing court is not bound by the agency's decision and need not defer to the agency's expertise. An agency's interpretation of legislative intent, while influential, cannot bind a court. * * * Nonetheless, "[w]hen the meaning of the statute is doubtful, courts should give great weight to a construction placed upon it by the department charged with its administration."

In re Minn. Joint Underwriting Ass'n, 408 N.W.2d 599, 605 (Minn.App. 1987) (citations omitted).

We construe the phrase "utility property and facilities" in terms of what society needs. The legislature has identified society's needs within assigned service area statutes:

> It is hereby declared to be in the public interest that, in order to encourage the development of coordinated statewide electric service at retail, to eliminate or avoid unnecessary duplication of electric utility facilities, and to promote economical, efficient, and adequate

electric service to the public, the state of Minnesota shall be divided into geographic service areas within which a specified electric utility shall provide electric service to customers on an exclusive basis. Minn.Stat. § 216B.37 (1990).

Underlying these policies is the idea that the public interest does not favor competition between or duplication of electric utilities. Rather, electric utilities are "natural monopolies." *See* Hamilton & Colacci, Economic Efficiency as the Primary Objective of State Utility Commission Policy, 8 Wm. Mitchell L.Rev. 309, 315 (1982). One commentator has explained this concept:

> The term "natural monopoly" suggests that most utility firms operate with a markedly decreasing cost function and have decreasing costs over a wide scale of operations. * * * In the long run, economies of large scale seem available to most utilities.
>
> * * *
>
> It is felt that society will be better served by a monopolistic type of organization if such an organization does indeed take advantage of these economies. This principle has long been recognized and has led to social preference for one utility in a given service area. It is further widely believed that utilities move "naturally" toward a monopolistic type of structure if allowed to operate without social controls. This tendency has been recognized in the literature of economics for more than a century, although some object to the use of the term "natural" to characterize this type of market structure.
>
> Controlled entry and operation only by permission of some agency of government are grounded in the concept that duplication of the large capital undertakings of utilities is socially wasteful and that competition among utility firms, which of necessity must use the public streets, is unduly disruptive. Under these circumstances it is logical to limit service to a single seller and thus avoid waste and disruption. Thus, local monopoly has become the predominant form of market structure.

M. Farris & R. Sampson, Public Utilities: Regulation, Management, and Ownership 156 (1973) (footnotes omitted).

Once it is recognized that electric utilities are natural monopolies, it follows that we must closely examine any alleged exceptions to exclusive service territory rights. In examining the exception to exclusive service rights for a utility's own "utility property and facilities," the Commission focused on the "utility" function. We agree that the function, rather than the ownership, of property or facilities is critical.

We also agree with the Commission's characterization of the utility function as that which is necessary for supplying electric power. *See* Minn.Stat. §§ 216B.02, subd. 4, 216B.38, subd. 5 (1990), (defining "electric utility" and "public utility" as entities operating, maintaining or controlling equipment or facilities used to furnish electric service). Thus, utility property and facilities would include, for example, power plants, substations, corporate headquarters, etc. Under this analysis, street lights do not serve a "utility" function.

* * *

DECISION

Principles of statutory construction and considerations of public policy support the Commission's conclusion that the city's municipal utility is prohibited from extending electric service to street lights in the Association's service territory.

Notes and Questions

1. In *City of Rochester*, the court articulates the traditional natural monopoly rationale. According to the court, without regulation: 1) there may be a duplication of facilities, and 2) citizens will end up paying more than they would if only one utility existed.

a. What do you think of this analysis? Do you normally believe you would be better off if your city had only one restaurant, for example, or one place to shop for clothing? Is there something about what we call a "natural monopoly" that makes the court's concern legitimate?

b. What makes selling electricity different from selling shoes? Sometimes the fear is that a new entrant to a natural monopoly market will "skim the cream" and leave the incumbent with just the customers who are expensive to serve. The idea is that the single firm is required to offer "universal service." For example, an electric utility is expected to serve customers in apartment complexes as well as customers living in isolated rural areas. If the newcomer enters, it will only compete for the apartment complex. What would the consequences of this be?

c. Similarly, concerns about "cut throat" competition are often expressed. Are you equally worried? Don't we welcome tough price competition in the sale of groceries? How can competition ever do anything other than benefit buyers? Are the firms we call "natural monopolies" sufficiently different from other sellers of goods and services that they deserve special treatment?

2. In *City of Rochester* the court defines "utility property and facilities" in a manner that is consistent with the economic function of the regulation. Another possibility would be a more literal definition. Do you agree with its methodology?

3. Is natural monopoly regulation primarily imposed to protect consumers or to protect investors in the regulated firms? Are those objectives necessarily incompatible? The following notes may help you think about these issues.

A NOTE ON PRICING BY MONOPOLIES IN GENERAL

The concept we are calling "natural monopoly" is a market condition in which the quantity demanded can be most efficiently produced by one firm. However "natural" it may be to want such productive efficiency, any time only one firm serves a market there is a concern consumers may not be well served.

The first step in understanding monopoly pricing is to think about how the costs of firms change as they increase output. You are already acquainted with the concept of marginal cost, which is the addition to total cost of production due to increasing output by one unit. More typically, one begins an examination of the costs of production by first noting that costs tend to be either fixed or variable. Fixed costs are those that do not change as the level of output increases. For example, the rental on a retail store may not change no matter how much is sold in the store. Or, the cost of the power plant or transmission lines may not vary with the level of electricity produced. Average fixed cost would just be the fixed cost divided by whatever level of output the firm was producing. If average fixed cost were plotted on a graph, it would look like Figure 5. Because fixed cost is the same regardless of the level of output, the average fixed cost steadily declines as output increases.

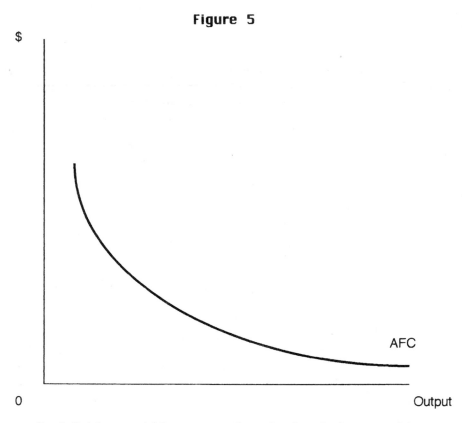

Figure 5

By definition, variable costs, on the other hand, change and increase as output increases. In most instances total variable cost does not increase in exact proportion with output. This is because as production increases the firm is likely to be increasingly efficient. That is, the firm gets more and more output per unit of variable input. After a while, though, the addition of units of an input will result in lower and lower increases in output. What this means is that average variable cost per unit of output will initially decline and then increase. This is plotted in Figure 6. Figure 6 also includes the average total cost curve (ATC). Average total cost is determined by dividing the total cost of production (fixed cost and average cost) by the level of output. Due to the influence of average variable cost, it too has a U shape. Finally, it is important to note that to an economist a "normal profit" is just another cost of production. A "normal profit" is just enough to keep investors satisfied with the return on their investment.

Figure 6 also includes the marginal cost curve (MC). Its placement on the graph relative to ATC and AVC is important. Remember, marginal cost is the extra cost of producing one more unit. Both average cost measures are averages for all units produced. Thus, as long as marginal cost is below either average cost, average cost will be declining.[1] This is because the addition of a lower cost single unit to the units already being produced will cause the average to fall. Of course, if the marginal cost exceeds either average cost, that average cost must be rising. Thus, when marginal cost is just equal to average cost, average cost must be stable. As a technical matter, this is exactly what is happening when average cost reaches its lowest level—for a very small increment it is neither rising nor falling.[2]

1. This applies to both average total cost and average variable cost.

2. Technically, even marginal cost is U-shaped, first declining and then rising. The declining portion is not pictured here because it is not relevant for decision making purposes.

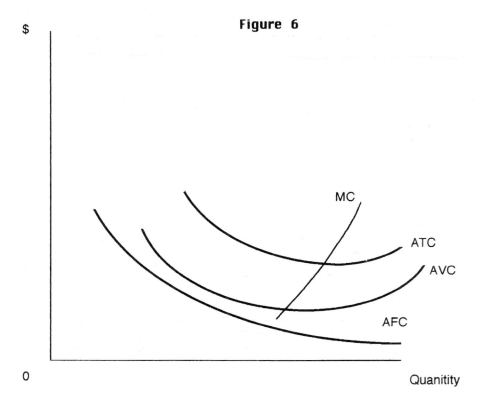

Figure 6

In order to fully appreciate the monopoly problem, one more piece of the puzzle must be introduced. In Chapter 1, you were introduced to the concept of demand. In the first two columns of Table 1, the demand from Table 1 in Chapter 1 is reproduced. A third column—marginal revenue—has been added. Marginal revenue is the extra revenue derived from selling one additional unit.

TABLE 1

Price	Quantity Demanded	Total Revenue	Marginal Revenue
$35	1	$35	$35
$30	2	$60	$25
$25	3	$75	$25
$20	4	$80	$ 5
$15	5	$75	− $ 5
$10	6	$60	− $15
$ 5	7	$35	− $25

Any firm would like to produce and sell a unit as long as the additional revenue (MR) from selling that unit of output exceeds the marginal cost (MC). To understand what this means, take a look at Figure 7. The cost curves are reproduced as well as demand and marginal revenue. Marginal revenue exceeds marginal cost for all units out until unit Qm. Thus, the profit maximizing firm will produce Qm units. The price it will sell those units for will be the highest price consistent with that number of units being purchased. In Figure 7, this can be determined by reference to the demand curve which tells us the price that is consistent with Qm units. Here it is Pm. Thus, the monopolist, or any firm with market power[3] will produce Qm units and sell them for price Pm.

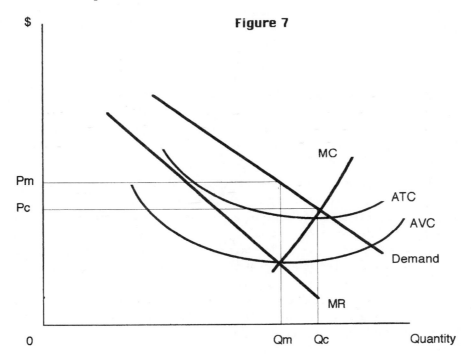

Figure 7

You can contrast this with the outcome under competitive conditions by recalling from Chapter 1 that under competitive conditions the level of output and price are determined by the intersection of supply and demand. The supply curve was the same as the marginal cost curve. In the market depicted in Figure 7, this means that the price would be Pc and the quantity Qc. Right away you can see some of the problems with a monopoly. Assuming nothing else changed in the market, the monopolist would charge a higher price and sell a lower quantity than would exist under competitive conditions. Also, remember that one of the appealing aspects of the intersection of supply and demand is that it is consistent with allocative efficiency. As Figure 7 shows, the monopolist would stop its production short of the allocatively efficient level.

---

3. "Market power" means that the firm has some ability to raise prices without losing all of its sales. In other words, the demand curve it faces is downward sloping.

THE UPSIDE–DOWN ECONOMICS
OF NATURAL MONOPOLIES

The *City of Rochester* court states that increased competition may lead to higher prices. This is counterintuitive until one considers the special character of the costs of production of a natural monopolist.

Imagine that a company in 1870 has built a railroad across the western mountains. It has sunk millions into that project and now the question is whether you as transportation planner should favor its carrying all the freight that is to go by rail, or whether some new firm should incur the expense of building a parallel set of tracks. It is not hard to see that in a highly capital-intensive industry such as railroading, once the capital was sunk for one firm, the marginal cost of running many trains across that track would be dramatically less than the cost of building a new set of tracks even if competition would thereby be increased. The amount of economic resources consumed in providing rail service would be substantially less if one firm carried the traffic than if two firms divided it between them.

When additional increments of service can be supplied less expensively by a single large producer instead of by additional producers, we say that production is subject to economies of scale. For example, it might be significantly less expensive to build one two-lane bridge across the Charles River than to build two one-lane bridges. Likewise, quadrupling the size of a gas pipeline before it is laid will not even double the cost of installing it. In such situations, it will take far less of society's resources to have one firm provide the large capacity rather than to have several firms each provide less. This is the economic phenomenon we call natural monopoly. Graphically, the position of the natural monopolist looks like Figure 8.

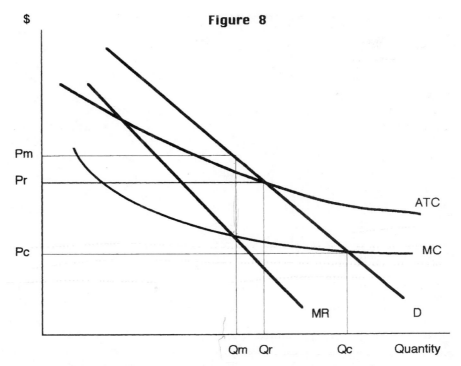

Figure 8

There's a lot of information in that picture, so let's take it step by step.

First, the graph illustrates the working definition of a natural monopoly, i.e. an industry and firm whose costs are falling over all relevant ranges of production. Notice that the cost decrease is faster over some production increases than others. You can also guess that ultimately marginal cost must turn up, i.e. sometime there will be a need for a second bridge or a larger pipeline. Over the range of production you as planner are considering, however, by definition one firm can always produce more cheaply than two if the industry is a natural monopoly.

Second, you can see from the graph that natural monopoly presents all of the opportunities for abuse of monopoly position discussed above. If there is only one railroad, and its price is not regulated, it will have every incentive to limit the number of trains it runs and to raise the price for rail service to the point which maximizes its profit. On the above graph, it would produce Qm and price at Pm. It still may be true that the monopolist will consume less economic resources in providing the service than firms in competition would have consumed, but it is not difficult to understand why pressure might build to require the monopolist to charge a lower price and make a lower profit, one that is more nearly the return that would have been available in a competitive industry.

On the other hand, if you look at the graph carefully you will see that the natural monopolist has a unique problem. Ask yourself what the price would be if a competing firm did enter. Notice that the natural monopolist's marginal cost is falling over all relevant ranges of output. In such a situation, the marginal cost will always be less than the average cost of producing any given level of output. That has an important consequence. If the firm prices its service at Pc, or at marginal cost generally, as competition will tend to make it do, it will never earn its average cost. Thus even though this price would be consistent with allocative efficiency, ultimately the firm will leave the industry, having "wasted" resources in the process. Regulation seeks to avoid this waste and guarantee the natural monopolist recovery of its variable costs and a stable, "fair" rate of return on its prudent investments.

Finally, the graph shows us what price lower than the monopoly price and quantity greater than the monopoly quantity will let a single firm produce profitably and at minimum cost to society. That price and quantity are shown on our graph as Pr and Qr respectively. If you were planning our society, that would come closest to the point you would pick, and you might see regulation as a valuable tool in your effort.

It is this seemingly inevitable movement toward a single firm that explains the label "natural monopoly." As the label suggests, the industry is only stable when a single firm remains. Whether an industry is a natural monopoly, however, depends on the state of technology. In other words, an industry that is not a "natural monopoly" may become one as technological changes make economics of scale possible. Or, technological developments may render previously high capital investments less necessary and competition correspondingly more practical. In the materials that follow, we look at industries going through this process of change and explore who bears the costs of deregulation. Labor and producers of other inputs, suppliers of capital, and parties who entered into long term contracts all may have done so based on the belief in these industries that regulation would never end.

The traditional concept of natural monopoly as explained here focuses on costs of production. Because costs decline throughout all relevant levels of production it makes sense to allow the market to be served by one regulated firm. In the 1990s economists and regulators began to examine another justification for single or few firm industries. You can understand this by thinking about the operating system of your computer. If your computer has the same operating system as many others, you are part of a "network." This is because you can readily communicate and share data with those who have systems that are compatible with your own. When a particular good or service becomes more useful to users as additional users also buy that good or service we say that there are "network effects." As you go through the cases that follow and examine some of the difficulties of deregulation, you should ask yourself whether the problem is one of deregulating industries that are natural monopolies, whether in fact there are substantial network effects at work, or both.

2. DEREGULATION OF NATURAL MONOPOLIES

During the last twenty-five years of the twentieth century many industries that had been viewed as natural monopolies were scrutinized very closely to determine if competitive alternatives were possible. Telecommunications, energy and transportation have all undergone changes in regulation. In the case of telecommunications, the Telecommunications Act of 1996 requires local exchange carriers to unbundle the various elements of their networks and to make them available to competitors. A similar unbundling strategy has been implemented in markets for natural gas. The idea is to promote competition without requiring new entrants to duplicate all the necessary facilities–something they are unlikely to do. The next two cases address the changes in telecommunications and energy. As you read them, think about whether they actually involve "deregulation" as you might have envisioned it before taking this course.

UNITED STATES TELECOM ASSOCIATION v. FEDERAL COMMUNICATIONS COMMISSION

United States Court of Appeals, District of Columbia Circuit, 2002.
290 F.3d 415.

Before EDWARDS AND RANDOLPH, CIRCUIT JUDGES, and WILLIAMS, SENIOR JUDGE

WILLIAMS, SENIOR CIRCUIT JUDGE:

Petitioners in these two cases—certain incumbent local exchange carriers ("ILECs") and the U.S. Telecom Association, representing approximately 1200 such carriers—seek review of two rulemaking orders of the Federal Communications Commission. One order requires ILECs to lease a variety of "unbundled network elements" ("UNEs") to competitive local exchange carriers ("CLECs"), and the other unbundles a portion of the spectrum of local copper loops so that CLECs can offer competitive Digital Subscriber Line ("DSL") internet access. We grant both petitions, and remand both rules to the Commission.

I. BACKGROUND

Congress passed the Telecommunications Act of 1996 * * * (the "1996 Act" or the "Act"), to "promote competition and reduce regulation in order to secure lower prices and higher quality services for American telecommunications consumers and encourage the rapid deployment of new telecommunications technologies." 1996 Act, preamble. In pursuit of that goal, § 251 of the Act requires that ILECs "unbundle" their network elements—that is, provide them on an individual basis to competitive providers on terms prescribed by the Commission. 47 U.S.C. § 251(c)(3). To guide the Commission in deciding which network elements are to be unbundled, the Act goes on to specify:

(2) Access standards

In determining what network elements should be made available for purposes of subsection (c)(3) of this section, the Commission shall consider, at a minimum, whether—

(A) access to such network elements as are proprietary in nature is necessary; and

(B) the failure to provide access to such network elements would *impair* the ability of the telecommunications carrier seeking access to provide the services that it seeks to offer.

47 U.S.C. § 251(d)(2) (emphasis added).

In its first effort at implementation, Implementation of the Local Competition Provisions in the Telecommunications Act of 1996, First Report and Order, CC Docket No. 96–98, 11 FCC Rcd 15499 (1996) ("First Local Competition Order"), the Commission gave this section the following reading:

The term "impair" means "to make or cause to become worse; diminish in value." We believe, generally, that an entrant's ability to offer a telecommunications service is "diminished in value" if the quality of the service the entrant can offer, absent access to the requested element, declines and/or the cost of providing the service rises. We believe we must consider this standard by evaluating whether a carrier could offer a service *using other unbundled elements within an incumbent LEC's network*.

In AT&T Corp. v. Iowa Utilities Board, 525 U.S. 366 [1999] the Supreme Court found the Commission's view far too broad, saying that under such a standard it was "hard to imagine when the incumbent's failure to give access to the element would not constitute an 'impairment.'" It specifically criticized the Commission's having "blind[ed] itself to the availability of elements outside the incumbent's network," including self-provisioning and leasing from other providers. It criticized the Commission's view that "*any* increase" in the competitor's cost (resulting from lack of access to an incumbent's element) would be an "impairment." *Id*. at 389–90, (emphasis in original). Summarizing the overall picture, it said that if "Congress had wanted to give blanket access to incumbents' networks," it "would simply have said (as the Commission in effect has) that whatever requested element can be provided must be provided." *Id*. at 390.

In *Iowa Utilities Board,* the Supreme Court also addressed the Act's provisions on rates for UNEs, reversing the Eighth Circuit's holding that the Commission had no authority to set such rates. * * * It accordingly returned the remaining rate issues to the Eighth Circuit, which on remand invalidated the Commission's rate-setting principle, known by the acronym TELRIC (for "total element long-run incremental cost"). * * *

Following the Supreme Court's remand on the "impairment" standard, the Commission again tackled that issue in the rulemakings now on review. In what we will call the "Local Competition Order," Implementation of the Local Competition Provisions of the Telecommunications Act of 1996, Third Report and Order and Fourth Further Notice of Proposed Rulemaking, 15 FCC Rcd 3696 (1999), it revised its definition of "impair" so as to require unbundling if, "taking into consideration the availability of alternative elements outside the incumbent's network, including self-provisioning by a requesting carrier or acquiring an alternative from a third-party supplier, *lack of access* to that element *materially diminishes* a requesting carrier's ability to provide the services it seeks to offer." * * * In weighing the availability of alternative network elements, the Commission noted that it would examine five factors— cost, effect on timeliness of entry, quality, ubiquity, and impact on network operations. * * * Finally, it said that beyond looking simply to "impairment," it would consider five factors that it believed would further the Act's goals, namely whether unbundling would lead to "rapid introduction of competition in all markets," promote "facilities-based competition, investment, and innovation," reduce regulatory obligations, promote certainty in the market, and be administratively practical. * * *

Of particular importance to this case, the Commission decided to make its unbundling requirements (except for two elements) applicable uniformly to all elements in every geographic or customer market.

    * * *

In what we call the "Line Sharing Order," In the Matters of Deployment of Wireline Services Offering Advanced Telecommunications Capability and Implementation of the Local Competition Provisions of the Telecommunications Act of 1996, Third Report and Order in CC Docket No. 98–147 and Fourth Report and Order in CC Docket No. 96–98, 14 FCC Rcd 20912 (1999), the Commission refined unbundling further. Copper loops have a range of spectrum in which the transmission of information is possible. Analog telephone service uses only the lower frequencies of that spectrum (typically 300 to 3400 hz), leaving higher frequencies unused. Recent technological development allows the provision of DSL high-speed internet access over the high-frequency (i.e., 20,000+ hz) spectrum. By fitting the loop with splitters (which split apart voice and digital signals) and DSLAMs (Digital Subscriber Line Access Multiplexers) (which send voice traffic to the circuit-switched telephone network and data traffic to the packet-switched data network), local carriers can provide both plain old telephone service and DSL internet access at the same time.

In the "Line Sharing Order" the Commission decided that the high frequency portion of copper loop spectrum should be unbundled as to those loops on which ILECs are currently providing telephone service. The Commission defined the "high frequency" portion as simply any frequency "above the voiceband on a copper loop facility used to carry analog circuit-switched voiceband transmissions." * * *

Such unbundling means, of course, that CLECs and ILECs would share the same copper loop to provide two different services at once.

* * * The Commission clarified that the unbundling obligation extends to only one competitor per line. * * *

The Commission also required ILECs to condition loops, that is, to remove loading coils, bridge taps, and other voiceband transmission enhancing equipment that tends to interfere with DSL service. * * * An ILEC can escape this obligation by demonstrating that conditioning would significantly degrade analog voice service. The Commission explicitly recognized that such a showing would be practically impossible for loops under 18,000 feet.

II. THE LOCAL COMPETITION ORDER

We note at the outset the extraordinary complexity of the Commission's task. Congress sought to foster competition in the telephone industry, and plainly believed that merely removing affirmative legal obstructions would not do the job. It thus charged the Commission with identifying those network elements whose lack would "impair" would-be competitors' ability to enter the market, yet gave no detail as to either the kind or degree of impairment that would qualify. We review the two orders with this in mind.

A. *Unvarying Scope*

As to almost every element, the Commission chose to adopt a uniform national rule, mandating the element's unbundling in every geographic market and customer class, without regard to the state of competitive impairment in any particular market. As a result, UNEs will be available to CLECs in many markets where there is no reasonable basis for thinking that competition is suffering from any impairment of a sort that might have the object of Congress's concern.

One reason for such market-specific variations in competitive impairment is the cross-subsidization often ordered by state regulatory commissions, typically in the name of universal service. This usually brings about undercharges for some subscribers (usually rural and/or residential) and overcharges for the others (usually urban and/or business). Petitioners' opening brief in the Local Competition Order case cites testimony of a former FCC Chairman for the proposition that 40% of telephone service is charged below cost and the Commission and its supporting intervenors do not demur. * * *

Competitors will presumably not be drawn to markets where customers are already charged below cost, unless either (1) the availability of UNEs priced well below the ILECs' historic cost makes such a strategy promising, or (2) provision of service may, by virtue of economies of scale and scope, enable a CLEC to sell complementary services (such as long distance or enhanced services) at prices high enough to cover incomplete recovery of costs in basic service. The Commission never explicitly addresses by what criteria want of unbundling can be said to impair competition in such markets, where, given the ILECs' regulatory hobbling, any competition will be wholly artificial. And, although it offers an explanation as to why it is desirable as a general matter that CLECs should have "ubiquitous" unimpaired access to network elements, * * * it never explains why the record supports a finding of material impairment where the element in question—though not literally ubiquitous—is significantly deployed on a competitive basis in those markets where there is no reason to suppose that rates are artificially low, compare * * *.

But it is in the other segments of the markets, where presumably ILECs must charge *above* cost (at least above average costs allocated in conventional regulatory fashion) in order to offset their losses in the subsidized markets, that the gap in the Commission's reasoning is greatest. In finding that the CLECs' lack of access to each of the many elements "materially diminish[ed]" their ability to provide service, the Commission nowhere appears to have considered the advantage CLECs enjoy in being free of any duty to provide underpriced service to rural and/or residential customers and thus of any need to make up the difference elsewhere. As a matter of pure language, perhaps, one might regard as an "impairment" any cost disadvantage that the CLECs suffer in markets where ILECs are hampered by regulatory redistribution, even if the disadvantage is fully offset by the exigencies faced by ILECs. But the Commission has never explained why such a view makes sense. Indeed, pointing to evidence of considerable investment by CLECs in facilities for service in what are evidently the relatively overcharged markets, * * * the petitioners argue that there has been little or no real net impairment. The Commission responds with an expression of doubt whether these "data accurately reflects [sic] the extent to which alternatives are actually available to competitors." * * * But because the Commission has loftily abstracted away all specific markets, and because its concept of impairing cost-differentials is so broad (an issue discussed below), we have no way of assessing the real meaning of that conclusion.

We now turn to the reasons offered by the Commission for adopting an undifferentiated national rule for each element (with narrow exceptions). Having found legal authority to adopt such a rule, it said that it would help achieve the goals of the Act, to wit: (1) rapid introduction of competition, (2) promotion of facilities-based competition, investment and innovation, (3) certainty in the marketplace, (4) administrative practicality and (5) reduced regulation. * * *

We first address the third and fourth justifications, both of which seemingly turn on how clear any non-universal rule can be. The Commission appears simply to assume that any such rule would be unpredictable and hard to apply. Yet the Commission itself, in regard to circuit switches, chose a partial rule, denying unbundling for local circuit switches serving customers with four or more lines in the highest-density zone in any of the top 50 Metropolitan Statistical Areas ("MSAs"). * * * The Commission's order has no explanation of why comparable differentiation was not available for other elements.

As to reduced regulation, the Commission says that a national list "will result immediately in reduced regulation." It does not elaborate on this counterintuitive proposition. It goes on to say that a national list is consistent with "the deregulatory goals of the Act":

> Reduced regulation will occur as we remove elements from the list as requesting carriers are no longer impaired without access to those elements, and it otherwise does not further the goals of the Act to continue requiring incumbent LECs to unbundle them.

Id. We understand that elimination of an entire universal mandate at one whack will achieve more deregulation than removal of a partial mandate. But imposition of a national mandate does not itself entail national elimination, and in any event we cannot see how imposition and then retraction of a national mandate is more deregulatory, overall, than imposition and retraction of a partial one.

This leaves the more substantive justifications—the ideas that universal rules would promote the goals of the Act by leading to rapid introduction of competition, and to promotion of facilities-based competition, investment, and innovation. Using certain definitions, the first point—more rapid introduction of competition—indeed follows automatically. If competition performed with ubiquitously provided ILEC facilities counts, the more unbundling there is, the more competition.

The Commission, here in unison with the ILEC petitioners, evidently assumes that the Commission-imposed prices are highly attractive to CLECs; on that assumption, universal rules encompassing as many elements as possible would indeed generate a rapid spread of "competition."

But the Commission never makes the argument in quite so stark a form, unwilling to embrace the idea that such completely synthetic competition would fulfill Congress's purposes. Thus it turns to the argument that universal rules promote investment and facilities-based competition.

The Commission says that "adoption of a national list" will "facilitate the deployment" of competitive facilities. There are plainly two sides to the effects on investment of ubiquitously available UNEs at Commission-mandated prices. On one side, the more widespread the availability of elements that can be more efficiently provided by the incumbent (presumably because of economies of scale and scope—an issue to which we'll return), the quicker competitors will set about providing the other elements and offering of complete competitive service, including long distance service. * * * Further, access to UNEs may enable a CLEC to enter the market gradually, building a customer base up to the level where its own investment would be profitable.

On the other side, the petitioners argued before the Commission that mandatory unbundling at Commission-mandated prices reduces the incentives for innovation and investment in facilities. Their reasoning, of course, is that a regulated price below true cost will reduce or eliminate the incentive for an ILEC to invest in innovation (because it will have to share the rewards with CLECs), and also for a CLEC to innovate (because it can get the element cheaper as a UNE). Indeed, many prices that *seem* to equate to cost have this effect. Some innovations pan out, others do not. If parties who have not shared the risks are able to come in as equal partners on the successes, and avoid payment for the losers, the incentive to invest plainly declines. * * * In any event, the Commission's own assumption that universal access to virtually all network elements would prove attractive (leading to rapid introduction of "competition") suggests that such a disincentive effect cannot be discounted a priori.

The Commission's only response is to point to evidence that both CLECs and ILECs have built facilities since passage of the 1996 Act (the same evidence invoked by the ILECs to show the existence of many markets where unbundling is unneeded), despite the Act's obviously having created a prospect of unbundling. * * * But the existence of investment of a specified level tells us little or nothing about incentive effects. The question is how such investment compares with what would have occurred in the absence of the prospect of unbundling * * *, an issue on which the record appears silent. Although we can't expect the Commission to offer a precise assessment of disincentive effects (a lack of multiple regression analyses is not ipso facto arbitrary and capricious), we can expect at least some confrontation of the issue and some effort to make reasonable trade-offs.

In the end, then, the entire argument about expanding competition and investment boils down to the Commission's expression of its belief that in this area more unbundling is better. But Congress did not authorize so open-ended a judgment. It made "impairment" the touchstone. The Commission argues that § 251(d)(2), directing it to consider necessity and impairment "at a minimum," clearly allows it to consider other elements. We assume in favor of the Commission that is so. But to the extent that the Commission orders access to UNEs in circumstances where there is little or no reason to think that its absence will genuinely impair competition that might otherwise occur, we believe it must point to something a bit more concrete than its belief in the beneficence of the widest unbundling possible.

Besides the analysis described above, the Commission addressed the question whether *Iowa Utilities Board* precluded its adoption of universal rules for each network element. It concluded that nothing in that opinion would require it "to determine, on a localized state-by-state or market-by-market basis which unbundled elements are to be made available." * * * We certainly agree that the Court's brief passage reversing the Commission on the impairment issue contained little detail as to the "right" way for the Commission to go about its work. But the Court's point that if "Congress had wanted to give blanket access to incumbents' networks," it "would simply have said (as the Commission in effect has) that whatever requested element can be provided must be provided," * * * suggests that the Court read the statute as requiring a more nuanced concept of impairment than is reflected in findings such as the Commission's—detached from any specific markets or market categories.

B. Kinds of Cost Disparities

Petitioners complain that the Commission myopically focused on "cost differences," thereby skewing its inquiry to produce the maximum unbundling.

Of course any cognizable competitive "impairment" would necessarily be traceable to some kind of disparity in cost. Indeed, the ILECs argued before the Commission and the Supreme Court that Congress intended that the impairment standard embody the criteria of the "essential facilities" doctrine, * * * which itself turns on concepts of cost. The doctrine's basic idea is that where one firm controls some facility (such as a bridge) that is essential for competition in a broader market, and it would make *no economic sense* for competitors to duplicate the facility, and certain other criteria are satisfied, see generally Phillip E. Areeda & Herbert Hovenkamp, 3A Antitrust Law ¶ ¶ 771–73 (1996), the owner may be compelled to share the facility with its competitors. The classic case where competitor duplication would make no economic sense is where average costs are declining throughout the range of the relevant market. * * * In such a case, duplication, even by the most efficient competitors imaginable, would only lead to higher unit costs for all firms, and thus for customers. * * * Thus the Supreme Court in *Verizon* observed that "entrants may need to share some facilities that are *very expensive to duplicate* (say, loop elements) in order to be able to compete in other, *more sensibly duplicable* elements (say, digital switches or signal-multiplexing technology)." *Verizon [Communications v. FCC]*, 535 U.S. at 510 n. 27, 122 S.Ct. at 1672 n. 27 (emphasis added). * * *

Petitioners' position here is fundamentally that the Commission relied on cost disparities that, far from being any indication that competitive supply would be wasteful, are simply disparities faced by virtually any new entrant in any sector of the economy, no matter how competitive the sector. * * * Indeed, the Commission's order does reflect an open-ended notion of what kinds of cost disparity are relevant.

For example, in the discussion of local switching, the Commission notes that there are economies of scale in switches, * * * and that it is cheaper to buy a 20,000–line switch than four increments of 5000 lines each * * *. The Commission refers explicitly to a CLEC's probable inability to enjoy scale economies comparable to ILECs' *"particularly in the early stages of entry."* * * * But average unit costs are necessarily higher at the outset for any new entrant into virtually any business. The Commission has in no way focused on the presence of economies of scale *"over the entire extent of the market."* * * * Without a link to this sort of cost disparity, there is no particular reason to think that the element is one for which multiple, competitive supply is unsuitable.

The Commission of course has recognized that marketplace changes and increases in competition may justify later reductions in unbundling mandates. But this acknowledgment doesn't respond to the analytical problem. To rely on cost disparities that are universal as between new entrants and incumbents in *any* industry is to invoke a concept too broad, even in support of an *initial* mandate, to be reasonably linked to the purpose of the Act's unbundling provisions.

Each unbundling of an element imposes costs of its own, spreading the disincentive to invest in innovation and creating complex issues of managing shared facilities. See *Iowa Utilities Board,* 525 U.S. at 428–29 (Breyer, J., concurring in part and dissenting in part). At the same time—the plus that the Commission focuses on single-mindedly—a broad mandate can facilitate competition by eliminating the need for separate construction of facilities where such construction would be wasteful. * * * Justice Breyer concluded that fulfillment of the Act's purposes therefore called for "balance" between these competing concerns. * * * A cost disparity approach that links "impairment" to universal characteristics, rather than ones linked (in some degree) to natural monopoly, can hardly be said to strike such a balance. The Local Competition Order reflects little Commission effort to pin "impairment" to cost differentials based on characteristics that would make genuinely competitive provision of an element's function wasteful.

Petitioners here do not explicitly attack the Commission for its refusal to incorporate the essential facilities doctrine, and we do not intend to suggest that the Act requires use of that doctrine's criteria. But what we do say is that cost comparisons of the sort made by the Commission, largely devoid of any interest in whether the cost characteristics of an "element" render it at all unsuitable for competitive supply, seem unlikely either to achieve the balance called for explicitly by Justice Breyer or implicitly by the Court as a whole in its disparagement of the Commission's readiness to find *"any"* cost disparity reason enough to order unbundling. * * *

Because the Commission's concept of "impairing" cost disparities is so broad and unrooted in any analysis of the competing values at stake in implementation of the Act, we cannot uphold even the two non-universal mandates adopted by the Commission (for circuit switches and packet switches).

　　　* * *

III.   The Line Sharing Order

Petitioners primarily attack the Line Sharing Order on the ground that the Commission, in ordering unbundling of the high frequency spectrum of copper loop so as to enable CLECs to provide DSL services, completely failed to consider the relevance of competition in broadband services coming from cable (and to a lesser extent satellite). We agree.

The Commission's own findings (in a series of reports under § 706 of the 1996 Act) repeatedly confirm both the robust competition, and the dominance of cable, in the broadband market. The first § 706 report found that "[n]umerous companies in virtually all segments of the communications industry are starting to deploy, or plan to deploy in the near future, broadband to the consumer market," including "cable television companies, incumbent LECs, some utilities, and 'wireless cable' companies." In the Matter of Inquiry Concerning the Deployment of Advanced Telecommunications Capability to All Americans in a Reasonable and Timely Fashion, and Possible Steps to Accelerate Such Deployment Pursuant to Section 706 of the Telecommunications Act of 1996, 14 FCC Rcd 2398, 2404 ¶ 12 (1999). The Commission also noted that the "most popular offering of broadband to residential consumers is via 'cable modems' * * * that "no competitor has a large embedded base of paying residential consumers," * * * and that the "record does not indicate that the consumer market is inherently a natural monopoly." The most recent § 706 Report (not in the record of this case) is consistent: As of the end of June 2001, cable companies had 54% of extant high-speed lines, almost double the 28% share of asymmetric DSL. * * * Even in the Local Competition Order on review in this case, the Commission said, "Competitive LECs and cable companies appear to be leading the incumbent LECs in their deployment of advanced services." * * *

Relying on the Commission's repeated findings, petitioners argue that it is "antithetical to the 1996 Act's language and deregulatory objectives" to mandate unbundling in a market that "already has intense facilities-based competition." They note the Supreme Court's observation that a proper "impairment" standard should be limited by the "goals of the Act."

The Commission's response to this argument is to say that it was "merely adhering" to the letter of the statute: Thus it quotes the instruction of § 251(d)(2)(B) that it consider whether "failure to provide access to such network elements would impair the ability of the telecommunications carrier seeking access to provide the services *that it seeks to offer.*" * * * On this theory the Commission believes it was justified in focusing solely on DSL because that is what "CLECs seek to offer when they request line sharing." The Commission thus appears to acknowledge that it adopted the Line Sharing Order with indifference to petitioners' contentions about the state of competition in the market.

The Commission's inference from § 251(d)(2)(B)'s allusion to the services the requester "seeks to offer" strikes us as quite unreasonable. * * * As Justice Breyer's separate opinion carefully explained, mandatory unbundling comes at a cost, including disincentives to research and development by both ILECs and CLECs and the tangled management inherent in shared use of a common resource. * * * And, as we said before, the Court's opinion in *Iowa Utilities Board,* though less explicit than Justice Breyer on the need for balance, plainly recognized that unbundling is not an unqualified good—thus its observation that the Commission must "apply *some* limiting standard, rationally related to the goals of the Act," and its point that the Commission "cannot, consistent with the statute, blind itself to the availability of elements outside the incumbent's network." In sum, nothing in the Act appears a license to the Commission to inflict on the economy the sort of costs noted by Justice Breyer under conditions where it had no reason to think doing so would bring on a significant enhancement of competition. The Commission's naked disregard of the competitive context risks exactly that result.

Accordingly, the Line Sharing Order must be vacated and remanded. Obviously any order unbundling the high frequency portion of the loop should also not be tainted by the sort of error identified in our discussion of the Local Competition Order and identified by petitioners here as well.

* * *

We grant the petitions for review, and remand both the Line Sharing Order and the Local Competition Order to the Commission for further consideration in accordance with the principles outlined above.

HISTORICAL NOTE ON TELECOMMUNICATIONS REGULATION

A complete examination of the telecommunications industry, its restructuring and deregulation would take an entire course—maybe a lifetime. The revolution began quietly enough when a Mr. Carter proposed to sell a "Carterphone" in which one placed a telephone receiver to permit direct communication with a police officer at the other end of a two-way radio. AT & T, then the only firm permitted to provide U.S. telecommunications services, objected that the Carterphone was a "foreign attachment." However, the Federal Communications Commission permitted its continued use so long as it could be shown not to damage the communications network. Matter of Carter v. AT & T, 13 F.C.C.2d 420 (1968).

Similarly, when an upstart midwestern firm called Microwave Communications, Inc. (MCI) asked permission to offer point-to-point microwave communications services only between Chicago and St. Louis, the Commission approved what one Commissioner called a way "to add a little salt and pepper of competition to the rather tasteless stew of regulatory protection that this Commission and Bell have cooked up." In re Applications of Microwave Communications, Inc., 18 F.C.C.2d 953 (1969) (Nicholas Johnson, concurring).

Due to delays resulting from further litigations and construction, MCI did not inaugurate its Chicago–St. Louis route until 1972. An issue left open was just how MCI and other long distance carriers were to connect with their actual customers. In *Specialized Common Carriers*[4] the Commission required AT & T to provide interconnect services between the specialized long distance carriers and their customers. See generally Gerald R. Faulhaber, Telecommunication in Turmoil: Technology and Public Policy 30–33 (1987).

4.   29 F.C.C.2d 870 (1971).

Another enormous boost toward deregulation was provided by an antitrust suit mounted by the Justice Department against AT & T in 1974. AT & T was charged with violating both Sections 1 & 2 of the Sherman Act, 15 U.S.C.A. §§ 1 & 2. It allegedly had monopolized and conspired to restrain trade in the market for telecommunications service and in the manufacture, sale and distribution of telecommunications equipment. After eight years, the suit culminated in a consent decree and a major restructuring of AT & T. The central feature of the decree was the requirement that AT & T divest itself of its Regional Bell Operating Companies (BOCs). In addition, the decree provided that each BOC would be the sole provider of local telephone service. The BOCs were also restricted, however, to specific "lines of business." For example, initially, BOCs were prohibited from competing in the market for equipment and in the market for long distance service as well as from providing information services. United States v. American Tel. & Tel., 552 F.Supp. 131 (D.D.C.1982), affirmed sub nom. Maryland v. United States, 460 U.S. 1001, 103 S.Ct. 1240, 75 L.Ed.2d 472 (1983).[5] As things turned out, the process of responding to requests for modifications, waivers and clarifications turned out to be virtually continuous.[6]

Critical to the consent decree dismantling AT & T was an emphasis away from seeing long distance service as a natural monopoly toward the view that the local systems were the only natural monopolies. The Telecommunications Act of 1996 represents an effort to inject competition even into those local markets.

Notes and Questions

1. Do you understand what went awry with the FCC's national standards? If the incumbent is overcharging some customers in order to undercharge others, which markets are new competitors likely to enter? How does one decide what is competitive in a context in which very few customers are being charged prices that would exist under competitive conditions? See generally, Reza Dibadj, "Competitive Debacle in Local Telephony: Is the 1996 Telecommunications Act to Blame," 81 Wash. U.L.Q. 1 (2003).

2. The issue of overcharging and undercharging is one of cross-subsidization. In effect, some customers are charged more so that others can be charged less. It is a subtle way states and their regulatory agencies "tax" some citizens in order to subsidize others. Do you see how this complicates the deregulation picture? Do you understand the court to be saying that less unbundling may be necessary when incumbents are required to engage in cross-subsidization.

---

5. See generally Constatine Kraus & Alfred W. Duerig, The Rape of Ma Bell, (1988); Peter Temin, The Fall of the Bell System, (1987); Warren G. Lavey & Dennis W. Carlton, Economic Goals and Remedies of the AT & T Modified Final Judgment, 71 Geo.L.J. 1497 (1983); Paul W. MacAvoy & Kenneth L. Robinson, Winning by Losing: The AT & T Settlement and Its Impact on Telecommunications, 1 Yale J. Reg. 1 (1983).

6. For a summary of a single year's activities see American Bar Association, 1991 Annual Report of the Section of Public Utilities, Communications and Transportation Law, pp. 117–119 (1991).

3.   In September 2003, the FCC announced the outcome of yet another effort to solve the unbundling puzzle. This time the Commission ruled that a requesting carrier is impaired "when lack of access to an incumbent LEC network element poses a barrier or barriers to entry, including operational and economic barriers, that are likely to make entry into a market uneconomic." Among the factors considered is specific marketplace evidence including whether entry has already occurred. The analysis is to take place on the bases of geographic markets, consumer classes, and the type and capacity of facilities to be used. See 68 Fed. Reg. 52276 at ¶ 5 (Sept. 2, 2003).

4.   Suppose local exchange carriers, having been ordered to unbundle, charge a price for the unbundled elements that allows them to undersell their new "competitors." Obviously, an unbundling requirement without some control over price is meaningless. In effect, deregulation did not mean escaping a rate-making process. The question of what that rate should be was addressed by the Supreme Court in Verizon Communications, Inc. v. Federal Communications Commission, 535 U.S. 467, 122 S.Ct. 1646, 152 L.Ed.2d 701 (2002), which is examined in Chapter 4.

5.   The concept of unbundling as a way of adding competitive pressures to a natural monopoly market is not limited to telecommunications. In the natural gas industry the process has been one that requires natural gas companies to make their pipelines available to those who wish to transport gas purchased from third parties. As you examine the following case, think about whether there are important distinctions between telecommunications and natural gas that make the unbundling process easier in one context than in the other.

UNITED DISTRIBUTION COMPANIES v. FEDERAL ENERGY REGULATORY COMMISSION

United States Court of Appeals, D.C. Circuit, 1996.
88 F.3d 1105.

Before WALD, SENTELLE and ROGERS, CIRCUIT JUDGES.

PER CURIAM:

In Order No. 636, the Federal Energy Regulatory Commission ("Commission" or "FERC") took the latest step in its decade-long restructuring of the natural gas industry, in which the Commission has gradually withdrawn from direct regulation of certain industry sectors in favor of a policy of "light-handed regulation" when market forces make that possible. * * *

I.

* * *

A.   BACKGROUND: NATURAL GAS INDUSTRY STRUCTURE

* * *

Federal regulation of the natural gas industry is * * * designed to curb pipelines' potential monopoly power over gas transportation. The enormous economies of scale involved in the construction of natural gas pipelines tend to make the transportation of gas a natural monopoly. Indeed, even with the expansion of the national pipeline grid, or network, in recent decades, many "captive" customers[7] remain served by a single pipeline.[8]

* * *

When a severe gas shortage developed in the 1970s, Congress enacted the Natural Gas Policy Act of 1978 (NGPA), 92 Stat. 3351 (codified as amended at 15 U.S.C. §§ 3301–3432 (1994)), which gradually phased out producer price regulation. Under the NGPA's partially regulated producer-price system, many pipelines entered into long-term contractual obligations, in what were known as "take-or-pay" provisions, to purchase minimum quantities of gas from producers at costs that proved to be well above current market prices of gas.

The problem of pipelines' take-or-pay settlement costs has plagued the industry and the Commission over the last fifteen years. * * *

B.   Order No. 436: Open-Access Transportation

In Order No. 436, the Commission began the transition toward removing pipelines from the gas-sales business and confining them to a more limited role as gas transporters. Under a new Part 284 of its regulations, the Commission conditioned receipt of a blanket certificate for firm transportation of third-party gas on the pipeline's acceptance of non-discrimination requirements guaranteeing equal access for all customers to the new service.[9] In effect, the Commission for the first time imposed the duties of common carriers upon interstate pipelines. By recognizing that anti-competitive conditions in the industry arose from pipeline control over access to transportation capacity, the equal-access requirements of Order No. 436 regulated the natural-monopoly conditions directly. In addition, every open-access pipeline was required to allow its existing bundled firm-sales customers to convert to firm-transportation service and, at the customer's option, to reduce its firm-transportation entitlement (its "contract demand"). * * *

* * *

Congress completed the process of deregulating the producer sales market by enacting the Natural Gas Wellhead Decontrol Act of 1989, 103 Stat. 157 (codified in scattered sections of 15 U.S.C.). As the House Committee on Energy and Commerce emphasized, the Commission's creation of open-access transportation was "essential" to Congress' decision completely to deregulate wellhead sales. The committee report

---

7. We use the term "captive customer" to refer to customers "who must use gas and can only obtain it from one provider." Mississippi Valley Gas Co. v. FERC, 68 F.3d 503, 506 (D.C. Cir. 1995). [Court's fn. 5]

8. As of 1985, 10% of gas deliveries were to LDCs served by four or more pipelines, 39.5% to LDCs served by three pipelines, 28% to LDCs served by two pipelines, and 22.5% to LDCs served by a single pipeline.

Stephen F. Williams, The Natural Gas Revolution of 1985, at 4 (1985). [Court's fn. 6]

9. Pipelines generally offer two forms of transportation service: firm transportation, for which delivery is guaranteed, and interruptible transportation, for which delivery can be delayed if all the capacity on the pipeline is in use. [Court's fn. 10]

declared also that "both the FERC and the courts are strongly urged to retain and improve this competitive structure in order to maximize the benefits of decontrol." The committee expected that, by ensuring that "all buyers [are] free to reach the lowest-selling producer," open-access transportation would allow the more efficient producers to emerge, leading to lower prices for consumers.

C.   Order No. 636: Mandatory Unbundling

In Order No. 636, the Commission declared the open-access requirements of Order No. 436 a partial success. The Commission found that pipeline firm sales, which in 1984 had been over 90 percent of deliveries to market, had declined by 1990 to 21 percent. On the other hand, only 28 percent of deliveries to market in 1990 were firm transportation, whereas 51 percent of deliveries used interruptible transportation. The Commission concluded that many customers had not taken advantage of Order No. 436's option to convert from firm-sales to firm-transportation service because the firm-transportation component of bundled firm-sales service was "superior in quality" to stand-alone firm-transportation service. In particular, the Commission found that stand-alone firm-transportation service was often subject to daily scheduling and balancing requirements, as well as to penalties for variances from projected purchases in excess of ten percent. Moreover, pipelines usually did not offer storage capacity on a contractual basis to stand-alone firm-transportation shippers. The result was that many of the non-converted customers used the pipelines' firm-sales service during times of peak demand but in non-peak periods bought third-party gas and transported it with interruptible transportation. The Commission found that "it is often cheaper for pipeline sales customers to buy gas on the spot market, and pay the pipeline's demand charge plus the interruptible rate, than to purchase the pipeline's gas." Because of the distortions in the sales market, these customers often paid twice for transportation services and still received an inferior form of transportation (interruptible rather than firm). Because of the anti-competitive effect on the industry, the Commission found that pipelines' bundled firm-sales service violated §§ 4(b) and 5(a) of the NGA.

The Commission's remedy for these anti-competitive conditions, and the principal innovation of Order No. 636, was mandatory unbundling of pipelines' sales and transportation services. By making the separation of the two functions mandatory, the Commission expects that pipelines' monopoly power over transportation will no longer distort the sales market. To replace the firm-transportation component of bundled firm-sales service, the Commission introduced the concept of "no-notice firm transportation," stand-alone firm transportation without penalties. Those customers who receive bundled firm-sales service have the right, during the restructuring process, to switch to no-notice firm-transportation service. Pipelines that did not offer bundled firm-sales service are not required to offer no-notice transportation; but if they do, they must offer no-notice transportation on a non-discriminatory basis.

In contrast to the continued regulation of the transportation market, the Commission essentially deregulated the pipeline sales market. The Commission issued every Part 284 pipeline a blanket certificate authorizing gas sales. Although acknowledging that "only Congress can 'deregulate,' the Commission 'instituted light-handed regulation', relying upon market forces at the wellhead or in the field to constrain unbundled pipeline sale for resale gas prices within the NGA's 'just and reasonable' standard." The Commission reasoned that open-access transportation, combined with its finding that "adequate divertible gas supplies exist in all pipeline markets," would ensure that the free market for gas sales would keep rates within the zone of reasonableness.

The Commission also undertook several measures to ensure that the pipeline grid, or network, functions as a whole in a more competitive fashion. First, open-access pipelines may not inhibit the development of "market centers," which are pipeline intersections that allow customers to take advantage of many more transportation routes and choose between sellers from different natural gas production areas. Similarly, open-access pipelines may not interfere with the development of "pooling areas," which allow the aggregation of gas supplies at a production area. Finally, as part of the move toward open-access transportation, the Commission required Part 284 pipelines to allow shippers to deliver gas at any delivery point without penalty and to allow customers to receive gas at any receipt point without penalty.

* * *

D.   Issues on Review and Conclusions

* * *

The petitioners do not challenge the mandatory unbundling remedy itself. At issue on review are numerous other aspects of Order No. 636 involving changes that the Commission undertook as part of its comprehensive restructuring of the natural gas industry. * * *

* * * We uphold the Commission's rule that customers must retain contractual firm-transportation capacity for which the pipeline receives no other offer. * * *

Part II.B [of this opinion] concerns the Commission's award of pregranted abandonment to long-term firm-transportation service, subject to the existing shipper's "right of first refusal" (ROFR). Under this provision of the rules, pipelines are no longer required to go through § 7 abandonment proceedings when a transportation contract expires. In return, the existing customer has the right to retain service if it matches the terms of a competing offer for that capacity. Such bids are capped at the maximum rate approved by the Commission for that service, and the contract length may not exceed twenty years. While we conclude that in its basic structure the right-of-first-refusal mechanism complies with § 7, we remand the right-of-first-refusal mechanism to the Commission for further explanation of why it adopted a twenty-year term-matching cap. We uphold the Commission's decision not to require pipelines to discount rates in the right-of-first-refusal process.

The Commission also re-visited its policies for the curtailment of gas in times of a supply shortage or a capacity interruption. Gas can be curtailed on an end-use basis, meaning that high-priority users have priority in times of curtailment, or on a pro rata basis, meaning that each user's deliveries are curtailed proportionally. The Commission found that it was statutorily obligated to require pipelines to adopt an end-use curtailment plan for shortages in the supply of pipeline gas. On the other hand, the Commission declined to require pipelines to adopt end-use curtailment for capacity interruption. In Part II.C, we affirm the Commission's decision that title IV of the NGPA requires end-use supply curtailment and conclude that the issue of curtailment compensation is not ripe for review. We also deny the petitions for review of the Commission's capacity-curtailment policies, but we do not examine whether pure pro rata capacity curtailment is always appropriate because the Commission has examined that issue on a pipeline-specific basis in the restructuring proceedings. Finally, we uphold the Commission's policies for supply shortages of third-party gas.

Part III addresses the Commission's adoption of a uniform capacity-release program—a regulated market that allows capacity-holders to re-sell the rights to pipeline firm-transportation capacity. An existing shipper that finds itself with excess capacity may list that capacity on the pipeline's electronic bulletin board (EBB), which functions as a central clearinghouse for the secondary capacity market. We uphold the Commission's jurisdiction to regulate the re-sale of interstate-transportation rights in general, as well as specifically its jurisdiction over LDCs who broker capacity to local end-users and over municipal LDCs. We also uphold the Commission's decision that state-authorized "buy/sell arrangements"[10] are pre-empted by the Commission's capacity-release program. Finally, we uphold the Commission's decision to exclude Part 157 shippers and conclude that other challenges to the substance of the capacity-release program are not ripe for review.

Part IV deals with the Commission's requirement that pipelines adopt a new rate-design methodology known as straight fixed/variable (SFV). Under SFV, pipelines must allocate fixed costs to the reservation charge, and variable costs to the usage charge. The Commission mandated SFV so that fixed costs, which vary greatly between pipelines, would no longer affect the usage charge and thus distort the national gas-sales market that Order No. 636 fosters. Because the shift from the previous modified fixed/variable (MFV) rate design would disadvantage low-load-factor customers,[11] the Commission adopted various SFV mitigation

---

10. A buy/sell arrangement is an agreement between an LDC and one of its local end-users under which (1) the end-user identifies (and sometimes purchases) gas held by a producer, (2) the LDC in turn purchases the identified gas and uses its firm-transportation capacity to transport the gas, and (3) the LDC sells the gas to the end-user. [Court's fn. 22]

11. A customer's load factor is the ratio between its average usage and its peak usage. Customers with seasonal usage fluctua-

measures to protect those customers. We uphold the Commission's authority under § 5 to adopt SFV rate design and conclude that substantial evidence supports the Commission's findings that MFV rate design distorted the producer sales market and that SFV is an appropriate rate-design methodology. * * *

Finally, as we explain in Part V, the Commission addressed the transition costs involved with implementing Order No. 636. The Commission allowed pipelines, whose role as gas merchants was greatly reduced, to pass through to transportation customers all the costs of reducing contractual purchase obligations from producers, known as gas-supply realignment (GSR) costs. Unlike the Order No. 500 equitable-sharing cost-recovery mechanism for take-or-pay costs from pipeline-producer contracts, Order No. 636 imposes all the costs of realigning unneeded producer-pipeline contracts on pipeline customers. The Commission authorized pipelines to recover 90% of the GSR costs from current firm-transportation customers * * * and 10% of the GSR costs from interruptible-transportation customers. We uphold the Commission's decision to allow pipelines to recover GSR costs from customers who converted to open-access transportation before Order No. 636, but remand the decision that pipelines must allocate 10% of GSR costs to interruptible-transportation customers for further explanation. We also remand the decision that pipelines can pass through all their GSR costs to customers for further consideration by the Commission in light of the equitable-sharing procedures in Order No. 500 and the general cost-spreading principles of Order No. 636. * * *

Notes and Questions

1. Order No. 636 is an important part of a nearly 20 year effort to deregulate the natural gas industry.

a. A key component of this effort was the "unbundling" of the gas itself from the pipeline. That meant that buyers and sellers of natural gas could interact in the market and then approach the pipeline for transportation services only. Indeed, notice that unbundling was by now so much a part of the natural gas industry that it was not even the subject of the appeal to the D.C. Circuit.

b. As Order No. 636 indicates, Order No. 436 had started this process but still left pipelines at a competitive advantage in the sale of natural gas. This was because pipelines could still sell a more integrated product consisting of gas, transportation and storage. The storage capacity made the pipelines preferred sellers to those for whom reliability in supply was essential. See generally, Adam D. Samuels, Reliability of Natural Gas Service for Captive End–Users Under the Federal Regulatory Commission's Order No. 636, 62 G.W. L. Rev. 718 (1994). Thus, Order No. 636 is also an effort to

---

tions, such as LDCs, have low load factors, whereas customers with constant usage throughout the year, such as industrial end-   users, have high load factors. [Court's fn. 26]

overcome the competitive advantage of natural gas pipelines by requiring that all of the services, including storage, be available to buyers separately.

c.   Notice as well that some of the biggest issues surrounding Order No. 636 seem to have been transitional, i.e., how preexisting contracts were to be treated under the new regime. Should pipelines be required to sell gas to existing buyers at old contract rates, for example, if a new customer is willing to pay more? Should the existing customer have a right to match the new customer's offer?

d.   Another problem is the differential effect of new policies and procedures on different classes of customers. Notice that FERC said it wanted no customer to be disadvantaged by its new Order. Is that possible? At the very least, are customers who made plans based on the earlier regulatory regime now at risk of bearing significant transition costs to convert to some other fuel?

2.   According to Order No. 636, gas pipelines remain natural monopolies and subject to rate regulation. Is that self-evidently desirable?

a.   Other commentators say:

> Pipelines are not natural monopolies, in spite of what the proponents of regulation have told us. They can be stripped of monopoly power in a network of interconnected pipelines that offers many distinct paths between markets. Both these things can be accomplished by making transmission an asset that can be traded in a market open to producers, distributors, customers, brokers, and others.

Arthur DeVany & W. David Walls, The Triumph of Markets in Natural Gas, 133 Public Utilities Fortnightly 21 (1995).

b.   Does the fact that large numbers of pipelines can be arranged into a variety of networks reduce the level of monopoly power possessed by any one pipeline? Obviously, it does. On the other hand, does the existence of a large number of pipelines mean that the industry is not subject to natural monopoly tendencies? For example, if there are a number of existing pipelines in place, what is the lowest price that could be charged for a unit of transmission? In a competitive pipeline transmission market, could all of the firms continue to survive?

3.   An obvious target for deregulation along the same lines as natural gas pipeline deregulation is electricity. In simple terms, the generation, transmission and retail sale of electricity would seem equally able to be unbundled and purchased separately from different sellers.[12]

a.   The analogies led FERC to issue a Notice of Proposed Rulemaking No. RM 95–8–000 in March 1995, and a final rule, Order No. 888, in April 1996 (61 Fed.Reg. 21540). The Commission found that:

> [F]unctional unbundling of wholesale services is necessary to implement non-discriminatory open access transmission * * *. * * * [F]unctional unbundling means three things:

---

12.   See, e.g., Robert W. Poole, Jr., Unnatural Monopolies: The Case for Deregulating Public Utilities (1985); William   Collins, Electric Utility Rate Regulation: Curing Economic Shortcoming Through Competition, 19 Tulsa L.J. 141 (1983).

(1) A public utility must take transmission services (including ancillary services) for all of its new wholesale sales and purchases of energy under the same tariff of general applicability as do others;

(2) A public utility must state separate rates for wholesale generation, transmission, and ancillary services;

(3) A public utility must rely on the same electronic information network that its transmission customers rely on to obtain information about its transmission system when buying or selling power.

We believe that these requirements are necessary to ensure that public utilities provide non-discriminatory service. These requirements also will give public utilities an incentive to file fair and efficient rates, terms, and conditions, since they will be subject to those same rates, terms, and conditions.

However, we recognize that additional safeguards are necessary to protect against market power abuses. Functional unbundling will work only if a strong code of conduct (including a requirement to separate employees involved in transmission functions from those involved in wholesale power merchant functions) is in place. * * *

Adoption of this code of conduct * * * is needed to ensure that the transmission owner's wholesale marketing personnel and the transmission customer's marketing personnel have comparable access to information about the transmission system.

* * * [A] further safeguard—section 206—is available if a public utility seeks to circumvent the functional unbundling requirements. Under section 206, any person is free to file a complaint with the Commission detailing any alleged misbehavior on the part of the public utility or its affiliates concerning matters subject to our jurisdiction under the FPA. Similarly, the Commission may, on its own motion, initiate a proceeding to investigate the practices of the public utility and its affiliates.

* * *

Finally, while we are not now requiring any form of corporate unbundling, we again encourage utilities to explore whether corporate unbundling or other restructuring mechanisms may be appropriate in particular circumstances. Thus, we intend to accommodate other mechanisms that public utilities may submit, including voluntary corporate restructurings (e.g., ISOs, separate corporate divisions, divestiture, poolcos), to ensure that open access transmission occurs on a non-discriminatory basis. We also will continue to monitor—and stand ready to work with parties engaging in—innovative restructuring proposals occurring around the country.

* * *

Finally, we will maintain our current practice of allowing market-based rates for existing generation to go into effect subject to refund. To the extent that either the applicant or intervenors in individual cases offer specific evidence that the relevant geographic market ought to be defined differently than under the existing test, we will examine such arguments through formal or paper hearings.

Because our goal is to develop more competitive bulk power markets, we will continue to monitor markets to assess the competitiveness of the market in existing generation, and we will modify our market rate criteria if and when appropriate. * * * The policies we put in place today to develop a smoothly functioning transmission access regime will provide useful experience and information for assessing the effects of generation concentration.

b.   What do you think of this proposal? Can you see any technical and structural differences between the industries that may make the transition in the electricity industry more difficult? How about the fact that electricity, unlike natural gas, cannot be easily stored and travels virtually instantly? See generally, Richard J. Pierce, Jr., The State of the Transition to Competitive Markets in Natural Gas and Electricity, 15 Energy L. J. 323 (1994); Elisabeth Pendley, Deregulation of the Energy Industry, 31 Land & Water L. Rev. 27 (1996).

c.   Furthermore, what will be the implications of the new world of electric power sales for the natural gas industry? Might it further exacerbate the transition problems we looked at there? Do you think it is significant that natural gas is the most important fuel used for low-cost, small-scale generation of electricity? See, e.g., Vinod K. Dar, The Electric and Gas Industries and Converging: What Does It Mean?, Public Utilities Fortnightly, April 1, 1995, p. 21; Richard D. Kinder, The Monolith is Cracking: Electric Restructuring and its Implications for Gas, Id., Sept. 15, 1995, p. 22.

d.   Finally, does the Commission's action look to you like real "deregulation"? Is the role of FERC likely to remain extremely significant in at least the transition years of the electric industry? Is this because the competitive concerns identified by the Commission are compelling? Is it an example of an agency that is reluctant to put itself completely out of business?

A NOTE ON MORE RECENT NATURAL GAS DEVELOPMENT

The demand for natural gas grew throughout the 1990s. This was in large part due to a decision by the Federal Energy Regulatory Commission to drop a prohibition on the use of natural gas for fueling electric generating facilities and the subsequent use of this relatively environmentally safe fuel for those purposes. The demand for natural gas for home heating also grew. Increases in demand were not followed by comparable increases in supply and the cost of natural gas has increased. With many industrial facilities dependent on natural gas, price increases can have implications for the economy more generally.

As you would expect there has been increased emphasis on developing greater domestic and foreign supplies. Recently attention has been turned to liquid natural gas (LNG). Liquid natural gas often enters the United States through import terminals and limitations on the number of terminals can slow the response of foreign suppliers to higher prices in the U.S. Interestingly, these facilities fell under Order No. 636 and, thus, had to be available to sellers of LNG other than companies investing in the import terminal. This was felt to be a disincentive to those willing to invest in these terminals because it might mean disfavoring their own affiliates. Thus, in late 2002, FERC dropped the open access requirements and allowed LGN import terminals to practice "non open access." In addition, access to the terminals will be on terms determined by terminal owners and those desiring access. The hope is that this will encourage LGN imports and relieve the pressure on domestic natural gas suppliers. See generally, James E. Vallee, "FERC Hackberry Decision Will Spur More US LNG Terminal Development, Oil and Gas Journal (November 10, 2003). In fact FERC is now engaged in a process of reevaluating parts of its natural gas policy in light of industry changes since Order No. 636. 67 Fed.Reg. 62918–01 (October 9, 2002).

Think back to the telecommunications industry. Do you think it is possible or likely that unbundling in that industry might lead to under-development of local access facilities?

A NOTE ON RAILROAD DEREGULATION

Rail transportation was the original subject of federal regulation when the Interstate Commerce Commission was created in 1887. The regulatory rationale was to control the natural monopoly character of a railroad. Enormous capital investment is required to complete a track before a single train can run. After that, however, the line can carry tons of freight at a comparatively low marginal cost. It is not surprising, then, that for close to a century, all aspects of transportation by rail—from rates to routes to services provided—were subject to pervasive regulation.

A change began in 1976 with the passage of the Railroad Revitalization and Regulatory Reform (or "4R") Act, Pub.Law 94–210, 90 Stat. 31 (1976). Basically, railroads were in significant financial trouble because the ICC had required them to charge rates that reflected their "fully distributed" or average costs instead of their "out-of-pocket" or marginal costs. See, e.g., American Commercial Lines, Inc. v. Louisville & Nashville Railroad Co., 392 U.S. 571, 88 S.Ct. 2105, 20 L.Ed.2d 1289 (1968). Being forced to charge rates that reflected a share of their fixed costs did not make the railroads richer; it meant that their share of the transportation business declined relative to that of trucks and barges that had lower fixed costs.

The 4R Act, followed by the Staggers Rail Act of 1980, Pub.Law 96–448, 94 Stat. 1895 (1980), gave railroads pricing flexibility so long as their rates covered operating, i.e., variable costs, and so long as a railroad lacked "market dominance" of a given route. Market dominance, in turn, was defined as the ability to sustain a rate of more than 180% of operating costs for the route. See 49 U.S.C. § 10709. The ICC retained authority to approve railroads' efforts to abandon service on particular lines, but strict time limits were imposed for ICC action. See 49 U.S.C. § 10903; Hayfield N. R.R. Co. v. Chicago & N.W. Transp. Co., 467 U.S. 622, 104 S.Ct. 2610, 81 L.Ed.2d 527 (1984).

As the materials in our next section suggest, deregulation of all aspects of surface transportation has proceeded apace and, ultimately, the Interstate Commerce Commission itself was abolished effective January 1, 1996. ICC Termination Act of 1995, Pub.Law 104–88, 109 Stat. 803 (1995).

Yet as we have tended to see, deregulation is rarely so final. Section 201 of the ICC Termination Act created a new Surface Transportation Board to be part of the Department of Transportation. "Except as otherwise provided in the ICC Termination Act * * * the Board shall perform all functions that, immediately before the effective date of such Act, were functions of the Interstate Commerce Commission * * *." 49 U.S.C. § 702. The Board's initial year's budget was less than half that in the last year of the ICC, but a number of former ICC employees apparently were simply transferred to jobs in the new agency.

Under the new regime, railroads are no longer required to file rate tariffs, 49 U.S.C. § 10701, but the Surface Transportation Board has the same jurisdiction the ICC had to determine market dominance, 49 U.S.C. § 10707, and to approve abandonment of service, 49 U.S.C. § 10903. See, e.g., Birt v. Surface Transportation Board, 90 F.3d 580 (D.C.Cir. 1996).

The Board also has authority over rail mergers, 49 U.S.C. §§ 11323–25. It is required to give "substantial weight" to views of the Attorney General about whether "the anticompetitive effects of [a merger] outweigh the public interest in meeting significant transportation needs," 49 U.S.C. § 11324(d), but even in its bureaucratic infancy, the Surface Transportation Board approved the merger of the Southern Pacific and Union Pacific Railroads over Justice Department objections that the country would be left with only two major western rail systems.

A NOTE ON CONTESTABILITY AS A WAY OF DEALING WITH NATURAL MONOPOLY

The central economic characteristic of natural monopoly—relatively large fixed costs—is obviously not subject to Congressional or Commission change. Even in industries where technological change has not made that characteristic a thing of the past, the theory of "contestable markets" offers a way to avoid some of the problems of monopoly without completely deregulating an industry.

Under this approach, only one firm would be allowed to serve the market, but competition would take place over which firm that will be. See Harold Demsetz, Why Regulate Utilities?, 11 J. L. & Econ. 55 (1968). The competition that takes place results in an auction in which competition determines which competitor will offer the best mix of prices and service. For example, every few years, firms might bid for the right to be the sole cable television supplier in a community. The city would establish service specifications and award the franchise to the company offering the lowest rates.

Such a process would preserve the benefits of natural monopoly production but retain some competitive pressure. However, the theory is not without its problems. For a firm to be willing to enter a market and make a large investment, for example, it might demand the right to serve the market for a relatively long period of time. This could necessitate periodic review of the contract terms the firm has with the reviewing agency. The process might look very much like a rate-hearing.

And, in any competition after the first, the incumbent firm will have a competitive advantage in that it will not have to incur the costs of newly entering the market. One way to reduce this advantage might be for any needed investment to be made by the granting authority, but that too would be costly for a government agency and ultimately the taxpayers paying the bill.

Whatever the structural arrangement, then, the contestable market approach is hardly problem free and may assume too much about the fungibility of monopoly producers. Are you better off with your present choice of three major long distance carriers, for example, or would you be equally happy being periodically reassigned by a Commission from one supplier to another? See generally, Kenneth Train, Optimal Regulation: The Economic Theory of Natural Monopoly (1991).

B. THE EXCESSIVE COMPETITION RATIONALE

"Excessive" or "destructive" competition may seem like an odd reason to regulate.[13] After all, there exists an entire body of law—the antitrust laws—aimed specifically at encouraging vigorous competition. It is important to remember, however, that political and social goals may not be those that competition can achieve. Moreover, groups or industries may have sufficient political clout to influence the creation of protective legislation.

You have already been introduced to one "excessive competition" rationale for regulation in the context of protecting a natural monopoly from competition. Other destructive competition situations raise concerns about distributive outcomes. For example, some industries, because of the ease of entry and the potential for high levels of competition, may be inherently unstable. You may think immediately of the restaurant industry, but the example shows that not every industry of that nature receives protection. At least in theory, one would hope that the only industries that are protected are those in which there is a broad public interest in increasing stability.

One industry traditionally regulated under the excessive competition rationale was the airline industry. In the 1930s, it was thought important to the country's economic development that cut-throat competition not snuff out a fledgling industry. Similarly, there was thought to be a

---

13. Justice Breyer has called this the "empty box" rationale for regulation, i.e., one that has no particular economic meaning or content. Stephen Breyer, Regulation and Its Reform 29–35 (1982).

public interest in having reliable airline service to at least all mid-size communities. Ultimately, however, the low fares observed in California's unregulated intrastate market helped convince federal regulators such as Civil Aeronautics Board Chairman Alfred Kahn that the industry would develop better without federal regulation. The C.A.B. was the first significant victim of the deregulation movement when it was abolished by the Airline Deregulation Act of 1978, 49 U.S.C. § 1301 et seq.

Deregulation has been proceeding apace in other kinds of industries originally regulated under an excessive competition rationale.

1. SURFACE TRANSPORTATION

The Motor Carrier Act of 1935, which restricted entry and rate competition among trucking common carriers, created one such regulatory scheme. The Interstate Commerce Commission had originally been created in 1887 to regulate railroad practices alleged to be burdening farmers and other producers. Railroads were among the classic natural monopolies.

Trucking regulation—and the regulation of interstate bus travel adopted the same year—can be seen from one perspective as a way of preserving the stability of an industry that might be important in times of national emergency. However, an equally compelling argument can be made that the purpose was to protect other common carriers—railroads and barge carriers—with relatively high fixed costs from competition by carriers—trucks and buses—with low fixed costs.[14]

Sometimes excessive competition is raised in the context of safety. One can envision a bleary-eyed, overworked truck driver speeding down the road in an overweight eighteen wheeler with bald tires or an airliner taking off after a sloppy maintenance check. The question is whether fierce competition can result in lapses in safety. As a matter of theory it should not. In principle, the trucking firm or airline is as interested in maximizing profit as any other firm. Thus, any profit-maximizing steps, including those that would avoid liability for accidents, would be taken even in a competitive environment. Whether this theory actually matches reality is an empirical question on which observers might differ.

The first great wave of deregulation of surface transportation came in the Railroad Revitalization and Regulatory Reform Act (the 4R Act) in 1976, Pub.Law 94–210, 90 Stat. 31 (1976), followed by the Staggers Rail Act of 1980, Pub.Law 96–448, 94 Stat. 1895 (1980), which gave railroads the right to lower their rates to any level above their marginal cost of transportation. The rate pressure thus put on trucks also led to the Motor Carrier Act of 1980, Pub.Law 96–296, 94 Stat. 793, 49 U.S. C. § 10101, et seq. Our next case arises in an industry in which regulation hung on only slightly longer.

14. See David Boies, Experiment in Mercantilism: Minimum Rate Regulation by the Interstate Commerce Commission, 68 Columbia L. Rev. 599 (1968); Jones, Interstate Trucking and the Legislative History of the Motor Carrier Act of 1935, 19 A.B.A. Antitrust Section Proc. 279 (1961).

HUDSON TRANSIT LINES, INC. v. INTERSTATE COMMERCE COMMISSION

United States Court of Appeals, Second Circuit, 1985.
765 F.2d 329.

CARDAMONE, CIRCUIT JUDGE.

Since the end of World War II Americans' overwhelming preference for the use of their private automobiles has been the primary cause of a seriously eroded public transport. As a result, the intercity passenger bus industry in the United States is in a state of decline that shows little sign of turning about. During the depths of the depression in the 1930's there was widespread concern over the creation of an oversupply of passenger transportation. To meet this concern, Congress in 1935 empowered the Interstate Commerce Commission to bring about equality of regulation between intrastate and interstate motor carriers to prevent such an oversupply. In the last decade the winds of deregulation have swirled through the legislature, first sweeping away the ICC's authority over rail and air travel, and then leading Congress to enact the Bus Regulatory Reform Act of 1982, designed to deregulate the ailing bus industry. Congress's new prescription for the financially ailing bus industry, embodied in the 1982 legislation, places a new emphasis on increased competition and aims to rejuvenate intercity bus travel.

These consolidated appeals are taken from decisions of the Interstate Commerce Commission (ICC or Commission) granting applicant bus companies unrestricted authority to transport passengers in the suburban New York City area and to Atlantic City, New Jersey. In the first group of cases an existing commuter service carrier has challenged the Commission's refusal to impose operating restrictions on its grant of certain licenses permitting applicants to provide service. In the second group of cases the State of New Jersey has challenged ICC orders that authorized two carriers to provide bus service to Atlantic City, claiming that such service would constitute prohibited special operations. These issues require us to analyze, for the first time, the Bus Regulatory Reform Act of 1982. Before analyzing these issues, it is necessary to review briefly Congress's involvement in the interstate bus industry.

I. REGULATORY BACKGROUND

Intercity bus transportation in the United States had its genesis around 1910. By 1930 virtually every state regulated the industry. Because of the Supreme Court's ruling in Buck v. Kuykendall, 267 U.S. 307 (1925), the scope of state regulation was limited to intrastate bus transportation, leaving unregulated the growing interstate bus industry. In the 1930's bus companies, trade associations, railroads, and state regulatory agencies called for federal legislation. The depression had undercut the financial stability of many carriers, and it was feared that competition would drive them out of business. Falling prices had caused many carriers to lower their service and safety standards.

In response Congress enacted the Motor Carrier Act of 1935 which led to the organization of a highly regulated, public utility-type bus industry. That Act empowered the Commission to control the number of carriers and the service provided. The Act's licensing provisions, which applied equally to motor carriers of property and passengers, required motor carriers to demonstrate to the ICC that they were "fit, willing, and able" to perform the proposed service, and that the service was "required by the present or future public convenience and necessity." Motor Carrier Act of 1935, amended by Bus Regulatory Reform Act of 1982. The Commission could issue a certificate only for operations over a "regular route and between specified places." Regular-route service involves scheduled transportation between fixed points over specific routes or highways. This type of service operates on a published timetable so that passengers can wait at a terminal or roadside stop on a designated route and be confident that sooner or later a bus will come along to collect them. The regular-route system eventually covered all of the United States, Canada, and Mexico and it is now possible to make a journey by bus from Alaska to Panama.

The Commission first established the test which it would use to apply the "public convenience and necessity" standard in Pan–American Bus Lines Operation, 1 M.C.C. 190, 203 (1936), stating: The question, in substance, is [1] whether the new operation or service will serve a useful public purpose, responsive to a public demand or need; [2] whether this purpose can and will be served as well by existing lines or carriers; and [3] whether it can be served by applicant with the new operation or service proposed without endangering or impairing the operations of existing carriers contrary to the public interest. To prevent an oversupply of transportation, the Commission applied this test for over 40 years.

By the early 1970's economists and administrators clamored for a change and urged the creation of a regulatory scheme that would abandon the protectionist system of the 1935 Act and encourage free market management of the industry. As a consequence, the ICC began more frequently to consider the benefits of competition in reaching its decisions. It shifted the burden with respect to the third part of the *Pan–American* guidelines to require the objectant to show that existing operations would be impaired in a way that would harm the public interest. and modified the *Pan–American* test by eliminating the second, and most "protectionist," criterion, see Assure Competitive Transportation, Inc. v. United States, 635 F.2d 1301, 1305–06 (7th Cir.1980) (finding it within the Commission's power to give more weight in its decisions to "the benefits of healthy competition and less to protecting existing carriers"). The Commission concluded that a more competitive market with easier entry would allow new carriers to provide efficient service using modern technology.

Thus, although the Commission had shifted its decision-making emphasis, the 1935 Act remained virtually unchanged until Congress enacted the Motor Carrier Act of 1980. This Act effected two major revisions. First, it eased entry into, and significantly reduced barriers to competition in, the trucking industry. The House Report, reprinted in 1980 U.S.Code Cong. & Ad.News 2283, 2285, stated:

> The legislation establishes a new Federal policy which is to promote a competitive and efficient motor carrier industry in order to accomplish certain goals. Those goals include meeting the needs of shippers, receivers, and consumers; allowing price flexibility; encouraging greater efficiency, particularly in the use of fuel; and providing service to small communities. Congress designed the 1980 Act "[to] increase[ ]opportunities for new carriers to get into the trucking business and for existing carriers to expand their services."

It virtually eliminated collective rate making in the trucking industry. Second, it revised the procedural handling of all motor carrier cases to expedite the proceedings before the Commission. The new procedures allowed the ICC to handle almost all of its cases without formal hearings or personal appearances by the parties. The 1980 Act did not affect the licensing of buses.

In 1982 Congress enacted the Bus Regulatory Reform Act (Bus Reform Act or Act), the statute before us on this appeal. Picking up where the Motor Carrier Act of 1980 left off, the Bus Reform Act was designed to facilitate entry into the intercity passenger carriage market by replacing the traditional "public convenience and necessity" test with a "public interest" test.

The procedure for obtaining authorization to operate regular-route service works as follows. First, an applicant must show the ICC that it is "fit, willing, and able to provide the transportation to be authorized by the certificate and to comply with [the Act] and regulations of the Commission." At this initial stage the ICC inquires about the applicant's safety record and whether it meets the minimum financial requirements. * * * After publication of the proposed service in the Federal Register, any motor carrier described in § 10922(c)(7) may protest the issuance of the certificate. The protestant has the burden of proving that the applicant is not fit, willing, and able to provide the proposed service, or that "the transportation to be authorized is not consistent with the public interest." § 10922(c)(1)(A).

In making its findings relating to public interest, the Act directs the Commission to consider the following factors: (A) "the transportation policy" of the Act; (B) the "value of competition to the traveling and shipping public;" (C) the effect of issuance of a certificate on "motor carrier of passenger service to small communities;" and (D) whether issuance of a certificate would impair the ability of any other motor carrier to provide service "except that diversion of revenue or traffic" from another motor carrier, in and of itself, will not be sufficient to support a finding that the grant of authority will impair the ability of the other carrier to operate. § 10922(c)(3). Congress outlined the "transportation policy" of the Act in § 10101, listing a number of interests. The Commission must continually balance the interest in economic efficiency and competition with the interest in safe and adequate service.

The importance of competition in bringing about efficient transportation services is the critical policy consideration that the Commission must weigh in resolving licensing protests that relate to public interest. In the view of Congress, competition between carriers brings about better wages for employees, lower rates for consumers, and more efficient use of technology, equipment, and fuel. The Act is designed to achieve these ends by limiting what the applicant must show to acquire a certificate and by expediting the licensing procedures in order to relax entry requirements. Its procedures are designed to promote service to intermediate points by removing restrictions on existing licenses, and to facilitate the granting of certificates for service along intrastate routes over which federal authority has been, or will be granted.

Congress did not plan to abandon all control of intercity bus travel and leave its fate in the hands of the marketplace. * * * Congress sought to maintain service to smaller communities, foster commuter service, and ensure adequate bus service to as many people as possible. With almost every licensing application, if a carrier protests the issuance of a certificate, the Commission must evaluate how the proposed service will affect smaller communities and existing commuter operations. In special cases involving bus service to isolated communities and service that will substitute for discontinued rail service or, in some cases, discontinued bus service, the Act presumes that the proposed service is in the public interest. In these cases all that the Act requires is that the applicant prove that it is fit, willing, and able to perform. With this review of the regulatory background, we turn to the first series of cases on this consolidated appeal.

II. COMMUTER OPERATIONS

A. *Background*

Pine Hill–Kingston Bus Corporation (Pine Hill) and Adirondack Transit Lines, Inc. (Adirondack) are affiliated bus companies that for several years have transported passengers over regular routes extending between New York City and points in northeastern New Jersey and New York State. Shortly after the Bus Reform Act became effective, Pine Hill and Adirondack filed applications with the ICC pursuant to § 10922(c) seeking Certificates of Public Convenience and Necessity over these routes. The proposed service was essentially the same in geographic scope and scheduling as the existing operations. The applications proposed to consolidate these existing routes and redescribe them so as to remove operating restrictions that prevented service at certain points. In accordance with the Act and ICC regulations the applicants submitted their insurance and safety records to show that they were "fit, willing, and able" to provide the requested service.

Many of the applicants' existing routes were between various cities in upstate New York and New York City along a commuter corridor that includes Bergen County in New Jersey and Rockland and Orange Counties in New York (commuter corridor). The old licenses did not permit the applicants to provide local service along the commuter corridor. For example, Pine Hill's and Adirondack's licenses did not permit them to pick-up or discharge passengers between Paramus, New Jersey and New York City or between Monroe or Suffern, New York and New York City. Consequently, Pine Hill and Adirondack historically served only long-haul intercity routes. The certificates for which they applied would grant them the right to provide unrestricted service at all points in the commuter corridor.

Pine Hill also requested unrestricted authority for a proposed Route (4) between Kingston, New York and Rockland County via Newburgh, New York along local highways. This route—when tacked to Pine Hill's other routes—would allow it to provide service between these bedroom communities and New York City. Pine Hill evidently held licenses for service along Route (4), but has made little use of it since the construction of the New York State Thruway.

A third carrier, Fugazy Express, Inc. (Fugazy), filed applications seeking authority to transport passengers between Rockland County and Atlantic City through New York City and between Goshen and Suffern, New York. Like Pine Hill and Adirondack, Fugazy has not provided commuter service along these routes. But by tacking an unrestricted Goshen–Suffern route to its Atlantic City route, Fugazy could provide any type of service, including commuter service, along much of the commuter corridor.

In response to these applications, Hudson Transit Lines (interstate service) and Hudson Transit Corporation (intrastate service) (Hudson), filed protests. Hudson is a commuter service carrier that transports passengers along the commuter corridor to New York City. It argued that because the applicants' proposed service duplicated existing commuter routes, a grant of unrestricted authority would adversely impact service on these routes and be inconsistent with the public interest. Hudson presented evidence of the number of passengers it carried, its seating capacity, and schedules, along with data for each of its principal routes. Protestant concluded that granting applicants unrestricted authority along the commuter corridor would divert over 20% of its operating revenue and force it to reduce both regular-route commuter service and service to smaller communities. It urged the ICC to restrict the grant of authority and to delete Route (4) from Pine Hill's route authority. Pine Hill and Adirondack filed a brief reply in which they reiterated that the purpose of their application was to consolidate all of their routes into one document. They explained that they would not oppose a restriction against "commuter operations" between New York City and those counties served by Hudson. Pine Hill also acquiesced in the deletion of its Route (4).

In separate written decisions the Commission Review Board (Board) granted each of the applications and issued unrestricted certificates. The Board concluded that each applicant was "fit, willing, and able to provide the transportation to be authorized by the certificate," within the meaning of § 10922(c)(6), and that protestant Hudson had not proved that "the transportation to be authorized is not consistent with the public interest." § 10922(c)(1)(A). The Board first concluded that the structure of the Act and the transportation policy evince a legislative intent that strongly disfavor the imposition of operating restrictions. It specifically found that the impetus behind filing these applications was the desire to eliminate restrictions in order to provide better service. It next concluded that after examining Hudson's evidence the unrestricted grants were consistent with the public interest. Although the Board recognized Congress's concern for the provision and maintenance of commuter bus operations, it characterized Hudson's fears for commuter service as "speculative" and concluded that the unrestricted grants would not adversely affect commuter operations or existing service to smaller cities. Hudson appealed the Board's determination to the Interstate Commerce Commission, which summarily affirmed the Board's decisions.

Hudson then petitioned the ICC for extraordinary relief. In denying the petition, the ICC expanded the explanation of its decision to grant the certificates. It pointed out again the policy against the imposition of restrictions. It found that the proposed commuter operations restrictions, at least to some extent, served no useful purpose, were unclear or confusing, and were unduly restrictive. It stated that the Act did not even permit restrictions on "commuter operations." Summarizing the data Hudson submitted, the ICC, like the Board, concluded that protestant had not shown that the impact of the proposed service would be contrary to the public interest. Hudson now seeks review of the ICC's refusal to prohibit Pine Hill, Adirondack, and Fugazy from performing commuter operations and to delete a portion of Pine Hill's application. Before discussing the merits, we focus briefly on the scope of review on an appeal from an Executive Branch agency.

B.   Scope of Review

A court reviewing a decision made by an administrative agency shall "hold unlawful and set aside agency action, findings, and conclusions found to be ... arbitrary, capricious, an abuse of discretion, or otherwise not in accordance with law." * * *

C.   Discussion

After carefully reviewing each opinion of the Board and the Commission in light of these precepts regarding our scope of review, we have concluded that the ICC's decisions to grant the Pine Hill and Adirondack applications and Fugazy's Goshen–Suffern route applications were not arbitrary and capricious. Congress structured the Act to facilitate entry into the bus industry and indicated its disfavor for the imposition of restrictions on grants of authority. Concededly, this creates an extremely difficult burden of proof for protestants like Hudson. But increased competition is the key to the Act. The protectionist goals of previous bus legislation have been abandoned. Thus, absent clear evidence that the issuance of an unrestricted certificate would be inconsistent with the public interest, we cannot set aside the Commission's actions. As just noted, a reviewing court's inquiry is limited to whether the ICC made a clear error of judgment. That we cannot say it has done.

1.   *Whether the ICC Decision Was Arbitrary and Capricious*

Hudson has not challenged the ICC's finding that each of the applicants is "fit, willing, and able" to provide the proposed service. Under the Act an applicant must prove only that it has a sufficient amount of insurance coverage, and that it is in compliance with applicable safety regulations. Hudson argues that the Commission acted in an arbitrary and capricious manner in determining that the proposed service is consistent with the public interest. * * *

In applying the public interest test, the Act requires the ICC to balance many interests, and a reviewing court may not overrule the balance achieved, unless the agency has acted clearly outside the Congressional mandate. The ICC based its decisions in these cases on the following conclusions: that the Act disfavors the imposition of operating restrictions, and that the protestant's assertions that the unrestricted grants would be inconsistent with the public interest were speculative. We affirm the Commission's determinations in these cases because "the path which it followed can be discerned."

The ICC interpreted the Act as signaling a legislative intent strongly disfavoring the imposition of operating restrictions. Although a broad policy against restrictions might reasonably provide some support for the ICC's conclusions, such cannot substitute for a reasoned analysis of the evidence presented. See RTC Transportation, Inc. v. ICC, 708 F.2d 617 (11th Cir.1983). In *RTC*, a trucking case, the court ordered the ICC to vacate its decision because it had acted "solely because of a policy against restrictions" without further explanation. Congress shouldered protestants with the difficult burden of proving that the public interest requires the imposition of an operating restriction; the burden is especially difficult in light of a restriction's inherently anticompetitive nature. Yet, as noted earlier, the legislature did not propose to make protestants' chances a charade.

Rejecting the parties' efforts to impose operating restrictions in this case, the Board cited "Congress' concern that motor carriers of passengers were unduly burdened with route restrictions which hampered the industry's ability to serve the public interest, and its desire for greater flexibility of service, increased competition, and improved operational and energy efficiency." Pine Hill–Kingston Bus Corp., No. MC–2060 (Sub–No. 18) (June 6, 1983). These factors are among the central policy concerns inherent in the Act and amply support the ICC's general policy against restrictions. In fact, the Act allows bus companies to use an abbreviated proceeding before the ICC in order to have intermediate point restrictions "automatically" removed from its routes.

The ICC also concluded that enforcing the proposed restrictions would present significant administrative difficulties. The imposition of operating restrictions as a practical matter will inevitably prompt numerous claims of their violation. A volume of such complaints would dramatically increase the ICC's investigatory and decision making responsibilities. Thus, it was proper for the ICC to consider, as a part of its analysis, the Act's firm policy against restrictions and the fact that imposing them would result in administrative burdens.

Hudson was also unable to convince the Commission that unrestricted grants of authority would have a significant adverse effect on commuter or small community service along the commuter corridor. The ICC viewed the evidence presented to prove this point as to speculative, apparently concluding that protestants' evidence was insufficient to permit an evaluation of the effect of the proposed service. The ICC also rejected Hudson's claims that the proposed routes would impair its ability to continue to serve its current routes. The Commission found that the protestant did not provide revenue or other figures that would substantiate such claims. The Act clearly provides that proof of diversion of traffic and passengers alone is not enough to demonstrate that the grant of authority is not consistent with the public interest. Rather, diversion could lead to "more quality and price options" for consumers and allow "the most productive use of equipment and energy resources." The newcomer may force the existing carrier to provide service that is faster, cheaper, more comfortable or better meets the needs of the community in order to keep its market share.

We note that the present application seeking a new route which might merely divert traffic from an existing bus route is different from one under which a new route might force a protesting carrier to abandon its existing service to a large number of small communities. For example, a protesting carrier might show that the proposed service will duplicate only one or two of its profitable routes, causing it to lose a substantial number of passengers and profits. From this the protestant could present evidence to the ICC that because of the structure of its entire system, any diminution of its profits along the duplicated routes would adversely affect the service provided to smaller communities. Proof of this direct impact could be developed from statements filed by the parties, affidavits of those with knowledge of the proposed new service, interviews and surveys to demonstrate loss of passengers, financial records, public records regarding bus usage in the affected communities, media reports and the like. Thus, in this way a protestant could demonstrate to the ICC that the proposed diversion of traffic would significantly and materially jeopardize its ability to provide service to a substantial portion of its entire regular-route system. At the same time, protestant might also demonstrate that the applicant's proposed service would result in no public benefit other than increased competition along the duplicated routes.

As discussed * * *, although Congress's main goal was to promote competition, service to smaller communities and commuters was not thereby to be substantially diminished. The Act envisioned some trade-off between the interests in efficiency and in service. But Congress left it to the ICC to achieve a proper balance between these competing interests. When a protestant is able to present proof that the trade-off will result only in a heavy reduction of service to passengers in small communities or commuters with little corresponding public benefit, the ICC must adhere to the statutory purpose and deny the applicant's request to provide the proposed service. In sum, while protestant's burden of proof is difficult, it is not impossible. Here, the ICC concluded that this application did not present such an extreme case. The duplicative proposed routes in the present case account for about 35% of Hudson's regular-route revenue; the new routes do not simply duplicate one or two of Hudson's profitable routes. The records also indicate that the proposed duplication of service will be minimal, as the applicants are long-haul carriers that have never been engaged in commuter operations. Further, the proposed unrestricted routes are logical extensions of the applicants' existing upstate New York routes. It was, therefore, not arbitrary or capricious for the ICC to determine that the proposed service would make the applicants' operations more efficient, while its adverse impact on existing service would not be great. Thus, the ICC's decision adequately reconciled the conflicting interests Congress confided to it under the Act. Since the agency's decision was not arbitrary and capricious, it should not be disturbed.

* * *

Accordingly, we affirm the grants of authority issued to Pine Hill, Adirondack, and Fugazy * * *.

* * *

Notes and Questions

1. This case provides you with the history of regulation and deregulation of motor carriers. This regulatory regime has all but disappeared and the I.C.C. itself was abolished at the end of 1995. Pub. Law 104–88, 109 Stat. 803 (1995). The remaining regulatory powers were transferred to the Department of Transportation. Some remaining rate regulation issues are discussed in Chapter 4. For another case that contains a similar history, this time of the trucking industry, see Central States Motor Freight Bureau v. I.C.C., 924 F.2d 1099 (D.C.Cir.1991).

2. Why does it seem regulation was first instituted in this industry? Was it seen as important to the nation that small communities not be left without any interstate bus service at all? Have conditions so changed that this is no longer true? Has deregulation of the airlines, for example, made air travel so inexpensive that people no longer ride the bus?

3. Who benefits most from the regulation of motor carrier entry and rates? Is it consumers? If not, what does that tell you about the politics of the decision to regulate? Who benefits from deregulation? Again, is it primarily consumers? If the regulated industry is the primary beneficiary, does that tell you who is more powerful in the "market for legislation?"[15] See

---

15. For an article arguing strenuously that the trucking industry was decidedly not helped by deregulation, see Paul S. Dempsey, Running on Empty: Trucking De-

generally, Alfred E. Kahn, Deregulation, Looking Backward and Looking Forward, 7 Yale J. Regulation 325 (1990).

4. We mentioned that the "excessive competition" rationale was also behind the regulation of airlines that ended with passage of the Airline Deregulation Act of 1978. Air transportation and its deregulation afford us an opportunity to assess whether deregulation really is superior to regulation in a particular industry.[16] The picture is somewhat mixed. Due to business failures and mergers the industry has become much more concentrated than it was immediately after deregulation. Airline hub-and-spoke policies have made some trips less convenient. On the other hand, there is clear evidence that fares are lower than they otherwise would be, and availability of service to some cities has increased.[17] Could the increase in concentration suggest that some air travel routes may be subject to natural monopoly forces? If so, what regulation would you propose, if any?

5. National transportation policy was historically designed to protect the "inherent advantage" of each mode of transportation against excessive competition from other modes. What do you think "inherent advantage" means? Are some modes of transportation better at specific things than others? If so, why wouldn't each such mode prevail in an unregulated market? Suppose truck transportation were so efficient (or so implicitly subsidized by the interstate highway system), that it completely displaced rail transportation and the latter ceased to exist. Would society be worse off if that happened?

2. THE FINANCIAL SERVICES INDUSTRY

Since at least the adoption of the Banking Act of 1933, Pub. Law No. 73–66, codified in scattered sections of 12 U.S.C.A., banking in the United States has been heavily regulated. Many Americans who lived through the Depression were convinced that the economic havoc was caused in large part by competition among banks that led them to engage in unsafe practices. First and foremost, regulation was imposed on entry into banking. The following is a classic case reviewing a grant of new entry well after the depression but while some of the concerns it raised continued to linger.

PLANTERS BANK v. T. M. GARROTT, JR.

Supreme Court of Mississippi, 1960.
239 Miss. 248, 122 So.2d 256.

KYLE, JUSTICE. This case is before us on appeal * * * from a decree of the Chancery Court of Tunica County, affirming the decision and order of the State Banking Board directing the Comptroller of banks to issue

---

regulation and Economic Theory, 43 Administrative L. Rev. 253 (1991).

16. Compare Brenner, Airline Deregulation—A Case Study in Public Policy Failure, 16 Trans. L. J. 179 (1988) with A. Kahn, Airline Deregulation—A Mixed Bag,

but a Clear Success Nonetheless, 16 Trans. L.J. 229 (1988).

17. See generally, S. Shapiro & J. Tomain, Regulatory Law and Policy 323–25 (1993).

to the * * * prospective incorporators, a certificate authorizing them to incorporate and organize a new bank in Tunica County * * *.

 * * *

The record in this case shows the following facts concerning the area in which the proposed bank is to be located: Tunica County has an area of 458 square miles lying wholly within the Mississippi Delta. The population of the county according to the 1950 census was 21,658 * * *. The total assessed valuation of taxable property in the county at the time of the hearing was $11,231,374. There is only one bank in the county, the appellant Planters Bank, which was chartered in 1912 and is domiciled in the Town of Tunica. The county is traversed from north to south by U. S. Highway No. 61, which is a heavily traveled paved highway, and by two lines of railroad, and three gas transmission lines. The chief source of income for the people of the county is agriculture. The value of the agricultural products produced and marketed during the year 1958 was approximately eleven million dollars. There are 26 cotton gins, two fertilizer distributing plants, one oil mill, five grain elevators, one cotton compress, two sawmills and one manufacturing plant in the county. There are two new automobile sales agencies, and several used car sales agencies, also the usual number of mercantile establishments, gasoline and oil distribution agencies and service stations. The record shows that there have been three bank failures in the county during the last 50 years. * * * There has been only one bank located in the county since 1926, the Planters Bank, which has been operated under capable management and has grown steadily during the last 40 years. * * * [At the close of business on December 31, 1958, t]he bank's deposits amounted to $5,448,548.46. The loans and discounts amounted to $1,477,514.08.

The appellees' evidence showed that the five prospective incorporators were men of good morals and sound business character, having a financial worth of $3,250,000; that there were 153 subscribers for stock in the new bank. * * * It was the opinion of the appellees' witnesses that there was a real public need in the county for the establishment of a new bank which would bring additional bank deposits into the county and help create new wealth. The prospective incorporators testified that, in their opinion, the new bank would bring into the county as much as one million dollars in deposits from out of state banks; that they had been assured of sufficient deposits to maintain a successful banking operation; that the county could support two banks; and that the new bank would not weaken the appellant bank.

T. M. Garrott testified that he knew that many residents of Tunica County carried sizeable bank deposits in Memphis banks, and some of that money would be deposited in the new bank if such bank were organized; that most of the deposits which he and the other incorporators expected to get for the new bank would come from banks outside of Tunica County. G. D. Perry testified that, in his opinion, another bank was badly needed in the county; that it was a matter of common knowledge that there was politics in the Planters Bank—"Everybody knows it." Perry stated that all of the presidents of the Planters Bank, all that he knew of, had been sheriff of the county, that there were two of the younger members of the Board of Directors whose fathers had held the office of sheriff. Perry stated that in his opinion the bank had not been rendering adequate service to meet the needs of the county. He stated that the new bank would probably have on deposit by the end of the first year $1,500,000; that he thought the bank would get one million dollars of that amount from banks outside of Tunica County; and that he hoped to get a half million dollars from Tunica. He stated that the Planters Bank was a strong financial institution and that a loss of 10 per cent of its deposits would not hurt it. J. W. Caperton testified that he was engaged in the implement business and the fire and casualty insurance business, in the Town of Tunica, and that 30 or 40 per cent of the checks which he received were drawn on banks located outside of Tunica County; and that people whom he knew who had money in other banks, had made the statement to him that if they had another bank "they would put their money back home." Sterling Owen testified that people were entitled to freedom of choice of the bank where they were doing business, and that there was every indication of a need for a second financial institution in the county because of the wide trade area of the county.

The appellees' evidence as a whole emphasized the fact that the appellant, being the only bank in Tunica County, had a monopoly of the banking business in the county; that there were many people in the county who did business with banks located outside of Tunica County; and that there was dissatisfaction among some of the people with the lending policy of the bank and with exchange charges made by the bank which continued in effect until July 1958, when the movement was launched to organize a new bank. There was also evidence which tended to show that the officers of the appellant bank were definitely identified with and actively participated in a political organization which sought to control the election of county officers.

The testimony of the witnesses offered on behalf of the appellant was to the effect that the appellant bank was fully capable of meeting the banking needs of the area, and that there was no real public necessity for the creation of another bank; that the economy of the county was almost wholly agricultural, and that 41 per cent of the privately-owned land was owned by nonresidents; that under the government crop control program there had been a steady decline during the last several years in the acreage planted in cotton; that the mechanization of farming in the Delta had reduced the need for an abundance of unskilled labor * * *. It was also shown that crop production loans to planters were usually made by the Production Credit Corporation and the Staple Discount Association, and that long-term loans were usually made by the Federal Land Bank or insurance companies. It was the opinion of the appellant's president and vice president that the appellant bank, during the last ten or fifteen years, had granted 99 ½ per cent of the loans for which applications had been received, and that there was no need for another bank in the county for money-lending purposes. The appellant offered in evidence a map which showed that there were 24 commercial banks, other than the appellant, located an average distance of 13.8 miles from the Tunica County line. It was also shown that the bank had in recent years erected a new bank building at a cost of approximately $160,000; and that, by virtue of its large capitalization, including surplus and undivided profits, the appellant had a maximum lending capacity to a single borrower of $63,000. It was the opinion of the appellant's witnesses that the organization of a new bank would result in withdrawal of substantial deposits from the appellant bank and a substantial weakening of the appellant's position as a banking institution. The appellant's witnesses denied the charge that the loan policies of the bank had been influenced by political considerations or a desire to promote the privately-owned business interests of the bank's officers and shareholders.

* * *

The State Banking Board in this case was the trier of the facts. It was an impartial tribunal legally constituted to determine the rights involved. Its findings were made upon due notice to the appellant and an opportunity to be heard. The appellant appeared and was represented throughout the hearing by able counsel, and the evidence which it offered was received and considered. * * *

We have not found, nor has there been called to our attention by counsel, a decision wherein there is a precise definition of "necessity" when used in a statute relative to the issuance of a bank charter. Decisions construing similar provisions in statutes pertaining to other fields of the law are not conclusive or particularly helpful to us in construing the statutory provision under consideration. In our opinion mere convenience is not sufficient to satisfy the statutory requisite of "necessity". But, as stated by the Michigan Court in Moran v. State Banking Commission, [33 N.W.2d 772 (1948),] when supplemented by proof of facts and circumstances which, as in the instant case, are persuasive of "necessity", it is proper to take into consideration testimony as to the element of convenience. We agree with the statement made by the Michigan Court in its opinion in the *Moran* case, that the meaning or import of "necessity", as the word is used in a statute such as we have here, is "a substantial or obvious need justifying the chartering of a new bank in view of the disclosed relevant circumstances."

The statute which we have under review was enacted in the exercise of the police power of the state, in the interest of the public, and as an aid to insure safe banking. Its purpose is not to deter competition or foster monopoly, but to guard the public and public interests against imprudent banking. By the enactment of the statute, the Legislature, in our opinion, did not intend that one or more established banks may keep out another merely because the banking facilities sufficiently take care of the banking business. The applicants for a charter were not required to show that the existing bank was not rendering adequate service to its customers, or that a new bank would be in a position to render better service to the public than the bank already in existence.

We find no reversible error in the record, and the decree of the lower court is therefore affirmed.

HALL, LEE, ETHRIDGE and GILLESPIE, JJ., concur.

McGEHEE, C. J., Dissenting:

I regret the necessity for so doing but I must respectfully dissent from the majority view in the decision of this case.

Following the "depression" years of the 1930's, the State Legislature realized that the laws governing the banking business in this State needed to be strengthened so as to prevent the location of more than one bank in a given area unless public necessity should require it. Prior to the enactment of Chapter 146, Laws of 1934, there was no restriction on the creation and incorporation of banks in this State, and a person desiring to open a new bank in any locality had only to make the proper application for that purpose.

    * * *

The appellant, Planters Bank of Tunica, Mississippi, was established in 1912 in the Town of Tunica in Tunica County, Mississippi, and it has increased its capital stock from $25,000 to nearly one-half million dollars and has recently expended approximately $160,000 for a new banking house, vault and other facilities, presumably with the approval and encouragement of the State Banking Department. Tunica County is one of the smallest counties in the State * * *. There are twenty-four commercial banks within approximately thirteen miles of the county line of this small county.

Pursuant to Section 5160, Code of 1942,[18] the State Comptroller of Banks made an examination and investigation as to whether or not the public necessity required the incorporation of a new bank in the county.

---

18. Editors' Note: At the time of this case, Miss.Ann.Stat. § 5160 specified the factors upon which the entry decision was to be made as:

    the number of unit banks and location thereof (excluding branch offices which branch offices shall not be considered as banks) then serving the area in which the proposed new bank is to be located, the ratio of capital funds to total deposits therein, the record of earnings and condition of existing banks and what effect, if any, a new unit bank would have on them, the number of previous bank failures in the area and their liquidation record and banking history generally in the area, the population of the area wherein the proposed bank will be located and relation to number of banks operating therein, reasonable prospects of growth of the area and its financial resources and whether the same are static, progressive or retrogressive, expectation of profitable operation of the proposed new bank, and the morals and business character of the prospective incorporators and * * * whether the public necessity requires that the proposed new bank should be chartered and permitted to operate.

The subsequent discussion by both the majority and dissent should be read in light of these factors.

* * * He recommended that the application for the charter for a new bank be denied. * * *

* * *

It was the theory of the appellees that the sixteen factors on which the statute contemplates that the Comptroller should make findings was complied with when the Board expressly found only one of such factors to exist, and that was that the proposed incorporators of the new bank were men of full age, and of good moral and business character. If this is to be the test, then every town in the State having only one bank, which may be adequately serving the needs of the community, could always find as many as five incorporators of full age and of good moral and business character, and thus the wholesome purpose of the Legislature in strengthening our banking structure so as to prevent too many banks would be effectually destroyed.

* * *

* * * If it be considered that there is a monopoly in banking anywhere in this State, the situation is such because public interest requires a limit on the number of banks for the protection of depositors. The existing bank has no such monopoly on the banking business, since it was shown that many deposits by citizens of Tunica County are kept in three large Memphis banks because of the fact that they have bond and trust departments and facilities for investment of funds and securities, which is not furnished by smaller banks, and there was no substantial proof to show that these depositors in the Memphis banks would bring their funds back to Tunica County, even if a new bank were established there * * *. I do not think that any of the fanciful theories of the appellees as to why a new bank is needed at Tunica were supported by substantial and competent evidence; and in my opinion the decision of the Board is against the overwhelming weight of the competent evidence.

* * *

To allow the chartering of a new bank in the Town of Tunica under the facts and circumstances of this case would, in my opinion, defeat the purpose and intention of the Legislature which * * * was designed to prevent the organization of more banks than needed in a particular locality. * * *

Notes and Questions

1. Are you convinced from the opinions that the Banking Board in fact considered the relevant statutory factors in deciding whether to charter the new bank? Were the criteria subject to precise analysis and subsequent judicial review or were they largely matters of experience and judgment?

2. The standards for authorizing a new national bank are even less specific than those in Mississippi. 12 U.S.C.A. § 27(a) simply directs the Comptroller of the Currency to grant a certificate to a new bank if after investigating "any * * * facts which may come to the knowledge of the

Comptroller, whether by means of a special commission appointed by him * * * or otherwise, it appears that such association is lawfully entitled to commence the business of banking * * *." The statute does not require the Comptroller to explain his decision and in practice he often says very little about them. See, e.g., Camp v. Pitts, 411 U.S. 138, 93 S.Ct. 1241, 36 L.Ed.2d 106 (1973).

3.   The criteria to be reviewed before a bank may receive federal deposit insurance from the FDIC are only somewhat more precise. They are (1) the financial history and condition of the bank, (2) the adequacy of its capital structure, (3) its future earnings prospects, (4) the general character of its management, (5) the likelihood the institution will have to be bailed out by the insurance fund, and (6) the convenience and needs of the community to be served. 12 U.S.C.A. § 1816. Denial of deposit insurance can as a practical matter, of course, cause a bank to elect not to open.

4.   What does dissenting Chief Justice McGehee believe the purpose of the regulation of bank entry was? How certain should the licensing authority have to have been that the new bank would survive and not seriously endanger the viability of existing banks? Is there a positive side to bank failure? Might making the industry too "safe" tend to perpetuate bad management and encourage high-risk investments because of confidence that the system will tend to protect banks from the consequences of their acts? See, e.g., A. Dale Tussing, The Case for Bank Failure, 10 J.Law & Econ. 129 (1967).

A NOTE ON SOME PERILS OF DEREGULATION: DISINTERMEDIATION AND THE SAVINGS AND LOAN CRISIS

Not only was bank entry regulated for many years so as to keep competitors few, but, under Regulation Q, banks were limited as to the interest rates they could pay on saving accounts. By reducing the price banks paid for an "input" which they then used to make loans, one of their "outputs," the industry was thought to be rendered more stable and economic growth more likely.

But the clash of market forces and regulation became increasingly evident during the 1960s and 1970s as the interest rates that banks and savings institutions were permitted to pay were insufficient to attract the savings of ordinary Americans. Moreover, state usury laws prevented the institutions from raising the price of their output—loans—to competitive levels. This led to "disintermediation," i.e., a decline in the importance of banks and savings and loans as go-betweens with respect to lenders and borrowers.

Pressure for deregulation grew throughout the 1970s and came in the form of both state and federal action. In essence, ceilings on the rates paid to savers and investors were lifted, state usury laws were preempted, and banks and thrifts were permitted to offer a variety of new "products" ranging from credits cards to access to money market funds. The principal events at the federal level were passage of the Depository Institutions Deregulation and Monetary Control Act of 1980,

Pub.Law No. 96–221, and passage of the Garn–St. Germain Act, Pub. Law No. 97–230, in 1982.

Even after deregulation, banks and savings and loans lived a somewhat sheltered life. Although they were permitted to respond to market forces, they were insulated somewhat from poor decisions by the fact that savings were insured up to $100,000 by the Federal Deposit Insurance Corporation. The premiums for that insurance, in turn, bore little relation to the risks taken by the insured institutions.

Deregulation set the stage for a tumultuous time in the industry as bankers learned about the realities of the market system the hard way. As buyers in the marketplace for loanable funds, they found themselves paying higher and higher "prices." They were also tempted to make riskier loans, which meant an increased risk of default. The incidence of bank failure increased dramatically. In the entire period from 1942 through 1980 there had been 198 bank failures. In 1989 and 1990 alone there were 362.[19]

Much harder hit were savings and loan associations that specialized in home mortgage loans. First, their historic advantage over commercial banks in terms of the interest they could pay savers was eliminated and they found themselves bidding for funds with others in a largely unregulated market. They also found themselves making loans, frequently ill-advised, in non-real estate markets in which they had little experience. Compounding matters was the fact that real estate markets, the traditional base of savings and loans, became much less reliable in the 1980s and the default rate of borrowers increased dramatically. Savings and loans tended to be more sensitive than commercial banks to these factors as they were, in general, more locally-based and dependent on local economic conditions for their welfare. Finally, much of the income of savings and loans continued to be based on interest rates charged on old, long-term mortgage agreements that had lagged well below current rates.

The "mismatch" between prices paid for money and income from lending money is largely responsible for what became known as the "savings and loan crisis" of the late 1980s and early 1990s. By then, the Federal government found itself in a very expensive effort to "bail out" savings and loans. The government not only made good on its promise to insure accounts up to $100,000; it also protected depositors whose accounts exceeded that amount. Under the Financial Institutions Reform, Recovery, and Enforcement Act of 1989 (FIRREA), Pub. Law 101–73, the Resolution Trust Corporation was created to acquire the assets of failed savings and loans and enter into the process of liquidating those assets.[20]

---

19. Timothy Canova, The Transformation of U.S. Banking and Finance: From Regulated Competition to Free–Market Receivership, 60 Brooklyn L. Rev. 1295, 1330 (1995).

20. We take up one of the innovative pre-RTC attempts to get "healthy" S & Ls to takeover "sick" ones in Chapter 5 of these materials.

A NOTE ON EXPANSION OF FINANCIAL INSTITUTIONS INTO OTHER FIELDS

Parallel to developments on the interest rate front, banks have received authority to increase the number and type of their outputs, i.e., to offer more kinds of financial products to their customers.

1. Section 16 of the Glass–Steagall Act, 12 U.S.C.A. § 24, for example, was another depression-era law that prohibited federally-chartered banks from "underwrit[ing] any issue of securities or stock." Sales of securities by bank affiliates were thought to have put depositors' funds at risk. Does that seem plausible to you? Was the speculation that allegedly brought down the securities markets at the beginning of the depression something that could have been avoided if non-bank securities dealers alone had sold stock? Were bankers more likely to lend money with which to buy securities sold by their affiliates than securities sold by other dealers? Is it likely that bankers were using bank deposits to support the price of the questionable stock that the bank's affiliates were trying to unload by selling it to the bank's depositors?

Practical erosion of Glass–Steagall prohibitions could be seen throughout the 1980s and 1990s as the Federal Reserve Board permitted banks to engage in securities financing through wholly-owned subsidiaries. See, e.g., Securities Industry Association v. Board of Governors of the Federal Reserve System, 839 F.2d 47 (2d Cir.1988).

Conversely, Travelers Group, a large insurance conglomerate, was permitted to buy Citicorp, Inc., a large bank holding company. Independent Community Bankers of America v. Board of Governors of the Federal Reserve System, 195 F.3d 28 (D.C. Cir.1999).

The death of Glass–Steagall was finally formalized in the Gramm–Leach–Bliley Act of 1999, Pub. Law No. 106–102, although some doubt that the new law eliminated all questions of bank safety. See, e.g., Jonathan R. Macey, The Business of Banking: Before and After Gramm–Leach–Bliley, 25 Iowa J. Corp. L. 691 (2000).

2. Next, ever since 1916, national banks have been specially permitted by federal law, 12 U.S.C.A. § 92, to sell insurance in towns with fewer than 5,000 inhabitants. Insurance agents believed the law was inconsistent with traditional state regulation of insurance, but in Barnett Bank of Marion County, N.A. v. Nelson, 517 U.S. 25, 116 S.Ct. 1103, 134 L.Ed.2d 237 (1996), the Supreme Court unanimously held that Congress expressly intended to preempt state law to give banks that authority, and held that Congress had not taken away the authority when it adopted an anti-preemption provision in the McCarran–Ferguson Act, 15 U.S.C.A. § 1012(b).

That result then opened the door to several preemption claims. In Bank One, Utah v. Guttau, 190 F.3d 844 (8th Cir.1999), for example, federal preemption was the basis for permitting an out-of-state national bank to install its ATMs in Iowa in violation of state law. And in Association of Banks in Insurance, Inc. v. Duryee, 270 F.3d 397 (6th Cir.

2001), the right of banks to sell insurance in small towns was again confirmed, citing not only *Barnett Bank* but also the Gramm–Leach–Bliley Act.

What do you think of these developments? Do you feel that your bank deposits are more at risk because your bank is engaging in multiple businesses? Are your deposits now in fact safer because your bank can now diversify its risk portfolio?

C. RESPONDING TO TRANSACTION COSTS

1. EXTERNALITIES AND THE COASE THEOREM

Externalities are costs or benefits of an activity that are not borne by the persons who decide whether or not to undertake the activity. External benefits, as the term implies, are benefits from an activity that do not accrue to the producer. In the case of external costs, the producer is able to escape paying some costs of production by imposing them on strangers.

In the case of external benefits, a "free rider" problem arises. This is a situation in which people do not contribute to the production of a good or service in hopes that others will produce it and they can enjoy the benefits without charge. One can understand why not being able to exclude others from the free enjoyment of a good would have a serious effect on the production and marketing of such goods.

Goods that give rise to such external benefits are sometimes called "public goods" and their production is frequently subsidized by government. Subsidization of medical care, education and public transportation can be defended using the "public goods" rationale.[21]

In the case of costs imposed on others, goods are produced in quantities that are too high. Focusing on the cost side of the picture and using an example of a familiar problem can give us a better understanding of how this problem relates to more technical economic concerns.

Groundwater is found in depletable underground reservoirs. There is not enough groundwater to supply all those who would like to use it. Suppose an industrial user, Poluto, Inc., shares a single groundwater basin with an agricultural user, Perfect Farms. Poluto produces bezels and determines the quantity to produce by comparing marginal cost and marginal revenue. In its marginal cost calculation it does not consider the external costs associated with forcing Perfect Farms to drill its own

---

21. Services like national defense or police protection, in which external benefits are especially high, are often directly produced or otherwise provided by government. Thus, the provision of external benefits goes beyond our principal concern with control of private business activities, and leaves interesting issues for courses in public finance, political science, and legislation. There are other circumstances, however, where a public goods rationale may best explain government intervention into the market, even though that is not its announced purpose. In this connection, the materials on the supply of information in Section C. 3 of this chapter should be considered. Ask yourself whether the regulations involved there can be supported using a public goods rationale.

well deeper each year as the supply of water is depleted and to import water when some of Poluto's toxic wastes seep into the common supply. Similarly, Poluto makes no conscious allowance for the fact that in 50 years the water will be used up.

In principle, too many bezels are produced because Poluto has not internalized all of the costs of production. If it had, the price of bezels would be higher and the quantity of bezels produced and sold would be lower. Another way of looking at the problem is that too much groundwater is used in the production of bezels because groundwater is underpriced to Poluto. Since it is underpriced it is not reserved only for the production of goods that can be sold for prices that cover *all* the costs of production. When a resource is not allocated to its most valuable use, we say there is a problem of allocative inefficiency.

Of course, maybe this scenario is not likely at all. For example, let's suppose that Poluto is legally entitled to all the groundwater it wants because it was the first to start drawing from the reservoir. Assume also that the cost incurred by Perfect Farms in drilling deeper and importing water is $100,000 per year. In other words, it is worth $100,000 per year to Perfect Farms to have the water now used by Poluto. Wouldn't it make sense for Perfect Farms to offer Poluto up to $100,000 per year to stop using the water and to dispose of its wastes in some other manner? Poluto would then compare the costs of taking the necessary actions with the $100,000 offered by Perfect Farms. If the costs are less than $100,000 the exchange will take place; the water is more valuable to Perfect Farms than to Poluto. Conversely, if the changes would cost Poluto more than $100,000, Poluto would not sell; the right to continue using the water is more valuable to Poluto than to Perfect Farms. In either case the water right would end up in the party placing the highest value on it and allocative efficiency with respect to the two parties would be achieved.

Now consider whether the fact that Poluto was the possessor of the right to use the water would make a difference in the outcome. Assume that the legal right to exclude Poluto from use of the water resides in Perfect Farms and that the damage caused by Poluto's use is still $100,000 per year. It would cost Poluto $200,000 to make the changes in its processes necessary to satisfy Perfect Farms. Who would end up possessing the right to use the water now, i.e., would Poluto buy the right from Perfect Farms? What would happen if Poluto's cost of making changes was only $50,000?

Notice that in this simple example the right to use the water ends up being possessed by the party valuing it most, regardless of the initial allocation. If that result is typical, the problem of externalities and allocative inefficiency may not be as severe as it would initially appear.

The general proposition that a particular interest will end up in the possession of the party placing the highest value on it regardless of the initial allocation is known as the "Coase Theorem."[22] Even in its original presentation in 1960, however, its author, Ronald Coase, recognized that the theorem only held under certain assumptions. In the Poluto and Perfect Farms example, the source of the "pollution" was well-known, as was a way to decrease it. There was an identifiable purchaser of the "right to pollute" who was able to come up with an offer to curtail the offensive conduct.

However, suppose there are 100 agricultural users, all of whom hold priority over Poluto in the use of the groundwater. Each agricultural user suffers from $1 to $1000 of damage if Poluto uses the water. Do you think Poluto is as likely to be able to negotiate an exchange even if the water is more valuable in industrial use than it is to all the agricultural users combined?

The problem is that the transaction itself is costly. That is, those who are buying and selling the right to use the water will have to have information in order to know how much the right is worth to each of them. There are transaction costs associated with bargaining, valuation, cooperation and just the mechanics of drawing up an acceptable contract and getting everyone to agree to it. Plus, in many such cases, they may not even know each other's identity.

These transaction costs may be so high that the gains from the exchange will be offset. The existence of externalities accompanied by high transaction costs is a major justification for regulations like those we are about to examine. Some regulations are designed to assist the market in achieving the efficient outcome. These regulations are a little like the oil on a stubborn door hinge. Of course, there is no guarantee that having government take an action will be less costly than leaving it to the private parties.[23]

In the rest of this section we focus on two specific aspects of the transaction cost problem. First, and perhaps most fundamentally, for the market to work there must be some basic givens. This may range from defining property rights to more detailed things like defining what certain words mean in an industry. Second, smooth operation of the market is dependent on information, the provision of which is itself often the object of regulation.

2. RATIONALIZING MARKETS

Efforts to rationalize markets can take a number of forms. The most fundamental is the definition of property rights: What does it mean to own something? A corollary question is how are these rights protected. These are the matters discussed in this section.

---

22. Ronald Coase, The Problem of Social Cost, 3 J.Law & Econ. 1 (1960). George Stigler describes the Coase Theorem as follows: "Under perfect competition private and social costs will be equal." G. Stigler, The Theory of Price 113 (3d ed. 1966).

23. Ronald Coase, supra note 22; See also Ronald Coase, The Firm, the Market and the Law (1988).

GARRET HARDIN, THE TRAGEDY OF THE COMMONS[24]

162 Science 1243 (1968).

* * *

The tragedy of the commons develops in this way. Picture a pasture open to all. It is to be expected that each herdsman will try to keep as many cattle as possible on the commons. Such an arrangement may work reasonably satisfactorily for centuries because tribal wars, poaching, and disease keep the numbers of both man and beast well below the carrying capacity of the land. Finally, however, comes the day of reckoning, that is, the day when the long-desired goal of social stability becomes a reality. At this point, the inherent logic of the commons remorselessly generates tragedy.

As a rational being, each herdsman seeks to maximize his gain. Explicitly or implicitly, more or less consciously, he asks, "What is the utility to me of adding one more animal to my herd?" This utility has one negative and one positive component.

The positive component is a function of the increment of one animal. Since the herdsman receives all the proceeds from the sale of the additional animal, the positive utility is nearly $+1$. The negative component is a function of the additional overgrazing created by one more animal. Since, however, the effects of overgrazing are shared by all the herdsmen, the negative utility for any particular decision-making herdsman is only a fraction of -1.

Adding together the component partial utilities, the rational herdsman concludes that the only sensible course for him to pursue is to add another animal to his herd. And another, and another ... But this is the conclusion reached by each and every rational herdsman sharing a commons. Therein is the tragedy. Each man is locked into a system that compels him to increase his herd without limit—in a world that is limited. Ruin is the destination toward which all men rush, each pursuing his own best interest in a society that believes in the freedom of the commons. Freedom in a commons brings ruin to all.

* * *

A NOTE ON THE TRAGEDY OF THE COMMONS

This classic article is a logical starting point for understanding the importance of property rights. If one lives in a world in which everything is part of the commons it is tempting not to worry about the harm one may do to others. Littering may seem perfectly sensible since individually one suffers no consequences. Even if you were civic minded, it might seem to make little sense to change your practices unless everyone else did.

Hence, the first and most critical step in making markets work is to create a system in which one can enjoy the benefits of his or her efforts but also incur the consequences of those same efforts. This marking out of rights means that an individual will be forced to weigh the costs of his or her activities against the benefits. It also means he or she can transfer those rights to those, and only to those, who have more "efficient" uses for those rights.

The problem of defining property rights may seem unimportant in modern times, but nothing could be further from the truth. Technological changes, as well as changes stemming from the imagination of individuals, means that we are involved in the never-ending process of defining the limits of rights.

The following case illustrates a modern "tragedy of the commons" and one response to it.

NEW YORK v. EVANS

United States District Court, E.D. New York, 2001.
162 F.Supp.2d 161.

GARAUFIS, DISTRICT JUDGE.

Plaintiffs have brought suit seeking invalidation of U.S. Department of Commerce (the "Secretary") final regulations implementing federal quotas for the summer 2000 and 2001 scup fisheries.[25] Plaintiffs intend by this lawsuit to compel the Secretary to allocate a specific percentage of the overall summer scup quota to each state participating in the fishery. * * *

I. STATUTORY BACKGROUND

The Secretary regulates the Atlantic Coast scup fishery pursuant to the Magnuson–Stevens Fishery Conservation and Management Act (the "Magnuson–Stevens Act"), 16 U.S.C. §§ 1801 et seq. The Magnuson–Stevens Act establishes an Exclusive Economic Zone ("Federal Waters"), extending from 3 miles seaward off the coastline to 200 nautical miles offshore. * * * The United States (with exceptions not relevant here) exercises "exclusive fishery management authority" over fisheries within Federal Waters, * * * through Fishery Management Plans ("FMPs"), * * *.

* * *

The Atlantic Coastal Fisheries Cooperative Management Act (the "Cooperative Act"), * * * permits Eastern Coastal states to participate in the management of Atlantic Ocean fisheries under a dual federal-state

---

25. Scup (also known as porgy) is a schooling fish species found in the Northwest Atlantic Ocean primarily between Cape Cod, Massachusetts, and Cape Hatteras, North Carolina. "Fishery" is defined under the Magnuson–Stevens Act as "(A) one or more stocks of fish which can be treated as a unit for the purposes of conservation and management and which are identified on the basis of geographical, scientific, technical, recreational and economic characteristics; and (B) any fishing for such stocks." 16 U.S.C. § 1802.

management regime. The Magnuson–Stevens Act expressly delegates exclusive regulatory authority within three miles of a state's coastline, traditionally recognized as state territorial waters ("State Waters"), to the individual states. * * * The Atlantic States Marine Fisheries Commission (the "States Commission"), which is comprised of representatives from the Eastern Coast states, prepares Coastal Fishery Management Plans ("CFMPs"). * * *

II. FACTUAL BACKGROUND

1. The Dual Regime

During the summer months, scup school primarily in State Waters and in Federal Waters during the winter months. In early 1995, the Fisheries Service concluded "that the scup stock is overexploited and at a low abundance level." In response, the Fisheries Service adopted a scup FMP (the "Federal Plan") proposed jointly by the Mid–Atlantic Fishery Management Council (the "Federal Council") and the States Commission, with input from the New England and South Atlantic Fishery Management Councils. The Federal Plan divided the fishing year into two winter periods and one summer period and set targets for fishing quotas to protect the fish stock. * * * The States Commission then adopted an identical plan as a scup CFMP (the "State Plan").

On May 22, 1997 the Secretary published final regulations implementing a regulatory amendment (the "Regulatory Amendment") allocating state-by-state on a percentage basis the summer period's overall federal scup quota. * * * Under the Regulatory Amendment the Secretary would announce in the Federal Register each state's attainment of its scup quota; the state would then close its scup fishery, thereby prohibiting vessels licensed to fish under state permits from selling scup to fish dealers. Upon attainment of every state's quota, the Secretary would close the scup fishery in Federal Waters and forbid vessels licensed to fish under federal permits from selling scup to fish dealers. * * * The States Commission adopted an addendum to the State Plan subdividing the overall summer quota into state-by-state allocations identical to the Regulatory Amendment. * * * Under this dual regime, any scup caught in either Federal or State Waters were counted against both the Federal Plan quota and the State Plan quota of the state where the fish were sold to fish dealers. * * *

2. Massachusetts Litigation

In June 1997, Massachusetts filed an action in federal district court to set aside the Secretary's Federal Plan to the extent that it established a state-by-state allocation of the summer quota. See Com. of Mass. by Div. of Marine Fisheries v. Daley, 10 F.Supp.2d 74 (D.Mass.1998). Massachusetts claimed that the state-by-state allocations were discriminatory. * * * The state argued that the data used to determine the allocations underestimated its appropriate share because scup caught and sold by small scale fishermen and dealers, who were not required to (and in fact did not) report amounts of scup caught and sold to the state or to the Fisheries Service, constituted 90% of the state's scup fishery. The district court set aside the federal state-by-state allocations of the summer quota as discriminatory to Massachusetts local fisherman.

In February 1999, the First Circuit affirmed the district court's decision on other grounds.

* * *

Even before the district court decision, Massachusetts had ignored the Federal and State Plan dual regime. In January 1998, the Fisheries Service determined that Massachusetts' 1997 summer scup landings exceeded its 1997 Federal Plan allocation by over one million pounds. * * * Subtracting Massachusetts' overages from the following year's allocation, the Fisheries Service determined that no commercial quota was available to Massachusetts for the 1998 summer period. * * * Under the procedures envisioned by the Federal Plan, the Secretary would have closed the Massachusetts scup fishery for the 1998 summer period.

Daley, however, invalidated the Federal Plan state-by-state allocations of the summer quota effectively prohibiting calculation and enforcement of Massachusetts' overages. Thus constrained, the Secretary regulated the summer scup fishery in 1998 exclusively through enforcement of the overall coastwide summer quota. When this quota had been met, the Secretary closed Federal Waters to further scup fishing. During the 1998 summer period, Massachusetts continued to ignore the Federal and State Plan conservation measures and landed almost 900,000 pounds of scup.

* * *

On June 23, 2000, New York filed this action, later joined by Rhode Island, seeking invalidation of the Federal Plan 2000 coastwide summer quota as arbitrary and capricious.

III. Discussion

* * *

2. *The Secretary's Coastwide Quota Is Adequately Supported in the Administrative Record*

It is well documented that scup are overfished, and the parties do not dispute that fact. Under the Magnuson–Stevens Act the Secretary must act to counteract the inimical effects of such overfishing. *See* 16 U.S.C. § 1854(e). The imposition of a coastwide quota is justified as a conservation measure which would allow for some fishing while rebuilding the fishery: "[t]he coastwide quota is a conservation measure, because it represents the maximum amount of fish that may be harvested while preventing overfishing and enabling this overfished resource to rebuild to its target level." * * * This rationale alone is sufficient to defeat Plaintiffs' motion. * * * Plaintiffs cannot show that the Federal Plan 2000 coastwide summer quota is without justification in the administrative record. Accordingly, this court must conclude that the regulation challenged here is not arbitrary and capricious.

3. The Challenges to the Secretary's Decision Lack Merit

Even though the Federal Plan 2000 coastwide summer quota finds ample justification in the administrative record, Plaintiffs argue on several grounds that the Secretary's decision to promulgate a coastwide quota in lieu of state-by-state allocations is nonetheless arbitrary and capricious. These arguments—that the state-by-state allocations were necessary to prevent overfishing, that there was adequate support in the administrative record for the state-by-state allocations, and that the Secretary had the power to enact the state-by-state allocations but failed to do so—bring to stark relief the lack of cooperative restraint and the absence of effective central leadership which together may well doom this troubled fishery to a tragedy of the commons.[26] Nonetheless, this court is constrained to do no more here than determine whether or not the Secretary entirely ignored important aspects of the problem, explained its decision in terms contrary to the evidence before it, or relied on factors that Congress did not intend for it to consider. * * * Plaintiffs have failed to show that the Secretary's promulgation of the Federal Plan 2000 coastwide summer quota was deficient under any of these tests.

a. The Secretary's Decision Entirely Ignores Important Aspects of the Problem

According to Plaintiffs, the Secretary entirely ignored the fact that a coastwide quota encourages a "derby-style"[27] summer fishing season and overfishing contrary to the conservation rationale of the Magnuson–Stevens Act. As early as July 21, 1999 the Fisheries Service asserted the need for new state-by-state allocations. The Secretary, through the Fisheries Service, explained the value of state-by-state allocations to the enforcement of the overall quota in the administrative record. Plaintiffs argue that the Fisheries Service's acknowledgment that state-by-state allocations are preferable to a coastwide quota renders the Secretary's failure to implement the former measures arbitrary and capricious. If the state-by-state allocations better conserve the fishery, Plaintiffs argue, any alternative is arbitrary and capricious as contrary to the Magnuson-Stevens Act's overarching conservation rationale.

---

26. *See* Garrett Hardin, *The Tragedy of the Commons,* 162 Science 1243 (1968). The tragedy ensues when "the rational but independent pursuit by each decisionmaker of its own self-interest leads to results that leave all decisionmakers worse off than they would have been had they been able to agree collectively on a different set of policies." *Natural Res. Def. Council, Inc. v. Costle,* 568 F.2d 1369, 1378 n. 19 (D.C.Cir. 1977).

27. "Derby-style" fishing is "a race to fish" in which fisherman are encouraged, due to limitations on a fishery, to attempt to catch as much of a species as quickly as possible in order to maximize their harvest before a season or fishery is closed. *See, e.g.,* ASMFC Fisheries Focus, Vol. 9, Issue 2, Feb. 2000, at 4.

This argument rests on the unfounded premise that state-by-state allocations are more effective than a coastwide quota. The first state-by-state allocations of the summer scup quota were ignored in 1997 and subsequently invalidated in 1998. In fact, there is no evidence in the administrative record that a state-by-state allocation of the summer scup quota has ever been effective. Furthermore, it is the states that have continued to allow fishing in State Waters after the Federal Plan's quota is reached and Federal Waters are closed; these states cannot now be heard to complain of a Federal Plan quota that does not guard against such overfishing, especially when the Secretary cannot enforce a Federal Plan quota in State Waters.

Moreover, even if Plaintiffs could show that federal state-by-state allocations are more effective, this fact alone would not warrant invalidation of the Secretary's action. * * * Plaintiffs' alternative to the coastwide quota only serves to call into doubt the wisdom of the Secretary's decision. Where a challenge to an agency action "fairly conceptualized, really centers on the wisdom of the agency's policy, rather than on whether it is a reasonable choice within a gap left open by Congress, the challenge must fail." *Chevron* [U.S.A., Inc. v. Natural Resources Defense Council, Inc.] 467 U.S. at 866, 104 S.Ct. 2778. * * * While the Secretary's lack of initiative in failing to re-establish state-by-state allocations may be lamentable, the Secretary did not ignore an aspect of the problem, and coastwide quota retains its presumption of validity based on the ample justification found in this administrative record.

b. The Secretary's Explanation Why State–By–State Allocations Were Not Justified Is Contrary to the Evidence

Plaintiffs next argue that the Secretary's decision to replace the state-by-state allocations, explained in terms of *Daley,* was contrary to the justification for the allocations based on the overfishing in the summer of 1999 in the administrative record. This is not the case. The First Circuit required that the justification for any federal state-by-state allocation "must demonstrate that the state-by-state quotas incorporate the best available scientific information and serve a conservation purpose. The administrative record must also show that if the new state-by-state quota system has some discriminatory effect among the states, any discrimination is necessary to conserve the scup resource." The overfishing in the summer of 1999 alone does not provide justification for federal state-by-state allocations. As discussed above, the overfishing occurred in State Waters after the Federal Plan 2000 quota was reached and Federal Waters were closed to scup fishing. It is unclear that federal state-by-state allocations can effectively address this problem. Because the administrative record in May of 2000 did not clearly satisfy this standard, the Secretary's decision not to implement state-by-state quotas until the record could be supplemented was merely cautious, not erroneous.

Further, ample justification for the Secretary's decision to opt against state-by-state allocations once again appears in the administrative record. * * * Plaintiffs fail to show that the Secretary relied upon an erroneous interpretation of *Daley,* or that state-by-state allocations were justified in the administrative record. There is, therefore, no basis for concluding that the decision to implement a coastwide quota was explained in terms contrary to the evidence before the Secretary.

   c.   The Secretary Relied on Factors Congress Did Not Intend For It To Consider

   Finally, Plaintiffs contend that the Secretary was prompted to reject state-by-state allocations and adopt a coastwide quota by an improper desire to avoid further litigation, and which is a factor Congress did not intend for the Secretary to consider. The administrative record clearly reflects that the Secretary took great pains to conform his actions to the *Daley* decisions. * * * There is no indication that apprehension of further litigation prompted agency action. In fact, the Secretary demonstrated a willingness to work toward future state-by-state allocations, despite the First Circuit's admonitions that they would be "subject to swift judicial review." This court will not equate adherence to court mandates with an impermissible formulation of agency regulations based on an aversion to litigation.

      * * *

                    IV.   CONCLUSION

   For the foregoing reasons Plaintiffs' motion for partial summary judgment is DENIED, and Plaintiffs' claim as to the summer 2000 scup regulations promulgated by the Secretary is DISMISSED. The parties are directed within 30 days to communicate to this court notice of the resolution of Plaintiffs' challenges to the summer 2001 scup regulations, or to make such motions as they deem appropriate.

                  Notes and Questions

   1.   As noted in the discussion of the "The Tragedy of the Commons," the definition of property rights can ensure that individuals internalize the costs of their activities. When resources are found in the wild, the problem is obvious. For example, those who fish for the scup enjoy a full and direct benefit. The cost in terms of depletion is spread haphazardly among members of the current and future generations.

   2.   In the case of fish it is impossible to assign property rights to the fish themselves. Instead an effort was made to limit the time and areas in which fishing could take place. This does not mean that the fishing industry actually internalizes the cost of overfishing, but it sets fishing limits roughly in accord with the levels that would exist if internalization did take place.

   3.   The states complain that by setting federal limits but not state limits the Secretary encourages "derby-style" fishing. Do you know what that means? Does it really encourage overfishing? If not, what do the states hope to gain from state-by-state allocations?

   4.   As already noted, the usual first step in rationalizing an industry is to define property rights. Defining these rights means that internalization

and meaningful exchange take place. It is, however, one thing to say that one "owns" something and quite another to describe exactly what that means. If you own your house, may you play your stereo there, for example? Does it matter how loudly you play it? May people freely walk across your yard? If not, what are the limits of your ability to discourage them?

5. Intellectual property rights are good examples of rationalizing mechanisms. They allow creative people to internalize the benefits of their efforts. Without this protection the incentive to be creative would be much less. Conversely, these rights mean that others must internalize the cost of using the creative efforts of others.

6. Defining what "property" one has leads to another important step in the rationalizing process. Just how are these rights protected and what are the consequences when they are violated? The next excerpt is from what is probably the best known article on the topic.

GUIDO CALABRESI & A. DOUGLAS MELAMED, PROPERTY RULES, LIABILITY RULES AND INALIENABILITY: ONE VIEW OF THE CATHEDRAL[28]

85 Harvard Law Review 1089, 1105–1111 (1972).

* * *

III. Rules for Protecting and Regulating Entitlements

Whenever society chooses an initial entitlement it must also determine whether to protect the entitlement by property rules, by liability rules, or rules of inalienability. In our framework, much of what is generally called private property can be viewed as an entitlement which is protected by a property rule. No one can take the entitlement to private property from the holder unless the holder sells it willingly and at the price at which he subjectively values the property. Yet a nuisance with sufficient public utility to avoid injunction has, in effect, the right to take property with compensation. In such a circumstance the entitlement to the property is protected only by what we call a liability rule: an external, objective standard of value is used to facilitate the transfer of the entitlement from the holder to the nuisance. Finally, in some instances we will not allow the sale of the property at all, that is, we will occasionally make the entitlement inalienable.

* * *

Why cannot a society simply decide * * * who should receive any given entitlement, and then let its transfer occur only through a voluntary negotiation? Why, in other words, cannot society limit itself to the property rule? To do this it would need only to protect and enforce the initial entitlements from all attacks, perhaps through criminal sanctions, and to enforce voluntary contracts for their transfer. Why do we need liability rules at all?

28. Copyright 1972 by the Harvard Law Review Association. Used with permission.

In terms of economic efficiency the reason is easy enough to see. Often the cost of establishing the value of an initial entitlement by negotiation is so great that even though a transfer of the entitlement would benefit all concerned, such a transfer will not occur. If a collective determination of the value were available instead, the beneficial transfer would quickly come about.

Eminent domain is a good example. A park where Guidacres, a tract of land owned by 1,000 owners in 1,000 parcels, now sits would, let us assume, benefit a neighboring town enough so that the 100,000 citizens of the town would each be willing to pay an average of $100 to have it. The park is Pareto desirable if the owners of the tracts of land in Guidacres actually value their entitlements at less than $10,000,000 or an average of $10,000 a tract. Let us assume that in fact the parcels are all the same and all the owners value them at $8,000. On this assumption, the park is, in economic efficiency terms, desirable—in values foregone it costs $8,000,000 and is worth $10,000,000 to the buyers. And yet it may well not be established. If enough of the owners hold-out for more than $10,000 in order to get a share of the $2,000,000 that they guess the buyers are willing to pay over the value which the sellers in actuality attach, the price demanded will be more than $10,000,000 and no park will result. The sellers have an incentive to hide their true valuation and the market will not succeed in establishing it.

An equally valid example could be made on the buying side. Suppose the sellers of Guidacres have agreed to a sales price of $8,000,000 (they are all relatives and at a family banquet decided that trying to hold-out would leave them all losers). It does not follow that the buyers can raise that much even though each of 100,000 citizens in fact values the park at $100. Some citizens may try to free-load and say the park is only worth $50 or even nothing to them, hoping that enough others will admit to a higher desire and make up the $8,000,000 price. Again there is no reason to believe that a market, a decentralized system of valuing, will cause people to express their true valuations and hence yield results which all would in fact agree are desirable.

Whenever this is the case an argument can readily be made for moving from a property rule to a liability rule. If society can remove from the market the valuation of each tract of land, decide the value collectively, and impose it, then the holdout problem is gone. Similarly, if society can value collectively each individual citizen's desire to have a park and charge him a "benefits" tax based upon it, the freeloader problem is gone. If the sum of the taxes is greater than the sum of the compensation awards, the park will result.

Of course, one can conceive of situations where it might be cheap to exclude all the freeloaders from the park, or to ration the park's use in accordance with original willingness to pay. In such cases the incentive to free-load might be eliminated. But such exclusions, even if possible, are usually not cheap. And the same may be the case for market methods which might avoid the holdout problem on the seller side.

Moreover, even if holdout and freeloader problems can be met feasibly by the market, an argument may remain for employing a liability rule. Assume that in our hypothetical, freeloaders can be excluded at the cost of $1,000,000 and that all owners of tracts in Guidacres can be convinced, by the use of $500,000 worth of advertising and cocktail parties, that a sale will only occur if they reveal their true land valuations. Since $8,000,000 plus $1,500,000 is less than $10,000,000 the park will be established. But if collective valuation of the tracts and of the benefits of the prospective park would have cost less than $1,500,000, it would have been inefficient to establish the park through the market—a market which was not worth having would have been paid for.

Of course, the problems with liability rules are equally real. We cannot be at all sure that landowner Taney is lying or holding out when he says his land is worth $12,000 to him. The fact that several neighbors sold identical tracts for $10,000 does not help us very much; Taney may be sentimentally attached to his land. As a result, eminent domain may grossly undervalue what Taney would actually sell for, even if it sought to give him his true valuation of his tract. In practice, it is so hard to determine Taney's true valuation that eminent domain simply gives him what the land is worth "objectively," in the full knowledge that this may result in over or under compensation. The same is true on the buyer side. "Benefits" taxes rarely attempt, let alone succeed, in gauging the individual citizen's relative desire for the alleged benefit. They are justified because, even if they do not accurately measure each individual's desire for the benefit, the market alternative seems worse. For example, fifty different households may place different values on a new sidewalk that is to abut all the properties. Nevertheless, because it is too difficult, even if possible, to gauge each household's valuation, we usually tax each household an equal amount.

The example of eminent domain is simply one of numerous instances in which society uses liability rules. Accidents is another. If we were to give victims a property entitlement not to be accidentally injured we would have to require all who engage in activities that may injure individuals to negotiate with them before an accident, and to buy the right to knock off an arm or a leg. Such pre-accident negotiations would be extremely expensive, often prohibitively so. To require them would thus preclude many activities that might, in fact, be worth having. And, after an accident, the loser of the arm or leg can always very plausibly deny that he would have sold it at the price the buyer would have offered. Indeed, where negotiations after an accident do occur—for instance pretrial settlements—it is largely because the alternative is the collective valuation of the damages.

It is not our object here to outline all the theoretical, let alone the practical, situations where markets may be too expensive or fail and where collective valuations seem more desirable. Economic literature has many times surrounded the issue if it has not always zeroed in on it in ways intelligible to lawyers. It is enough for our purposes to note that a very common reason, perhaps the most common one, for employing a liability rule rather than a property rule to protect an entitlement is that market valuation of the entitlement is deemed inefficient, that is, it is either unavailable or too expensive compared to a collective valuation.

We should also recognize that efficiency is not the sole ground for employing liability rules rather than property rules. Just as the initial entitlement is often decided upon for distributional reasons, so too the choice of a liability rule is often made because it facilitates a combination of efficiency and distributive results which would be difficult to achieve under a property rule. As we shall see in the pollution context, use of a liability rule may allow us to accomplish a measure of redistribution that could only be attained at a prohibitive sacrifice of efficiency if we employed a corresponding property rule.

More often, once a liability rule is decided upon, perhaps for efficiency reasons, it is then employed to favor distributive goals as well. Again accidents and eminent domain are good examples. In both of these areas the compensation given has clearly varied with society's distributive goals, and cannot be readily explained in terms of giving the victim, as nearly as possible, and objectively determined equivalent of the price at which he would have sold what was taken from him.

It should not be surprising that this is often so, even if the original reason for a liability rule is an efficiency one. For distributional goals are expensive and difficult to achieve, and the collective valuation involved in liability rules readily lends itself to promoting distributional goals. This does not mean that distributional goals are always well served in this way. Ad hoc decision-making is always troublesome, and the difficulties are especially acute when the settlement of conflicts between parties is used as a vehicle for the solution of more widespread distributional problems. Nevertheless, distributional objectives may be better attained in this way than otherwise.

Thus far we have focused on the questions of when society should protect an entitlement by property or liability rules. However, there remain many entitlements which involve a still greater degree of societal intervention: the law not only decides who is to own something and what price is to be paid for it if it is taken or destroyed, but also regulates its sale—by, for example, prescribing preconditions for a valid sale or forbidding a sale altogether. Although these rules of inalienability are substantially different from the property and liability rules, their use can be analyzed in terms of the same efficiency and distributional goals that underlie the use of the other two rules.

While at first glance efficiency objectives may seem undermined by limitations on the ability to engage in transactions, closer analysis suggests that there are instances, perhaps many, in which economic efficiency is more closely approximated by such limitations. This might occur when a transaction would create significant externalities—costs to third parties.

For instance, if Taney were allowed to sell his land to Chase, a polluter, he would injure his neighbor Marshall by lowering the value of Marshall's land. Conceivably, Marshall could pay Taney not to sell his land; but, because there are many injured Marshalls, freeloader and information costs make such transactions practically impossible. The state could protect the Marshall and yet facilitate the sale of the land by giving the Marshalls an entitlement to prevent Taney's sale to Chase but only protecting the entitlement by a liability rule. It might, for instance, charge an excise tax on all sales of land to polluters equal to its estimate of the external cost to the Marshalls of the sale. But where there are so many injured Marshalls that the price required under the liability rule is likely to be high enough so that no one would be willing to pay it, then setting up the machinery for collective valuation will be wasteful. Barring the sale to polluters will be the most efficient result because it is clear that avoiding pollution is cheaper than paying its costs—including its costs to the Marshalls.

* * *

Notes and Questions

1.   What is the difference between a property rule and a liability rule? In a sense, property rules afford more protection for the owner than liability rules.[29] Do you see why? What do Calabresi and Melamed suggest should determine which kind of rule should be found to exist?

2.   In very general terms, property rules may impede the efficient allocation of resources when transactions are high. In these instances, liability rules permit the "buyer" to avoid many transaction costs by simply taking the property of others without permission and then compensating them. Do you think the various costs identified by Calabresi and Melamed should be the determinants of when to apply a property rule or a liability rule? What about the type of property? For example, suppose the property is something that someone attaches value to in excess of the market value? Is it fair to protect that property with a liability rule? Why or why not?

3.   Suppose you were a legislator in the State of Florida and you were asked how you would vote on a plan that would permit the state to acquire the property of sugar growers who have been damaging the environment by the use of chemicals and the diversion of the natural flow of water. Suppose most of the sugar growers were families and had been in business for generations. First, if the citizens of the state value less environmental degradation more than the sugar growers value continued operation, why wouldn't the market solve the "misallocation"? How would you vote if you were from a sugar growing district? How would you vote if you were from a district that was dependent on tourism? Is the decisive factor here really your desire to be reelected?

---

29.   For a more recent economic analysis of this distinction, see Louis Kaplow & Steven Shavell, Property Rules versus Liability Rules: An Economic Analysis, 109 Harvard L. Rev. 713 (1996).

4. Calabresi and Melamed also refer to some entitlements that are protected by rules of inalienability. We return to those issues in Section D of this Chapter.

3.   REGULATING THE SUPPLY OF INFORMATION

One of the more intriguing topics under the rubric of transaction costs is information. Information is something people value and you would expect it to be produced by the market. In fact, there is a great deal of advertising and a great many publications (e.g., Consumer Reports) that specialize in selling information. On the other hand, some types of information may not be readily available and some information that is available may be misleading. The following case illustrates a response to such a problem.

ASSOCIATION OF NATIONAL ADVERTISERS, INC. v. LUNGREN

United States Court of Appeals, Ninth Circuit, 1994.
44 F.3d 726.

Before HERBERT Y.C. CHOY, JOHN T. NOONAN, JR., CIRCUIT JUDGES and ALFREDO C. MARQUEZ, DISTRICT JUDGE.

CHOY, CIRCUIT JUDGE:

Appellants, the Association of National Advertisers, Inc., et al. (Trade Associations), appeal the district court's grant of summary judgment upholding the constitutionality of California Business and Professions Code § 17508.5.[30] * * * [W]e affirm.

30. § 17508.5. It is unlawful for any person to represent that any consumer good which it manufactures or distributes is "ozone friendly," or any like term which connotes that stratospheric ozone is not being depleted, "biodegradable," "photodegradable," "recyclable," or "recycled" unless that consumer good meets the definitions contained in this section, or meets definitions established in trade rules adopted by the Federal Trade Commission. For the purposes of this section, the following words have the following meanings:

(a) "Ozone friendly," or any like term which connotes that stratospheric ozone is not being depleted, means that any chemical or material released into the environment as a result of the use or production of a product, will not migrate to the stratosphere and cause unnatural and accelerated deterioration of the ozone.

(b) "Biodegradable" means that a material has the proven capability to decompose in the most common environment where the material is disposed within one year through natural biological processes

into nontoxic carbonaceous soil, water or carbon dioxide.

(c) "Photodegradable" means that a material has the proven capability to decompose in the most common environment where the material is disposed within one year through physical processes, such as exposure to heat and light, into nontoxic carbonaceous soil, water, or carbon dioxide.

(d) "Recyclable" means that an article can be conveniently recycled, as defined in Section 40180 of the Public Resources Code, in every county in California with a population over 300,000 persons. For the purposes of this subdivision, "conveniently recycled" shall not mean that a consumer good may be recycled in a convenience zone as defined in Section 14909.4 of the Public Resources Code.

(e) "Recycled" means that an article's contents contain at least 10 percent, by weight, postconsumer material, as defined in subdivision (b) of Section 12200 of the Public Contract Code.

(f) "Consumer good" means any article which is used or bought for use primarily

I. FACTUAL AND PROCEDURAL BACKGROUND

Section 17508.5 makes it unlawful for a manufacturer or distributor of consumer goods to represent that its products are "ozone friendly", "biodegradable", "photodegradable", "recyclable" or "recycled" unless their goods meet the statute's definitions of those terms. In 1990, the California Legislature enacted this statute in the wake of a report on environmental advertising issued by a ten-state task force of state attorneys general (the Task Force). This report summarized the findings of the Task Force from a public meeting it convened in March 1990 to address the potential for abuse raised by the increasing popularity of what the attorneys general characterized as "green marketing . . . the marketing craze of the 1990's."

The Task Force found disparities in the usage of these terms by different firms and noted the assertions of environmental groups and business representatives that there was "growing confusion surrounding many environmental marketing claims" creating a "fertile ground for abusive business practices." The Task Force further discerned a "wide degree of consensus among business and environmental groups" on the need for "development of national standards, guidelines or definitions to guide business in making environmental claims and to help consumers understand the claims made." Section 17508.5 is an attempt to implement these findings at the state level.

In February 1992, the Trade Associations responded to the passage of section 17508.5 by bringing suit in the Northern District of California against the attorney general of California, Appellee Daniel Lungren (Lungren or California). The Trade Associations sought a declaration that section 17508.5 impermissibly restricts both commercial and non-commercial speech and is unconstitutionally vague. They also pursued a permanent injunction against the statute's enforcement. Appellees, the Californians Against Waste and the Environmental Defense Fund (collectively referred to as "CAW"), intervened.

The district court held that the statute was adequately tailored to further substantial state interests in consumer and environmental protection and, accordingly, complied with the First Amendment. The Trade Associations appeal this ruling here on the basis that (1) the district court erred in concluding that section 17508.5 regulates only commercial speech; (2) the district court erroneously analyzed the statute under an intermediate standard of scrutiny inapplicable to non-commercial speech, or to commercial speech inextricably intertwined with more privileged expression; and (3) the district court misapplied intermediate scrutiny by ignoring far less restrictive alternatives to section 17508.5 and mistakenly finding that the statute directly advances a substantial governmental interest.

for personal, family, or household purposes.

(g) For the purposes of this section, a wholesaler or retailer who does not initiate a representation by advertising or by placing the representation on a package shall not be deemed to have made the representation. [Appendix to the Court's opinion]

II. Discussion

A. *Intermediate scrutiny governs section 17508.5.*

The Trade Associations contend that the district court erred in holding that section 17508.5 regulates only commercial speech. They further assert that as a result the district court applied to the statute an unduly deferential standard of review, the intermediate scrutiny governing commercial speech. We disagree.

* * *

We agree with the district court that "the messages regulated by section 17508.5 possess the three characteristics recognized by the Court as constitutive of commercial speech" in Bolger v. Youngs Drug Products Corp., 463 U.S. 60, 77 L.Ed.2d 469, 103 S.Ct. 2875 (1983). In *Bolger*, the Court struck down a federal statute prohibiting the mailing of unsolicited advertisements for contraceptives under the First Amendment. In doing so, the Court set out three characteristics which, in combination, supported its conclusion that the informational pamphlets at issue constituted commercial speech, including (i) their advertising format, (ii) their reference to a specific product, and (iii) the underlying economic motive of the speaker.

Here, the district court reasonably found all three of these factors present. * * *

* * *

We bear in mind that "[a] statute, of course, is to be construed, if such a construction is fairly possible, to avoid raising doubts of its constitutionality." The district court's interpretation is more than "fairly possible". As the district court observed, the preamble specifies that only representations pertaining to the speaker's own products give rise to potential liability. In addition, the district court reasonably attributed some significance to the California legislature's placement of section 17508.5 in the middle of Part 3, Chapter 1 of the code, entitled "Advertising", and, more specifically, in Article 1 of Chapter 1, entitled "False Advertising in General". In conjunction with the three *Bolger* factors analyzed by the district court and the limiting language in the statute's preface, the placement of section 17508.5 amidst provisions more generally governing advertising and, in particular, false advertising, betokens the statute's commercial subject matter and the California legislature's intent to regulate misrepresentations made in a commercial context exclusively.

* * *

* * * With the exception of the term "recyclable", deemed unduly vague, the district court satisfied itself after thorough analysis that section 17508.5 would neither stifle non-commercial expression by manufacturers and distributors nor create unconstitutionally excessive uncertainty for such merchants in their use of the regulated terms in commercial speech.

In addition, the district court correctly determined that section 17508.5 escapes strict scrutiny because it does not embrace non-commercial messages inextricably linked with commercial speech. Where commercial and non-commercial speech are inseparable, strict scrutiny is required. * * * [T]he district court reasonably concluded that editorializing was not essential to product advertising. "[W]hile statements that a firm supports recycling, for instance, are undoubtedly included in advertisements as a marketing tool and may in fact augment sales, firms can nevertheless sell their wares without editorializing about the environment". Conversely, the district court persuasively reasoned that a firm can editorialize about the environment, lambast the statute or laud recycling without advertising or otherwise making commercial representations about one of its products. Insofar as these activities are severable and separately treated under section 17508.5, the district court appropriately selected intermediate scrutiny.

* * *

In sum, we conclude that the district court established the basis for intermediate scrutiny by determining correctly that section 17508.5 is directed only at commercial speech and does not collaterally stifle more privileged speech.

B. *Section 17508.5 withstands intermediate scrutiny.*

The Trade Associations assert that section 17508.5 fails to withstand intermediate scrutiny, even assuming its applicability, because the statute prohibits truthful and accurate commercial speech, fails to advance directly any alleged government interest, and is more restrictive than necessary to serve its supposed interests. We disagree.

* * *

The Trade Associations offer two purportedly far less restrictive alternatives: case-by-case prosecution of spurious environmental claims under existing false advertising statutes or adoption of a statute or regulations mandating qualifying or explanatory language to clarify use of the regulated terms not conforming with section 17508.5. The possibility of a case-by-case approach under existing statutes governing false advertising, previously opposed but newly advocated by the Trade Associations, does not undermine section 17508.5 * * *. The district court rejected this alternative on the basis that "nothing prevents a legislative body from adopting a specific law simply because a more general law already exists."

* * * The prohibitions of false advertising in sections 17500 and 17508 of the Business and Professional Code require reference to vague, unspecified standards as opposed to section 17508.5's numerically exact thresholds, to ascertain liability. These alternative statutes are less precise and, as the district court noted, potentially more inhibiting of truthful environmental representations. Moreover, these statutes promote a narrower range of state interests than section 17508.5, insofar as they fail to create the same incentives for environmentally substandard firms to improve the ecological attributes of their products rather than merely harmonize their claims with production and disposal realities. * * *

The second suggested alternative, a statute requiring "more speech", runs headlong into the Court's rejection of such an approach to fourth prong analysis in *Fox*. * * *[31]

* * * [A]s the district court observed, these and other potential alternatives—including prescreening, format and content guidelines and added detail—were not clearly less burdensome than adherence to uniform definitions. In addition, * * * it is not apparent that use of the regulated terms with qualifiers would advance California's second asserted interest, environmental protection.

     * * *

To be sure, there is inevitably a degree of arbitrariness in the legislative determination of where along the continuum of recycled content percentages or decomposition timetables a product becomes "recycled" or "biodegradable". But [we have] scant judicial latitude to disturb such legislative determinations where, as here, the thresholds drawn do not appear unduly prohibitive and leave considerable room for both more privileged editorial commentary and, in the commercial context, alternative expressions conveying perfectly well information about the modest environmental attributes of products not measuring up under section 17508.5 (e.g., "this product contains x% [reused/recaptured] materials," in lieu of "recycled"; "these trash bags will decompose in two years under x conditions," in lieu of "biodegradable"). Accordingly, we affirm the district court's ruling that "the California legislature has stayed within constitutional parameters in restricting commercial expression."

NOONAN, CIRCUIT JUDGE, dissenting:

I accept the majority's conclusion that the speech made criminal by this statute is commercial speech. I follow the doctrine of the Supreme Court that commercial speech is, ordinarily, more subject to state regulation than noncommercial speech. I have no doubt at all that untrue or deceptive advertising can be outlawed. I see no problem in the government prescribing precise labels for what cures our bodies or goes into them, or goes into a gas tank. But I have great difficulty in seeing this statute as anything other than a zealous and unconstitutional intrusion by a state government into an area where technologies are developing, the free play of ideas is important, and the free speech of everyone, including manufacturers and distributors, is essential to the develop-

---

31. In Board of Trustees of State Univ. of N.Y. v. Fox, 492 U.S. 469, 106 L.Ed.2d 388, 109 S.Ct. 3028 (1989), the Court ruled that the Second Circuit erred in requiring the district court to apply a least-restrictive-means test to a state university's regulation banning private commercial enterprises from its facilities. While the Court in *Fox* instructed that a narrowly tailored regulation on less privileged commercial speech would logically pass muster it also indicated that an even more flexible standard governs such "hardy, less likely to be chilled" expression. [Footnote by editors quoting from earlier portion of Court's opinion]

ment of a healthy environment. Tested by our Bill of Rights, the statute is defective.

To begin with, several of the definitions imposed on manufacturers and distributors under criminal penalties are unconstitutionally vague. Three definitions have a common deficiency: the use of nature as an intelligible standard in an environment and economy where there is scarcely any "nature" independent of human intervention. "Ozone-friendly" and "any like term" (a bit of extra vagueness) are defined as a chemical or material that "will not migrate to the stratosphere and cause unnatural and accelerated deterioration of the ozone." What is unnatural deterioration of the ozone? How is unnaturalness to be determined? What state of the universe is assumed to be the natural state as far as ozone is concerned? The statute affords no guidance. It compels the advertiser to determine at the peril of criminal penalties that the product advertised does not have this elusive metaphysical quality.

Less obviously, because "natural" may seem less problematic than "unnatural," but just as effectively, the statutory definitions of biodegradable and photodegradable are vague in their use of nature as the standard for the products advertised. To be biodegradable under the criminal law of California the product must be decomposable through "natural processes." What is a "natural process"? Is it one in which there is no human intervention? Is the implicit assumption of the statute that nature is one thing and human activity another, so that if human intelligence intervenes the process is no longer natural? The same questions are latent in the definition of photodegradable in terms of ability to decompose by "physical processes, such as exposure to heat and light," where "physical" is a stand-in for "natural." The advertiser is left to speculate what degree of human intervention will sully the natural and so lead to noncompliance with the statutory command.

As for "recyclable" and "recycled", what is recyclable should eventually be recycled. One would expect the definition of the two terms to be in tandem. The statute, however, adopts one definition of "recyclable" and another of "recycled", so that what is "recyclable" will not necessarily be "recycled" when re-use is made. "Recyclable" has now been held to be defined in a fashion incomprehensible to a manufacturer or distributor of ordinary intelligence. Does striking it from the statute make "recycled" more intelligible by removing the statute's inconsistency? Arguably, yes, although a lingering doubt remains about the surviving definition which in its origin was so flawed.

* * *

The statute has other constitutional infirmities. The district court noted that to avoid the reach of the First Amendment the words that the statute defined must be "sufficiently deceptive." As to whether the words were in fact "sufficiently deceptive," the district court candidly acknowledged that it found "no easy answer." The strongest thing the district court could say about the restricted words was that, without the state's help, they were "potentially misleading." To substantiate that characterization the district court cited a letter from the attorney general's office to the governor which "opined" that there had been "an increase" in "questionable 'environmental' advertising." No actual instances of deception were cited; the letter was written as advocacy for enactment of the statute. * * * The true basis for this far-reaching conclusion, on which the majority opinion so heavily relies, is speculation. Speculation is no basis on which to support a criminal law licensing speech.

Even if, contrary to the record in this case, the presumption were indulged that a factual predicate of potential deceptiveness had been established, such facts would not justify the state's invasion of freedom of speech. A variety of words are commonly used in American advertising, all of which are potentially misleading. For example:

antique

bargain

economical

environmentally sound

naturally good

A paternalistic government might decide to protect consumers by criminalizing all advertising containing these words if the product advertised failed to conform with the state's own definition. That the terms defined were capable of misleading use would be incontestable. That a criminal law of this character would violate the First Amendment would be equally incontestable. Potential misuse "does not satisfy the State's heavy burden of justifying a categorical prohibition against the dissemination of accurate factual information." The difference between this hypothetical statute and the California criminal law at issue here is not a difference in kind or in degree. The only difference is that the California law has chosen a different set of speculatively misleading words to define and criminalize.

Why have these particular words been made the subject of legislation? Why have Californians Against Waste and the Environmental Defense Fund been allowed to enter the case on the side of the state with the status of intervenors? Why do these intervenors defend the district court's decision with such skill, tenacity and vigor? Plainly because, as the intervenors declare, the words defined are "key environmental terms." In the Green Movement the words are powerful, evocative, almost sacred. There is a sense that they should not be profaned by casual usage. The legislation embodies a clear conviction that there are those who can be trusted to use them and those who cannot be trusted; for the legislation singles out commercial advertisers as the untrustworthy and leaves unregulated and trusted the nonprofits who believe the terms are key.

Such a distinction between speakers, made by a legislature, has a name: viewpoint discrimination. Such a distinction has a constitutional destiny, to be held a violation of the First Amendment unless, strictly scrutinized, it is shown to be narrowly tailored to serve a compelling state interest. A legislature cannot privilege one set of speakers as the good guys, while restraining another set of speakers as the baddies. When the speakers use the same language, it's not difference enough that one speaks for profit and the other for "nature."

This broad-brush, speculatively-justified statute cannot survive the test of rationality, let alone strict scrutiny. To the state's present embarrassment, the state argued in its Points and Authorities to the district court that the plaintiffs would not violate the statute if their advertising qualified the restricted terms appropriately. This argument, of course, rewrote the statute, was ignored by the district court, and is abandoned by the state on this appeal. But the abandoned argument does point to the obvious, that with a minimum of effort the legislature could have provided that qualified use of the terms was acceptable. The legislature tacitly conceded as much by accepting in the statute itself any definitions "established in trade rules adopted by the Federal Trade Commission." If potential misuse was the problem, it would have been possible to do as the FTC may sometime do and as Maine in fact does do, provide a governmental definition of "recycled content," but permit any "properly qualified statement of fact" addressed to consumers. Maine Rev. Stat.Ann., Title 38, § 2141.2. When such means could be used to attain the legislative end, the present fit is too rough to be rational.

In summary, the statute in question, criminalizing the use of specific words in commercial speech, is vague in the standard set; has a rough and speculative relation to the interests of the state; and discriminates among speakers. The statute is incompatible with the freedom assured by the First Amendment.

Notes and Questions

1. The standards examined in the case were adopted in 1990. In 1992 the Federal Trade Commission announced its own guidelines for environmental labeling. The FTC guidelines can and have been enforced under section 5 of the Federal Trade Commission Act which prohibits "unfair means of competition." Several states, including California, have now adopted the FTC guidelines. Cal. Bus. & Prof. Code § 17580.5 (2003). See generally, Jeremy Rosen, "Requirements for Environmental Marketing Claims Under the Federal Trade Commission's Guides," 4 Environmental Lawyer 241 (1997).

2. Accurate information about environmental effects of products obviously has value to many consumers. Perhaps it was produced in sufficient quantities before this regulation. Do you think so? If not, what barriers would keep it from being produced in sufficient quantities?

3. If a market is competitive, wouldn't you expect sellers to attempt to lower the search costs of consumers by supplying them with any information that is inexpensive for sellers to provide and that buyers would find rele-

vant? Does this mean that a failure to disclose reflects a lack of competition in the market for retail goods?

4.   The availability of information is likely to lower the search costs of consumers, increase competition, and result in lower prices. With increased competition, firms in an industry may experience lower profits and pay shareholders lower dividends. Do laws like the California law considered here result in the subsidization of consumers by shareholders? Is this the kind of "taking" of the companies' rights for which compensation should be mandated?

5.   Could consumers soon be subject to "information overload"? Assume that if average consumers were supplied with ten items of information, they might use of all ten; however, if they were supplied with twenty items of information, they might tend to use only five. Would you require sellers who were supplying "too much" information to reduce the supply to the "optimal" level for the average consumer? Cf. Jeffrey Davis, Protecting Consumers from Overdisclosure and Gobbledygook: An Empirical Look at the Simplification of Consumer–Credit Contracts, 63 Virginia L. Rev. 841 (1977); Lars Noah, The Imperative to Warn: Disentangling the "Right to Know" from the "Need to Know" about Consumer Hazards, 11 Yale J. Regulation 293 (1994).

6.   Many mandated disclosures concern possible health hazards. Cigarette manufacturers must report the tar and nicotine content of their products and soft drink manufacturers must warn of the possible health consequences of consuming saccharin in diet beverages. Why require these disclosures? Isn't the common law system of contract and tort law sufficiently robust to encourage manufacturers to disclose the hazardous nature of their products? Would the common law system insure that consumers had access to information concerning ingredients or the salt and fat content of foods? See Howard Beales, Richard Craswell & Steven C. Salop, The Efficient Regulation of Consumer Information, 24 J. L. & Econ. 491 (1981); Alan Schwartz & Louis L. Wilde, Intervening in Markets on the Basis of Imperfect Information: A Legal and Economic Analysis, 127 U. Pennsylvania L. Rev. 630 (1979); George Stigler, The Economics of Information, 69 J. Political Economy 213 (1961).

7.   In addition to product labeling, one form of controlling the cost of information is through regulating what is introduced into the market. For example, various licensing requirements provide information to consumers that individuals possess the minimum qualifications to practice medicine or law as we have seen. In the case of medications, the Food and Drug Administration determines whether new drugs are "safe and effective." Thus, the drug approval process is one that indirectly provides information and probably means that information is produced in a more systematic way than it would be in an unregulated market.

8.   If there is a "market for legislation" does it surprise you that the California legislation was produced? How would this demand be manifested? Do you agree with Judge Noonan that creation of an inventory of "good" environmental words is a form of unconstitutional thought control?

9.   In issuing a regulation requiring the manufacturers of insulation to provide R-value information, the Federal Trade Commission noted:

Since many consumers do not know what R-value means, an advertisement that focuses on R-value is often simply another advertisement to buy insulation. Thus, the R-value information in the ad often does not benefit the advertiser. In fact, an ad that attempts boldly to educate consumers about R-value may inure as much to the benefit of competitors as it does to the advertiser; a competitor with comparable R-value material will be able to exploit the consumer education paid for by the advertiser. This risk, one which no reasonable advertiser wishes to take alone, encourages industry members to focus instead on product features that consumers will understand. 44 Fed. Reg. 50218 (1979).

a. Is production of R-value information thus like production of works of art or new inventions? Does it result in positive externalities that will be generated in less than optimal amounts unless the government either helps manufacturers capture the economic value of the effort, mandates its production by the manufacturers, or produces the information itself?

b. If the government requires manufacturers of insulation to provide the information, will that tend to reduce the quantity of insulation produced and raise its price? Why or why not?

10. Now consider the opposite problem. May the government prohibit the transmission of truthful information? Should protecting consumers from the annoyance of answering the telephone be enough to justify doing so? These are the kinds of issues considered in the next case.

FEDERAL TRADE COMMISSION v. MAINSTREAM MARKETING SERVICES, INC.

United States Court of Appeals, Tenth Circuit, 2003.
345 F.3d 850.

Before SEYMOUR, EBEL, and HENRY, CIRCUIT JUDGES

PER CURIAM.

The Federal Trade Commission (Petitioner) ("FTC") challenges an order of the United States District Court for the District of Colorado permanently enjoining the FTC from implementing provisions in its amended Telemarketing Sales Rule creating a national do-not-call list. The Rule created a federal registry of telephone numbers of consumers who have indicated that they do not wish to receive unsolicited telephone calls from commercial telemarketers, and it prohibits those telemarketers from making sales calls to consumers on the list. The Federal Communications Commission (FCC), in coordination with the FTC, has also ordered the establishment of a national do-not-call list. The only issue to be decided at this time is the FTC's request for a stay of the district court's order pending this Court's decision on the merits.

I. STANDARD FOR GRANTING STAY

The FTC's request for a stay is governed by Federal Rules of Appellate Procedure 8 and 18. To obtain a stay under these rules, the FTC must address the following factors: (1) the likelihood of success on appeal; (2) the threat of irreparable harm if the stay or injunction is not granted; (3) the absence of harm to opposing parties if the stay or injunction is granted; and (4) any risk of harm to the public interest. * * *

II. LIKELIHOOD OF SUCCESS ON THE MERITS

The Supreme Court has identified a 3–step test to analyze First Amendment challenges to restrictions applied to lawful and non-misleading commercial speech. Regulation of such commercial speech passes constitutional muster if (1) the government asserts a substantial interest to be achieved by the restrictions; (2) the restriction directly advances that governmental interest; and (3) the restriction is narrowly tailored to meet that interest. Central Hudson Gas & Elec. Corp. v. Pub. Serv. Comm'n of N.Y., 447 U.S. 557, 566, 100 S.Ct. 2343, 65 L.Ed.2d 341 (1980). Together, the final two factors in the *Central Hudson* analysis require that there be a "fit between the legislature's ends and the means chosen to accomplish those ends." United States v. Edge Broad. Co., 509 U.S. 418, 427–28, 113 S.Ct. 2696, 125 L.Ed.2d 345 (1993).

For purposes of First Amendment analysis, to show a reasonable fit the government must "demonstrate that the harms it recites are real and that its restriction will in fact alleviate them to a material degree." Rubin v. Coors Brewing Co., 514 U.S. 476, 486–87, 115 S.Ct. 1585, 131 L.Ed.2d 532 (1995). However, in response to a First Amendment challenge to a regulation, the government is not limited in the evidence it may use to support the asserted harms; it may demonstrate its justification with anecdotes, history, consensus, and simple common sense. * * * Moreover, while the fit must be reasonable and in proportion to the interest served, it need not be a perfect fit or the best fit. * * * "Within the bounds of the general protection provided by the Constitution to commercial speech, we allow room for legislative judgments." *Edge Broad. Co.*, 509 U.S. at 434, 113 S.Ct. 2696. We do not require "that the Government make progress on every front before it can make progress on any front." *Id.*

A. Substantial Governmental Interest

The FTC's do-not-call list includes commercial telemarketers but specifically excludes calls from charitable organizations. The FTC has asserted that this distinction between commercial and non-commercial speech is justified by (1) a greater risk of abusive practices associated with commercial calls, and (2) commercial solicitation's greater impact on consumer privacy, based both on the greater number of commercial calls and upon the less welcome nature of commercial calls. The district court found, and Mainstream Marketing Services does not dispute, that these asserted interests in preventing abusive practices and protecting residential privacy are substantial under the first prong of *Central Hudson*.

The Supreme Court has held that there is undoubtedly a substantial governmental interest in the prevention of abusive and coercive sales practices. * * * The prevention of intrusions upon privacy in the home is another paradigmatic substantial governmental interest. In Rowan v. United States Post Office Department, the Supreme Court held that protecting individual privacy is an important governmental interest, especially in the context of the home. * * * The Court recognized "the right of a householder to bar, by order or notice, solicitors, hawkers, and peddlers from his property." * * * "The ancient concept that 'a man's home is his castle' into which 'not even the king may enter' has lost none of its vitality." In the context of telephone solicitations, this privacy interest is not limited to the ringing of the phone; rather, how invasive a phone call may be is also influenced by the manner and substance of the call.

Therefore, the FTC's justifications of preventing abusive and coercive sales practices and protecting privacy are substantial governmental interests. We turn now to analyzing whether the FTC has established a likelihood of success on its contention that the do-not-call list bears a reasonable fit with these interests.

B. Reasonable Fit

1. Relevant Factors in Analyzing Reasonable Fit

Although a regulation may draw a line between commercial and non-commercial speech, that distinction must bear a relationship to the legitimate interests the government seeks to achieve. * * * For example, a distinction between commercial and non-commercial speech could be justified by reference to the differing impact those categories of speech have on esthetics, safety, privacy, or the like. In contrast, the distinction may not be justified on a perceived "low value" of commercial speech.

In [Cincinnati v.] Discovery Network, the Supreme Court struck down a city ordinance banning freestanding commercial newsracks on grounds that the restriction was not narrowly tailored. 507 U.S. at 412, 430, 113 S.Ct. 1505. The Court recognized that the city had substantial interests in esthetics and safety that were impaired by freestanding newsracks, but concluded that there was no reasonable fit between those goals and the city's policy of banning only commercial newsracks while leaving similar non-commercial newsracks undisturbed. Although the Court recognized that there may be situations where "differential treatment of commercial and noncommercial newsracks" could be justified by a reasonable fit with the government's interest in esthetics and safety, it held that the government had failed to make any such showing in that case. Id. * * *

Whether a commercial solicitation restriction meets the "reasonable fit" test depends in part on the existence of private choice on the part of homeowners. In Martin v. City of Struthers, the Supreme Court struck down a city ordinance banning door-to-door canvassing because it took the right to decide whether to receive visitors away from the individual's own private choice. 319 U.S. 141, 148–49 (1943). While recognizing the government's interest in protecting privacy, the Court held that the ordinance swept too broadly because the dangers of door-to-door canvassing easily could have been controlled by giving the householder the right to decide whether to receive visitors.

Rowan [v. U.S. Post Office Dept., 397 U.S. 728 (1970)] demonstrates that the element of private choice in an opt-in feature is relevant for purposes of analyzing "reasonable fit." In *Rowan,* the Court upheld an opt-in do-not-mail list system in which a homeowner could require that a commercial advertiser remove his or her name from its mailing list if the homeowner determined in his or her "sole discretion" that the material received was erotically arousing or provocative. In finding the privacy regulation reasonable, the Court emphasized the element of private choice, stating that the homeowner was the "exclusive and final judge of what will cross his threshold."

* * *

In sum, a regulation drawing a line between commercial and non-commercial speech must have a reasonable fit with substantial governmental interests. The "reasonable fit" analysis will at least partially depend upon whether the initiation of the solicitation restriction is at the hands of private citizens or the government. Additionally, we will consider the extent to which the regulatory scheme will materially advance the governmental interest and the disparity in treatment between commercial and non-commercial speech.

   2.   *The FTC's Record Evidence Supporting a Reasonable Fit Between the National Do–Not–Call List and its Asserted Justifications*

In light of the above legal standards, we must review the record to determine the FTC's asserted rationales for applying its national do-not-call restrictions only to commercial sales calls, and the evidence to support those rationales. Here, the FTC attempts to justify this distinction by showing that commercial telemarketing is more abusive and coercive than charitable telemarketing and constitutes a greater intrusion upon consumer privacy. We are mindful that these rationales overlap to some extent.

* * *

   a.   *Telephone Consumer Protection Act (TCPA)*

In the TCPA, Congress found that unrestricted telemarketing can be an intrusive invasion of privacy and that many consumers are outraged by the proliferation of intrusive calls to their homes from telemarketers. Therefore, Congress in the TCPA authorized the FCC to establish a national database of residential subscribers who object to receiving "telephone solicitations." A "telephone solicitation" was defined as a "telephone call or message for the purpose of encouraging the purchase or rental of, or investment in, property, goods, or services," excluding, inter alia, calls from a tax exempt nonprofit organization. This definition excluded charitable telemarketers.

According to the legislative history accompanying the TCPA, "the record suggests that most unwanted telephone solicitations are commercial in nature. Complaint statistics show that unwanted commercial calls are a far bigger problem than unsolicited calls from political or charitable organizations." * * * The House Report cited statistical data from several states reporting that consumer complaints were directed mostly at commercial sales calls. Moreover, the Committee found that non-commercial calls were less intrusive to consumers because they are more expected and because there is a lower volume of non-commercial calls. It concluded that "the two main sources of consumer problems—high volume of solicitations and unexpected solicitations—are not present in solicitations by nonprofit organizations. . . . It is on this basis that the Committee believes that the scope of the regulation is a workable 'commercial speech' distinction consistent with Supreme Court precedent." This distinction between commercial and non-commercial telemarketing, justified in the TCPA, persists in all subsequent legislation and administrative rules regulating telemarketing calls.

   b. Telemarketing and Consumer Fraud and Abuse Prevention Act (TCFPA)

   In the TCFPA, Congress directed the FTC to prescribe rules prohibiting deceptive and abusive telemarketing acts and practices, including calls that a reasonable consumer would consider coercive or abusive of such consumer's right to privacy. Congress found that consumers lose an estimated $40 billion each year in "telemarketing" fraud and are victimized by other forms of "telemarketing" deception and abuse. Significantly, Congress in the TCFPA defined the term "telemarketing" as calls "conducted to induce purchases of goods or services,"—e.g., commercial calls. This is the Act under which the FTC enacted the national do-not-call regulations challenged in this case.

   c. 1995 Telemarketing Sales Rule

   In 1995, acting pursuant to the TCFPA, the FTC established a company-specific do-not-call provision, which prohibited telemarketers from making sales calls to persons who had previously stated their desire not to receive such calls from that solicitor. * * * This rule did not apply to an entity such as a charitable organization that was not "organized to carry on business for its own profit or that of its members." Accordingly, the distinction between commercial and non-commercial speech, first enacted in the TCPA, was present in the initial FTC Telemarketing Sales Rule. In justifying this rule, the FTC relied in part on the TCFPA and its legislative history, which emphasized that sellers of goods and services regularly subjected consumers to deception and abuse infringing upon their privacy rights. Moreover, the FTC later explained that when enacting this original Telemarketing Sales Rule it also considered the TCPA (which as noted above explicitly drew a distinction between commercial and non-commercial solicitations in its legislative history) and related FCC action.

   d. 2003 Amended Telemarketing Sales Rule

   In its amended Rule (the subject of the instant litigation), the FTC established a national do-not-call registry that allowed individuals to block all commercial sales calls, with certain exceptions. * * * Most significantly to this case, the FTC preserved the distinction between commercial and non-commercial calls by limiting "coverage of the national registry to telemarketing calls made by or on behalf of sellers of goods or services, thus exempting telemarketing calls on behalf of charitable organizations." The "sellers of goods or services" limit relates back to Congress' findings in the TCFPA, which had documented a history of abuses specifically committed by telemarketers selling goods or services.

Importantly, the amended FTC Telemarketing Sales Rule did subject charitable organizations to the company-specific do-not-call provision. In this amended Rule, the FTC retained the basic distinction between commercial and non-commercial calls already present in the earlier version of the Telemarketing Sales Rule, although the amended rule resulted in stricter requirements for both categories of calls.

The FTC found that the original Rule's company-specific do-not-call list was inadequate to prevent the type of abusive commercial sales calls it was intended to prohibit. The FTC concluded that "[T]he registry is . . . designed to cure the inadequacies as a privacy protection measure that became apparent in the company-specific 'do-not-call' provisions included in the original Rule." For example, the FTC referred to complaints that commercial telemarketers ignored consumers' repeated requests to be placed on company-specific do-not-call lists. It concluded that the national do-not-call list will also prevent fraud or abuse in some cases by protecting vulnerable consumers from exploitative telemarketers.

Furthermore, the FTC specifically found that "fundamental differences between commercial solicitations and charitable solicitations may confer upon the company-specific 'do-not-call' requirements a greater measure of success with respect to preventing a pattern of abusive calls from a fundraiser to a consumer than it was able to produce in the context of commercial fundraising." Specifically, it reasoned that in an advocacy call, such as a charitable solicitation, a significant purpose of the call is to "sell" a cause, not simply to receive a donation. Therefore, the FTC found that it would be self-defeating for a non-commercial caller to engage in abusive telemarketing practices that invade personal privacy because such conduct could alienate the recipient against the cause the caller was attempting to promote. "When a pure commercial transaction is at stake, callers have an incentive to engage in all the things that telemarketers are hated for. But non-commercial speech is a different matter." In enacting these provisions, the FTC cited both the TCFPA and the TCPA, noting that "Congress knowingly put the FTC on the same path that the FCC had trod."

e. *2003 FCC Rules and Regulations*

Finally, in July 2003, the FCC enacted regulations to "establish, with the Federal Trade Commission (FTC) a national do-not-call registry." Similar to the FTC's do-not-call regulations, the FCC list was not designed to apply to charitable callers. Citing the legislative history to the TCPA (which, as noted before, contained a congressional justification for distinguishing between commercial and non-commercial calls), the FCC reaffirmed that most unwanted telephone solicitations are commercial in nature and that charitable calls are less intrusive to consumers. The FCC rule also provided for a company-specific do-not-call system for consumers who elect not to register for the national list.

f. Summary

Congress expressly made factual findings in the TCFPA that telemarketing calls "conducted to induce purchases of goods or services" have subjected consumers to substantial fraud, deception, and abuse. Consequently, in enacting a national do-not-call registry, the FTC "decided to limit coverage of the national registry to telemarketing calls made by or on behalf of sellers of goods or services." * * * Furthermore, the FTC's revised Telemarketing Sales Rule states that the agency relied on TCPA and FCC authority when it initially endorsed the distinction between commercial and non-commercial calls. *Id.* at 4591. The legislative history accompanying the TCPA, citing complaint statistics, found that commercial telemarketing intrudes upon personal privacy more than non-commercial telemarketing.

3. The FTC's Likelihood of Success

In light of this record, it appears that the FTC is likely to succeed on its argument that the distinction in the Amended Telemarketing Sales Rule between commercial and non-commercial phone solicitation passes muster under *Central Hudson*'s reasonable fit analysis. The line between these two types of speech is not drawn solely on the basis of the lesser degree of scrutiny applied to commercial speech. Rather, we examine the constitutionality of the distinction under the *Central Hudson* test with reference to the substantial governmental interest in preventing the greater risk of privacy invasion and abusive sales practices correlated with commercial telemarketing.

We find it relevant that the national do-not-call list is of an opt-in nature, which provides an element of private choice and thus weighs in favor of a reasonable fit. The list is not invoked until the homeowner makes a private decision to invoke it. * * * We also find it relevant that the FTC has not exempted non-commercial speech totally from all regulation, as consumers are also given some mechanism to block non-commercial solicitations by means of company-specific objections to solicitations by charitable organizations. And it is permissible for the FTC to act now to fix a problem upon which it has record support (the inadequacy of company-specific do-not-call lists to prevent invasion of privacy and abusive practices in the context of commercial calls) without waiting until it can develop experience on whether or not a company-specific do-not-call list will be effective to prevent such abuses in the context of non-commercial telemarketing. * * *

In the context of analyzing whether to stay the district court's injunction, we conclude there is a substantial likelihood that the FTC will be able to show a reasonable fit between the substantial governmental interests it asserted and the national do-not-call list or, in other words, that the list directly advances the government's substantial interests and is narrowly tailored. * * *

III. CONCLUSION

In light of our conclusions as to the three harm factors addressed above, we will stay the district court's order only if the FTC shows substantial likelihood of success on the merits. After reviewing the record and the parties' submissions, we are satisfied the FTC has met its burden.

Notes and Questions

1.   Things moved quickly in the latter half of 2003 with respect to the do-not-call rules. On September 23, 2003, a federal court held that the FTC did not have authority to create a do-not-call list. U.S. Security v. Federal Trade Commission, 282 F.Supp.2d 1285 (W.D. Okla. 2003). Two days later, by an overwhelming vote, Congress granted the FTC specific authority to create the list. On that day, another federal court held that the do-not-call list violated the First amendment. The case excerpted here is an appeal from that decision.

2.   Is this a case in which there is a clash in interests between privacy and information? Or is it a clash between privacy and expression? If it is the former, isn't the solution easy? The right to privacy and the right to more information are both supposed to be beneficial to the same parties. Why not allow them to choose to forgo information in the interest of protecting their privacy? On the other hand, if the clash is between privacy and expression the analysis is more difficult because the interests are favored by different people.

3.   Suppose, however, that if enough people put their names on a do-not-call list it means that it becomes uneconomical for some telemarketers to operate. This may sound fine but some people may like receiving the calls of telemarketers. Should people who prefer not to receive information have the "right" to interfere with the ability of others to get it?

4.   The do-not-call lists apply to commercial solicitations. Are charitable solicitations any less disruptive? How can they be distinguished in order to justify different treatment?

5.   Does it make sense to apply an economic analysis to the rule in question here. For example, supposedly a person who adds his or her name to a do-not-call list understands that it may mean not receiving important information. The value of that information, however, is less than the value of privacy. The "price" of privacy is the value of the forgone information. On the other hand, the price of screening for valuable information by receiving calls is less privacy. If you look at it this way, isn't the do-not-call list simply a type of market through which preferences are expressed?

6.   In 1991 the Consumer Telephone Protection Act became law. The statute prohibits the unsolicited sending of faxes for commercial purposes. Isn't a fax less intrusive than an unwanted telephone call? The recipient

could decide to ignore them all or look through them once a week yet the recipient must pay for the paper and toner used to print the unwanted message. Does this mean that the Act is more likely to be unconstitutional than the do-not-call provisions discussed in the case? The Act allows for a private right of action against those sending unwanted faxes. See Paul J. Batista, The Perils of Telemarketing Under the Consumer Telephone Protection Act: Sending Unwanted Faxes Costs Dallas Cowboys $1.73 Million, Leave Dallas Mavericks Under Full Court Pressure, 25 COM/ENT 232 (2003).

D. ALLOCATION OF INHERENTLY SCARCE RESOURCES

The entire discipline of economics is devoted to the allocation of scarce resources. Typically, this process is left to markets. Indeed, allocation of scarce resources is precisely what markets are for. On the other hand, the government sometimes steps in when the resource is said to be "inherently scarce."

Just because a resource is "inherently scarce" does not mean that a regulatory structure is necessary. Take the traditional example of broadcast frequencies. Since there is limited space on the broadcast spectrum and the use of one frequency can interfere with use of others, it was thought necessary to assign broadcast rights to specific entities or individuals. This assignment could have been done in any method from a raffle to an auction. As long as broadcast property rights were clear, systems of private tort and contract law could have been adapted to solve the "inherently scarce resource" problem. In fact, as we saw in the preceding Section of this Chapter, perhaps the single most important thing a government can do in terms of assuring the wise use of resources is to make sure that property rights are clearly delineated.

If one views the sum a potential user would bid as a measure of the value to her of the productive use she can make of the resources, then it follows that an auction technique would tend to allocate the scarce resources to the most valuable or productive uses. The requirement of bidding would also tend to reduce the monopoly profit that the grantee of the scarce resource could otherwise earn.

In fact, everything from human organs for life-saving transplants to available seats in law school could be allocated through the market system. In the case of a kidney for transplant purposes, one could view the amount bidders are willing to pay as investments. These investments, in theory, will be tied to the money they are likely to earn. Thus, the highest bidders arguably would be the ones whose services are the most valued by society.[32]

---

32. In examining instances in which the market system is not used as an allocative tool, it is interesting to note how technological change affects the "inherently scarce resource" issue. As noted above broadcast frequencies were traditionally cited as representing an inherently scarce resource; the number of frequencies was limited in an

But there are a number of reasons why this sort of reasoning may make one uncomfortable. For example, the bidder for the life-saving organ may be a spoiled college student who has a rich relative and who will spend his or her life smoking marijuana and listening to the Red Hot Chili Peppers. The low bidder may be someone with great artistic talent, but whose creations will not be recognized as great until three generations in the future. The market is inherently unable to take all factors into consideration.

Indeed, sometimes, non-market allocations reflect a belief that not all valuable uses of a resource can be transmitted through the market. Suppose we were to conclude, for example, that the ultimate social benefit to be derived from a future attorney's practice is not correlated all that closely with the price a law school applicant could pay for admission. Might that explain why most law schools today allocate rights to admission based on factors other than price.[33]

Do you see any problems with such extra-market systems of allocating rights? Is the "social benefit" really measured by society? Is it instead determined in a political process that has its own built-in biases as the Public Choice theorists suggest? Should the Constitution limit at least some of the factors that might be considered in such allocations? These are some of the issues we consider in this Section.

1. ALLOCATION OF ACCESS TO CABLE TELEVISION SYSTEMS

As suggested above, allocation of rights to pieces of the broadcast spectrum has been one of the most important traditional examples of the "scarce resources" rationale. With the advent of cable and its almost unlimited number of available channels, the problem might have been thought to go away. However, the following case suggests that is not entirely so.

TURNER BROADCASTING SYSTEM, INC. v. FEDERAL COMMUNICATIONS COMMISSION

Supreme Court of the United States, 1997.
520 U.S. 180, 117 S.Ct. 1174, 137 L.Ed.2d 369.

JUSTICE KENNEDY delivered the opinion of the Court, except as to a portion of Part II–A–1.

absolute sense and an overuse of the spectrum could actually render the resource useless. Now, although nothing has happened to the actual spectrum, the opportunities to communicate to others through other technologies have largely eliminated the "inherently scarce resource" problem. On the other hand we know that resources like air, water, the ozone layer and rain forests, which were taken for granted— even referred to in economics texts as "free goods"—are the inherently scarce resources for this generation.

33. One more issue may be noted. Suppose certain resources are allocated politically, but then are freely transferrable to anyone by a willing seller. One might ask, why not just sell it to the highest bidder in the first place. One of the important consequences of assigning the resource to one party who then sells it to the highest bidder is distributive. Although the highest bidder ends up with the particular resource, another party is also made wealthier.

Sections 4 and 5 of the Cable Television Consumer Protection and Competition Act of 1992 require cable television systems to dedicate some of their channels to local broadcast television stations. Earlier in this case, we held the so-called "must-carry" provisions to be content-neutral restrictions on speech, subject to intermediate First Amendment scrutiny under United States v. O'Brien, 391 U.S. 367, 377, 88 S.Ct. 1673, 1679, 20 L.Ed.2d 672 (1968). A plurality of the Court considered the record as then developed insufficient to determine whether the provisions were narrowly tailored to further important governmental interests, and we remanded the case to the District Court for the District of Columbia for additional factfinding.

On appeal from the District Court's grant of summary judgment for appellees, the case now presents the two questions left open during the first appeal: First, whether the record as it now stands supports Congress' predictive judgment that the must-carry provisions further important governmental interests; and second, whether the provisions do not burden substantially more speech than necessary to further those interests. We answer both questions in the affirmative, and conclude the must-carry provisions are consistent with the First Amendment.

* * *

II

We begin where the plurality ended in *Turner* [Broadcasting System, Inc. v. Federal Communications Commission, 512 U.S. 622 (1994)] applying the standards for intermediate scrutiny enunciated in *O'Brien*. A content-neutral regulation will be sustained under the First Amendment if it advances important governmental interests unrelated to the suppression of free speech and does not burden substantially more speech than necessary to further those interests. * * * As noted in *Turner,* must-carry was designed to serve "three interrelated interests: (1) preserving the benefits of free, over-the-air local broadcast television, (2) promoting the widespread dissemination of information from a multiplicity of sources, and (3) promoting fair competition in the market for television programming." We decided then, and now reaffirm, that each of those is an important governmental interest. We have been most explicit in holding that " 'protecting noncable households from loss of regular television broadcasting service due to competition from cable systems' is an important federal interest." Forty percent of American households continue to rely on over-the-air signals for television programming. Despite the growing importance of cable television and alternative technologies, " 'broadcasting is demonstrably a principal source of information and entertainment for a great part of the Nation's population.' " * * * We have identified a corresponding "governmental purpose of the highest order" in ensuring public access to "a multiplicity of information sources," * * *. And it is undisputed the Government has an interest in "eliminating restraints on fair competition . . ., even when the individuals or entities subject to particular regulations are engaged in expressive activity protected by the First Amendment." * * *

On remand, and again before this Court, both sides have advanced new interpretations of these interests in an attempt to recast them in forms "more readily proven." * * * The Government downplays the importance of showing a risk to the broadcast industry as a whole and suggests the loss of even a few broadcast stations "is a matter of critical importance." * * * Taking the opposite approach, appellants argue Congress' interest in preserving broadcasting is not implicated unless it is shown the industry as a whole would fail without must-carry, * * * and suggest Congress' legitimate interest in "assuring that the public has access to a multiplicity of information sources," * * * extends only as far as preserving "a minimum amount of television broadcast service," * * *.

These alternative formulations are inconsistent with Congress' stated interests in enacting must-carry. The congressional findings do not reflect concern that, absent must-carry, "a few voices," would be lost from the television marketplace. In explicit factual findings, Congress expressed clear concern that the "marked shift in market share from broadcast television to cable television services," Cable Act § 2(a)(13), note following 47 U.S.C. § 521, resulting from increasing market penetration by cable services, as well as the expanding horizontal concentration and vertical integration of cable operators, combined to give cable systems the incentive and ability to delete, reposition, or decline carriage to local broadcasters in an attempt to favor affiliated cable programmers. §§ 2a(2)–(5), (15). Congress predicted that "absent the reimposition of [must-carry], additional local broadcast signals will be deleted, repositioned, or not carried," § 2(a)(15); see also § 2(a)(8)(D), with the end result that "the economic viability of free local broadcast television and its ability to originate quality local programming will be seriously jeopardized," § 2(a)(16).

At the same time, Congress was under no illusion that there would be a complete disappearance of broadcast television nationwide in the absence of must-carry. Congress recognized broadcast programming (and network programming in particular) "remains the most popular programming on cable systems," § 2(a)(19). Indeed, reflecting the popularity and strength of some broadcasters, Congress included in the Cable Act a provision permitting broadcasters to charge cable systems for carriage of the broadcasters' signals. * * * Congress was concerned not that broadcast television would disappear in its entirety without must-carry, but that without it, "significant numbers of broadcast stations will be refused carriage on cable systems," and those "broadcast stations denied carriage will either deteriorate to a substantial degree or fail altogether." * * *

Nor do the congressional findings support appellants' suggestion that legitimate legislative goals would be satisfied by the preservation of a rump broadcasting industry providing a minimum of broadcast service to Americans without cable. We have noted that " 'it has long been a basic tenet of national communications policy that "the widest possible dissemination of information from diverse and antagonistic sources is essential to the welfare of the public." ' " *Turner,* 512 U.S., at 663–664, 114 S.Ct., at 2470 * * *. Consistent with this objective, the Cable Act's findings reflect a concern that congressional action was necessary to prevent "a reduction in the number of media voices available to consumers." § 2(a)(4). Congress identified a specific interest in "ensuring [the] continuation" of "the local origination of [broadcast] programming," § 2(a)(10), an interest consistent with its larger purpose of promoting multiple types of media, § 2(a)(6), and found must-carry necessary "to serve the goals" of the original Communications Act of 1934 of "providing a fair, efficient, and equitable distribution of broadcast services," § 2(a)(9). In short, Congress enacted must-carry to "preserve the existing structure of the Nation's broadcast television medium while permitting the concomitant expansion and development of cable television." 512 U.S., at 652, 114 S.Ct., at 2464.

Although Congress set no definite number of broadcast stations sufficient for these purposes, the Cable Act's requirement that all cable operators with more than 12 channels set aside one-third of their channel capacity for local broadcasters, § 4, 47 U.S.C. § 534(b)(1)(B), refutes the notion that Congress contemplated preserving only a bare minimum of stations. Congress' evident interest in "preserv[ing] the existing structure," * * * of the broadcast industry discloses a purpose to prevent any significant reduction in the multiplicity of broadcast programming sources available to noncable households. To the extent the appellants question the substantiality of the Government's interest in preserving something more than a minimum number of stations in each community, their position is meritless. It is for Congress to decide how much local broadcast television should be preserved for noncable households, and the validity of its determination " 'does not turn on a judge's agreement with the responsible decisionmaker concerning' ... the degree to which [the Government's] interests should be promoted." * * *

The dissent proceeds on the assumption that must-carry is designed solely to be (and can only be justified as) a measure to protect broadcasters from cable operators' anticompetitive behavior. * * * Federal policy, however, has long favored preserving a multiplicity of broadcast outlets regardless of whether the conduct that threatens it is motivated by anticompetitive animus or rises to the level of an antitrust violation. * * * Broadcast television is an important source of information to many Americans. Though it is but one of many means for communication, by tradition and use for decades now it has been an essential part of the national discourse on subjects across the whole broad spectrum of speech, thought, and expression. * * * Congress has an independent interest in preserving a multiplicity of broadcasters to ensure that all households have access to information and entertainment on an equal footing with those who subscribe to cable.

A

* * *

1

We have no difficulty in finding a substantial basis to support Congress' conclusion that a real threat justified enactment of the must-carry provisions. We examine first the evidence before Congress and then the further evidence presented to the District Court on remand to supplement the congressional determination.

As to the evidence before Congress, there was specific support for its conclusion that cable operators had considerable and growing market power over local video programming markets. Cable served at least 60 percent of American households in 1992, see Cable Act § 2(a)(3), and evidence indicated cable market penetration was projected to grow beyond 70 percent. * * * As Congress noted, § 2(a)(2), cable operators possess a local monopoly over cable households. Only one percent of communities are served by more than one cable system. * * * Even in communities with two or more cable systems, in the typical case each system has a local monopoly over its subscribers. * * *

Evidence indicated the structure of the cable industry would give cable operators increasing ability and incentive to drop local broadcast stations from their systems, or reposition them to a less-viewed channel. Horizontal concentration was increasing as a small number of multiple system operators (MSO's) acquired large numbers of cable systems nationwide. § 2(a)(4). The trend was accelerating, giving the MSO's increasing market power. In 1985, the 10 largest MSO's controlled cable systems serving slightly less than 42 percent of all cable subscribers; by 1989, the figure was nearly 54 percent. * * *

Vertical integration in the industry also was increasing. As Congress was aware, many MSO's owned or had affiliation agreements with cable programmers. § 2(a)(5); Senate Report, at 24–29. Evidence indicated that before 1984 cable operators had equity interests in 38 percent of cable programming networks. In the late 1980's, 64 percent of new cable programmers were held in vertical ownership. * * * Congress concluded that "vertical integration gives cable operators the incentive and ability to favor their affiliated programming services," * * *. Extensive testimony indicated that cable operators would have an incentive to drop local broadcasters and to favor affiliated programmers. * * *

        * * *

In addition, evidence before Congress, supplemented on remand, indicated that cable systems would have incentives to drop local broadcasters in favor of other programmers less likely to compete with them for audience and advertisers. Independent local broadcasters tend to be the closest substitutes for cable programs, because their programming tends to be similar * * * and because both primarily target the same type of advertiser: those interested in cheaper (and more frequent) ad spots than are typically available on network affiliates. * * * The ability of broadcast stations to compete for advertising is greatly increased by cable carriage, which increases viewership substantially. * * * With expanded viewership, broadcast presents a more competitive medium for television advertising. Empirical studies indicate that cable-carried broadcasters so enhance competition for advertising that even modest increases in the numbers of broadcast stations carried on cable are correlated with significant decreases in advertising revenue to cable systems. * * *

Cable systems also have more systemic reasons for seeking to disadvantage broadcast stations: Simply stated, cable has little interest in assisting, through carriage, a competing medium of communication. As one cable-industry executive put it, " 'our job is to promote cable television, not broadcast television.' " Hearing on Competitive Issues, at 658 (quoting Multichannel News, Channel Realignments: United Cable Eyes Plan to Bump Network Affils to Upper Channels, Nov. 3, 1986, p. 39); * * *. Congress could therefore reasonably conclude that cable systems would drop broadcasters in favor of programmers—even unaffiliated ones—less likely to compete with them for audience and advertisers. The cap on carriage of affiliates included in the Cable Act, 47 U.S.C. § 533(f)(1)(B); 47 CFR § 76.504 (1995), and relied on by the dissent, is of limited utility in protecting broadcasters.

* * *

It was more than a theoretical possibility in 1992 that cable operators would take actions adverse to local broadcasters; indeed, significant numbers of broadcasters had already been dropped. The record before Congress contained extensive anecdotal evidence about scores of adverse carriage decisions against broadcast stations. * * * Even assuming that every station dropped or denied coverage responded to the survey, it would indicate that nearly a quarter (21 percent) of the approximately 1,356 broadcast stations then in existence had been denied carriage. The same study reported 869 of 4,303 reporting cable systems had denied carriage to 704 broadcast stations in 1,820 instances and 279 of those stations had qualified for carriage under the prior must-carry rules. A contemporaneous study of public television stations indicated that in the vast majority of cases, dropped stations were not restored to the cable service.

* * *

2

The harm Congress feared was that stations dropped or denied carriage would be at a "serious risk of financial difficulty," * * * and would "deteriorate to a substantial degree or fail altogether," * * * Congress had before it substantial evidence to support its conclusion. Congress was advised the viability of a broadcast station depends to a material extent on its ability to secure cable carriage. * * * One broadcast industry executive explained it this way:

"Simply put, a television station's audience size directly translates into revenue—large audiences attract larger revenues, through the sale of advertising time. If a station is not carried on cable, and thereby loses a substantial portion of its audience, it will lose revenue. With less revenue, the station can not serve its community as well. The station will have less money to invest in equipment and programming. The attractiveness of its programming will lessen, as will its audience. Revenues will continue to decline, and the cycle will repeat." Hearing on Competitive Issues, at 526–527 (statement of Gary Chapman) (App.1600).

* * * Empirical research in the record before Congress confirmed the " 'direct correlation [between] size in audience and station [advertising] revenues,' " and that viewership was in turn heavily dependent on cable carriage.

Considerable evidence, consisting of statements compiled from dozens of broadcasters who testified before Congress and the FCC, confirmed that broadcast stations had fallen into bankruptcy. * * * The record also reflected substantial evidence that stations without cable carriage encountered severe difficulties obtaining financing for operations, reflecting the financial markets' judgment that the prospects are poor for broadcasters unable to secure carriage. * * * Evidence before Congress suggested the potential adverse impact of losing carriage was increasing as the growth of clustering gave MSO's centralized control over more local markets. Congress thus had ample basis to conclude that attaining cable carriage would be of increasing importance to ensuring a station's viability. We hold Congress could conclude from the substantial body of evidence before it that "absent legislative action, the free local off-air broadcast system is endangered."

The evidence assembled on remand confirms the reasonableness of the congressional judgment. Documents produced on remand reflect that internal cable industry studies:

"clearly establis[h] the importance of cable television to broadcast television stations. Because viewership equates to ratings and in turn ratings equate to revenues, it is unlikely that broadcast stations could afford to be off the cable system's line-up for any extended period of time." Memorandum from F. Lopez to T. Baxter re: Adlink's Presentations on Retransmission Consent, dated June 14, 1993.

Another study prepared by a large MSO in 1993 concluded that "[w]ith cable penetration now exceeding 70% in many markets, the ability of a broadcast television station to easily reach its audience through cable television is crucial." The study acknowledged that even in a market with significantly below-average cable penetration, "[t]he loss of cable carriage could cause a significant decrease in a station's ratings and a resulting loss in advertising revenues." For an average market "the impact would be even greater." The study determined that for a popular station in a major television market, even modest reductions in carriage could result in sizeable reductions in revenue. A 5 percent reduction in cable viewers, for example, would result in a $1.48 million reduction in gross revenue for the station.

* * *

We think it apparent must-carry serves the Government's interests "in a direct and effective way." Ward [v. Rock Against Racism], 491 U.S., at 800, 109 S.Ct., at 2759. Must-carry ensures that a number of local broadcasters retain cable carriage, with the concomitant audience access and advertising revenues needed to support a multiplicity of stations. Appellants contend that even were this so, must-carry is broader than necessary to accomplish its goals. We turn to this question.

B

The second portion of the *O'Brien* inquiry concerns the fit between the asserted interests and the means chosen to advance them. Content-neutral regulations do not pose the same "inherent dangers to free expression," * * * that content-based regulations do, and thus are subject to a less rigorous analysis, which affords the Government latitude in designing a regulatory solution. * * * Under intermediate scrutiny, the Government may employ the means of its choosing " 'so long as the . . . regulation promotes a substantial governmental interest that would be achieved less effectively absent the regulation,' " and does not " 'burden substantially more speech than is necessary to further' " that interest. *Turner,* 512 U.S., at 662, 114 S.Ct., at 2469.

The must-carry provisions have the potential to interfere with protected speech in two ways. First, the provisions restrain cable operators' editorial discretion in creating programming packages by "reduc[ing] the number of channels over which [they] exercise unfettered control." *Turner,* 512 U.S., at 637, 114 S.Ct., at 2456. Second, the rules "render it more difficult for cable programmers to compete for carriage on the limited channels remaining."

Appellants say the burden of must-carry is great, but the evidence adduced on remand indicates the actual effects are modest. Significant evidence indicates the vast majority of cable operators have not been affected in a significant manner by must-carry. Cable operators have been able to satisfy their must-carry obligations 87 percent of the time using previously unused channel capacity, * * * 94.5 percent of the 11,628 cable systems nationwide have not had to drop any programming in order to fulfill their must-carry obligations; the remaining 5.5 percent have had to drop an average of only 1.22 services from their programming, and cable operators nationwide carry 99.8 percent of the programming they carried before enactment of must-carry.

We do not understand appellants to dispute in any fundamental way the accuracy of those figures, only their significance. * * * They note national averages fail to account for greater crowding on certain (especially urban) cable systems,* * *. Appellants argue that the rate of growth in cable programming outstrips cable operators' creation of new channel space, that the rate of cable growth is lower than claimed and that must-carry infringes First Amendment rights now irrespective of future growth * * *. Finally, they say that regardless of the percentage of channels occupied, must-carry still represents "thousands of real and individual infringements of speech."

While the parties' evidence is susceptible of varying interpretations, a few definite conclusions can be drawn about the burdens of must-carry. It is undisputed that broadcast stations gained carriage on 5,880 channels as a result of must-carry. While broadcast stations occupy another 30,006 cable channels nationwide, this carriage does not represent a significant First Amendment harm to either system operators or cable programmers because those stations were carried voluntarily before 1992, and even appellants represent that the vast majority of those channels would continue to be carried in the absence of any legal obligation to do so. * * * The 5,880 channels occupied by added broadcasters represent the actual burden of the regulatory scheme. Appellants concede most of those stations would be dropped in the absence of must-carry, so the figure approximates the benefits of must-carry as well.

Because the burden imposed by must-carry is congruent to the benefits it affords, we conclude must-carry is narrowly tailored to preserve a multiplicity of broadcast stations for the 40 percent of American households without cable. * * * Congress took steps to confine the breadth and burden of the regulatory scheme. For example, the more popular stations (which appellants concede would be carried anyway) will likely opt to be paid for cable carriage under the "retransmission consent" provision of the Cable Act; those stations will nonetheless be counted toward systems' must-carry obligations. Congress exempted systems of 12 or fewer channels, and limited the must-carry obligation of larger systems to one-third of capacity, 47 U.S.C. § 534(b)(1); see also §§ 535(b)(2)–(3); allowed cable operators discretion in choosing which competing and qualified signals would be carried, § 534(b)(2); and permitted operators to carry public stations on unused public, educational, and governmental channels in some circumstances, § 535(d).

* * *

The judgment of the District Court is affirmed.

It is so ordered.

* * *

Justice Breyer, concurring in part.

I join the opinion of the Court except insofar as Part II–A–1 relies on an anticompetitive rationale. I agree with the majority that the statute must be "sustained under the First Amendment if it advances important governmental interests unrelated to the suppression of free speech and does not burden substantially more speech than necessary to further those interests." * * * I also agree that the statute satisfies this standard. My conclusion rests, however, not upon the principal opinion's analysis of the statute's efforts to "promot[e] fair competition," but rather upon its discussion of the statute's other objectives, namely, " '(1) preserving the benefits of free, over-the-air local broadcast television,' " and " '(2) promoting the widespread dissemination of information from a multiplicity of sources'."

* * *

"The statute's basic noneconomic purpose is to prevent too precipitous a decline in the quality and quantity of programming choice for an ever-shrinking non-cable-subscribing segment of the public. This purpose reflects what "has long been a basic tenet of national communications policy," namely that "the widest possible dissemination of information from diverse and antagonistic sources is essential to the welfare of the public." *Turner.* That policy, in turn, seeks to facilitate the public discussion and informed deliberation, which, as Justice Brandeis pointed out many years ago, democratic government presupposes and the First Amendment seeks to achieve. Whitney v. California, 274 U.S. 357, 375–376, 71 L.Ed. 1095, 47 S.Ct. 641 (1927) (Brandeis, J., concurring). * * *

With important First Amendment interests on both sides of the equation, the key question becomes one of proper fit. That question, in my view, requires a reviewing court to determine both whether there are significantly less restrictive ways to achieve Congress' over-the-air programming objectives, and also to decide whether the statute, in its effort to achieve those objectives, strikes a reasonable balance between potentially speech-restricting and speech-enhancing consequences. The majority's opinion analyzes and evaluates those consequences, and I agree with its conclusions in respect to both of these matters.

In particular, I note (and agree) that a cable system, physically dependent upon the availability of space along city streets, at present (perhaps less in the future) typically faces little competition, that it therefore constitutes a kind of bottleneck that controls the range of viewer choice (whether or not it uses any consequent economic power for economically predatory purposes), and that *some* degree—at least a limited degree—of governmental intervention and control through regulation can prove appropriate when justified under *O'Brien* (at least when not "content based"). * * *

Finally, I believe that Congress could reasonably conclude that the statute will help the typical over-the-air viewer (by maintaining an expanded range of choice) more than it will hurt the typical cable subscriber (by restricting cable slots otherwise available for preferred programming). The latter's cable choices are many and varied, and the range of choice is rapidly increasing. The former's over-the-air choice is more restricted; and, as cable becomes more popular, it may well become still more restricted insofar as the over-the-air market shrinks and thereby, by itself, becomes less profitable. In these circumstances, I do not believe the First Amendment dictates a result that favors the cable viewers' interests.

[JUSTICES O'CONNOR, SCALIA, THOMAS, and GINSBURG dissented.]

Notes and Questions

1. In *Turner Broadcasting,* regulatory issues once again have constitutional dimensions. The Court takes pains to distinguish the constitutional basis for regulating over-the-air broadcasting from that for cable regulation, but at the end of the day, on what basis does the Court justify imposing regulations on cable companies that it would be unconstitutional to impose on newspapers?

2. What Public Interest arguments could be made in favor of requiring the carriage of local broadcast stations? Is the interest only one of the broadcasters in having an outlet for their product? Do cable subscribers also have an interest in access to local stations that cannot be satisfied by unplugging the cable when they want to watch the local news?[34]

3. Was at least part of the need for these regulations the fact that cable television has been treated as a natural monopoly within each community? That is, if there were multiple cable systems in a locality, each competing to attract subscribers, would all likely choose to exclude the local broadcast stations from their offerings? Is it not likely that most if not all would offer local stations so as to meet the consumer demand the FCC perceived?

4. Even assuming a local monopoly of cable, were transaction costs so high that local stations could not have purchased access to cable systems? Remember what the Coase Theorem said about the effects of private contracting to produce an optimal result? The local stations wanted to be carried free, of course, but was the problem here really one of access or simply the price of access? Should your answer to that question affect your judgment of the constitutionality of the access rules?

5. Who likely favored requiring carriage of local stations on the cable systems? Might one group have been political candidates wanting to maximize their local exposure and acquire the good will of local broadcasters? Might some beneficiaries even have been Members of Congress who reviewed the budget of the FCC? Should such political realities cut in favor of or against the constitutionality of the legislation?

6. Now that we know that cable television offerings are subject to at least some regulation, should Congress be able to require cable operators to segregate "patently offensive" programming to a single channel that can only be unblocked after a viewer's specific request? May Congress require prohibition of such content on "public access channels?" See Denver Area Educational Telecommunications Consortium, Inc. v. Federal Communications Commission, 518 U.S. 727, 116 S.Ct. 2374, 135 L.Ed.2d 888 (1996) (striking down such regulations on First Amendment grounds).

7. Might the same kinds of concerns about diversity in broadcasting also justify regulation of the number of stations or cable systems a particular operator may own? Would such regulation raise different First Amendment issues? Our next case examines such concerns.

---

34. Section 301 the Telecommunications Act of 1996 alters the must carry rules only slightly. Pub.Law 104–104, 110 Stat. 116.

FOX TELEVISION STATIONS, INC. v. FEDERAL COMMUNICATIONS COMMISSION

United States Court of Appeals, District of Columbia Circuit, 2002.
280 F.3d 1027.

Before GINSBURG, CHIEF JUDGE, EDWARDS and SENTELLE, CIRCUIT JUDGES

GINSBURG, CHIEF JUDGE:

Before the court are five consolidated petitions to review and one appeal from the Federal Communications Commission's 1998 decision not to repeal or to modify the national television station ownership rule * * * and the cable/broadcast cross-ownership rule. * * * Petitioners challenge the decision as a violation of both the Administrative Procedure Act (APA) * * * and § 202(h) of the Telecommunications Act of 1996. * * * They also contend that both rules violate the First Amendment to the Constitution of the United States. The network petitioners—Fox Television Stations, Inc., National Broadcasting Company, Inc., Viacom Inc., and CBS Broadcasting Inc.—address the national television ownership rule, while petitioner Time Warner Entertainment Company, L.P. addresses the cable/broadcast cross-ownership rule. The National Association of Broadcasters (NAB), the Network Affiliated Stations Alliance (NASA), the Consumer Federation of America (CFA), and the United Church of Christ, Office of Communications, Inc. (UCC) have intervened and filed briefs in support of the Commission's decision to retain the national television station ownership rule.

We conclude that the Commission's decision to retain the rules was arbitrary and capricious and contrary to law. We remand the national television station ownership rule to the Commission for further consideration, and we vacate the cable/broadcast cross-ownership rule because we think it unlikely the Commission will be able on remand to justify retaining it.

I. BACKGROUND

In the Telecommunications Act of 1996 the Congress set in motion a process to deregulate the structure of the broadcast and cable television industries. The Act itself repealed the statutes prohibiting telephone/cable and cable/broadcast cross-ownership and overrode the few remaining regulatory limits upon cable/network cross-ownership. In radio it eliminated the national and relaxed the local restrictions upon ownership and eased the "dual network" rule. In addition, the Act directed the Commission to eliminate the cap upon the number of television stations any one entity may own and to increase to 35 from 25 the maximum percentage of American households a single broadcaster may reach.

Finally, and most important to this case, in § 202(h) of the Act, the Congress instructed the Commission, in order to continue the process of deregulation, to review each of the Commission's ownership rules every two years. * * * The Commission first undertook a review of its owner-ship rules pursuant to this mandate in 1998. * * *

A.   The National Television Station Ownership (NTSO) Rule

The NTSO Rule prohibits any entity from controlling television stations the combined potential audience reach of which exceeds 35% of the television households in the United States. As originally promulgated in the early 1940s, the Rule prohibited common ownership of more than three television stations; that number was later increased to seven. * * *

In 1984 the Commission considered the effects of technological changes in the mass media and repealed the NTSO Rule subject to a six-year transition period during which the ownership limit was raised to 12 stations. The Commission determined that repeal of the NTSO Rule would not adversely affect either the diversity of viewpoints available on the airwaves or competition among broadcasters. It concluded that diversity should be a concern only at the local level, as to which the NTSO Rule was irrelevant, and that "looking at the national level [the Rule was unnecessary because] the U.S. enjoys an abundance of indepen-dently owned mass media outlets." The Commission also concluded that group owners were not likely to impose upon their stations a "monolith-ic" point of view. * * *

Implementation of the *1984 Report* was subsequently blocked by the Congress. The Commission thereupon reconsidered the matter and pro-hibited common ownership (1) of stations that in the aggregate reached more than 25% of the national television audience, and (2) of more than 12 stations regardless of their combined audience reach. * * * These limitations remained in place until 1996, when the Congress * * * directed the Commission to eliminate the 12–station rule and to raise to 35% the cap upon audience reach, both of which actions the Commission promptly took.

B.   The Cable/Broadcast Cross–Ownership (CBCO) Rule

The CBCO Rule prohibits a cable television system from carrying the signal of any television broadcast station if the system owns a broadcast station in the same local market. In conjunction with certain "must-carry" requirements to which cable operators are subject, *see Turner I* (1994), the Rule has the effect of prohibiting common owner-ship of a broadcast station and a cable television system in the same local market.

The Commission first promulgated the CBCO Rule in 1970 along with a rule banning network ownership of cable systems. In 1984 the Congress codified the CBCO Rule but not the network ownership ban.

In 1992 the Commission repealed the rule prohibiting network ownership of cable systems. The Commission also revisited the CBCO Rule and concluded that "the rationale for an absolute prohibition on broadcast-cable cross-ownership is no longer valid in light of the ongoing changes in the video marketplace." Because the Congress had imposed a similar prohibition by statute, however, the Commission did not repeal the Rule; instead, the Commission recommended that the Congress repeal the statutory prohibition. In the 1996 Act the Congress did just that without, however, requiring the Commission to repeal the CBCO Rule.

* * *

III. The NTSO Rule

Having found no obstacle to our adjudication of this dispute, we turn at last to the merits. The networks assert that the Commission's decision to retain the NTSO Rule was contrary to § 202(h) and arbitrary and capricious in violation of the APA; alternatively they contend the Rule violates the First Amendment.

A. Section 202(h) and the APA

The networks argue that the Commission's decision not to repeal the NTSO Rule was arbitrary and capricious and contrary to § 202(h) for three reasons: (1) the Rule is fundamentally irrational, and the Commission's justifications for retaining it are correlatively flawed; (2) the Commission failed meaningfully to consider whether the Rule was "necessary" in the public interest; and (3) the Commission failed to explain why it departed from its previous position that the Rule should be repealed.

1. Is the Rule irrational?

The networks advance three reasons for thinking that retention of the NTSO Rule was irrational: The 35% cap is if anything less justified than the aggregate limitation upon cable system ownership we held a violation of the First Amendment in Time Warner Entertainment Co., L.P. v. FCC, 240 F.3d 1126 (D.C.Cir.2001) (*Time Warner II*); the Commission has provided no persuasive reason to believe retention of the Rule is necessary in the public interest; and retention of the Rule is inconsistent with some of the Commission's other recent decisions.

Time Warner II. According to the networks, "[t]he logic of *Time Warner II* applies with even greater force here." They contend that the television station ownership cap of 35% is more severe than the cable system ownership cap of 30% struck down in *Time Warner II,* because unlike cable systems "broadcasters face intense competition from numerous stations in each local market" and the 35% cap is measured in terms of homes potentially rather than actually served. In response, the Commission, supported by intervenors NAB and NASA, notes two distinctions between *Time Warner II* and this case: The 30% cap in *Time Warner II* was set by the Commission whereas the 35% cap at issue here was set by the Congress; and the provision of the Cable Act at issue in the prior case limited the extent to which the Commission could regulate in furtherance of diversity, whereas § 202(h) mandates that a rule necessary "in the public interest"—including the public interest in diversity—be retained.

The networks are right, of course, that a broadcaster faces more local competition than does a cable system. We must also acknowledge that under the cap expressed in terms of a "potential audience reach" of 35%, an owner of television stations cannot in practice achieve an audience share that approaches 35% of the national audience. Nonetheless, we find the networks' reliance upon *Time Warner II* less than convincing for two reasons, one advanced by the Commission and one not. As the Commission points out, we concluded in *Time Warner II* that the 1992 Cable Act limited the agency's authority to impose regulations solely in order to further diversity in programming, * * * whereas no such limitation is at work in this case. Additionally, in *Time Warner II* we reviewed the challenged regulations under first amendment "intermediate scrutiny," which is more demanding than the arbitrary and capricious standard of the APA. * * * In sum, although *Time Warner II* does give the court a point of reference, it is not controlling here.

The Commission's reasons: competition, diversity, et al. The networks next argue that neither safeguarding competition nor promoting diversity generally can support the Commission's decision to retain the NTSO Rule. They then take on the specific reasons given by the Commission in support of its 1998 decision.

As to competition, the networks note that there is no evidence "that broadcasters have undue market power," such as to dampen competition, in any relevant market. The Commission attempts to rebut the point, but to no avail. In its brief the agency cites a single, barely relevant study by Phillip A. Beutel et al., entitled Broadcast Television Networks and Affiliates: Economic Conditions and Relationship—1980 and Today (1995). Insofar as there is any point of tangency between that study and the matter at hand, it is in the authors' conclusion that "the available evidence tends to refute the proposition that affiliates have gained negotiating power since ... 1980." The study plainly does not, however, suggest that broadcasters have undue market power. The only other evidence to which the Commission points is a table said to show that "many group owners have acquired additional stations and increased their audience reach since the Telecom Act's passage." As the networks point out, however, "such figures alone, without some tangible evidence of an adverse effect on the market, are insufficient to support retention of the Cap." * * * Consequently, we must conclude, as the networks maintain, that the Commission has no valid reason to think the NTSO Rule is necessary to safeguard competition.

As to diversity, the networks contend there is no evidence that "the national ownership cap is needed to protect diversity" and that in any event § 202(h) does not allow the Commission to regulate broadcast ownership "in the name of diversity alone." The Commission, again supported by intervenors NAB and NASA, persuasively counters the statutory point: In the context of the regulation of broadcasting, "the public interest" has historically embraced diversity (as well as localism), * * * and nothing in § 202(h) signals a departure from that historic scope. The question, therefore, is whether the Commission adequately justified its retention decision as necessary to further diversity or local-ism. In the *1998 Report* the Commission mentioned national diversity as a justification for retaining the NTSO Rule but never elaborated upon the point. This justification fails for two reasons. First, the Commission failed to explain why it was no longer adhering to the view it expressed in the *1984 Report* that national diversity is irrelevant. Second, the Commission's passing reference to national diversity does nothing to explain why the Rule is necessary to further that end. The Commission did, however, discuss at some length fostering local diversity by strength-ening the bargaining position of affiliates vis-a-vis their networks, a justification to which we shall come shortly.

As to the Commission's three more specific reasons for retaining the NTSO Rule, the networks contend that each is inadequate. The Commis-sion stated that retaining the cap was necessary so it could: (1) observe the effects of recent changes in the rules governing local ownership of television stations; (2) observe the effects of the national ownership cap having been raised to 35%; and (3) preserve the power of local affiliates to bargain with their networks in order to promote diversity of program-ming. We agree with the networks that these reasons cannot justify the Commission's decision.

The first reason is insufficient because there is no obvious relation-ship between relaxation of the local ownership rule—which now permits a single entity to own two broadcast stations in the same market in some situations * * * and retention of the national ownership cap, and the Commission does nothing to suggest there is any non-obvious relation-ship. Furthermore, as the networks point out, neither the first nor the second reason is responsive to § 202(h): The Commission's wait-and-see approach cannot be squared with its statutory mandate promptly—that is, by revisiting the matter biennially—to "repeal or modify" any rule that is not "necessary in the public interest."

The Commission, with the support of intervenors NAB and NASA, argues that it was required to defer to the decision of the Congress to set the initial ownership cap in the 1996 Act at 35%. For this the Commis-sion relies upon both the House and the Senate having rejected a proposal to raise the cap to 50%, and upon the statement of Congress-man Markey, ranking minority Member of the relevant subcommittee of the House, that the Congress's choice of the 35% cap "should settle the issue for many years to come." This legislative history is no basis whatever for the Commission's decision. First, the choice of 35% rather than any other number determined only the starting point from which the Commission was to assess the need for further change. * * * In this instance, moreover, the congressman did not even purport to interpret the statute; he merely offered his own prediction that competitive conditions would not warrant a change in the Rule anytime soon. Maybe yes, maybe no. The statute says that is for the Commission to decide. Consequently, the first two reasons given by the Commission do nothing to support its decision.

Nor does the Commission's third reason—that the Rule is necessary to strengthen the bargaining power of network affiliates and thereby to promote diversity of programming—have sufficient support in the present record. Although we do not agree with the networks that this reason is unresponsive to § 202(h)—as we have said, that section allows the Commission to retain a rule necessary to safeguard the public interest in diversity—we must agree that the Commission's failure to address itself to the contrary views it expressed in the *1984 Report* effectively undermines its present rationale. In the *1998 Report* the Commission asserted that independently-owned affiliates play a valuable role by "counterbalancing" the networks' strong economic incentive in clearing all network programming "because they have the right ... to air instead" programming more responsive to local concerns. In the *1984 Report,* however, the Commission said it had "no evidence indicating that stations which are not group-owned better respond to community needs, or expend proportionately more of their revenues on local programming." The later decision does not indicate the Commission has since received such evidence or otherwise found reason to repudiate its prior conclusion.

In sum, we agree with the networks that the Commission has adduced not a single valid reason to believe the NTSO Rule is necessary in the public interest, either to safeguard competition or to enhance diversity. Although we agree with the Commission that protecting diversity is a permissible policy, the Commission did not provide an adequate basis for believing the Rule would in fact further that cause. We conclude, therefore, that the 1998 decision to retain the NTSO Rule was arbitrary and capricious in violation of the APA.

　　* * *

B. The First Amendment

The networks contend that the NTSO Rule violates the First Amendment because it prevents them from speaking directly—that is, through stations they own and operate—to 65% of the potential television audience in the United States. They would have the court subject the Rule to "intermediate scrutiny," rather than to rationality review, on the grounds that: (a) in today's populous media marketplace the "scarcity" rationale associated with Red Lion Broadcasting Co. v. FCC, 395 U.S. 367 (1969)—but in fact, we note, first set forth in National Broadcasting Co. v. United States, 319 U.S. 190, 226–27 (*NBC*)—"makes no sense" as a reason for regulating ownership; (b) even if scarcity is still a valid concern, the NTSO Rule, which does not prevent an entity from owning more than one station in the same local market, does nothing to mitigate the effect of scarcity; and (c) FCC v. League of Women Voters, 468 U.S. 364, 104 S.Ct. 3106, 82 L.Ed.2d 278 (1984), which postdates *Red Lion,* mandates heightened scrutiny for all restrictions on broadcast speech. In the alternative, the networks argue that even if the NTSO Rule is subject only to review for mere rationality—the least demanding type of first amendment scrutiny—then it is still unconstitutional because it "severely restricts [their] free speech rights and fails to advance any countervailing public interest."

The Commission urges the court to accord the NTSO Rule more deference than is accorded under intermediate scrutiny on the ground that the Supreme Court upheld similar ownership rules in *NCCB* and *NBC* upon determining they were merely reasonable. * * *

In *NCCB* the court upheld the newspaper/broadcast crossownership rule stating: "The regulations are a reasonable means of promoting the public interest in diversified mass communications; thus they do not violate the First Amendment rights of those who will be denied broadcast licenses pursuant to them." * * * In *NBC* the court upheld a regulation that prohibited a network from owning more than one radio station in a market and from owning any station in a market with few stations. * * * As in *NCCB,* the Court in *NBC* held the regulation to be consistent with the First Amendment because it was based upon network practices deemed contrary to the public interest and not upon the applicants' "political, economic or social views, or upon any other capricious basis." * * *

The networks offer no convincing reason why those cases should not control. First, contrary to the implication of the networks' argument, this court is not in a position to reject the scarcity rationale even if we agree that it no longer makes sense. The Supreme Court has already heard the empirical case against that rationale and still "declined to question its continuing validity." *Turner I,* 512 U.S. 622, 638 (1994).

Second, contrary to the networks' express protestations, the scarcity rationale is implicated in this case. The scarcity rationale is based upon the limited physical capacity of the broadcast spectrum, which limited capacity means that "there are more would-be broadcasters than frequencies available." *Turner I,* 512 U.S. at 637. In the face of this limitation, the national ownership cap increases the number of different voices heard in the nation (albeit not the number heard in any one market). But for the scarcity rationale, that increase would be of no moment.

Third, we do not think *League of Women Voters* mandates heightened scrutiny in this case. That case involved a prohibition upon editorializing by noncommercial broadcasters that received government money under the Public Broadcasting Act, which prohibition the Court concluded was a content-based restriction upon speech. * * * The Court applied heightened scrutiny, noting that restrictions placed upon broadcasters in order to "secure the public's First Amendment interest in receiving a balanced presentation of views on diverse matters of public concern," such as the fairness doctrine at issue in *Red Lion,* 395 U.S. at 386, 89 S.Ct. at 1804, "have been upheld only when we were satisfied that the restriction is narrowly tailored to further a substantial government interest." * * * The Court did not question, however, the continued propriety of deferential scrutiny of structural regulations. The NTSO Rule, unlike the ban upon editorializing at issue in *League of Women*

Voters, is not a content-based regulation; it is a regulation of industry structure, like the newspaper/broadcast cross-ownership rule the Court concluded was content-neutral in *NCCB,* and like the network ownership restriction upheld in *NBC.* * * * For these reasons, the deferential review undertaken by the Supreme Court in *NCCB* and *NBC* is also appropriate here.

The networks * * * argue that the Rule fails even rationality review because "[p]ermitting one entity to own many stations can foster ... more programming preferred by consumers." They also suggest that but for the Rule "buyers with superior skills [could] purchase stations where they may be able to do a better job" of meeting local needs even as they realize economies of scale.

This paean to the undoubted virtues of a free market in television stations is not, however, responsive to the question whether the Congress could reasonably determine that a more diversified ownership of television stations would likely lead to the presentation of more diverse points of view. By limiting the number of stations each network (or other entity) may own, the NTSO Rule ensures that there are more owners than there would otherwise be. An industry with a larger number of owners may well be less efficient than a more concentrated industry. Both consumer satisfaction and potential operating cost savings may be sacrificed as a result of the Rule. But that is not to say the Rule is unreasonable because the Congress may, in the regulation of broadcasting, constitutionally pursue values other than efficiency—including in particular diversity in programming, for which diversity of ownership is perhaps an aspirational but surely not an irrational proxy. Simply put, it is not unreasonable—and therefore not unconstitutional—for the Congress to prefer having in the aggregate more voices heard, each in roughly one-third of the nation, even if the number of voices heard in any given market remains the same.

C. Remedy

* * *

We * * * remand this case to the Commission for further consideration whether to repeal or to modify the NTSO Rule.

IV. THE CBCO RULE

Time Warner's principal contention is that the CBCO Rule is an unconstitutional abridgment of its first amendment right to speak. Time Warner also argues that the Commission's decision to retain the Rule was arbitrary and capricious and contrary to § 202(h). Because we agree that the retention decision was arbitrary and capricious as well as contrary to § 202(h), and that this requires us to vacate the Rule, we do not reach Time Warner's first amendment claim.

A. Section 202(h) and the APA

Time Warner raises a host of objections to the Commission's decision to retain the CBCO Rule. The Commission is largely unresponsive to these arguments; to the extent it is responsive, it is unpersuasive.

First, Time Warner argues that the Commission impermissibly justified retaining the Rule on a ground, namely that cable/broadcast combines might "discriminate against unaffiliated broadcasters in making cable-carriage decisions," different from the one it gave when it promulgated the Rule, namely, that "cable should be protected" from acquisition by networks bent upon pre-empting new competition. The Commission does not respond but even so we think the argument is clearly without merit. Nothing in § 202(h) suggests the grounds upon which the Commission may conclude that a rule is necessary in the public interest are limited to the grounds upon which it adopted the rule in the first place.

Next, Time Warner argues that the Commission applied too lenient a standard when it concluded only that the CBCO Rule "continues to serve the public interest," and not that it was "necessary" in the public interest. Again the Commission is silent, but this time we agree with Time Warner; the Commission appears to have applied too low a standard. The statute is clear that a regulation should be retained only insofar as it is necessary in, not merely consonant with, the public interest.

Finally, Time Warner attacks the specific reasons the Commission gave for retaining the Rule. All three reasons relate either to competition or to diversity, and we have grouped them below accordingly.

1. Competition

The Commission expressed concern that a cable operator that owns a broadcast station: (1) can "discriminate" against other broadcasters by offering cable/broadcast joint advertising sales and promotions; and (2) has an incentive not to carry, or to carry on undesirable channels, the broadcast signals—including the forthcoming digital signals—of competing stations. Addressing the first concern, Time Warner argues that the Commission failed both to explain why joint advertising rates constitute "discrimination—which is simply a pejorative way of referring to economies of scale and scope"—and to "point to substantial evidence that such 'discrimination' is a nonconjectural problem." Addressing the second concern (in part), Time Warner contends that refusals by cable operators to carry digital signals must not be a significant problem because the Commission has declined to impose must-carry rules for duplicate digital signals. * * * Both of Time Warner's points are plausible—indeed the first is quite persuasive—and we have no basis upon which to reject either inasmuch as the Commission does not respond to them.

Next, Time Warner gives four reasons for which the Commission's concern about discriminatory carriage of broadcast signals is unwarranted. First, must-carry provisions already ensure that broadcast stations have access to cable systems; indeed, the Commission pointed to only one instance in which a cable operator denied carriage to a broadcast station (Univision). Second, competition from direct broadcast satellite (DBS) providers makes discrimination against competing stations unprofitable.

Third, the Commission failed to explain why it departed from the position it took in the *1992 Report,* where it said that the CBCO Rule was not necessary to prevent carriage discrimination. Fourth, because a cable operator may lawfully be co-owned with a cable programmer or a network, the Rule does little to cure the alleged problem of cable operators having an incentive to discriminate against stations that air competing programming.

In response the Commission concedes it did not address Time Warner's second and third points—competition from DBS services and the contradiction of the *1992 Report*: "Since the Commission did not address any of these issues in the *1998 Report,* counsel for the Commission are not in a position to respond to Time Warner's claims concerning these issues." The same might have been said of Time Warner's fourth point. These failings alone require that we reverse as arbitrary and capricious the Commission's decision to retain the CBCO Rule. * * *

The only argument to which the Commission does respond is that the Univision incident alone cannot justify retention of the Rule: The Commission first points to its predictive judgment that there would be more discrimination without the CBCO Rule and then, citing *Time Warner I,* 211 F.3d at 1322–23, points out that the availability of behavioral remedies does not necessarily preclude it from imposing a structural remedy. We acknowledge that the court should ordinarily defer to the Commission's predictive judgments, and we take the Commission's point about remedies. In this case, however, the Commission has not shown a substantial enough probability of discrimination to deem reasonable a prophylactic rule as broad as the cross-ownership ban, especially in light of the already extant conduct rules. A single incident since the must-carry rules were promulgated—and one that seems to have been dealt with adequately under those rules—is just not enough to suggest an otherwise significant problem held in check only by the CBCO Rule.

We conclude that the Commission has failed to justify its retention of the CBCO Rule as necessary to safeguard competition. The Commission failed to consider competition from DBS, to justify its change in position from the *1992 Report,* and to put forward any adequate reason for believing the Rule remains "necessary in the public interest."

2. Diversity

As for retaining the Rule in the interest of diversity, the Commission had this to say: "Cable/TV combinations ... would represent the consolidation of the only participants in the video market for local news and public affairs programming, and would therefore compromise diversity." *1998 Report* ¶ 107. Time Warner argues that this rationale is contrary to § 202(h), as well as arbitrary and capricious, for essentially three reasons.

First, Time Warner contends that § 202(h), by virtue of its exclusive concern with competition, plainly precludes consideration of diversity and that, in any event, it should be so interpreted in order to avoid the constitutional question raised by the burden the CBCO Rule places upon the company's right to speak. Second, Time Warner argues that the increase in the number of broadcast stations in each local market since the promulgation of the CBCO Rule in 1970 renders any marginal increase in diversity owing to the operation of the Rule too slight to justify retaining it. Finally, Time Warner asserts that the decision to retain the Rule cannot be reconciled with the *TV Ownership Order,* in which the Commission concluded that a single entity may own two local television stations as long as there are eight other stations in the market and one of the two stations coming under common ownership is not among the four most watched stations. * * *

The Commission responds feebly. First, it does not address Time Warner's argument that diversity may not be considered under § 202(h), but that is of little moment because it adequately addressed essentially the same argument when it was presented by the networks in connection with the NTSO Rule: A rule may be retained if it is necessary "in the public interest"; it need not be necessary specifically to safeguard competition. Second, the Commission concedes that it decided to retain the Rule without considering the increase in the number of competing television stations since it had promulgated the Rule in 1970. The Commission gives no explanation for this omission, yet it is hard to imagine anything more relevant to the question whether the Rule is still necessary to further diversity.

Finally, the Commission makes no response to Time Warner's argument that the concern with diversity cannot support an across-the-board prohibition of cross-ownership in light of the Commission's conclusion in the *TV Ownership Order* that common ownership of two broadcast stations in the same local market need not unduly compromise diversity. The Commission does object that Time Warner failed to raise this argument before the agency, but it appears that Time Warner did what it could to bring the argument to the Commission's attention. The *TV Ownership Order* was issued in August, 1999, after the close of the comment period, but almost a year before the *1998 Report* was issued (in June, 2000). A few months thereafter Time Warner proffered supplemental comments raising this point but the Commission declined to consider them. For this reason, we find the Commission's forfeiture argument unpersuasive. Even if it was proper for the agency to refuse to accept the comments, however, it does not follow that the agency was free to ignore its own recently issued *TV Ownership Order.* Yet the Commission made no attempt in the *1998 Report* and makes no attempt in its brief to harmonize its seemingly inconsistent decisions.

In sum, the Commission concedes it failed to consider the increased number of television stations now in operation, and it is clear that the Commission failed to reconcile the decision under review with the *TV Ownership Order* it had issued only shortly before. We conclude, therefore, that the Commission's diversity rationale for retaining the CBCO Rule is woefully inadequate.

B.   Remedy

* * *

Because the probability that the Commission would be able to justify retaining the CBCO Rule is low and the disruption that vacatur will create is relatively insubstantial, we shall vacate the CBCO Rule.

Notes and Questions

1.   In light of this opinion it was back to the drawing board for the FCC. 68 Fed. Reg. 46286 (August 5, 2003). The Commission announced that it had raised the cap on national ownership from 35% to 45%. In addition, rules were announced regulating the number of television stations that can be owned by a single entity in the same market, the number of radio stations that can be owned in the same market, and cross ownership. The term cross ownership refers to ownership in more than one form of media. For example, in areas with three or fewer television stations, the owner of a newspaper, radio or television station may not also own another type of media outlet. As the number of television stations increases, cross ownership is less restricted. If an area has between 4 and 8 televisions stations, an entity may own a television station, a newspaper and up to half of the radio stations. These rules are currently being appealed.

2.   Prominent among the goals announced by the FCC are "localism" and "diversity." The idea is that news and programing about local concerns are of greatest interest to viewers and listeners and that it is in the public interest for a diversity of views to be heard. The Commission specifically notes the importance of minorities and women in bringing diversity to the airways. Why not let the market determine all media ownership and content? If people want localism and diversity why wouldn't broadcasters offering those qualities emerge in an unregulated market?

3.   Suppose a community does not have a conservative talk radio station or a good country music station. Is that the type of diversity the Commission is likely to be concerned about? Is the Commission essentially trying to promote certain types of diversity?

4.   Broadcast regulation started from the idea that there were an inherently limited number of broadcast frequencies. Without regulation something like a "broadcast tragedy of the commons" would occur as competing broadcasters interfered with each other. Does that problem still exist? If not, isn't the FCC simply trying to regulate what "products" are sold in a market that, at least as a technical matter, allows unlimited participation?

5.   The problem of scarcity as it affects broadcasting has resurfaced in the area of direct broadcast satellites. These satellites are placed in the geosynchronous zone that is approximately 22,300 miles from the earth's surface and travel at approximately the same speed as the rotation of the earth. Thus, they are "stationary" vis-a-vis the earth's surface and capable of transmitting video signals directly into individual homes without elaborate earthbound transmission equipment. The geosynchronous zone has limited capacity and there is already evidence of crowding. Allocation of

space in the zone is a highly sensitive process that carries with it huge international implications. Especially difficult issues arise with respect to international spillovers of broadcast signals and the treatment of countries that have not yet developed the technology to employ direct broadcast satellites. For a thorough discussion see Lawrence D. Roberts, "A Lost Connection: Geostationary Satellite Networks and the International Telecommunications Union," 15 Berkeley Tech. L.J. 1095 (2000).

2. ALLOCATION OF SCARCE NATURAL RESOURCES

McDOWELL v. ALASKA

Supreme Court of Alaska, 1989.
785 P.2d 1.

MATTHEWS, CHIEF JUSTICE.

This case challenges chapter 52 SLA 1986 which grants a preference to rural residents to take fish and game for subsistence purposes. The only requirement to be met by a subsistence fisherman or hunter is residency in a rural area of the state.

The rural preference is challenged under several provisions of the Alaska Constitution: the common use clause, article VIII, section 3; the no exclusive right of fishery clause, article VIII, section 15; the uniform application clause, article VIII, section 17; the equal rights clause, article I, section 1; and the due process clause, article I, section 7. In addition, violation of the equal protection and due process clauses of the United States Constitution is claimed. For the reasons that follow, we hold that the rural preference violates article VIII, sections 3, 15 and 17 of the Alaska Constitution.

FACTUAL AND PROCEDURAL SETTING

The 1986 act defines subsistence fishing and hunting as activities which can be undertaken only "by a resident domiciled in a rural area of the state. . . ." Subsistence uses are also defined in terms of residency in rural areas:

> "Subsistence uses" means the noncommercial, customary and traditional uses of wild, renewable resources by a resident domiciled in a rural area of the state for direct personal or family consumption as food, shelter, fuel, clothing, tools, or transportation, for the making and selling of handicraft articles out of non-edible by-products of fish and wildlife resources taken for personal or family consumption, and for the customary trade, barter, or sharing for personal or family consumption. AS 16.05.940(30).

> A "rural area" is defined as "a community or area of the state in which the noncommercial, customary, and traditional use of fish or game for personal or family consumption is a principal characteristic of the economy of the community or area." AS 16.05.940(25).

Appellants are Alaska residents who have engaged in subsistence hunting and fishing in the past and wish to continue to do so. Under the 1986 act, they are disqualified as subsistence users because they reside in areas classified as non-rural by the joint Boards of Fisheries and Game. Appellants McDowell and Mahle reside in Anchorage, Bondurant resides in Cooper Landing, and Eastwood resides in the community of McKinley Park.

The 1986 act requires the Board of Fisheries and the Board of Game to decide what portion of each fish stock and game population can be harvested consistent with the principle of sustained yield. Next the Boards must determine how much of the harvestable portion is needed to satisfy subsistence needs. If the harvestable portion of any stock or population is not sufficient to accommodate all consumptive uses—sport, personal use, and commercial—then subsistence uses shall be accorded a preference over other consumptive uses, and the regulations shall provide a reasonable opportunity to satisfy the subsistence uses. If the harvestable portion is sufficient to accommodate the subsistence uses of the stock or population, then the Boards may provide for other consumptive uses of the remainder of the harvestable portion. AS 16.05.258(c). If the harvestable portion of a stock or population is insufficient to satisfy all subsistence needs, all non-subsistence uses are barred, and the Boards are required to distinguish among subsistence users by applying three criteria: "(1) customary and direct dependence on the fish stock or game population as the mainstay of livelihood; (2) local residency; and (3) availability of alternative resources." Id.

* * *

Appellants' basic objection to the 1986 act is that by excluding from eligibility as subsistence users all urban dwellers and by including all rural dwellers, the act unfairly excludes some urban residents who have lived a subsistence lifestyle and desire to continue to do so, while needlessly including numerous rural residents who have not engaged in subsistence hunting and fishing. Appellants claim, in other words, that the urban/rural criterion is both unfairly under-inclusive, because it excludes deserving urban residents, and over-inclusive, because it includes undeserving rural residents. Appellants instead suggest that the right to subsistence should depend upon individual needs and traditions, not on one's place of residence.

The record supports the appellants' claim that there are substantial numbers of urban subsistence users. A state study of subsistence use patterns found that of some 255 holders of subsistence salmon permits for the 1980 Tanana River fishery, approximately 20% exhibited the attributes commonly associated with a traditional subsistence lifestyle, even though they all resided in the urban Fairbanks area. The report states:

Despite their residence in or near populated areas of the Fairbanks North Star Borough, these households generally participated in the wage economy on a seasonal basis and had longer histories of participation in the fishery, lower cash incomes, and somewhat larger household sizes than the majority of users. Some of these households have longstanding cultural ties to the subsistence fishery. For these more intensive users, fishing in sub-district Y–6C was less a recreational outing than an integral component of their way of life in Interior Alaska. Their residence in an area which is currently defined by regulation as urban, coupled with escalating demands upon the resource base, however, raise questions about whether these more intensive uses can continue in the future.

Similarly, in the city of Homer, an urban area under the regulations, the study reports that 38.2% of the city residents obtained at least one-half of their meat and fish supply from personal hunting and fishing activities.

Likewise, the study documents the fact that numerous Alaskans who live in areas classified by the regulations as rural do not engage in subsistence activities. For example, in the City of Sitka, which is classified as rural, although it has a population of 7,803, some 26% of the households sampled did no hunting and 7% did no fishing. Similarly, in the City of Nome, population 3,249, which is also rural under the regulations, some 5% of all households use no locally taken fish or game.

The study also amply supports the critical importance of subsistence hunting and fishing to residents of the numerous small and remote villages of our state. For example, in the Wade Hampton census area of Western Alaska, the average annual per capita cash income was only $2,737 (1979), and the average household harvested 4,597, dressed weight, pounds of fish and game each year.

The Article VIII Clauses—History and Analysis

A.

Section 15 of article VIII of the Alaska Constitution provides:

No exclusive right or special privilege of fishery shall be created or authorized in the natural waters of the State. This section does not restrict the power of the State to limit entry into any fishery for the purposes of resource conservation, to prevent economic distress among fishermen and those dependent upon them for a livelihood and to promote the efficient development of aquaculture in the State. Section 3 of article VIII provides: Wherever occurring in their natural state, fish, wildlife, and waters are reserved to the people for common use.

Section 17 of article VIII provides:

Laws and regulations governing the use or disposal of natural resources shall apply equally to all persons similarly situated with reference to the subject matter and purpose to be served by the law or regulation.

* * *

We * * * conclude that the requirement contained in the 1986 subsistence statute, that one must reside in a rural area in order to participate in subsistence hunting and fishing, violates sections 3, 15, and 17 of article VIII of the Alaska Constitution.

* * *

B.

The conclusion we have reached does not mean that everyone can engage in subsistence hunting or fishing. We do not imply that the constitution bars all methods of exclusion where exclusion is required for species protection reasons. We hold only that the residency criterion used in the 1986 act which conclusively excludes all urban residents from subsistence hunting and fishing regardless of their individual characteristics is unconstitutional.

* * *

Reversed and Remanded.

Notes and Questions

1. *McDowell v. Alaska* presents two facets of the "inherently scarce resources" rationale. First, it is clear that over-fishing and hunting could eventually eliminate the resources altogether. Thus, the State Board of Fisheries and Board of Game was charged with determining how much of the resources could be "consumed" each year. Second, having decided that access to the resources must be limited, the issue was how to ration them among those who would like to have access. It is important to note that these are different issues. For example, the State could institute limitations on fishing and hunting and simply sell them to the highest bidders. Obviously the State of Alaska did not adopt an approach of auctioning off rights to those who were willing to pay the most. What approach did it take?

2. The market is itself one rationing mechanism. Once the market is taken out of the picture as the way of allocating rights, can you think of a substitute method of allocation? One might be to ration the scarce resource to people on the basis of "need." For example, during World War II, many staples were allocated on the basis of family size. Having the necessary cash was but one requirement to be met to purchase certain items. In addition, it was necessary to have a coupon that entitled one to purchase the item.

3. Should the right to fish or hunt be allocated on the basis of need? How would you compare how much a poor person needs to be able to fish and hunt compared to how much a wealthier person needs the right to do so?

4. What appears to be the principle, if any, underlying the favored treatment afforded "subsistence" uses? Do you think the less privileged citizens of Alaska would rather have fishing licenses or money? For example, suppose the fishing licenses were auctioned off to the highest bidders and the receipts used to build schools in rural areas.

5.   Consider the following scenarios.

a.   All licenses are freely transferrable. Under one plan they are sold at an auction and five years later the original purchasers still own them. Does this mean those people value the licenses more than others?

b.   Under another plan, they are allocated to those people who can demonstrate a past dependence on fishing and hunting for food. Five years later—and after many attempts by others to purchase their licenses at very high prices—the same people own the licenses.

Would one conclude that these licensees value their fishing rights more than any others? Empirical tests suggest that the answer is yes in both cases. See J. Hammack & G. Brown, Waterfowl and Wetlands: Toward Bioeconomic Analysis (1974). Does this mean that the fishing licenses are simply more highly valued by those who get them first? Does it say anything about the market as a way to determine who attributes the highest value to an item?

6.   The Alaska Supreme Court was able to decide *McDowell* without reaching the due process and equal protections issues under the U.S. Constitution. But frequently, courts confront state or municipal efforts to regulate scarce resources, e.g., water during a drought, and cannot avoid these questions. It may be relatively easy to sustain limitations on the use of swimming pools in drought periods, but how about restrictions on washing cars that put small car washes out of business. Should such businesses have a right to compensation for the "taking" of their property? How about at least a right to a hearing? See, e.g., the *Londoner/Bi–Metallic* distinction discussed in Note 5 after the *Dolan* case in Chapter 2. See also, Richard Pierce, Sidney Shapiro & Paul Verkuil, Administrative Law and Process (4th ed. 2004), at § 6.3.2.

3.   SCARCITY AND INALIENABLE INTERESTS

In the cases of telecommunications and natural resources, there was nothing about the fact of scarcity that ruled out the use of a market to determine how the resources would be allocated. Television stations and wildlife would simply go to the highest bidders. Economists would argue that this is very often likely to result in an efficient outcome. This solution also would be similar to the usual case in which we allow the market to mediate between demanders and suppliers. In both of those instances, however, there was something about a highest-bidder allocation that policy makers evidently felt was not efficient or that was inconsistent with goals beyond efficiency.

The sense that the market solution is not always the best way to determine the ultimate solution to problems of scarcity is at the heart of the following case. As you read it, think of other instances in which the operative regulation is one that's principal goal is to displace the market. You might also ask yourself how effective those efforts ultimately are.

IN THE MATTER OF BABY M

Supreme Court of New Jersey, 1988.
109 N.J. 396, 537 A.2d 1227.

WILENTZ, C.J.

* * *

In February 1985, William Stern and Mary Beth Whitehead entered into a surrogacy contract. It recited that Stern's wife, Elizabeth, was infertile, that they wanted a child, and that Mrs. Whitehead was willing to provide that child as the mother with Mr. Stern as the father.

The contract provided that through artificial insemination using Mr. Stern's sperm, Mrs. Whitehead would become pregnant, carry the child to term, bear it, deliver it to the Sterns, and thereafter do whatever was necessary to terminate her maternal rights so that Mrs. Stern could thereafter adopt the child. Mrs. Whitehead's husband, Richard, was also a party to the contract; Mrs. Stern was not. Mr. Whitehead promised to do all acts necessary to rebut the presumption of paternity under the Parentage Act. [Under the terms of the contract, Mrs. Whitehead was to receive $10,000.]

* * *

INVALIDITY AND UNENFORCEABILITY OF SURROGACY CONTRACT

We have concluded that this surrogacy contract is invalid. Our conclusion has two bases: direct conflict with existing statutes and conflict with the public policies of this State, as expressed in its statutory and decisional law.

* * *

Public Policy Considerations

The surrogacy contract's invalidity, resulting from its direct conflict with * * * statutory provisions, is further underlined when its goals and means are measured against New Jersey's public policy. The contract's basic premise, that the natural parents can decide in advance of birth which one is to have custody of the child, bears no relationship to the settled law that the child's best interests shall determine custody. * * *

The surrogacy contract guarantees permanent separation of the child from one of its natural parents. Our policy, however, has long been that to the extent possible, children should remain with and be brought up by both of their natural parents. That was the first stated purpose of the previous adoption act, codified at N.J.S.A. 9:3–17 (repealed): "it is necessary and desirable (a) to protect the child from unnecessary separation from his natural parents...." While not so stated in the present adoption law, this purpose remains part of the public policy of this State. This is not simply some theoretical ideal that in practice has no meaning. The impact of failure to follow that policy is nowhere better shown than in the results of this surrogacy contract. A child, instead of starting off its life with as much peace and security as possible, finds itself immediately in a tug-of-war between contending mother and father.

The surrogacy contract violates the policy of this State that the rights of natural parents are equal concerning their child, the father's right no greater than the mother's. "The parent and child relationship extends equally to every child and to every parent, regardless of the marital status of the parents." N.J.S.A. 9:17–40. As the Assembly Judiciary Committee noted in its statement to the bill, this section establishes "the principle that regardless of the marital status of the parents, all children and all parents have equal rights with respect to each other." The whole purpose and effect of the surrogacy contract was to give the father the exclusive right to the child by destroying the rights of the mother.

The policies expressed in our comprehensive laws governing consent to the surrender of a child stand in stark contrast to the surrogacy contract and what it implies. Here there is no counseling, independent or otherwise, of the natural mother, no evaluation, no warning.

The only legal advice Mary Beth Whitehead received regarding the surrogacy contract was provided in connection with the contract that she previously entered into with another couple. Mrs. Whitehead's lawyer was referred to her by the Infertility Center, with which he had an agreement to act as counsel for surrogate candidates. His services consisted of spending one hour going through the contract with the Whiteheads, section by section, and answering their questions. Mrs. Whitehead received no further legal advice prior to signing the contract with the Sterns.

Mrs. Whitehead was examined and psychologically evaluated, but if it was for her benefit, the record does not disclose that fact. The Sterns regarded the evaluation as important, particularly in connection with the question of whether she would change her mind. Yet they never asked to see it, and were content with the assumption that the Infertility Center had made an evaluation and had concluded that there was no danger that the surrogate mother would change her mind. From Mrs. Whitehead's point of view, all that she learned from the evaluation was that "she had passed." It is apparent that the profit motive got the better of the Infertility Center. Although the evaluation was made, it was not put to any use, and understandably so, for the psychologist warned that Mrs. Whitehead demonstrated certain traits that might make surrender of the child difficult and that there should be further inquiry into this issue in connection with her surrogacy. To inquire further, however, might have jeopardized the Infertility Center's fee. The record indicates that neither Mrs. Whitehead nor the Sterns were ever told of this fact, a fact that might have ended their surrogacy arrangement.

Under the contract, the natural mother is irrevocably committed before she knows the strength of her bond with her child. She never makes a totally voluntary, informed decision, for quite clearly any decision prior to the baby's birth is, in the most important sense, uninformed, and any decision after that, compelled by a pre-existing contractual commitment, the threat of a lawsuit, and the inducement of a $10,000 payment, is less than totally voluntary. Her interests are of little concern to those who controlled this transaction.

Although the interest of the natural father and adoptive mother is certainly the predominant interest, realistically the only interest served, even they are left with less than what public policy requires. They know little about the natural mother, her genetic makeup, and her psychological and medical history. Moreover, not even a superficial attempt is made to determine their awareness of their responsibilities as parents.

Worst of all, however, is the contract's total disregard of the best interests of the child. There is not the slightest suggestion that any inquiry will be made at any time to determine the fitness of the Sterns as custodial parents, of Mrs. Stern as an adoptive parent, their superiority to Mrs. Whitehead, or the effect on the child of not living with her natural mother.

This is the sale of a child, or, at the very least, the sale of a mother's right to her child, the only mitigating factor being that one of the purchasers is the father. Almost every evil that prompted the prohibition on the payment of money in connection with adoptions exists here.

The differences between an adoption and a surrogacy contract should be noted, since it is asserted that the use of money in connection with surrogacy does not pose the risks found where money buys an adoption. Katz, "Surrogate Motherhood and the Baby–Selling Laws," 20 Colum.J.L. & Soc.Probs. 1 (1986).

First, and perhaps most important, all parties concede that it is unlikely that surrogacy will survive without money. Despite the alleged selfless motivation of surrogate mothers, if there is no payment, there will be no surrogates, or very few. That conclusion contrasts with adoption; for obvious reasons, there remains a steady supply, albeit insufficient, despite the prohibitions against payment. The adoption itself, relieving the natural mother of the financial burden of supporting an infant, is in some sense the equivalent of payment.

Second, the use of money in adoptions does not produce the problem—conception occurs, and usually the birth itself, before illicit funds are offered. With surrogacy, the "problem," if one views it as such, consisting of the purchase of a woman's procreative capacity, at the risk of her life, is caused by and originates with the offer of money.

Third, with the law prohibiting the use of money in connection with adoptions, the built-in financial pressure of the unwanted pregnancy and the consequent support obligation do not lead the mother to the highest paying, ill-suited, adoptive parents. She is just as well-off surrendering the child to an approved agency. In surrogacy, the highest bidders will presumably become the adoptive parents regardless of suitability, so long as payment of money is permitted.

Fourth, the mother's consent to surrender her child in adoptions is revocable, even after surrender of the child, unless it be to an approved agency, where by regulation there are protections against an ill-advised surrender. In surrogacy, consent occurs so early that no amount of advice would satisfy the potential mother's need, yet the consent is irrevocable.

The main difference, that the unwanted pregnancy is unintended while the situation of the surrogate mother is voluntary and intended, is really not significant. Initially, it produces stronger reactions of sympathy for the mother whose pregnancy was unwanted than for the surrogate mother, who "went into this with her eyes wide open." On reflection, however, it appears that the essential evil is the same, taking advantage of a woman's circumstances (the unwanted pregnancy or the need for money) in order to take away her child, the difference being one of degree.

In the scheme contemplated by the surrogacy contract in this case, a middle man, propelled by profit, promotes the sale. Whatever idealism may have motivated any of the participants, the profit motive predominates, permeates, and ultimately governs the transaction. The demand for children is great and the supply small. The availability of contraception, abortion, and the greater willingness of single mothers to bring up their children has led to a shortage of babies offered for adoption. The situation is ripe for the entry of the middleman who will bring some equilibrium into the market by increasing the supply through the use of money.

Intimated, but disputed, is the assertion that surrogacy will be used for the benefit of the rich at the expense of the poor. See, e.g., Radin, "Market Inalienability," 100 Harv.L.Rev. 1849, 1930 (1987). In response it is noted that the Sterns are not rich and the Whiteheads not poor. Nevertheless, it is clear to us that it is unlikely that surrogate mothers will be as proportionately numerous among those women in the top twenty percent income bracket as among those in the bottom twenty percent. Put differently, we doubt that infertile couples in the low-income bracket will find upper income surrogates.

In any event, even in this case one should not pretend that disparate wealth does not play a part simply because the contrast is not the dramatic "rich versus poor." At the time of trial, the Whiteheads' net assets were probably negative—Mrs. Whitehead's own sister was foreclosing on a second mortgage. Their income derived from Mr. Whitehead's labors. Mrs. Whitehead is a homemaker, having previously held part-time jobs. The Sterns are both professionals, she a medical doctor, he a biochemist. Their combined income when both were working was about $89,500 a year and their assets sufficient to pay for the surrogacy contract arrangements.

The point is made that Mrs. Whitehead agreed to the surrogacy arrangement, supposedly fully understanding the consequences. Putting aside the issue of how compelling her need for money may have been, and how significant her understanding of the consequences, we suggest that her consent is irrelevant. There are, in a civilized society, some things that money cannot buy. In America, we decided long ago that merely because conduct purchased by money was "voluntary" did not mean that it was good or beyond regulation and prohibition. West Coast Hotel Co. v. Parrish, 300 U.S. 379, 57 S.Ct. 578, 81 L.Ed. 703 (1937). Employers can no longer buy labor at the lowest price they can bargain for, even though that labor is "voluntary," 29 U.S.C. § 206 (1982), or buy women's labor for less money than paid to men for the same job, 29 U.S.C. § 206(d), or purchase the agreement of children to perform oppressive labor, 29 U.S.C. § 212, or purchase the agreement of workers to subject themselves to unsafe or unhealthful working conditions, 29 U.S.C. §§ 651 to 678 (Occupational Safety and Health Act of 1970). There are, in short, values that society deems more important than granting to wealth whatever it can buy, be it labor, love, or life. Whether this principle recommends prohibition of surrogacy, which presumably sometimes results in great satisfaction to all of the parties, is not for us to say. We note here only that, under existing law, the fact that Mrs. Whitehead "agreed" to the arrangement is not dispositive.

　　　　* * *

Beyond that is the potential degradation of some women that may result from this arrangement. In many cases, of course, surrogacy may bring satisfaction, not only to the infertile couple, but to the surrogate mother herself. The fact, however, that many women may not perceive surrogacy negatively but rather see it as an opportunity does not diminish its potential for devastation to other women.

In sum, the harmful consequences of this surrogacy arrangement appear to us all too palpable. In New Jersey the surrogate mother's agreement to sell her child is void. Its irrevocability infects the entire contract, as does the money that purports to buy it.

[The Court granted custody to Mr. Stern based an analysis of the best interests of the child. It voided the termination of Mrs. Whitehead's parental rights and the adoption of the child by Mrs. Stern.]

Notes and Questions

1.   Obviously there is both a demand for and a supply of babies or, at least, the child bearing services of women. In an unregulated market, exchanges would be made. The transaction costs of these exchanges would be decreased by the existence of agencies that would match buyers with sellers. If both sellers and buyers are better off, why object to this scheme?

2.   The Court distinguishes adoption from the surrogacy contract in the case. Does this mean that if Mrs. Whitehead had simply given the child to the Sterns the interests the court seeks to protect would be properly protected? What connection do you see between the payment of money and the welfare of the child? If someone is willing to pay a large sum for a child and someone is willing to take the money, why isn't it likely that the child

would be better off with the person who was willing to pay for it rather than the person who was willing to sell it?

3. Note the Court's phrasing of its reasoning and its obvious aversion to market transactions of this sort. For example, unlike adoption, in a surrogacy case the use of money is said to produce a problem. The use of money means "taking advantage of a woman's circumstances * * * *in order to take away her child.*" (emphasis added). What makes this situation different from one in which someone "takes advantage" of your circumstances to buy a copy of your notes for this course?

4. Should it be relevant in a case like this that Mr. Stern is the biological father? Should the case come out differently if Mrs. Stern's egg had been used in the process and Mrs. Whitehead had "incubated" the fertilized egg? Do any of those factual distinctions address the best interests of the child?

5. Is the real concern in a case like this one of class distinctions and the possibility of taking advantage of women? Did that seem to be a problem here? Should the result had come out differently if Mrs. Whitehead had had her own lawyer and had received five times as much money? Would that have offended the Court even more? Should the Court have been offended?

GUIDO CALABRESI & A. DOUGLAS MELAMED, PROPERTY RULES, LIABILITY RULES AND INALIENABILITY: ONE VIEW OF THE CATHETRAL

85 Harvard Law Review 1089 (1972).

* * * [E]xternal costs may justify inalienability * * * when [they] do not lend themselves to collective measurement which is acceptably objective and nonarbitrary. * * * Such external costs are often called moralisms.

If Taney is allowed to sell himself into slavery, or to take undue risks of becoming penniless, or to sell a kidney, Marshall may be harmed, simply because Marshall is a sensitive man who is made unhappy by seeing slaves, paupers, or persons who die because they have sold a kidney. Again Marshall could pay Taney not to sell his freedom to Chase the slaveowner; but again, because Marshall is not one but many individuals, freeloader and information costs make such transactions practically impossible. Again, it might seem that the state could intervene by objectively valuing the external cost to Marshall and requiring Chase to pay that cost. But since the external cost to Marshall does not lend itself to an acceptable objective measurement, such liability rules are not appropriate.

In the case of Taney selling land to Chase, the polluter, they were inappropriate because we knew that the costs to Taney and the Marshalls exceeded the benefits to Chase. Here, though we are not certain of how a cost-benefit analysis would come out, liability rules are inappropriate because any monetization is, by hypothesis, out of the question. The state must, therefore, either ignore the external costs to Marshall, or if it judges them great enough, forbid the transaction that gave rise to them by making Taney's freedom inalienable.

Obviously we will not always value the external harm of a moralism enough to prohibit the sale. And obviously also, external costs of the other than moralisms may be sufficiently hard to value to make rules of inalienability appropriate in certain circumstances; this reason for rules of inalienability, however, does seem most often germane in situations where moralisms are involved.

There are two other efficiency reasons for forbidding the sale of entitlements under certain circumstances: self paternalism and true paternalism. Examples of the first are Ulysses tying himself to the mast or individuals passing a bill of rights so that they will be prevented from yielding to momentary temptations which they deem harmful to themselves. This type of limitation is not in any real sense paternalism. It is fully consistent with Pareto efficiency criteria, based on the notion that over the mass of cases no one knows better than the individual what is best in the long run rather than in the short run, even though that choice entails giving up some short run freedom of choice. Self paternalism may cause us to require certain conditions to exist before we allow a sale of an entitlement; and it may help explain many situations of inalienability, like the invalidity of contracts entered into when drunk, or under undue influence or coercion. But it probably does not fully explain even these.

True paternalism brings us a step further toward explaining such prohibitions and those of broader kinds—for example the prohibitions on a whole range of activities by minors. Paternalism is based on the notion that at least in some situations the Marshalls know better than Taney what will make Taney better off. Here we are not talking about the offense to Marshall from Taney's choosing to read pornography, or selling himself into slavery, but rather the judgment that Taney was not in the position to choose best for himself when he made the choice for erotica or servitude. The first concept we called a moralism and is a frequent and important ground for inalienability. But it is consistent with the premises of Pareto optimality. The second, paternalism, is also an important economic efficiency reason for inalienability, but it is not consistent with the premises of Pareto optimality: the most efficient pie is no longer that which costless bargains would achieve, because a person may be better off if he is prohibited from bargaining.

Finally, just as efficiency goals sometimes dictate the use of rules of inalienability, so, of course, do distributional goals. Whether an entitlement may be sold or not often affects directly who is richer and who is poorer. Prohibiting the sale of babies makes poorer those who can cheaply produce babies and richer those who through some nonmarket device get free an "unwanted" baby. Prohibiting exculpatory clauses in product sales makes richer those who were not injured and who paid more for the product because the exculpatory clause was forbidden. Favoring the specific group that has benefited may or may not have been the reason for the prohibition on bargaining. What is important is that, regardless of the reason for barring a contract, a group did gain from the prohibition.

This should suffice to put us on guard, for it suggests that direct distributional motives may lie behind asserted nondistributional grounds for inalienability, whether they be paternalism, self-paternalism, or externalities. This does not mean that giving weight to distributional goals is undesirable. * * * The danger may be, however, that what is justified on, for example, paternalism grounds is really a hidden way of accruing distributional benefits for a group whom we would not otherwise wish to benefit. For example, we may use certain types of zoning to preserve open spaces on the grounds that the poor will be happier, though they do not know it now. And open spaces may indeed make the poor happier in the long run. But the zoning that preserves open space also makes housing in the suburbs more expensive and it may be that the whole plan is aimed at securing distributional benefits to the suburban dweller regardless of the poor's happiness.

Notes and Questions

1. Where does *Baby M* fit in the framework presented by Calabresi and Melamed? Who is being protected by the Court—the child, Mrs. Whitehead or both? What is the rationale? Note that Calabresi and Melamed attempt to connect inalienability rules with efficiency or distributive concerns. Are there other bases for having rules of inalienability?

2. Some sales do have third party effects that would be difficult to force the actor to internalize. These range from the discomfort we may feel knowing that a destitute woman sells a baby to more quantifiable values like the cost that society generally may bear if tenants of rental property are permitted to sell back to the landlord their right not to have an exculpatory provision included in their rental agreement.

3. Perhaps more intriguing are the examples of self-paternalism and true paternalism. Self-paternalism suggests that we may have preferences that we would prefer not to have and that we protect ourselves by passing laws that prohibit us from acting in a manner that are consistent with the lower order preferences. Can you think of any example of a regulation on alienability that seems based on self-paternalism?

4. True paternalism is perhaps more difficult to justify since it involves tying the hands of others. Moreover, the implication is that the individuals are either not able to act in conformity with their preferences or that their preferences are not legitimate. Who should make these decisions? Are they consistent? In this country alcohol and tobacco are, with some limitations, readily available, but many other drugs are not. Does this mean that what determines alienability is political power?

5. It may appear that a rule prohibiting the sale of something is a preemptive type of regulation that basically eliminates a market. One view of inalienability is that it does not prohibit the sale of anything—it just raises the price. Thus, prostitution exists and there is a "black market" for babies.

In fact, the inalienability rules applied in some markets may mean that only the very well-to-do will acquire the property.

6.   Inalienability rules have been applied when it comes to the sale of human organs. For example, under federal law it is "unlawful for anyone to acquire, receive or otherwise transfer any human organ for valuable consideration . . ." 42 U.S.C.§ 274e. This prohibition even applies to cadaveric organs. In other words, it would be illegal for you to agree in advance, and for payment, to transfer an organ at the time of your death.[35] Where do you think this prohibition fits in with the rationales explained by Calabresi and Melamed? Is it simply a way of avoiding making some hard choices? As the next section illustrates, we are beginning an era of making similar "hard choices."

4. THE ALLOCATION OF SCARCE HEALTH CARE RE-SOURCES

There seems to be little doubt that during the next fifty years the most pressing issues under the scarce resource rationale will concern various health care resources. The questions will range from highly technical to deeply philosophical. In a sense, this is the ultimate regulatory issue since there will never be enough life, longevity, or comfort to satisfy everyone.

This regulation is especially complicated due to a number of factors. First, the health care industry is really composed of a number of quite different sectors with different economic characteristics requiring different regulatory approaches. Second, the health care industry can be viewed as selling a virtually infinite number of products ranging from surgical procedures to physical and psychological therapy to nutritional information. Third, a great deal of the payment for health care is made through third party payers meaning that the actual recipients of care are not as price sensitive as they otherwise would be. Finally, even if consumers were price sensitive, they face the additional barrier of not being able to fully assess the products offered due to their technical nature and rapid changes in technology.

This is not to say that the health or medical care industry is not already heavily regulated. In fact a great number of these regulations fall under the rationales you have already seen. For example, the licensing of physicians serves the purpose of providing information to consumers and rationalizing the industry. Regulation by the Food and Drug Administration lowers the transaction costs of obtaining accurate information about the safety and efficacy of prescription drugs. Hospital construction is often regulated by states through the requirement that a certificate of need be obtained before construction. In theory, this requirement can be seen as being linked to both the natural monopoly rationale and the transaction costs rationale. Hospital mergers are also regulated under the antitrust laws as are the types of agreements that can be entered

35. See Roger D. Blair & David L. Kaserman, The Economics and Ethics of Alternative Cadaveric Procurement Policies, 8 Yale J. Regulation 403 (1991).

into by health care providers. Finally, insurance providers are also heavily regulated.

These regulations are, for the most part, uncoordinated efforts to respond to relatively narrow issues raised in specific parts of the health care industry. Future regulations will be the product of two basic determinations. First, there is a shortage of care relative to some undetermined level of what would be acceptable. This is already reflected in the public subsidization of health care delivery and research. The second general conclusion is that access to medical care should not be allocated on an ability to pay basis. This too is already reflected in public subsidization of the elderly through Medicare and of the indigent through Medicaid.

These are by no means conclusions to be taken lightly. In order to understand why, consider what the quantity and distribution of health care might look like if unregulated—aside from the relatively narrow industry-by-industry regulations noted above. The amount of health care and its character would be entirely market driven. Research by a pharmaceutical company, for example, would be determined exclusively by what private parties or their insurers would be willing and able to pay for drugs. There might be billions of dollars spent on a "cure" for baldness and little invested in research aimed at eliminating a relatively rare, but deadly disease. Likewise, physician specialties would be market driven. Specialties that are "needed" by the relatively well-to-do would be more attractive than those that disproportionately serve those suffering from ailments associated with malnutrition, poor prenatal care or poverty generally.

The decision to produce more or different health care than the market would otherwise deliver and to distribute it differently, leads to several questions like:

    a.   How much should a society invest in health care?

    b.   Who will benefit from this investment?

    c.   Who will pay for this investment?

    d.   How will a comprehensive health care policy be administered?

As the following suggests, these questions are not only complex, but interrelated.

    a. How great a health care investment?

Once a market determination of the level of health care investment is abandoned, we are faced with the very complex and controversial issue of deciding as a matter of public policy how much should be spent on health care. There is likely to be little agreement on how great the need is, whether it is quantifiable or whether it is even morally right to attempt to quantify it. The issues are not always subject to the type of public interest analysis you have already seen. For example, what is the goal? More particularly, what is health care? Is it just medical treatment or does it extend to things like better nutrition and highway safety? Is the goal to make people live as long as possible? Is it to enable them to live as comfortably as possible? If so, how would you distinguish a pain-relieving medication from liposuction for someone who is self-conscious about being overweight? Are the needs of future generations to be included in the analysis?

One major difficulty that arises in addressing these issues is that the reactions are highly subjective. Indeed, both religious beliefs and super-stition can play a role. For example, note the material above about the sale of human organs. The idea to some may seem so far-fetched as to be a joke—even macabre. Yet, it is no different in principle than the decision to pursue one type of potentially life-saving research over another. If you look at the issue closely can you come up with a sound basis for not permitting the sale of organs? If your answer is that only the rich will be able to afford to buy organs, the next question is whether a market that permits access only by the rich is worse than a policy of denying access to everyone.

One thing that basic economics tells us is that addressing a per-ceived shortage of health care means not using resources for some other purpose. For example, increased investment might mean less public investment in education or the arts. In determining how far to go, how would you feel about a health care investment program that only recognized shortages when the money spent would be more than offset by increases in Gross Domestic Product?

b.   Who benefits?

If you accept the notion that addressing a health care shortage means something less than solving every perceived health care problem, then general hand-wringing must give way to specific issues of how relatively scarce resources are to be allocated. Some identifiable groups will still not have their needs met. One possibility would be to maintain the status quo with respect to the proportionate share of health care investment by simply increasing the amounts devoted to each need. On the other hand, consider the following: in 1996 breast cancer was responsible for the deaths of nearly 45,000 women and prostate cancer killed over 40,000 men. AIDS was responsible for a similar number of deaths. At the same time, there are currently over 34,000 studies being conducted on breast cancer, 5,000 on prostate cancer and 85,000 on AIDS.[36] The number of dollars devoted to each area of research reflects the same ranking. How can this type of allocation be explained? One likely possibility is political influence stemming from better organization of advocates for and more publicity of those diseases receiving higher funding.

This sort of "Public Choice" explanation, if true, may not seem fair to you. If so, with what would you replace it? Should these decisions be made on some kind of risk-benefit basis that takes into consideration the education, age and future productivity of the individual and weighs it

36. Health, 133 Fortune Magazine, No. 9, May 13, 1996.

against the cost of treatment and the probability of successful treatment?[37] Should investments be made in children over adults? Would you favor investments in prevention over treatment of existing serious illness?[38] In this regard, one politician is reported to have said that the elderly "have a duty to die and get out of the way."[39]

The distributive issue can be reframed not as "who gets what," but as "what is the proper methodology for making this decision."[40] For example, if a cost benefit analysis makes you feel squeamish, how about a distribution decision made behind the Rawlsian "veil of ignorance?" Put differently, think right now of the system of allocation you would favor. Then think about the system you would consider "fair" if you knew nothing about yourself. You would not know your age, gender, race, or medical condition. Behind this "veil of ignorance" would you choose the same rationing priorities? Which construct should we assume when determining health care allocations?[41]

c. Who pays?

Obviously, a system that is designed to increase the amount of health care over that which would be produced under market driven conditions means that there will be a need for subsidization of some groups by others. The beginning proposition might seem to be that the relatively healthy and wealthy will subsidize the poor and unhealthy. Of course, programs with this goal often undergo subtle adjustments in the legislative process so that healthy poor and middle class Americans end up subsidizing the unhealthy poor.

More importantly, the question of subsidization cannot be addressed in the abstract. For example, suppose that a health care proposal requires a contribution from you in the form of additional insurance premiums or taxes. Suppose further that this decrease in your disposable income makes that face-lift or liposuction treatment you have been wanting just out of reach.

How would you feel about your contribution if funds were spent on a "Stop Smoking" campaign? How about abortions? Liver transplants for

---

37. See Susan D. Goold, Allocating Health Care: Cost–Utility Analysis, Informed Democratic Decision Making or the Veil of Ignorance? 21 J. Health Policy & Law 69 (1996).

38. These are some of the trends developing in an effort by the State of Oregon to ration medical care in the context of its Medicaid program. See Caitlin J. Halligan, "Just What the Doctor Ordered": Oregon's Medicaid Rationing Process and Public Participation in Risk Regulation, 83 Georgetown L. J. 2697 (1995).

39. Gov. Lamm Asserts Elderly, If Very Ill, have a "Duty to Die," The New York Times, March 29, 1984, p. 16, col. 5. But see, Richard D. Lamm, Long Time Dying:

When "Miracle Cures" Don't Cure, 191 The New Republic 20, August 27, 1984. Whatever else one can say about this proposition, it surely seems to contradict the Public Choice view of political behavior since the elderly vote and children do not. Or do they?

40. See generally David Orentlicher, Destructuring Disability: Rationing of Health Care and Unfair Discrimination Against the Sick, 31 Harv. Civ. Rights–Civ. Liberties L. Rev. 49 (1996).

41. See generally, Einer Elhauge, Allocating Health Care Morally, 82 California L. Rev. 1449 (1994); Dieter Geissen, A Right to Health Care?: A Comparative Perspective, 4 Health Matrix 277 (1994).

alcoholics? Therapy for people who suffer from stage fright? Should the "Stop Smoking" campaign be paid for by the tobacco industry and the liver transplant by the alcoholic beverage industry?

The issue of "who pays" raises an obvious question of equity. That is not the only important issue, however. Consider, for example, legislation proposed by the Clinton Administration in 1993. Under that proposal, revenue would be generated by taxes on employers, employees and specific industries like tobacco. Obviously, all of these sources of revenue find their way back to individuals in the form of higher prices, lower wages or lower dividends. Still, there is an obvious disconnection between those who pay for health care and those who consume it.[42] Put differently, those most able to control high-risk behavior may not be provided with incentives to do so. Thus, when addressing the question of "who pays," can an argument be made that, to the extent possible, those engaging in high-risk behavior should be the ones who pay to have health care available?

d.   Administering a Health Care Plan

Should a program be administered by the federal government? Should private insurance firms remain the primary insurers with premium payments subsidized by the government? Should there be incentives to encourage people to rely on one provider systems—say HMOs—over the typical pay-as-you-go system? Hovering over these decisions is the question of just how involved the government should be in what are traditionally personal choices, sometimes even involving the decision of whether to live or die.

These decisions have and will be affected by the actions of interest groups ranging from physicians and pharmaceutical companies to those affected by a particular illness.[43] Reflect on the materials you have seen concerning the transportation and telecommunications industries as they moved from highly regulated to relatively "deregulated." Do you foresee health care going through the same cycle? Do you see it perhaps going the other way?

---

42.   See generally, John J. Kang, Perpetuating Market Misallocations in Health Care Through Employer Insurance Mandates, 12 American J. of Tax Policy 513 (1995).

43.   For more on the "realities" of health care reform see generally, W. John Thomas, The Clinton Health Care Reform Plan: A Failed Dramatic Presentation, 7 Stanford L. & Policy Rev. 83 (1996).

Chapter 4

RATE REGULATION IN
A DEREGULATION
ENVIRONMENT

As we have seen, prices in most American industries are regulated by market forces unleashed by competition. In public utilities, however, and other industries in which there was only one provider of services, rate regulation was often seen as a bulwark against the provider's wish to exploit its monopoly position. Conversely, the regulators were also required to protect the regulated firm against rates so low that they would constitute an unconstitutional taking of the company's assets.

Misconceptions about the reliability and effects of such regulation sometimes led to a naive reliance on regulation as a sure way to achieve results. Realistically, rate regulation cannot reproduce the incentives for quality, efficiency or price that are created by competition. Nor can it make possible the quick responses to competitive pressures that are so characteristic of a competitive economy. The most that probably can be said is that rate regulation seeks to assure that the regulated firm does not make an "excessive" profit.

The first part of this Chapter reviews traditional rate regulation, both because it still exists in some industries and because it helps one understand current efforts to look for different ways to protect consumers. The rest of the Chapter examines some of those current efforts.

A. AN OVERVIEW OF THE TRADITIONAL RATE–MAKING PROCESS

1. AN INTRODUCTION TO PROCEDURE

It is important to understand that in most regulatory schemes, the initiative for establishing rates is taken by the regulated firms. The regulatory agency normally does not itself initiate a proceeding to change the status quo. Instead, a regulated firm will publish a rate schedule or "tariff" in the same way an unregulated firm would publish

250

a price list. The new tariff will then normally be subject to suspension by the agency while the agency determines whether it is reasonable, i.e., whether it will lead to an excessive return to the company and whether it distributes the charges for service fairly across all customers.

The typical procedure has been summarized as follows:

> Company X files for a rate increase. The company, with the concurrence of the commission or its staff, will generally select a "test period," frequently the latest 12–month period for which complete data are available. The purposes of such a test period are as follows. In the first place, the commission must examine company expenses. Only reasonable expenses are allowed for rate-making purposes. In the second place, the commission must have a basis for estimating future revenue requirements. This estimate is, perhaps, the most difficult problem in a rate case. A commission is setting rates for the future, but it has only past experience (expenses, cost, and demand conditions) to use as a guide. Frequently, future estimates of expenses will be made, thereby resulting in either an increase or decrease of the test period expenses. But the commissions have been hesitant to make future forecasts of consumer demand, often preferring instead to assume that the test period demand conditions will hold in the immediate future. For this reason, the actual rate of return earned by a regulated company may turn out to be quite different from the rate allowed by the commission in a particular rate case.

> The case will be set down on the commission's docket for public hearings, and due notice will be given. When the case is called, testimony—sometimes oral and sometimes written ("canned")—will be presented by the company, the commission's staff, and interveners (interested parties). Such testimony is usually presented by outside experts, as well as by both company and staff personnel. All witnesses are sworn, the evidence is recorded, and witnesses may be questioned by the examiner or commission and cross-examined by counsel for opposing parties. In some instances, hearings will be held in the community or communities affected. At the federal level, the examiner will then issue his decision (the "initial decision") on the case. The decision must be written and accompanied by formal findings of fact and conclusions of law. It is then subject to review by the full commission, and the commission's decision, in turn, may be appealed to the courts.

> It is not uncommon for important cases to require several sets of hearings and to take from one to five years before a final commission order is issued. When a decision is appealed to the courts, another two to four years may be added.[1]

1. Charles F. Phillips, Jr., The Economics of Regulation 136–37 (Rev. Ed. 1969). Copyright 1969, Richard D. Irwin, Inc. Reprinted by permission.

Other overviews of the process include William K. Jones, An Example of a Regulatory Alternative to Antitrust: New York Utilities in the Early Seventies, 73 Colum-

Notes and Questions

1. Is the process described here designed to come up with a "fair" price for the regulated firm's service? In what sense is the price "fair"?

   a. Should it be relevant that many consumers believe the cost of the service is "too high"? What is the justification for allowing a utility to charge rates that, say, seventy-five per cent of consumers polled believe are excessive?

   b. Is there any point in the process at which someone steps back and asks whether the price dictated by the firm's cost figures is "reasonable"? Should Commissioners be entitled to intervene if they conclude that rates determined by the process are simply more than they believe consumers can afford to pay?

2. Does the rate-making process suggest anything about the possible "capture" of regulatory agencies by the firms they regulate? In what sense is capture inevitable? Who has the information with which the regulatory body must work? In what posture does the regulatory agency tend to find itself in rate-making? Might "teamwork" between company and agency understandably seem more efficient and pleasant than constant warfare? What are the problems with "teamwork" in the regulatory context?

2. THE FORMULA FOR DETERMINING ALLOWABLE REVENUE

Contrary to stockbroker rhetoric, no regulated firm is "guaranteed" a profit. Each regulated firm is simply guaranteed a right to sell its product or service at a prescribed schedule of rates. If the regulatory agency's crystal ball has been perfect, the firm will receive total revenues which just equal the figure the agency has determined is proper. Of course in reality, actual earnings may be more or less, but determining the target revenue figure, which we will call "R", is the ultimate objective of a rate hearing.

The formula for determining "R" is simply stated:[2]

$$R = C + I \times r$$

Those letters represent a shorthand way of saying that the total revenue (R) which a regulated firm should be entitled to earn is equal to the regulated firm's expected costs (C) during the relevant period for goods and services consumed during that period, plus a reasonable rate

bia L. Rev. 462 (1973); Louis Kohlmeier, The Regulators 29–35 (1969); Richard Posner, Natural Monopoly and its Regulation, 21 Stanford L. Rev. 548, 592–93 (1969); Ralph S. Spritzer, Uses of the Summary Power to Suspend Rates: An Examination of Federal Regulatory Agency Practices, 120 U. Pennsylvania L. Rev.39 (1971).

2. There are many ways to state this formula and no consensus as to the best has emerged. Common additions to the formula are terms to reflect that depreciation for the test period has been reflected as part of C and that total depreciation on the fixed assets has been subtracted to get the value of I. Such treatment of depreciation is assumed in the formula used here.

of return (r) figured on the capital invested (I) in assets used but not consumed by the business.[3]

Conceptually, that formula is clear, but as we shall see, factual and legal issues arise with respect to each of its elements. Furthermore, as deregulation produces conditions in which an increasing portion of the output of regulated firms is sold in competition with unregulated firms, the problems of applying this formula become even more complex.

3. ISSUES ARISING IN THE DETERMINATION OF OPERATING COSTS (C)

Obviously, any rate-hearing will contain numerous examples of costs applicable to the test period. Such things as the cost of supplies and materials used, and wages and salaries paid, will inevitably be part of the calculation. As to most of these costs, there will be little or no question of allowability. However, some expenses seem continually to raise issues. In perspective, some of the dollar amounts at stake may be relatively low, but the principles they help illustrate can give us an insight into very basic concerns that underlie the determination of which costs, if any, should be excluded from "C" in rate-making.[4]

a. Advertising Expenditures and Charitable Contributions

BOSTON GAS COMPANY v. DEPARTMENT OF PUBLIC UTILITIES

Supreme Judicial Court of Massachusetts, 1989.
405 Mass. 115, 539 N.E.2d 1001.

WILKINS, J. The Boston Gas Company (company), by this appeal from an order of the Department of Public Utilities (department), challenges those aspects of the department's 1988 rate decision that disallowed certain advertising expenses and all charitable contributions as costs of service that could be recognized in the company's rates charged to its customers. * * *

      * * *

1. The department was warranted in disallowing, as a cost of service to be reflected in the company's rates, institutional advertising, advertising that is designed to improve the image of the company and that contains no information which might be directly helpful or beneficial to the company's customers.

Our opinion in the *New England Tel.* case [360 Mass. 443 (1971)] was written at a time when it was generally believed * * * that a utility

---

3. "I" is the firm's so-called "rate base."

4. In the cases that follow, some will speak of "allowing an expense" and others of "allowing deductions from income." These are just different accounting formats for raising the same issue. We will speak throughout of allowing or disallowing an expense. The other format simply acts as though the basic formula were R–C = Ir. That is, it establishes an appropriate return to the firm and the revenue necessary to earn it, treating all expenditures as "deductions from income" actually received. Don't be confused. Nothing turns on the format chosen; it's purely a matter of terminology.

should be encouraged to foster growth and that growth would benefit consumers and shareholders alike. We concluded that a utility was "entitled to expend reasonable sums in an effort to retain its current customers, to acquire additional customers, and to sell to all such customers as many of its services as it has available for sale." Id. at 483. We said that the utility's managers should make the decision whether institutional advertising is helpful to its business and, if so, what amounts the company should spend. * * * We concluded that the department had attempted without warrant to interfere with the prerogatives of the utility's business managers and thus had acted beyond its authority.

Almost ten years later, the Legislature enacted a statute disallowing as a cost of service amounts expended by gas and electric companies for promotional (and political) advertising, subject to certain exclusions. This expression of public policy for such companies substantially undercuts the basis for the court's treatment of advertising expenses in the *New England Tel.* case. Section 33A * * * is concerned with discouraging gas and electric companies from promoting the use of gas and electricity, respectively. The language of § 33A was taken largely from the Federal Public Utility Regulatory Policies Act of 1978. The object of the Federal act was to promote energy conservation by federally regulated utilities in response to the nationwide energy crisis and to encourage States to adopt similar regulations. If the use of energy was not encouraged by promotional advertising, it was assumed that less energy would be used.

This case, of course, does not involve promotional advertising. * * * * * *

The *New England Tel.* case espoused a broad principle of managerial prerogative concerning advertising for the benefit of the company. That reasoning, which no longer fully obtains at least as to gas and electric companies, may explain why a utility should be allowed to advertise to promote its image, but it does not explain why ratepayers, as opposed to shareholders, should shoulder the expense of advertising that does not benefit them in any fairly discernible and direct way. We thus agree with the department, and the strong trend of judicial decisions issued since our opinion in the *New England Tel.* case, that the cost of institutional or image advertising may be treated as a cost of service only if it benefits ratepayers directly.

* * *

2. The department disallowed charitable contributions as a cost of service because the company did not establish on the record "that its corporate charitable giving is reasonable and provides some clear benefit to ratepayers that is essential to serving them." * * *

* * *

We accept the department's view that amounts given to charities may be included in the cost of service if they provide some clear benefit to ratepayers. The concept of direct or essential benefit to ratepayers must, however, be given appropriate interpretation.

In the test year used as a base for determining costs of service in this proceeding, the company provided $20,000 in matching funds to supplement charitable gifts made by its employees. Reasonable fringe benefits for employees help to attract and retain employees. As fringe benefits that promote employee good will, assuming the plan is reasonable in scope, the company's charitable gifts made to match its employees' gifts seem to benefit ratepayers directly and, if they do, they should be recognized as a cost of service. The test is not what the charity is. It is that matching charitable gifts by the company fall in the category of employee benefits. On remand the department should consider whether to recognize this form of charitable gifts as a cost of service.

Other charitable gifts may be less clearly includible in the cost of service. Two-thirds of the company's charitable gifts during the test year went to the United Way. It is not obvious on this record whether such a gift, even though made to charities largely serving within the company's area of service, provides any benefit to ratepayers sufficiently direct to warrant inclusion of the expense in the cost of service.

* * *

3. The department's decision is vacated in so far as it concerns advertising expenses and charitable gifts as a cost of service, and the proceeding is remanded to the department for further consideration in light of this opinion.

Notes and Questions

1. Are distinctions between kinds of advertising analytically useful? Are the distinctions of any practical use? Is it often hard to distinguish the types in concrete cases? For example, would you allow the cost of an ad showing a worried driver lost in a strange neighborhood who takes comfort knowing that she has a phone in the car with which to call for help?

2. As noted in *Boston Gas*, the Public Utility Regulatory Policies Act (PURPA) of 1978 covers a wide range of regulatory matters. Title I is of particular interest because it sets federal standards for electric utilities.[5] The

5. The five other Titles are as follows: Title II, Certain Federal Energy Regulatory Commission and Department of Energy Authorities (including various amendments to the Federal Power Act relative to wheeling, interconnection and cogeneration) is contained in 16 U.S.C.A. §§ 791a, 796 823a, 824, 824a–824a–4 824d, 824i, 824i, 825d. Title III, Retail Policies for Natural Gas Utilities (enacted to conserve energy supplied by gas utilities, encourage efficient use of facilities and equitable rates for consumers) is found at 15 U.S.C.A §§ 3201–3211. Title IV, Small Hydroelectric Power Projects, (establishing programs to encourage various entities to develop small projects in connection with existing dams not being used to generate electricity) is codified in 16 U.S.C.A. §§ 2701–2708. Title V, Crude Oil Transportation Systems (including a method for providing delivery systems to alleviate impending oil shortages) is contained in 43 U.S.C.A. §§ 2001–2012, and Title VI, Miscellaneous Provisions, (including amendments to various energy-related acts already existing) is scattered among 15 U.S.C.A. § 717x–717z, 16 U.S.C.A. §§ 824a–4, 2621, 2645, and 30 U.S.C.A. §§ 1311, 1316 (1976 F.Supp. 11, 1978). In 1982, Titles I and III of the PURPA were

purposes of Title I are "to encourage (1) conservation of energy supplied by electric utilities; (2) the optimization of the efficiency of use of facilities and resources by electric utilities; and (3) equitable rates to electric consumers."

Title I contains federal standards concerning methods of determining rates, load management techniques, master metering, automatic adjustment clauses, the provision of information to consumers and procedures for termination of service. A particular standard is to be applied by both state regulated and unregulated electric utilities if the state regulatory agency or the utility itself, if unregulated, determines that the standard is consistent with the purposes of the Title.

The only standard that is directly relevant for the determination of allowable expenses concerns advertising. According to the Act, "No electric utility may recover from any person other than the shareholders (or other owners) of such utility any direct or indirect expenditure by such utility for promotional or political advertising. * * * "[6] Promotional advertising is "any advertising for the purpose of encouraging any person to select or use the service or additional service of an electric utility or the selection or installation of any appliance or equipment designed to use such utility's service."[7] Political advertising is defined as "any advertising for the purpose of influencing public opinion with respect to legislative, administrative, or electoral matters, or with respect to any controversial issue of public importance."[8]

3. Should a regulated firm have to use the least expensive form of advertising?

a. If the U.S. Postal Service becomes an "Olympic Sponsor", for example, or buys ads on Super Bowl telecasts, should those costs be factored into the next round of increases in the price of first class stamps?

b. Might one permit the expense of a utility's printing an insert for inclusion with a utility bill but not permit reimbursement for television advertising? Suppose reputable studies show that people do not read inserts in utility bills?

4. Does regulation of communications with ratepayers raise constitutional questions? For example, should an electric utility be prohibited from advocating that it be given the right to produce nuclear power? See Consolidated Edison Co. of New York, Inc. v. Public Service Commission of New York, 447 U.S. 530, 100 S.Ct. 2326, 65 L.Ed.2d 319 (1980); Jeffrey L. Harrison, Public Utilities in the Marketplace of Ideas: A Fairness Solution For a Competitive Imbalance, 1982 Wisconsin L. Rev. 43.

5. Are different questions presented by permitting a regulated company to include its charitable expenditures in the calculation of its allowable rates?

held not to be in violation of the Tenth Amendment to the U.S. Constitution. Federal Energy Regulatory Commission v. Mississippi, 456 U.S. 742, 102 S.Ct. 2126, 72 L.Ed.2d 532 (1982).

6. 16 U.S.C.A. § 2623(b)(5).

7. 16 U.S.C.A. § 2625(h)(1)(C).

8. 16 U.S.C.A. § 2625(h)(1)(B). See generally, Note, The Constitutionality and Effectiveness of the Electric Regulatory Policies Act of 1978, 47 George Washington L. Rev. 787 (1979).

a.   Is it persuasive to argue that if utilities did not contribute to private charities, the ratepayers would have to support the charitable functions through public expenditures?

b.   Are a state's ratepayers the same individuals as the state's taxpayers? Are they likely to contribute to social service costs as taxpayers in the same proportion that they contribute as ratepayers? Do charitable contributions through utility rates likely constitute a progressive or a regressive "tax"?

AN ASIDE ON THE ECONOMICS OF PASSING COSTS ON TO THE CONSUMER

An important question underlying the allowability of advertising and charitable spending, as well as all other questions of cost reimbursement, is the regulated firm's ability to pass costs on to the ultimate consumer. One sometimes reads that any business will "pass on" its cost increases, but for most firms the process is not that simple.

Imagine a firm in perfect competition. It can only sell its product for the market price, say $6.00. It is producing the quantity of that product at which its marginal and average costs equal $6.00. Now assume that the firm gives $250.00 to charity. Who will bear the impact of that $250.00 gift? Do you see that the entire amount will be borne by the firm's stockholders? Under the circumstances we have posed, the firm was exactly breaking even. It will not be able to increase the price of the product because it is sold in perfect competition. The same thing would be true if the gift were of $1.00 per unit of output. That would change the firm's marginal cost and perhaps affect its quantity produced, but only it would bear the cost. In short, any cost incurred by a firm in perfect competition which is not incurred by the rest of the firms in the industry will be borne by the firm itself. It cannot "pass it on."[9]

Now assume that the firm is a monopolist and that demand for its product is inelastic, i.e., as the price of the firm's product is increased a given percentage, the quantity demanded falls by less than that percentage. Now what will be the effect of a lump-sum contribution of $250.00? Here again the monopolist will bear the entire amount because its marginal cost and marginal revenue will be unaffected. To complicate the problem, however, assume that the charitable contribution is $1.00 per unit. Figure 11 may be of help. The $1.00 per unit increase is represented by the vertical shift from MC to MC1.

As this graph suggests, the price increase, from P to P1 is less than $1.00. This is not because the monopolist is generous. It simply was charging what the traffic would bear before the contribution and its new point of profit maximization will not be high enough to let it recover the full $1.00. Although the amount the monopolist bears will depend on the shape of the particular curves, the point is fundamental and important.

9. What would be the effect of a cost increase which affected all competitive firms equally? See, e.g., Armen Alchian & William R. Allen, University Economics 325–27 (3d Ed. 1972).

Even a monopolist will pay a price in lost profits if it runs up costs, so it has some incentive to avoid doing so.

Figure 11

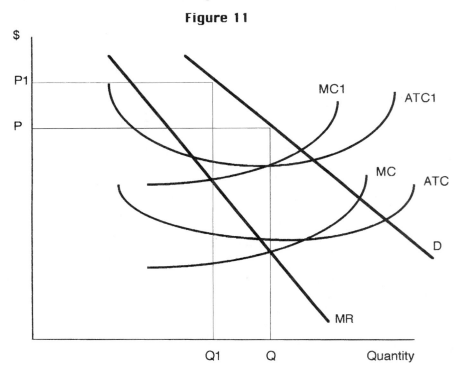

But contrast the case of the rate-regulated firm. Assume its cost curves are precisely those of the unregulated monopolist, as indicated in Figure 12 on the following page.[10] Here the shift from MC to MC1 is equal to the increase from P to P1.

Of course the regulated firm has not been permitted to maximize its profits. Such regulation may have some public benefits, but encouragement of cost cutting is not one of them. The regulated firm is entitled to pass on the full amount of an allowable cost and can do so easily out of the difference between the regulated price and what it could charge as a *monopolist*. The regulated firm will then presumably be forced to cut its output as people tend to do without service at the higher price. Indeed, average cost may go up as quantities are reduced and the price increase may have to exceed the $1.00 per unit the firm is seeking to recover.

---

10. It can persuasively be argued that a regulated firm would not have the same cost curves as an unregulated one precisely because of the phenomenon we are describing. That would not change the principles we are discussing but it would reduce the spread between the price charged under regulation and that charged by an unregu-lated monopolist. Indeed, if the costs of a regulated firm exceed those of a firm in competition, the loss in productive efficiency may outweigh the gains in allocative efficiency from keeping the price below the monopoly level. See Oliver Williamson, Economies as an Antitrust Defense Revisited, 125 U. Pennsylvania L. Rev. 699 (1977).

Figure   12

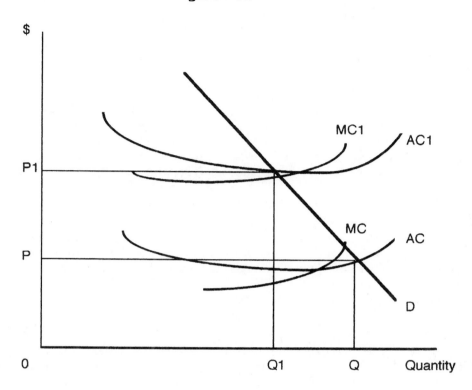

What this analysis suggests is that "passing on" by a regulated firm is inherently more of a blank check than it is in the case of a competitive firm or an unregulated monopolist. It is thus not surprising that citizens and regulators become moderately paranoid about the levels of cost incurred by regulated firms. It also helps explain why an increase in the price of any basic component of cost, Middle Eastern oil for example, can contribute to a dramatic increase in a utility's rates.

The "passing on" issue discussed here arises with respect to allowable expenses. A related and equally important issue is raised when a utility incurs expenses which are not allowable for rate-making purposes. The obvious initial impact is that revenue available for payment to holders of equity will decline. The expense is, in effect, absorbed by shareholders. Less obvious, however, is the eventual impact this may have on ratepayers as investment in the utility comes to be viewed as increasingly risky. This secondary or indirect "passing on" issue is discussed later in this Chapter in connection with the determination of a reasonable rate of return.

b. Intra–Corporate Transfers

ROCHESTER TELEPHONE CORP. v. PUBLIC SERVICE COMMISSION

Court of Appeals of New York, 1995.
87 N.Y.2d 17, 637 N.Y.S.2d 333, 660 N.E.2d 1112.

SMITH J.:

In July 1993, the Public Service Commission ("PSC") reduced the permissible utility rate Rochester Telephone Company ("RTC") could charge its ratepayers by imputing revenue to RTC in the form of a 2% royalty arising out of improper cost-shifting and uncompensated transfers of RTC's intangible assets between RTC and its subsidiaries and affiliates. * * * We affirm * * * because we conclude that the royalty and the rebuttable presumption are rational means for achieving just and reasonable utility rates.

In 1983, staff members of the Department of Public Service proposed imputing revenues to RTC in the form of a royalty to compensate ratepayers for the free transfer of intangible assets to RTC's affiliate, Rotelcom, and improper cost-shifting from Rotelcom to RTC. PSC called for hearings on the need for and the propriety of levying such a royalty. After the completion of hearings in June 1985, the Administrative Law Judge concluded that PSC had the legal authority to impose a royalty.

In 1990, PSC reopened the record to receive additional evidence on the propriety of imposing a royalty on RTC based on RTC's dealings with its subsidiaries and affiliates, and the appropriate level of such a royalty. * * * In July 1993, * * * PSC issued Opinion 93–11 which imposed a 2% royalty on RTC and created a rebuttable presumption of a 2% royalty for ratemaking purposes whenever a utility invests in competitive enterprises. * * *

RTC filed an article 78 proceeding, in which various interested utilities intervened, questioning PSC's authority to levy a royalty and challenging the royalty as an irrational means of achieving state interests. * * *

　　　* * *

The royalty at issue contains two components, a regulated value assurance mechanism (the "RVAM") and a positive benefits element. The RVAM was designed to compensate the ratepayers for the imprudent, uncompensated use of RTC's intangible assets, such as its name and reputation, while the positive benefits aspect, a misnomer, was designed to address the improper shifting of costs from the unregulated subsidiaries and affiliates to the regulated utility.

* * * Appellants contend that the RVAM improperly permits ratepayers to benefit from a non-ratemaking asset because the utility does not earn a rate of return on the utility's name and reputation. Appellants also argue that the record does not contain any finding of impru-

dence on the part of the utility and that diversification did not impose any costs on ratepayers. Appellants further argue the record contains no basis for the quantification of the 2% royalty.

The Legislature has granted the PSC broad regulatory authority over various public utilities in the highly technical field of setting just and reasonable rates. The PSC's determinations, within the ambit of its authority, are entitled to deference and may not be set aside unless they are without rational basis or without reasonable support in the record.

We have held that the PSC may not deny a utility a reasonable rate of return on its investment in the exercise of its ratemaking power. The PSC is also charged with the duty of ensuring that a telephone utility charges just and reasonable rates to its customers. In determining whether a utility has set reasonable rates, we have held that the PSC must evaluate the economic consequences of a utility's actions so that ratepayers may be protected from the utility's imprudent acts.

We conclude that the PSC had a rational basis for the RVAM element of the royalty. The record contains support for PSC's conclusion that RTC's name and reputation have value. RTC sought to exploit these intangible assets by closely associating itself with its affiliates in various advertising campaigns. It is undisputed that the unregulated subsidiaries and affiliates did not pay for the use of RTC's logo and name.

Where a utility derives benefit from the use of a non rate-based asset paid for by the ratepayers, we have held that the PSC may allocate part of the cost borne by the ratepayers to the shareholders. * * *

Insofar as the ratepayers have borne the costs for creating value in RTC's name and reputation, the ratepayers are entitled to a prudent use of those assets. The RVAM properly compensates ratepayers for RTC's imprudence in allowing the free use of its intangible assets rather than impermissibly granting ratepayers a direct interest in those assets. As noted by the PSC * * *, RTC ratepayers have funded the salaries, training, advertising and other activities that generate good will. Ratepayers have also paid for capital investments which have contributed positively to RTC's name and reputation. Moreover, a utility is able to establish widespread name recognition because the monopoly nature of the utility industry provides a widespread, captive ratepayer base in which to instill the name recognition. These ratepayers cannot obtain the same services from a competitor because no competitor exists.

Appellants' repeated protestations that PSC failed to make an imprudence finding in Opinion 93–11 are unpersuasive. A fair reading of Opinion 93–11 indicates that the PSC concluded that RTC acted imprudently by permitting its subsidiaries and affiliates to use valuable intangible assets, i.e. RTC's name and logo, free of charge. For example, PSC states the following in Opinion 93–11.

    * * *

A utility in an arms-length transaction could be expected to receive revenues for allowing the use of its employees or goodwill ... (p. 38).

A utility should make [a reasonable level of off-system electric] sales and receive such revenues [from directory publishing]; if it chooses not to, the revenue (and return) shortfall is its own fault. Similarly, a utility should receive reasonable remuneration when its affiliates benefit from it ... (p.41).

Because ratepayers have funded the salaries, training, advertising, and other activities that generate good will, they are entitled to rate recognition of revenues received by the utility in exchange for the use of that asset by an affiliate or otherwise (p.37).

Assets should be devoted to serving ratepayers and not dissipated for shareholders' benefit ... (p.66).

The PSC also considered the prudence standard in making its determinations. It observed that various methods for determining just and reasonable rates could be used and that "Traditionally, regulation has proceeded by allowing for recovery of reasonable, prudent costs, plus a fair profit ..." (p.66).

* * *

It is reasonable to conclude, as PSC did from this record, that a utility that permits its subsidiaries and affiliates to exploit valuable intangible assets for free, acts imprudently. Moreover, the imputation of the royalty does not result in an automatic obligation to pay the royalty. Utilities will have the opportunity to demonstrate that the RVAM component does not apply to their individual cases. The record indicates that the PSC had a rational basis for adopting the RVAM component of the rebuttable presumption.

The positive benefits component of the royalty is also supported by the record. The record contains evidence of actual costs imposed on ratepayers as a result of RTC's diversification and evidence of RTC's abundant incentive to shift costs from its unregulated subsidiaries and affiliates to its monopoly operations. A parent utility has an incentive to support its subsidiaries by entering into non-arms length transactions, and pass off any additional expense which may result to the parent's ratepayers. For example, RTC bought AT & T switching equipment from Rotelcom, an RTC subsidiary, at a mark-up from AT & T prices, when RTC could have bought the equipment directly from AT & T without paying the mark-up.

Regulated utilities also subsidize their subsidiaries and affiliates when the expertise and experience of the utilities' employees are placed at the disposal of the subsidiaries and affiliates for consultation and advice. Since ratepayers have paid for these human resources through training, salaries, bonuses and other incentive programs, the diversion of employee resources on subsidiary and affiliate matters imposes costs on the ratepayers. The record reflects that RTC did not adequately track and/or compensate its ratepayers for the costs of permitting its subsidiaries and affiliates access to RTC employees.

When a utility guarantees the bank debt of a subsidiary or affiliate, higher costs will be imposed on the guaranteeing utility's ratepayers if a bailout of that subsidiary or affiliate becomes necessary. For example, RTC guaranteed loans for RCI, a subsidiary. Consequently, RCI's lenders have recourse against RTC in the event of a default by RCI. RTC also invested over $40 million in RCI, to prevent the subsidiary from defaulting, when RCI could not meet the financial criteria set forth in a loan agreement.

The foregoing is not meant to be an exhaustive listing, but sets forth some of the various cost factors associated with the positive benefits component of the royalty. Given the complexity of the relationships between various utilities and their subsidiaries and affiliates, as well as the volume of transactions that must be scrutinized, PSC's conclusions that certain costs could not be adequately quantified and that current oversight systems could not capture all cases of improper cost-shifting, were rational and supported by the record.

We also reject appellants' claim that PSC's exercise of discretion in setting the royalty level at 2% lacked a rational basis. Ratemaking is a highly technical field within the special expertise of the PSC. In quantifying the royalty, PSC applied the expertise it had acquired in the context of previous settlements, where the amount of rate adjustments could not be precisely or objectively determined. The record also contained evidence that the PSC had previously imputed a percentage in quantifying objectively unascertainable items such as reasonably anticipated productivity improvements and allowances for certain types of advertising.

The 2% royalty was designed to compensate ratepayers for the uncompensated use of RTC's intangible assets and the costs of diversification, without imposing a penalty on RTC. PSC's exercise of judgment in this highly technical field was reasonable, especially given the ability of individual utilities to rebut the 2% figure. As recognized by the Appellate Division, the PSC envisioned situations in which individual utilities would be required to pay a different or no royalty percentage. This built-in flexibility renders the rebuttable presumption rational because any royalty ultimately imposed will be tailored to the individual circumstances of particular utilities.

        * * *

Accordingly, the judgment of the Appellate Division should be affirmed, with costs.

Notes and Questions

1. Ratemaking when a firm has both regulated and unregulated elements has been a long-standing problem.

   a. One kind of problem arises when the regulated entity buys an input—say coal for electricity generation—from a related entity at a price higher than the one that would prevail under competitive conditions. In general, even in a time of shortage where the related entity is a secure source of supply, the regulated firm will not be permitted to pass on to ratepayers any price higher than the price offered generally by firms in the industry. See, e.g., Application of Montana–Dakota Utilities Co., 278 N.W.2d 189 (S.D.1979).

b.   In *Rochester Telephone*, of course, the question is whether the unregulated entity has appropriated a valuable asset of the regulated firm without adequately paying for it. Do you agree that it has?

2.   A recurring issue, no matter how the issue arises, has been the appropriate allocation of joint costs between regulated and unregulated parts of a company. How should the company's office building be allocated, for example? How about the company parking lot? The point is that there are many expenditures that benefit all parts of the company and that would be incurred almost without regard to whether the other parts of the company existed. Almost any allocation thus can be accused of being arbitrary.

3.   What solution to the problem of joint costs did the Commission come up with here? Do you agree that a 2% royalty for use of the company name is appropriate to require of the unregulated operations? Did the unregulated sales increase the regulated firm's costs to create or advertise the name? Is it enough to say that the name was valuable and thus that it was "imprudent" for the regulated firm not to charge for its use?

4.   Was a 2% royalty high enough? Too high? Is any figure simply a tax on owning shares in a regulated firm? As more and more aspects of a regulated firm's activities are "deregulated," more and more forms of these questions are going to require answers.

c.   Depreciation and Tax Credits

A third difficult issue of costs incurred by a regulated firm is presented by the issue of how much depreciation to allow in a given year and how to account for tax credits.

Notes and Questions

1.   Is depreciation the same as the other costs we have been considering? Does it represent cash actually expended during the test period? Does it represent facilities actually consumed during the period? Is there a single objectively right way to handle depreciation?

2.   What method of calculating depreciation would you use in your own business to give you the most helpful information as to your true cost of doing business? What method most directly accounts for the impact, if any, of inflation on the firm's true costs?

3.   Does accelerated depreciation accurately reflect the phenomenon of asset exhaustion? Does it cause the "cost" to be overstated in early years and understated later? If the total depreciation charged over the life of an asset is reasonable, should it matter when specific sums are claimed? Why?

4.   If you were a regulatory official, would you want the utility to show a depreciation figure that was high or low? Would you want it to be

computed differently for tax purposes than it is for regulatory purposes? The level of depreciation taken has a three-way impact on rates—it makes (a) costs go up, (b) taxes go down, and (C) the rate base on which a return is earned (a process we discuss shortly) go down. Some examples may be helpful in seeing these relationships.

Example 1: Assume straight-line depreciation of $1,000.00 for both tax and rate-making purposes. Assume further that the tax rate is 50 per cent and the allowed rate of return is 10 per cent. Costs will rise $1,000.00, taxes fall $500.00 and "return" will fall 10 per cent x $1,000.00 or $100.00. The net impact for rate-making purposes thus will be to raise costs $400.00.

Example 2: Assume accelerated depreciation of $2,000.00 for both purposes. Costs will rise $2,000.00, taxes fall $1,000.00 and return falls 10 per cent x $2,000.00 or $200.00. Net impact thus will be $800.00. Under this example, rates would tend to be higher than under example 1, and agency critics would be calling for your resignation.

Example 3: Assume accelerated depreciation for tax but not rate-making purposes. Costs will rise $1,000.00, taxes falls $1,000.00 and return falls $100.00. The net impact will be to *reduce* costs (and ultimately rates) $100.00. You will now be hailed as a regulatory genius.

5. Can an argument be made that a utility should not pay any income taxes at all? Can you argue that a regulated firm is only a tax collector and not a taxpayer? Is the tax burden passed on through higher utility rates a progressive or regressive form of taxation? If utilities were exempted from taxes and utility rates thus reduced, would consumers be stimulated to demand more than an optimal amount of utility services?

d. The Problem of Bad Judgment

Running through all cases on allowability of costs is the requirement that an expense have been incurred "prudently." Wasteful expenditures are to be borne by the utility, not the ratepayers. That principle is easy to state but often hard to apply, particularly where decisions requiring a long time to implement turn out other than as expected. On top of that problem, our next case illustrates the possibility of federal preemption of a state's prudence determination.

MISSISSIPPI POWER & LIGHT CO. v. MISSISSIPPI EX REL. MOORE

Supreme Court of the United States, 1988.
487 U.S. 354, 108 S.Ct. 2428, 101 L.Ed.2d 322.

JUSTICE STEVENS delivered the opinion of the Court.

On July 1, 1985, Grand Gulf Unit 1, a major nuclear power plant located in Port Gibson, Mississippi, began commercial operations. An order entered by the Federal Energy Regulatory Commission (FERC) required Mississippi Power and Light Company (MP & L) to purchase 33% of the plant's output at rates determined by FERC to be just and reasonable. The Mississippi Public Service Commission (MPSC) subsequently granted MP & L an increase in its retail rates to enable it to recover the cost of its purchases of Grand Gulf power. On appeal, the Mississippi Supreme Court held that it was error to grant an increase in retail rates without first examining the prudence of the management decisions that led to the construction and completion of Grand Gulf 1. * * * [W]e conclude that the state proceedings are pre-empted [by the FERC proceedings] and therefore reverse.

I

MP & L is one of four operating companies whose voting stock is wholly owned by Middle South Utilities (MSU), a public utility holding company. The four companies are engaged both in the wholesale sale of electricity to each other and to companies outside the MSU system and in the retail sale of electricity in separate service areas in Louisiana, Arkansas, Missouri, and Mississippi. Through MSU the four companies operate as an integrated power pool, with all energy in the entire system being distributed by a single dispatch center located in Pine Bluff, Arkansas. Wholesale transactions among the four operating companies historically have been governed by a succession of three "System Agreements," which were filed with FERC in 1951, 1973, and 1982. The System Agreements have provided the basis for planning and operating the companies' generating units on a single-system basis and for equalizing cost imbalances among the four companies.

The retail sales of each of the operating companies are regulated by one or more local regulatory agencies. For example, Arkansas Power and Light Company (AP & L) sells in both Arkansas and Missouri and therefore is regulated by both the Arkansas Public Service Commission and the Missouri Public Service Commission. MP & L's retail rates are subject to the jurisdiction of the MPSC.

Through the 1950's and into the 1960's, most of the MSU system's generating plants were fueled with oil or gas. In the late 1960's, the MSU system sought to meet projected increases in demand and to diversify its fuel base by adding coal and nuclear generating units. It was originally contemplated that each of the four operating companies would finance and construct a nuclear power facility. Consistent with this scheme, MP & L was assigned to construct two nuclear power facilities at Port Gibson, Mississippi, Grand Gulf 1 and 2. The Grand Gulf project, however, proved too large for one operating company to finance. MSU therefore formed a new subsidiary, Middle South Energy, Inc. (MSE), to finance, own, and operate Grand Gulf. MSE acquired full title to Grand Gulf, but hired MP & L to design, construct, and operate the facilities.

In April 1974, MSE and MP & L applied to MPSC for a certificate of public convenience and necessity authorizing the construction of the plant. The State Commission granted the certificate, noting that MP & L was part of "an integrated electric system" and that "the Grand Gulf Project [would] serve as a major source of base load capacity for the company and the entire Middle South System pooling arrangement."

By the late 1970's it became apparent that system wide demand in the ensuing years would be lower than had been forecast, making Grand Gulf's capacity unnecessary. Moreover, regulatory delays, additional construction requirements, and severe inflation frustrated the project. Management decided to halt construction of Grand Gulf 2, but to complete Grand Gulf 1, largely on the assumption that the relatively low cost of nuclear fuel would make the overall cost of Grand Gulf power per kilowatt hour lower than that of alternative energy sources. As it turned out, however, the cost of completing Grand Gulf construction was about six times greater than had been projected.[11] Consequently, the wholesale cost of Grand Gulf's power greatly exceeds that of power produced in other system facilities.

The four operating companies considered various methods of allocating the cost of Grand Gulf's power. In 1982 MSU filed two agreements with FERC. The first was a new System Agreement, which set forth the terms and conditions for coordinated operations and wholesale transactions among the four companies, including a scheme of "capacity equalization payments," which were designed to ensure that each company contribute proportionately to the total costs of generating power on the system. * * * The second agreement filed with FERC was the Unit Power Sales Agreement (UPSA), which provided wholesale rates for MSE's sale of Grand Gulf 1 capacity and energy. Under the UPSA, AP & L was not obligated to purchase any of Grand Gulf's capacity; LP & L was obligated to purchase 38.57%, NOPSI 29.8%, and MP & L 31.63%.

THE FERC PROCEEDINGS

    * * *

The Commission affirmed and adopted the findings of the Administrative Law Judges that MSU is a highly integrated and coordinated power pool. It concluded that the result of this integration and coordination was "planning, construction, and operations which [were] conducted primarily for the system as a whole." Because it found that nuclear units on the System had been "planned to meet overall System needs and objectives," it concluded "that some form of equalization of nuclear plant costs [was] necessary to achieve just, reasonable, and non-discriminatory rates among the MSU operating companies." The Commission agreed with the judges that the 1982 System Agreement and the UPSA as filed would not together produce proper cost allocation, but concluded that the 1982 System Agreement in conjunction with ALJ Liebman's allocation of capacity costs associated with Grand Gulf would "achieve just and reasonable results." Thus FERC affirmed the allocation of 33% of Grand Gulf's capacity costs to MP & L as just and reasonable.

---

11. It was originally estimated that the cost per kilowatt of capacity would be about $500; by the time commercial operations began, that cost amounted to $2,933. The original estimate for the cost of two nuclear units at Port Gibson was approximately $1.2 billion. Regulatory delays, additional construction requirements imposed after the Three Mile Island disaster, and severe inflation, however, ran up Grand Gulf costs to more than $3 billion for the single unit. See Mississippi Industries v. FERC, 808 F.2d 1525, 1531 (1987). [Court's fn. 5]

Although it did not expressly discuss the "prudence" of constructing Grand Gulf and bringing it on line, FERC implicitly accepted the uncontroverted testimony of the MSU executives who explained why they believed the decisions to construct and to complete Grand Gulf 1 were sound, and approved the finding that "continuing construction of Grand Gulf Unit No. 1 was prudent because Middle South's executives believed Grand Gulf would enable the Middle South system to diversify its base load fuel mix and, it was projected, at the same time, produce power for a total cost (capacity and energy) which would be less than existing alternatives on the system."

The Commission later * * * rejected contentions that its exercise of jurisdiction would destroy effective state regulation of retail rates. * * * FERC went on to reject the argument that allocation of Grand Gulf costs should be based on whether individual companies needed Grand Gulf capacity. Since Grand Gulf had been constructed to meet the needs and serve the goals of the entire system, FERC reasoned that "the allocation of Grand Gulf power must rest not on the 'needs' of an individual company, but rather on the principles of just, reasonable, non-discriminatory, and non-preferential rates." * * *

On review, the United States Court of Appeals for the District of Columbia Circuit affirmed * * *.

THE STATE PROCEEDINGS

On November 16, 1984, before the FERC proceedings were completed, MP & L filed an application for a substantial increase in its retail rates. The major portion of the requested increase was based on the assumption that MP & L would be required to purchase 31.63% of the high-cost Grand Gulf power when the unit began operating on July 1, 1985, in accordance with the terms of the UPSA. * * * [T]he Mississippi Commission entered an order allowing MP & L certain additional revenues, but denying MP & L any retail rate relief associated with Grand Gulf Unit 1.

* * * As expected, Grand Gulf went on line on July 1, 1985, and MP & L became obligated consistent with FERC's allocation to make net payments of about $27 million per month for Grand Gulf capacity. After public hearings * * *, the MPSC found that MP & L would become insolvent if relief were not granted and allowed a rate increase to go into effect to recover a projected annual revenue deficiency of about $327 million. The increase was predicated entirely on the company's need for revenues to cover the purchased power expenses associated with Grand Gulf 1.

* * *

The Attorney General of Mississippi and certain other parties representing Mississippi consumers appealed to the Mississippi Supreme Court. * * * The appealing parties charged, inter alia, that the MPSC had exceeded the scope of its authority by adopting "retail rates to pay Grand Gulf expenses without first determining that the expenses were prudently incurred." The State Supreme Court agreed, rejecting the argument that requiring the MPSC to review the prudence of incurring costs associated with Grand Gulf would violate the Supremacy Clause of the United States Constitution. The court concluded that MP & L and its sister and parent companies were "using the jurisdictional relationship between state and federal regulatory agencies to completely evade a prudency review of Grand Gulf costs" by either state or federal agencies and remanded the case to the MPSC for further proceedings. The court held that FERC's determination that MP & L's assumption of a 33% share of the costs associated with Grand Gulf would be fair to its sister operating companies did not obligate the State to approve a pass-through of those costs to state consumers without a prudence review.[12]

* * *

II

* * *

In this case as in Nantahala [Power & Light Co. v. Thornburg, 476 U.S. 953 (1986)], we hold that "a state utility commission setting retail prices must allow, as reasonable operating expenses, costs incurred as a result of paying a FERC-determined wholesale price.... Once FERC sets such a rate, a State may not conclude in setting retail rates that the FERC-approved wholesale rates are unreasonable. A State must rather give effect to Congress' desire to give FERC plenary authority over interstate wholesale rates, and to ensure that the States do not interfere with this authority." Thus we conclude that the Supremacy Clause compels the MPSC to permit MP & L to recover as a reasonable operating expense costs incurred as the result of paying a FERC-determined wholesale rate for a FERC-mandated allocation of power.

* * *

There "can be no divided authority over interstate commerce ... the acts of Congress on that subject are supreme and exclusive." Consequently, a state agency's "efforts to regulate commerce must fall when they conflict with or interfere with federal authority over the same activity." Mississippi's effort to invade the province of federal authority must be rejected. The judgment of the Mississippi Supreme Court is reversed.

---

12. The court pointed out that approval to build Grand Gulf in the State of Mississippi had been secured on the strength of certain assumptions: "the first unit was to be operational in 1980, the two units were to cost $1.227 billion, and Mississippi ratepayers were not to pay for any more of its capacity than they needed." Reliance on these assumptions proved unjustified: "Unit 1 began operation in July, 1985; the cost of Unit 1 alone, was over $3.5 billion; and the MSU-controlled operating companies agreed, among themselves that Mississippians should pay for ⅓ of its cost." Of course, the failure of the assumptions made by both MP & L and the State at the time construction of Grand Gulf was approved has little to do with the pre-emption question before us. We note, however, that the failure was not the result of any deception on the part of MP & L, MSU, or MSE. At the time construction of Grand Gulf was initiated, no one anticipated the enormous cost overruns that would be associated not only with that plant but also with virtually every nuclear power facility being constructed in the United States. [Court's fn. 9]

[The opinion of JUSTICE SCALIA, concurring in the judgment, is omitted.]

JUSTICE BRENNAN, with whom JUSTICE MARSHALL and JUSTICE BLACKMUN join, dissenting.

This case involves two separate prudency issues: one is governed by Nantahala Power & Light Co. v. Thornburg, the other is not. The first issue is whether the state utility commission has jurisdiction to determine whether, treating appellant's participation in the Grand Gulf project as a given, it was imprudent for appellant to purchase such a high amount of expensive Grand Gulf power. I agree with the Court that the portions of the Mississippi Supreme Court's opinion suggesting that the state commission does have this jurisdiction are in error. * * *

That issue is distinct, however, from the issue whether, to the extent appellant's decision to participate in the Grand Gulf project involved the purchase decision of a retail utility, a state utility commission has jurisdiction to review the prudency of that purchase. This issue cannot be resolved by simple reference to *Nantahala*, for FERC did not order appellant to participate in the Grand Gulf project, and although FERC's order determines the allocation of the costs incurred in the project, the question remains whether appellant imprudently incurred those costs in the first place. I am convinced that the state utility commission does have jurisdiction over this prudency issue, and thus I would affirm the Mississippi Supreme Court's judgment remanding for a prudency determination. * * *

* * *

The state utility commissions have jurisdiction to determine, for example, that the retail utility does not need the power or could obtain power from other sources at a lower cost. Thus, although a state utility commission cannot decide that a retail utility should have bought wholesale power from a given source at other than the FERC-approved wholesale rate, it can decide that the utility should not have bought power from that source at all. In short, the reasonableness of charging a rate as a wholesaler is distinct from the reasonableness of incurring that charge as a purchaser.

* * *

* * * I see no reason why FERC's review should bar States from applying state-law standards of prudency to the purchase decisions that are an integral part of a member retail utility's participation in an interstate pool. FERC's interpretation of the Act would divest States of authority to determine the prudence of costs incurred by retail utilities whenever those utilities belong to an interstate pool—a result that I do not think can be squared (particularly given FERC's shaky jurisdictional foundation) with the clear intent of Congress to preserve the authority of States to regulate retail utilities. Moreover, allowing only FERC review of interstate pool decisions would effectively allow retail utilities that either belong to interstate pools or span more than one State to pick and

choose between state and federal regulation by deciding whether to form subsidiaries to operate their generating facilities and sell them "wholesale" electricity.

* * *

Notes and Questions

1. Who should bear the burden of bad judgment? If a company in a perfectly competitive industry makes what in retrospect was a serious mistake, who will bear the consequences of its bad judgment? Will an unregulated monopolist similarly be forced to bear at least a portion of the consequences of its error? Is the correct conclusion, then, that the regulatory agency should be vigorous in its review of firm judgments and should disallow the costs of bad decisions?

2. What problems suggest themselves if an agency engages in such review? Will it always be clear what is bad judgment and what is bad luck? Can the agency avoid relying on hindsight in its evaluation of the firm's decisions?

3. Will the disallowance of particular bad judgments necessarily always work to the benefit of the public? For example, can uncertainty as to the amount of earnings the utility will get to pay to its shareholders fail to have an impact on the price of the firm's stock? What will the increased risk reflected in a lower stock price mean in terms of the rate of return required on the firm's common stock and perhaps even its bonds?

For a good discussion of many of these problems, see Richard J. Pierce, Jr., The Regulatory Treatment of Mistakes in Retrospect: Canceled Plants and Excess Capacity, 132 U. Pennsylvania L. Rev. 497 (1984).

e. The Task of Creating an Incentive for Economy

As we have seen, operating a regulated firm has many of the attributes of credit card living. If someone can pass expenses on to others, he or she has little incentive to keep those expenses low. So, too, with regulated firms. The problem then becomes to design a system that will allow reimbursement of expenses but build in an incentive to control those expenses. Can you think of some techniques you might try?

First, you could try to reward the efficient firm and penalize the inefficient. Why should an efficient firm receive the same profit as a managerial disaster? That surely isn't the case in the unregulated sector. You might give a "good" firm a high rate of return. Allow it to keep part of any cost savings it can make. Expand its service area when the time comes to award new certificates of convenience and necessity.[13]

---

13. This approach was taken or suggested in several cases, e.g., Re General Telephone Co. of California, 80 P.U.R.3d 2, 58–59 (Cal.P.U.C.1969); Re New York Telephone Co., 95 P.U.R.3d 333, 335 (N.Y.P.S.C.1972); Western Union Telegraph Co., 27 FCC 2d 515, 541–49, 21 R.R.2d 81, 107–16 (1971). But consider the doubt expressed in Richard Posner, Natural Monopoly and Its Regulation, 21 Stanford L. Rev. 548, 627–32 (1969).

The initial appeal of such an approach, though, begins to wane when one reflects upon the institutional as well as technical difficulties. First, it requires regulatory agencies with members who possess a high degree of expertise in economics and finance. Second, it requires the availability of some kind of sound yardstick upon which to base comparisons.[14] Thus, the "excessive" cost of one utility might be a function of the costs of construction, the market in which it hires labor and the load characteristics of its customers rather than any real lack of diligence. Finally, the very process of penalizing the less efficient firm creates uncertainty among investors and may actually increase the costs the firm incurs to raise capital even further.[15]

Second, even if you could not effectively review all aspects of a firm's efficiency, you might try to identify areas of particular weakness. A disturbing number of railroad accidents, for example, have apparently been caused by the railroads' failure to provide sufficient maintenance of their tracks. Poor roadbed has likewise contributed to reduced speed, poor service and lost business. Is there anything you as a regulator could do about the situation?

One response has been the allowance of rate increases specifically allocable to particular future expenditures. This targeted-expenditure approach has obvious limitations. If they use it too often, regulatory officials will find themselves running the company. On the other hand, when the regulated firm would seek to defer long-range needs and short-run service because of inefficient management or a desire to increase short-run earnings, this approach may provide a useful technique for control.

Third, probably the most common form of control is the phenomenon of "regulatory lag." Regulatory lag simply recognizes that rate adjustments are not necessarily made every year. During the period of time between one rate adjustment and the next, the utility must live within its income and in fact bears the cost of a failure to do so. Thus if rates are adjusted every three years, the firm which lets its costs get out of hand during the second year will not get those costs back. To some extent, its bad experience will be reflected in higher rates for the future, but not on a dollar-for-dollar compensatory basis.

The problems with relying on lag, however, once again are apparent. Regulatory lag is an arbitrary and unpredictable phenomenon that can have the same adverse effect on investor risk and required rate of return that we suggested earlier. Furthermore, in a period of inflation, the delay is a serious burden on a regulated firm. In fact, the increase in investors' risk associated with delays in obtaining approval for rate increases during an inflationary period may increase costs and off-set

---

14. See F.M. Scherer, Industrial Market Structure and Economic Performance 527–28 (1970).

15. For a suggested way out of this dilemma see William J. Baumol, "Productivi-

ty Incentive Clauses and Rate Adjustment," 110 Public Utilities Fortnightly 11 (July 22, 1982). But see, Phillip S. Cross, Performance–Based Ratemaking, 123 Public Utilities Fortnightly 44 (July 15, 1995).

whatever savings the delay may encourage.[16] This has led to the use of automatic adjustment measures which allow utilities to immediately pass on increases in operating expenses as well as attempts to estimate future expenses.

Automatic adjustment clauses, however, bring the issue full circle and once again present the issue of incentives. Utilities may not be as inclined to search as carefully for the lowest cost suppliers of inputs if those costs can be relatively easily passed on to consumers.[17] Similarly, if the automatic adjustment applies only to fuel, as is typically the case, the utility may invest in a particular technology, not because it is the most efficient, but because it is fuel-intensive.[18]

Finally, the best incentive for economy is competition. Obviously, if competition were wholly effective in a given situation there would be no need for rate regulation in the first place. On the other hand, the incentive for efficiency is one important reason for the desire to reduce barriers to entry to the minimum truly necessary and to develop periodic competition for the right to be the monopolist. In any event, an effect similar to competition can be achieved through the process of setting "average" rates. Here we have in mind setting the rates for several similar firms based on an average of all their costs. Such a process provides a greater incentive than usual to "beat the average." If my firm is more efficient than the median of the firms being averaged, I may take home a larger than average profit. No outside observer need evaluate my performance; the market will render a trustworthy verdict. As all firms seek to beat the average, ideally the average cost will itself decline and the "credit card" phenomenon of regulated living will be reduced if not eliminated.

Although the average rate approach may lower administrative expenses and provide a useful incentive, it also is not without side effects. An average price is, after all, a price ceiling. Both economic theory and experience demonstrate that price ceilings may result in a shortage of the regulated good or service and the need to develop a rationing mechanism other than the market system.[19]

16. For discussion of the general impact of regulation on the cost of capital, see Stephen H. Archer, "The Regulatory Effects on Cost of Capital in Electric Utilities," 107 Public Utilities Fortnightly 36 (Feb. 26, 1981); Kern, "Inflation, Regulation and Utility Stock Prices," 7 Bell J. 268 (1976). The impact of regulation on unit costs is considered in Peterson, "Empirical Test of Regulatory Effects," 6 Bell J. 111 (1975). The cost and benefits of regulatory lag to various parties is considered in Spann, "The Regulatory Cobweb: Inflation, Deflation, Regulatory Lags and the Effects of Alternative Administrative Rules in Public Utilities," 43 Southern Econ. J. 827 (1976).

17. See Kaserman and Tepel, "The Impact of the Automatic Adjustment Clause on Fuel Purchase and Utilization Practices in the U.S. Electric Utility Industry," 48 Southern Econ.J. 687 (Jan.1982).

18. See Blair and Kaserman, "Automatic Fuel Cost Adjustment Clauses: Issues and Evidence," 110 Public Utilities Fortnightly 27 (November 25, 1982).

19. See Jeffrey L. Harrison and John P. Formby "Regional Distortions in Natural Gas Allocations: A Legal and Economic Analysis," 57 North Carolina L. Rev. 57 (1978).

The most recent effort to "regulate" through the use of competition has occurred in the telecommunications industry. As you saw in Chapter 3, local exchange carriers that own the actual transmission equipment are now required to "unbundle" and allow competitors to have access to the elements of the incumbents' networks. The objective is to encourage competition without requiring costly duplication of facilities. At this point the success of this venture is still up in the air. Certainly local exchange carriers will feel pressures to economize, but the process of change is likely to be an administratively costly one.

4. CALCULATION OF THE ALLOWABLE RETURN ON IN-VESTED CAPITAL (I X R)

Although more dollars are often involved in the determination of allowable costs (C) than in determination of the allowed return on capital (I x r), the latter has attracted more attention from regulatory commissions and the courts. There are probably at least three reasons for this.

First, as we have seen, allowable costs consist of thousands, indeed often millions, of individual transactions. The Commission cannot possibly review all of them. About the most it can do is structure a system that will seek to encourage efficiency.

Second, since rate-regulated industries tend to have high capital requirements, the "I" factor may be large in absolute terms and have a significant impact on the total allowable earnings. Further, since high-capital firms often need to keep going to capital markets for additional funds, the return they are allowed can have a significant effect on their ability to raise those funds.

Finally, rate of return on investment has been equated in the public mind with "profits," and since limitation of profits is often seen to be one of the prime objectives of regulation, this factor understandably has assumed special importance.

a. Determination of the Elements of Invested Capital (I)

It might seem easy to determine the value of "I." Accountants do something similar each year in their preparation of the firm's balance sheet. After listing assets of the firm and its liabilities, the difference between the two is often said to represent "capital." This figure is made up of contributions from stockholders for capital stock and reinvested income of the firm. If this balance sheet concept of stockholder investment were used by regulatory commissions, the process of calculating the total investment would be simplified or eliminated, although of course there would still have to be some rules for the accounting underlying the balance sheet.

However, the concept of investment as used by regulatory commissions is somewhat different. We have seen that in the calculation of C, all the goods and services consumed within the test period are included, including an allowance for depreciation. The investment, then, consists of all those assets of the firm which are not consumed during the test period. It includes not only those assets financed by stock purchases or reinvested income, but also those assets financed by bonds.

As is true with annual costs, many elements of invested capital—e.g. land, buildings, equipment—are uncontested. However, in high fixed cost businesses where construction takes a long time, an important question arises concerning when the value of construction work in progress should be included in the rate base. One solution is to simply include these expenses as they are incurred (CWIP). An alternative is to wait until the project is completed and then add both accumulated financing expenses and the actual costs of construction to the rate base. This is called the allowance for funds used during construction method (AFUDC). The following case explores which approach is preferable.

LEGISLATIVE UTILITY CONSUMERS' COUNCIL v. PUBLIC SERVICE CO.

Supreme Court of New Hampshire, 1979.
119 N.H. 332, 402 A.2d 626.

BOIS, JUSTICE.

* * *

The most important issue that this appeal presents for our review is whether it is legal under existing statutory law for the Commission to order the inclusion of CWIP in a public utility rate base. The LUCC argues that the Commission's inclusion of $111,258,428 of CWIP in the Company's rate base contravenes the "used and useful" requirement of RSA 378:27, which is applicable to the present case under RSA 378:28, and the "just and reasonable" principle basic to all the provisions of RSA ch. 378.

    * * *

We consider first the LUCC's argument that the Commission's inclusion of CWIP in the Company's rate base violates the "used and useful" requirement of RSA 328:27. We have * * * previously allowed property held for future use to be included in the rate base. See e.g., Pub. Serv. Co. v. State, 113 N.H. 497, 311 A.2d 513 (1973).

* * * Whether CWIP is "used and useful" is a determination that must be made by the Commission based on a careful case-by-case analysis. The Commission should consider whether the CWIP asked to be included in the rate base represents the cost of money expended for raising capital to finance construction that is undertaken upon sound business judgment and in accordance with a definite plan to meet the needs of future utility consumers. We have recognized that a public utility must be able to earn revenue sufficient "to maintain its credit and attract the necessary capital to meet increased demands for improvement and extension of its service[s]." Allowing the Commission flexibility in applying the "used and useful" test serves to promote the public interest by allowing an energy policy that can achieve an adequate and reliable supply of electric power. * * *

The factual determination that the Commission had to make in its used and useful analysis was whether the Company's CWIP represents an expenditure incurred in raising capital to finance a reasonable construction program that will inure to the benefit of energy consumers by assuring a future supply of electricity.

Five years ago, on January 29, 1974, the Commission specifically found that construction of the Seabrook nuclear powered generating facility was necessary to meet the present and future demand for electric power in this State. The Commission's expert witness, Donald J. Trawicki, testified that the Company's load growth for the ten-year period ending in 1977 was approximately eight percent annually, and that it had reached as high as twelve percent in 1975. Trawicki commented that the Company's projection of a 7.3 percent annual load growth over the next ten years, a projection provided by Company witness D.N. Merrill and filed exhibits, "appear[s] somewhat conservative." * * *

The Commission examined a filed exhibit outlining the Company's projected construction costs for Seabrook and allied projects. The exhibit * * * showed that the two-year projection was $296,601,000, or 63% of the total utility plant at original cost of the Company at year-end 1976. Evidence showed that the estimated construction cost to the Company of its share of Seabrook and other generating facilities would be over one billion dollars through 1984. The LUCC made no substantial allegation that these projected expenditures were wasteful, and the Commission's expert Trawicki, upon his analysis of the expenditures, strongly recommended the annual inclusion of $111,258,428 of CWIP in the rate base. We hold that LUCC has not sustained its burden of showing "by a clear preponderance of the evidence," that the Commission erroneously found that the Company's CWIP is "used and useful."

We next consider the LUCC's argument that inclusion of CWIP in the Company's rate base violates the basic "just and reasonable" principle of RSA ch. 378. The thrust of the LUCC's position is that including CWIP in the rate base forces present ratepayers to pay costs that should fall on future ratepayers who will actually benefit from the plant under construction when it comes on line. The LUCC argues that the traditional AFUDC [Allowance for Funds Used During Construction] treatment of CWIP, whereby it is capitalized and collected from future ratepayers via inclusion in the rate base over the period of the useful life of the plant when it comes on line, is required by the "just and reasonable" principle. The LUCC suggests that "the inclusion of CWIP [in the current rate base] is detrimental to present consumers while providing a windfall to future consumers."

We reject the LUCC's contention that AFUDC treatment of CWIP is mandated by law. The Commission's decision to include CWIP in the rate base instead of capitalizing it in an AFUDC account is a factual one to be made on a case by case basis. * * *

We have held that a public utility must be given the opportunity to earn revenue "sufficient to assure the investor's confidence in the financial soundness of the utility and enough to maintain and support its credit so that it will be sold to raise money necessary to improve and expand its service." The building of a nuclear powered generating facility requires very substantial lines of bank credit for the early construction stages. Immediate financing must be available. If credit is not forthcoming, the construction program will be jeopardized. Because it is fundamental that ratemaking must take into account the need for the utility to maintain the confidence of investors, the Commission properly exercised its regulatory function by allowing the Company to prove the necessity of including its CWIP in the rate base.

> * * *

We hold that the Commission's decision represents a reasonable balancing of the interests of present ratepayers, future ratepayers, and the Company's investors. The decision is a policy determination that we will not disturb in exercising our appellate function even if we might have come to a different conclusion.

The LUCC next argues that by allowing inclusion of CWIP in the rate base, the Commission violates the fundamental test year matching principle. The LUCC bases its assertion upon the fact that the Commission ordered no revenue adjustment to offset the inclusion of CWIP in the rate base. We feel that the LUCC's reasoning is misguided.

We have recognized the validity of applying the principle that revenue and expenses must be matched over a given test year. Nevertheless, we have also noted that when considering the issue of inclusion in the rate base of property held for future use, "obviously the expense" could not be matched with revenue from the plant for the same period, since there was none. The argument that the matching principle bars the Commission from including CWIP in the rate base elevates form over substance. To adopt it would unduly restrict the wide regulatory discretion that the Legislature delegated to the Commission in RSA ch. 378.

* * *

* * * Ultimately, under either a CWIP inclusion approach or an AFUDC accumulation approach, the Company's revenues are evenly matched with its expenses. The Commission has the authority to select one approach or the other in its sound judgment. * * *

We next address the LUCC's argument that including CWIP in the rate base is inequitable because it casts the current ratepayer in the role of a forced investor who is not entitled to a return on his investment. * * * Including CWIP in the rate base does not place ratepayers in the role of suppliers of capital. Rather, it requires them to pay a return on capital contributions of investors and the cost of money prior to the completion of the facility under construction.

Ratepayers will be charged the Company's CWIP under either the CWIP inclusion approach or the AFUDC accumulation approach. As the

LUCC concedes in its brief, the issue is only "[t]he timing of the recovery of those financing costs." The ratepayers always pay all the costs of utility investment and never are afforded a return on their money.

The Commission made a policy decision to allocate the recovery of the Company's CWIP to present ratepayers. The Commission balanced the equities and, while recognizing that a small percentage of present ratepayers would suffer inequity because they might die or leave New Hampshire before the Company's construction program is completed, decided that the public interest in the completion of the plant demanded the inclusion of CWIP in the rate base.

Ratepayers like taxpayers come and go but ratepayers like taxpayers cannot expect to be charged solely on the basis of their individual benefits. Schools and other public buildings are benefiting the taxpayers today but were fully paid for by taxpayers of yesterday. Previous ratepayers have paid for plant construction now producing electricity being used by present ratepayers. Moreover, over a five year period, the basic body of ratepayers will not change significantly. * * *

* * * [T]he Commission exercised its discretion in arriving at a ratemaking procedure it regarded as imposing the least burden on the New Hampshire energy consumer over the next several years while assuring the completion of the Company's construction program. We will not substitute our judgment for that of the Commission.

Notes and Questions

1. Who benefits from present expansion to meet future needs? Is expansion intended to meet the needs of future customers or the future needs of present customers? Can anyone know? Should it matter?

2. What would be the effect on rates of including CWIP in the rate base? Would the size of individual rate increases be moderated? What would tend to be the effect on service consumption in years before the new capacity becomes available?

3. Are the CWIP and AFUDC approaches equally good? If you were a ratepayer, which would you prefer? As an investor, which would you prefer? Why might reliance on AFUDC increase the difficulty of finding investors and consequently raise the cost of capital?

b. Determining the Appropriate Value to Be Placed on Assets

Once we have determined what the appropriate elements of the firm's rate base are, we must determine their dollar value. That may seem a straightforward enough issue, but it turns out to be one of the most troublesome and basic in the entire rate-making calculation. The two basic alternatives are suggested in the following cases.

SMYTH v. AMES

Supreme Court of the United States, 1898.
169 U.S. 466, 18 S.Ct. 418, 42 L.Ed. 819.

value as as reproduction costs

MR. JUSTICE HARLAN * * * delivered the opinion of the court.

A corporation maintaining a public highway, although it owns the property it employs for accomplishing public objects, must be held to have accepted its rights, privileges and franchises subject to the condition that the government creating it, or the government within whose limits it conducts its business, may by legislation protect the people against unreasonable charges for the services rendered by it. * * * But it is equally true that the corporation performing such public services and the people financially interested in its business and affairs have rights that may not be invaded by legislative enactment in disregard of the fundamental guarantees for the protection of property. The corporation may not be required to use its property for the benefit of the public without receiving just compensation for the services rendered by it. How such compensation may be ascertained, and what are the necessary elements in such an inquiry, will always be an embarrassing question. * * *

We hold, however, that the basis of all calculations as to the reasonableness of rates to be charged by a corporation maintaining a highway under legislative sanction must be the fair value of the property being used by it for the convenience of the public. And in order to ascertain that value, the original cost of construction, the amount expended in permanent improvements, the amount and market value of its bonds and stock, the present as compared with the original cost of construction, the probable earning capacity of the property under particular rates prescribed by statute, and the sum required to meet operating expenses, are all matters for consideration, and are to be given such weight as may be just and right in each case. We do not say that there may not be other matters to be regarded in estimating the value of the property. What the company is entitled to ask is a fair return upon the value of that which it employs for the public convenience. On the other hand, what the public is entitled to demand is that no more be exacted from it for the use of a public highway than the services rendered by it are reasonably worth.

MISSOURI EX REL. SOUTHWESTERN BELL TELEPHONE CO. v. PUBLIC SERVICE COMMISSION

value at original cost.

Supreme Court of the United States, 1923.
262 U.S. 276, 43 S.Ct. 544, 67 L.Ed. 981.

[The majority opinion has been deleted.]

MR. JUSTICE BRANDEIS, with whom MR. JUSTICE HOLMES concurs.

* * *

The so-called rule of Smyth v. Ames is, in my opinion, legally and economically unsound. The thing devoted by the investor to the public use is not specific property, tangible and intangible, but capital embarked in the enterprise. Upon the capital so invested the federal Constitution guarantees to the utility the opportunity to earn a fair return.

* * *

The doubts and uncertainties incident to the [determination] can be eliminated, or lessened, only by redefining the rate base, called value, and the measure of fairness in return, now applied under the rule of Smyth v. Ames. The experience of the 25 years since that case was decided has demonstrated that the rule there enunciated is delusive. In the attempt to apply it insuperable obstacles have been encountered. It has failed to afford adequate protection either to capital or to the public. It leaves open the door to grave injustice. To give to capital embarked in public utilities the protection guaranteed by the Constitution, and to secure for the public reasonable rates, it is essential that the rate base be definite, stable, and readily ascertainable, and that the percentage to be earned on the rate base be measured by the cost, or charge, of the capital employed in the enterprise. * * *

The rule of Smyth v. Ames sets the laborious and baffling task of finding the present value of the utility. It is impossible to find an exchange value for a utility, since utilities, unlike merchandise or land, are not commonly bought and sold in the market. Nor can the present value of the utility be determined by capitalizing its net earnings, since the earnings are determined, in large measure, by the rate which the company will be permitted to charge, and thus the vicious circle would be encountered. So, under the rule of Smyth v. Ames, it is usually sought to prove the present value of a utility by ascertaining what it actually cost to construct and install it, or by estimating what it should have cost, or by estimating what it would cost to reproduce or to replace it. To this end an enumeration is made of the component elements of the utility, tangible and intangible; then the actual, or the proper, cost of producing, or of reproducing, each part is sought; and finally it is estimated how much less than the new each part, or the whole, is worth. That is, the depreciation is estimated. Obviously each step in the process of estimating the cost of reproduction, or replacement, involves forming an opinion, or exercising judgment, as distinguished from merely ascertaining facts. And this is true, also, of each step in the process of estimating how much less the existing plant is worth than if it were new. There is another potent reason why, under the rule of Smyth v. Ames, the room for difference in opinion as to the present value of a utility is so wide. The rule does not measure the present value either by what the utility cost to produce, or by what it should have cost, or by what it would cost to reproduce, or to replace it. Under that rule the tribunal is directed, in forming its judgment, to take into consideration all those and also other elements, called relevant facts.

* * *

The efforts of courts to control commissions' findings of value have largely failed. The reason lies in the character of the rule declared in Smyth v. Ames. The rule there stated was to be applied solely as a means of determining whether rates already prescribed by the Legislature were confiscatory. It was to be applied judicially after the rate had been made, and by a court which had had no part in making the rate. * * * But the commissions undertook to make the rule their standard for constructive action. They used it as a guide for making or approving rates, and the tendency developed to fix as reasonable the rate which is not so low as to be confiscatory. Thus the rule which assumes that rates of utilities will ordinarily he higher than the minimum required by the Constitution has, by the practice of the commissions, eliminated the margin between a reasonable rate and a merely compensatory rate, and, in the process of rate-making, effective judicial review is very often rendered impossible. * * *

The adoption of present value of the utility's property, as the rate base, was urged in 1893 on behalf of the community, and it was adopted by the courts, largely, as a protection against inflated claims, based on what were then deemed inflated prices of the past.

    * * *

Reproduction cost, as the measure, or as evidence, of present value, was also pressed then by representatives of the public, who sought to justify legislative reductions of railroad rates. The long depression which followed the panic of 1893 had brought prices to the lowest level reached in the nineteenth century. Insistence upon reproduction cost was the shippers' protest against burdens believed to have resulted from watered stocks, reckless financing, and unconscionable construction contracts. Those were the days before state legislation prohibited the issue of public utility securities without authorization from state officials, before accounting was prescribed and supervised, when outstanding bonds and stocks were hardly an indication of the amount of capital embarked in the enterprise, when depreciation accounts were unknown, and when book values, or property accounts, furnished no trustworthy evidence either of cost or of real value. Estimates of reproduction cost were then offered, largely as a means, either of supplying lacks in the proof of actual cost and investment, or of testing the credibility of evidence adduced, or of showing that the cost of installation had been wasteful. For these purposes evidence of the cost of reproduction is obviously appropriate.

At first reproduction cost was welcomed by commissions as evidence of present value. Perhaps it was because the estimates then indicated values lower than the actual cost of installation; for, even after the price level had begun to rise, improved machinery and new devices tended for some years to reduce construction costs. Evidence of reproduction costs was certainly welcomed, because it seemed to offer a reliable means for performing the difficult task of fixing, in obedience to Smyth v. Ames, the value of a new species of property to which the old tests—selling price or net earnings—were not applicable. The engineer spoke in figures—a language implying certitude. His estimates seemed to be free of the infirmities which had stamped as untrustworthy the opinion evidence of experts common in condemnation cases. Thus, for some time, replacement cost, on the basis of prices prevailing at the date of the valuation, was often adopted by state commissions as the standard for fixing the rate base. But gradually it came to be realized that the definiteness of the engineer's calculations was delusive, that they rested upon shifting theories, and that their estimates varied so widely as to intensify, rather than to allay doubts.

When the price levels had risen largely, and estimates of replacement cost indicated values much greater than the actual cost of installation, many commissions refused to consider valuable what one declared to be assumptions based on things that never happened and estimates requiring the projection of the engineer's imagination into the future and methods of construction and installation that have never been and never will be adopted by sane men. * * * The conviction is widespread that a sound conclusion as to the actual value of a utility is not to be reached by a meticulous study of conflicting estimates of the cost of reproducing new the congeries of old machinery and equipment, called the plant, and the still more fanciful estimates concerning the value of the intangible elements of an established business.

The adoption of the amount prudently invested as the rate base and the amount of the capital charge as the measure of the rate of return would give definiteness to these two factors involved in rate controversies which are now shifting and treacherous, and which render the proceedings peculiarly burdensome and largely futile. Such measures offer a basis for decision which is certain and stable. The rate base would be ascertained as a fact, not determined as matter of opinion. It would not fluctuate with the market price of labor, or materials, or money. It would not change with hard times or shifting populations. It would not be distorted by the fickle and varying judgments of appraisers, commissions, or courts. It would, when once made in respect to any utility, be fixed, for all time, subject only to increases to represent additions to plant, after allowance for the depreciation included in the annual operating charges. The wild uncertainties of the present method of fixing the rate base under the so-called rule of Smyth v. Ames would be avoided, and likewise the fluctuations which introduce into the enterprise unnecessary elements of speculation, create useless expense, and impose upon the public a heavy, unnecessary burden.

* * * About 75 per cent. of the capital invested in utilities is represented by bonds. He who buys bonds seeks primarily safety. If he can obtain it, he is content with a low rate of interest. Through a fluctuating rate base the bondholder can only lose. He can receive no benefit from a rule which increases the rate base as the price level rises; for his return, expressed in dollars, would be the same, whatever the income of the company. That the stockholder does not in fact receive an increased return in time of rapidly rising prices under the rule of Smyth

v. Ames, as applied, the financial record of the last six years demonstrates. But the burden upon the community is heavy, because the risk makes the capital cost high.

The expense and loss now incident to recurrent rate controversies is also very large. The most serious vice of the present rule for fixing the rate base is not the existing uncertainty, but that the method does not lead to certainty. Under it, the value for rate-making purposes must ever be an unstable factor. Instability is a standing menace of renewed controversy. The direct expense to the utility of maintaining an army of experts and of counsel is appalling. The indirect cost is far greater. The attention of officials high and low is, necessarily, diverted from the constructive tasks of efficient operation and of development. The public relations of the utility to the community are apt to become more and more strained, and a victory for the utility may in the end prove more disastrous than defeat would have been. * * *

What is now termed the prudent investment is, in essence, the same thing as that which the court has always sought to protect in using the term present value. Twenty-five years ago, when Smyth v. Ames was decided, it was impossible to ascertain with accuracy, in respect to most of the utilities, in most of the states in which rate controversies arose, what it cost in money to establish the utility; or what the money cost with which the utility was established; or what income had been earned by it; or how the income had been expended. It was, therefore, not feasible, then, to adopt, as the rate base, the amount properly invested or, as the rate of fair return, the amount of the capital charge. Now the situation is fundamentally different. These amounts are, now, readily ascertainable in respect to a large, and rapidly increasing, proportion of the utilities. The change in this respect is due to the enlargement, meanwhile, of the powers and functions of state utility commissions. The issue of securities is now, and for many years has been, under the control of commissions, in the leading states. Hence the amount of capital raised (since the conferring of these powers) and its cost are definitely known * * *. The amount and disposition of current earnings of all the companies are also known. It is, therefore, feasible now to adopt as the measure of a compensatory rate—the annual cost, or charge, of the capital prudently invested in the utility. And, hence, it should be done.

Notes and Questions

1. What is the "rule of Smyth v. Ames" to which Justice Brandeis refers? Is it easy to summarize that "rule"? Did Justice Harlan define a process rather than a formula for determining the rate?

2. What is the basis of the "rule"? Is there a constitutional right to a fair return? What theory underlies such a right? Whose right is involved? The company's? The investors'? Both?

3. What troubles Justice Brandeis about the approach taken in Smyth v. Ames? Do you share Justice Brandeis' concern about the differences of

opinion possible under it? Do you share his concern about the difficulty of reviewing the exercise of agency discretion? Do you believe that a return is likely to be excessive if it is based on a figure higher than original cost?

The alternatives being considered in the preceding two cases can be highlighted by the following problem.

Problem, Questions and Note

A regulated firm has capital assets with a book value (original cost) adjusted for depreciation of $1,000,000.00. To replace those goods with goods of comparable quality, depreciated as much as the present goods, would cost $2,000,000.00. The cost of building a plant to perform another, functionally comparable service, i.e. to provide gas instead of electricity, would be $2,500,000.00. The company has been permitted a return of $150,000.00 per year at a time when general interest rates are 10%.[20] Because the goods are specialized for the business of the particular firm, their only alternative value is as scrap which would bring $200,000.00.

What value should the assets be given for purposes of rate making?

a.   Which figure represents the true economic cost to the firm of continuing to use the assets in the current way?

b.   If one were allowing competition for the right to perform the functions of the regulated firm, what sale price should be set on the existing firm's assets when selling them to the winning firm? Put another way, if you were the buying firm, what would you be willing to pay for the assets?

c.   What value should be placed on the assets in order to return to the investors most nearly that sum which they expected to receive when they made their investments?

d.   Which figure is the most objective measure of the real economic cost of providing the service which the firm is offering?

e.   Which approach is calculated to provide the lowest current rates for the service?

f.   Which approach most accurately reflects what the service is "worth" to the consumers?

The conflicting answers to these questions suggest the complexity involved in determining the appropriate valuation for assets. The "opportunity cost" of current investors, i.e. what they could otherwise get for the assets, is only $200,000.00. In an important sense, that is the "cost" to the firm of using the assets to provide the service in question. On the other hand, if opportunity cost were the sole measure of the value of assets, it would likely seriously discourage investment in the type of assets required by most utilities—assets which tend to have little value for alternative uses.

The $1,000,000 depreciated original cost of the assets tends to provide, as Justice Brandeis argued, the most accurate measure of what the original investors paid for them. On the other hand, this figure is not an accurate measure of what another utility would think they were "worth" and indeed

20.   This is much too crude a measure of   The problem is considered more fully in the
the cost of capital but it will do for now.   next section of this chapter.

would be willing to pay to buy them. Depreciated original cost, then, may be higher than salvage value of the assets, but it arguably is not a "fair value."

The projected earnings flow may be the most realistic measure of what a firm would pay for this business. Here a firm would pay $1,500,000 to get $150,000 per year. But the company's earnings are themselves a product of the regulatory process, and it would be circular indeed to use those earnings to determine the "fair" value of the assets.

The cost of providing an alternative source of service provides a good measure of what the present service is "worth" to consumers. But regulation presupposes that rates will not be set at "all the traffic will bear", so while $2,500,000 might be a maximum value it is not necessarily the "correct" one.

Finally, the replacement value of the assets both tends to measure what a new firm would pay for them to avoid building its own, and tends to reflect most accurately the cost of providing *additional* service. Rates set on the basis of replacement cost valuation therefore tend, better than rates based on original cost, to provide accurate cues to consumers as to how much of the service they ought to demand.[21] On the other hand, computing rates based on replacement cost tends to provide a windfall to the existing investors. That is, a rate of return of five per cent on $2,000,000.00 is the equivalent of ten per cent on the actual investment of $1,000,000.00.

The regulator, then, may find himself or herself torn between conflicting pressures to (a) give investors a "fair" but not "excessive" rate of return, (b) set rates at a level which does not encourage uneconomic use of service, (c) keep rates as low as possible so as to permit relatively poor persons to consume the service, (d) keep rates at a level which will encourage maximum productive use of the facilities that have already been constructed, and (e) provide a sufficiently consistent and secure measure of return that investors will not discount the price they are willing to pay for the firm's securities. It is a fascinating intellectual exercise to try to resolve these conflicting objectives at this point. It may be more productive, however, to wait until we have also discussed setting the rate of return. Our next case illustrates that process.

c. *Setting the Rate of Return to be Allowed (r)*

Determining the rate of return "r" that a company should be allowed is harder than it looks. The first problem is that rate of return is ultimately a single figure, but it is calculated as the weighted average of other numbers.

The cost of financing by use of debt securities is relatively easy to calculate. It is simply the interest the company has to pay on the debt. Preferred stock is treated like debt if it has a fixed dividend. Thus, that dividend is the "cost" of preferred stock, even if the board of the company could vote not to pay a dividend, because it is assumed that the

---

21. In other words, rates based on original cost valuation may be so low as to encourage uneconomic use of the utility's services and may therefore tend to cause rates to go up sharply when expansion of the utility at current cost occurs.

regulators are trying to allow the company sufficient earnings to cover a "fair" return to shareholders.

Of course, even these questions are not without controversy. Why shouldn't a company be entitled to earn the current cost of issuing debt securities on all its debt securities, including those issued at a lower rate of interest? Indeed, why should we treat facilities financed by debt as part of "I" at all? Why not make interest charges an element of "C", let "I" represent only equity capital, and "r" only the cost of equity?

At first blush, determining the cost of equity capital seems no more complicated than determining the cost of debt. Money is money. However, in practice, the processes are quite different.

TENNESSEE GAS PIPELINE CO. v. FEDERAL ENERGY REGULATORY COMMISSION

United States Court of Appeals, District of Columbia Circuit, 1991.
926 F.2d 1206.

Before WALD, WILLIAMS and THOMAS, CIRCUIT JUDGES.

WILLIAMS, CIRCUIT JUDGE.

In its Opinion No. 240, the Federal Energy Regulatory Commission picked the figure 15.1% as the return on equity for Tennessee Gas Pipeline Company for the period June 1, 1982 through January 31, 1983. Because of a serious methodological error—FERC had derived one of the key ingredients in its calculation from a logically irrelevant prior period—we reversed and remanded * * *. On remand, the Commission again picked 15.1%. Tennessee argues * * * that the decision on remand is arbitrary and capricious * * *. We agree * * *.

In the early 1980s Tennessee filed a number of general rate increases under § 4 of the Natural Gas Act, which the Commission consolidated. A major issue, and the one that survives through to this case, was choosing the appropriate rate of return on equity, an inevitable component of cost-of-service ratemaking. Recognizing that utility investors must be allowed an opportunity to earn returns sufficient to "attract capital," and "to compensate [the] investors for the risks assumed," the Commission endeavors to set a utility's rate of return on equity at its cost of equity capital. * * *

In Opinion No. 190, the Commission addressed the two periods immediately preceding the present one and set the cost of equity capital (and hence the return on equity) at 15.95%. It reached this number by taking the midpoint of a "zone of reasonableness." The Commission evidently found the lower bound of this zone in its staff's recommendation of 15%,[22] and the upper bound in a discounted cash flow ("DCF")[23] analysis of Tennessee's parent company, Tenneco, Inc.

22. The methodology behind this figure is unclear, but in adopting it the Commission noted "the relatively high yields on risk-free U.S. Treasury bonds during this period (which averaged 13.8%), the recommendations of the parties (Staff's 15% and Tennessee's 17%), and the returns we recently allowed for pipelines," and concluded "that the zone of reasonableness ... is 15.0% to 16.9%...." [Court's fn. 1]

23. The Discounted Cash Flow model

Opinion No. 190 did not reach the period at issue here, but an Administrative Law Judge sought to apply its methodology to the period. She believed that the 15% lower bound had been the result of risk premium analysis, which typically takes the risk-free rate of return on U.S. government bonds and adds an estimated premium for the greater risk of the particular stock. Accordingly, she used a kind of "reverse engineering" to arrive at a lower bound of 13.2%.[24] She set the upper bound at 16.93%, the unrevised DCF figure from Opinion No. 190. Finally, she chose the midpoint of this zone of reasonableness, 15.1%.

In Opinion No. 240, the Commission expressly adopted the ALJ's analysis and conclusion, noting "the close proximity of the issuance of Opinion No. 190 to [the ALJ's] decision." On Tennessee's request for rehearing, the Commission rejected Tennessee's argument that it was improper to use DCF figures from prior periods. We found the use of obsolete data arbitrary and capricious, and reversed and remanded.

On remand, the Commission again used the ALJ's reverse-engineered risk premium figure of 13.2% as its lower bound and used an updated DCF figure of 18.79% as its upper bound. While recognizing that the midpoint of this zone of reasonableness was 15.99%, it instead chose its old favorite, 15.1%. To justify choosing well below the midpoint, the Commission noted that the price of Tenneco's stock rose in the six months following the end of the relevant period, so that its dividend yield (dividend divided by price) fell. Use of this out-of-period data would, the Commission noted, result in a DCF or upper limit of only 16.84%. (Explicit use of that figure as the upper bound would have yielded a midpoint of 15.02%, a rate quite similar to what the Commission adopted.)

On Tennessee's request for rehearing, the Commission * * * explained that its reference to the out-of-period data was "made only to show the existence of a lag in the decline in dividend yields following the decline in interest rates." On the basis of this supposed lag, the Commission explained that it made a "pragmatic adjustment." Thus the supposed lag—the proposition that investors are not able to account fully for

---

flows from the classical valuation theory "that the value of a financial asset is determined by its ... ability to generate future cash flows." Roger A. Morin, Utilities' Cost of Capital 74 (1984). Thus, "the fundamental value of [any] asset is the discounted sum of all future income flows that will be received by the owner of the asset." [Court's fn. 2]

24. She took the lower bound of 15% from Opinion No. 190 and subtracted the then prevailing government bond rate of 13.8%, to arrive at an implicit "risk premium" of 1.2%. She then added this risk premium to the 12.0% government bond rate prevailing in the disputed period. The resulting 1.2% premium is far lower than normal ones. See, e.g., Morin, Utilities' Cost of Capital 181 (risk premium in electric utility industry ranged from 2.36% to 5.26% between 1974 and 1983 with an average equity risk premium of 3.78%); Frank K. Reilly, Investment Analysis and Portfolio Management 46 (1989), citing Roger G. Ibbotson and Rex A. Sinquefield, Stocks, Bonds, Bills, and Inflation: 1987 Yearbook (average equity risk premium of stocks over long-term government bonds for the period 1926–1987 of 5.6%). [Court's fn. 3]

the effects of a decline in interest rates on their investment alternatives until some six months or more after those rates are published—is the sole basis for the Commission's use of a rate of return below the midpoint.

* * *

The Commission's approach to estimating the cost of equity capital appears to be a two-step process, in which it first frames a zone of reasonableness with the estimation tools of its choice. Then, in the absence of evidence that leads the Commission to prefer one estimate over the other, it sets the rate of return at the average of those boundary figures. If "other factors" warrant a preference one way or the other, the Commission makes a suitable "pragmatic adjustment".

We have no quarrel with this general methodology. Even if we did, we have no authority to insist that the Commission use "any single formula or combination of formulae." But the notion of lawfulness requires insistence that the chosen framework not collapse in practice into a standardless exercise of Commission discretion resting on no more than an assertion of "expertise". We therefore turn to an evaluation of the "pragmatism" behind the adjustment.

The trend of Tenneco's dividend yield diverged from the trend of interest rates during the disputed period. One held steady, the other fell. The Commission introduced its "lag" theory as the explanation. That solution, however, disregards the evidence and violates the principles underlying the Commission's own methodology.

As the Commission noted, there is a direct relationship between interest rates and dividend yields. Everything else being equal, a decline in interest rates means a decline in dividend yields, as stocks and bonds compete for investors' capital. A "drastic drop in interest rates attract[s] capital away from bonds and into stocks, causing a rise in stock prices and a decline in dividend yields...."

* * *

Thus, implicit in the Commission's assertion that the "decline [in interest rates] was not yet reflected in the relevant [dividend yield] data" is a finding of fact that nothing (save interest rates) changed during the disputed period. Under the Natural Gas Act the Commission's factual findings are conclusive only "if supported by substantial evidence." The Commission has not pointed to any evidence that would support this finding.

Indeed, the evidence offered by Tennessee strongly suggests changes in company-specific risk. First, the spread between Tenneco's bond yields and the risk-free yield increased substantially, indicating that investors thought Tenneco was becoming riskier. While that may have been due to components of Tenneco's business other than Tennessee, Tennessee also offered evidence of stiffening competition from oil as a result of declining oil prices (which declined in price from \$31.74 to \$29.49) and from other gas suppliers, with a concomitant likelihood that

Tennessee would run up greater liability under the "take-or-pay" contracts by which it secured its gas. It is thus hard to imagine how the Commission could support a finding that interest rates were the only relevant dynamic force in an otherwise static world. In any event, Tennessee did offer evidence of countervailing risk factors, and it had "a right to have its proof either accepted or appropriately refuted."

Even if there were no direct evidence of changing risks for Tennessee, however, the Commission's lag theory would still be in intolerable conflict with the principles the Commission has endorsed in adopting the DCF method itself. DCF analysis works from the proposition that the price of a stock is the current value of all expected future cash flows, discounted at the rate of return.[25] The key equation, $r=D[1]/P[0] + g$, employs the current price of the utility, because that price is understood to represent the best possible assessment of the available information about the utility. If the market is in fact unable to promptly reflect information so widely publicized as risk-free interest rates, DCF theory collapses.

More generally, the Commission's lag theory implies a frontal assault on "the cornerstone of modern investment theory," the Efficient Market Hypothesis. In its "semi-strong" form, the hypothesis says that stock prices will react promptly to new public releases of information and thus "fully reflect all public information." Frank K. Reilly, Investment Analysis and Portfolio Management 215 (1989). If, as the Commission urges, the market cannot promptly digest information about interest rates, it must be quite inefficient.

In fact, if the stock market is such a laggard as the members of the Commission say, they would do well to abandon their regulatory work and turn to exploitation of their theory. At the conclusion of any sharp change in interest rates, they could buy stocks or sell them short, as appropriate, and then await the market's leisurely response—the Commission claims it may take more than six months. That investors can have been so obtuse as to miss this opportunity—and thus compete away the resulting profits—strains credulity.

* * *

Of course the Commission is free to adopt a minority position in the financial and economic communities. Tennessee does not argue that the 14th Amendment enacted the Efficient Market Hypothesis, or DCF for that matter. Nor, indeed, does it claim the Natural Gas Act or the Administrative Procedure Act did so. If the Commission proposes to reject either the Efficient Market Hypothesis or DCF methodology, we therefore assume that it is free to do so. But it must say so, and, if the rejection is inconsistent with prior decisions, explain the change.

25. This can be stated as $P[0] = D[1]/(r-g)$, i.e., the price of a stock equals the value of next year's dividends divided by the cost of capital net of the steady future growth rate of dividends. See Kolbe, The Cost of Capital 54; Morin, Utilities' Cost of Capital 82. This can then be restated to focus on what the regulator is seeking to discover, the cost of capital: $r = D[1]/P[0] + g$. [Court's fn. 6]

In fact, the Commission appears quite wedded to DCF analysis and to efficient market theory as its theoretical mainstay. * * *

Indeed, if there is any method on which the Commission has recently frowned, it is risk premium analysis. Thus in *Montaup Electric Co.*, it said, "Because a risk-premium analysis can accentuate erratic market conditions and tends to over-emphasize recent market changes by producing too high a return when capital costs are steeply rising and too low a return when they are steeply falling, this type of analysis must be used with caution." * * *

* * *

Thus the Commission's theory for departing from use of the midpoint of the zone of reasonableness is inconsistent with its basic and strongly held ratemaking theories. We are not saying that there are no legitimate bases for departing from the midpoint; we are merely saying that this is not one. In fact, the theory on which the parties seem to regard the midpoint as the proper norm—that Tennessee is "of average risk"—is a bit puzzling to us. Both boundaries of the zone of reasonableness, the 13.2% "risk premium" figure and the 18.79% DCF calculation, are estimates of Tennessee's cost of equity capital. Neither is a measure of industry rate of return or of Tennessee's relative risk within the industry. Thus it is unclear why a Commission assessment of Tennessee's risk in relation to other natural gas companies is helpful in choosing a place within the zone of reasonableness. The existence of the zone of reasonableness range reflects the lack of precision of the estimation tools, not variability within the industry.

A better reason for treating the midpoint as a starting place is that an average is an obvious place to begin when there is no information that would incline the decisionmaker to prefer one estimate over another. Without some reasoned basis for such a preference, any departure from the midpoint is arbitrary. There may well be valid reasons for a departure, but the Commission has not shown us any.

* * *

The case is remanded for proceedings consistent with this opinion.

Notes and Questions

1. Which approach to determining the cost of equity did the Commission try to use here? Did the Commission persuade you that it had properly calculated the risk premium over government bonds?

2. Do you agree with the court's preference for assuming that the stock market is efficient and will properly price the risk associated with a stock? Is part of the problem with that theory in the case of a regulated firm the fact that one of the principal "risks" as to the firm's earnings is what the Commission will allow it to earn?

3. Might there be any appropriate concern about the ratio of debt financing to equity financing used by the corporation? Is there a single debt-

equity ratio that would be best for the company to have? What standards would you use to determine what that is? See Joseph R. Rose, Cost of Capital in Rate Regulation, 43 Virginia L. Rev. 1079, 1082–89, 1098–1100 (1957). Why might firms seem to prefer a different ratio?[26]

4. Another issue concerning the appropriate rate of return can arise from the practice of "double leveraging." For example, suppose a regulated utility has a capital structure consisting of 50% debt at 8% and 50% equity at 12% resulting in a cost of capital of 10%. It is said to be "leveraged" because the cost of debt is lower than the cost of capital and holders of equity receive a return that is higher than the firm's cost of capital.

Now suppose the utility becomes a wholly owned subsidiary of a firm which is funded by 50% debt at 8% and 50% equity at 10%. The cost of capital for the parent is, therefore, 9%. This is the second level of leveraging and gives rise to the issue of whether the regulated subsidiary's cost of equity should be regarded as 10%, the open market cost of equity, or 9%, the actual cost of the capital which the parent has invested in the subsidiary. Do you see how this problem is analogous to the problem of intracorporate transfers discussed earlier? See Mountain States Telephone & Telegraph Co. v. Department of Public Service, 191 Mont. 331, 624 P.2d 481 (1981); New England Telephone & Telegraph Co. v. Public Utilities Commission, 390 A.2d 8 (Me.1978).

A NOTE ON THE AMBIGUOUS COST OF EQUITY CAPITAL

A regulatory body, of course, cannot *set* the cost of equity capital. The market does that; the regulator can merely try to see that the company is entitled to earn enough to cover that "cost." Furthermore, in making that calculation, no single cost of equity capital can confidently be declared correct. Justice Holmes put the issue this way:

> An adjustment of this sort under a power to regulate rates has to steer between Scylla and Charybdis. On the one side if the franchise is taken to mean that the most profitable return that could be got, free from competition, is protected by the Fourteenth Amendment, then the power to regulate is null. On the other hand if the power to regulate withdraws the protection of the Amendment altogether, then the property is nought. This is not a matter of economic theory, but of fair interpretation of a bargain. Neither extreme can have been meant. A midway between them must be hit. Cedar Rapids Gas Light Co. v. City of Cedar Rapids, 223 U.S. 655, 32 S.Ct. 389, 56 L.Ed. 594 (1912).

26. Miller and Modigliani argued that the debt-equity ratio should have no effect on the total cost of capital. Investors will price the risk of the debt and the risk of the equity separately, but the sum of the prices of the various securities should always be the same figure, i.e. the cost of capital to the company. See Franco Modigliani & Merton H. Miller, The Cost of Capital, Corporation Finance & the Theory of the Firm, 48 American Econ. Rev. 261 (1958). See also the Comments by Joseph R. Rose, 49 Id. 638 (1959), and David Durand 49 Id. 639 (1959). Empirical results and a review of the literature can be found in Irwin Friend and Marshall Puckett, Dividends & Stock Prices, 54 American Econ. Rev 656 (1964). See also, Joseph E. Stiglitz, On the Irrelevance of Corporate Financial Policy, 64 American Econ. Rev 851 (1974).

A detailed treatment of the ambiguities and complexities in measuring or even defining the cost of capital is more than we need to undertake. Two different approaches, however, based on the twin themes of Bluefield Waterworks & Improvement Co. v. Public Service Commission, 262 U.S. 679, 43 S.Ct. 675, 67 L.Ed. 1176 (1923), will suggest the nature of the problems.[27]

First, the "return * * * equal to that * * * made * * * in other business * * * attended by corresponding risks" language of *Bluefield* has led to the so-called "comparable earnings" standard. This approach says that the regulator should determine and allow the actual rate of return earned by investors on "comparable" investments.[28] This technique is initially attractive because it recognizes that investors have other opportunities, the returns on which represent the cost of staying with one's investment in the regulated firm. However, practical difficulties with this approach abound. What company, for example, is "comparable" to a regulated waterworks? If the answer is some other regulated firm, the process becomes circular. One regulated firm's rates are set in terms of the regulatory body's conclusions as to capital costs. When one looks beyond regulated firms, the problem of finding companies of comparable risk or potential becomes even more difficult. Thus other techniques for measurement have been sought.

The "return * * * adequate * * * to maintain * * * its credit and enable it to raise * * * money" language of *Bluefield* underlies the so-called "earnings-price" approach. Proponents observe that the cost of raising equity capital can best be determined, not by theorizing about "comparability", but from the company's own stock, specifically its price on the stock exchange. A simple version of this approach would say that if a utility's own stock is selling for ten times earnings, the appropriate rate of return would be ten per cent because that represents the market's impartial report of the return which people are willing to accept in order to buy the stock today.[29] However this approach, too, is not without problems. In the long run, the stock market may reflect the company's fundamentals and the true cost of capital, but short run stock prices often seem to be affected by rumor, speculation and general economic expectations. A rate case looking at a short test period thus might get a distorted view of the proper return. Further, the price at

27. A much more extensive treatment of these issues may be found in J.C. Bonbright, Principles of Public Utility Rates 238–83 (1961); Alfred E. Kahn, The Economics of Regulation, Vol. I, 42–54 (1970); Charles F. Phillips, Jr., The Economics of Regulation 260–302 (1969); Solomon, Alternative Rate of Return Concepts and their Implication for Utility Regulation, 1 Bell J. 65 (1970).

28. Two articles systematically developing and defending this approach are Harold Leventhal, Comparable Earnings Standard for Regulation of Utilities in a Growth Economy, 74 Yale L.J. 989 (1965), and

Myers, The Application of Finance Theory to Public Utility Rate Cases, 3 Bell J. 58 (1972).

29. A well-developed treatment of this approach is contained in Note, An Earnings–Price Approach to Fair Rate of Return in Regulated Industries, 20 Stanford L. Rev. 287 (1969). See also, Bierman, Investment Decisions and Regulated Firms, in R. Salmonson, Ed., Public Utility Accounting: Models, Mergers, Information Systems 53 (1971); Leland, Regulation of Natural Monopolies & the Fair Rate of Return, 5 Bell J. 3 (1974).

which a stock sells on the stock exchange may reflect expectations as to future earnings as much as it does the objective determination of what is "necessary." Thus if investors expect the commission to be "tough" they may demand a high rate of return, and vice versa.

Both approaches reflect important perceptions about determining the cost of capital. Further, they may not be the polar extremes their proponents would sometimes maintain. To see that, and to try to more explicitly define the "true" or "fair" cost of capital, it seems useful to ask, "If it were wholly up to you, would you want to allow utilities a 'fair' rate of return on their investment?" It would take a low rate indeed before the firm would find it attractive to sell its plant for scrap, even if it were permitted to do so. You could apparently be a hero to all consumers if you slashed the return on utility investment in half. Would you do so if you could?

Would you be afraid the firm could not sell securities if a "confiscatory" rate were set? You will read that rationale from time to time, primarily in literature published by utilities, but ask yourself whether it is so. Suppose, for example, a "tough" regulatory commission allowed only three per cent return on debt when the market demanded ten per cent. Would the bonds sell? If you think they would not, look at the financial page of any newspaper and see the current price for old bonds, many of which pay three per cent or less. They sell briskly; they simply do not sell at face value. The same holds true for stock in firms which haven't earned a profit in years; it sells, but at lower prices than if earnings were high.

Who then gets hurt if the return is set too low? Think about it. It's the holders of existing equity securities. Holders of debt get their contracted-for interest, and as long as it is paid they have no cause for complaint. Equity holders, however, are vulnerable. If they bought at $50 per share when earnings on equity were $2.50 a share and a fair return was five per cent, when the fair return goes to ten per cent and earnings stay the same, their stock will only sell for something like $25. They will feel, and *be,* poorer. The requirement of a "fair" return, then, in constitutional terms, would seem to mean that there is a limit to what a state regulatory body can do to the value of a utility stock.

But being hard-headed about it, does such solicitude for equity holders serve any public purpose? Is there any sense in which the public is hurt by a too-low rate of return? Can't the firm simply issue cheap securities until it raises the capital it requires to meet the public's needs? Analytically, probably so, but the practical ability to raise capital may genuinely be impaired. Regulated firms must sell securities in a market in which investors have alternatives. The risks in economic activity are assumed and priced by investors every day, but investors might understandably demand a large price discount for buying something as "risky" as a stock whose price depends on the whims of a regulatory body. It might take such a large issue of new securities, and such a dilution of existing holders' interests, to raise a needed sum that the firm would reasonably conclude it could or should not do so. A guarantee of a "fair" return, then, can help bring order to the marketing of utility securities and itself tend to reduce the cost of capital.

Can one devise a formula that will protect equity holders' investment and permit the utility to raise capital effectively without giving investors a windfall? One approach would seem to be to allow that level of earnings that is necessary to keep the market value of the stock at or near book value. Why book value? That represents, as Justice Brandeis saw, a close approximation of the sum that investors contributed to the corporation and that they can reasonably argue should be "protected" by the company's earnings. That, too, represents a sufficiently discernable sum that prospective or current investors can know what they are getting into and what the future of their investment is likely to be. As conditions change, whether price levels generally or stock prices in particular, earnings would be allowed to change as well—up or down. The process would thus be self-correcting and allowable earnings would be relatively straightforward both to allow and review.

This approach is most nearly related to the earnings-price analysis because it makes a great deal turn on the market's evaluation of the particular stock.[30] But the comparable earnings test need not be eliminated altogether. Comparable situations can help define the limits of reasonableness within which company management can be judged and "errors" of the stock market discerned. If the rate of return required by the market for one utility's securities is higher than that for comparable firms, the commission can have some indication that some changes are in order. Some reduction in earnings may be appropriate for a time to "discipline" management and encourage better performance. Taken together, however, the comparable earnings approach and the earnings-price approach can give some framework to the otherwise unstructured process of determining the cost of equity.

THE EFFECT ON SERVICE RATES OF A RISE IN THE COST OF CAPITAL

It is easy to assume that a rise or fall of a few points in allowed rate of return may make little overall difference to the ratepayers. However, the following example may dispel that notion.

Assume a firm with annual costs (C) of $1 million, and that pays income taxes at a 50% rate. Assume it has $2 million in investment

---

30. This proposal is consistent with J.C. Bonbright, Principles of Public Utility Rates 246–56 (1961), and Note, An Earnings Price Approach to Fair Rate of Return in Regulated Industries, 20 Stanford L. Rev. 287 (1968). A short but good statement of the limitations of the proposal is contained in Leonard M. Ross, Comments on the Earnings–Price Note, 21 Stanford L. Rev. 644 (1969). Harold Somers advocated such an "end result" approach for many years. See Harold Somers, "Cost of Money" as the Determinant of Public Utility Rates, 4 Buffalo L. Rev. 289 (1955); Harold Somers, The "End Result" Approach to Public Utility Regulation, 16 Buffalo L. Rev. 689 (1967); Harold Somers, Rate of Return and Misallocation of Resources, in Haring & Humphrey, Eds., Utility Regulation During Inflation 37 (1971). The FCC spoke approvingly of and apparently relied heavily on a similar approach in Re American Telephone & Telegraph Co., 9 F.C.C.2d 30, 66–68, 87, 70 P.U.R.3d 129, 173–76, 195–96 (1967).

assets (I), half financed by debt and half by equity. Assume the interest rate on debt starts at five per cent and equity at ten per cent. The firm's allowed earnings thus will be:

R = C + I/2–r (debt) + I – r (equity) (doubled to cover income tax liability)

R = $1 m + $1 m @ 5% + $2 m @ 10%

R = $1.25 million

Now assume the prevailing interest rate on equity increases by five percentage points to fifteen per cent. Assume that the interest on debt also rises five percentage points but only twenty per cent of it needs to be refinanced this year so that the effective rate is six per cent. Now our calculation is as follows:

R = $1 m + $1 m @ 6% + $2 m @ 15%

R = $1.36 million

These have been reasonably conservative assumptions and yet we have seen that to cover a rise of five percentage points in interest rates, the rates charged consumers will have to rise $11/$125 or about nine per cent. (Consider again the argument for exempting a utility from income taxes.) If we assume such a rise in charges will cause a drop in consumption and the consequent necessity for an even larger rise in rates, it is not hard to understand how "tight money" in the economy will have a magnified effect on utility rates. Even ignoring all other increases in the firm's costs, a rise of five percentage points in the cost of money can easily mean a ten to fifteen per cent increase in the firm's charges for service.

THE AVERCH–JOHNSON HYPOTHESIS

What consequences other than "excessive" rates might flow from allowing too high a rate of return? In 1962, Professors Averch and Johnson developed an intuitively reasonable model suggesting that there will be an undesirable effect on the company's pattern of investment.[31]

Suppose someone would let you borrow money at five per cent interest which you could invest in assets producing a return of ten per cent. Would you make the investment? The answer, of course, is yes.

---

31. Harvey Averch and Leland L. Johnson, Behavior of the Firm Under Regulatory Constraint, 52 American Econ. Rev. 1052 (1962). A similar conclusion was reached almost concurrently in Wellisz, Regulation of Natural Gas Pipeline Companies: An Economic Analysis, 71 J. Political Economy 30 (1963). Analytic statements of the hypothesis are provided in Fred M. Westfield, Regulation & Conspiracy, 55 American Econ. Rev. 424 (1965); Akira Takayama, Behavior of the Firm Under Regulatory Constraint, 59 American Econ. Rev. 255 (1969); and William C. Baumol & Alvin Klevorick, Output Choices and Rate-of-Return Regulation. An Overview of the Discussion, 1 Bell J. 162 (1970). Considerable doubt about the validity of the A–J effect has been expressed in Corey, The Averch and Johnson Proposition: A Critical Analysis, 2 Bell J. 358 (1971). See also, Leland L. Johnson, Behavior of the Firm Under Regulatory Constraint: A Reassessment, 63 American Econ. Rev. (No. 2) 90 (1973). The analysis is explained further in Alfred E. Kahn, The Economics of Regulation, Vol. II, pp. 49–59, 106–108 (1971).

This is the concept of leveraging, and presumably you would buy all of the productive assets you could until the marginal cost of borrowing just equaled the marginal return you were getting from the new investment.

Professors Averch and Johnson reasoned that if a regulated firm is allowed a rate of return on its invested capital which is greater than the actual cost of raising that capital, it, too, will have an incentive to invest in capital goods. As in our example, if the regulatory agency will allow the firm ten per cent return on assets that it can purchase with five per cent money, the utility will have an incentive to build new buildings, lay new lines, buy new equipment, etc. Because the return allowed is by definition "too high," the observed investment can be presumed to be "too great."

Not surprisingly, economists have sought to find evidence supporting or impeaching this hypothesis. Professor Scherer has offered the following comments:

> The model probably applies poorly to those regulated industries in which price levels are set through joint actions encompassing a number of firms. Railroading is the prime example. The most important Interstate Commerce Commission rate of return determination decisions are addressed to broad commodity groups and geographic territories, and these decisions are commonly implemented by changes affecting many carriers. A particular carrier must be wary of letting its costs rise through excessive capital investment, for if other carriers fail to behave symmetrically, it may obtain no price relief from the ICC, and this fear blunts its incentive to distort its investment. Obversely, the companies most certain to secure price relief when costs rise are those who have no direct or close competitors and whose rates of return and prices are determined on a case-by-case basis. Prime candidates include the electric power and natural gas utilities, the telephone companies, and private urban transit lines. It seems almost certain that latent or active incentives for investment decision distortion exist within this latter group. Allowed rates of return vary widely from state to state. In 1966, net income after taxes as a percentage of stockholders' equity among the 50 largest U.S. electric, gas, and communications utilities ranged as high as 19 per cent from a mean of 10.2 per cent, with 17 companies earning returns of 12 per cent or more. Utilities allowed to earn returns exceeding their cost of new capital should tend to operate more capital-intensive processes than less privileged compatriots, *ceteris paribus*. And since the implications of the distortion model are symmetric, we should expect firms allowed a rate of return *below* the cost of capital to adopt processes which are less than optimally capital-intensive. This hypothesis is eminently testable. Unfortunately, no quantitative tests had been published at the time of writing. We are forced to fall back upon qualitative observations.
>
> Crude and plainly tenuous support for the Averch–Johnson hypothesis might be drawn from observing the office and factory

buildings of the American Telephone & Telegraph Co. They tend to be unusually massive, durable structures, with lavish reinforced brickwork—the kind of thing erected only when one's discount rate (reflecting the implicit cost of capital) is low. Indeed, they may be among the few 20th century industrial artifacts surviving into the 30th century—a source of wonder to economic anthropologists of that (hopefully) enlightened era.

However, we should not expect all A.T. & T. investments to exhibit this bias. Because intrastate telephone service rates are set on a state-by-state basis, the Bell System's allowed rate of return varies with the local regulatory climate. In a private communication, an A.T. & T. financial executive indicated that state-by-state variation in returns has a definite impact on the outcome of decisions to build certain facilities. To illustrate one case cited, suppose two coaxial cables are needed, one immediately and the other only in 10 years. The two can be buried simultaneously for an outlay of $25,000 per mile. Alternatively, one cable can be buried today at a cost of $20,000 per mile and then the trench can be re-opened 10 years hence to bury the second cable at an incremental cost of $10,000 per mile. Which alternative is more economical? It depends upon the discount rate, as the following comparison shows:

Discounted Value of the Cost per Mile of Cable

Discount Rate	Bury Both Cables Simultaneously	Bury One Today One in Ten Years
0%	$25,000	$30,000
2%	25,000	28,203
4%	25,000	26,756
6%	25,000	25,584
7%	25,000	25,084
8%	25,000	24,632
10%	25,000	23,855

At discount rates of seven per cent and less, burying both cables simultaneously is the low-cost alternative; the opposite is true over 7 per cent. According to the A.T. & T. executive, there is a tendency in states with low allowed rates of return (and hence high implicit capital cost) to choose the sequential strategy, though company officials believed that the simultaneous cable-laying alternative would more often be optimal if evaluated at true capital cost rates. Of course, the socially optimal choice depends upon cost and demand conditions which vary from case to case. It is possible (although this variant was not stressed by the A.T. & T. executive) that in states allowing generous rates of return, the simultaneous strategy might be chosen when the sequential strategy would entail lower costs at correctly imputed market discount rates.

In a less speculative vein, there is solid evidence that A.T. & T. favored coaxial cable over much less capital-intensive microwave radio relay systems to transmit television signals between major cities during the first few years following World War II. But when several other firms began developing potentially competing microwave relay networks, A.T. & T. accelerated its microwave program and cut back its planned coaxial cable installations by 33 per cent. This example suggests that competitive pressures may serve as a check against Averch–Johnson investment biases.[32]

Notes and Questions

1. Are you persuaded that examples of the Averch–Johnson phenomenon can be observed? Can you think of some not mentioned by Professor Scherer? Are there "innocent" explanations for the examples Professor Scherer has chosen?

2. What would be the effect of regulatory lag on the likelihood of the Averch–Johnson effect being observed? Even if money is "cheap," can one argue that regulated firms rarely have surplus dollars lying around to invest?[33]

3. What would Averch and Johnson say about the wisdom of allowing firms to invest now in capital goods only required sometime in the future? Under what conditions would the firm have an incentive to do so? Will it have that incentive if there is no current return from investment in the capital asset?[34]

4. If you were to err in setting rates, would you want to err too high or too low? Given that either error will lead to less than optimal results, which predicted consequences are the most difficult to live with? Which are easiest to correct by other means?

5. FITTING THE THREE ELEMENTS TOGETHER

Having looked at the three basic components of computing "I" times "r", the return to be allowed on investment, we may now understand some of the complexity and ambiguity in its calculation. All three

---

32. F.M. Scherer, Industrial Market Structure and Economic Performance 533–35 (1970). Copyright © 1970, Rand McNally & Company. Reprinted with permission. The comments about A.T. & T. refer to the period in which it was the sole provider of telephone service in the United States—both local and long distance.

Since Professor Scherer wrote, some articles have come out tending to support the A–J effect in the case of electric utilities. See Spann, Rate of Return Regulation and Efficiency in Production: An Empirical Test of the Averch–Johnson Thesis, 5 Bell J. 38 (1974); Conville, Regulation and Efficiency in the Electric Utility Industry, 5 Id. 53, 46 P. 1022 (1974); Petersen, An Empirical Test of Regulatory Effects, 6 Bell J. 111 (1975). It has been suggested that because of the A–J Effect, electric utilities were reluctant or at least not encouraged to resist the price

fixing conspiracy of electrical equipment manufacturers. Fred M. Westfield, Regulation and Conspiracy, 55 American Econ. Rev. 424 (1965). The empirical evidence for that conclusion has proved inconclusive, however. Emery, Regulated Utilities and Equipment Manufacturers' Conspiracies in the Electrical Power Industry, 4 Bell J. 322 (1973).

33. See Bailey & Coleman, The Effect of Lagged Regulation in an Averch–Johnson Model, 2 Bell J. 278 (1971).

34. See Zajac, Note on "Gold Plating" or "Rate Base Padding," 3 Bell J. 311 (1972), which concludes that while the A–J effect will cause investment in assets with less than optimal return, it will tend not to cause investment in wholly unproductive capital.

elements—the composition of the rate base, its valuation, and the rate of return—help determine the total figure to be allowed for rate making, and an "error" in one direction on one factor may be offset by an "error" in the other direction on some other factor.

Thus an attorney representing a regulated firm will seek to have the maximum number of items included in the "rate base." He or she will also seek to value those items as nearly at replacement cost as the commission will allow. The attorney will then take another bite at the apple by seeking to get the highest-possible rate of return allowed. If the commission wishes to appear tough, on the other hand, it may set an arbitrarily low rate of return but compensate by valuing the assets more nearly at replacement cost than it otherwise would have done.

With this perspective, we can perhaps better understand the message of the next case—probably the leading single case on rate determination.

FPC v. HOPE NATURAL GAS CO.

Supreme Court of the United States, 1944.
320 U.S. 591, 64 S.Ct. 281, 88 L.Ed. 333.

Mr. Justice Douglas delivered the opinion of the Court.

The primary issue in these cases concerns the validity under the Natural Gas Act of 1938 of a rate order issued by the Federal Power Commission reducing the rates chargeable by Hope Natural Gas Co. * * *

Hope is a West Virginia corporation organized in 1898. It is a wholly owned subsidiary of Standard Oil Co. (N.J.). Since the date of its organization, it has been in the business of producing, purchasing and marketing natural gas in that state. It sells some of that gas to local consumers in West Virginia. But the great bulk of it goes to five customer companies which receive it at the West Virginia line and distribute it in Ohio and in Pennsylvania. In July, 1938, the cities of Cleveland and Akron filed complaints with the Commission charging that the rates collected by Hope from East Ohio Gas Co. (an affiliate of Hope which distributes gas in Ohio) were excessive and unreasonable. * * *

On May 26, 1942, the Commission entered its order and made its findings. Its order required Hope to decrease its future interstate rates so as to reflect a reduction, on an annual basis of not less than $3,609,857 in operating revenues. And it established "just and reasonable" average rates per m.c.f. for each of the five customer companies.

The Commission established an interstate rate base of $33,712,526 which, it found, represented the "actual legitimate cost" of the company's interstate property less depletion and depreciation and plus unoperated acreage, working capital and future net capital additions. The Commission, beginning with book cost, made certain adjustments not necessary to relate here and found the "actual legitimate cost" of the plant in interstate service to be $51,957,416, as of December 31, 1940. It deducted accrued depletion and depreciation, which it found to be $22,328,016 on an "economic-service-life" basis. And it added $1,392,021 for future net capital additions, $566,105 for useful unoperated acreage, and $2,125,000 for working capital. * * *

Hope introduced evidence from which it estimated reproduction cost of the property at $97,000,000. It also presented a so-called trended "original cost" estimate which exceeded $105,000,000. The latter was designed "to indicate what the original cost of the property would have been if 1938 material and labor prices had prevailed throughout the whole period of the piece-meal construction of the company's property since 1898." Hope estimated by the "per cent condition" method accrued depreciation at about 35% of reproduction cost new. On that basis Hope contended for a rate base of $66,000,000. The Commission refused to place any reliance on reproduction cost new, saying that it was "not predicated upon facts" and was "too conjectural and illusory to be given any weight in these proceedings." It likewise refused to give any "probative value" to trended "original cost" since it was "not founded in fact" but was "basically erroneous" and produced "irrational results." In determining the amount of accrued depletion and depreciation the Commission * * * based its computation on "actual legitimate cost".

* * *

Hope contended that it should be allowed a return of not less than 8%. The Commission found that an 8% return would be unreasonable but that 6½% was a fair rate of return. That rate of return, applied to the rate base of $33,712,526, would produce $2,191,314 annually, as compared with the present income of not less than $5,801,171.

The Circuit Court of Appeals set aside the order of the Commission for the following reasons. (1) It held that the rate base should reflect the "present fair value" of the property, that the Commission in determining the "value" should have considered reproduction cost and trended original cost, and that "actual legitimate cost" (prudent investment) was not the proper measure of "fair value" where price levels had changed since the investment. * * * (3) It held that accrued depletion and depreciation and the annual allowance for that expense should be computed on the basis of "present fair value" of the property not on the basis of "actual legitimate cost".

* * *

Order Reducing Rates. Congress has provided in § 4(a) of the Natural Gas Act that all natural gas rates subject to the jurisdiction of the Commission "shall be just and reasonable, and any such rate or charge that is not just and reasonable is hereby declared to be unlawful." * * * Congress, however, has provided no formula by which the "just and reasonable" rate is to be determined. It has not filled in the details of the general prescription[35] of § 4(a) and § 5(a). It has not expressed in a specific rule the fixed principle of "just and reasonable".

35. Sec. 6 of the Act comes the closest to supplying any definite criteria for rate making. It provides in subsection (a) that, "The Commission may investigate and as-

When we sustained the constitutionality of the Natural Gas Act in the *Natural Gas Pipeline Co.* case, we stated that the "authority of Congress to regulate the prices of commodities in interstate commerce is at least as great under the Fifth Amendment as is that of the states under the Fourteenth to regulate the prices of commodities in intrastate commerce." Rate-making is indeed but one species of price-fixing. The fixing of prices, like other applications of the police power, may reduce the value of the property which is being regulated. But the fact that the value is reduced does not mean that the regulation is invalid. It does, however, indicate that "fair value" is the end product of the process of rate making not the starting point as the Circuit Court of Appeals held. The heart of the matter is that rates cannot be made to depend upon "fair value" when the value of the going enterprise depends on earnings under whatever rates may be anticipated.[36] We held in Federal Power Commission v. Natural Gas Pipeline Co., [315 U.S. 575, 62 S.Ct. 736, 86 L.Ed. 1037 (1942)], that the Commission was not bound to the use of any single formula or combination of formulae in determining rates. Its ratemaking function, moreover, involves the making of "pragmatic adjustments." And when the Commission's order is challenged in the courts, the question is whether that order "viewed in its entirety" meets the requirements of the Act. Under the statutory standard of "just and reasonable" it is the result reached not the method employed which is controlling. * * * It is not theory but the impact of the rate order which counts. If the total effect of the rate order cannot be said to be unjust and unreasonable, judicial inquiry under the Act is at an end. The fact that the method employed to reach that result may contain infirmities is not then important. Moreover, the Commission's order does not become suspect by reason of the fact that it is challenged. It is the product of expert judgment which carries a presumption of validity. And he who would upset the rate order under the Act carries the heavy burden of making a convincing showing that it is invalid because it is unjust and unreasonable in its consequences.

* * *

The rate-making process under the Act, i.e., the fixing of "just and reasonable" rates, involves a balancing of the investor and the consumer interests. Thus we stated in the *Natural Gas Pipeline Co.* case that "regulation does not insure that the business shall produce net reve-

---

certain the actual legitimate cost of the property of every natural-gas company, the depreciation therein, and, when found necessary for rate-making purposes, other facts which bear on the determination of such cost or depreciation and the fair value of such property." Subsection (b) provides that every natural-gas company on request shall file with the Commission a statement of the "original cost" of its property and shall keep the Commission informed regarding the "cost" of all additions, etc. [Court's fn. 8]

36. We recently stated that the meaning of the word "value" is to be gathered "from the purpose for which a valuation is being made. Thus the question in a valuation for rate making is how much a utility will be allowed to earn. The basic question in a valuation for reorganization purposes is how much the enterprise in all probability can earn." Institutional Investors v. Chicago, M., St. P. & P. R. Co., 318 U.S. 523, 540, 63 S.Ct. 727, 738. [Court's fn. 9]

nues." But such considerations aside, the investor interest has a legitimate concern with the financial integrity of the company whose rates are being regulated. From the investor or company point of view it is important that there be enough revenue not only for operating expenses but also for the capital costs of the business. These include service on the debt and dividends on the stock. By that standard the return to the equity owner should be commensurate with returns on investments in other enterprises having corresponding risks. That return, moreover, should be sufficient to assure confidence in the financial integrity of the enterprise, so as to maintain its credit and to attract capital. See State of Missouri ex rel. Southwestern Bell Tel. Co. v. Public Service Commission (Mr. Justice Brandeis concurring). The conditions under which more or less might be allowed are not important here. Nor is it important to this case to determine the various permissible ways in which any rate base on which the return is computed might be arrived at. For we are of the view that the end result in this case cannot be condemned under the Act as unjust and unreasonable from the investor or company viewpoint.

We have already noted that Hope is a wholly owned subsidiary of the Standard Oil Co. (N.J.). * * * On an average invested capital of some $23,000,000 Hope's average earnings have been about 12% a year. And during this period it had accumulated in addition reserves for depletion and depreciation of about $46,000,000. Furthermore, during 1939, 1940 and 1941, Hope paid dividends of 10% on its stock. And in the year 1942, during about half of which the lower rates were in effect, it paid dividends of 7½%. From 1939–1942 its earned surplus increased from $5,250,000 to about $13,700,000, i.e., to almost half the par value of its outstanding stock.

As we have noted, the Commission fixed a rate of return which permits Hope to earn $2,191,314 annually. In determining that amount it stressed the importance of maintaining the financial integrity of the company. It considered the financial history of Hope and a vast array of data bearing on the natural gas industry, related businesses, and general economic conditions. It noted that the yields on better issues of bonds of natural gas companies sold in the last few years were "close to 3 per cent". It stated that the company was a "seasoned enterprise whose risks have been minimized" by adequate provisions for depletion and depreciation (past and present) with "concurrent high profits", by "protected established markets, through affiliated distribution companies, in populous and industrialized areas", and by a supply of gas locally to meet all requirements, "except on certain peak days in the winter, which it is feasible to supplement in the future with gas from other sources." The Commission concluded, "The company's efficient management, established markets, financial record, affiliations, and its prospective business place it in a strong position to attract capital upon favorable terms when it is required."

In view of these various considerations we cannot say that an annual return of $2,191,314 is not "just and reasonable" within the meaning of the Act. Rates which enable the company to operate successfully, to maintain its financial integrity, to attract capital, and to compensate its investors for the risks assumed certainly cannot be condemned as invalid, even though they might produce only a meager return on the so-called "fair value" rate base. * * * Since there are no constitutional requirements more exacting than the standards of the Act, a rate order which conforms to the latter does not run afoul of the former.

* * *

Reversed.

Notes and Questions

1. Does Hope give a blank check to a regulatory agency to come up with whatever result it believes is "just and reasonable"? Recall Justice Brandeis' concern about the ability of a Court to review the Commission's work. Would he have necessarily disagreed with the Court's statement that, "It is not theory but the impact of the rate order which counts"?[37]

2. Does the opinion as a whole give content to the Court's concept of the appropriate lines of inquiry? What facts does it deem important in determining that the result reached here by the Commission was correct?

3. How should a Commission go about "balancing * * * the investor and consumer interests"? Is the Court suggesting there is an objective test of when rates are "too high"? Is it saying there is no objective test for when rates are "too low"? Is any argument still available that rates are "confiscatory"?

4. Might one conclude that the inquiry today should be more functional than mathematical? That is, may one properly ask the "revenue needs" of the firm rather than the level of income that is "just"? May one argue that if the firm has enough revenue to pay its current bills, including its interest on debt, and enough left over to assure that investors will supply the firm's future capital needs, its rates are by definition "just and reasonable" regardless of its "rate of return" by whatever measure that may be computed?

5. Duquesne Light Co. v. Barasch, 488 U.S. 299, 109 S.Ct. 609, 102 L.Ed.2d 646 (1989), helped answer such questions. Several electric utilities had been part of a group that planned to build nuclear generating facilities. After the Three Mile Island disaster, those plans were scrapped, but only after Duquesne Light had expended almost $35 million. It wanted to amortize that expenditure over 10 years, but the Pennsylvania Supreme Court held that state law did not permit recovery of sums spent for facilities that were never used to produce electricity. Duquesne and others appealed to the U.S. Supreme Court, which held:

37. In his lengthy and well-reasoned dissent in *Hope*, Justice Jackson writes, "The Court sustains this order as reasonable, but what makes it so or what could possibly make it otherwise, I cannot learn." His opinion is worth reading for his detailed analysis of the difficulty of rate making in the natural gas industry, a problem which we consider in Mobil Oil Exploration & Producing Southeast Inc. v. United Distribution Companies, *infra*.

Forty-five years ago in the landmark case of FPC v. Hope Natural Gas Co., this Court abandoned the rule of Smyth v. Ames, and held that the "fair value" rule is not the only constitutionally acceptable method of fixing utility rates. * * * We also acknowledged in that case that all of the subsidiary aspects of valuation for ratemaking purposes could not properly be characterized as having a constitutional dimension, despite the fact that they might affect property rights to some degree. Today we reaffirm these teachings of *Hope Natural Gas* * * *. [Hope], of course, does not dispense with all of the constitutional difficulties when a utility raises a claim that the rate which it is permitted to charge is so low as to be confiscatory: whether a particular rate is "unjust" or "unreasonable" will depend to some extent on what is a fair rate of return given the risks under a particular ratesetting system, and on the amount of capital upon which the investors are entitled to earn that return. At the margins, these questions have constitutional overtones.

Pennsylvania determines rates under a slightly modified form of the historical cost/prudent investment system. Neither Duquesne nor Penn Power alleges that the total effect of the rate order arrived at within this system is unjust or unreasonable. In fact the overall effect is well within the bounds of *Hope*, even with total exclusion of the CAPCO costs. Duquesne was authorized to earn a 16.14% return on common equity and an 11.64% overall return on a rate base of nearly $1.8 billion. Its $35 million investment in the canceled plants comprises roughly 1.9% of its total base. * * *

"Given these numbers, it appears that the PUC would have acted within the constitutional range of reasonableness if it had allowed amortization of the CAPCO costs but set a lower rate of return on equity with the result that Duquesne and Penn Power received the same revenue they will under the instant orders on remand. The overall impact of the rate orders, then, is not constitutionally objectionable. No argument has been made that these slightly reduced rates jeopardize the financial integrity of the companies, either by leaving them insufficient operating capital or by impeding their ability to raise future capital. Nor has it been demonstrated that these rates are inadequate to compensate current equity holders for the risk associated with their investments under a modified prudent investment scheme.

        * * *

" * * * We therefore hold that * * * the rate order at issue does not result in a constitutionally impermissible rate."

6. The question of what is "just and reasonable" remains a relevant question with answers that may surprise you. Regulations coming in the wake of the Telecommunications Act of 1996 are especially interesting. Justice Souter reviews the history of the Supreme Court's responses to rate making—and Congress and the agencies' reactions to them—in the following case.

VERIZON COMMUNICATIONS, INC. v. FEDERAL COMMUNICATIONS COMMISSION

Unites States Supreme Court, 2002.
535 U.S. 467, 122 S.Ct. 1646, 152 L.Ed.2d 701.

JUSTICE SOUTER delivered the opinion of the Court.

[The Court considered a challenge to the pricing methodology of the FCC which required local exchange carriers to unbundle network elements and make them available to competitors at a price which reflects "the most efficient telecommunications technology currently available and the lowest cost network configuration."]

    * * *

Companies providing telephone service have traditionally been regulated as monopolistic public utilities. At the dawn of modern utility regulation, in order to offset monopoly power and ensure affordable, stable public access to a utility's goods or services, legislatures enacted rate schedules to fix the prices a utility could charge. See * * * Munn v. Illinois, 94 U.S. 113, 134, 24 L.Ed. 77 (1877). As this job became more complicated, legislatures established specialized administrative agencies, first local or state, then federal, to set and regulate rates. The familiar mandate in the enabling Acts was to see that rates be "just and reasonable" and not discriminatory.

All rates were subject to regulation this way: retail rates charged directly to the public and wholesale rates charged among businesses involved in providing the goods or services offered by the retail utility. Intrastate retail rates were regulated by the States or municipalities, with those at wholesale generally the responsibility of the National Government, since the transmission or transportation involved was characteristically interstate.[38]

Historically, the classic scheme of administrative ratesetting at the federal level called for rates to be set out by the regulated utility companies in proposed tariff schedules, on the model applied to railroad carriers under the Interstate Commerce Act of 1887, 24 Stat. 379. After interested parties had had notice of the proposals and a chance to comment, the tariffs would be accepted by the controlling agency so long as they were "reasonable" (or "just and reasonable") and not "unduly discriminatory." Hale, Commissions, Rates, and Policies, 53 Harv. L.Rev. 1103, 1104–1105 (1940). See, e.g., Southern Pacific Co. v. ICC, 219 U.S. 433, 445, 31 S.Ct. 288, 55 L.Ed. 283 (1911). * * *

---

38. The first noteworthy federal rate-regulation statute was the Interstate Commerce Act of 1887, 24 Stat. 379, which was principally concerned with railroad rates but generally governed all interstate rates. It was the model for subsequent federal public-utility statutes like the Federal Power Act of 1920, 41 Stat. 1063, the Communi- cations Act of 1934, 48 Stat. 1064, the Natural Gas Act of 1938, 52 Stat. 821, and the Civil Aeronautics Act of 1938, 52 Stat. 973. The Communications Act of 1934 created the FCC and was the first statute to address interstate telephone regulation in an independent and substantive way. * * * [Court's fn. 2]

The way rates were regulated as between businesses (by the National Government) was in some respects, however, different from regulation of rates as between businesses and the public (at the state or local level). In wholesale markets, the party charging the rate and the party charged were often sophisticated businesses enjoying presumptively equal bargaining power, who could be expected to negotiate a "just and reasonable" rate as between the two of them. Accordingly, in the Federal Power Act of 1920 * * * and again in the Natural Gas Act of 1938 * * * . Congress departed from the scheme of purely tariff-based regulation and acknowledged that contracts between commercial buyers and sellers could be used in ratesetting, * * *. When commercial parties did avail themselves of rate agreements, the principal regulatory responsibility was not to relieve a contracting party of an unreasonable rate, * * * but to protect against potential discrimination by favorable contract rates between allied businesses to the detriment of other wholesale customers. * * * This Court once summed up matters at the wholesale level this way:

> "[W]hile it may be that the Commission may not normally impose upon a public utility a rate which would produce less than a fair return, it does not follow that the public utility may not itself agree by contract to a rate affording less than a fair return or that, if it does so, it is entitled to be relieved of its improvident bargain. In such circumstances the sole concern of the Commission would seem to be whether the rate is so low as to adversely affect the public interest—as where it might impair the financial ability of the public utility to continue its service, cast upon other consumers an excessive burden, or be unduly discriminatory." [Federal Power Commission v.] Sierra Pacific Power Co., [350 U.S. 348], at 355, 76 S.Ct. 368[, 100 L.Ed. 388 (1956)] (citation omitted).

Regulation of retail rates at the state and local levels was, on the other hand, focused more on the demand for "just and reasonable" rates to the public than on the perils of rate discrimination. Indeed, regulated local telephone markets evolved into arenas of state-sanctioned discrimination engineered by the public utility commissions themselves in the cause of "universal service." * * * In order to hold down charges for telephone service in rural markets with higher marginal costs due to lower population densities and lesser volumes of use, urban and business users were charged subsidizing premiums over the marginal costs of providing their own service.

These cross subsidies between markets were not necessarily transfers between truly independent companies, however, thanks largely to the position attained by AT & T and its satellites. This was known as the "Bell system," which by the mid–20th century had come to possess overwhelming monopoly power in all telephone markets nationwide, supplying local-exchange and long-distance services as well as equipment. * * * The same pervasive market presence of Bell providers that made it simple to provide cross subsidies in aid of universal service, however, also frustrated conventional efforts to hold retail rates down.

* * * Before the Bell system's predominance, regulators might have played competing carriers against one another to get lower rates for the public, * * * but the strategy became virtually impossible once a single company had become the only provider in nearly every town and city across the country. This regulatory frustration led, in turn, to new thinking about just and reasonable retail rates and ultimately to these cases.

The traditional regulatory notion of the "just and reasonable" rate was aimed at navigating the straits between gouging utility customers and confiscating utility property. FPC v. Hope Natural Gas Co., 320 U.S. 591, 64 S.Ct. 281, 88 L.Ed. 333 (1944). More than a century ago, reviewing courts charged with determining whether utility rates were sufficiently reasonable to avoid unconstitutional confiscation took as their touchstone the revenue that would be a "fair return" on certain utility property known as a "rate base." The fair rate of return was usually set as the rate generated by similar investment property at the time of the rate proceeding, and in Smyth v. Ames, 169 U.S. [466], at 546, 18 S.Ct. 418, [42 L.Ed. 819,] the Court held that the rate base must be calculated as "the fair value of the property being used by [the utility] for the convenience of the public." In pegging the rate base at "fair value," the Smyth Court consciously rejected the primary alternative standard, of capital actually invested to provide the public service or good. The Court made this choice in large part to prevent "excessive valuation or fictitious capitalization" from artificially inflating the rate base lest " '[t]he public . . . be subjected to unreasonable rates in order simply that stockholders may earn dividends.' " * * *

But Smyth proved to be a troublesome mandate, as Justice Brandeis, joined by Justice Holmes, famously observed 25 years later. Missouri ex rel. Southwestern Bell Telephone Co. v. Public Serv. Comm'n of Mo., 262 U.S. 276, 292, 43 S.Ct. 544, 67 L.Ed. 981 (1923) (dissenting opinion). The Smyth Court itself had described, without irony, the mind-numbing complexity of the required enquiry into fair value, as the alternative to historical investment:

> "[I]n order to ascertain [fair] value, original cost of construction, the amount expended in permanent improvements, the amount and market value of its bonds and stock, the present as compared with the original cost of construction, the probable earning capacity of the property under particular rates prescribed by statute, and the sum required to meet operating expenses, are all matters for consideration, and are to be given such weight as may be just and right in each case. We do not say that there may not be other matters to be regarded in estimating the value of the property." 169 U.S., at 546–547, 18 S.Ct. 418.

To the bewildered, Smyth simply threw up its hands, prescribing no one method for limiting use of these numbers but declaring all such facts to be "relevant." Southwestern Bell Telephone Co. (Brandeis, J., dissenting). What is more, the customary checks on calculations of value in other circumstances were hard to come by for a utility's property; its costly facilities rarely changed hands and so were seldom tagged with a price a buyer would actually pay and a seller accept, * * * . Neither could reviewing courts resort to a utility's revenue as an index of fair value, since its revenues were necessarily determined by the rates subject to review, with the rate of return applied to the very property subject to valuation. * * *

     * * *

The upshot of *Smyth*, then, was the specter of utilities forced into bankruptcy by rates inadequate to pay off the costs of capital, even when a drop in value resulted from general economic decline, not imprudent investment; while in a robust economy, an investment no more prescient could claim what seemed a rapacious return on equity invested. Justice Brandeis accordingly advocated replacing "fair value" with a calculation of rate base on the cost of capital prudently invested in assets used for the provision of the public good or service, and although he did not live to enjoy success, his campaign against *Smyth* came to fruition in FPC v. Hope Natural Gas Co. * * *

In *Hope Natural Gas*, this Court disavowed the position that the Natural Gas Act and the Constitution required fair value as the sole measure of a rate base on which "just and reasonable" rates were to be calculated. * * * In the matter under review, the Federal Power Commission had valued the rate base by using "actual legitimate cost" reflecting "sound depreciation and depletion practices," and so had calculated a value roughly 25 percent below the figure generated by the natural-gas company's fair-value methods using "estimated reproduction cost" and "trended original cost." * * * The Court upheld the Commission. "Rates which enable the company to operate successfully, to maintain its financial integrity, to attract capital, and to compensate its investors for the risks assumed certainly cannot be condemned as invalid, even though they might produce only a meager return on the so-called 'fair value' rate base." Although *Hope Natural Gas* did not repudiate everything said in *Smyth*, since fair value was still "the end product of the process of rate-making," federal and state commissions setting rates in the aftermath of *Hope Natural Gas* largely abandoned the old fair-value approach and turned to methods of calculating the rate base on the basis of "cost." A. Kahn, Economics of Regulations: Principles and Institutions 40–41 (1988).

"Cost" was neither self-evident nor immune to confusion, however; witness the invocation of "reproduction cost" as a popular method for calculating fair value under *Smyth*, and the Federal Power Commission's rejection of "trended original cost" (apparently, a straight-line derivation from the cost of capital originally invested) in favor of "actual legitimate cost," * * *. Still, over time, general agreement developed on a method that was primus inter pares, and it is essentially a modern gloss on that method that the incumbent carriers say the FCC should have used to set the rates at issue here.

The method worked out is not a simple calculation of rate base as the original cost of "prudently invested" capital that Justice Brandeis assumed, presumably by reference to the utility's balance sheet at the time of the rate proceeding. * * * Rather, "cost" came to mean "cost of service," that is, the cost of prudently invested capital used to provide the service. Bonbright[, Principles of Public Utility Rates (1961) at] 173; P. Garfield & W. Lovejoy, Public Utility Economics 56 (1964). This was calculated subject to deductions for accrued depreciation and allowances for working capital, * * * naturally leading utilities to minimize depreciation by using very slow depreciation rates (on the assumption of long useful lives), and to maximize working capital claimed as a distinct rate-base constituent.

This formula, commonly called the prudent-investment rule, addressed the natural temptations on the utilities' part to claim a return on outlays producing nothing of value to the public. It was meant, on the one hand, to discourage unnecessary investment and the "fictitious capitalization" feared in *Smyth* * * * and so to protect ratepayers from supporting excessive capacity, or abandoned, destroyed, or phantom assets. * * * At the same time, the prudent-investment rule was intended to give utilities an incentive to make smart investments deserving a "fair" return, and thus to mimic natural incentives in competitive markets (though without an eye to fostering the actual competition by which such markets are defined). In theory, then, the prudent-investment qualification gave the ratepayer an important protection by mitigating the tendency of a regulated market's lack of competition to support monopolistic prices.

But the mitigation was too little, the prudent-investment rule in practice often being no match for the capacity of utilities having all the relevant information to manipulate the rate base and renegotiate the rate of return every time a rate was set. The regulatory response in some markets was adoption of a rate-based method commonly called "price caps," * * * as, for example, by the FCC's setting of maximum access charges paid to large local-exchange companies by interexchange carriers, In re Policy and Rules Concerning Rates for Dominant Carriers, 5 FCC Rcd. 6786, 6787, ¶ 1 (1990).

The price-cap scheme starts with a rate generated by the conventional cost-of-service formula, which it takes as a benchmark to be decreased at an average of some 2–3 percent a year to reflect productivity growth, subject to an upward adjustment if necessary to reflect inflation or certain unavoidable "exogenous costs" on which the company is authorized to recover a return. * * * Although the price caps do not eliminate gamesmanship, since there are still battles to be fought over the productivity offset and allowable exogenous costs, * * * they do give companies an incentive "to improve productivity to the maximum extent possible," by entitling those that outperform the productivity offset to keep resulting profits Ultimately, the goal, as under the basic prudent-investment rule, is to encourage investment in more productive equipment.

Before the passage of the 1996 Act, the price cap was, at the federal level, the final stage in a century of developing ratesetting methodology. What had changed throughout the era beginning with Smyth v. Ames was prevailing opinion on how to calculate the most useful rate base, with the disagreement between fair-value and cost advocates turning on whether invested capital was the key to the right balance between investors and ratepayers, and with the price-cap scheme simply being a rate-based offset to the utilities' advantage of superior knowledge of the facts employed in cost-of-service ratemaking. What is remarkable about this evolution of just and reasonable ratesetting, however, is what did not change. The enduring feature of ratesetting from Smyth v. Ames to the institution of price caps was the idea that calculating a rate base and then allowing a fair rate of return on it was a sensible way to identify a range of rates that would be just and reasonable to investors and ratepayers. Equally enduring throughout the period was dissatisfaction with the successive rate-based variants. From the constancy of this dissatisfaction, one possible lesson was drawn by Congress in the 1996 Act, which was that regulation using the traditional rate-based methodologies gave monopolies too great an advantage and that the answer lay in moving away from the assumption common to all the rate-based methods, that the monopolistic structure within the discrete markets would endure.

* * *

For the first time, Congress passed a ratesetting statute with the aim not just to balance interests between sellers and buyers, but to reorganize markets by rendering regulated utilities' monopolies vulnerable to interlopers, even if that meant swallowing the traditional federal reluctance to intrude into local telephone markets. The approach was deliberate, through a hybrid jurisdictional scheme with the FCC setting a basic, default methodology for use in setting rates when carriers fail to agree, but leaving it to state utility commissions to set the actual rates.

While the Act is like its predecessors in tying the methodology to the objectives of "just and reasonable" and nondiscriminatory rates, it is radically unlike all previous statutes in providing that rates be set "without reference to a rate-of-return or other rate-based proceeding," * * * . The Act thus appears to be an explicit disavowal of the familiar public-utility model of rate regulation (whether in its fair-value or cost-of-service incarnations) presumably still being applied by many States for retail sales, * * * in favor of novel ratesetting designed to give aspiring competitors every possible incentive to enter local retail telephone markets, short of confiscating the incumbents' property.

[The Court went on to uphold the Commission's pricing methodology.]

Notes and Questions

1. In *Verizon*, the Court approves a "forward looking" cost approach to pricing the services that existing firms will have to provide new entrants. Justice Souter's detailed analysis is presented later in this Chapter. Do you agree that such an approach would be "just and reasonable" even if it means the incumbent will not cover its costs? If the incumbent cannot cover costs, does that mean the investment by the incumbent was necessarily imprudent?

2. A dramatic change made in *Verizon* is from linking prices to some measure of the value of assets actually in use to basing prices on the cost to produce with possibly hypothetical future facilities. According to the Court this is, in part, a reaction to the ability of utilities to rig the system in one way or another. Under the new system, do you think new entrants will be in the driver's seat? Isn't there a potential that new entrants will be able to rig the system by virtue of the imprecision of the idea of "most efficient technology currently available?"

3. The Court reasons that "monopoly" is an assumption of rate-based methodologies and that the FCC's "answer lay in moving away from the assumption * * * that the monopolistic structure within the discrete markets would endure." Does this mean that local telephone service is actually not monopolistic? Or, is the Court suggesting that the FCC is trying to create competitive pressures even though the industry has natural monopoly characteristics?

4. In Chapter 3 you were introduced to the concept of "contestable markets." The idea was that firms could compete for the right to be the sole provider of a service. Is that what is going on with respect to local telephone service in the new world of deregulation?

5. Think about the issues this way. Suppose local exchange facilities were owned by states or cities rather than local exchange carriers. If the state or city then leased the right to use those facilities to private companies, what price do you think would be appropriate? One based on the cost of the facilities or one based on the most efficient technology currently available?

B. ALLOCATION OF CHARGES TO PARTICULAR CUSTOMERS

In this section we assume that the regulatory agency has determined the total revenue that the firm will be entitled to earn. It then becomes the agency's task to approve a structure of rates that will permit the firm to earn that income. To some extent, the two tasks go hand in hand. However, while the determination of the revenue ceiling is largely a policing function, the design of rates gives the agency substantially greater latitude to work in partnership with the firm both to help it earn its revenue and to indulge particular preferences as to non-economic objectives which may be furthered by the ratesetting process.

An example may help illustrate. Suppose that a regulated firm has the capacity to produce 1,000,000 units of an item in a given year and is entitled to earn $1,000,000. What should be its charge per unit? Too easy for you? Should it be $1.00 per unit? If you think about the problem again, you will realize that you cannot reach that conclusion with confidence. From the facts given, you have no idea how many units of the product would be demanded at $1.00 per unit. For all you know, the company might not sell all 1,000,000 at $1.00 each. On the other hand, at that price, the quantity demanded may be so in excess of 1,000,000 units that there would be shortages and great public inconvenience.

Putting the problem on a smaller scale, we can again see the problem of rate design. Suppose there are only two customers, you and me. Total allowed revenue is $2.00. You will not pay $1.00 for a unit but I will. Therefore, at a price of $1.00, the company can only sell one of its two units. Suppose, however, that you would pay $.90 for the item and that, if pressed, I would pay $1.10. What might a regulator wish to have the firm charge us in order to earn its $2.00? Of course. If the agency lets it charge you $.90 and me $1.10, that will permit it to earn its $2.00 and we both will be happy—at least until I find out how little you paid.

Conversely, and more realistic in practice, in almost any case there is more than one form of rate design that will permit the regulated firm to earn its allowed revenue. If we assume that the firm is permitted to earn less than it could have earned had it not been subject to regulation, then it will be charging less than profit-maximizing prices for its various services. It is evident, therefore, that there will be several combinations of prices of services that will lead to the allowed total revenue. The choice among the possible rate designs will depend on the agency's choice of what other values will be maximized. Will the agency require the firm to serve senior citizens at a lower price than others, for example? Will it favor small towns over big cities, or vice versa? Exploration of such questions is the subject of this part of the Chapter.[39]

1. REFLECTING COST DIFFERENCES IN SETTING RATES: AVERAGE v. MARGINAL COST PRICING

In asking the "proper" way for a regulated firm to do anything, we traditionally begin by asking how an unregulated firm in competition would tend to behave. Let's say you have gone into business to sell ice cream sundaes. It costs you $150.00 to buy the glasses, rent the store, etc. At that point you can make each additional ice cream sundae for 50 cents worth of materials. You believe that you can sell 300 sundaes for $1.00 each. As you can see, your business will exactly break even. You will sell 300 sundaes, take in $300.00 and will have spent $300.00.

---

39. The area of rate design is treated intensively and extensively in economic literature, usually at a level of refinement that is unnecessary for the lawyer. Good analyses can be obtained, however, in J.C. Bonbright, Principles of Public Utility Rates 287–406 (1961), and Alfred E. Kahn, The Economics of Regulation, Vol. I., pp. 63–199 (1970). See also, Abba Lerner, Conflicting Principles of Public Utility Rate Regulation, and William C. Baumol, Reasonable Rules for Rate Regulation: Plausible Policies for an Imperfect World, both in Paul W. MacAvoy, ed., The Crisis of the Regulatory Commissions (1970).

Now assume someone whom you did not expect to be one of your 300 customers offers to buy 100 sundaes for 80 cents each (suppose you can use the glassware and other supplies at no additional cost). Will you sell the 100 sundaes? Notice that the total cost of producing 400 sundaes will be $350.00. That means that your average cost per sundae will be 88 cents. Therefore, you might argue that you could not afford to sell a sundae for 80 cents.

On the contrary! Under the assumptions stated here, you would jump at the chance. You would see that the additional 100 sundaes would cost you $50.00 to make but would earn you $80.00. Thus your total cost for selling 400 sundaes would be $350.00, your total receipts $380.00, and you would make $30.00 additional profit. This example is nothing more nor less than an illustration of the fundamental point made earlier that a business person will want to produce as long as the marginal revenue from additional sales exceeds the marginal cost. Average cost is an utterly irrelevant feature of this kind of calculation.

Now transpose the situation in this way. Suppose that there is more than one ice cream store in town and that when you offer your sundaes for $1.00, you find that all your customers are going across the street where the sundaes are sold for 90 cents. What will you do? You have already spent $150.00 for glassware and initial supplies. While they might bring something at a distress sale, you want to sell ice cream. Even if your well-considered initial projections indicated that a price of $1.00 was possible, you now find that reality is different. Will you as a reasonable business person cut your price to 90 cents? Of course you will. You will recognize that on each sundae you sell at that price you are earning 40 cents above your marginal cost. This will go toward repayment of your initial expenditure. Conceivably, you won't earn back the full $150.00, but you certainly will have a better chance of doing so than if you sell no ice cream at all. How low will you cut your price in order to get business? On the facts as described, presumably you could cut your price nearly to 50 cents per sundae. As long as you are making anything more than your out-of-pocket costs of selling sundaes, you are making some contribution toward your fixed costs.

In its detailed analysis of the marginal vs. average cost issue, one agency concluded:

> The record in this proceeding abounds with arguments over the relevance, the calculation, and the practicability and applicability of marginal costs in connection with electric rate structures. There is no disagreement, however, about its underlying theoretical rationale, as set forth in the following testimony by Dr. Paul Joskow (associate professor of economics at the Massachusetts Institute of Technology, a witness proffered by the seven electric utility companies), which provides a suitable starting point:
>
> > "We can define marginal cost very generally as the cost of society's scarce resources which must be used to produce one additional unit of some commodity or the value of resources

that would be saved by producing one less unit of that commodity. As long as our goal is economic efficiency, the notion that prices should be equal to marginal cost is a general economic principle having nothing in particular to do with electricity. The principle derives from the basic operation of an economy where production and consumption decisions are decentralized. Consumers decide how they will divide their incomes among different commodities by looking at the relative prices of these commodities. Prices act as signals to consumers indicating the cost to them of additional consumption of various commodities. To the extent that commodity prices are equal to the marginal social costs of production, these pricing signals indicate simultaneously the cost of commodities to individual consumers and the cost of producing such commodities from the viewpoint of society as a whole. With prices set equal to marginal cost, consumers' decisions regarding the trade-offs associated with the consumption of different commodities are guided by signals which reflect the actual production of these commodities.

"For example, if the price for some commodity like electricity is set below its marginal cost, consumers will think it is cheaper to purchase an additional unit than it really costs society to produce it. The consumer will then be led to expand his consumption to the point where the * * * value of an additional unit of the commodity is equal to its price. But since the price has been set below the marginal cost, the value of the last unit of consumption to the consumer is less than what it costs society to produce it. More resources are being devoted to the production of this commodity than is socially efficient.

"There is, I submit, no real argument about whether marginal cost pricing is right or wrong. If our goal is economic efficiency, it is almost definitional that the prices of commodities must reflect the marginal social cost of supplying these commodities."[40]

The fundamental conclusion from this analysis is that any reasonable business person will tend to price at marginal cost and that a regulated firm "should" do so. Indeed it is fashionable in working through this reasoning to belittle those uninitiated who fall into the "ignorant" fallacy of pricing at average cost.

But the analysis should begin, not end, there. Figure 13 is reproduced from Chapter III. It illustrates what we learned there about the cost curves of a natural monopolist. Remember that the natural monopoly rationale suggested that the dominant characteristic of a natural monopoly was that its marginal cost of providing additional service was constantly falling over all relevant ranges of production. Thus, in the figure the marginal cost price of Pc is always below the average cost price of Pa.

40. Re Rate Design For Electric Corporations, 15 P.U.R.4th 434 (N.Y.P.S.C.1976).

There will be a revenue "gap." Our ice cream producer will always earn the cost of the ice cream but never the cost of his glassware, initial remodeling, and the like. Unless some technique is devised for reimbursing those expenses as well, the word will spread quickly throughout the economy that one is a fool to make those expenditures.

Figure 13

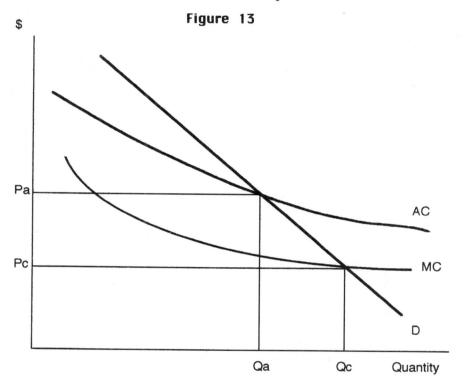

The typical electric utility finds itself in precisely the situation of our hypothetical ice cream store. It has incurred extensive capital expenses in order to be able to provide the first unit of power. The marginal cost of providing that power is low, but if the firm does not have some way of recovering those capital expenditures, it will not be willing to undertake them. And, as we have seen, in the calculation of the total revenue which the firm is entitled to earn, a provision for recovering at least a reasonable rate of return on those investments is included.

There are basically four techniques by which a regulatory agency can seek to deal with the inherent "gap" between a natural monopolist's marginal cost and its average cost. First, the company can simply be directed to price at or near average cost. We have already discussed the problems that can create. Some people would be willing and eager to buy the service at marginal cost but will be denied the service at average cost. Firms which would rationally want to meet that demand will be forbidden to do so. Indeed, strict average cost pricing might result in the company earning less than its total costs. On the other hand, average cost pricing tends to avoid price discrimination. It is "fair" in the sense that persons tend to be charged the same price for the same service. Furthermore, average cost often is, at least compared to some other techniques, relatively easy to calculate.

Second, the company might seek appropriations to have the taxpaying public bear some or all of the fixed costs. For example, one could conceive of a system in which railroad roadbeds were publicly-owned in the same manner as highways are. The effect of this type of action would be to reduce the spread between marginal and average cost and thus make marginal-cost pricing, or something closely approximating it, substantially more practical. On the other hand, the taxes in many cases would presumably be levied against people who would never take advantage of the service being subsidized. This would not only be a transfer of wealth from some persons to others, but it might well stimulate consumption of an apparently low-cost service which in reality was costing the taxpayers a great deal.

Third, the company might use multi-part pricing. This is a system that would say that people should pay a one-time charge for the right to buy a service at marginal cost. In our example, 100 people might each pay $1.50 for the right to buy sundaes for 50 cents. This is really a private version of the taxing scheme mentioned above and would have the obvious advantage of meeting the firm's needs, assessing costs to those who are benefitted, and pricing at marginal cost. However, if marginal cost varied with output, pricing might become a marketing nightmare. Further, persons who would be willing to purchase the service at or above marginal cost might not be willing to pay the one-time charge, and therefore they would be denied the service as much as under average cost pricing.

Fourth, the firm might be permitted to engage in some form of price discrimination. Some of the examples suggested above have incorporated this approach and suggested its apparent rationality. That is, if one purchaser would be willing to pay $1.10 for a service but another would be willing to pay only 90 cents, perhaps they should be charged different prices in order that the firm may earn its $2.00. In reality, what this tends to mean is that some purchasers will pay marginal cost and it will be left to other persons, who for various reasons are more willing to do so, to make up the "gap."

This kind of price discrimination may seem to make sense initially, but there is historical evidence that the practice of such discrimination was one of the evils sought to be avoided by regulation. The following excerpt from a report of the ICC is illustrative.

I.C.C. BUREAU OF STATISTICS, INTERSTATE COMMISSION COMMERCE COMMISSION ACTIVITIES 1887–1937

Pp. 26–28 (1937).

The financial methods that accompanied the growth of the railway for the several decades after the Civil War are generally familiar. Trickery and piracy in railway finance early became prominent, as in the manipulation of Erie securities by Drew, Fiske and Gould, in the sixties, and were widely publicized. * * *

While railway finance aroused both suspicion and indignation, rate abuses produced even greater unrest because of their more far-reaching effects, and hence played a more important part in bringing about regulatory measures. Railroad rates were affected by the strange malady of being at once both too high and too low. The early railway, being short, competed directly with the highway and sometimes with the waterway, and undoubtedly patterned its charges with relation to both. As the railway lengthened, it was able to furnish a service beyond the capacity of the highway and often beyond the reach of a waterway, giving it a monopolistic position in certain traffic. In the latter situation, the railway not only could exact a monopoly price for its services but could supply transportation in the manner and amount it wished. The other extreme was encountered when two or more lines were completed between important areas. Rates were then lowered sharply and suddenly and devious methods were employed to secure traffic that might go to the competing carrier. As it was not possible for railway service to be duplicated in every instance, much traffic was free from any competitive influence. Hence, in such instances relatively low rates were published for shipments between common markets and high rates, intended to offset the lower competitive charges, were quoted on the local traffic.

The traffic manager's command to get competitive tonnage at any price resulted probably from an extreme interpretation by railway officials of the principle that additional business is desirable as long as out-of-pocket costs are covered and something is added for the fixed costs. In many cases it is doubtful that the rates followed any principle. In the late sixties, cattle were moved from Buffalo to New York for $1 per car. Between 1866 and 1870 the first class rate for shipments from Chicago to New York varied between 25 cents and $2.15 per 100 pounds, and in some instances the first four classes took the same rate. It is asserted, however, that the rate wars really did not start until the seventies. During that decade it is recorded that cattle moved free of charge from Chicago to Pittsburgh, and for $5 per car from Chicago to New York. Nor was the cut-throat game which continued into the eighties confined to freight traffic as is indicated by the dollar rate for immigrants traveling from New York to Chicago and by other examples. Although attempts were made by the carriers to reach agreements from time to time, these apparently served merely as recuperation periods in their constant warfare. Moreover, the public which had developed a fear of monopoly vigorously opposed any kind of railroad combination.

One of the results of these conditions has been stated as follows:

In some sections of the country, if rates were maintained as they were at the time the interstate commerce law took effect, it would have been practically impossible for a new town, however great its natural advantages, to acquire the prosperity and the strength which would make it a rival of the towns which were specially favored in rates; for the rates themselves would establish for it indefinitely a condition of subordination and dependence to "trade centers."

Discrimination between places was accompanied by another form of evil in discrimination between persons. Rebates, special rates, underbilling, and free passes were among the weapons the traffic solicitor always held in readiness as he made the rounds of his patrons. He varied their use according to severity of competition, volume of shipment, and personal considerations. Shippers often entered into the scheme and exerted pressure for their own gains. The result was not merely a wide difference between competitive and noncompetitive rates but a great variety of such competitive rates. It was only natural that discontent should be general since many shippers received no privileges at all while, as between the favored shippers, some received more than others.

————

Does the railroad's practice of charging less on routes in which there was competition surprise you? Does it illustrate that the traffic managers were "evil" people? Would you have expected them, acting rationally, to have priced any other way?

Who got hurt by the kind of practices described here? Why should anyone care about the alleged injury to cities served by only one mode of transportation? Notice that the economic effects would tend to be self-correcting in the sense that land values in the less-favored towns would tend to be lower to counterbalance the increased costs of transportation. If that would simply mean that people could make a tradeoff of cheap land and high-cost transportation versus expensive land and low-cost transportation, who would get hurt? Obviously the landowners in the smaller, more remote towns would be unhappy, but should we be concerned about landowners? Even if the abstract image of a landowner does not trigger an emotional response, remember that these landowners are very often homeowners, small business persons, and people who would otherwise be employed in businesses which elect to leave the area because of high transportation costs. In short, the consequences of high transportation costs may spill over and touch many lives. As a result, it probably should not be surprising to find that political pressure built to require that price discrimination not be the technique chosen for making up the gap between marginal and average cost.

The perception of unfairness, regardless of its abstract soundness, has led to statutory prohibitions of "discrimination." The Interstate Commerce Act, for example, prohibits discrimination among "persons," commodities or localities.[41] Similar provisions exist in the statutes creating state utility commissions. See Kenneth C. Dam, The Economics and Law of Price Discrimination: Herein of Three Regulatory Schemes, 31 U. Chicago L. Rev. 1 (1963).

However, statutory prohibitions of discrimination cannot eliminate the problem "gap" between marginal cost and average cost. Nor can they eliminate the temptation of a politically-appointed group to favor some persons, areas and interests over others. Thus the twin problems of rate design have become to identify (1) when a pattern of rates is discriminatory and (2) when a discriminatory pattern is so unjust as to be illegal.

The potential problems with marginal cost pricing do not end there. It is easy to say that one should price services at their marginal cost or at least accurately reflect marginal cost differences in pricing. However that objective is easier to articulate than to accomplish for additional reasons.

1. Definition of the marginal unit. So far we have spoken of ice cream sundaes and railroad flat cars, both small, relatively-discrete units of measurement. These are far from typical, however, and the problem of defining the unit of production is central to many rate structure issues.

What is the basic unit of telephone service, for example? Is it the "call"? Is it the "telephone instrument"? Is it the "phone line," i.e. the capacity to have calls come in and out, regardless of the number of calls made or extension phones attached to the line? Is it one minute of line use? Is "directory assistance" a separate unit of service that should be priced separately? The answer is that there is no inherently right measure of phone service. Some measures are more useful than others; each is probably useful in some contexts. Indeed the pricing units for local and long distance service are different.

What is the basic unit of airline service? Is it the "seat"? Is it the single "flight," the take-off on one day from point A and landing at point B? Is it the "passenger-mile," a factor which relates the number of seats to the distance the flight covers? Is it the "scheduled flight," the availability of a flight on a given day regardless whether or not the flight is full? In which of these units do individuals plan? In which units do airlines plan, i.e. what is an airline in a realistic position to add or delete? Once again, how one defines the marginal unit is crucial to how one calculates the marginal cost and economic theory cannot tell us exactly what the marginal unit is in many cases.

2. Long-run vs. short-run time perspective. What is the marginal cost to a bus company of allowing one bus to be chartered for one trip

---

41. 24 Stat. 379 (1887), as amended, 49 U.S.C.A. § 1 et seq. The key provisions against discrimination are sections 1(4), 1(6), 2, 3(1), 3(4), and 4(1).

when it would not otherwise be in use? One can identify the costs of driver salary and gasoline for which the company will pay almost immediately. Are those the only costs, however? Presumably the bus will need an oil change sooner than usual and perhaps the tires will show more wear. Any proper calculation of marginal cost should account for these longer-range expenses as well. It may even be that the bus will bring less at trade-in time because of the extra mileage. Even this long-term cost should be deemed marginal because it is attributable to the trip in question, yet the problems of specifying such costs accurately are often great.

The problem of long-term marginal cost is important in another sense as well. There may be costs associated with entering the charter business which are hard to associate with a given trip. New buses may have to be bought which are used only in part for charter work. Insurance rates may go up. A new garage may be needed to house the new buses. An attempt to translate such costs into cents-per-mile may be necessary but can be seen to be inherently arbitrary. The costs are not incurred per mile; they are large scale and long duration. They are "marginal costs," but they are long-term costs rather than short-term.

In a sense, of course, the problems of defining the marginal unit and defining the proper time perspective are the same. It is easy to specify in theory that incremental or marginal cost should be the standard for rate making but the practical problems of such an approach can be great indeed.

Finally, look at Figure 14. Here the marginal cost curve does not decline throughout the relevant levels of production. As a result, the marginal cost price of Pc is higher than the average cost price of Pa. Could this happen? Sure, during a highly inflationary period such as the late 70s, it happened often. Fixed costs were likely to be stable and tied to long-term contracts or represented goods bought at lower prices. Marginal costs, however, are inherently more likely to reflect current input prices. Thus, the marginal cost strategy in this instance would result in the "worst" of all regulatory worlds, a state of excess revenue.

Figure 14

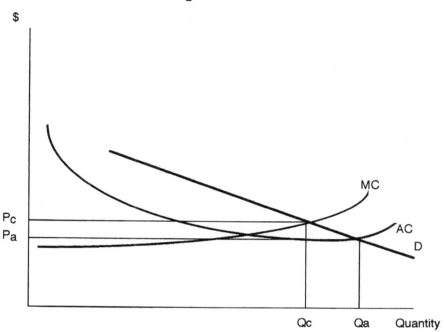

What could you do in this state of affairs? Sure, price at average cost. But are you convinced that such a course would send consumers the right signals as to how much of the service to demand?[42]

Keep these problems in mind, then, as you look at the later cases. Ask whether the court or commission is even addressing the issues we have raised. Real-life rate making often involves compromises and conscious choices to set some rates on some basis other than marginal cost. Often, such ratesetting will take elasticity of demand into account.

A NOTE ON DEMAND ELASTICITY

Basic economics and common sense indicate that when prices increase the amount of a commodity demanded will decline. Conversely, when prices fall, the quantity demanded will increase. As important to economists and ratemakers as this basic law of demand, however, is the issue of *how much* quantity demanded changes in response to a price change.

Figures 15 and 16 show two possible demand curves for product X and illustrate why the degree of responsiveness is so important. In Figure 1 the demand curve is purposely drawn to be relatively flat; in

---

42. Consider also the "problem of second best." It says that marginal cost pricing is socially optimal as long as other goods and services also have marginal cost prices. How could the application of marginal cost pricing to one good while others are priced at average cost actually be less efficient than average cost pricing? See F.M. Scherer, Industrial Market Structure and Economic Performance 24–29 (1970).

Figure 2 the curve is steep. In both graphs the original price is $1.00 and the quantity demanded is 20. Now suppose the price increases to $2.00. Note that this is the same price increase in both graphs. In Figure 15 the quantity demanded drops to 8 units. In Figure 16 though, it only falls to 15 units. Thus, even though the direction of the changes in price and quantity are consistent with economic theory, just knowing the basic principle of demand tells one very little about a particular demand.

Figure 15   Figure 16

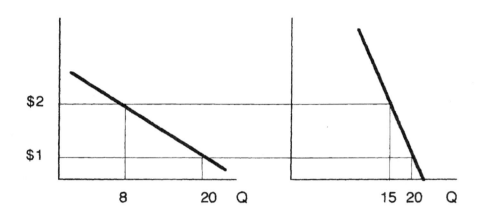

The measure of responsiveness of quantity demanded to price is called "demand elasticity."[43] It can be expressed as percentage *change* in quantity/percentage *change* in price (Q/P). When the absolute value of elasticity is greater than one, demand is said to be elastic; when it is less than one, demand is inelastic.[44] The data provided in the graphs enables you to calculate the actual elasticities. To do so, though, requires a small refinement in the equation. The elasticity associated with a change in price should be the same whether price is moving from $1 to $2 or from $2 to $1. After all, the responsiveness in demand is the same. The problem is that the change in price is 100% if we move from $1 to $2, and only 50% if we move from $2 to $1. In short, the calculation of elasticity may be affected by our starting point. A method of overcoming this problem is to take an average of the price and quantity values. This results in the following equation:

$$\frac{Q2 - Q1}{Q2 + Q1} \Big/ \frac{P2 - P1}{P2 + P1}$$

43. The term elasticity is used to describe the relationship between any independent and dependent variable. For example, one could measure the response in the quantity demanded of product X to changes in the price of product Y. This is called cross elasticity.

44. When the percentage changes are equal, the demand is unitary elastic.

Plugging the values from the figures into this equation you should be able to calculate an elasticity of 1.29 for the change in Figure 15 and .43 for Figure 16.[45] The calculation of demand elasticity in some respects just confirms what is evident from inspection of the graphs; demand is more responsive to price changes in Figure 15 than in Figure 16.

Not only is the demand in Figure 15 more elastic than the demand in Figure 16, the calculations indicate that Figure 15 elasticity is greater than 1 and, therefore, elastic in an absolute sense while demand in Figure 16 is inelastic. This information is important because it enables one to predict what will happen to total revenue when price changes. For example, in both Figures 15 and 16, total revenue—the price times the quantity sold—is initially $20. After the change in price to $2, the total revenue in Figure 15 is $16, while the total revenue in Figure 16 is $30. In the inelastic situation, prices increased but so did total revenue. Do you see why this occurred? Why might this be important for a regulatory commission to know?

A common approach to setting rates is to vary rates inversely with elasticity. See J. Bonbright, Principles of Public Utility Rates 378 (1961). In short, prices are based on "what the traffic will bear." The practice is typically called "value-of-service" pricing.

1. Does "value-of-service" pricing inevitably constitute price discrimination? If so, is it necessarily unreasonable or arbitrary? What problem is it seeking to overcome?

2. Does such discrimination present the same kinds of problems that the ICC was worried about in the report quoted earlier? That is, can one design a system of rates without putting one area or industry at a competitive disadvantage with respect to another? Does value-of-service pricing minimize those consequences at all?

3. Is it fair to say that at least some of the pressure for entry into a regulated industry may be caused by the regulators themselves when they price a service at a rate so far in excess of marginal cost that new entrants want to provide the service?

2. THE PRINCIPLE OF PEAK–LOAD PRICING: A COST–BASED APPROACH?

METROPOLITAN WASHINGTON BOARD OF TRADE v. PUBLIC SERVICE COMMISSION OF THE DISTRICT OF COLUMBIA

District of Columbia Court of Appeals, 1981.
432 A.2d 343.

GALLAGHER, ASSOCIATE JUDGE, Retired:

The Apartment and Office Building Association of Metropolitan Washington (AOBA) and the Metropolitan Washington Board of Trade

---

45. This is actually the average elasticity for the segment of demand bounded by the two price-quantity points chosen. It is technically called arc elasticity. Point elasticity would be the elasticity of demand at one point on the demand curve.

(Board of Trade) bring consolidated petitions for review of the Final Opinion and Order issued by the Public Service Commission in Formal Case No. 680. In Formal Case No. 680, the Commission considered and adopted marginal cost based, time-of-day (TOD) pricing for large demand customers of Potomac Electric Power Company (PEPCO).

The marginal cost based, TOD pricing system adopted by the Commission reflects a recognition that demand for electricity varies from hour to hour and from season to season and that capital costs and fuel costs generally vary with the level of demand. Marginal cost based, TOD pricing attempts to allocate costs to customers who consume electricity during peak periods, when the cost of providing electricity is high, by charging higher prices per unit of electricity during these peak periods. In theory, marginal cost based, TOD pricing should discourage consumers from using electricity during peak periods and, in so doing, should result in the conservation of energy and in the reduction of capital and fuel expenditures. The Commission, then, adopted the marginal cost based, TOD pricing system, which is challenged by petitioners in this case, in order to promote three goals: (1) rate equity, (2) maximization of efficiency in facility and resource use by electric utilities, and (3) conservation of energy. * * *

* * * We uphold the decision of the Commission.

* * *

III. ROLE OF THE COMMISSION, SCOPE OF REVIEW, AND THE PURPA MANDATE

* * *

In order to define the reasonableness requirement of § 40301, in the specific context of this case, the Commission appropriately has looked to the recent expression of Congressional policy contained in the Public Utility Regulatory Policies Act of 1978 (PURPA). Title I of PURPA, 16 U.S.C. §§ 2611–2644, requires each state regulatory authority to consider implementing several specified ratemaking standards if it finds that the standards would achieve one of three explicit goals—conservation of electricity, maximization of efficiency in facility and resource use by electric utilities, and assurance of equitable rates to consumers—without undermining the other goals. * * * The PURPA standards require, *inter alia*, that rates charged by any electric utility to each class of consumers reflect as well as possible the cost of providing the service to the class; and that time-of-day rates be used unless shown to be cost-ineffective for the class under consideration.

* * *

In this case, the Commission specifically found that TOD rates would further rate equity and potentially would further the other two PURPA goals as well. Having made this threshold finding of reasonableness, the Commission then determined that TOD rates would not be cost-ineffective for the class under consideration—that is, PEPCO's large commercial customers. The Commission therefore found that it is "reasonable" and "appropriate," to implement PURPA's TOD standard for this class of customers.

Petitioners, to meet their burden in the context of this case, must establish "clearly and convincingly a fatal flaw" in the Commission's decision to adopt what is essentially an experimental marginal cost based, TOD ratemaking scheme. * * *

IV.   Adequacy of the Commission's Consideration
of the Consumers' Interests

* * *

A.   Theory and Objectives of Marginal Cost Based, Time–of–Day Pricing

Marginal cost based, TOD pricing is based on two fundamental observations: that demand for electricity varies from hour to hour and from season to season, and that capital costs and fuel costs generally vary with the level of demand. An increase in demand during peak consumption periods may result in increased capital costs, for electric utility companies must have sufficient generation, transmission, and distribution capacity to meet the maximum aggregate demand placed on their systems at any given time. Therefore, even if much of the capacity needed to meet the maximum aggregate demand during peak consumption periods lies idle for substantial periods of time, electric utility companies still must incur the additional capital costs necessary to meet the demand for electricity during these peak periods. An increase in demand during peak consumption periods is also likely to result in higher fuel costs, for electric utility companies normally have their most fuel efficient generators in service almost continuously and use their less efficient and more costly equipment only as demand increases.[46]

* * *

The first goal of marginal cost based, TOD pricing—rate equity— generally is achieved by designing a rate scheme that aligns a customer's rates as closely as possible with the costs that this customer actually imposes on the system. Under a rate system that is not designed to align customers' rate with the costs that these customers impose on the system, the customers may think it is cheaper to produce an additional unit of electricity than it really is and consequently be led to expand their consumption beyond the point that is socially efficient or desirable. Marginal cost based, TOD pricing, by definition, requires that the price of a unit of electricity reflect the cost of producing and distributing that unit of electricity. Under a marginal cost based, TOD pricing system, then, the consumers should receive accurate price signals. These price

---

46. In the words of Richard Galligan, an expert witness who testified before the Commission: Some generating units use less expensive fuel, such as nuclear fuel or coal, than other generating units, which may use residual fuel oil or diesel oil. And even for generating units that use the same type of fuel, some units make more efficient use of that fuel than other units. The result is that some generating units have higher fuel costs per kilowatt-hour than other generating units. [Court's fn. 17]

signals should enable consumers to recognize the costs they are imposing upon society and to decide whether to alter their consumption patterns or pay the price.

The second goal of a marginal cost based, TOD pricing system—maximization of efficiency in facility and resource use by electric utilities—is based on the theory that, if the price of a unit of electricity reflects the cost of producing and distributing that unit of electricity, consumers will be induced to shift their load from peak periods to off-peak periods. The cost of producing and distributing that unit of electricity, as we have just observed, generally varies depending upon the level of demand. An additional unit of electricity is most expensive if capital expenditures are required to meet the new level of demand, but marginal costs also increase during peak-load periods if the existing, less fuel-efficient generators must be utilized. Therefore, a utility could save both fuel and capital expenditures if it could reduce its system peak by transferring or "shifting" a portion of its peak load to an off-peak period. Many authorities agree that an effective way to reduce peak level consumption is to implement marginal cost based, TOD pricing.

The third goal of a marginal cost based, TOD ratemaking system is the conservation of energy, that is, an overall reduction in electricity consumption. The theory is that if consumers are given the proper price signals—if prices during the peak period are based on the costs of producing energy during that period—these consumers will be induced to consume less than if the price of electricity were based on non-TOD averaging techniques.

These three goals are interrelated to a degree. At the same time, however, each goal is essentially independent of the other goals and important in itself. Thus, although maximization of efficiency in facility and resource use through load-shifting is one important goal, many TOD pricing advocates would not be disturbed if load-shifting does not occur. Rate equity still can be achieved, for consumers will be faced with the appropriate costs in determining their consumption patterns. Conservation of energy can occur by a simple reduction in consumption, and, therefore, this goal also can be achieved regardless of whether load shifting occurs.

B.   The Commission's Cost–Benefit Analysis

* * *

Petitioners make two basic arguments attacking the adequacy of the benefit portion of the Commission's cost-benefit analysis. Petitioner AOBA focuses almost entirely on the fact that there is inadequate evidence of record to indicate that PEPCO's large commercial customers will alter their electricity consumption patterns so that load-shifting will occur and that, therefore, there is inadequate evidence that marginal cost based, TOD pricing will further one of the Commission's articulated goals—maximization of efficiency and resource use by electric utilities.

* * *

The fundamental problem with petitioner AOBA's argument, then, is that it completely ignores the possibility that the other two goals—conservation of energy and rate equity—will be achieved through the implementation of the Commission's TOD rate-making scheme. Even if maximization of efficiency in facility and resource use by electric utilities through load shifting does not occur, as the Commission noted, TOD rates will encourage energy conservation through a simple reduction in consumption effectuated by the installation of pre-cooling devices or of more efficient electricity consuming equipment.

* * *

Petitioner Board of Trade takes a different tack and focuses on the Commission's consideration of its stated, primary goal—rate equity. Board of Trade's principal argument is that TOD rates cannot possibly promote rate equity in the District of Columbia, for the fundamental prerequisite for TOD rates—that the cost of providing service varies by the time of day—is not present. This fundamental prerequisite is not present, petitioner argues, because PEPCO currently has substantial excess generating capacity. Petitioner maintains that if a utility already has too much capacity and increased customer usage does not require new capacity construction, there is no capacity-related loss to the utility from that usage. Therefore, Board of Trade argues, the generation costs necessary to support a TOD generation demand charge do not exist. Petitioner concludes that a TOD rate structure which relies on such non-existent costs will not promote rate equity, but rather will promote rate inequity.

We find this argument puzzling. We note that PEPCO's revenue requirement is recovered through four basic charges: (1) the energy charge, which covers the cost of running the electricity producing generators—principally the cost of fuel; (2) the demand charge associated with generation (or production) and transmission, which covers the costs of constructing, operating, and maintaining the utility's generation and transmission facilities, exclusive of fuel; (3) the demand charge for distribution costs, which covers the cost of transmitting electricity from power substations to the customer's premises, including all costs associated with construction, maintenance, and repair of the utility's distribution system; and (4) the customer charge, which covers the costs of attaching a customer to the system and maintaining a readiness to serve the customer, including the costs associated with meter reading, customer accounting and billing, and service lines and meter installations on the customer's premises. Surplus generation capacity is relevant to a determination of how much of PEPCO's revenue requirement, if any, should be recovered through one of the four charges delineated above—the generation and transmission charge. Surplus generating capacity, however, has no direct effect on the cost of fueling and running the generators to produce electricity.

There is ample evidence in the record that PEPCO's fuel costs increase during peak periods, for PEPCO uses their less efficient and

more costly generating equipment only during periods of high demand.
* * * Contrary to Board of Trade's broad assertion, then, there is ample
evidence that the cost of providing service varies by time of day and by
season, even if PEPCO does not incur construction costs in the near
future to meet increasing demands for electricity.

More importantly, it is clear to this court that the Commission
considered both the variation of fuel costs and the existence of excess
capacity when it adopted its TOD ratemaking principles and methodology. The energy charge, which recovers fuel costs, was designed to vary
depending on whether the electricity was used during peak, intermediate, or off-peak periods. The Commission then considered whether a
portion of PEPCO's revenue requirement should be recovered through a
charge for generating capacity. After careful consideration, the Commission rejected the argument that excess capacity should preclude PEPCO
from charging for generating capacity. The Commission observed:

> * * * While at the present time PEPCO may have a large generat-
> ing capacity reserve, it would be unreasonable to assume that this
> condition will prevail indefinitely. When PEPCO does add new
> generating capacity, the commission would have to include that
> capacity in the demand charges. This could cause sharp rate increas-
> es at that time. The commission believes that the better course is to
> include generating capacity now and thereby smooth out PEPCO's
> rates in the long term.

Having given reasoned consideration to the excess capacity argument, the Commission did not find that TOD rates would lead to rate
inequities due to PEPCO's excess generating capacity. The Commission
explained "fully and carefully" why TOD rates were needed to promote
its primary goal of rate equity and why a generation charge is needed.
Petitioner Board of Trade has demonstrated no "fatal flaw" with respect
to this aspect of the Commission's decision.

* * *

Recognizing the experimental nature of TOD rates and our circumscribed scope of review, we conclude that the Commission's adoption of
the TOD ratemaking principles articulated in Orders 7002 and 7034
represents a reasonable step toward implementing a potentially effective
TOD pricing system and that the Commission's decision finds substantial support in the record. Petitioners have failed to demonstrate that
the Commission's decision contains a "fatal flaw." We therefore affirm
the decision of the Commission.

Notes and Questions

1. The Public Utility Regulatory Policies Act required adoption of time
of day rates if they were (1) consistent with the objectives of the Act, and (2)
the costs of implementing the programs do not offset the benefits. Are time
of day rates the same as marginal cost rates? Why or why not?

2. In *Metropolitan Washington,* why is the cost of fuel not simply allocated on a volumetric basis regardless of the time of day? Why would the cost of fuel vary with the time of day the energy is actually produced?

3. Professor Kahn states that the peak-load pricing principle "is absolutely clear: if the same type of capacity serves all users, capacity costs as such should be levied only on utilization at the peak. * * * No part of those costs as such should be levied on off-peak users." A.E. Kahn, The Economics of Regulation, Vol. I, p. 89 (1970). What are capacity costs? Are they the same as fixed costs? Is Professor Kahn saying that all fixed costs should be allocated to those using the system at its peak?

4. What is the marginal cost of a unit of power during the off-peak period? Do you see why it is close to zero? Does it follow that therefore it is inappropriate to allocate any of the fixed costs of the system to off-peak customers? What is the marginal cost of a unit of power at the peak period? Can you argue that it is no higher than off-peak? Indeed, can you argue that there is very little cost to produce any additional power except that production which requires that the system be physically altered?

5. What sort of marginal cost does question 4 presuppose is relevant? Might long-term marginal costs show a greater degree of difference? Suppose an electric utility has generators that come into use only for peak loads. Would those constitute what Kahn called "capacity costs as such"? Can you think of any other examples of true marginal costs attributable only to peak-load service?[47]

6. Suppose a utility acquires additional generating capacity specifically to meet the mid-August demands of residential customers. Who should pay for this increase in capacity? Now suppose that over the years the mid-August peak declines but is replaced by a mid-January peak created by new industrial users. Who, if anyone, should be charged for the generating capacity acquired earlier? Is the critical question who actually "caused" the need for the capacity? See, e.g., Fort Pierce Utilities Authority v. Federal Energy Regulatory Comm'n, 730 F.2d 778 (D.C.Cir.1984).

7. If the decline in the mid-August peak were not offset by any increases in demand, the utility would have excess capacity. Would it be equitable to continue to charge the class giving rise to the original expansion (which may in fact include none of the individuals originally in that class) for the capacity they no longer use? If not, is it fair to spread the cost across all ratepayers? Which approach, if either, is consistent with marginal cost pricing? Which approach was adopted in *Metropolitan Washington?*

8. What is rate equity? Suppose the energy needs of an impoverished group of consumers coincides with the time of the system peak and they are unable to shift their demand to a less expensive period? Is the rate charged efficient? Is it equitable?

AN APPROACH TO DETERMINING PROPER PEAK AND OFF–PEAK RATES

What has been suggested by the preceding questions is that, in spite of some rhetoric, peak-load pricing has very little to do with what we

---

47. The desire to expand peak capacity is called the "Wellisz effect" and is often considered a corollary to the Averch–Johnson principle. See Wellisz, Regulation of Natural Gas Pipeline Companies: An Economic Analysis, 71 J.Pol.Econ. 30 (1963).

have been calling marginal cost. However, it has a great deal to do with encouraging optimal use of fixed resources. Peak-load consumers are not "responsible" for the size of the physical plant in any actual or moral sense, but charging them more than off-peak consumers may make practical sense. The question then becomes how much more they should pay.

A persuasive argument can be made that absolute peak-load pricing, i.e. putting all fixed costs into peak-load rates, will often tend to make pipelines or other capital facilities less than optimal size. One can see this better by recognizing that a single pipeline provides benefits to both the peak-load and off-peak users, e.g., winter and summer users of gas. We will assume now for simplicity that because these users consume at different times, they are not competitive. That is, peak users can be served without affecting the capacity to serve or demand from off-peak users and vice versa. Thus, the demand for service can be drawn as two separate demand curves.

Figure 17

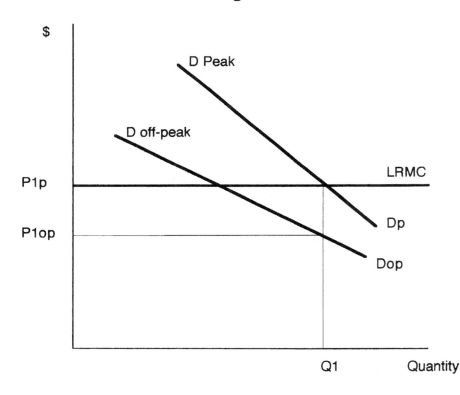

These lines show first that at any given price, more will be demanded at peak periods than off-peak, and second, that the factors that lead to peak demand will cause people to be willing to pay more for any given quantity than at off-peak periods. The LRMC or supply curve represents the long-run additional cost of making a pipeline progressively larger. There is only one such curve because the single pipe is meeting both demands.

Do you see what size the pipeline would be applying a peak-load pricing formula that put all capacity costs on peak users? That's right, Q1 is the size at which the marginal benefit to the public represented by the peak-load demand just equals the marginal cost of providing more service. Put another way, at price P1p and quantity Q1 the pipe would be just large enough to carry the peak-load demand and more than large enough to carry the off-peak demand at that price.

However, could the pipeline carry the entire off-peak demand if the off-peak price were zero? No. There would be "too much" demand for gas at that price and the price would have to be set at P1op for the pipeline to be full but not too full. Yet if the price is P1op, the total received (P1p + P1op) will exceed the firm's costs. Something seems to be wrong.[48]

Consider the following analogy. Suppose a refinery produces oil and gas in fixed proportions. Oil is the more valuable product but the gas has willing customers as well. Would the size of your refinery be set at the point at which the marginal cost of increasing the size equaled the marginal revenue from oil alone? Would your relevant demand curve be the sum of the demand for oil and that for gas?

Should the same be true where the pipeline produces two products, peak and off-peak service? Consider how that graph would look.

---

48. Notice that if the off-peak demand at zero price *could* all be carried in the existing pipeline, then peak load users *would* properly bear the entire capacity cost.

Figure 18

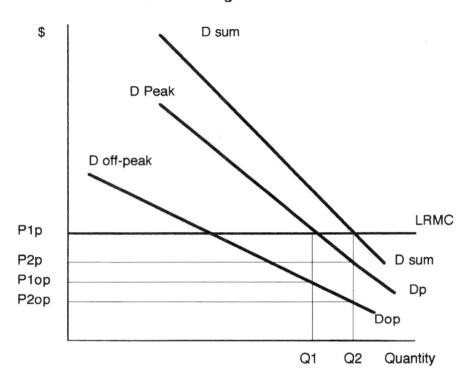

Now how big would you make your pipeline? What prices would you set for peak and off-peak service respectively? Are your prices discriminatory? Are they based on the marginal cost of the respective services? Are the rates arbitrary? Is either service "subsidizing" the other?[49]

Notes and Questions

1. Can you think of other industries in which a peak-load pricing structure might be appropriate?

49. This model is the same one economists have used for the pricing of jointly-produced products, i.e. situations in which two or more products are produced in fixed proportions so that the producer wants to maximize the return from the sale of each. The peak-load pricing literature is extensive. See the texts cited earlier, as well as Oliver Williamson, Peak–Load Pricing and Optimal Capacity Under Indivisibility Constraints, 56 American Econ. Rev. 810 (1966); Vickery, Responsive Pricing of Public Utility Services, 2 Bell J. 337 (1971); Criffin, The Effects of Higher Prices on Electricity Consumption, 5 Bell J. 515 (1974). For a debate on a closely analogous issue, see Harold Demsetz, The Private Production of Public Goods, 13 J. L. & Econ. 293 (1970), Robert B. Ekelund, Jr. & Joe R. Hulett, Joint Supply, The Taussig–Pigou Controversy, and the Competitive Provision of Public Goods, 16 J. L. & Econ. 369 (1973); Harold Demsetz, Joint Supply and Price Discrimination, 16 J. L. & Econ. 389 (1973); Earl A. Thompson, The Private Production of Public Goods: A Comment, 16 J. L. & Econ. 407 (1973).

a. The taxi drivers in your community have proposed a "rainy weather fare" in lieu of a general fare increase. They propose that whenever it rains hard enough to require windshield wipers, the fare will go up 50%. Do you see any problems with such a plan? Is it consistent with good "peak-load pricing" theory?

b. Are the same issues presented by the telephone company's decision to price calls made at night and on weekends at a substantially lower price than daytime calls? Does the analysis differ greatly when the decision as to price tends to shift the peak rather than simply reflect two distinct demand schedules?

c. Do discount fares on commuter trains reflect the same concerns? Can you argue that such discounts directly violate the principles we have been discussing? How would you argue the other way?

2. What practical problems can you imagine arising from introduction of peak-load pricing where it is not now employed? Do gas and electric meters commonly in use measure time of consumption or only quantity, for example? How would someone know when the peak demand was on a given day and thus what rate he or she was being charged? Is it likely that our knowledge of demand curves is sophisticated enough to know what any given structure of rates will do to demand patterns?

3. Do you think that maximum efficiency in the use of fixed resources should be the main criterion in rate making? What will be the effect on off-peak demand if it is assigned little or no fixed costs? Would it matter to you who the off-peak users were?

ELIZABETHTOWN GAS CO. v. FEDERAL ENERGY REGULATORY COMMISSION

United States Court of Appeals, D.C. Circuit, 1993.
10 F.3d 866.

Before EDWARDS, D.H. GINSBURG, and RANDOLPH, CIRCUIT JUDGES.

D.H. GINSBURG, CIRCUIT JUDGE: The petitioners, a group of industrial gas consumers and a local distribution company (LDC), challenge orders of the Federal Energy Regulatory Commission approving two settlements between the Transcontinental Gas Pipeline Corporation (Transco) and its customers. The petitioners are Transco customers that did not join in the settlements. They contend that the agreements are inconsistent with the Natural Gas Act (NGA), the Natural Gas Policy Act (NGPA), and the Commission's own policies. We reject these contentions in large part, but remand the case for the Commission to reconsider whether the customers that benefit from the priority curtailment provision in one of the agreements should be required to compensate the customers that are harmed by virtue of that provision.

I. BACKGROUND

The Restructuring Settlement calls for Transco to "unbundle" its regulated transportation service from its natural gas sales or merchant service, which by the terms of the settlement is to be priced at market rates. The Transportation Settlement establishes the rates, terms, and conditions of transportation service on the Transco pipeline, using cost-based pricing principles.

A. The Restructuring Settlement

Under the Restructuring Settlement, Transco will no longer sell gas bundled with transportation service (i.e., delivered gas); instead it will sell gas at the wellhead or pipeline receipt point, to be transported as the buyer sees fit. Transco's sales are to be market-based; that is, the rates are to be negotiated or arbitrated between Transco and its customers. In approving the Restructuring Settlement, the FERC determined that Transco's markets are sufficiently competitive to preclude the pipeline from exercising significant market power in its merchant function and to assure that gas prices are "just and reasonable" within the meaning of the NGA § 4. Therefore, in the settlement, the FERC authorized Transco in advance "to establish and to change" individually negotiated rates free of customer challenge under § 4 of the NGA; the "only further regulatory action" possible under the settlement is the Commission's review of Transco's prices under § 5 of the Act, upon the Commission's own motion or upon the complaint of a customer that is not a party to the settlement.

As initially submitted to the FERC, the Restructuring Settlement also contained a "pro rata curtailment provision," which provided that in times of supply shortage Transco would reduce its deliveries "in proportion to each customer's daily entitlement to Transco gas." The Commission rejected this provision on the ground that it did not protect certain high-priority customers (e.g., agriculturalists) "to the maximum extent practicable," as required by Title IV of the NGPA. On rehearing, petitioner Elizabethtown Gas Company challenged this conclusion; in the alternative it argued that if priority distribution is to be permitted then high priority customers should at least be required to compensate lower priority customers for their loss of gas. The FERC rejected these arguments on the ground that such "policy arguments do not overcome the legal requirements under NGPA § 401(a) to give curtailment priority to certain high priority users."

* * *

II. ANALYSIS

* * *

A. Market-based pricing

The petitioners contend that the FERC's approval of market-based pricing for Transco's merchant service constitutes "virtual deregulation" and is "utterly at odds with its NGA obligation to insure that rates are cost-based so that consumers will be protected from abuse at the hands of natural gas companies." Pointing to the Supreme Court's statement that "the prevailing price in the market cannot be the final measure of 'just and reasonable' rates mandated by the Act," the petitioners maintain that the FERC was required to adhere to its historical policy of basing rates upon the cost of providing service plus a fair return on invested capital.

* * *

Here the Commission specifically found that "Transco's markets are sufficiently competitive to preclude it from exercising significant market power in its merchant function...." In support of this conclusion, the FERC noted that "Transco will be providing comparable transportation service with respect to all gas supplies whether purchased from Transco or its competitors" and that "adequate divertible gas supplies exist" to assure that Transco will have to sell at competitive prices. The petitioners point to no record evidence to the contrary. It appears, therefore, that Transco will not be able to raise its price above the competitive level without losing substantial business to rival sellers. Such market discipline provides strong reason to believe that Transco will be able to charge only a price that is "just and reasonable" within the meaning of § 4 of the NGA.

* * *

C. Pro rata curtailment provision

Elizabethtown Gas contends that by insisting upon priority curtailment, rather than pro rata curtailment as provided in the original Restructuring Settlement, and by refusing to require compensation for low priority users, the Commission misinterpreted § 401(a) of the NGPA, and acted in an arbitrary and capricious manner. First, Elizabethtown claims that the original pro rata plan was proper under the terms of § 401(a) because it provided the greatest "practicable" protection for high priority users, such as agriculturalists. Greater protection for those users is not practicable because, we are told, Transco's firm sales are greatly reduced under the Restructuring Settlement and "Transco will cease to be the dominant firm supplier" to its LDC customers. This argument makes no sense to us. Even if Transco supplies a smaller share of the gas bought by each of the LDCs, the gas it does deliver to them could still in times of shortage go first to "high-priority users." Accordingly, it seems entirely "practicable" to increase the level of protection for high priority users above that provided by the pro rata plan.

* * *

Elizabethtown [argues] * * * that the FERC should have required high priority customers to compensate low priority customers if the former group benefits at the expense of the latter during a period of curtailment. Responding in its order on rehearing, the Commission stated only that "the petitioners' policy arguments do not overcome the legal requirement under NGPA § 401(a) to give curtailment priority to certain high priority users. Until Congress changes the statute, the statutory priority must be observed."

As Elizabethtown points out, however, this court has clearly held that a compensation provision is not necessarily inconsistent with § 401(a). In Consolidated Edison Co. v. FERC, 676 F.2d 763 (D.C.Cir. 1982), we said that "there is nothing inherently inconsistent about allocating natural gas to those who are most in need of it while requiring the beneficiaries of such a plan to compensate those who must purchase more expensive alternative supplies." Therefore, the FERC's conclusion that § 401 disables it from requiring curtailment compensation seems plainly incorrect.

* * * Because it is clear that the petitioner preserved its argument on rehearing, we remand this aspect of the case to the agency for it to do what it should have done in the first instance—consider on the merits the petitioner's request for a curtailment compensation scheme.

* * *

Notes and Questions

1. How should "capacity costs" be allocated between customers who have a right to the natural gas at all times and those who can be terminated in periods of peak demand? Is this simply another form of the question of peak-load pricing? Was the pipeline size determined solely by the demand of the priority customers?

2. What did you think of Judge Ginsburg's suggestion that the Commission might make the preferred customers pay the terminated ones if the priority claims are ever exercised? Does that seem a way to share the true cost and benefits inherent in the different status? Would determination of the correct level of compensation necessarily be so arbitrary that no firm could rely on being fairly treated?

3. Is there a deeper question of social policy involved here? Suppose the terminable customers are industrial plants with alternative sources of power while the priority customers are households without such alternatives. Does that argue for not allowing compensation? Should the agency care less about terminable business customers' welfare?

What is wrong with one group being asked to cross-subsidize another in society? That issue is explored in our next cases.

4. WHO PAYS FOR STRANDED COSTS?

Perhaps the most difficult issue—both theoretically and practically—in the transition from pervasively regulated rates to more competition in the supply of utility services is the issue known as "stranded costs." As you now understand, rate-regulated firms have not been permitted to amortize investments and pass costs on to consumers any faster than commissions would permit. The firms thus often have high cost assets, e.g., nuclear-fueled power plants, that they had expected to have in their rate base for years to come.

When a firm sells in a competitive environment, however, customers do not ask: "What do I owe you for what you sold me at below-cost prices last year." They ask instead: "Who will sell me the cheapest service tomorrow?" Firms caught in this transition are said to face the problem of "stranded costs," i.e., costs for which no one in the competitive environment wants to pay.

CAJUN ELECTRIC POWER COOPERATIVE, INC. v. FEDERAL ENERGY REGULATORY COMMISSION

United States Court of Appeals, District of Columbia Circuit, 1994.
28 F.3d 173.

Before MIKVA, CHIEF JUDGE, and SILBERMAN and BUCKLEY, CIRCUIT JUDGES.

PER CURIAM:

Cajun Electric Power Cooperative, Inc., and other wholesale and retail customers of Entergy Corporation (Entergy) petition for review of three electric power tariffs filed by Entergy and approved by the Federal Energy Regulatory Commission. * * * In combination, they were designed to permit Entergy—a monopolist of transmission services in the relevant market—to engage in market-based pricing in the generation market, while simultaneously introducing competition to that market through the unbundling of generation sales from transmission services. * * *

The record reveals disputed issues of material fact concerning the impact of the "open-access" transmission tariff on Entergy's market power. We find that the Commission failed to adequately address these and other concerns raised by the petitioners and conclude that it was arbitrary and capricious in declining to conduct hearings. We grant the petition and remand for reconsideration consistent with this opinion.

I. BACKGROUND

Entergy is a public utility holding company, whose various wholly-owned subsidiaries collectively deal in both the transmission and generation of electric power. On August 2, 1991, one of its subsidiaries, Entergy Services, Inc., submitted three tariffs to the Commission for approval pursuant to section 205 of the Federal Power Act. Two were rate schedules which provided for the wholesale sale of power at negotiated, market-based rates. These represented a departure from the regulated, cost-based rates that Entergy was then applying. The third tariff was a rate schedule which purported to provide open access to Entergy's transmission system. This transmission service tariff (TST) provided that any eligible electric utility could purchase transmission service over Entergy's lines at cost-based rates. It also included a provision under which Entergy could recover its "stranded investment costs," which are the costs Entergy incurs due to any surplus in generation (or other) facilities resulting from the introduction of open access to its transmission services; i.e., Entergy's current customers might take advantage of open access to purchase power from competing entities and thereby leave Entergy with excess capacity and the costs which that entails. Entergy's filing—although lengthy—was not supported by either testimony or affidavits.

* * *

II. DISCUSSION

The critical issue in this case involves Entergy's move from regulated to market pricing for its wholesale sales of electric power. As both parties agreed at oral argument, the primary source of Entergy's market power in generation sales is its bottleneck monopoly in transmission services. Given this market power, a classic tying problem exists: Entergy could use its monopoly over transmission services to eliminate competition in the market for generation services.

When faced with these kinds of concerns, FERC only approves market-based rates when a utility demonstrates that its market power is sufficiently mitigated in the relevant markets. Hence, the core question here is whether the open-access transmission tariff truly mitigates Entergy's market power; accordingly, FERC approved Entergy's tariffs only after concluding that Entergy "will not dominate generation in any relevant market" and "will have adequately mitigated its market power in transmission" after having implemented the TST.

In declining to hold a hearing or request additional evidentiary submissions before rendering its decision, FERC concluded that the petitioners had not demonstrated in their intervention motion that there were any genuine issues of material fact that required a trial-type hearing. FERC believed that by granting competitors access to Entergy's transmission services, the TST would "provide sufficient assurance that Entergy will not exercise market power under the new tariffs." The idea was that "open access" to Entergy's transmission grid would effectively mitigate production-related market power. To facilitate this result, FERC modified Entergy's proposed TST. For example, FERC required Entergy to file all transmission service requests with FERC, to maintain an electronic bulletin board of available transmission capacity and requests for transmission service, and to submit an updated market analysis every three years. FERC also permitted customers to file complaints under section 206 of the Federal Power Act if they believed that Entergy was exercising market power. Finally, FERC also required that any stranded investment costs levied against users of Entergy's transmission grid be "legitimate and verifiable." Satisfied with these adjustments, FERC declined to conduct hearings on the TST, and maintained that a "hearing would only speculate about what Entergy might do in the future."

* * * We review FERC's decision to deny an evidentiary hearing for an abuse of discretion. Notwithstanding this deferential standard of review, we conclude that FERC erred in summarily approving Entergy's tariffs.

The petitioners proffered several facts that raise serious doubts concerning the mitigation of Entergy's market power—doubts that FERC has not adequately addressed and upon which an evidentiary hearing may shed light. Although FERC's analysis of Entergy's market power was not cursory, we think its determination that the TST would sufficiently mitigate Entergy's market power is seriously flawed. The petitioners raised several factual issues which indicate that Entergy might retain significant market power notwithstanding the TST.

The most problematic of these involves the "stranded investment" provision, concerning which the Commission stated as follows:

> The Commission believes that Entergy should be able to recover legitimate and verifiable stranded investment costs and that such cost recovery does not constitute the collection of monopoly rents. By filing the open access transmission tariff in this proceeding, Entergy provided an opportunity for wholesale power market participants in its relevant market area to trade with each other more easily. However, this opportunity may result in certain transition problems, such as Entergy's stranded investment. Entergy negotiated its existing power contracts with Captive Cities and Individual Cities when these entities were its full and partial requirements customers respectively. They had limited, if any, options other than purchasing Entergy's generation services. By offering the open access transmission tariff, Entergy has now expanded the supply options available to these customers so that they can, in many cases, purchase their requirements elsewhere as soon as the tariff becomes effective. If Entergy has made investment decisions based on a contractual commitment or a reasonable expectation at that time that it would continue to serve these customers, it should be able to recover from them the legitimate and verifiable costs invested on their behalf.

Section 9a of the TST provides that Entergy may recover its stranded investment costs from certain competitors who use its transmission services. These costs—which must be generation-related since the customer will be employing Entergy's transmission services in any case—are to be included in the rates charged for the transmission service. In other words, if Entergy loses a customer of generation capacity to a competitor but the customer continues to employ Entergy's transmission grid, the charge for the transmission will include not only costs directly associated with it, but also the cost of Entergy's generation capacity idled by the switch. "[T]he customer's cost liability for stranded investment" is, however, limited to "what the customer would have contributed to fixed costs under its existing rate had the customer remained on Entergy's system."

This is, in essence, a tying arrangement, and it might be fine if the purpose of the arrangement were not to cabin Entergy's market power. The Commission argues that this is not a tying arrangement because it "is not a situation in which Entergy is requiring a customer to purchase generation in the future in exchange for transmission in the future." But if a company can charge a former customer for the fixed cost of its product whether or not the customer wants that product, and can tie this cost to the delivery of a bottleneck monopoly product that the customer must purchase, the products are as effectively tied as they would be in a traditional tying arrangement. By analogy, suppose a certain Company A both owned the roads and sold cars. Section 9a of the TST is equivalent to a rule whereby former car customers of Company A, who decide instead to purchase a car from Company B, must pay a toll for road use that covers not only the cost of the road, but also the cost of the displaced productive capacity that would have built the cars they no longer buy from Company A. At any rate, it is hard to imagine that such limited and costly access to the "roads"—that is, to Entergy's transmission grid—will serve to effectively mitigate its market power, especially in the context of electricity generation where fractions of a cent per kilowatt hour can make the difference among competitors.

Permitting a transmission monopolist to impose generation-related charges on competitors who seek only transmission services may actually serve to increase the entity's market power, for it creates an odd asymmetry. That is, while Entergy can compete for generation sales outside its transmission grid without concern for a stranded investment charge, Entergy's competitors cannot compete for the customers on its transmission system on the same basis.

As a theoretical matter, then, the petitioners would appear to be correct that the stranded investment provision is anti-competitive. The Commission admitted as much at oral argument * * * . The question of how much competition in fact is dampened goes to the heart of the complicated issues the Commission faces in these tariffs. The petitioners adequately flagged this issue for the Commission as a specific disputed material issue of fact. We think that there should have been an evidentiary hearing to address it.

      * * *

* * * [T]he Commission argues that the issue of whether stranded investment cost will reduce access to transmission is not susceptible of final resolution by a hearing at this point, because legitimate and verifiable stranded investment can only properly be determined on a case-by-case basis and appropriate procedures have been made available for doing just that.

But central to the Commission's approval of the tariffs was its finding that Entergy's market power would be mitigated by the TST upon its implementation. It follows that the question of whether Entergy's recovery of stranded investment cost precludes mitigation of its market power must be faced squarely by the Commission at this juncture. * * * Assurances that stranded investment cost is legitimate, verifiable and accurately calculated do not in themselves resolve whether the imposition of such production-related costs on transmission services precludes the mitigation of Entergy's market power.

Moreover, the procedures themselves hang over any prospective deal like the sword of Damocles. To be forced to litigate to determine the price of a product introduces deal-killing transactional costs and uncertainties. * * *

What is inescapably before the Commission at this juncture is its validation of the concept of stranded investment, because—not surprisingly really—its view on this matter may itself dictate market structure. The Commission must address whether the TST's provision of a process for recovery of stranded investment costs is itself a deal killer that, perhaps ironically, precludes genuine open access to Entergy's transmission system. In short, the question that must be asked now is whether the TST allows for "meaningful access to alternative suppliers."

Petitioners argue that the concept of stranded investment has no meaning in a competitive market, since a surplus of productive capacity can always be readily eliminated simply by lowering price. That is, a price can always be found that is low enough that it increases demand sufficiently to eliminate any excess in productive capacity. In the instant case, Entergy always has the option to reemploy any temporarily unemployed productive resources by making off-system sales at market-based prices. Hence, there really is no such thing as stranded investment, only a failure to compete. Of course, the point of introducing competition is to reap the benefits associated with just such market forces. In this sense, a stranded investment provision is the antithesis of competition.

* * *

Taken as a whole, the TST seems to provide Entergy with the means to stifle the very competition it purports to create. * * * At the very least, Entergy's ability to determine whether and when it has surplus transmission capability creates an uncertainty that impedes competition. Any competitor willing to bear this uncertainty, moreover, is then confronted with another: the potentially high stranded investment costs that it might have to bear in using Entergy's transmission services. No competitor could be but somewhat leery of depending on the TST in light of these concerns.

* * *

The Commission suggests that the stranded investment provision is necessary to lure Entergy into competition: "[a]ny utility would be reluctant to open its transmission system voluntarily if it meant being subjected to self-inflicted stranded investment." There are two answers to this. First, while the Commission argues that the stranded investment charge "provides an equitable recovery of costs from the parties for which the costs were incurred," this is irrelevant if the tariffs do not mitigate Entergy's market power sufficiently that the resulting market-based prices will be "just and reasonable" under section 205 of the Federal Power Act. 16 U.S.C. § 824d (1988).

Second, this case may take on a different cast in light of recent amendments to the Federal Power Act. Specifically, the Commission can now order transmission services pursuant to the Energy Policy Act of 1992. See 16 U.S.C.A. §§ 824j and 824k (1992). As the legislative history explains:

> [T]he title clarifies FERC's authority to order utilities to provide transmission service. It directs FERC to require wheeling that is in the public interest, maintains system reliability, and serves one or more additional goals—including the promotion of wholesale competition, conservation, efficiency, and the prevention of discriminatory practices. The transmitting utility is entitled to payment for the cost of providing such service, plus a reasonable rate of return.

III.   CONCLUSION

In light of the substantial controversies evoked by Entergy's tariff filing, the Commission's failure to conduct an evidentiary hearing was arbitrary and capricious. Moreover, the substantive decision is flawed in that the Commission failed to adequately explain its approval of the stranded investment provision, among others. Accordingly, we grant the petition for review and remand this matter to the Commission to conduct further proceedings.

Notes and Questions

1.   What was FERC trying to do here to deal with the problem of stranded costs? Did it permit the company to impose charges on customers that wanted to switch to other electricity suppliers? Is such a plan consistent with a principle of encouraging competition in production, transmission and sale of electricity? Is it a necessary way to deal with the transition problem that is inherent in any such move to competition? See generally, William J. Baumol & J. Gregory Sidak, Transmission Pricing and Stranded Costs in the Electric Power Industry (1995).

2.   The problem of stranded costs arises from the fact that some costs are fixed or common—they do not disappear with the customer or even with the elimination of a service. *Cajun Electric* deals with one variation of the stranded cost problem. Consider some other possibilities.

a.   Suppose the new entrant had never been a customer of the incumbent. Should the incumbent be permitted to include in its charges some portion of its stranded costs—fixed costs it had incurred expecting that they would be paid for by customers that it has now lost to the new entrant? If not, isn't the incumbent simply being required to turn the market over to the new entrant?

b.   Suppose a firm in one market seeks to enter another. In its original market, it has stranded or fixed costs. Should the rate it charges in the new market reflect those costs? If not, is it subsidizing its competition in one market with the rates charged in another which do reflect those stranded costs?

3.   Notice that the Court's principal focus was not on the justice of allowing stranded costs or even the transition to competition; it was on whether Entergy had excessive market power. Was FERC disingenuous in

suggesting that the market power had been dissipated? Was the Court right to believe FERC was letting Entergy exploit at least some of its remaining monopoly power so as to generate returns that would cover the stranded costs? Indeed, without significant market power, could stranded costs ever be recovered?

4. The Court criticizes FERC for failure to hold a hearing, but was a lack of information the real problem? Did the real issue have as much to do with the specific elements of Entergy's tariffs as it did with the overall wisdom of the move to competitive pricing and the policy choices raised by that transition? If the latter, would rulemaking be a better way to make those policy choices than case-by-case tariff approval hearings?

Chastened by this opinion but confident of its basic direction, FERC took up the issue of stranded costs in its so-called MEGA–NOPR for the electric power industry. On the issue of stranded costs, it ultimately concluded in part:

ORDER NO. 888—RECOVERY OF STRANDED COSTS BY PUBLIC UTILITIES

Federal Energy Regulatory Commission, 1996.
61 Fed.Reg. 21540, 21628–38.

* * *

1. JUSTIFICATION FOR ALLOWING RECOVERY OF STRANDED COSTS

In the Supplemental Stranded Cost NOPR, the Commission noted that the Open Access Rule would give a utility's historical wholesale customers greatly enhanced opportunities to reach new suppliers. This would affect the way in which utilities have recovered costs under the traditional regulatory system that, on the one hand, imposed an obligation to serve, and, on the other hand, permitted recovery of all prudently incurred costs. We noted that if customers leave their utilities' generation systems without paying a share of these costs, the costs will become stranded unless they can be recovered from other customers. The Commission stated in the NOPR that we must address the costs of the transition to a competitive industry by allowing utilities to recover their legitimate, prudent and verifiable stranded costs simultaneously with any final rule we adopt requiring open access transmission.

* * *

We reaffirm our preliminary determination that the recovery of legitimate, prudent and verifiable stranded costs should be allowed. * * * [W]e continue to believe that utilities that entered into contracts to make wholesale requirements sales under an entirely different regulatory regime should have an opportunity to recover stranded costs that occur as a result of customers leaving the utilities' generation systems through Commission-jurisdictional open access tariffs or FPA section 211 orders, in order to reach other power suppliers. * * * While * * * there has always been some risk that a utility would lose a particular customer, in the past that risk was smaller. It was not unreasonable for the

utility to plan to continue serving the needs of its wholesale requirements customers and retail customers, and for those customers to expect
the utility to plan to meet future customer needs. With the new open
access, the risk of losing a customer is radically increased. If a former
wholesale requirements customer or a former retail customer uses the
new open access to reach a new supplier, we believe that the utility is
entitled to recover legitimate, prudent and verifiable costs that it incurred under the prior regulatory regime to serve that customer.

We learned from our experience with natural gas that, as both a
legal and a policy matter, we cannot ignore these costs. During the 1980s
and early 1990s, the Commission undertook a series of actions that
contributed to the impetus for restructuring of the gas pipeline industry.
The introduction of competitive forces in the natural gas supply market
as a result of the Natural Gas Policy Act of 1978 and the subsequent
restructuring of the natural gas industry left many pipelines holding
uneconomic take-or-pay contracts with gas producers. When the Commission initially declined to take direct action to alleviate that burden,
the U.S. Court of Appeals for the District of Columbia Circuit faulted the
Commission for failing to do so. [citing Associated Gas Distributors v.
FERC, 824 F.2d 981, 1021 (D.C.Cir.1987)] * * *

* * * [T]he court's reasoning in the gas context applies to the
current move to a competitive bulk power industry. * * * Once again,
we are faced with an industry transition in which there is the possibility
that certain utilities will be left with large unrecoverable costs or that
those costs will be unfairly shifted to other (remaining) customers. That
is why we must directly and timely address the costs of the transition by
allowing utilities to seek recovery of legitimate, prudent and verifiable
stranded costs. At the same time, however, this Rule will not insulate a
utility from the normal risks of competition, such as self-generation,
cogeneration, or industrial plant closure, that do not arise from the new
availability of non-discriminatory open access transmission. Any such
costs would not constitute stranded costs for purposes of this Rule.

* * *

2. CAJUN ELECTRIC POWER COOPERATIVE, INC. v. FERC

* * *

We * * * do not interpret the *Cajun* court decision as barring the
recovery of stranded costs. The court in that case * * * instead found
that the Commission had not provided adequate proceedings and had not
fully explained its decision. The Commission had failed to hold an
evidentiary hearing concerning whether the inclusion of a stranded cost
recovery provision in a particular utility's transmission tariff, along with
other provisions in the tariff, resulted in the adequate mitigation of
Entergy's market power so as to justify market-based rates. * * * [W]e
have addressed * * * all of the *Cajun* court's concerns.

Our interpretation of *Cajun* is bolstered by a recent opinion of the
Court of Appeals for the D.C. Circuit * * *. In Western Resources, Inc.

v. FERC, [72 F.3d 147 (D.C.Cir.1995)] the court affirmed the Commission's decision to allow the recovery of costs stranded in the transition of the natural gas industry to a competitive market. We believe that, by this decision, the court has again affirmed the Commission's ability to allow stranded cost recovery, as long as we follow adequate procedures and explain our decision.

We are providing in this proceeding the evidentiary record to support our decision to allow the recovery of legitimate, prudent and verifiable stranded costs on a generic basis. We also are ensuring the "meaningful" access to alternative suppliers that was identified as a concern of the *Cajun* court. The Open Access Final Rule is designed to attack one essential element of market power—namely, control over transmission access. The standard we are adopting for transmission service is far stricter than the standard we used at the time *Cajun* was decided; we now require non-discriminatory open access transmission, as well as a code of conduct and non-discriminatory sharing of transmission information * * *. The collective effect of these actions is that public utilities that own, control or operate interstate transmission facilities will not be able to favor their own generation and will have to compete on an equal basis with other suppliers. All public utilities that own, control or operate facilities used for transmitting electric energy in interstate commerce will have tariffs on file that offer to any eligible customer any transmission services that the public utility could provide to itself, and under comparable terms and conditions.

We note that the *Cajun* court identified several provisions in Entergy's proposed tariff as potentially restraining competition: Entergy's retention of sole discretion to determine the amount of transmission capability available for its competitors' use; the point-to-point service limitation; the failure to impose reasonable time limits on Entergy's response to requests for transmission service; and Entergy's reservation of the right to cancel service in certain instances, even where a customer had paid for transmission system modifications. These types of provisions, which have the potential to restrain competition, will not be allowed under the Open Access Rule. * * *

We also have addressed the *Cajun* court's concern over the method of recovery. In that case, Entergy proposed to include a charge in the departing customer's transmission rate to recover its stranded investment costs. The court said that this might constitute an anticompetitive tying arrangement. * * * [T]he stranded cost recovery procedure we prescribe in this Rule is a transitional mechanism only that is intended to enable utilities to recover costs prudently incurred under a different regulatory regime. * * * Although * * * stranded cost recovery may delay some of the benefits of competitive bulk power markets for some customers, such transition costs must nevertheless be addressed at an early stage if we are to fulfill our regulatory responsibilities in moving to competitive markets. * * * In the long term, the Commission's rule will result in more competitive prices and lower rates for consumers.

    * * *

Several commenters (and the *Cajun* court) express concern for the need to provide as much certainty as possible for departing customers concerning their potential stranded cost obligation. Without some certainty, customers may be unable to shop for alternative suppliers. In response to these concerns, we have modified the stranded cost recovery mechanism to include a formula for calculating a departing customer's potential stranded cost obligation. * * * [This] formula is designed to provide certainty for departing customers and to create incentives for the parties to address stranded cost claims between themselves without resort to litigation.

* * *

3. Responsibility for Wholesale Stranded Costs (Whether to Adopt Direct Assignment to Departing Customers)

* * *

We reaffirm our decision that direct assignment of stranded costs to the departing wholesale generation customer through either an exit fee or a surcharge on transmission is the appropriate method for recovery of such costs. We believe it is appropriate that the departing generation customer, and not the remaining generation or transmission customers (or shareholders), bear its fair share of the legitimate and prudent obligations that the utility undertook on that customer's behalf.

In reaching this decision, we have carefully weighed the arguments supporting direct assignment of stranded costs against those supporting a more broad-based approach, such as spreading stranded costs to all transmission users of a utility's system. * * *

One of the main reasons to adopt direct assignment of stranded costs is that direct assignment is consistent with the well-established principle of cost causation, namely, that the party who has caused a cost to be incurred should pay it. Direct assignment of stranded costs to departing generation customers is particularly appropriate given the nature of the stranded cost recovery mechanism contained in this Rule, which links the incurrence of stranded costs to the decision of a particular generation customer to use open access transmission to leave the utility's generation system and shop for power, and which bases the prospect of stranded cost recovery on the utility's ability to demonstrate that it incurred costs with the reasonable expectation that the customer would remain on its generation system.

A broad-based approach, in contrast, would violate the cost causation principle by shifting costs to customers (such as transmission users of the utility's system) that had no responsibility for stranding the costs in the first place. In addition, if the Commission were to adopt a broad-based approach, it would have to determine whether to base the transmission surcharge on all users of a utility's transmission system on a one-time, up-front estimate of stranded costs (that is, each utility claiming stranded costs would make a one-time, comprehensive determination of stranded costs for the utility as a whole) or on an as-realized basis (the surcharge would be based on actual customer departures and would be adjusted each time a customer departs). Each option would have disadvantages that are not present in the direct cost causation approach we are adopting.

For example, a major disadvantage of an up-front, broad-based transmission surcharge is that it in effect would charge customers for costs before the costs are incurred (i.e., before customers have even decided to leave the utility's generation system) and could charge for costs that may never be incurred (e.g., some customers may decide to stay on the utility's system as requirements customers). The other option, a broad-based transmission surcharge that would be adjusted as customers leave the utility's system, also has disadvantages. While this option might recover stranded costs that are closer to the actual amount incurred by the utility, it could produce variability in transmission rates every time stranded costs from a newly-departed customer are included in the transmission surcharge and, in turn, could possibly hamper efficient power supply choices and efficient generator location decisions. These disadvantages are not present in the direct assignment approach.

Direct assignment will result in a more accurate determination of a utility's stranded costs than would an up-front, broad-based transmission surcharge. This is because the stranded cost for any customer is finally determined only if that customer actually leaves a utility. Moreover, there is no stranded cost unless the then-current market price of power for the period that the utility reasonably expected to continue serving the customer is below the utility's cost. Thus, because the circumstances of each departing customer will be known, the amount of any stranded cost liability can be determined with reasonable accuracy. Further, if a customer does not leave the utility or leaves at some future time when the utility's costs are competitive, the issue need not be addressed.

* * *

Direct assignment by means of an exit fee or a transmission surcharge that is not dependent on any subsequent power or transmission purchases by the customer is also an economically efficient way to collected stranded costs. The customer may make a lump-sum stranded cost payment, amortize the lump-sum payment, or spread the payment as a surcharge in addition to its transmission rate. The total amount of stranded costs that the directly-assigned customer ultimately pays would not depend on how much transmission service it takes and thus would not influence the customer's subsequent transmission purchase decisions.

With a broad-based surcharge (which could be demand-or usage-based), on the other hand, the surcharge for transmission users would depend on how much transmission service the users take. A broad-based approach also would be inefficient as it would raise the price of transmission service for all customers, thereby potentially cutting off some beneficial power trading that would otherwise occur for all unbundled transmission customers. The surcharge also could convert some profitable existing power purchase contracts into unprofitable contracts. In addition, it could reduce economy trading because the surcharge would be added to the price of economy transmission. In this manner, a broad-based surcharge would constitute a cross-subsidy that could distort the market.

We recognize that direct assignment is not without its potential drawbacks. For example, when compared to an up-front, broad-based transmission surcharge approach, direct assignment may entail a longer stranded cost recovery period. * * *

      * * *

In addition, * * * the departing generation customer may see little or no savings in the short-term by switching power suppliers once its stranded cost exit fee is added to its lower power price from a new supplier. Direct assignment may leave the customer uncertain about the benefits of shopping for power because of the customer's potential stranded cost liability and, in turn, may bias the customer toward staying with its existing power supplier.

In the case of a broad-based approach, in contrast, much of the customer's direct assignment stranded costs are spread to others through a transmission surcharge. As a result, the departing generation customer's power cost savings may more than offset the customer's stranded cost transmission surcharge. The customer may therefore see earlier power cost savings if a broad-based approach were adopted. Once again, however, we believe that this potential benefit to a broad-based approach is outweighed by a significant countervailing disadvantage. In particular, the potential power cost savings to the departing generation customer would be realized only by shifting costs (that are directly attributable to the departing generation customer) to the other users of the utility's transmission system. We believe that this negative aspect of a broad-based approach—its violation of the cost causation principle—is too great a price to pay for allowing a departing generation customer to realize power cost savings as early as possible.

      * * *

Although this direct assignment approach is different from the approach taken in the natural gas industry, we believe that the difference is justified. The transition of the electric industry to an open transmission access, competitive industry * * * is different in a number of respects from the natural gas industry's transition to open access transportation service by interstate natural gas pipelines. The gas industry underwent a long period of open access transition. * * *

      * * *

* * * [B]ecause of the changes in contractual relationships that had already occurred among pipelines and their customers, it was no longer possible for the Commission to follow a strict cost causation approach to recovering take-or-pay costs. The Commission-prescribed remedy for the

recovery of transition costs in the natural gas industry thus was tailored to fit the needs of that industry given the stage of development at the time.

However, such a broad-based approach to recovery of natural gas transition costs was an exception to the time-honored principle that rates should reflect cost causation, and because of this it was necessary for the Commission to justify its departure from that principle. As the court said in K N Energy v. FERC, [968 F.2d 1295, 1300–01 (D.C.Cir. 1992) (quoting Alabama Electric Cooperative, Inc. v. FERC, 684 F.2d 20, 27 (D.C.Cir.1982))]: "[i]t has been this Commission's long standing policy that rates must be cost supported. Properly designed rates should produce revenues from each class of customers which match, as closely as practicable, the costs to serve each class or individual customer." In that case, the court found the Commission's departure from cost-causation justified "given the unusual circumstances surrounding the take-or-pay problem, and the limited nature—both in time and scope—of the Commission's departure from the cost-causation principle." It continues to be Commission policy to follow the cost-causation principle to the extent possible.

The factors described above are not present in the electric industry. At this time, the vast majority of customers remain on their bundled suppliers' systems and generation is not yet fully competitive. Because the situation facing the electric industry today is different from that which the natural gas industry faced, the Commission must tailor its approach differently. * * * We thus are able to use the cost causation approach that has been fundamental to our regulation since 1935.

    * * *

Notes and Questions

1. Has the Commission convinced you it has properly resolved the dilemmas inherent in the problem of stranded costs? In approving the imposition of an exit charge on current customers, has FERC made it unlikely that customers will search for new sources of supply? Will simplifying customers' ability to know what the exit cost will be at least make the search more practical? Is it likely that—given the significant dollar amounts inherent in power transactions—search problems will be relatively minor in the transition to competition?

2. Are you convinced that imposing costs on departing customers is a better course than simply letting the utilities charge new and existing customers rates that include an amount to recover the costs in question? Is the decisive argument the Commission's insight that regulated rates have long been based on the cost of providing service? While that argument should sound familiar by now, is it persuasive in a competitive rather than a rate-regulated environment?

3. Elsewhere in the Order, FERC decided to permit imposing this stranded cost burden only on wholesale customers on whose large orders the

utility had come to rely. Does that make more plausible the argument that those customers were "responsible" for the costs?

4. Even in a regulated setting, did we see the regulators use cost-based rhetoric but demand-based pricing? (Remember "peak-load pricing"?) Is the decision to impose costs on departing customers simply a concession that if the costs were imposed on new or existing customers the firms most in need of the revenue would tend to experience the quickest loss of business?

5. Did the Commission adequately answer the Court's concerns in *Cajun Electric* about the market power of firms that would be able to impose a charge for stranded costs? Do you agree that adding a charge for unused generating services to a charge for transmission services should be seen as an illegal "tying" arrangement? Was the Court right that there is no such thing as a producing firm's "excess" power; there is just some power that is overpriced?

6. If you were a member of the D.C. Circuit, would you approve this approach to stranded costs when the issue is before you on review? See Transmission Access Policy Study Group v. F.E.R.C., 225 F.3d 667 (2000) Has the Commission satisfied the concerns expressed in *Cajun Electric*? Should the Court defer to the Commission's judgment of how best to make the transition to a new, more competitive electric power industry? Would you have doubts whether even the objective of that transition was sound?

7. As it has turned out, different regions of the country have very different experiences with stranded costs. What this means is that different sellers of electricity who choose to buy it on the open market may incur different exit charges. Does this mean that a seller's competitive plight may be determined by the economics of the company from whom it used to buy electricity as opposed to its own efficiencies. If so, are market outcomes determined by current efficiencies or historical happenstance? See generally, Laura R. Starling, Don't Be Shocked: Electric Utility Regulation Can Benefit Low–Cost States, 74 Tulane L. Rev. 1519 (2000).

8. Another element of the stranded cost problem is determining the amount of stranded cost. Presumably it is not simply excess capacity or amounts the utility invested imprudently. The issue is important because the party who pays for a particular cost may vary with whether it is a stranded cost, temporary excess capacity or investment resulting from a bad decision.

5. THE ISSUE OF CROSS–SUBSIDIZATION

A perennial concern in the pricing of regulated services is the problem of "cross-subsidization." This term simply means that one user pays more than cost so that another might pay less. It can occur, for example, when a high-valued product pays more than the "cost" of carrying it and a low-valued product pays less. It can also occur when two persons are provided service at the same price but the costs of serving them are different.[50] For example, it may be very costly to serve a

---

50. An analogous political issue is presented, of course, whenever more public   resources are devoted to one group of citizens than to another in an arguably analo-

remote farmhouse with telephone service, but that home owner may pay no more than the resident of an apartment building where the telephone company's costs of service are comparatively low.

Richard Posner has aptly described cross-subsidization as "taxation by regulation." He correctly reviews the phenomenon as the same as taxing the person paying more than cost and making an income transfer to the person paying less.[51] Seen in that light, it seems that the decision when and what, if anything, to cross-subsidize should be made at least as openly and explicitly as decisions on taxation.

Two harder questions, however, remain. First, what constitutes cross-subsidization? Put another way, how does one properly allocate costs? When is a cost allocation unequal but not arbitrary? Second, is there a better way to provide support for desirable public objectives? Is direct taxation always preferable to "taxation by regulation"? We have laid the analytic groundwork for an answer to these questions in what has come before. Now we apply those insights to important current factual settings.

Should a railroad line be obliged to keep operating at a loss so as to guarantee *some* rail service to particular shippers and communities? Should citizens of other communities have to make up that loss? Such issues are implicit in our next case.

a. *Rail Service*

SOUTHERN PACIFIC TRANSPORTATION CO. v. INTERSTATE COMMERCE COMMISSION

United States Court of Appeals, Ninth Circuit, 1989.
871 F.2d 838.

Before BROWNING, BEEZER and KOZINSKI, CIRCUIT JUDGES.

JAMES R. BROWNING, CIRCUIT JUDGE:

The Interstate Commerce Commission rejected Southern Pacific's application to abandon its 38.573–mile Placerville Branch serving El Dorado County, California, near Lake Tahoe, essentially on the ground that abandonment would be premature. Southern Pacific petitions for review pursuant to 28 U.S.C. §§ 2321(a) and 2342(5). We deny the petition.

I.

Southern Pacific claimed that present and estimated future traffic levels did not justify continued operation of the Placerville Branch. The

gous position. In some communities, more money is spent on meeting the needs of physically and mentally disabled children, for example, than on artistically-gifted children. We tend to acknowledge those choices as subject only to a test of rationality; should we do the same for choices made by utilities and their regulatory commissions?

51. Richard Posner, Taxation by Regulation, 2 Bell J. 22 (1971).

railroad reported that a steady decline in the lumber industry and the loss of traffic from two major business concerns had resulted in a decline in traffic from 2,500 carloads in 1975 to 548 a decade later and to only 64 in the first six months of 1987.

Southern Pacific acknowledged that despite the traffic decline the Placerville Branch continuously earned a net profit, totaling $165,616 in 1984, $231,240 in 1985 and $184,019 in the base year of July 1986 through June 1987. However, the carrier projected a continuation of the traffic decline and an increase in the cost of necessary repair and maintenance, and predicted a one-year operating loss of $121,735, which abandonment would avoid. Southern Pacific also claimed abandonment would save the railroad an annual opportunity cost of more than $1.442 million.[52]

El Dorado County vigorously disputed Southern Pacific's estimated operating loss and opportunity costs. The County projected increases in traffic more than sufficient to generate a profit even after accounting for future repair and maintenance costs. These estimates were supported by affidavits from executives of two new companies, which had supplanted the two shippers lost to Southern Pacific, pledging future shipments exceeding those of the businesses they replaced; and by forecasts from lumber company officials that use of the Branch would increase substantially because of the anticipated economic recovery of that industry. The County offered evidence that Southern Pacific's opportunity costs were premised upon greatly inflated land appraisals, and that the true costs were closer to $144,000 annually, or one-tenth Southern Pacific's figure. Most importantly, the County offered evidence that abandonment would devastate the local economy and frustrate future planned development because alternative means of transporting freight into and out of El Dorado were not economically feasible.

The ICC denied Southern Pacific's application. The Commission noted it was required to balance the interests of those served by the line against the interests of Southern Pacific and the transportation system, and could grant the application only if Southern Pacific proved that present or future convenience or necessity permitted abandonment. The ICC concluded Southern Pacific had failed to carry its burden of proving abandonment of the Placerville Branch at this time would serve the public convenience or necessity.

The ICC emphasized that Southern Pacific's own "revenue and cost data indicate operation of the line has produced substantial profits and would remain profitable even if [the railroad] performed the short-term maintenance it says is necessary to keep the line at its present condition."

---

52. "Opportunity cost" represents the economic loss sustained by the railroad from foregoing a more profitable alternative use of its assets. Southern Pacific calculated it could realize $6,787,275 by selling the land under the tracks and $968,837 by sal-

vaging portions of the line. This net liquidation value of $7,756,112, multiplied by an 18.6% rate of return, resulted in an annual opportunity cost of $1,442,637. [Court's fn. 2]

The Commission accorded less weight to Southern Pacific's project-ed long-term repair costs because they were "speculative." The Commis-sion also gave limited effect to the loss of the two major shippers on the ground the railroad's evidence was not sufficient to discount the Coun-ty's showing that these operations had been acquired recently by new owners who anticipated substantial use of the railroad.

The Commission noted that the abandonment would have a signifi-cant impact on El Dorado County shippers and the community generally; that the County had raised legitimate concerns about the effects of loss of rail service to the area; and that the railroad had failed to substantiate its assertions that alternative means of transportation were economically feasible.

The Commission did not resolve the dispute over the level of opportunity costs, because it concluded that "even accepting the [rail-road's] figures, those costs would not constitute a reason to grant the abandonment." In reaching this conclusion, the ICC pointed out that opportunity costs were not dispositive, and that in this case "the documented profitability of the line, the lack of any showing that alternative transportation services are economically feasible, and the adverse impact of the abandonment on shipper and community interests weigh against a grant of the abandonment application." Considering all relevant factors, the ICC concluded that, "on balance, the public conven-ience and necessity do not support abandonment."

Southern Pacific filed an administrative appeal, which the ICC rejected. The Commission adhered to its conclusion that Southern Pacif-ic had not provided adequate data reflecting current operations. It gave no weight to Southern Pacific's projected losses on the Placerville Branch because the railroad's claim that operating costs would increase was based on a steady or accelerated flow of traffic while its assertions that revenues would decrease was premised on a significant decline in use. The ICC also rejected the railroad's contention that the Commission erred by not calculating the exact level of opportunity costs:

> We found that, under either the [Southern Pacific] or County methodology, [Southern Pacific] would incur a substantial opportu-nity cost.... [But] other factors, including the profitability of the line, lack of feasible alternative transportation service, and adverse impact on the community outweighed the opportunity cost to [the railroad]. Weighing the burdens of continued rail service on the carrier against the burden of the abandonment on the affected shippers and community is the means used to determine whether to permit abandonment. [The railroad] has not convinced us that we erred in balancing those burdens in this case.

The ICC concluded, in essence, that Southern Pacific's application was premature because it was clear abandonment would adversely affect El Dorado County, but it was unclear that continued operation would burden Southern Pacific or the railroad system. * * *

The railroad petitioned for review.

II.

Congress has endowed the Interstate Commerce Commission "with broad power to regulate a carrier's permanent or temporary cessation of service"; the Commission's jurisdiction over abandonments is "exclusive" and "plenary." Our function in reviewing the Commission's determination whether to permit abandonment is accordingly narrow * * *.

* * *

III.

Southern Pacific claims the ICC "ignored" Southern Pacific's evidence of a decline in traffic and increase in operating costs that together would create future losses. As our summary of the Commission's decision demonstrates, the ICC considered these factors in detail and stated clearly why the Commission concluded they did not justify abandonment at this time.

The ICC predicted that shipments from two new companies, combined with increased traffic from the local lumber industry as it emerged from a cyclical decline, would more than offset the loss of traffic from the two major shippers the new companies replaced.[53] Such predictive judgments, when based upon credible evidence, are best left to the expertise of the administrative agency familiar with the industry.

The Commission acted within its discretion in concluding this evidence was not undercut by the failure of the predicted traffic to materialize during the course of the abandonment proceedings, in view of the County's showing that Southern Pacific downgraded service on the Placerville Branch after filing the application to abandon. According to the County's evidence, Southern Pacific adopted an "adversarial attitude toward the line" by severely delaying pick ups, cutting service in half and imposing a $750–per carload surcharge. The president of one company labeled Southern Pacific's actions "tantamount to a de facto embargo, suspension, and abandonment of service on this line without the approval or authorization of the Interstate Commerce Commission.... Shippers are literally being driven off this Branch by the railroad."

The Commission found Southern Pacific's evidence insufficient to establish future operating costs would render the line unprofitable. The railroad's own "revenue and cost data indicate operation of the line has produced substantial profits and would remain profitable even if applicant performed the short-term maintenance it says is necessary to keep the line at its present condition."[54] Moreover, the Commission noted,

---

53. Two new companies, P.W. Pipe and Cornett, together promised shipments exceeding those of the businesses they replaced. P.W. Pipe's president anticipated shipping in at least 250 carloads annually of raw materials. Cornett's president predicted annual shipments of up to 1,000 cars. In contrast, during the 2 years prior to Southern Pacific's application, the two defunct

shippers, Certainteed Corp. and Placerville Lumber, accounted for a total of only 585 carloads. Longtime shippers also pledged increased traffic as a consequence of recovery in the lumber industry. [Court's fn. 5]

54. Even if traffic did not increase at all over base year levels, the line would still earn a $49,000 profit after short term re-

Southern Pacific's short term cost-revenue projections, forecasting future losses, were flawed by discrepancies.[55] The Commission also declined to base its decision on Southern Pacific's projection of long term losses—the railroad conceded that most of the $3.237 million in projected long term track repair need not be undertaken in the next two-to-three years, and the ICC refused to speculate as to whether the level of traffic at that time would produce revenues sufficient to cover the added expense.

The Commission concluded it was too soon to tell with sufficient certainty whether the line would become a burden on Southern Pacific or would remain profitable, and invited Southern Pacific to reapply for abandonment if the promised increase in traffic did not materialize. We do not believe the ICC's pragmatic approach was arbitrary or capricious. A cautious approach was justified under the circumstances. A grant of abandonment under section 10903 is normally irrevocable. If abandonment were approved, the Commission would be powerless, absent extraordinary circumstances, to order rail service reinstated even if the need forecast by the County and its shippers proved to be accurate.

IV.

Southern Pacific contends the ICC's decision is fatally flawed by the Commission's failure to calculate the value of Southern Pacific's opportunity costs. The Commission declined to resolve the discrepancy between the railroad's estimate and that of the County because it concluded that even if Southern Pacific's estimate was accurate, "those costs would not constitute a reason to grant the abandonment." "Other factors, including the profitability of the line, lack of feasible alternative transportation service, and adverse impact on the community," the Commission concluded, "outweighed the opportunity cost...."

The ICC was not required to resolve a subsidiary issue irrelevant to the ultimate outcome. Moreover, by treating Southern Pacific's estimate of opportunity costs as if it were correct, the Commission accorded it as much weight as the Commission could without treating it as dispositive, which the Commission could not do. "Opportunity cost is just one of the factors that must be taken into consideration in determining whether abandonment is justified. Merely because a railroad could earn greater revenue by investing its assets elsewhere does not mean that public convenience and necessity requires abandonment."

V.

Southern Pacific challenges the ICC's findings regarding adverse community impact and lack of alternative means of transportation. The

---

pair costs—$93,182 for crossing repairs and $42,000 for bridge replacement—are subtracted from net revenues. [Court's fn. 7]

55. Southern Pacific projected a loss by predicting a need for "considerably higher" maintenance costs—reflecting an increase from $47,486 in the base year to $160,631—while simultaneously predicting a drastic decline in revenues—from $1.021 million to $336,000. As the ICC recognized, these two projections are inconsistent, since Southern Pacific conceded the higher maintenance costs were only required if traffic remained steady or increased, but the railroad's dramatic drop in revenues was based on a 67% decline in traffic. [Court's fn. 8]

ICC, which is required by statute to consider whether abandonment will create "serious adverse impact on rural and community development," 49 U.S.C. § 10903(a), had before it evidence that abandonment would threaten current industry and jobs and would derail plans for future development because alternative means of transportation were not economically feasible.

Southern Pacific pointed out that trucking and off-branch service are available to El Dorado County businesses. "If the phrase 'alternative' is to have any meaning," however, "it must be interpreted to include transportation both logistically and economically feasible." As the Commission concluded, "[a] mere statement that alternatives are available is insufficient to establish in this case that these alternatives were feasible." The Commission's conclusion is particularly well taken in light of affidavits offered by the County that the "alternatives" suggested by Southern Pacific would increase shippers' costs by as much as 30 percent and decrease revenues by as much as 10 percent—enough to force some of them out of business.

VI.

Where the question facing the ICC in an abandonment case is whether the injury to the affected communities outweighs the burden on the carrier, the Supreme Court has instructed the Commission to answer this question by balancing the competing interests "to decide what fairness to all concerned demands." The Commission decided that fairness in this case demanded denying abandonment until the County and its shippers had an opportunity to fulfill their pledge to increase shipments to a level sufficient to justify continued operation. On the record before the Commission, we cannot say this was error.

Accordingly, Southern Pacific's petition for review is denied.

KOZINSKI, CIRCUIT JUDGE, concurring.

I join Judge Browning's excellent opinion, which correctly resolves this case according to established principles of administrative law. I write separately to comment on a more general problem raised by Judge Beezer's thoughtful dissent.

Judge Beezer is concerned that the ICC has accorded more weight to intangible factors (the community's future need for rail transportation) than to hard financial data (the fact that Southern Pacific could earn a greater return by investing its money elsewhere). He is also troubled because the ICC has failed to provide "a thorough explanation of why the factors of continued profitability, adverse community and shipper impact, and alternate transportation services outweigh an opportunity cost to SPT of $1,442,637 per year." Judge Beezer's concern is well-founded, but the problem he raises is not unique to this case; it accompanies all judicial review of economic regulation.

If there were no ICC, railroads would abandon lines when they decided that they could make more money investing their resources elsewhere. Such market-based decisions allocate resources to their highest-valued use. Almost by definition, an ICC decision not to permit abandonment will be inefficient; if economic efficiency were our only concern, we would let the railroads do whatever they think best.

Once we abandon efficiency as the benchmark, it becomes very difficult, if not impossible, to come up with objectively verifiable criteria by which to review ICC decisions. The Commission must make an apples-and-oranges comparison: The community's needs and the railroad's balance sheet cannot be measured against a common standard. There is no way to tell whether an ICC decision is right or wrong unless it is extremely wrong; indeed, the labels right and wrong lose most of their meaning. Whenever the government intervenes in the economy, government officials must weigh the benefits to one group against the harms to another. It is a rare case when the objects in the balance can be made commensurable.

This is why the courts can play only a limited role in this process. We defer to the judgment of the ICC in part because of the Commissioners' expertise, but even more so because the types of policy judgments the ICC makes are quite unlike those that courts are equipped to make. We have no standards by which to judge the ICC's determination that, in a given case, the needs of the community outweigh the railroad's interests. Accordingly, we do not—cannot—second-guess the judgment of the ICC; more active review would embroil the federal courts in questions of interest-group balancing reserved for the political branches of government.

* * *

BEEZER, CIRCUIT JUDGE, dissenting:

* * * I would reverse and remand, on the grounds that the ICC's decision failed to establish a rational link between facts found and decision made on two issues: Opportunity costs, and prospects for growth in traffic.

I

From Folsom Junction, California, near Sacramento, a branch railroad line winds some thirty-eight miles into the foothills of Sierra Nevada mountains to the small town of Placerville. A century ago, the line carried gold-seekers into the hills. Today, it carries more prosaic cargoes of lumber. Approximately two freight trains per week use the Placerville branch, which is serviced by SPT.

Traffic on the line has declined precipitously, from 2,500 carloads of freight in 1975 to 341 in 1986. Believing the decline irreversible, SPT filed an application with the ICC to abandon the line * * *. * * * SPT made a profit on the Placerville branch of $184,019 in the base year of July 1985 through July 1986.

SPT foresaw major losses in the future for several reasons * * *. First, several of its most important customers had recently ended operations or shifted entirely to trucking. Second, major maintenance was needed to keep the line operating. Third, SPT calculated large "opportunity costs." Opportunity cost is the economic loss incurred by committing assets to an inefficient use, when they could be used for other purposes generating a higher rate of return. SPT calculated its opportunity cost of continuing to operate the Placerville branch at $1,442,637 per year. SPT further asserted that the loss to Placerville businesses of abandoning service would be minimal, since Placerville enjoys good highway access, allowing goods to be trucked to (or from) Placerville directly to customers, or to the Sacramento railhead for transshipment. In short, SPT argued that it should not be required to operate an inefficient and unnecessary rail line indefinitely.

* * *

The general thrust of the ICC's opinion was that the burden of proof was on SPT and that SPT had failed to assert sufficient facts regarding its projected losses, the availability of alternate transport, and the lack of adverse community impact to meet its burden. The ICC considered opportunity costs, noting that the costs as calculated by SPT and by the protestants varied by a factor of ten, due primarily to disputes over the value of the roadbed land. The ICC did not venture into this morass to attempt to calculate opportunity cost itself; accepting SPT's figure for the purpose of argument, the ICC held that even this cost did not outweigh the factors adverse to abandonment. Two commissioners sharply dissented on all the issues.

* * *

III

* * *

[The Commission's] treatment of opportunity cost was arbitrary and capricious. First, it is unclear, despite the ICC's apparent acceptance of SPT's figures, which ones it really relied upon, based on its continued emphasis of the protestants' lower figures and its lumping together of the various positions as "substantial." True as this may be, there is a major difference between an opportunity cost less than base year profit, and one approximately eight times greater. The factual basis for the decision was so unclear as to require reversal and remand for a better explanation of which opportunity cost was used.

Second, assuming that the ICC did accept SPT's figure of $1.4 million, the decision was not grounded by a rational explanation of its factual basis. The ICC is correct in stating that a consideration of opportunity cost need not involve a precise numerical weighing of the cost against all other factors. Data accepted by the ICC that indicate an opportunity cost of $1.4 million per year, however, require more than a conclusory response that they are "outweighed" by intangible (and, in fact, quite speculative) factors. Such a "consideration" is, in fact, no consideration at all.

The only thing making this a close case is the deferential standard of review, which counsels due respect for the ICC's authority at every turn. But the ICC has failed to articulate the rational connection between facts and decision that we require to perform our reviewing function. * * *

IV

SPT argues that the ICC improperly ignored its evidence regarding the loss of major customers, and the resulting prospect of major financial losses. The Michigan–California Lumber Co. shipped 96 cars on the Placerville branch in 1985. In September 1986, it abandoned its spur line to the branch and began shipping exclusively by truck. The Certainteed Corp. received 266 carloads of plastic pellets in 1985, nearly half of the branch line traffic. The plant has since closed. SPT argues that these losses ripped the heart out of its business.

In response, certain of the protestants projected replacement use of the line. The Certainteed plant had been purchased by the PW Pipe Co. ("PW") and had resumed operations. PW forecast possible use of 275 carloads of freight per year. In addition, the Cornett Co. had purchased the Placerville Lumber Co. Cornett projected possible shipment of a remarkable total of 1,000 carloads annually. Its predecessor, Placerville Lumber Co., shipped exactly three carloads in 1985.

The ICC accepted these projections more or less at face value. In so doing, the ICC failed to make even a minimal determination of credibility. * * * The companies projecting massive future shipments are under no financial obligation actually to live up to their promises. It is in their interest to require the line to be kept open by regulatory means for their possible future use, because they incur no costs by doing so. The ICC failed to explain why it gave these extraordinarily speculative predictions the same credence as projections backed up by a clear economic interest and by historical data.

The ICC held that SPT had failed to meet its burden of showing that these projections were inaccurate. It is difficult to see how SPT ever could do so to the ICC's satisfaction. SPT pointed out the obvious fact that these projections were pure pie-in-the-sky speculation * * *.

* * *

We defer to predictions based upon an agency's expertise. It is apparent from the record, however, that these predictions were not based on anyone's expertise. They were sheer speculation, unsupported by any evidence that they would ever come to pass. * * *

* * *

I would reverse and remand on the issues of opportunity costs and projections of growth. * * *

Notes and Questions

1. In what sense was the term "not profitable" used in this case? If the revenue derived from this line had covered the marginal costs of running the trains here, but no part of the fixed or "sunk" costs, would it have been proper to say that service was being provided at a "loss"?

2. If this service were paying its marginal cost, would the other service unfairly be forced to "subsidize" it? Would there be a subsidy if this service were paying less than marginal cost? Why? What is the economic argument against requiring that service be provided at less than marginal cost? Where should "opportunity cost" fit into the analysis?

3. If cross-subsidization is in fact going on here, who is being subsidized by whom? Are owners of the industries in the area served being subsidized by other business persons shipping on other SPT lines? Are SPT employees being subsidized? By whom?

4. Doesn't government often "subsidize" desirable activities which cannot pay their own way? What is different between direct subsidization through tax revenues and "cross-subsidization" as illustrated here? Would you as a legislator vote to levy a ton-mile "tax" on railroad freight service generally, the proceeds of which would be used to subsidize this service? Why would you impose the tax on freight service rather than, say, on gasoline? Why would you subsidize this rail service at all?

5. Can you distinguish the economic effects of this decision from the economic effects of unemployment compensation or the distribution of food stamps or "free" food? Are there valuable noneconomic distinctions?

6. Is there a practical problem created by pricing some services below marginal cost? Is there likely to be a limit to what the railroad may charge on even its "lucrative" routes? Is there contemporary evidence from which to conclude that railroads cannot continue indefinitely to provide freight service, for example, to remote communities which "need" and "demand" the service but are unable or unwilling to pay even the marginal cost?

7. Suppose the federal agency permits abandonment and the state does not choose to subsidize the service but instead creates a private damage remedy against the railroad on behalf of all those damaged by the loss of service. Is the damage remedy preempted? See Chicago & North Western Transportation Co. v. Kalo Brick & Tile Co., 450 U.S. 311, 101 S.Ct. 1124, 67 L.Ed.2d 258 (1981) (answering yes).

8. Should wealthier customers be forced to cross-subsidize delivery of service to poor customers? Should some customers receive at least a basic amount of the company's service at little or no cost at all? Such issues are presented even more directly by our next case.

b. Lifeline Rates

RE INVESTIGATION INTO RATE STRUCTURES OF ELECTRIC UTILITIES

Oregon Public Utility Commission, 1980.
38 P.U.R. 4th 409.

By the COMMISSIONER:

* * *

HISTORY OF THE PROCEEDING

On August 8, 1979, I issued Order No. 79–556 instituting an investigation into rate structures of electric utilities and rate-making standards as required under the Public Utility Regulatory Policies Act of 1978 (PURPA).

The subject of this order is to determine whether a lifeline rate should be implemented.

FINDINGS OF FACT AND CONCLUSIONS OF LAW

CRITERIA FOR MAKING A DETERMINATION ON LIFELINE RATES

In Order No. 79–556, issued August 8, 1979, I set forth the criteria by which lifeline rates would be measured. That order states:

The commissioner will adopt lifeline rates if he finds from the record that lifeline rates encourage:

1. Conservation of electric energy supplied by electric utilities;

2. Efficient use of facilities and resources by electric utilities; and

3. Equitable rates to electric consumers.

The central issue in this proceeding is whether a lifeline rate will promote conservation. Efficiency and equity effects of a lifeline rate will be considered after the benefits from conservation are demonstrated.

DEFINITION OF LIFELINE RATES

In Order No. 79–556, lifeline rates were defined as "rates for the essential needs of residential electric customers." Rates designed to meet this definition were proposed by three parties to the proceeding. * * *

Staff proposal. Staff proposes that the lifeline rate be limited to a customer charge plus the first 200 kwh of electricity. Staff believes that 200 kwh per month would approximate the electric usage for food refrigeration and lighting. They argue that there should be no charge for these kilowatt-hours because there is no feasible alternative for electric hookup, refrigeration, and lighting.

Mr. Schaye's proposal. Mr. Schaye suggests lifeline rates for the following end uses: 400 kwh for lighting, cooking, and food refrigeration; 400 kwh for water heating; 1,120 kwh for space heating in the western zone of the state between October 26th and April 25th; and 1,420 kwh per month for space heating in the eastern zone for the same period. Mr. Schaye proposes that the lifeline rate be set at the lowest possible rate, not higher than rates presently in effect. He also proposes a lifeline rate structure for small businesses.

Mr. Schaye would protect the lifeline rates from future rate increases.

Southwest Oregon Community Action Committee proposal. Southwest Oregon Community Action Committee offers a lifeline rate which includes 250 kwh at 50 per cent of the non lifeline rate, 500 kwh for water heating at 25 per cent of the non lifeline rate, 750 kwh for space heating in the eastern zone of the state at 25 per cent of the non lifeline rate, and 500 kwh for space heating in the western zone of the state at 25 per cent of the non lifeline rate. Staff, Mr. Schaye, and SWOCAC propose shifting at least a portion of the revenue loss created by the new rate from the residential to the industrial classes. All three parties also propose eliminating the monthly customer charge.

I am rejecting lifeline rate proposals which require the utility to identify the type of water and space heat the customer uses. A lifeline rate keyed to a particular use of electricity encourages the use of electricity for which there is a discount. This effect encourages customers to use electricity for heating rather than convert to natural gas or some other form of energy.

Each of the three parties defines "essential needs" according to a predetermined number of kilowatt-hours tied to end uses. These proposals assume (1) an arbitrarily set number of kilowatt-hours will meet essential needs, and (2) that one can identify what the ratepayer's essential needs are. Neither of these assumptions are supported in the record. In fact, PP & L witness Shue testified that on average, individual electric consumption varies by 275 kilowatt-hours from month to month. Presumably, even "essential needs" would vary monthly depending on temperature, amount of time spent at home, number of loads of wash, and other factors.

CONSERVATION EFFECT OF LIFELINE RATES

During this proceeding, there was much debate about whether a lifeline rate would promote conservation. The industrial intervenors and PP & L argued that the customer responds to average price, not marginal price, in making consumption decisions. Staff, SWOCAC, and Mr. Schaye argued that customers respond to marginal price.

It has been the policy of this agency since 1974 that marginal costs are the relevant costs to be used in making pricing decisions. Because of the difficulty in computing short-run marginal costs, incremental costs were found to constitute a logical, practical substitute for short run marginal costs. This policy was discussed extensively during the 1977–78 rate investigation of PP & L and PGE which led to the adoption of seasonal rates for all customers and time-of-day rates for large commercial and industrial customers.

The evidence in this proceeding reaffirms the policy that marginal costs should be used in pricing decisions. Mr. White of the PUC staff and Mr. Burgess, a witness for PGE, both argued on theoretical grounds that consumers respond to marginal price. Mr. Shue of PP & L argued persuasively that customers respond to total monthly bill size, not the marginal price of each kilowatt-hour consumed. Mr. Shue admits, however, that customers would respond to marginal price if the differences between blocks, or if the differences in total bill from month to month, were dramatic enough.

As pointed out by Mr. Schaye's witness, Dr. Power, whether the consumer responds to total bill size or to the price of electricity at the margin, the effects are identical.

> When the [customers] respond to one, they are responding to the other. The thing that changes the total bill is the price at the margin. One determines what the marginal price is, if somebody didn't whisper it in your ear, by seeing how your total bill has changed. There is no inconsistency in the assertion that the total bill is what people watch and the economists' assertion that what is important is price. Those two are perfectly consistent. One necessarily implies the other.

When Dr. Power was asked whether people respond to total bill size or not, he responded that people respond to *changes* in total bill size. I adopt staff witness Hellman's and Dr. Power's assertion that it is not necessary for the residential customer to know precisely what the price of electric energy is in order to react to marginal price. It is sufficient for the customer to notice that the bills are going up and to realize that in order to keep them from going up higher in the future, he will have to take some affirmative action to conserve.

Common sense tells us that even though a customer may not know the cost of burning a light bulb for one hour, the customer does know that the price of electricity has increased dramatically in recent years and the cost of a light bulb burning in an empty room will have a greater impact on his or her bill than it did a few years ago. In other words, as a result of increases in total bill over the last ten years, customers are increasingly aware of the cost of the marginal nonessential or wasteful uses of electricity.

* * *

ECONOMIC EFFICIENCY EFFECTS OF LIFELINE RATES

Staff witness White argued that, by definition, when marginal cost is greater than average cost, encouraging conservation will lead to an efficient use of resources. I find that resources are wasted, "used inefficiently," when the price paid by the consumer for the next kilowatt-hour used is less than the cost of producing that kilowatt-hour. If a rate is imposed that sets marginal price equal to marginal cost, or marginal price progressively closer to marginal cost as consumption increases, consumers will be more likely to use each succeeding kilowatt-hour of electricity wisely.

EQUITY EFFECTS OF LIFELINE RATES

Equity in electric rates to consumers should be considered from several perspectives.

As a starting point we should determine whether there should be a redistribution of the cost of electricity according to socioeconomic criteria. That is, should the poor and elderly receive cheaper electricity than the affluent customer? In 1975, the commissioner instituted an investigation to determine whether to reduce rates for energy consumed by poor persons and senior citizens (Order No. 76–39, January 16, 1976). The commissioner concluded that he was forbidden under Oregon law from imposing rate classifications which discriminate on the basis of customer age or income level. The commissioner found the legislative assembly to be the government agency most appropriate and able to address the needs of the poor and the elderly.

A serious concern is that an inverted rate may have serious *adverse* effects on low income individuals. The record in this proceeding indicates that this concern is well founded. Mr. Schaye's witness, Dr. Power, cited a 1975 study which asserted that perhaps 15 per cent of the poor consume more than the average amount of electricity, while electricity consumption of some 20 per cent of the upper middle income or more affluent customers is considerably below the average. Staff witness Taussig demonstrated that, over the long run, households tend to increase electricity consumption as their income increases. However, Mr. Taussig warns that this result holds only in the aggregate and that no conclusion can be drawn about individual households. Even though scope and magnitude of the adverse effects on the poor are not established, the record does raise a concern that some low income persons would be victims rather than beneficiaries of lifeline rate.

Two other views of equity are fully consistent with inverted rates. One perspective says that electricity is priced equitably if the same price schedule applies to all consumers, and no consumer is required to pay more for the same amount of electricity than any other consumer. Under this definition of equity, any rate is equitable as long as it is applied consistently to all consumers. This view is unacceptable. Consistency without consideration of other policies such as cost or value of service can lead to arbitrary and unjust rates. Consistency is an important factor in defining equity, but it is not the end of the inquiry.

Another view of equity tolerant of inverted rates is based on the relative burden of each class in bearing the marginal cost of electricity. If customer A is not paying a rate equal to marginal cost, he cannot be subsidizing customer B who is also paying less than marginal cost, even though B's rate is less than A's for the same or similar service. Only by paying full marginal cost may a consumer pay "an equitable" price. To accept this definition, you must equate economic efficiency with equity. I will not sacrifice fairness and justice to an abstract economic theory.

One final view of equity would preclude shifting the cost burden of providing energy between customer classes. Equity may result when customers pay the cost that their electric consumption imposes on the supplying utility. This view requires careful metering and costing procedures and would preclude cost subsidies between customer classes.

Shifting revenues from one customer class to another would be unfair and inequitable. The cost of serving the residential class should be raised from the residential class. Without convincing evidence that there are differences in demand elasticity between the classes, I cannot find a satisfactory justification for subsidizing one class at the expense of another.

I conclude subsidies from one class to another would be inequitable. I also find that a lifeline rate without a revenue shift imposes an unacceptably high burden on the residential customer. Under staff's proposal, with the entire revenue loss collected from the residential class, December, January, and February monthly bills for average usage would increase by over 21 per cent, 24.3 per cent, and 23 per cent, respectively. Summer bills for average PGE single-family, space-heating, customer usage would decrease. The impact of such a large winter bill increase would have a severe adverse effect on the average customer. The impact would be especially severe on low income consumers of an above average number of kilowatt-hours.

Shifting the revenue burden from one class to another would also be detrimental to meeting the conservation criterion. The residential class would have far more of an incentive to conserve electricity if the lost revenues from the lower ranges of kilowatt-hour usage were shifted to the upper ranges of a progressive rate structure.

Conclusion

As appealing as lifeline rates are to promote conservation, the proposed rates by staff, Mr. Schaye, and SWOCAC all fail because of the inequitable or burdensome effects they impose on various classes of customers. None of the proposed rates promote sufficient conservation or other benefits to outweigh the costs to the public imposed by the onerous or inequitable operation of the rates.

Notes and Questions

1. Low rates designed to benefit the poor are typically called "lifeline" rates. Can you think of good reasons for permitting lifeline rates?

2. The Oregon Commission was precluded by precedent from adopting an approach that would have focused on a specific class of needy consumers. Re Rate Concessions to Poor Persons and Senior Citizens, 14 P.U.R. 4th 87 (1976). Consequently, all the proposals considered were based on an across-the-board lifeline rate and the use of an inverted rate structure in which rates increase with the level of consumption.

3. Why is the issue of whether consumers respond to marginal rates or to their total monthly bill critical to the determination of whether the rate structures considered here are consistent with conservation? Do you agree with the expert relied upon by the Commissioner? What is your personal experience?

4. What is the Commissioner's reasoning for not permitting cross-subsidization between classes? Is he saying that cross-subsidization between classes would be equitable if there were a difference in demand elasticity? Why?

5. According to the Commissioner, the lifeline proposal of the staff would result in an over 20% increase in monthly bills during the winter months for the average residential customer even though the first 200 kwh are free. Because this is an average, some users will experience even greater increases.

a. Do you think this phenomenon can be explained by the different uses various consumers have for electricity? Is it safe to assume that the proposal was one under which consumers using electricity for heating would be subsidizing those using other energy sources for heat regardless of income?

b. Could this inequity be eliminated by adopting one of the proposals that would increase the amount of electricity available at lifeline rates depending upon the type of heating used by a consumer? What was the demand distortion that led the Commissioner to reject these proposals? Is this quandary inherent in the across the board approach to lifeline rates?

6. Suppose the Oregon utility were pricing at marginal cost and marginal cost were higher than average cost, resulting in a revenue surplus. Consequently, implementation of lifeline rates did not raise the rates of any consumers but eliminated some of the surplus. Would it be correct to say that, under these circumstances, cross-subsidization did not exist? Do you think lifeline rates are more equitable when there is a revenue surplus than when there is a revenue "gap" or when the utility is pricing at average cost? Why?

7. Instead of lifeline rates, suppose "energy stamps" were distributed to the indigent by the government on the basis of family size. The stamps could then be used to pay for any kind of energy at the normal price and redeemed by the utility receiving them. In what ways is this a better approach? Would the source of the subsidy change?

C. RATEMAKING IN A COMPETITIVE ENVIRONMENT

The current environment of deregulation has done much to cast doubt on the premises underlying rate regulation. However, you have also seen that "deregulation" does not mean that all regulation disappears. Again as you have seen, one strategy designed to increase competition is "unbundling." This leads to complex questions of what the regulated firm may charge for the unbundled elements of a system. In some cases those charges will be to ultimate consumers of the firm's services. In other cases, users will be companies who want to compete with the regulated firm to serve those consumers.

Earlier in this Chapter, we saw the Supreme Court looking at some of those issues in the context of whether particular rates were confiscatory and thus unconstitutional. In this part of the same case, we see the Court evaluate the FCC's ratemaking methodology in terms of the Commission's mandate to introduce competition into local telephone markets.

1. RATES IN THE CONTEXT OF UNBUNDLING

VERIZON COMMUNICATIONS INC v. FEDERAL COMMUNICATIONS COMMISSION

Supreme Court of the United States, 2002.
535 U.S. 467, 122 S.Ct. 1646, 152 L.Ed.2d 701.

JUSTICE SOUTER delivered the opinion of the Court.

These cases arise under the Telecommunications Act of 1996. Each is about the power of the Federal Communications Commission to regulate a relationship between monopolistic companies providing local telephone service and companies entering local markets to compete with the incumbents. Under the Act, the new entrants are entitled, among other things, to lease elements of the local telephone networks from the incumbent monopolists. The issues are whether the FCC is authorized (1) to require state utility commissions to set the rates charged by the incumbents for leased elements on a forward-looking basis untied to the incumbents' investment, and (2) to require incumbents to combine such elements at the entrants' request when they lease them to the entrants. We uphold the FCC's assumption and exercise of authority on both issues.

I

The 1982 consent decree settling the Government's antitrust suit against the American Telephone and Telegraph Company (AT & T) divested AT & T of its local-exchange carriers, leaving AT & T as a long-distance and equipment company, and limiting the divested carriers to the provision of local telephone service. United States v. American Telephone & Telegraph Co., 552 F.Supp. 131 (D.D.C.1982), aff'd. *sub nom.* Maryland v. United States, 460 U.S. 1001, * * * (1983).

The decree did nothing, however, to increase competition in the persistently monopolistic local markets, which were thought to be the root of natural monopoly in the telecommunications industry. * * * These markets were addressed by provisions of the Telecommunications Act of 1996 (1996 Act or Act) * * * that were intended to eliminate the monopolies enjoyed by the inheritors of AT & T's local franchises; this objective was considered both an end in itself and an important step toward the Act's other goals of boosting competition in broader markets and revising the mandate to provide universal telephone service. * * *

Two sets of related provisions for opening local markets concern us here. First, Congress required incumbent local-exchange carriers to share their own facilities and services on terms to be agreed upon with new entrants in their markets. * * * Second, knowing that incumbents and prospective entrants would sometimes disagree on prices for facilities or services, Congress directed the FCC to prescribe methods for state commissions to use in setting rates that would subject both incumbents and entrants to the risks and incentives that a competitive market would produce. § 252(d). The particular method devised by the FCC for setting rates to be charged for interconnection and lease of network elements under the Act, § 252(d)(1),] and regulations the FCC imposed to implement the statutory duty to share these elements, § 251(c)(3), are the subjects of this litigation, which must be understood against the background of ratemaking for public utilities in the United States and the structure of local exchanges made accessible by the Act.

A

* * *

Under the local-competition provisions of the Act, Congress called for ratemaking different from any historical practice, to achieve the entirely new objective of uprooting the monopolies that traditional rate-based methods had perpetuated. * * * A leading backer of the Act in the Senate put the new goal this way:

> "This is extraordinary in the sense of telling private industry that this is what they have to do in order to let the competitors come in and try to beat your economic brains out. . . .

> "It is kind of almost a jump-start. . . . I will do everything I have to let you into my business, because we used to be a bottleneck; we used to be a monopoly; we used to control everything.

> "Now, this legislation says you will not control much of anything. You will have to allow for nondiscriminatory access on an unbundled basis to the network functions and services of the Bell operating companies network that is at least equal in type, quality, and price to the access [a] Bell operating company affords to itself." 141 Cong. Rec. 15572 (1995) (remarks of Sen. Breaux (La.) on Pub.L. 104–104).

For the first time, Congress passed a ratesetting statute with the aim not just to balance interests between sellers and buyers, but to reorganize markets by rendering regulated utilities' monopolies vulnerable to interlopers, even if that meant swallowing the traditional federal reluctance to intrude into local telephone markets. The approach was deliberate, through a hybrid jurisdictional scheme with the FCC setting a basic, default methodology for use in setting rates when carriers fail to agree, but leaving it to state utility commissions to set the actual rates.

While the Act is like its predecessors in tying the methodology to the objectives of "just and reasonable" and nondiscriminatory rates, 47 U.S.C. § 252(d)(1), it is radically unlike all previous statutes in providing that rates be set "without reference to a rate-of-return or other rate-based proceeding," § 252(d)(1)(A)(I). The Act thus appears to be an explicit disavowal of the familiar public-utility model of rate regulation (whether in its fair-value or cost-of-service incarnations) presumably still being applied by many States for retail sales, * * * in favor of novel ratesetting designed to give aspiring competitors every possible incentive to enter local retail telephone markets, short of confiscating the incumbents' property.

B

The physical incarnation of such a market, a "local exchange," is a network connecting terminals like telephones, faxes, and modems to other terminals within a geographical area like a city. From terminal network interface devices, feeder wires, collectively called the "local loop," are run to local switches that aggregate traffic into common "trunks." The local loop was traditionally, and is still largely, made of copper wire, though fiber-optic cable is also used, albeit to a far lesser extent than in long-haul markets. Just as the loop runs from terminals to local switches, the trunks run from the local switches to centralized, or tandem, switches, originally worked by hand but now by computer, which operate much like railway switches, directing traffic into other trunks. A signal is sent toward its destination terminal on these common ways so far as necessary, then routed back down another hierarchy of switches to the intended telephone or other equipment. A local exchange is thus a transportation network for communications signals, radiating like a root system from a "central office" (or several offices for larger areas) to individual telephones, faxes, and the like.

It is easy to see why a company that owns a local exchange (what the Act calls an "incumbent local exchange carrier," 47 U.S.C. § 251(h)) would have an almost insurmountable competitive advantage not only in routing calls within the exchange, but, through its control of this local market, in the markets for terminal equipment and long-distance calling as well. A newcomer could not compete with the incumbent carrier to provide local service without coming close to replicating the incumbent's entire existing network, the most costly and difficult part of which would be laying down the "last mile" of feeder wire, the local loop, to the thousands (or millions) of terminal points in individual houses and businesses. The incumbent company could also control its local-loop plant so as to connect only with terminals it manufactured or selected, and could place conditions or fees (called "access charges") on long-distance carriers seeking to connect with its network. In an unregulated world, another telecommunications carrier would be forced to comply with these conditions, or it could never reach the customers of a local exchange.

II

The 1996 Act both prohibits state and local regulation that impedes the provision of "telecommunications service," § 253(a), and obligates incumbent carriers to allow competitors to enter their local markets, § 251(c). Section 251(c) addresses the practical difficulties of fostering local competition by recognizing three strategies that a potential competitor may pursue. First, a competitor entering the market (a "requesting" carrier, § 251(c)(2)) may decide to engage in pure facilities-based competition, that is, to build its own network to replace or supplement the network of the incumbent. If an entrant takes this course, the Act obligates the incumbent to "interconnect" the competitor's facilities to its own network to whatever extent is necessary to allow the competitor's facilities to operate. §§ 251(a) and (c)(2). At the other end of the spectrum, the statute permits an entrant to skip construction and instead simply to buy and resell "telecommunications service," which the incumbent has a duty to sell at wholesale. §§ 251(b)(1) and (c)(4). Between these extremes, an entering competitor may choose to lease certain of an incumbent's "network elements," which the incumbent has a duty to provide "on an unbundled basis" at terms that are "just, reasonable, and nondiscriminatory." § 251(c)(3).

Since wholesale markets for companies engaged in resale, leasing, or interconnection of facilities cannot be created without addressing rates, Congress provided for rates to be set either by contracts between carriers or by state utility commission rate orders. §§ 252(a)–(b). Like other federal utility statutes that authorize contracts approved by a regulatory agency in setting rates between businesses, * * * the Act permits incumbent and entering carriers to negotiate private rate agreements. * * * State utility commissions are required to accept any such agreement unless it discriminates against a carrier not a party to the contract, or is otherwise shown to be contrary to the public interest. §§ 252(e)(1) and (e)(2)(A). Carriers, of course, might well not agree, in which case an entering carrier has a statutory option to request mediation by a state commission, § 252(a)(2). But the option comes with strings, for mediation subjects the parties to the duties specified in § 251 and the pricing standards set forth in § 252(d), as interpreted by the FCC's regulations, § 252(e)(2)(B). These regulations are at issue here.

As to pricing, the Act provides that when incumbent and requesting carriers fail to agree, state commissions will set a "just and reasonable" and "nondiscriminatory" rate for interconnection or the lease of network elements based on "the cost of providing the ... network element," which "may include a reasonable profit." § 252(d)(1). In setting these rates, the state commissions are, however, subject to that important limitation previously unknown to utility regulation: the rate must be "determined without reference to a rate-of-return or other rate-based proceeding." * * * The attack today is on the legality and logic of the particular methodology the Commission chose.

       * * *

As for the method to derive a "nondiscriminatory," "just and reasonable rate for network elements," the Act requires the FCC to decide how to value "the cost ... of providing the ... network element [which] may include a reasonable profit," although the FCC is (as already seen) forbidden to allow any "reference to a rate-of-return or other rate-based proceeding," § 252(d)(1). Within the discretion left to it after eliminating any dependence on a "rate-of-return or other rate-based proceeding," the Commission chose a way of treating "cost" as "forward-looking economic cost," 47 CFR § 51.505 (1997). * * * In Rule 505, the FCC defined the "forward-looking economic cost of an element [as] the sum of (1) the allocation total element long-run incremental cost of the element [TELRIC]; [and] (2) a reasonable allocation of forward-looking common costs," § 51.505(a), common costs being "costs incurred in providing a group of elements that "cannot be attributed directly to individual elements," § 51.505(c)(1). Most important of all, the FCC decided that the TELRIC "should be measured based on the use of the most efficient telecommunications technology currently available and the lowest cost network configuration, given the existing location of the incumbent['s] wire centers." § 51.505(b)(1).

"The TELRIC of an element has three components, the operating expenses, the depreciation cost, and the appropriate risk-adjusted cost of capital." * * * A concrete example may help. Assume that it would cost $1 a year to operate a most-efficient loop element; that it would take $10 for interest payments on the capital a carrier would have to invest to build the lowest cost loop centered upon an incumbent carrier's existing wire centers (say $100, at 10 percent per annum); and that $9 would be reasonable for depreciation on that loop (an 11–year useful life); then the annual TELRIC for the loop element would be $20.

The Court of Appeals understood § 252(d)(1)'s reference to "the cost . . . of providing the . . . network element" to be ambiguous as between "forward-looking" and "historical" cost, so that a forward-looking ratesetting method would presumably be a reasonable implementation of the statute. But the Eighth Circuit thought the ambiguity afforded no leeway beyond that, and read the Act to require any forward-looking methodology to be "based on the incremental costs that an [incumbent] actually incurs or will incur in providing . . . the unbundled access to its specific network elements." 219 F.3d, at 751–753. Hence, the Eighth Circuit held that § 252(d)(1) foreclosed the use of the TELRIC methodology. In other words, the court read the Act as plainly requiring rates based on the "actual" not "hypothetical" "cost . . . of providing the . . . network element," and reasoned that TELRIC was clearly the latter. * * * The Eighth Circuit added, however, that if it were wrong and TELRIC were permitted, the claim that in prescribing TELRIC the FCC had effected an unconstitutional taking would not be "ripe" until "resulting rates have been determined and applied."

* * *

Before us, the incumbent local-exchange carriers claim error in the Eighth Circuit's holding that a "forward-looking cost" methodology (as opposed to the use of "historical" cost) is consistent with § 252(d)(1), and its conclusion that the use of the TELRIC forward-looking cost methodology presents no "ripe" takings claim. The FCC and the entrants, on the other side, seek review of the Eighth Circuit's invalidation of the TELRIC methodology * * * . We * * * affirm on the issues raised by the incumbents, and reverse on those raised by the FCC and the entrants.

III

A

The incumbent carriers' first attack charges the FCC with ignoring the plain meaning of the word "cost" as it occurs in the provision of § 252(d)(1) that "the just and reasonable rate for network elements . . . shall be . . . based on the cost (determined without reference to a rate-of-return or other rate-based proceeding) of providing the . . . network element. . . ." The incumbents do not argue that in theory the statute precludes any forward-looking methodology, but they do claim that the cost of providing a competitor with a network element in the future must be calculated using the incumbent's past investment in the element and the means of providing it. They contend that "cost" in the statute refers to "historical" cost, which they define as "what was in fact paid" for a capital asset, as distinct from "value," or "the price that would be paid on the open market." * * * They say that the technical meaning of "cost" is "past capital expenditure," and they suggest an equation between "historical" and "embedded" costs, which the FCC defines as "the costs that the incumbent LEC incurred in the past and that are recorded in the incumbent LEC's books of accounts," 47 CFR § 51.505(d)(1) (1997). The argument boils down to the proposition that "the cost of providing the network element" can only mean, in plain language and in this particular technical context, the past cost to an incumbent of furnishing the specific network element actually, physically, to be provided.

The incumbents have picked an uphill battle. At the most basic level of common usage, "cost" has no such clear implication. A merchant who is asked about "the cost of providing the goods" he sells may reasonably quote their current wholesale market price, not the cost of the particular items he happens to have on his shelves, which may have been bought at higher or lower prices.

* * *

What is equally important is that the incumbents' plain-meaning argument ignores the statutory setting in which the mandate to use "cost" in valuing network elements occurs. First, the Act uses "cost" as an intermediate term in the calculation of "just and reasonable rates * * *. Second, it would have been passing strange to think Congress tied "cost" to historical cost without a more specific indication, when the very same sentence that requires "cost" pricing also prohibits any reference to a "rate-of-return or other rate-based proceeding" * * * .

The fact is that without any better indication of meaning than the unadorned term, the word "cost" in § 252(d)(1), as in accounting generally, is "a chameleon," Strickland v. Commissioner, Maine Dept. of Human Services, 96 F.3d 542, 546 (C.A.1 1996), a "virtually meaningless" term, R. Estes, Dictionary of Accounting 32 (2d ed.1985). As Justice BREYER put it in *Iowa Utilities Bd.,* words like "cost" "give ratesetting commissions broad methodological leeway; they say little about the 'method employed' to determine a particular rate." 525 U.S., at 423, 119 S.Ct. 721 (opinion concurring in part and dissenting in part). * * *

B

The incumbents' alternative argument is that even without a stern anchor in calculating "the cost ... of providing the ... network element," the particular forward-looking methodology the FCC chose is neither consistent with the plain language of § 252(d)(1) nor within the zone of reasonable interpretation subject to deference under Chevron U.S.A. Inc. v. Natural Resources Defense Council, *Inc.,* 467 U.S. 837, 843–845, 104 S.Ct. 2778, 81 L.Ed.2d 694 (1984). This is so, they say, because TELRIC calculates the forward-looking cost by reference to a hypothetical, most efficient element at existing wire centers, not the actual network element being provided.

1

The short answer to the objection that TELRIC violates plain language is much the same as the answer to the previous plain-language argument, for what the incumbents call the "hypothetical" element is simply the element valued in terms of a piece of equipment an incumbent may not own. This claim, like the one just considered, is that plain language bars a definition of "cost" untethered to historical investment, and as explained already, the term "cost" is simply too protean to support the incumbents' argument.

2

Similarly, the claim that TELRIC exceeds reasonable interpretative leeway is open to the objection already noted, that responsibility for "just and reasonable" rates leaves methodology largely subject to discretion. * * * The incumbents nevertheless field three arguments. They contend, first, that a method of calculating wholesale lease rates based on the costs of providing hypothetical, most efficient elements may simulate the competition envisioned by the Act but does not induce it. Second, they argue that even if rates based on hypothetical elements could induce competition in theory, TELRIC cannot do this, because it does not provide the depreciation and risk-adjusted capital costs that the theory compels. Finally, the incumbents say that even if these objections can be answered, TELRIC is needlessly, and hence unreasonably, complicated and impracticable.

A

The incumbents' (and Justice Breyer's) basic critique of TELRIC is that by setting rates for leased network elements on the assumption of perfect competition, TELRIC perversely creates incentives against competition in fact. The incumbents say that in purporting to set incumbents' wholesale prices at the level that would exist in a perfectly competitive market (in order to make retail prices similarly competitive), TELRIC sets rates so low that entrants will always lease and never build network elements. And even if an entrant would otherwise consider building a network element more efficient than the best one then on the market (the one assumed in setting the TELRIC rate), it would likewise be deterred by the prospect that its lower cost in building and operating this new element would be immediately available to its competitors; under TELRIC, the incumbents assert, the lease rate for an incumbent's existing element would instantly drop to match the marginal cost of the entrant's new element once built. * * * According to the incumbents, the result will be, not competition, but a sort of parasitic free riding, leaving TELRIC incapable of stimulating the facilities-based competition intended by Congress.

We think there are basically three answers to this no-stimulation claim of unreasonableness: (1) the TELRIC methodology does not assume that the relevant markets are perfectly competitive, and the scheme includes several features of inefficiency that undermine the plausibility of the incumbents' no-stimulation argument; (2) comparison of TELRIC with alternatives proposed by the incumbents as more reasonable are plausibly answered by the FCC's stated reasons to reject the alternatives; and (3) actual investment in competing facilities since the effective date of the Act simply belies the no-stimulation argument's conclusion.

(1)

The basic assumption of the incumbents' no-stimulation argument is contrary to fact. As we explained, the argument rests on the assumption that in a perfectly efficient market, no one who can lease at a TELRIC rate will ever build. But TELRIC does not assume a perfectly efficient wholesale market or one that is likely to resemble perfection in any foreseeable time. The incumbents thus make the same mistake we attributed in a different setting to the FCC itself. In *Iowa Utilities Bd.*, we rejected the FCC's necessary-and-impair rule, 47 CFR § 51.319 (1997), which required incumbents to lease any network element that might reduce, however slightly, an entrant's marginal cost of providing a telecommunications service, as compared with providing the service using the entrant's own equivalent element. 525 U.S., at 389–390, 119 S.Ct. 721. "In a world of perfect competition, in which all carriers are providing their service at marginal cost, the Commission's total equating of increased cost (or decreased quality) with 'necessity' and 'impairment' might be reasonable, but it has not established the existence of such an ideal world." *Id.*, at 390, 119 S.Ct. 721.

Not only that, but the FCC has of its own accord allowed for inefficiency in the TELRIC design in additional ways affecting the likelihood that TELRIC will squelch competition in facilities. First, the Commission has qualified any assumption of efficiency by requiring ratesetters to calculate cost on the basis of "the existing location of the incumbent['s] wire centers." 47 CFR § 51.505(b)(1) (1997). This means that certain network elements, principally local-loop elements, will not be priced at their most efficient cost and configuration to the extent, say, that a shorter loop could serve a local exchange if the incumbent's wire centers were relocated for a snugger fit with the current geography of terminal locations.

Second, TELRIC rates in practice will differ from the products of a perfectly competitive market owing to built-in lags in price adjustments. In a perfectly competitive market, retail prices drop instantly to the marginal cost of the most efficient company. * * * As the incumbents point out, this would deter market entry because a potential entrant would know that even if it could provide a retail service at a lower marginal cost, it would instantly lose that competitive edge once it entered the market and competitors adjusted to match its price. * * * Wholesale TELRIC rates, however, are set by state commissions, usually by arbitrated agreements with 3– or 4–year terms, * * * and no one claims that a competitor could receive immediately on demand a TELRIC rate on a leased element at the marginal cost of the entrant who introduces a more efficient element.

But even if a competitor could call for a new TELRIC rate proceeding immediately upon the introduction of a more efficient element by a competing entrant, the competitor would not necessarily know enough to make the call; the fact of the element's greater efficiency would only become apparent when reflected in lower retail prices drawing demand away from existing competitors (including the incumbent), forcing them to look to lowering their own marginal costs. In practice, it would take some time for the innovating entrant to install the new equipment, to engage in marketing offering a lower retail price to attract business, and to steal away enough customer subscriptions (given the limited opportunity to capture untapped customers for local telephone service) for competitors to register the drop in demand.

Finally, it bears reminding that the FCC prescribes measurement of the TELRIC "based on the use of the most efficient telecommunications technology currently available," 47 CFR § 51.505(b)(1) (1997). Owing to that condition of current availability, the marginal cost of a most-efficient element that an entrant alone has built and uses would not set a new pricing standard until it became available to competitors as an alternative to the incumbent's corresponding element.

       * * *

(2)

Perhaps sensing the futility of an unsupported theoretical attack, the incumbents make the complementary argument that the FCC's choice of TELRIC, whatever might be said about it on its own terms, was unreasonable as a matter of law because other methods of determining cost would have done a better job of inducing competition. Having considered the proffered alternatives and the reasons the FCC gave for rejecting them, * * * we cannot say that the FCC acted unreasonably in picking TELRIC to promote the mandated competition.

The incumbents present three principal alternatives for setting rates for network elements * * *. The arguments that one or another of these methodologies is preferable to TELRIC share a basic claim: it was unreasonable for the FCC to choose a method of setting rates that fails to include, at least in theory, some additional costs beyond what would be most efficient in the long run, because lease rates that incorporate such costs will do a better job of inducing competition. The theory is that once an entrant has its foot in the door, it will have a greater incentive to build and operate its own more efficient network element if the lease rates reflect something of the incumbents' actual and inefficient marginal costs. And once the entrant develops the element at its lower marginal cost and the retail price drops accordingly, the incumbent will have no choice but to innovate itself by building the most efficient element or finding ways to reduce its marginal cost to retain its market share.

The generic feature of the incumbents' proposed alternatives, in other words, is that some degree of long-run inefficiency ought to be preserved through the lease rates, in order to give an entrant a more efficient alternative to leasing. Of course, we have already seen that TELRIC itself tolerates some degree of inefficient pricing in its existing wire-center configuration requirement and through the ratemaking and development lags just described. This aside, however, there are at least two objections that generally undercut any desirability that such alternatives may seem to offer over TELRIC.

The first objection turns on the fact that a lease rate that compensates the lessor for some degree of existing inefficiency (at least from the perspective of the long run) is simply a higher rate, and the difference between such a higher rate and the TELRIC rate could be the difference that keeps a potential competitor from entering the market. * * *

The second general objection turns the incumbents' attack on TELRIC against the incumbents' own alternatives. If the problem with TELRIC is that an entrant will never build because at the instant it builds, other competitors can lease the analogous existing (but less efficient) element from an incumbent at a rate assuming the same most efficient marginal cost, then the same problem persists under the incumbents' methods. For as soon as an entrant builds a more efficient element, the incumbent will be forced to price to match, and that rate will be available to all other competitors. The point, of course, is that things are not this simple. As we have said, under TELRIC, price adjustment is not instantaneous in rates for a leased element corresponding to an innovating entrant's more efficient element; the same would presumably be true under the incumbents' alternative methods, though they do not come out and say it.

    * * *

(3)

At the end of the day, theory aside, the claim that TELRIC is unreasonable as a matter of law because it simulates but does not produce facilities-based competition founders on fact. The entrants have presented figures showing that they have invested in new facilities to the tune of $55 billion since the passage of the Act * * * . The FCC's statistics indicate substantial resort to pure and partial facilities-based competition among the three entry strategies: as of June 30, 2001, 33 percent of entrants were using their own facilities; 23 percent were reselling services; and 44 percent were leasing network elements (26 percent of entrants leasing loops with switching; 18 percent without switching). * * * The incumbents do not contradict these figures, but merely speculate that the investment has not been as much as it could have been under other ratemaking approaches, and they note that investment has more recently shifted to nonfacilities entry options. We, of course, have no idea whether a different forward-looking pricing scheme would have generated even greater competitive investment than the $55 billion that the entrants claim, but it suffices to say that a regulatory scheme that can boast such substantial competitive capital spending over a 4–year period is not easily described as an unreasonable way to promote competitive investment in facilities.

B

The incumbents' second reason for calling TELRIC an unreasonable exercise of the FCC's regulatory discretion is the supposed incapacity of this methodology to provide enough depreciation and allowance for capital costs to induce rational competition on the theory's own terms. This challenge must be assessed against the background of utilities' customary preference for extended depreciation schedules in ratemaking (so as to preserve high rate bases), * * * we have already noted the consequence of the utilities' approach, that the "book" value or embedded costs of capital presented to traditional ratemaking bodies often bore little resemblance to the economic value of the capital. * * * TELRIC seeks to avoid this problem by basing its valuation on the market price for most efficient elements; when rates are figured by reference to a hypothetical element instead of an incumbent's actual element, the incumbent gets no unfair advantage from favorable depreciation rates in the traditional sense.

This, according to the incumbents, will be fatal to competition. Their argument is that TELRIC will result in constantly changing rates based on ever cheaper, more efficient technology; the incumbents will be unable to write off each new piece of technology rapidly enough to anticipate an even newer gadget portending a new and lower rate. They will be stuck, they say, with sunk costs in less efficient plant and equipment, with their investment unrecoverable through depreciation, and their increased risk unrecognized and uncompensated.

The argument, however, rests upon a fundamentally false premise, that the TELRIC rules limit the depreciation and capital costs that ratesetting commissions may recognize. In fact, TELRIC itself prescribes no fixed percentage rate as risk-adjusted capital costs and recognizes no particular useful life as a basis for calculating depreciation costs. * * *

Finally, as to the incumbents' accusation that TELRIC is too complicated to be practical, a criticism at least as telling can be leveled at traditional ratemaking methodologies and the alternatives proffered. "One important potential advantage of the T[E]LRIC approach, however is its relative ease of calculation. Rather than estimate costs reflecting the present [incumbent] network—a difficult task even if [incumbents] provided reliable data—it is possible to generate T[E]LRIC estimates based on a 'green field' approach, which assumes construction of a network from scratch." * * * To the extent that the traditional public-utility model generally relied on embedded costs, similar sorts of complexity in reckoning were exacerbated by an asymmetry of information, much to the utilities' benefit. * * * And what we see from the record suggests that TELRIC rate proceedings are surprisingly smooth-running affairs, with incumbents and competitors typically presenting two conflicting economic models supported by expert testimony, and state commissioners customarily assigning rates based on some predictions from one model and others from its counterpart. * * * At bottom, battles of experts are bound to be part of any ratesetting scheme, and the FCC was reasonable to prefer TELRIC over alternative fixed-cost schemes that preserve home-field advantages for the incumbents.

* * *

We cannot say whether the passage of time will show competition prompted by TELRIC to be an illusion, but TELRIC appears to be a reasonable policy for now, and that is all that counts. See *Chevron,* 467 U.S., at 866, 104 S.Ct. 2778. The incumbents have failed to show that TELRIC is unreasonable on its own terms, largely because they fall into the trap of mischaracterizing the FCC's departures from the assumption of a perfectly competitive market (the wire-center limitation, regulatory and development lags, or the refusal to prescribe high depreciation and capital costs) as inconsistencies rather than pragmatic features of the TELRIC plan. Nor have they shown it was unreasonable for the FCC to pick TELRIC over alternative methods, or presented evidence to rebut the entrants' figures as to the level of competitive investment in local-exchange markets. In short, the incumbents have failed to carry their burden of showing unreasonableness to defeat the deference due the Commission. We therefore reverse the Eighth Circuit's judgment insofar as it invalidated TELRIC as a method for setting rates under the Act.

* * *

The judgment of the Court of Appeals is reversed in part and affirmed in part, and the cases are remanded for further proceedings consistent with this opinion.

Notes and Questions

1. Do you understand "forward looking" to mean the costs incurred by the incumbent in the future? If not, what does it mean?

2. Suppose an incumbent has invested a certain amount of money in its facilities and that amount is used in determining its own rates. For example it may have invested $20 million in its local exchange network and incurs obligations to investors for that amount. In order to meet these obligations, its rates must reflect its historical investment.

On the other hand, if the incumbent were starting up today, it would invest differently in order to provide the same service. In fact, lower cost materials and newer construction methods may mean that its local exchange network could be created for $10 million. When required to allow a new entrant to use its facilities, which cost is relevant under the Commission's ruling?

3. Does TELRIC seem fair to incumbents? What if their investments are the result of bad business judgments. Should the new entrants and consumers be saddled with these bad decisions forever?

4. The incumbents argue that the TELRIC will actually discourage competition. The logic is that new entrants who are permitted to gain access by paying a price equal to what would exist under ideal conditions have little reason to make their own investments. What do you make of the Court's response to this argument? Is it an argument that, ironically, has as its premise that competitive conditions do not, in fact, exist?

5. In Chapter 3, in the context of the deregulation of natural gas, you may recall that the demand over the last ten years has outstripped supply so much so that regulatory officials are revisiting the unbundling policy. One theory is that companies are more likely to invest in fixed facilities if they are permitted to deny access (rebundle). Can the same eventually be true in the context of local exchange service?

2. SETTING RATES IN COMPETITIVE MARKETS

NATIONAL ASSOCIATION OF GREETING CARD PUBLISHERS v. UNITED STATES POSTAL SERVICE

Supreme Court of the United States, 1983.
462 U.S. 810, 103 S.Ct. 2717, 77 L.Ed.2d 195.

JUSTICE BLACKMUN delivered the opinion of the Court.

This case arises out of the most recent general postal ratemaking proceeding, the fifth under the Postal Reorganization Act. At issue is the extent to which the Act requires the responsible federal agencies to base postal rates on cost-of-service principles.

I

A

When, in 1970, Congress enacted the Postal Reorganization Act (Act), 84 Stat. 719, 39 U.S.C. § 101 *et seq.*, it divested itself of the control it theretofore had exercised over the setting of postal rates and fees. The Act abolished the Post Office Department, which since 1789 had administered the Nation's mails. See Act of Sept. 22, 1789, ch. 16, 1 Stat. 70. In its place, the Act established the United States Postal Service as an independent agency under the direction of an eleven-member Board of Governors. The Act also established a five-member Postal Rate Commission (Rate Commission) as an agency independent of the Postal Service.

Basic to the Act is the principle that, to the extent "practicable," the Postal Service's total revenue must equal its costs. Guided by this principle, the Board of Governors, when it deems it in the public interest, may request the Rate Commission to recommend a new rate schedule. After receiving the request, the Rate Commission holds hearings and formulates a schedule, Section 3622(b) provides that the Rate Commission shall recommend rates for the classes of mail[57] in accordance with nine factors, the third of which is "the requirement that each class of mail or type of mail service bear the direct and indirect postal costs attributable to that class or type plus that portion of all other costs of the Postal Service reasonably assignable to such class or type." The Governors may approve the recommended rate schedule, may allow it under protest, may reject it, or, in limited circumstances, may modify it. The Governors' decision to order new rates into effect may be appealed to any United States court of appeals.

Questions confronting us in this case are whether the Rate Commission must follow a two-tier or a three-trier process in setting rates, and

---

57. Section 3622(b) provides in relevant part:

"(b) Upon receiving a request [from the Postal Service], the [Rate] Commission shall make a recommended decision ... in accordance with the policies of this title and the following factors:

"(1) the establishment and maintenance of a fair and equitable schedule;

"(2) the value of the mail service actually provided each class or type of mail service to both the sender and the recipient, including but not limited to the collection, mode of transportation, and priority of delivery;

"(3) the requirement that each class of mail or type of mail service bear the direct and indirect postal costs attributable to that class or type plus that portion of all other costs of the Postal Service reasonably assignable to such class or type;

"(4) the effect of rate increases upon the general public, business mail users, and enterprises in the private sector of the economy engaged in the delivery of mail matter other than letters;

"(5) the available alternative means of sending and receiving letters and other mail matter at reasonable costs;" (6) the degree of preparation of mail for delivery into the postal system performed by the mailer and its effect upon reducing costs to the Postal Service;

"(7) simplicity of structure for the entire schedule and simple, identifiable relationships between the rates or fees charged the various classes of mail for postal services;

"(8) the educational, cultural, scientific, and informational value to the recipient of mail matter; and

"(9) such other factors as the Commission deems appropriate." [Court's fn. 2]

the extent to which the Rate Commission must base rates on estimates of the costs caused by providing each class of mail service.

B

In its first two ratemaking proceedings under the Act, the Rate Commission determined that § 3622(b) establishes a two-tier approach to allocating the Postal Service's total revenue requirement. Under this approach, the Rate Commission first must determine the costs caused by ("attributable to") each class of mail, and on that basis establish a rate floor for each class. The Rate Commission then must "reasonably assign," the remaining costs to the various classes of mail on the basis of the other factors set forth in § 3622(b).

In the first proceeding, the Rate Commission concluded that the Act does not dictate the use of any particular method of identifying the costs caused by each class. Without committing itself to any theory for the future, it chose to attribute those costs shown to vary with the volume of mail in each class over the "short term"—the period of a single year. Although it considered other methods, it found the short-term approach to be the only feasible one, given the limited data developed by the Postal Service.

In the second proceeding, the Rate Commission again viewed the choice of a costing system as within its discretion. Although the Postal Service contended that short-term costs should again control attribution, the Rate Commission determined that it could reliably attribute more costs through a long-term variable costing analysis. That method attributes costs by identifying cost variations associated with shifts in mail volume and with shifts in the Postal Service's capacity to handle mail over periods of time longer than one year. The Rate Commission did not go beyond attributing long-run variable costs, because the statute forbids attribution based on guesswork and because the Rate Commission was unable to find "any other reliable principle of causality on [the] record". The Rate Commission urged the development of improved data for future proceedings, so that it could identify more causal relationships, and thereby attribute more costs.[58]

C

Reviewing the second proceeding, the United States Court of Appeals for the District of Columbia Circuit rejected the Rate Commission's approach. National Assn. of Greeting Card Publishers v. United States Postal Service, 186 U.S.App.D.C. 331, 569 F.2d 570 (1976) (*NAGCP I*), vacated on other grounds, 434 U.S. 884 (1977). The court held that the Act's principal goals of eliminating price discrimination among classes of mail and curtailing discretion in ratesetting, * * * require the Rate Commission "to employ cost-of-service principles to the fullest extent

---

58. The Rate Commission attributed 50% of the Postal Service's total revenue requirement in the first proceeding, and in the second the data provided by the Postal Service had improved enough to support a rate floor consisting of 52.5% of total postal costs. * * * [Court's fn. 6]

possible." * * * Therefore, the court stated, the Act mandates not only attribution of variable costs, but also "extended attribution" of costs that, "although not measurably variable," can reasonably be determined to result from handling each class of mail. * * * The court required the Rate Commission to allocate some costs on the basis of "cost accounting principles." * * * This involves apportioning costs on the basis of "distribution keys," such as the weight or cubic volume of mail, notwithstanding the lack of proof that such factors play a causative role.[59]

The Court of Appeals, citing the language and purposes of the statute, also required the Rate Commission to follow a three-tier, rather than a two-tier, procedure in setting rates. In the court's view, the first two tiers—attribution and assignment—are to proceed on a cost-of-service basis.[60] * * * Only those "residual costs" that cannot be attributed or assigned on the basis of reasonable inferences of causation may be distributed, in the third tier, among the classes of mail on the basis of § 3622(b)'s noncost, discretionary factors.

Despite its doubts about *NAGCP I,* the Rate Commission attempted to comply in the fourth ratemaking proceeding. It adhered to its view that variability is the key to attribution, because only with "some showing of volume variability over the long run" could it have reasonable confidence that particular costs were the consequence of providing the service. Because the data on long-run costs had improved, the Rate Commission found that its long-run analysis satisfied *NAGCP I*'s requirement of "extended attribution" without resort to mere "inferences of causation."

Turning to the intermediate assignment tier created by *NAGCP I,* the Rate Commission found a group of nonvariable "Service Related Costs" to be reasonably assignable to first class and certain categories of second class mail. Service Related Costs were defined as the fixed delivery costs incurred in maintaining the current six-day-a-week delivery schedule for those classes, rather than a hypothetical three-day-a-week schedule.

D

The current controversy began on April 21, 1980, when the Postal Service requested from the Rate Commission a fifth increase in postal rates. Following extensive hearings, the Rate Commission recommended continued assignment of Service Related Costs in order to comply with the Court of Appeals' three-tier approach. The Rate Commission also made clear that while it did not consider variability analysis to be the sole statutory basis for attribution, only long-run variability analysis had

---

59. Such accounting principles are used in utility ratemaking proceedings that employ "fully allocated costing" systems. Under such systems, a specific cause is assigned to every cost incurred by a utility. The Post Office employed such a system prior to the Act. [Court's fn. 7]

60. The court said that attributable and assignable costs are distinguishable in that "the latter concept permits a greater degree of estimation and connotes somewhat more judgment and discretion than the former." [Court's fn. 8]

been shown to be accurate enough to permit attribution. * * * The Governors, under protest, permitted these rates to go into effect.[61]

On petitions for review, the United States Court of Appeals for the Second Circuit held that Congress had not intended to require the maximum possible use of cost-of-service principles in postal ratesetting. Newsweek, Inc. v. United States Postal Service, 663 F.2d 1186 (2d Cir.1981). The Second Circuit stated that although the Rate Commission is free to use the approach the District of Columbia Circuit had required, the Act permits the use of other approaches as well, including the Rate Commission's original two-tier approach to ratesetting. Under the Second Circuit's construction, § 3622(b)(3) requires that the rate floor for each class consist of attributable costs based, at a minimum, on short-term variability; reasonable assignment may proceed on the basis of the other factors set forth in § 3622(b). The court remanded to the agencies for reconsideration.

Because of the inconsistencies in the holdings of the Second and District of Columbia Circuits, we granted certiorari. * * *

II

As a threshold matter, it is useful to set forth what is, and what is not, at issue in this litigation. Of the factors set forth in § 3622(b), only subsection (b)(3) is styled a "requirement." With the approval of both Courts of Appeals, the Rate Commission has concluded that notwithstanding its placement as the third of nine factors, this distinction dictates that "attribution" and "assignment" define the framework for ratesetting. In addition, the Rate Commission takes the view that "causation is both the statutory and the logical basis for attribution." The parties do not dispute these premises, and we see no reason to question them.

At issue is the Rate Commission's consistent position that the Act establishes a two-tier structure for ratesetting, and that the Act does not dictate or exclude the use of any method of attributing costs, but requires that all costs reliably identifiable with a given class, by whatever method, be attributed to that class. * * *

III

In *NAGCP I*, the Court of Appeals for the District of Columbia Circuit discerned in the Act an overriding purpose to minimize the Rate Commission's discretion by maximizing the use of cost-of-service principles. According to the Court of Appeals, the Rate Commission's failure to use "cost accounting principles" to attribute costs, and its failure to "assign" costs on the basis of extended inferences of causation as a middle ratesetting tier, frustrated these congressional goals. Animating the court's view was the fact that Congress, in passing the Act, was

---

61. More than 64% of total costs were attributed by this method. * * * [Court's fn. 12]

disturbed about the influence of lobbyists on Congress' discretionary ratemaking and the resulting discrimination in rates among classes of postal service; in the Act, Congress sought to "get 'politics out of the Post Office.' " * * *

Without doubt, Congress did have these problems in mind, but we agree with the Second Circuit that the District of Columbia Circuit misunderstood Congress' solution. Congress did not eliminate the rate setter's discretion; it simply removed the rate-setting function from the political arena, by removing postal funding from the budgetary process * * * and by removing the Postal Service's principal officers from the President's direct control. * * * In addition, Congress recognized that the increasing economic, accounting, and engineering complexity of ratemaking issues had caused Members of Congress, "lacking the time, training, and staff support for thorough analysis," to place too much reliance on lobbyists. Consequently, it attempted to remove undue price discrimination and political influence by placing ratesetting in the hands of a Rate Commission, composed of "professional economists, trained rate analysts, and the like". * * * There is no suggestion in the legislative history that Congress viewed the exercise of discretion as an evil in itself. Congress simply wished to substitute the educated and politically insulated discretion of experts for its own.

IV

We turn now to the narrower contentions about the meaning of § 3622(b)(3). In determining whether the Rate Commission's two-tier approach to ratesetting is contrary to the mandate of the Act or frustrates its policies, we begin with the statute's language. * * * Once the Rate Commission has allocated all attributable costs, § 3622(b)(3) directs that each class must bear, in addition, "that portion of all other costs ... reasonably assignable" to it. While the verb "attribute" primarily connotes causation, the verb "assign" connotes distribution on any basis. On its face, therefore, the section suggests one ratemaking tier based on causation, and a second based on other factors. We see no justification for the interposition of an intermediate causation-based assignment tier. The Rate Commission's two-tier approach is consistent with the statutory language.

* * *

V

We now turn to the nature of the first tier, the statutory requirement of attribution.

A

* * *

We agree with the Rate Commission's consistent position that Congress did not dictate a specific method for identifying causal relationships between costs and classes of mail, but that the Act "envisions consideration of all appropriate costing approaches." * * * The Rate Commission has held that, regardless of method, the Act requires the establishment of a sufficient causal nexus before costs may be attributed. The Rate Commission has variously described that requirement as demanding a "reliable principle of causality," or "reasonable confidence" that costs are the consequence of providing a particular service or a "reasoned analysis of cost causation." Accordingly, despite the District of Columbia Circuit's interpretation, the Rate Commission has refused to use general "accounting principles" based on distribution keys without an established causal basis. But the Rate Commission has gone beyond short-term costs in each rate proceeding since the first.

B

Section 3622(b)(3) requires that all "attributable costs" be borne by the responsible class. In determining what costs are "attributable," the Rate Commission is directed to look to all costs of the Postal Service, both "direct" and "indirect." In selecting the phrase "attributable costs," Congress avoided the use of any term of art in law or accounting. In the normal sense of the word, an "attributable" cost is a cost that may be considered to result from providing a particular class of service. On its face, there is no reason to suppose that § 3622(b)(3) denies to the expert ratesetting agency, exercising its reasonable judgment, the authority to decide which methods sufficiently identify the requisite causal connection between particular services and particular costs.

The legislative history supports the Rate Commission's view that when causal analysis is limited by insufficient data, the statute envisions that the Rate Commission will "press for . . . better data," rather than "construct an 'attribution'" based on unsupported inferences of causation. * * *

     * * *

* * * The Rate Commission, therefore, acted consistently with the statutory mandate and Congress' policy objectives in refusing to use distribution keys or other accounting principles lacking an established causal basis.[62]

C

The Postal Service contends that Congress intended long-term and short-term variable costs to be attributed, but that Congress did not direct attribution of costs, apart from fixed costs incurred by a particular class, that do not vary directly or indirectly with volume. We agree that, because the Rate Commission has decided that these methods reliably indicate causal connections between classes of mail and postal rates, the

---

62. Petitioner United Parcel Service argues that extended use of cost-of-service principles is necessary to avoid subsidization of those classes of mail for which the Postal Service has competition, such as parcel post, by other classes of mail for which the Postal Service enjoys a statutory monopoly, such as first class. Congress' concern about such cross-subsidies, of course, was one motive for including the rate floor established in § 3622(b)(3). * * * [Court's fn. 24]

Act requires that they be employed. But the Act's language and legislative history support the Rate Commission's position that Congress did not intend to bar the use of any reliable method of attributing costs.

     * * *

D

The Second Circuit found controlling the definition of "attributable" costs contained in the Statement of the Managers on the Part of the House, appended to the Conference Report on the Act, H.R.Conf.Rep. No. 91–1363, pp. 79–90 (1970). Newsweek, Inc. v. United States Postal Service, 663 F.2d, at 1199–1200. The House Managers stated that the conference substitute established a rate floor for each class of mail "equal to costs . . . *that vary over the short term* in response to changes in volume of a particular class or, even though fixed rather than variable, are the consequence of providing the specific service involved." H.R.Conf.Rep. No. 91–1363, at 87 (emphasis supplied), U.S.Code Cong. & Admin.News 1970, p. 3720. The Rate Commission specifically addressed and rejected this argument when it was advanced by the Postal Service in the first two ratemaking proceedings, see PRC Op. R74–1, pp. 101–102, 126–127; PRC Op. R71–1, pp. 42–46, and even the Postal Service since has abandoned it. The statute's plain language and prior legislative history, discussed above, indicate that Congress' broad policy was to mandate a rate floor consisting of all costs that could be identified, in the view of the expert Rate Commission, as causally linked to a class of postal service. We cannot say that the House Managers' statement alone demonstrates that the Rate Commission's view is "inconsistent with the statutory mandate or . . . frustrate[s] the policy that Congress sought to implement." Federal Election Commission v. Democratic Senatorial Campaign Committee, 454 U.S., at 32, 102 S.Ct., at 42.

VI

We hold that the Rate Commission has reasonably construed the Act as establishing a two-tier ratesetting structure. First, all costs that in the judgment of the Rate Commission are the consequence of providing a particular class of service must be borne by that class. The statute requires attribution of any cost for which the source can be identified, but leaves it to the Commissioners, in the first instance, to decide which methods provide reasonable assurance that costs are the result of providing one class of service.

For this function to be performed, the Postal Service must seek to improve the data on which causal relationships may be identified as the Rate Commission remains open to the use of any method that reliably identifies causal relationships. In our view, the Rate Commission conscientiously has attempted to find causal connections between classes of service and all postal costs—both operating costs and "overhead" or "capacity" costs—where the data is sufficient. The Rate Commission is to assign remaining costs reasonably on the basis of the other eight factors set forth by § 3622(b).

Inasmuch as the rates at issue were established according to the District of Columbia Circuit's erroneous view of the Act, we agree with the Second Circuit that this matter must be remanded to the agencies. While we do not agree with all that the Second Circuit said in its opinion, we affirm its judgment in remanding the cases. The remand will be for further proceedings consistent with this opinion.

Notes and Questions

1. Do you understand the disagreement the Supreme Court sought to resolve? Take a look at footnote 57. Any costs not assigned under subsection (3) are to be assigned on the basis of the other 8 factors. What difference does this make and what sorts of people are likely to be concerned?

2. One of the features of the Postal Reorganization Act is that the costs and revenues of the Postal Service are supposed to be equal to the extent practical. Does this necessarily lead to the requirement in subsection (3)? If not, why have the requirement in subsection (3)?

3. Would you describe the methodology adopted here as a form of marginal cost pricing?

4. Once a type of mail has been assigned the cost that can be traced to that service, how would you assign the remaining costs? Should it be assigned to mail based on the elasticity of demand? In other words should demanders of mail service who have no alternatives be expected to pay a bigger share of the unassigned costs? Suppose this means that those people who buy medication end up paying more. Does that seem fair? Should people who buy glossy high end magazines be expected to pay a larger or smaller share?

5. Item 8 is "the educational, cultural, scientific, and informational value to the recipient of mail matter." How is one to determine this? How would you define "cultural value"? Is it the same for Playboy and National Geographic?

6. As you might expect, the assignment of costs can have important competitive implications. This is illustrated in the next case.

UNITED PARCEL SERVICE, INC. v. UNITED STATES POSTAL SERVICE

United States Court of Appeals, District of Columbia Circuit, 1999.
184 F.3d 827.

Before GINSBURG, HENDERSON and ROGERS, CIRCUIT JUDGES

PER CURIAM:

The petitioners raise five challenges to the May 11, 1998 Opinion and Recommended Decision of the United States Postal Rate Commission (Commission), as approved by the United State Postal Service Board of Governors (Governors) on June 29, 1998. For the reasons set out below, we reject each of the challenges and deny the petitions for review.

I. BACKGROUND

Under the Postal Reorganization Act (Act), "the Governors are authorized to establish reasonable and equitable classes of mail and reasonable and equitable rates of postage and fees for postal services" subject to the over-all "break even" limitation that "[p]ostal rates and fees shall provide sufficient revenues so that the total estimated income and appropriations to the Postal Service will equal as nearly as practicable total estimated costs of the Postal Service." 39 U.S.C. § 3621 (1994). * * * The United States Postal Service * * * initiates a ratemaking proceeding by requesting that the Commission "submit a recommended decision on changes in a rate or rates of postage or in a fee or fees for postal services." Id. § 3622 (a).

* * *

The Commission has construed section 3622(b) to establish a "two-tier approach to allocating the Postal Service's total revenue requirement" under which the Commission "first must determine the costs caused by ('attributable to') each class of mail, § 3622(b)(3), and on that basis establish a rate floor for each class" (the "attributable" costs) and "then must 'reasonably assign,' see § 3622(b)(3), the remaining costs to the various classes of mail on the basis of the other factors set forth in § 3622(b)" (the "institutional" costs). National Ass'n of Greeting Card Publishers v. USPS, 462 U.S. 810, 814–15, 103 S.Ct. 2717, 77 L.Ed.2d 195 (1983). * * *

II. DISCUSSION

As noted above, the petitioners challenge the Commission's rate-making decision on five grounds. We examine each ground separately.

* * *

C. *Alaskan Parcel Post Air Costs*

United Parcel Service (UPS) first challenges the amount of the Commission's attributable costs for Parcel Post mail on the ground that the Commission improperly excluded from them a substantial portion of air transportation costs attributable to delivering Parcel Post mail to the remote Alaskan "bush country." Because the Alaskan bush country is accessible only by air, all mail delivered there, including nonpreferential Parcel Post mail, which is usually carried by ground transport, must be delivered by air, inflating considerably the costs of delivering Parcel Post mail to the area. The Commission elected to attribute only a portion of the air delivery costs to the Parcel Post subclass, however, concluding the remainder was attributable to the Act's "universal service obligation," which the Commission found to be the primary cause of the air costs. (providing Postal Service "shall provide prompt, reliable, and efficient services to patrons in *all* areas and shall render postal services to *all* communities") (emphasis added). Because the statutory term "attributable" is ambiguous, we defer to the Commission's reasonable interpretation of it and uphold its consequent decision to attribute only a portion of Alaskan air costs to the Parcel Post subclass.

As noted above, section 3622(b)(3) requires "that each class of mail or type of mail service bear the direct and indirect postal costs attributable to that class or type." Thus, "all costs that in the judgment of the Rate Commission are the consequence of providing a particular class of service must be borne by that class." * * * In this ratemaking, as in past ratemakings, the Commission generally attributed costs under the "volume variability" methodology, which classifies a cost as "volume variable" and therefore attributable to a particular class if the cost rises as the volume of the particular class of mail rises. * * * Here, however, the Commission elected to deviate from strict volume variable causation because of the unusual and constraining geographical circumstances of Alaskan Parcel Post service.

In its decision the Commission applied a "premium costing approach" under which the attributable costs of delivering Alaskan Parcel Post were "calculated based on the nationwide average costs of [ ] highway transportation," while "[t]he remaining portion, approximately $70 million for the last year, is transferred to the institutional cost pool and recovered through the markup procedure pursuant to the Act." The Commission's decision explained this attribution only briefly:

> The costs of serving areas without road access, the so-called Bush Country of Alaska, are considerably higher than the costs of providing service to other areas in the United States. Since the Postal Service's universal service obligation extends to citizens of all regions of the United States, it would not be appropriate to recover all these costs from the nonpreferential classes carried by intra–Alaska–Air.

Id. The Commission explained its reasoning more clearly and extensively in the 1990 postal ratemaking decision in which, as the Commission specifically noted here, for the first time "a portion of the costs of intra-Alaskan transportation costs ... ha[d] been considered institutional, although they are recognized as being volume variable in nature." *Id*. * * *

> In the 1990 ratemaking the Commission determined:

> The record supports a finding that nonpriority Alaska air costs are attributable only to the extent that they substitute for the surface costs that would be incurred if that transportation service were available. The remaining costs, which we refer to as the "universal service obligation premium," are institutional. These costs are caused by the Postal Service's statutory obligation to serve the entire nation.

Id. at III–195. The Commission defended its use of the "premium costing approach" as reasonable under the circumstances:

> Our approach is the one supported by the record before us. The evidence shows that the costs are being overattributed, and it is our

statutory duty to be as accurate as possible in attributing costs. Over-attribution can be just as much an error as the under-attribution proscribed by section 3622(b)(3). Our approach is a better reflection of reality. And, as this record shows, the potential to support the rate design and rate schedules of two subclasses, parcel post and Priority Mail, requires that the costing method be improved.

Id. at III–212. The Commission also explained why it considered the Alaskan air costs caused by and therefore attributable to the Postal Service's universal mail obligation:

In considering these costs and the mail which is being carried on both mainline and bush transportation, we look for the true causal connection. Regardless of how these costs might actually vary with volume, we find that the premium is caused by the statutory obligation to provide universal service rather than the mail volumes. It is true that if none of this mail existed, the costs would not be incurred. It is difficult to believe, however, that this nonpreferential mail would be incurring these very high air costs in the absence of a statutory mandate to serve the entire nation. The Postal Service interprets its duty as one to offer its basic services to every part of the country, and not to deny the lower priced parcel post service to people who live in remote areas which have only expensive transportation available.

Id. at III–213 to –14 (footnote & record citation omitted). The Commission's reasoning adequately supports its bifurcated attribution of Alaskan air costs.

Nevertheless, UPS contends the Commission's use of the premium cost approach violates the Act because it either (1) fails to allocate to Parcel Post the Alaskan air costs that the Commission has found attributable to that subclass or (2) fails in the first instance to find that such costs are attributable to Parcel Post even though the Commission acknowledged the costs "are recognized as being volume variable in nature." UPS's first objection is easily answered: the Commission specifically found that the "premium" air delivery costs are attributable not to Parcel Post service but to the statutory universal service obligation. As for the second, although the Commission has generally used volume variability to attribute costs, the Act itself does not require any specific cost method or define the term "attributable," which, as the Commission's analysis demonstrates, can have various meanings that support various attribution methods. * * *

Instead, the Act "leaves it to the Commissioners, in the first instance, to decide which methods provide reasonable assurance that costs are the result of providing one class of service." * * * Based on its analysis in the 1990 ratemaking decision, we conclude that the Commission's choice of the premium methodology reflects a reasonable construction of the Act and must therefore be upheld.

D. Priority Mail Institutional Costs

UPS next challenges the Commission's allocation of Priority Mail institutional costs. The Commission assigns institutional costs by establishing a separate markup for each class of mail and then applying the markup to the class's attributable costs. In this ratemaking the Commission recommended an institutional markup for Priority Mail of 66.1%. UPS contends this markup is artificially low and shifts to First Class mail institutional costs reasonably assignable to Priority Mail in violation of section 3622(b)(3). We conclude the institutional costs for Priority Mail are, as the statute requires, "reasonably assignable" to the subclass and we therefore uphold them.

As we noted above, once the Commission has established attributable costs under its two-tier cost methodology, it must then allocate institutional costs by " 'reasonably assign[ing]' the remaining costs to the various classes of mail on the basis of the other factors set forth in § 3622(b)." *National Ass'n of Greeting Card Publishers*, 462 U.S. at 815. In assigning Priority Mail institutional costs, the Commission relied heavily on the second statutory factor included in section 3622(b): "the value of the mail service actually provided each class or type of mail service to both the sender and the recipient, including but not limited to the collection, mode of transportation, and priority of delivery." 39 U.S.C. § 3622(b)(2). The Commission cited testimony that Priority Mail has a high "intrinsic value of service," which might justify a higher share of institutional costs, but also noted that it has a "high own-price elasticity," meaning that rate increases might drive away customers despite the high intrinsic value, therefore calling for a lower markup. The Commission further pointed to testimony questioning the value of Priority Mail's service because (1) it often falls short of one- and two-day delivery benchmarks, (2) its service will deteriorate further with implementation of a new processing network service, (3) its market share has been decreasing, and (4) it lacks enhancements available with private priority delivery services, such as automatic insurance coverage, billing, payment and rate options and guaranteed delivery. Based on its perception of the value of Priority Mail service and of the deleterious effect a price increase might have, the Commission concluded that a "reduction in the proportional contribution by Priority Mail is not unreasonable," especially since even the lower markup the Commission recommended led to a rate increase for Priority Mail that exceeded the systemwide average. UPS challenges the 66.1% Priority Mail markup primarily on two grounds. We find neither one persuasive.

First, UPS contends that in the 1997 ratemaking the Commission impermissibly "changed course" without explanation because for the first time it assigned a lower markup to Priority Mail than to regular First Class mail. This argument misapprehends the Commission's institutional cost assignment process. The Commission has not, in this ratemaking or previous ones, assigned the Priority Mail markup based on its relationship to the First Class markup, as is manifest from the widely varying gaps between the two markups in each of the ten ratemakings conducted under the Act. *See* JA vol. I 706. Instead, the Commission assigned the markup here, as before, based on consideration of the mandatory statutory factors. It was these factors, and the second one in particular, that led the Commission to assign lower institutional costs to Priority Mail.

UPS also argues that consideration of the fourth and fifth statutory factors ("the effect of rate increases upon the general public, business mail users, and enterprises in the private sector of the economy engaged in the delivery of mail matter other than letters" and "the available alternative means of sending and receiving letters and other mail matter at reasonable costs," 39 U.S.C. § 3622(b)(4),(5)) requires that the Commission assign lower universal costs to the monopoly regular First Class mail than to Priority Mail because those factors were intended to protect the interests of First Class customers, who have no private alternative, and of Priority Mail competitors, each of which will be harmed by higher First Class and lower Priority Mail rates. We disagree. While the Commission must " 'take into account all the relevant factors and no others,' " *Mail Order Ass'n*, 2 F.3d at 426 (quoting *Association of Am. Publishers,* 485 F.2d at 775), it need not give each factor equal weight. " '[U]nder familiar jurisdictional principles,' " we " 'may not, and under human limitations generally could not, reassess the weights given by a rate-making agency to different factors, absent a legislative direction as to precisely what gravity each factor bears.' " *Id*. (quoting *Association of Am. Publishers,* 485 F.2d at 774–75). Given that the Act provides no such direction, we cannot fault the Commission's determination that the second factor is the decisive one here. In any event, UPS's reading of the statutory provisions it invokes is unduly narrow. By its terms, § 3622(b)(4) allows the Commission to consider lowering rates in order to protect "the general public [and] business mail users," as well as raising them in the interests of "enterprises in the private sector ... engaged in the delivery of mail matter." As to § 3622(b)(5), the Commission has consistently, and reasonably, held that it authorizes a reduction in rates to maintain the position of the Postal Service as a competitor in the mail delivery industry.

* * *

For the preceding reasons, the petitions for review are *Denied*.

Notes and Questions

1.   Think back to the telecommunications cases and the FCC requirement that unbundled facilities be available at prices that reflect the most efficient technology. Would that standard be appropriate in setting postal rates? Could Congress tell the Postal Service that when competing with private carriers it must charge prices that reflect the most efficient technology for handling mail and messages? What might those technologies be?

2.   The Postal Service has long made the allocation of rates to classes of mail on the basis of demand elasticity. What are its assumptions about the

demand elasticity for priority mail? With the growth of e-mail, fax and overnight services, are those assumptions still valid today?

3. The Postal Service has an obligation to provide universal service. Does this mean it must not charge some customers the costs of serving them? If people living in the bush country need not pay the full cost of serving them, who should pay it? What is the logical connection, if any, between universal service and the cost assignment adopted by the Postal Service?

4. What difference does it make to UPS if the Postal Service includes some of the costs of serving people in the bush country of Alaska in institutional costs that are spread throughout the system? Does that amount to taxing some postal customers in order to subsidize others? Why does UPS care what the cost assignment is to priority mail?

5. Looking back at this case and the previous one, what do you make of the effort to use a political process to decide the prices that will be charged in competition with private firms like UPS? Can we have it both ways? Can competition between a regulated firm and an unregulated one ever duplicate what would happen in the market?

3. RATEMAKING ACROSS AN ENTIRE INDUSTRY OR INDUSTRIES

One method of avoiding the complexities of firm-by-firm rate regulation is to set maximum prices or rates on a national or regional scale. In its most expansive form, the price ceiling approach was applied nationwide in the early 1970s to all prices, rents, wages and salaries as an element of macroeconomic policy designed to curb inflation. A smaller scale but especially instructive recent experience with price ceilings concerned the field price of natural gas.

MOBIL OIL EXPLORATION v. UNITED DISTRIBUTION COMPANIES

Supreme Court of the United States, 1991.
498 U.S. 211, 111 S.Ct. 615, 112 L.Ed.2d 636.

JUSTICE WHITE delivered the opinion of the Court.

These cases involve the validity of two orders promulgated by the Federal Energy Regulatory Commission (Commission) to make substantial changes in the national market for natural gas. On petitions for review, a divided panel of the Court of Appeals for the Fifth Circuit vacated the orders as exceeding the Commission's authority under the Natural Gas Policy Act of 1978 (NGPA). In light of the economic interests at stake, we granted certiorari * * *. For the reasons that follow, we reverse and sustain the Commission's orders in their entirety.

I

The Natural Gas Act of 1938 (NGA) was Congress' first attempt to establish nationwide natural gas regulation. Section 4(a) mandated that the present Commission's predecessor, the Federal Power Commission, ensure that all rates and charges requested by a natural gas company for the sale or transportation of natural gas in interstate commerce be "just and reasonable." Section 5(a) further provided that the Commission order a "just and reasonable rate, charge, classification, rule, regulation, practice, or contract" connected with the sale or transportation of gas whenever it determined that any of these standards or actions were "unjust" or "unreasonable."

Over the years the Commission adopted a number of different approaches in applying the NGA's "just and reasonable" standard. * * * Initially the Commission, construing the NGA to regulate gas sales only at the downstream end of interstate pipelines, proceeded on a company-by-company basis with reference to the historical costs each pipeline operator incurred in acquiring and transporting gas to its customers. The Court upheld this approach in FPC v. Hope Natural Gas Co. [320 U.S. 591 (1944)], explaining that the NGA did not bind the Commission to "any single formula or combination of formulae in determining rates."

The Commission of necessity shifted course in response to our decision in Phillips Petroleum Co. v. Wisconsin [347 U.S. 672 (1954)]. *Phillips* interpreted the NGA to require that the Commission regulate not just the downstream rates charged by large interstate pipeline concerns, but also upstream sales rates charged by thousands of independent gas producers. Faced with the regulatory burden that resulted, the Commission eventually opted for an "area rate" approach for the independent producers while retaining the company-by-company method for the interstate pipelines. First articulated in 1960, the area rate approach established a single rate schedule for all gas produced in a given region based upon historical production costs and rates of return. Each area rate schedule included a two-tiered price ceiling: the lower ceiling for gas prices established in "old" gas contracts and a higher ceiling for gas prices set in "new" contracts. The new two-tiered system was termed "vintage pricing" or "vintaging." Vintaging rested on the premise that the higher ceiling price for new gas production would provide incentives that would be superfluous for old gas already flowing because "price could not serve as an incentive, and since any price above average historical costs, plus an appropriate return, would merely confer windfalls." Permian Basin Area Rate Cases [390 U.S. 747 (1968)]. The balance the Commission hoped to strike was the development of gas production through the "new" gas ceilings while ensuring continued protection of consumers through the "old" gas price limits. At the same time the Commission anticipated that the differences in price levels would be "reduced and eventually eliminated as subsequent experience brings about revisions in the prices in the various areas." We upheld the vintage pricing system in *Permian Basin*, holding that the courts lacked the authority to set aside any Commission rate that was within the "zone of reasonableness."

By the early 1970's, the two-tiered area rate approach no longer worked. Inadequate production had led to gas shortages which in turn had prompted a rapid rise in prices. Accordingly, the Commission abandoned vintaging in favor of a single national rate designed to encourage production. Refining this decision, the Commission prescribed a single national rate for all gas drilled after 1972, thus rejecting an earlier plan to establish different national rates for succeeding biennial vintages. But the single national pricing scheme did not last long either. In 1976 the Commission reinstated vintaging with the promulgation of Order No. 770. At about the same time, in Order No. 749, the Commission also consolidated a number of the old vintages for discrete areas into a single nationwide category for all gas already under production before 1973. Despite this consolidation, the Commission's price structure still contained 15 different categories of old gas, each with its own ceiling price. Despite all these efforts, moreover, severe shortages persisted in the interstate market because low ceiling prices for interstate gas sales fell considerably below prices the same gas could command in intrastate markets, which were as yet unregulated.

Congress responded to these ongoing problems by enacting the NGPA, the statute that controls this controversy. The NGPA addressed the problem of continuing shortages in several ways. First, it gave the Commission the authority to regulate prices in the intrastate market as well as the interstate market. Second, to encourage production of new reserves, the NGPA established higher price ceilings for new and hard-to-produce gas as well as a phased deregulation scheme for these types of gas. Finally, to safeguard consumers, §§ 104 and 106 carried over the vintage price ceilings that happened to be in effect for old gas when the NGPA was enacted while mandating that these be adjusted for inflation. Congress, however, recognized that some of these vintage price ceilings "may be too low and authorized the Commission to raise [them] whenever traditional NGA principles would dictate a higher price." * * * The only conditions that Congress placed on the Commission were, first, that the new ceiling be higher than the ceiling set by the statute itself and, second, that it be "just and reasonable" within the meaning of the NGA.

The new incentives for production of new and difficult-to-produce gas transformed the gas shortages of the 1970's into gas surpluses during the 1980s. One result was serious market distortions. The higher new gas price ceilings prevented the unexpected oversupply from translating into lower consumer prices since the lower, vintage gas ceilings led to the premature abandonment of old gas reserves. Accordingly, the Secretary of Energy in 1985 formally recommended that the Commission issue a notice of proposed rulemaking to revise the old gas pricing system. After conducting two days of public hearings and analyzing approximately 113 sets of comments, the Commission issued the two orders under dispute in this case: Order No. 451, promulgated in June 1986, and Order No. 451–A, promulgated in December 1986, which reaffirmed the approach of its predecessor while making certain modifications.

The Commission's orders have three principal components. First, the Commission collapsed the 15 existing vintage price categories of old gas into a single classification and established an alternative maximum price for a producer of gas in that category to charge, though only to a willing buyer. The new ceiling was set at $2.57 per million BTU's, a price equal to the highest of the ceilings then in effect for old gas (that having the most recent, post–1974, vintage) adjusted for inflation. When established the new ceiling exceeded the then-current market price for old gas. The Commission nonetheless concluded that this new price was "just and reasonable" because, among other reasons, it generally approximated the replacement cost of gas based upon the current cost of finding new gas fields, drilling new wells, and producing new gas. * * *

The second principal feature of the orders establishes a "Good Faith Negotiation" (GFN) procedure that producers must follow before they can collect a higher price from current pipeline customers. The GFN process consists of several steps. Initially, a producer may request a pipeline to nominate a price at which the pipeline would be willing to continue purchasing old gas under any existing contract. At the same time, however, this request is also deemed to be an offer by the producer to release the purchaser from any contract between the parties that covers the sale of old gas. In response, the purchaser can both nominate its own price for continuing to purchase old gas under the contracts specified by the purchaser and further request that the producer nominate a price at which the producer would be willing to continue selling any gas, old or new, covered under any contracts specified by the purchaser that cover at least some old gas. If the parties cannot come to terms, the producer can either continue sales at the old price under existing contracts or abandon its existing obligations so long as it has executed a new contract with another purchaser and given its old customer 30–days' notice. The Commission's chief rationale for the GFN process was a fear that automatic collection of the new price by producers would lead to market disruption given the existence of numerous gas contracts containing indefinite price-escalation clauses tied to whatever ceiling the agency established. * * *

* * *

A divided panel of the Court of Appeals for the Fifth Circuit vacated the orders on the ground that the Commission had exceeded its statutory authority. * * * We granted certiorari, and now reverse and sustain the Commission's orders.

II

Section 104 (a) provides that the maximum price for old gas should be * * * priced as it was prior to the enactment of the NGPA, but increased over time in accordance with an inflation formula. This was the regime that obtained under the NGPA until the issuance of the orders at issue here. Section 104(b)(2), however, plainly gives the Commission authority to change this regulatory scheme applicable to old gas * * *.

* * * [T]he statute states that the Commission may increase the ceiling price for "any natural gas (or category thereof, as determined by the Commission)." Likewise, § 104(b)(2) allows the Commission to "prescribe a ceiling price" applicable to any natural gas category. Insofar as "any" encompasses "all," this language enables the Commission to set a single ceiling price for every category of old gas. * * *

Respondents counter that the structure of the NGPA points to the opposite conclusion. Specifically, they contend that Congress could not have intended to allow the Commission to collapse all old gas vintages under a single price where the NGPA created detailed incentives for new and difficult-to-produce gas on one hand, yet carefully preserved the old gas vintaging scheme on the other. We disagree. The statute's bifurcated approach implies no more than that Congress found the need to encourage new gas production sufficiently pressing to deal with the matter directly, but was content to leave old gas pricing within the discretion of the Commission to alter as conditions warranted. The plain meaning of § 104(b)(2) confirms this view.

* * *

Far from binding the Commission, the "just and reasonable" requirement accords it broad ratemaking authority that its decision to set a single ceiling does not exceed. The Court has repeatedly held that the just and reasonable standard does not compel the Commission to use any single pricing formula in general or vintaging in particular. * * *

Respondents contend that even if the statute allows the Commission to set a single old gas ceiling, the particular ceiling it has set is unjustly and impermissibly high. * * * We disagree. There is nothing incompatible between the belief that a price is reasonable and the belief that it ought not to be imposed without prior negotiations. We decline to disallow an otherwise lawful rate because additional safeguards accompany it.

We likewise reject respondents' more fundamental objection that no order "deregulating" the price of old gas can be deemed just and reasonable. The agency's orders do not deregulate in any legally relevant sense. The Commission adopted an approved pricing formula, set a maximum price, and expressly rejected proposals that it truly deregulate by eliminating any ceiling for old gas whatsoever. Nor can we conclude that deregulation results simply because a given ceiling price may be above the market price.

* * *

V

* * * Accordingly, we reverse the judgment of the Court of Appeals and sustain Orders No. 451 and 451–A in their entirety.

Notes and Questions

1. As the Court suggests, the context of the program reviewed in *Mobil Oil* case is important. Congress adopted the Natural Gas Act in 1938 and clearly allowed regulation of gas sold by interstate pipelines to consumers. Indeed, Federal Power Commission v. Hope Natural Gas was such a case. But until 1954, the price of natural gas that the pipelines bought from independent producers at the wellhead was unregulated.

2. As discussed in Chapter 3, supra, all that changed when in Phillips Petroleum Co. v. Wisconsin, 347 U.S. 672, 74 S.Ct. 794, 98 L.Ed. 1035 (1954), the Supreme Court asserted that Congress meant to have the Federal Power Commission regulate wellhead prices of such gas.

a. How should the FPC have undertaken that task? Should it have opened a rate case for each well owner? Does natural gas vary significantly in quality from well to well? If A's costs and hence regulated price had been 10% higher than what became the market price, could A have sold much gas? If B's production costs were 10% lower than other producers and B had paid correspondingly more for the land as a result, should B be forced to charge below-market rates?

b. The fungibility of natural gas and the inevitability of a de facto market price for gas, plus the fact that even the first round of review of the over 11,000 rates on file would have taken an estimated 80 years, led the FPC to adopt "area rates" applicable to all producers in a particular part of the country. The practice was approved in the Permian Basin Area Rate Cases, 390 U.S. 747, 88 S.Ct. 1344, 20 L.Ed.2d 312 (1968).

c. Also in *Permian Basin*, the Court approved a system whereby producers were limited to a rate based on historic costs for "old" gas, i.e., gas produced from already open wells. In order to create an incentive to open new wells, however, a higher rate could be charged for the "new" gas produced from those wells.

3. It is the regime that followed those pre–1970 developments that the Court reviews in *Mobil Oil*.

a. Would you expect a two-tier pricing system to work well in practice? Can one tell old gas from new just by smelling it, for example? Does it come out of the ground with a label? Would you expect firms to put "old" gas in "new" tanks and try to sell it at "new" prices?

b. What problems would you expect to see arise if the Commission set gas prices higher than the costs of drilling required? Would you expect to see "the gas shortages of the 1970s [become] the gas surpluses during the 1980s"?

c. Do you agree with the Court that the Commission did not "deregulate" the price of old gas when it set the ceiling price above the market price? In what meaningful sense is gas still regulated under such a regime? Is the Court in effect simply conceding that the attempt to set the price of gas itself—as opposed to its transportation—was a bad idea?

d. Indeed, might the Court reasonably conclude that the "energy crisis" of the 1970s was itself partly caused by the attempt to regulate the extraordinarily diverse world of domestic oil and gas production? The economics of mistakes in such regulation is suggested in the following note.

A NOTE ON PRICE CEILINGS AND SHORTAGES

THE ECONOMIC THEORY OF PRICE CEILINGS

Figure 19 illustrates the traditional price ceiling model. D1 is the initial demand and S is supply. If the market is free to adjust to these supply and demand conditions, the equilibrium price will be P1 and the equilibrium quantity will be Q1. Price works as a market clearing mechanism. All those willing to pay P1 are able to obtain as much of the good as they want.

Figure 19

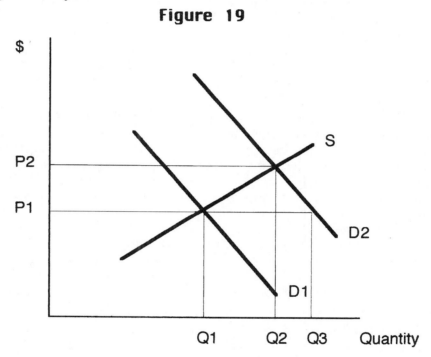

Now suppose demand increases to D2. This might be a result of a number of factors including a change in tastes or preferences or a decrease in the availability of a substitute good. The consequences are fairly clear. If the market is permitted to adjust, the new equilibrium price will be P2 and the new equilibrium quantity will be Q2.

What happens, though, if regulatory officials decide to limit the price to the original level? The quantity demanded at this price is Q3. The quantity supplied, however, is only Q1. The effect of the price ceiling is to create a shortage. In effect, price has failed to be a market clearing device; some of those willing to pay P1 are not able to obtain as much of the good as they want.

THE NATURAL GAS SHORTAGE

The result suggested by economic theory was precisely what happened in the aftermath of area and nationwide price ceilings on natural gas. During the 1970s, environmental legislation increased the attractiveness of natural gas as an industrial fuel. At the same time, actions by OPEC caused the price of crude oil to soar and the demand for natural gas swelled even further. The increased demand, in the context of price ceilings, led to a severe shortage.[63]

Whenever there is a price ceiling induced shortage, another critical problem arises: who is to get the relatively scarce commodity? Since the market has been preempted as a rationing mechanism, the allocation process must be handled administratively. In the case of natural gas, the problem was one of determining which consumers would be required to curtail their use. The choice was between pro rata curtailment with all users absorbing an equal percentage cutback and end-use curtailment with an agency determination of which uses were important enough to be sheltered from the shortage.[64]

Reasoning that it was inconsistent with the public interest to ignore the actual end use of natural gas in devising a curtailment plan, the FPC developed a list of priorities giving highest priority to residential users and lowest priority to large interruptible users where alternatives were available.[65] The rationing problem, however, was far from solved. The curtailment plan was administered on a pipeline-by-pipeline basis and different pipelines had different amounts of natural gas available. Thus, consumers with exactly the same use were subject to different curtailment levels depending upon the pipeline serving their area. Similarly, low priority users in one area were able to obtain gas while higher priority users in other areas were severely curtailed.[66] In effect, the agency's attempt to favor some users over others was far from successful.

Throughout the 1990s the demand for natural gas grew. Supply did not keep pace and the result is an increase in natural gas prices. As an economic matter do you think there is a difference between the "shortages" of the 1970s and the increases in price over the past few years? As a technical matter, as long as price is permitted to allocate what natural gas there is, there is no shortage.

The most recent chapter of this regulatory struggle involves efforts to increase the supply of liquid natural gas by providing incentives to construct facilities suitable for receiving imported liquid natural gas.

63. See Jeffrey L. Harrison and John P. Formby, Regional Distortions in Natural Gas Allocations, 57 North Carolina L. Rev. 57, 67–68 (1978).

64. Arkansas Louisiana Gas Co., 49 F.P.C. 53 (1973), *remanded for further consideration sub nom.* Arkansas Power and Light Co. v. F.P.C., 517 F.2d 1223 (D.C.Cir. 1975), *certiorari denied* 424 U.S. 933, 96 S.Ct. 1146, 47 L.Ed.2d 341 (1976).

65. Order No. 467, 49 F.P.C. 85 (1973).

66. Harrison and Formby, note 63 supra, at 81–86.

WAGE AND PRICE CONTROLS

For a three year period beginning in August 1971 and ending when statutory authorization expired in April 1974, the United States engaged in a much broader program of price controls.[67] The program, designed to curb general inflationary pressures in the economy, started with a 90 day freeze on prices, rent, wages and salaries. Subsequent phases of the program were characterized by less stringency with price increases tied to cost increases.[68]

This experiment with price ceilings as a tool of macroeconomic policy has been extensively studied and compared with earlier wartime controls.[69] The results of the program were mixed. The evidence suggests that the program was initially successful in lowering the rate at which prices increased.[70] As the program progressed, however, the controls became less effective. This was probably due in part to laxity in enforcement.[71] In any case, not surprisingly, shortages occurred, exports increased and the end of the control period was marked by inflation far in excess of precontrol levels. The experience led one commentator to observe that, "We have learned a lot about wage and price controls but not how to control wages and prices."[72]

Since there is not much serious controversy about the basic static theory of controls, why do reputable economists differ over whether controls should be instituted in a given situation? Presumably it is because some economists believe that controls are better than alternative policies and that the problems created by controls are less serious than the consequences of not imposing them.

What was it the congressional majority seemed to believe controls would accomplish? First, they seem to have been arguing that the public would perceive controls as "doing something" about the problem of inflation. Relying on the belief that public confidence is an important element in economic health, one might make the argument that doing something is better than doing nothing.

Second, the argument was made that controls would be less likely than some other measures, i.e. tight money or a deflationary fiscal policy, to stifle or depress economic activity in the country. That is, if

---

67. The program was authorized by Economic Stabilization Act of 1970, Public Law 91–379, 84 Stat. 799, August 15, 1970 (lapsed April 30, 1970).

68. Phase II, (November 14, 1971–January 11, 1973) 6 CFR § 300.11; Phase III, (January 11, 1973–June 13, 1973) 6 CFR § 130.13; Phase IV, (August 12, 1973–April 30, 1974) 6 CFR § 150.73.

69. For an excellent collection of studies see Wage and Price Controls: The U.S. Experiment, (J. Kraft & B. Roberts, eds. 1975); Symposium, Two Years of Wage–Price Controls, 64 Am. Econ. Rev. (No. 2) 82 (1974). See also F.M. Scherer, Industrial Market Structure and Economic Performance 476–80 (2nd ed. 1980).

70. See Robert F. Lanzillotti and Blaine Roberts, The Legacy of Phase II Price Controls, 64 American Econ. Rev. 82, No. 2 (May 1974).

71. See Askin, Wage–Price Controls in Administrative and Political Perspective: The Case of the Price Commission During Phase II, in Wage and Price Controls: The U.S. Experiment 22 (J. Kraft & B. Roberts, eds. 1975).

72. Jones, The Lessons of Wage and Price Controls, in Wage and Price Controls: The U.S. Experiment, supra note 69, at 1.

something is to be done, it is arguably best to use the technique which will cause the least harm.

Finally, it can be argued that controls will help slow the "inflationary psychology" that can build in a time of rising prices. That is, people may tend to buy today in the belief that prices will be higher tomorrow. Because there are only a given number of goods and services available today, that increase in demand may tend to move prices higher in the short run than they would go without this psychology. If people can be given the assurance that prices will *not* be higher tomorrow, then the pattern of demand may assume more nearly a rational long-run level. On our graph, Figure 19, supra, that would be shown as less of a shift in the demand curve toward the right. An economist might say, then, that although the shortage that we described would be present to some extent, it would not be as bad as that which our graph tended to indicate.

4. THE EFFORT TO RELAX RATE REGULATION IN POTENTIALLY COMPETITIVE INDUSTRIES

The move to deregulate rates has not always gone smoothly. In the following case, the Supreme Court called at least a temporary halt to one such effort.

MAISLIN INDUSTRIES v. PRIMARY STEEL INC.

Supreme Court of the United States, 1990.
497 U.S. 116, 110 S.Ct. 2759, 111 L.Ed.2d 94.

JUSTICE BRENNAN delivered the opinion of the Court.

Under the Interstate Commerce Act (Act), motor common carriers must file their rates with the Interstate Commerce Commission (ICC or Commission), and both carriers and shippers must adhere to these rates. This case requires us to determine the validity of a policy recently adopted by the ICC that relieves a shipper of the obligation of paying the filed rate when the shipper and carrier have privately negotiated a lower rate. We hold that this policy is inconsistent with the Act.

I

A

The ICC regulates interstate transportation by motor common carriers to ensure that rates are both reasonable and nondiscriminatory. * * *

The Act requires a motor common carrier to "publish and file with the Commission tariffs containing the rates for transportation it may provide." 49 U.S.C. § 10762(a)(1) (1982 ed.). The Act also specifically prohibits a carrier from providing services at any rate other than the filed (also known as the tariff) rate. * * * Deviation from the filed rate may result in the imposition of civil or criminal sanctions on the carrier or shipper.[73]

As the Court has frequently stated, the statute does not permit either a shipper's ignorance or the carrier's misquotation of the applicable rate to serve as a defense to the collection of the filed rate. * * *

In *Negotiated Rates I* [3 I.C.C.2d 99 (1986)], the Commission adverted to a growing trend in the motor carrier industry whereby carriers and shippers negotiate rates lower than those on file with the ICC, and the shippers are billed for and remit payment at the negotiated rate. In many instances, however, the negotiated rate is never filed with the ICC. In some of those cases, the carrier subsequently files for bankruptcy and the trustee bills the shipper for the difference between the tariff rate and the negotiated rate, arguing that § 10761 compels the collection of the filed rather than negotiated rate. The Commission concluded that, under such circumstances, "it could be fundamentally unfair not to consider a shipper's equitable defenses to a claim for undercharges." The Commission reasoned that the passage of the Motor Carrier Act of 1980, which significantly deregulated the motor carrier industry, justified the change in policy, for the new competitive atmosphere made strict application of § 10761 unnecessary to deter discrimination. Moreover, the Commission asserted that it had authority under § 10701 to determine whether the collection of the undercharge in a particular case would constitute an unreasonable practice.[74]

      * * *

B

This case involves the application of the Commission's new Negotiated Rates policy. It arises from an action by petitioner Maislin Industries, U.S., Inc. (Maislin), to recover freight undercharges for 1,081 interstate shipments performed for a shipper, respondent Primary Steel (Primary), by petitioner's subsidiary, Quinn Freight Lines (Quinn). From 1981 to 1983, Quinn, a motor common carrier certificated by the ICC, privately negotiated rates with Primary that were lower than Quinn's rates then on file with the ICC. Quinn never filed the negotiated rates with the ICC.

---

73. Section 11902 provides that a shipper who knowingly receives a rebate or offset against the filed rate is liable to the Government for a civil penalty in an amount equal to three times the rebate. Section 11903 (a) states that any person who "knowingly offers, grants, gives, solicits, accepts, or receives" service at less than the filed rate "shall be fined at least $1,000 but not more than $20,000, imprisoned for not more than 2 years, or both." A carrier who willfully fails to file and publish its tariffs is subject to the same penalty. See § 11903(b); see also § 11904 (corporate liability). [Court's fn. 2]

74. The Commission stated that its new policy did not "abrogate Section 10761. Rather, we emphasize that carriers must continue to charge the tariff rate, as provided in the statute. The issue here is simply whether we have the authority to consider all the circumstances surrounding an undercharge suit." The Commission rejected a proposal by the National Industrial Transportation League (NITL) that would have declared the negotiated rate to be the maximum reasonable rate. The Commission concluded that the proposal conflicted with § 10761 because it created a "per se determination that, as a matter of law, the negotiated rate would apply." [Court's fn. 3]

In 1983, Maislin filed for bankruptcy, and a post petition audit of its accounts revealed undercharges of $187,923.36 resulting from billing Primary at the negotiated, rather than filed, rates. The agents of the bankrupt estate, pursuant to the authorization of the Bankruptcy Court, issued balance due bills to Primary for these undercharges. When Primary refused to pay the amounts demanded, the estate brought suit in the United States District Court for the Western District of Missouri * * * for the difference between the filed rates and the negotiated rates.

In its answer, Primary alleged that since the parties had negotiated lower rates, rebilling at the tariff rates would constitute an unreasonable practice in violation of § 10701; that the tariff rates themselves were not "reasonable" within the meaning of § 10701; and that the asserted tariff rates were otherwise inapplicable to the shipments at issue. The District Court, finding these matters to be within the primary jurisdiction of the ICC, stayed the proceeding at Primary's request and referred the case to the Commission.

The ICC ruled in Primary's favor, rejecting Maislin's argument that the Commission lacked the statutory power to release a shipper from liability for such undercharges. Relying on *Negotiated Rates I*, the ICC reiterated that § 10701 authorized it to "consider all the circumstances surrounding an undercharge suit" to determine whether collection of the filed rate would constitute an unreasonable practice. In the Commission's view, its role was "to undertake an analysis of whether a negotiated but unpublished rate existed, the circumstances surrounding assessment of the tariff rate, and any other pertinent facts." With respect to the instant controversy, the ICC concluded that Quinn and Primary had negotiated rates other than the tariff rates and that Primary had relied on Quinn to file the rates with the ICC. * * *

The case returned to the District Court where both parties moved for summary judgment. The court granted summary judgment for Primary, rejecting Maislin's argument that the ICC's new policy was, in effect, an impermissible recognition of equitable defenses to the application of the filed rate. The District Court concluded that the ICC's policy of determining case by case whether the collection of undercharges would be an unreasonable practice under § 10701 was based on a permissible construction of the Act. The court also determined that the ICC's finding that Maislin had engaged in an unreasonable practice was supported by substantial evidence.

The Court of Appeals for the Eighth Circuit affirmed, agreeing that the approach taken by the ICC was consistent with the Act. The court reasoned that "[s]ection 10761(a), which mandates the collection of tariff rates, is only part of an overall regulatory scheme administered by the ICC, and there is no provision in the [Act] elevating this section over section 10701, which requires that tariff rates be reasonable." The court concluded: "[T]he proper authority to harmonize these competing provisions is the ICC.... The approach taken by the ICC does not abolish the filed rate doctrine, but merely allows the ICC to consider all of the circumstances, including equitable defenses, to determine if strict adherence to the filed rate doctrine would constitute an unreasonable practice.'' Because the Courts of Appeals have disagreed on the important issue whether the ICC's Negotiated Rates policy is consistent with the Act, we granted certiorari.

II

* * * This Court has long understood that the filed rate governs the legal relationship between shipper and carrier. In Keogh v. Chicago & Northwestern R. Co., 260 U.S. 156, 163 (1922), the Court explained:

> "The legal rights of shipper as against carrier in respect to a rate are measured by the published tariff. Unless and until suspended or set aside, this rate is made, for all purposes, the legal rate, as between carrier and shipper. The rights as defined by the tariff cannot be varied or enlarged by either contract or tort of the carrier. . . . This stringent rule prevails, because otherwise the paramount purpose of Congress—prevention of unjust discrimination— might be defeated.'' (Citations omitted.)

The duty to file rates with the Commission, see § 10762, and the obligation to charge only those rates, see § 10761, have always been considered essential to preventing price discrimination and stabilizing rates. "In order to render rates definite and certain, and to prevent discrimination and other abuses, the statute require[s] the filing and publishing of tariffs specifying the rates adopted by the carrier, and ma[kes] these the legal rates, that is, those which must be charged to all shippers alike.'' Arizona Grocery Co. v. Atchison, T. & S. F. R. Co., 284 U.S. 370, 384 (1932).

Given the close interplay between the duties imposed by §§ 10761– 10762 and the statutory prohibition on discrimination, this Court has read the statute to create strict filed rate requirements and to forbid equitable defenses to collection of the filed tariff. The classic statement of the "filed rate doctrine,'' as it has come to be known, is explained in Louisville & Nashville R. Co. v. Maxwell, 237 U.S. 94 (1915). In that case, the Court held that a passenger who purchased a train ticket at a rate misquoted by the ticket agent did not have a defense against the subsequent collection of the higher tariff rate by the railroad.

> "Under the Interstate Commerce Act, the rate of the carrier duly filed is the only lawful charge. Deviation from it is not permitted upon any pretext. Shippers and travelers are charged with notice of it, and they as well as the carrier must abide by it, unless it is found by the Commission to be unreasonable. Ignorance or misquotation of rates is not an excuse for paying or charging either less or more than the rate filed. This rule is undeniably strict and it obviously may work hardship in some cases, but it embodies the policy which has been adopted by Congress in the regulation of interstate commerce in order to prevent unjust discrimination.''

This rigid approach was deemed necessary to prevent carriers from intentionally "misquoting" rates to shippers as a means of offering them rebates or discounts. * * *

The filed rate doctrine, however, contains an important caveat: The filed rate is not enforceable if the ICC finds the rate to be unreasonable. * * *

  * * *

In the instant case, the Commission did not find that the rates were unreasonable, but rather concluded that the carrier had engaged in an unreasonable practice in violation of § 10701 that should preclude it from collecting the filed rates. The Commission argues that under the filed rate doctrine, a finding that the carrier engaged in an unreasonable practice should, like a finding that the filed rate is unreasonable, disentitle the carrier to collection of the filed rate. We have never held that a carrier's unreasonable practice justifies departure from the filed tariff schedule. But we need not resolve this issue today because we conclude that the justification for departure from the filed tariff schedule that the ICC set forth in its Negotiated Rates policy rests on an interpretation of the Act that is contrary to the language and structure of the statute as a whole and the requirements that make up the filed rate doctrine in particular.

Under the Negotiated Rates policy, the ICC has determined that a carrier engages in an unreasonable practice when it attempts to collect the filed rate after the parties have negotiated a lower rate. The ICC argues that its conclusion is entitled to deference because § 10701 does not specifically address the types of practices that are to be considered unreasonable and because its construction is rational and consistent with the statute. See Chevron U.S.A. Inc. v. Natural Resources Defense Council, Inc., 467 U.S. 837, 843 (1984).

We disagree. For a century, this Court has held that the Act, as it incorporates the filed rate doctrine, forbids as discriminatory the secret negotiation and collection of rates lower than the filed rate. By refusing to order collection of the filed rate solely because the parties had agreed to a lower rate, the ICC has permitted the very price discrimination that the Act by its terms seeks to prevent. * * *

  * * *

  * * * Labeling the carrier's conduct an "unreasonable practice" cannot disguise the fact that the ICC is justifying deviation from the filed rate purely on the ground that the carrier and shipper have privately negotiated a lower rate. Stripped of its semantic cover, the Negotiated Rates policy and, more specifically, the Commission's interpretation of "unreasonable practices" thus stand revealed as flatly inconsistent with the statutory scheme as a whole, and §§ 10761 and 10762 in particular.

  * * *

The ICC maintains, however, that the passage of the Motor Carrier Act of 1980 (MCA), justifies its Negotiated Rates policy. The MCA substantially deregulated the motor carrier industry in many ways in an effort to "promote competitive and efficient transportation services." In addition to loosening entry controls, the MCA also created a zone of reasonableness within which carriers can raise rates without interference from the ICC. More importantly, the MCA also allows motor carriers to operate as both common carriers and contract carriers. A contract carrier transports property under exclusive agreements with a shipper, see § 10102(14), and the Commission has exempted all motor contract carriers from the requirements of §§ 10761 and 10762. The Commission has also relaxed the regulations relating to motor common carriers, most significantly, by allowing decreased rates to go into effect one day after the filing of a tariff. In *Negotiated Rates I and II*, the Commission concluded that in light of the more competitive environment, strict adherence to the filed rate doctrine "is inappropriate and unnecessary to deter discrimination today." According to the Commission, "the inability of a shipper to rely on a carrier's interpretation of a tariff is a greater evil than the remote possibility that a carrier might intentionally misquote an applicable tariff rate to discriminate illegally between shippers."

We reject this argument. Although the Commission has both the authority and expertise generally to adopt new policies when faced with new developments in the industry, it does not have the power to adopt a policy that directly conflicts with its governing statute. Nothing in the MCA repeals §§ 10761 and 10762 or casts doubt on our prior interpretation of those sections. Generalized congressional exhortations to "increase competition" cannot provide the ICC authority to alter the well-established statutory filed rate requirements. * * *

Accordingly, the judgment of the Court of Appeals is reversed, and the cause is remanded for further proceedings consistent with this opinion.

JUSTICE SCALIA, concurring.

I join the Court's opinion but add a few words in response to Justice Stevens' assertion that the Court has "fail[ed] to adhere today to the teaching of *Chevron*."

In my view, the Court correctly relies upon our prior "filed rate" decisions, which were based not on the "regulatory scheme as a whole,"—by which Justice Stevens appears to mean the regulatory climate within which the statute then operated—but rather on the text of the statute. * * *

        * * *

* * * Justice Stevens points to changes in the motor carrier industry occasioned in part by 1980 amendments to the statute, which amendments he says "represented a fundamental policy choice in favor of deregulation." But the only amendments of any relevance to the

requirement of § 10761(a) that a carrier collect no rate other than the filed rate are those that remove certain pre-existing barriers to motor contract carriage—which amendments have the practical effect of making more carriers eligible for the pre-existing exception to the filing requirement of § 10761(a), permitting the Commission to exempt them under certain circumstances, § 10761(b). While this plainly reflects an intent to deregulate, it reflects an intent to deregulate within the framework of the existing statutory scheme. Perhaps deregulation cannot efficiently be accomplished within that framework, but that is Congress' choice and not the Commission's or ours. It may well be, as Justice Stevens thinks, that after the 1980 amendments and the various administrative changes that the Commission has made by rule, " '[t]he skeleton of regulation remains; the flesh has been stripped away.' " But it is the skeleton we are construing, and we must read it for what it says.

JUSTICE STEVENS, with whom THE CHIEF JUSTICE joins, dissenting.

The "filed rate doctrine" was developed in the 19th century as part of a program to regulate the ruthless exercise of monopoly power by the Nation's railroads. Today the Court places an interpretation on that doctrine even more strict than the original version. In doing so, the Court misreads the text of the Interstate Commerce Act (Act), ignores the history of motor carrier regulation in this country, and gives no deference to the sensible construction of the Act by six Courts of Appeals and the administrative agency responsible for its enforcement. Most significantly, the majority fails to appreciate the significance of the "sea change" in the statutory scheme that has converted a regime of regulated monopoly pricing into a highly competitive market. Even wearing his famous blinders, old Dobbin would see through the tired arguments the Court accepts today.

* * *

The action of the Commission in this case faithfully tracks its statutory grant of authority. After considering all of the relevant evidence, the Commission determined "that it would be an unreasonable practice now to require Primary to pay undercharges for the difference between the negotiated rates and the tariff rates." That determination was unquestionably consistent with the plain language of the statute governing the Commission's authority. A carrier's failure to file negotiated rates obviously does not make it reasonable for the carrier to quote low rates and collect higher ones; the Commission is free to find, as it has done, that a practice of misquotation, failure to file, and subsequent collection is unreasonable under § 10701(a).

The Court offers no reason whatsoever to doubt this conclusion. Indeed, the Court's discussion of the statutory text consists almost entirely of vague references to some unarticulated interplay between §§ 10761(a) and 10762(a)(1), an interplay which the Court contends would be "render[ed] nugatory" if carriers are not permitted to obtain payment of the filed rate when they have led shippers to rely upon a lower negotiated rate. For the reasons I have already stated, the text of those provisions does not generate any "interplay" capable of sustaining so rigid an inference. * * *

     * * *

II

Because no particular provision of the statute supports the Court's position, its principal argument must be that the agency's construction of the Act is inconsistent with the regulatory scheme as a whole. There are, of course, important differences between markets in which prices are regulated, either by private cartels or by public authority, and those in which prices are the product of independent decisions by competitors. Rules requiring adherence to predetermined prices are characteristic of regulated markets, but are incompatible with independent pricing in a competitive market. The "filed rate doctrine" has played an important role, not just in the segments of the transportation industry regulated by the Commission, but in other regulated markets as well. It requires the courts to respect the public agency's control over market prices and industry practices; moreover, it significantly reduces the temptation of regulated parties to deviate from the market-wide rules formulated by the agency.

The filed rate doctrine has been a part of our law during the century of regulation of the railroad industry by the Commission. In 1935, when Congress decided to impose economic regulation on the motor carrier industry, partly if not primarily in order to protect the railroads from too much competition,[75] the filed rate doctrine was applied to their rates just as it had previously applied to the railroads. It had the same regulatory purpose.[76] In its applications during the period of regulatory control over

---

75. "Though identical statutory standards govern both motor carrier and rail consolidations, their legislative backgrounds differ. The demand for motor carrier regulation came, not from shippers, as in railroads, but from the roads themselves, who urged that virtually unregulated motor carrier competition threatened railroad financial stability. * * * [T]he Commission was empowered to establish minimum as well as maximum rates. And this minimum rate power was soon utilized by the Commission both to protect the railroads from motor carrier competition as well as to safeguard the motor carrier industry from 'destructive' competition within its own ranks. Indeed, from the inception of motor carrier regulation to the present day, the power to fix minimum rates has been more significant than the authority to fix maximum charges." Report of the Attorney General's National Committee to Study the Antitrust Laws 265 (1955). [Dissent fn. 10]

76. "To understand the purpose of the filed-rate doctrine and hence the Commission's recent efforts to relax it, one must

understand the history of federal regulation of common carriers. Railroads have heavy fixed costs, and in their heyday faced little effective competition from other modes of transportation. Naturally they tended to load the fixed costs onto those shippers who had poor competitive alternatives and to charge low prices to those shippers who had good alternatives by reason of (for example) being big enough to induce two or more railroads to serve their plants. This created a disparity in transportation costs painful to shippers who paid high railroad rates and were competing with shippers who paid low rates, and it also undermined the railroads' efforts to cartelize railroad transportation. The confluence of interests between railroads and weak shippers resulted in a regulatory scheme in which railroads were forbidden both to price off tariff and to refuse service to any shipper at the tariffed rate. The scheme would have been undermined if carriers had been permitted to negotiate secret discounts with favored shippers. To deter this was the office of the filed-rate doctrine. It authorized carriers to

motor carrier rate-making, the doctrine was for the most part applied to reinforce the policies and the decisions of the regulatory agency.

After years of debate over whether it was sound policy to substitute regulation for competition in the motor carrier industry, Congress decided to eliminate the regulatory barriers to free entry and individual ratemaking. The 1980 amendments to the Act represented a fundamental policy choice in favor of deregulation. Overnight the application of the filed rate doctrine in that market became an anachronism. As Judge Posner has explained:

> Many years later came deregulation, which has changed the trucking industry beyond recognition. As a result of amendments made to the Motor Carrier Act in 1980 and their interpretation by the Commission, the present regime is essentially one of free competition. No longer does the ICC seek to nurture and protect cartel pricing and division of markets. A motor carrier that wants to lower its price can file a new tariff effective the following day. No longer does the Commission seek to limit the number of motor carriers, which has more than doubled in less than a decade. Most important, a carrier and shipper who want to get out from under tariff regulation altogether have only to negotiate a contract of carriage, and then the lawful price is the price in the contract rather than in any filed tariff. There used to be all sorts of restrictions on contract carriage, which greatly limited it as an escape hatch from regulation. There are no longer. The skeleton of regulation remains; the flesh has been stripped away.

Orscheln Bros. Truck Lines, Inc. v. Zenith Electric Corp., 899 F.2d 642, 644 (7th Cir.1990).

The significance of these fundamental changes was also noted and explained by Judge Alarcon:

> A variety of practices that previously would have been considered discriminatory are now allowed. For example, the ICC has recently ruled that volume discount rates are not per se unlawful and may be justified by cost savings to the carrier. Moreover, carriers may impose geographic or product line restrictions that must be met to obtain rate reductions.
>
> In addition to increased competitive pressures, statutory changes, and a relaxed regulatory climate, the ICC's Negotiated Rates decisions are a practical response to the information costs faced by shippers. The ease of filing tariffs and the sheer number filed no longer makes it appropriate to allocate the burden of discovering a

recover the discounts regardless, which meant that the shipper could not count on being able to keep any discount that the railroad might dangle before it. Motor carriers do not have heavy fixed costs, but they do not like competition any more than railroads do, so when in 1935 they were brought under federal regulation (in major part to protect the railroads from their competition) they were placed under the filed-rate doctrine too." Orscheln Bros. Truck Lines, Inc. v. Zenith Electric Corp., 899 F.2d, at 643–644. [Dissent fn. 11]

filed rate to the shipper in all cases. Reduced tariff rates may now be filed to become effective on one day's notice.

West Coast Truck Lines, Inc. v. Weyerhaeuser Co., 893 F.2d 1016, 1026 (9th Cir.1990).

The Court catalogs these reforms, but fails to analyze their implications for the "reasonableness" requirement of § 10701(a) and, consequently, for the provisions of § 10761(a). What the Court now misses has been succinctly set forth by Judge Alarcon:

> The ICC's determination that the collection of undercharges constitutes an unreasonable practice if the shipper is unaware of the filed rate is also a reflection of changing legislative goals. Congress modified national transportation policy when it amended 49 U.S. C. § 10101(a) in the Motor Carrier Act of 1980. Section 10101(a)(2) now directs the Commission, 'in regulating transportation by motor carrier, to promote competitive and efficient transportation services in order to (A) meet the needs of shippers, receivers, passengers, and consumers; [and] (B) allow a variety of quality and price options to meet changing market demands and the diverse requirements of the shipping and traveling public. . . .' In addition, § 10101(a)(1)(D) directs the ICC to encourage the establishment of reasonable transportation rates without 'unfair or destructive competitive practices.' 49 U.S.C. § 10101(a)(1)(D) (1982). * * *

> Section 10701(a) provides the ICC with the mechanism to put into effect Congress' restated goals of national transportation policy. By declaring the adherence to filed rates unreasonable under the circumstances presented in this case, the ICC has demonstrated its intention to prevent carriers from engaging in unfair competitive practices.

Weyerhaeuser, 893 F.2d, at 1026–1027.

Despite the Court's puzzling suggestion that the filed rate doctrine is essential to the "core purposes of the Act," the doctrine is instead, as the Court elsewhere seems to concede, "an anachronism in the wake of the [Motor Carrier Act of 1980]." If plain text is a poor basis for the Court's holding, statutory purpose is altogether worse. As Judge Posner has explained:

> Counsel for the carrier in this case—which is to say for the carrier's trustee in bankruptcy—conceded at argument that the motor carrier industry is today highly competitive. But if so, the filed-rate doctrine has lost its raison d'etre. * * *

> * * * Firms in a competitive market cannot discriminate against weak shippers, for even the weak shipper has, by definition of competition, alternative sources of supply to which to turn if one of his suppliers tries to make a monopoly profit off him. 'In the more competitive, more flexible pricing atmosphere created by [deregulation], there is little likelihood of carriers using a rate misquotation as a means to discriminate in favor of particular shippers.' And since

it is no longer the policy of Congress or the ICC to foster monopoly pricing in the motor carrier industry, no public object is served by forcing carriers to adhere to published price schedules regardless of circumstances. * * *

Orscheln, 899 F.2d at 644–45.

Judge Posner's conclusion that strict mechanical adherence to the filed rate doctrine produces absurd results and serves no social purpose, is one that I share. It is likewise shared by the agency charged with administration of the Act.

* * *

IV

Finally, I must express my emphatic agreement with the Commission's conclusion, that an unreasonable practice would result if the carrier in this case were rewarded for violating its duty to file a new rate promptly. There is no evidence of discrimination in this record; nor is there any reason to believe that any shipper or any competing motor carrier was harmed by the negotiated rate or by the failure to file it. The only consequence of today's misguided decision is to produce a bonanza for the bankruptcy bar. "Now that off-tariff pricing is harmless to the (de)regulatory scheme, the only purpose served by making the statutory obligation to price in conformity with published tariffs draconian is to provide windfalls for unsecured creditors in bankruptcy." *Orscheln*, 899 F.2d, at 646.

As Justice Black said more than 30 years ago in similar circumstances, "I am unable to understand why the Court strains so hard to reach so bad a result." T.I.M.E. Inc. v. United States, 359 U.S. 464, 481 (1959) (dissenting opinion). The Court's analysis is plausible only if read as a historical excursus about a statute that no longer exists. Nothing more than blind adherence to language in cases that have nothing to do with the present situation supports today's result.

Notes and Questions

1. Who has the better of the economic merits in this case, the majority or Justice Stevens? Are negotiated rates the only practical way to compete in an economy where shippers have as many alternatives as they do in ours?

2. Were the negotiated rates consistent with I.C.C. policy? Was there any I.C.C. policy that these rates violated?

3. Were other carriers complaining? Was this a case in which someone who had won in the legislative arena was saying that the prize had been taken away by an agency that was not following the law?

4. Most of the cases seeking back rates seem to have been filed in bankruptcy by trustees who were little interested in preserving future good relations with the shippers. See, e.g., Reiter v. Cooper, 507 U.S. 258, 113 S.Ct. 1213, 122 L.Ed.2d 604 (1993) (there is no firm rule as to whether trial

court should defer ruling on claim for filed rates until ICC determines reasonableness of those rates); Security Services, Inc. v. K Mart Corporation, 511 U.S. 431, 114 S.Ct. 1702, 128 L.Ed.2d 433 (1994) (may not collect back rate that had been filed but that was void under ICC regulations). Why should the Court bail out unsecured creditors in this way? Are they among those whom rate regulation is designed to benefit? Was the case simply an occasion for the Court to slow down a deregulatory process that might have seemed to be ignoring the law?

5. In response to the uncertainty that followed these cases, Congress passed the Negotiated Rates Act of 1993, Pub.Law 103–180, 107 Stat. 2044, 49 U.S.C. §§ 10701 et seq. The constitutionality of the Act has been upheld against several challenges, e.g., In re Jones Truck Lines, Inc., 57 F.3d 642 (8th Cir.1995); In re Transcon Lines, 58 F.3d 1432 (9th Cir.1995); Matter of Lifschultz Fast Freight Corp., 63 F.3d 621 (7th Cir.1995); In re Bulldog Trucking, Inc., 66 F.3d 1390 (4th Cir.1995); Hargrave v. United Wire Hanger Corp., 73 F.3d 36 (3d Cir.1996).

Other developments, this time in the energy industry, also produced important new law.

5. THE QUEST FOR FLEXIBLE PRICING

ENVIRONMENTAL ACTION v. FEDERAL ENERGY REGULATORY COMMISSION

United States Court of Appeals, District of Columbia Circuit, 1993.
996 F.2d 401.

Before RUTH BADER GINSBURG, BUCKLEY, and HENDERSON, CIRCUIT JUDGES.

BUCKLEY, CIRCUIT JUDGE:

Petitioners seek review of two orders of the Federal Energy Regulatory Commission approving the Western System Power Pool. Their principal claim is that the Commission erred in allowing a flexible pricing arrangement for the sale and exchange of energy and energy transmission services among the members of the Pool while not requiring that they provide each other with access to their transmission lines at cost. Finding the Commission's action soundly reasoned and substantially supported, we deny the petitions.

I. BACKGROUND

For almost a decade, the Federal Energy Regulatory Commission ("FERC") has been experimenting with power pooling arrangements capable of delivering surplus electricity on a flexible, market-priced basis. In this case, we are asked to review two FERC rulings that authorized, apparently for the first time, the permanent operation of such a pool.

The Commission's interest in the market pricing of electric power traded between utilities dates from its approval of the so-called Southwest Bulk Power Experiment in 1983. In that two-year test, FERC abandoned its traditional practice of linking the price of bulk electricity to cost. It agreed to permit market pricing instead, on the condition that the experiment's six participating utilities would sell transmission services to one another at a pre-specified rate, and that no sale of power would be priced at more than twice the cost-based rate. FERC believed the transmission requirement was crucial to the promotion of competition, as it would enable participants to trade bulk power with all participating utilities, not just those with which they were directly interconnected.

In 1987, FERC approved the Western System Power Pool ("WSPP" or "Pool") as a follow-up to the Southwest Bulk Power Experiment and required the participants to retain independent consultants to monitor and report on the Pool's operation. The new pool began with 15 utilities serving 40 million customers in ten western states, and membership was opened to all utilities connected to the existing members by transmission lines. The terms of the Pool Agreement differed in significant respects from those involved in the Southwest Bulk Power Experiment. The Agreement provided for the more liberal capping of energy prices, which were to be based on the costs of the highest-cost participant. It did not mandate open access to transmission services at cost; rather, these services, like various categories of energy, were to be sold or exchanged at flexible rates.

The most important feature of the Agreement was its establishment of a "hub" or "electronic bulletin board" to provide WSPP members with information about trading opportunities. The hub consisted of a centralized computer that received daily offers to buy or sell energy and transmission services, incorporated them into a standard form, and transmitted the information electronically to all WSPP members. Although the hub itself did not execute sales or exchanges, it provided information about trading possibilities that interested participants could follow up and negotiate directly.

During the WSPP's experimental period, FERC approved market-priced sales of various categories of energy or transmission "products." The energy products traded were "economy energy," "unit commitment service," and "firm system capacity/energy sale or exchange service"; the transmission products were "non-firm service," "standby service," and "firm (or priority) service." The differences between these products are defined by the firmness of the seller's pledge to provide the promised energy or transmission. Nonfirm transmission is interruptible during the next scheduled hour; standby transmission is interruptible subject to an agreed-upon notice period; and firm service is ordinarily not interruptible. Turning to the energy services, economy energy is energy subject to immediate interruption upon notification; unit commitment service is service from a specified generating unit for a specified period; and firm system capacity/energy sale or exchange service is an agreement for selling or exchanging system capacity backed by reserves. The energy products, together, are sometimes referred to as coordination services.

Throughout the experimental period, FERC emphasized that one of the Pool's primary purposes was to reduce costs through coordination— that is, to ensure that electricity is always generated by the least expensive means available, then moved through purchase or exchange to where it is needed.

On December 31, 1990, the Strategic Decision Group ("SDG"), the consulting firm retained by WSPP, issued its report. SDG described the Pool as "an unqualified success," and determined that it had saved consumers $71 million through increased competition and the coordination of trades among the member utilities. SDG calculated the savings by subtracting the dollar value of trades (both sales and exchanges) made possible by the WSPP from the buyers' costs of obtaining electricity in the absence of the Pool. SDG found that the Pool promoted efficiency principally by providing utilities with both information and a flexible regulatory environment. Finally, it estimated that approximately one percent of all the electricity generated by WSPP members was exchanged through trades made possible by the WSPP.

Upon publication of the consultant's report, Pacific Gas and Electric Company, on behalf of the other WSPP participants, petitioned FERC to allow the Pool to operate permanently. By that time, the WSPP had grown to 40 members representing one quarter of the nation's electrical generating capacity, and it covered most of a wedge stretching from Louisiana to British Columbia and west to the Pacific. Of the 40 members, 21 were subject to FERC's jurisdiction, while 19 (government-owned utilities) were not. The WSPP sought to continue its existing arrangement allowing for price flexibility beneath a cap based on the costs of the highest-cost WSPP member.

By the time of the WSPP application, however, prior FERC orders had expressed uneasiness over the high experimental price ceilings and the possibility that sellers of services under the Pool Agreement could wield "market power" to the disadvantage of buyers. In particular, FERC appeared to be concerned about the WSPP's "transmission-dependent" utilities, namely those whose links to the nation's electrical grid are controlled by a single entity. In PG & E II, it specifically requested that the Pool address, in the context of its upcoming request to operate permanently, issues of transmission access and market power.

In response, the WSPP application proposed the so-called "Exhibit C transmission principles." These "principles" required member utilities to provide transmission services to other members on reasonable terms. In theory, such access would open new markets for transmission-dependent utilities, break the monopoly power of those controlling transmission facilities, and eliminate exorbitant prices. After the WSPP application was docketed, petitioners * * * intervened in the proceedings.

On April 23, 1991, FERC accepted the WSPP's application with major modifications. Most importantly, it found that Exhibit C did not go far enough in opening access to transmission lines, providing trading opportunities, and mitigating market power. It found as well that ordering more stringent transmission-access requirements would jeopardize the continued existence of the Pool because of its members' opposition to such commitments.

Accordingly, on its own initiative and as an alternative to the WSPP's system of caps based on the costs of its highest cost participants, FERC developed and published uniform energy and transmission rate ceilings. These were designed to reflect the costs of a "hypothetical" average utility and were set at about half the level of the ceilings in force during the experiment. FERC established the ceilings on the basis of data filed with the Commission by the Pool's FERC-regulated members.

Finally, on rehearing, the Commission modified and clarified its April 23 order. Most significantly, it required that quarterly WSPP transaction reports be filed by FERC-regulated utilities so that both FERC and the WSPP membership could guard against excessive or discriminatory pricing, and it permitted the WSPP to rescind the Exhibit C principles on the ground that they were unnecessary in light of the cost-based ceilings. The Clarification Order also denied petitioners' request for company-specific and product-specific price regulation. These petitions followed.

II.   Discussion

B.   *The Merits*

1.   *Flexible Pricing in the Absence of Transmission Access*

Petitioners' principal contention is that FERC improperly failed to order either open access to transmission lines or company-specific, product-specific pricing within the WSPP. Their theory is that prices must closely track costs of service, whether through the indirect compulsion of the market or the direct command of the Commission. * * *

a.   *Just and Reasonable Rates*

Section 205(a) of the Federal Power Act ("FPA"), 16 U.S.C. § 824d(a) (1988), provides that:

> all rates and charges made ... in connection with the transmission or sale of electric energy subject to the jurisdiction of the Commission, and all rules and regulations affecting or pertaining to such rates or charges shall be just and reasonable....

Petitioners contend that FERC acted arbitrarily and capriciously in finding the ceiling rates it imposed to be just and reasonable. We recently affirmed the following standard for reviewing such claims:

> Issues of rate design are fairly technical and, insofar as they are not technical, involve policy judgments that lie at the core of the regulatory mission. Not surprisingly, therefore, our review is deferential. In determining whether the FERC's decision that a rate design is "just and reasonable," we require only that the agency have made a reasoned decision based upon substantial evidence in the record.

Town of Norwood, Mass. v. FERC, 962 F.2d 20, 22 (D.C.Cir.1992).

We begin with the crucial first step in FERC's own reasoning. In accepting the modified Pool Agreement, FERC reiterated its support for the objective of the WSPP: "to capture economic benefits which were not already covered under existing agreements." To appreciate this statement, one must understand that the Pool provides a mechanism by which member utilities may seize opportunities to trade that would otherwise be uneconomical or difficult to identify. These opportunities vary constantly according to patterns of usage, equipment availability, and weather conditions. The continual communication of basic data among the member utilities enables them to take instant advantage of often short-lived opportunities. Thus, a utility experiencing an unexpected, short-term lull in demand may sell capacity to another experiencing an unexpected, short-term run on electricity. Moreover, such transactions may occur over substantial distances, involve multiple parties, and include various services. In February 1989, for example, the Pacific Northwest experienced an unusual, region-wide cold snap and needed to import power. Several WSPP members serving the region used the hub to locate and purchase excess power from other areas. These utilities told the SDG consultants that without the WSPP mechanism, they would have had to resort to expensive, emergency supply arrangements to meet the demands of their customers.

The orders we review today exemplify FERC's determination to streamline its regulatory processes to keep pace with advances in information technology. Ratemaking is a time-consuming process. Before the Commission accepted the Pool Agreement, as modified by its orders, the member utilities were required to secure FERC's acquiescence in each transaction they undertook. Were they still obliged to petition FERC, or to wait 60 days, every time they wished to consummate a new transaction, they could not take advantage of a host of short-lived opportunities made available by advances in information technology.

By accepting the WSPP Agreement, FERC has approved one set of rate ceilings to apply to all sales of energy products and another for all sales of transmission services. In effect, then, it has pre-approved countless trading arrangements, relying on market forces to keep most individual prices at reasonable levels. The only limitations on these arrangements are that the trades be short-term (lasting one year or less), and that they be priced at or below the pre-set ceilings. Not surprisingly, "ease of contracting with new partners" was the aspect of the Pool cited as "most valuable" by a plurality of the WSPP utilities.

Petitioners complain, first, that FERC declined to order open access to transmission lines at cost-based rates to spur competition within the WSPP. The Exhibit C principles that FERC rejected constituted a pledge by WSPP members to employ specified "building blocks" in reaching bilateral or multilateral transmission agreements. Because WSPP membership is available to all qualifying utilities, Exhibit C represented a giant step toward the conversion of private transmission facilities into common carriers. Not surprisingly, the WSPP filing emphasized repeatedly the unwillingness of its members to go any further than Exhibit C in guaranteeing open access to transmission lines.

On determining that Exhibit C did not go far enough, FERC declined to condition its approval of the WSPP on the WSPP members' agreement to extend it still farther because it was satisfied that the members would not do so. By demanding that the WSPP approval be conditioned on still more stringent access requirements, petitioners would have FERC wager the Pool's proven efficiencies in a gamble to create an even better market. Given the WSPP's unquestioned benefits and the evidence that stronger transmission commitments could not be obtained, we do not find FERC's refusal to accede either arbitrary or unreasonable.

Petitioners' second and more substantial contention is that FERC acted arbitrarily by choosing a system of pricing flexibility over one fixed by regulation on a company-by-company, product-by-product basis. FERC offered three reasons for choosing pricing flexibility over greater pricing regulation.

First, FERC invoked the "administrative benefits" of flexible pricing. The Commission described the "umbrella nature" of the WSPP agreement as an element "essential" to its success. It pointed to SDG's findings regarding "ease of contracting with new partners," which was named by a plurality of the WSPP membership as the "most valuable" aspect of the arrangement. And it specifically declined to order product-specific pricing, saying it wanted to allow participants the flexibility to buy and sell services with varying characteristics.

Although FERC did not expand further on these themes, we think its meaning is apparent. The administrative work involved in establishing and adhering to product and company-specific rates is both extensive and expensive; thus, it would constitute a disincentive both to joining and to using the Pool. And this expense, significant in any case, could be redoubled here. Petitioners have asked FERC not only to establish cost-based rates, but also to scrutinize costs to ensure that the approved rates reflect only that share of actual costs that was "prudently" incurred. It is true, of course, that the company- and product-specific rates petitioners advocate would be pre-approved, and thus that they would retain some of the benefits of the scheme approved by FERC. Still, the administrative burdens of establishing and implementing petitioners' complicated rate structure would be substantial.

Second, FERC noted that it had been its "consistent practice, in evaluating ceilings to be used to price transactions that will occur from time to time without Commission review," to adopt cost-based uniform ceilings applicable to all services, whether firm or nonfirm. In this manner, utilities would have "the greatest flexibility ... to negotiate prices that reflect the service characteristics that will vary from time to time," while capping prices at reasonable levels. It also noted that this policy was based on the presumption "that differences in the quality of the service will, in fact, be reflected in the discount below the ceiling offered by the supplier, i.e., nonfirm services will be offered at prices lower than firm services," adding that if this presumption were not vindicated in practice, interested parties could register their complaints with the Commission under section 206 of the Federal Power Act. FERC admitted that the Pool ceilings were a compromise, but it found them reasonable because they were based on the average fixed costs of the facilities used by the WSPP members in providing their services.

This approach to price regulation may have reflected a fear on FERC's part that the more rigid approach to pricing urged by petitioners would have robbed the pooling arrangement of much of its efficiency. In its analysis of the Southwest Bulk Power Experiment, FERC recognized that regulation by product can sometimes distort the marketplace, as trades are structured to take advantage of higher price ceilings rather than to meet the needs of utilities. For instance, where prices are capped by product, and where demand for economy energy service outstrips supply, two utilities wishing to trade economy energy at higher-than-ceiling prices might agree to trade power on a firm basis instead, just to take advantage of the higher price cap that would apply to such a trade. Under a product-specific pricing regime, then, trades may occur either because the parties wish to purchase and sell the product involved, or because they wish to avail themselves of that product's price ceiling. Where trade occurs for the latter reason, the regulatory regime, not the needs of the utilities involved, has determined what product was traded; and one may rightly say that the pattern of trading in the market has been distorted by regulation.

Finally, FERC feared that stricter regulation would foreclose transaction opportunities, reducing the efficiency savings to be realized through the WSPP. Because WSPP transactions are consummated between willing and informed buyers and sellers, one may assume that transactions within the Pool promote efficiency. Buyers presumably buy from others only when doing so is less costly than the alternative, such as generating the extra power themselves. Therefore, in the absence of monopoly power, price ceilings will impinge on efficiency by forbidding sales that can occur only at higher-than-ceiling rates. Because the more restrictive pricing policy favored by petitioners would effect a net reduction in FERC-ordered rate ceilings, which are currently based on the cost of the most valuable product traded, firm energy, the adoption of product-based rates could only diminish the effectiveness achieved by WSPP.

Similarly, company-specific ceilings, while they would be higher in some cases and lower in others, would also be likely to decrease efficiency. FERC found that the steep cuts it ordered in the experimental Pool-wide rate ceilings (about 38 percent for firm transmission and approximately 46 to 66 percent for firm energy) would reduce transaction volumes for both energy and transmission services by approximately ten percent. It appears from this that transactions occur most frequently toward the low end of the currently permissible price range. If so, then lowering the current ceilings for low-cost companies could be expected to foreclose many more transactions than raising the ceilings for high-cost companies would allow.

Petitioners' complaint, in essence, is that FERC struck the wrong balance between promoting efficiency and ensuring that efficiency gains are widely distributed. They do not dispute that the regulation they seek could compromise overall efficiency through greater administrative burdens, distorted trading patterns, and foreclosed transaction opportunities. Rather, they argue that such regulation, even with its attendant losses, is needed to prevent monopoly returns from being reaped in certain transactions. FERC allowed a large degree of pricing flexibility, while forbidding trades above rates that it thought unreasonable in most circumstances. It ordered disclosure of all transaction prices, thus putting WSPP members on notice that their transactions would be monitored. At the same time, it reminded the participating utilities that in the event of any abuses of the latitude allowed them, the Commission and interested parties could seek redress under section 206. In sum, FERC sought to preserve the Pool's efficiencies even as it guarded against price gouging. On the facts in evidence, we find no basis for concluding it acted unreasonably.

b. Discriminatory Rates

The FPA forbids public utilities from "maintaining any unreasonable difference in rates ... either as between localities or as between classes of service." Petitioners argue that flexible pricing will lead to unreasonable price differences at the expense of utilities that are dependent on a single entity for access to the national electrical grid. Again, we disagree.

In previous cases, we have upheld the Commission in outlawing pool rates that would inevitably impose disproportionate burdens on certain utilities. We have also overturned the Commission where a rate design on its face produced discriminatory cross-subsidizations of some customers by others. What is alleged here, however, is not discrimination that "seems clear from the [rate's] formulation," but potential discrimination made possible by pricing flexibility. Under like circumstances in the context of natural gas regulation, we have recognized FERC's authority to police potential price discrimination through broad monitoring and individualized enforcement, so long as doing so does not "carry such a risk of allowing undue discrimination or preferences as to be arbitrary and capricious." Because the relevant provisions of the Federal Power and Natural Gas Acts are "substantially identical," we apply the same standards here.

The factors bearing on FERC's willingness to accept a certain risk of price discrimination are akin to those supporting its finding that the price ceilings are just and reasonable. FERC apparently accepted SDG's conclusion that only the most disadvantageously positioned of the transmission-dependent utilities (the so-called "captives") would be significantly affected by any abuses of market power. This group consisted of only five of the 40 WSPP members. FERC also noted that the transaction reporting requirements would make it easier for any victim of discriminatory pricing to seek relief under section 206 of the FPA.

We acknowledge that the flexible pricing that fosters trading among the members of the Pool also permits price discrimination, especially against captive utilities. Yet given the benefits of this trading, the limited number of captive members, and the provisions for monitoring transactions and remedying any abuses of market power, we do not find that the Commission acted arbitrarily when it approved the use of flexible prices, despite their admitted risks.

* * *

In view of the foregoing, the petitions for review of FERC's decision are denied.

Notes and Questions

1. What was the purpose of this pooling arrangement? Was it a logical step toward eliminating the treatment of electrical utilities as natural monopolies altogether? Such plans do seem to be popular among regulators trying to help the industry run efficiently.

2. How was the scheme to work? Did anyone have to look over the firms' shoulders and determine whether their purchase and sale decisions were "prudent"? Were all the buyers and sellers in the industry likely sophisticated enough to deal at arm's length without having someone take advantage of their need or inexperience?

3. Who were the potential losers from this arrangement? Were there some "captive" users or resellers who would always wind up paying the highest prices? What defenses, if any, would they have to prevent "abuse" by the pool members?

4. How, if at all, does this case relate to *Maislin Industries*, supra? Was this Court stretching to find that FERC had authority to approve the flexible dealing permitted within this pool?

5. The Supreme Court continues to be less willing than the courts of appeal to allow the agencies flexibility to experiment with granting waivers of their procedures as they try to introduce competition into an industry. See, e.g., MCI Telecommunications Corp. v. American Telephone & Telegraph Co., 512 U.S. 218, 114 S.Ct. 2223, 129 L.Ed.2d 182 (1994) (FCC action in excusing non-dominant carriers like MCI from filing tariffs was improper as more than a "modification" of the 120–day advance filing requirement imposed on AT & T, the largest carrier in the industry).

Chapter 5

CREATIVE APPROACHES TO REGULATION: COST–BENEFIT ANALYSIS, SELF–REGULATION AND PRIVATIZATION

Throughout this book we have stressed the reasons for regulation and the ways in which the decision to regulate may be influenced by them. But the fact that markets may be technically imperfect or may produce outcomes that are not uniformly viewed as desirable does not mean that regulation should be imposed. Spotting a problem can be a quite different exercise from deciding what should be done about it. It is easy to imagine a situation in which regulation could produce a worse outcome than the imperfect status quo. Regulatory techniques are instruments to achieve public good. They are best handled like scalpels in the hands of surgeons, rather than broadswords in the hands of crusaders.

In Chapter 3, our analysis was built upon traditional Public Interest grounds for regulation. This Chapter raises emerging issues of Public Administration—how to govern better or even how to "reinvent government."[1] Justice Stephen Breyer, for example, while still an academic, called for "matching" regulatory responses to market realities, so as to use incentives rather than coercion to encourage public-private solutions.[2] Later, Professors Ayres and Braithwaite argued for government to enforce self regulation of the private sector as a way of reaching elusive public goals.[3] And, recently, Professor Freeman has argued for a process of "publicization" that would infuse privatization proposals with democratic norms of accountability.[4]

---

1. See, e.g., David Osborne & Ted Gaebler, Reinventing Government—How the Entrepreneurial Spirit is Transforming the Public Sector (1992). An important new procedure for considering regulatory options—"negotiated rulemaking" or "Reg–Neg"—has been codified in the Negotiated Rulemaking Act of 1990, 5 U.S.C. §§ 581–90. See note, infra at section C.

2. Stephen Breyer, Regulation and Its Reform (1982). Justice Antonin Scalia, while an academic, likewise highlighted many weaknesses in regulation as editor of *Regulation* magazine.

3. Ian Ayres & John Braithwaite, Responsive Regulation (1992).

Proposals for reform have established an important agenda for government leaders.[5] Perhaps the most difficult issue is one of measuring inputs and outputs. Since government does not produce "products" that have a "price" in the marketplace, how can citizens know when government is producing benefits that justify the resources government consumes? Thus, while deregulation and privatization have become popular ideas, disagreement still arises over what functions are best performed by government and at what levels.[6]

A less controversial approach to improving the process is to require government agencies to be more accountable and strategic. For example, the Government Results and Performance Act of 1993[7] requires performance-based budgeting and provides "a new focus on results, service quality, and customer satisfaction." When coupled with approaches to minimize regulatory burdens such as transferable rights to pollute and programs of self regulation discussed in this Chapter, performance accountability in budgeting may offer a hopeful first step toward more intelligent regulation.

For the most part, the materials in this Chapter deal with instances in which there are externalities and high transaction costs. It is in these contexts that parties are unable to use private agreements to overcome inefficiencies. Thus, one way to approach these materials is to ask whether the outcome is the same as that the affected parties would have reached in the absence of transaction costs.

It may also be useful to approach the materials from the perspective of a government regulator who must "balance" not only costs and benefits, but the often opaque regulatory directives of Congress, the sometimes inflexible demands of a concerned public, and the frequently antagonistic responses of a skeptical if not hostile business sector. In this setting, clear thinking on transactional—let alone non-transactional—costs and benefits is understandably in short supply.

For example, assume that you are on the staff of the OMB's Office of Information and Regulatory Affairs (OIRA) whose task it is to monitor, review and, where feasible, improve the regulatory and cost-benefit analysis of federal agencies. You are governed by Executive Order 12,866 which was issued in the Clinton Administration but has not been changed by President Bush. It is hardly a complete guide to the balancing choices you will be called upon to make, but it does recommend cost-benefit analysis as a regulatory default principle.[8] To further assist you, a blue-ribbon panel of economists has offered the following guidance:[9]

4. Jody Freeman, Extending Public Law Norms Through Privatization, 116 Harv. L. Rev. 1285 (2003).

5. See, e.g., Paul Verkuil, Is Efficient Government an Oxymoron?, 43 Duke L.J. 1221 (1994).

6. See, e.g., Donald K. Kettl & John J. DiIulio, Jr., Cutting Government (1995)

(trying to answer these questions in a preliminary way).

7. Pub. Law 103–62, 107 Stat. 285 (1993).

8. See Cass R. Sunstein, Cost–Benefit Default Principles, 99 Mich. L. Rev. 1651 (2002) (describing a common law regulatory review principle that defaults to cost-benefit analysis).

Benefit-cost analysis should be required for all major regulatory decisions, but agency heads should not be bound by a strict benefit-cost test. Instead, they should be required to consider available benefit-cost analyses and to justify the reasons for their decision in the event that the expected costs of a regulation far exceed the expected benefits. Agencies should be encouraged to use economic analysis to help set regulatory priorities. Economic analyses prepared in support of particularly important decisions should be subjected to peer review both inside and outside government.

Benefits and costs of proposed major regulations should be quantified wherever possible. Best estimates should be presented along with a description of the uncertainties. Not all benefits or costs can be easily quantified, much less translated into dollar terms. Nevertheless, even qualitative descriptions of the pros and cons associated with contemplated action can be helpful. Care should be taken to assure that quantitative factors do not dominate important qualitative factors in decisionmaking.

With that guidance in hand, are you prepared for your task? What puzzles do you still face? In the materials that follow, consider both how far cost-benefit analysis has come and also how far it still has to go. And keep in mind that CBA is viewed as a controversial practice since it sets (and trades off) safety and health benefits against financial costs.[10]

A. THE EVOLUTION OF COST–BENEFIT ANALYSIS

In very general terms, if the costs or risks of a regulation are greater than the expected benefits, the regulation should not be undertaken. In other words—paraphrasing the Hippocratic Oath—we should not adopt regulatory programs that do more harm than good. Of course, underlying this simple statement are a host of complex issues, the most general of which is what costs and benefits count? Moreover, as the next case illustrates, to some, the question of which costs and benefits are to be considered is one for legislators and judges, not one for economic experts. After the "proper umpire" issue is resolved comes the challenge of giving weight to each of the costs and benefits and deciding which predominate. As we will see, these questions can be at least equally controversial.

9. Kenneth Arrow, et al., Benefit–Cost Analysis in Environmental, Health, and Safety Regulation—A Statement of Principles 3 (1996). We use the term cost-benefit analysis (or CBA) in this casebook for consistency.

10. See W. Kip Viscusi, Corporate Risk Analysis: A Reckless Act? 52 Stan. L. Rev. 547, 586–88 (2000) (mock jurors were more likely to award punitive damages against manufacturers who engaged in CBA).

1. WHEN IS A COST A RELEVANT COST?

METROPOLITAN EDISON CO. v. PEOPLE AGAINST NUCLEAR ENERGY

Supreme Court of the United States, 1983.
460 U.S. 766, 103 S.Ct. 1556, 75 L.Ed.2d 534.

JUSTICE REHNQUIST delivered the opinion of the Court.

The issue in these cases is whether petitioner Nuclear Regulatory Commission (NRC) complied with the National Environmental Policy Act, 42 U.S.C. § 4321 et. seq. (NEPA), when it considered whether to permit petitioner Metropolitan Edison Co. to resume operation of the Three Mile Island Unit 1 nuclear power plant (TMI–1). The Court of Appeals for the District of Columbia Circuit held that the NRC improperly failed to consider whether the risk of an accident at TMI–1 might cause harm to the psychological health and community well-being of residents of the surrounding area. We reverse.

Metropolitan owns two nuclear power plants at Three Mile Island near Harrisburg, Pennsylvania. Both of these plants were licensed by the NRC after extensive proceedings, which included preparation of Environmental Impact Statements (EIS). On March 28, 1979, TMI–1 was not operating; it had been shut down for refueling. TMI–2 was operating and it suffered a serious accident that damaged the reactor. Although, as it turned out, no dangerous radiation was released, the accident caused widespread concern. The Governor of Pennsylvania recommended an evacuation of all pregnant women and small children, and many area residents left their homes for several days.

After the accident, the NRC ordered Metropolitan to keep TMI–1 shut down until it had an opportunity to determine whether the plant could be operated safely. The NRC then published a notice of hearing specifying several safety related issues for consideration. The notice stated that the Commission had not determined whether to consider psychological harm or other indirect effects of the accident or of renewed operation of TMI–1. It invited interested parties to submit briefs on this issue.

Petitioner People Against Nuclear Energy (PANE), intervened and responded to this invitation. PANE is an association of residents of the Harrisburg area who are opposed to further operation of either TMI reactor. PANE contended that restarting TMI–1 would cause both severe psychological health damage to persons living in the vicinity, and serious damage to the stability, cohesiveness, and well-being of the neighboring communities.[11]

---

11. Specifically, PANE contended:

"1.) Renewed operation of ... TMI–1 would cause severe psychological distress to PANE's members and other persons living in the vicinity of the reactor. The accident at [TMI–2] has already impaired the health and sense of well being of these individuals, as evidenced by their feelings of increased anxiety, tension and fear, a sense of helplessness and such physical disorders as skin rashes, aggravated ulcers, and skeletal and muscular problems. Such manifestations of psychological distress have been seen in the aftermath of other disasters. The possibility that [TMI–1] will reopen severely aggravates these problems. As long as this possibility exists, PANE's members and other person's living in the communities around the plant will be unable to resolve

The NRC decided not to take evidence concerning PANE's contentions. PANE filed a petition for review in the Court of Appeals, contending that both NEPA and the Atomic Energy Act, 42 U.S.C. § 2011 et seq., require the NRC to address its contentions. Metropolitan intervened on the side of the NRC.

The Court of Appeals concluded that the Atomic Energy Act does not require the NRC to address PANE's contentions. It did find, however, that NEPA requires the NRC to evaluate "the potential psychological health effects of operating" TMI–1 which have arisen since the original EIS was prepared. It also held that, if the NRC finds that significant new circumstances or information on the subject, it shall prepare a "supplemental [EIS] which considers not only the effects on psychological health but also effects on the well being of communities surrounding Three Mile Island." We granted certiorari.

All the parties agree that effects on human health can be cognizable under NEPA, and that human health may include psychological health. The Court of Appeals thought these propositions were enough to complete a syllogism that disposes of the case: NEPA requires agencies to consider effects on health. An effect on psychological health is an effect on health. Therefore, NEPA requires agencies to consider the effects on psychological health asserted by PANE. PANE, using similar reasoning, contends that because psychological health damage to its members would be caused by a change in the environment (renewed operation of TMI–1), NEPA requires the NRC to consider that damage. Although these arguments are appealing at first glance, we believe they skip over an essential step in the analysis. They do not consider the closeness of the relationship between the change in the environment and the "effect" at issue.

Section 102(C) of NEPA, 42 U.S.C. § 4332(C), directs all federal agencies to

and recover from the trauma from which they have suffered. Operation of [TMI–1] would be a constant reminder of the terror which they felt during the accident, and of the possibility that it will happen again. The distress caused by this ever present specter of disaster makes it impossible . . . to operate TMI–1 without endangering the public health and safety.

"2.) Renewed operation of TMI–1 would cause severe harm to the stability, cohesiveness and well being of the communities in the vicinity of the reactor. Community institutions have already been weakened as a result of loss of citizen confidence in the ability of these institutions to function properly and in a helpful manner during a crisis. The potential for a reoccurrence of the accident will further stress the community infrastructure, causing increased loss of confidence and a breakdown of the social and political order. Sociologists such as Kai Erikson have documented similar phenomena in other communities following disasters.

"The perception, created by the accident, that the communities near Three Mile Island are undesirable locations for business and industry, or for the establishment of law or medical practice, or homes compounds the damage to the viabilities of the communities. Community vitality depends upon the ability to attract and keep persons, such as teachers, doctors, lawyers, and businesses critical to economic and social health. The potential for another accident, should TMI–1 be allowed to operate, would compound and make permanent damage, trapping the residents in disintegrating and dying communities and discouraging * * * essential growth." [Court's fn. 2]

include in every recommendation or report on proposals for legislation and other major Federal actions significantly affecting the quality of the human environment, a detailed statement by the responsible official on—

> (i) the environmental impact of the proposed action, [and]

> (ii) any adverse environmental *effects* which cannot be avoided should the proposal be implemented * * *

To paraphrase the statutory language in light of the facts of this case, where an agency action significantly affects the quality of the human environment, the agency must evaluate the "environmental impact" and any unavoidable adverse environmental effects of its proposal. The theme of § 102 is sounded by the adjective "environmental": NEPA does not require the agency to assess *every* impact or effect of its proposed action, but only the impact or effect on the environment. If we were to seize the word "environmental" out of its context and give it the broadest possible definition, the words "adverse environmental effects" might embrace virtually any consequence of a governmental action that some one thought "adverse." But we think the context of the statute shows that Congress was talking about the physical environment—the world around us, so to speak. NEPA was designed to promote human welfare by alerting governmental actors to the effect of their proposed actions on the physical environment.

The statements of two principal sponsors of NEPA, explaining to their colleagues the Conference Report that was ultimately enacted, illustrate this point:

> What is involved [in NEPA] is a declaration that we do not intend as a government or as a people to initiate actions which endanger the continued existence or the health of mankind: That *we will not intentionally initiate actions which do irreparable damage to the air, land, and water* which support life on earth. 115 Cong.Rec. 40416 (1969) (Remarks of Sen. Jackson) (emphasis supplied).

> [W]e can now move forward to *preserve and enhance our air, aquatic, and terrestrial environments* * * * to carry out the policies and goals set forth in the bill to provide each citizen of this great country a healthful environment. 115 Cong.Rec. 40924 (1969) (remarks of Senator Dingell) (emphasis supplied).

Thus, although NEPA states its goals in sweeping terms of human health and welfare,[12] these goals are ends that Congress has chosen to pursue by means of protecting the physical environment.

---

12. For example, § 2 of NEPA, 42 U.S.C.§ 4321, provides:

"The purpose, of this chapter are: To declare a national policy which will encourage productive and enjoyable harmony between man and his environment; to promote efforts which will prevent or eliminate damage to the environment and biosphere and stimulate the health and welfare of man; to enrich the understanding of the ecological systems and natural resources important to the Nation; and to establish a Council on Environmental Quality." [Court's fn. 6]

To determine whether § 102 requires consideration of a particular effect and the change in the physical environment caused by the major federal action at issue. For example, if the Department of Health and Human Services were to implement extremely stringent requirements for hospitals and nursing homes receiving federal funds, many perfectly adequate hospitals and homes might be forced out of existence. The remaining facilities might be so limited or so expensive that many ill people would be unable to afford medical care and would suffer severe health damage. Nonetheless, NEPA would not require the Department to prepare an EIS evaluating that health damage because it would not be proximately related to a change in the physical environment.

Some effects that are "caused by" a change in the physical environment in the sense of "but for" causation, will nonetheless not fall within § 102 because the causal chain is too attenuated. For example, residents of the Harrisburg area have relatives in the other parts of the country. Renewed operation of the TMI–1 may well cause psychological health problems for these people. They may suffer "anxiety, tension and fear, a sense of helplessness," and accompanying physical disorders because of the risk that their relatives may be harmed in a nuclear accident. However, this harm is simply too remote from the physical environment to justify requiring the NRC to evaluate the psychological health damage to these people that may be caused renewed operation of TMI–1.

Our understanding of the congressional concerns that led to the enactment of NEPA suggests that the terms "environmental effect" and "environmental impact" in § 102 be read to include a requirement of a reasonably close casual relationship between a change in the physical environment and the effect at issue. This requirement is like the familiar doctrine of proximate cause from tort law. See generally W. Prosser, Law of Torts Ch. 7 (4th ed. 1971).[13] The issue before us, then, is how to give content to this requirement. This is a question of first impression in this Court.

The federal action that affects the environment in this case is permitting renewed operation of TMI–1. The direct effects on the environment of this action include release of low-level radiation, increased fog in the Harrisburg area (caused by operation of the plant's cooling towers), and the release of warm water into the Susquehanna River. The NRC has considered each of these effects in its EIS, and again in the EIA. Another effect of renewed operation is a risk of a nuclear accident. The NRC has also considered this effect.[14]

---

13. In drawing this analogy, we do not mean to suggest that any cause-effect relation too attenuated to merit damages in a tort suit would also be too attenuated to merit notice in an EIS; nor do we mean to suggest the converse. In the context of both tort law and NEPA, courts must look to the underlying policies or legislative intent to draw a manageable line between those casual changes that may make an actor re-

sponsible for an effect and those that do not. [Court's fn. 7]

14. The NRC concluded that the risk of an accident had not changed significantly since the EIS for TMI–1 was prepared in 1972.

We emphasize that in this case we are considering effects caused by the risk of an accident. The situation where an agency is

PANE argues that the psychological health damage it alleges "will flow directly from the risk of [a nuclear] accident." But a *risk* of an accident is not an effect of the physical environment. A risk is, by definition, unrealized in the physical world. In a causal chain from renewed operation of TMI–1 to psychological health damage, the element of risk and its perception by PANE's members are necessary middle links.[15] We believe that the element of risk lengthens the causal chain beyond the reach of NEPA.

Risk is a pervasive element of modern life; to say more would belabor the obvious. Many of the risks we face are generated by modern technology, which brings both the possibility of major accidents and opportunities for tremendous achievements. Medical experts apparently agree that risk can generate stress in human beings, which in turn may rise to the level of serious health damage. For this reason among many others, the question whether the gains from any technological advance are worth its attendant risks may be an important public policy issue. Nonetheless, it is quite different from the question whether the same gains are worth a given level of alteration of our physical environment or depletion of our natural resources. The latter question rather than the former is the central concern of the NEPA.

Time and resources are simply too limited for us to believe that Congress intended to expand NEPA as far as the Court of Appeals has taken it. See Vermont Yankee Nuclear Power Corp. v. NRDC, 435 U.S. 519, 551, 98 S.Ct. 1197, 1215, 55 L.Ed.2d. 460 (1978). The scope of the agency's inquiries must remain manageable if NEPA's goal of "ensur[ing] a fully informed and well considered decision," is to be accomplished.

If contentions of psychological health damage caused by risk were cognizable under NEPA, agencies would, at the very least, be obliged to expend considerable resources developing psychiatric expertise that is not otherwise relevant to their congressionally assigned functions. The available resources may be spread so thin that agencies are unable adequately to pursue protection of the physical environment and natural resources. As we said in another context in United States v. Dow, 357 U.S. 17, 25, 78 S.Ct. 1039, 1046, 2 L.Ed.2d. 1109 (1958), "[w]e cannot attribute to Congress the intention to * * * open the door to such obvious incongruities and undesirable possibilities."

This case bears strong resemblance to other cases in which plaintiffs have sought to require agencies to evaluate the risk of crime from the operation of a jail or other public facility in their neighborhood. See e.g., Como–Falcon Coalition, Inc. v. Department of Labor, 609 F.2d 342

---

asked to consider effects that will occur if a risk is realized, for example, if an accident occurs at TMI–1, is an entirely different case. The NRC considered, in the original EIS and in the most EIA for TMI–1, the possible effects of a number of accidents that might occur at TMI–1. [Court's fn. 9]

15. This risk can be perceived differently by different people. Indeed, it appears that the members of PANE perceive much greater risk of another nuclear accident at Three Mile Island than is perceived by the NRC and its staff. [Court's fn. 10]

(C.A.8 1979) (Job Corps Center); Nucleus of Chicago Homeowners Association v. Lynn, 524 F.2d 225 (C.A.7 1975) (low income housing); First National Bank of Chicago v. Richardson, 484 F.2d 1369 (C.A.7 1973) (jail). The plaintiffs in these cases could have alleged that the risk of crime (or their dislike of the occupants of the facility) would cause severe psychological health damage.[16] The operation of the facility is an event in the physical environment, but the psychological health damage to neighboring residents resulting from unrealized risks of crime is too far removed from that event to be covered by NEPA. The psychological health damage alleged by PANE is no closer to an event in the environment or to environmental concerns.

The Court of Appeals thought PANE's contentions are qualitatively different from the harm at issue in the cases just described. It thought PANE raised an issue of health damage, while those cases presented questions of fear or policy disagreement. We do not believe this line is so easily drawn. Anyone who fears or dislikes a project may find himself suffering from "anxiety, tension, fear, [and] a sense of helplessness," Neither the language nor the history of NEPA suggest that it was intended to give citizens a general opportunity to air their policy objections to proposed federal actions. The political process, and not NEPA, provides the appropriate forum in which to air policy disagreements.[17]

We do not mean to denigrate the fears of PANE's members, or to suggest that the psychological health damage they fear could not, in fact, occur. Nonetheless, it is difficult for us to see the differences between someone who dislikes a government decision so much that he suffers anxiety and stress, someone who fears the effects of that decision so much that he suffers similar anxiety and stress, and someone who suffers anxiety and stress that "flow directly," from the risks associated with the same decision. It would be extraordinarily difficult for agencies to differentiate between "genuine" claims of psychological health damage and claims that are grounded solely in disagreement with a democratically adopted policy. Until Congress provides a more explicit statutory instruction than NEPA now contains, we do not think agencies are obliged to undertake the inquiry.

The Court of Appeals' opinion seems at one point to acknowledge the force of these arguments, but seeks to distinguish the situation suggested by the related cases. First, the Court of Appeals thought the harm alleged by PANE is far more severe than the harm alleged in other

16. Although these cases involved similar facts, they presented different legal issues. They did not consider allegations that risk of crime would lead to psychological health damage. They did hold that the risk of crime, or the plaintiffs' concern about crime, do not constitute environmental effects. Of course, these holdings are not at issue in this case. [Court's fn. 11]

17. PANE's original contention seems to be addressed as much to the symbolic significance of continued operation of TMI-

1 as to the risk of an accident. NEPA does not require consideration of stress caused by the symbolic significance individuals attach to federal actions. Psychological health damage caused by a symbol is even farther removed from the physical environment, and more closely connected with the broader political process, than psychological health damage caused by risk. [Court's fn. 12]

cases. It thought that the severity of the harm is relevant to whether NEPA requires consideration of an effect. This cannot be the case. NEPA addresses environmental effects of federal actions. The gravity of harm does not change its character. If a harm does not have a sufficiently close connection to the physical environment, NEPA does not apply.

Second, the Court of Appeals noted that PANE's claim was made "in the wake of a unique and traumatic nuclear accident." We do not understand how the accident at TMI–2 transforms PANE's contentions into "environmental effects." The Court of Appeals "cannot believe that the psychological aftermath of the March 1979 accident falls outside" NEPA. On the contrary, NEPA is not directed at the effects of past accidents and does not create a remedial scheme for past federal actions. It was enacted to require agencies to assess the future effects of future actions. There is nothing in the language or the history of NEPA to suggest that its scope should be expanded "in the wake of" any kind of accident.

For these reasons, we hold that the NRC need not consider PANE's contentions. NEPA does not require agencies to evaluate the effects of risk, *qua* risk. The judgment of the Court of Appeals is reversed, and the case is remanded with the instructions to dismiss the petition for review.

[The brief concurring opinion of JUSTICE BRENNAN is omitted.]

Notes and Questions

1. NEPA is the primary source of federal regulation of externalities associated with environmental decisions. Section 102(C) of the Act (partially quoted in the *Metropolitan Edison* opinion) requires all federal agencies in actions significantly affecting the quality of the human environment, to prepare environmental impact statements that identify unavoidable adverse environmental effects. It does not direct agencies to disallow such actions if adverse effects are present, but only to consider and presumably ameliorate those adverse consequences. In this regime how would you measure external costs? Would you offset them against external benefits of the proposed action? If so, how would you measure those benefits? Compare the legislative solution proposed in the Endangered Species Act, discussed in the next case.

2. What, if any, limits should be placed upon the Environmental Protection Agency (EPA) in its efforts to require industries to internalize the externalities associated with environmental injury? Should external benefits produced, e.g. jobs, be considered as well as external costs, e.g. dirty air?

3. In *Metropolitan Edison*, Justice Rehnquist asserts that the adverse effects on psychological health are cognizable under NEPA. In light of the decision, however, can you describe the situations in which such injuries are required to be considered in the future?

4. Justice Rehnquist suggests an example to explain the necessary relationship between environmental effect and change in the physical environment. His point is that some actions, such as Department of Health and Human Services (HHS) subsidies for hospitals, create too tenuous a relationship between health and change in the physical environment. Can you turn

Justice Rehnquist's hypothetical around? Suppose a certain number of hospitals will close without federal subsidies. Is there any reason not to impose upon HHS an EIS responsibility for such a change in the physical environment if it leads to demonstrable health effects? Suppose the Public Health Service intends to close (or open) a hospital in a given community; should its action be subject to an EIS? What is the practical difference between its action and HHS's?

5.   The effects of delay have their own adverse environmental consequences. Since society's need for energy is a given, isn't it possible that the type of fuel likely to be called upon to replace nuclear will raise equally troubling environmental concerns? If so, should one require consideration of the "opportunity cost" of delaying the use of nuclear fuel? See Stephen Breyer, Vermont Yankee and the Court's Role in the Nuclear Power Controversy, 91 Harv. L. Rev. 1833 (1978) (describing the environmental problems inherent in the use of coal and other alternative fuels).

6.   Much of what is going on in *Metropolitan Edison* may stem from the Court's long-standing objections to the D.C. Circuit's ostensible use of procedural controls to delay the coming on line of nuclear power plants. See Vermont Yankee Nuclear Power Corp. v. NRDC, 435 U.S. 519, 98 S.Ct. 1197, 55 L.Ed.2d 460 (1978); Baltimore Gas & Electric v. NRDC, 462 U.S. 87, 103 S.Ct. 2246, 76 L.Ed.2d 437 (1983). In the Three Mile Island situation, expanding the EIS inquiry had the necessary effect of delaying the reopening of an already completed plant. This is one reason why Justice Rehnquist emphasizes that it is to the political process that those who fear the risks of nuclear power must turn. Judge Wilkey adverted to this problem in his dissent below:

> We have thus come a long way in fifty years, from a time when the President of the United States was widely and enthusiastically applauded for declaring: "The only thing we have to fear is fear itself." Now the fear itself necessitates an environmental assessment. All risky activity must grind to a halt in the interim. Inaction has become epidemic, and delay is maximized. I do not believe that the Congress intended NEPA to constrain federal action on these psychological and emotional bases.

Does Judge Wilkey have a point? How *do* you inquire into psychological factors relating to fear of nuclear power without in effect making a political choice? On the other hand, the EIS process itself creates an inevitable source of delay. Is it ever clear whether judicial remands to NRC (or any other agency) to make adequate EIS inquiries are based upon legal rather than political factors? Or does this overstate matters? Doesn't Congress always invite this possibility when it provides for judicial review?

A NOTE ON THE *CHEVRON* DOCTRINE

No discussion of judicial review of agency action can take place without considering Chevron, U.S.A. Inc. v. Natural Resources Defense Council, 467 U.S. 837, 104 S.Ct. 2778, 81 L.Ed.2d 694 (1984), which was decided the year after *Metropolitan Edison*. The *Chevron* doctrine reflects the Court's concern that political decisions were being subverted by judicial policymaking. In cases like Vermont Yankee Nuclear Power Corp. v. NRDC, 435 U.S. 519, 98 S.Ct. 1197, 55 L.Ed.2d 460 (1978), the

Court earlier warned against creative and expansive notions of judicial review. See also Motor Vehicle Manufacturers Ass'n v. State Farm, 463 U.S. 29, 103 S.Ct. 2856, 77 L.Ed.2d 443 (1983) (leaving policy decisions on seat belts to the Department of Transportation so long as it engaged in "reasoned analysis"). In *Chevron* the Court established a default principle that left to agencies (and not the courts on review) most questions of congressional intent. This principle was designed to delegate issues of policy to the "political" branches. It has become the most cited case on judicial review in the federal courts.[18] And it has also affected the affirmance rates of rules on judicial review.[19]

Chevron involved the question whether the EPA was free to choose, through rulemaking, a regulatory strategy for controlling airborne emissions within plants (the "bubble" concept), a concept that was not clearly contemplated by its authorizing legislation. Thus, the case deals with the tension between the ability of administrative agencies to reflect political choices of the Executive branch and the requirements that the agencies stay within boundaries established by Congress. In practice, it is about when courts must defer to an agency's interpretation of its own authority.

Chevron "deference" requires that the reviewing courts follow a "two-step" process:

First, if Congress has spoken directly about a matter, neither the agency nor the court has authority to change the position Congress has adopted;

But second, if Congress has not spoken directly, the only question for the court is "whether the agency decision is based on a permissible construction of the statute."

Applying these steps is a continuing challenge, not only for the lower courts but for the Justices who created them. For example, how formally must the agency have spoken (i.e., through rulemaking or adjudication?) See United States v. Mead Corp., 533 U.S. 218, 121 S.Ct. 2164, 150 L.Ed.2d 292 (2001). How clearly must Congress have spoken, and who is to judge what Congress said? Further, to which "executive" interpretation is deference to be given? The agency's? The Office of Management and Budget's? The Justice Department's (when, for example, it is asked to give an antitrust perspective to agencies like the FCC)? Or the President's? Our next case, Babbitt v. Sweet Home Chapter, raises several of these issues. *Chevron* makes the court ask in each case what responsibility the political decisionmakers have been given and how much respect their decisions should be entitled to on review. In essence,

18. See Peter Strauss, et al., Gellhorn & Byse's Administrative Law 1033 (10th Ed.2003). This is not the place to evaluate the *Chevron* case in detail; we leave that task to the judicial review sections of the Administrative Law course.

19. Peter H. Schuck & E. Donald Elliott, To the *Chevron* Station: An Empirical Study of Administrative Law, 1990 Duke L.J. 984 (affirmance rates moved from 71% to 81% over a three year period after Chevron); See also Orin S. Kerr, Shedding Light on *Chevron*: An Empirical Study of the *Chevron* Doctrine in the U.S. Courts of Appeals, 15 Yale J. on Reg. 1 (1998).

while *Chevron* is a doctrine of judicial review, it asks fundamental separation of powers questions about the intended relationships of the three branches of government to each other.

2. WHEN ARE VALUES COMPARABLE?

Executive Order 12,866, which requires agencies like EPA to engage in cost-benefit analysis (except where Congress has specifically provided to the contrary), requires agencies to select among the regulatory alternatives those that "maximize net benefits (including potential economic, environmental, public health and safety, and other advantages, distributive impacts, and equity)" and produce the "least net cost to society." 58 Fed. Reg. 51735 (Sept. 30, 1993), as amended by Executive Order 13, 258, 67 Fed. Reg. 9385 (Feb. 26, 2002).

Even when one engages in some version of comparing the costs and benefits of regulation, there are additional issues to consider. Two of these are addressed in the following cases. The first issue is whether all costs and benefits are comparable. More generally, is there a scale upon which sources of well-being can be weighed opposite each other? It may seem that this is the case, but sometimes an interest is so powerful that it is said to have lexical priority. This means that its value is simply not comparable to the things that can be exchanged in markets. This is not to say that the interest "trumps" all others. For example, you may decide that there is not enough money in the world for you either to take the life of another person or to kill the last remaining members of an endangered species. On the other hand, some people might wipe out a species in order to protect the lives of human beings.

The second issue is less philosophical but has huge practical and political importance. In many instances the government regulation instructs the agency in charge not to engage in a conventional cost-benefit analysis but to adopt a measure as long as it is "feasible" or "reasonable." Obviously, this is a vague target, but it would be a mistake to think that all of the problems encountered are related to imprecise legislative guidance. In fact, even when the analysis is seemingly "objective," much subjectivity is involved.

BABBITT v. SWEET HOME CHAPTER

Supreme Court of the United States, 1995.
515 U.S. 687, 115 S.Ct. 2407, 132 L.Ed.2d 597.

JUSTICE STEVENS delivered the opinion of the Court.

The Endangered Species Act of 1973, 87 Stat. 884, 16 U.S.C. § 1531 (1988 ed. and Supp. V) (ESA or Act), contains a variety of protections designed to save from extinction species that the Secretary of the Interior designates as endangered or threatened. Section 9 of the Act makes it unlawful for any person to "take" any endangered or threatened species. The Secretary has promulgated a regulation that defines the statute's prohibition on taking to include "significant habitat modification or degradation where it actually kills or injures wildlife." This case presents the question whether the Secretary exceeded his authority under the Act by promulgating that regulation.

I

Section 9(a)(1) of the Endangered Species Act provides the following protection for endangered species:[20]

> Except as provided in sections 1535(g)(2) and 1539 of this title, with respect to any endangered species of fish or wildlife listed pursuant to section 1533 of this title it is unlawful for any person subject to the jurisdiction of the United States to:

> (B) take any such species within the United States or the territorial sea of the United States[.] 16 U.S.C § 1538(a)(1).

Section 3(19) of the Act defines the statutory term "take":

> The term "take" means to harass, harm, pursue, hunt, shoot, wound, kill, trap, capture, or collect, or to attempt to engage in any such conduct. 16 U.S.C. § 1532(19).

The Act does not further define the terms it uses to define "take." The Interior Department regulations that implement the statute, however, define the statutory term "harm":

> *Harm* in the definition of 'take' in the Act means an act which actually kills or injures wildlife. Such act may include significant habitat modification or degradation where it actually kills or injures wildlife by significantly impairing essential behavioral patterns, including breeding, feeding, or sheltering. 50 CFR § 17.3 (1994).

> This regulation has been in place since 1975.[21]

A limitation on the § 9 "take" prohibition appears in § 10(a)(1)(B) of the Act, which Congress added by Amendment in 1982. That section authorizes the Secretary to grant a permit for any taking otherwise prohibited by § 9(a)(1)(B) "if such taking is incidental to, and not the purpose of, the carrying out of an otherwise lawful activity." 16 U.S.C. § 1539(a)(1)(B).

In addition to the prohibition on takings, the Act provides several other protections for endangered species. Section 4, 16 U.S.C. § 1533, commands the Secretary to identify species of fish or wildlife that are in danger of extinction and to publish from time to time lists of all species he determines to be endangered or threatened. Section 5, 16 U.S.C.

---

20. The Act defines the term "endangered species" to mean "any species which is in danger of extinction throughout all or a significant portion of its range other than a species of the Class Insecta determined by the Secretary to constitute a pest whose protection under the provisions of this chapter would present an overwhelming and overriding risk to man." 16 U.S.C. § 1532(6). [Court's fn. 1]

21. The Secretary, through the Director of Fish and Wildlife Service, originally promulgate the regulation in 1975 and amended it in 1981 to emphasize that actual death or injury of a protected animal is necessary for a violation. See 40 Fed. Reg. 44416 (1975); 46 Fed. Reg. 54748, 54750 (1981). [Court's fn. 2]

§ 1534, authorizes the Secretary, in cooperation with the States, see 16 U.S.C. § 1535, to acquire land to aid in preserving such species. Section 7 requires federal agencies to ensure that none of their activities, including the granting of licenses and permits, will jeopardize the continued existence of endangered species "or result in the destruction or adverse modification of habitat of such species which is determined by the Secretary to be critical." 16 U.S.C. § 1536(a)(2).

Respondents in this action are small landowners, logging companies, and families dependent on the forest products industries in the Pacific Northwest and in the Southeast, and organizations that represent their interests. They brought this declaratory judgment action against petitioners, the Secretary of the Interior and the Director of the Fish and Wildlife Service, in the United States District Court for the District of Columbia to challenge the statutory validity of the Secretary's regulation defining "harm," particularly the inclusion of habitat modification and degradation in the definition.[22] Respondents challenged the regulation on its face. Their complaint alleged that application of the "harm" regulation to the red-cockaded woodpecker, an endangered species,[23] and the northern spotted owl, a threatened species,[24] had injured them economically.

Respondents advanced three arguments to support their submission that Congress did not intend the word "take" in § 9 to include habitat modification, as the Secretary's "harm" regulation provides. First, they correctly noted the language in the Senate's original version of the ESA would have defined "take" to include "destruction, modification, or curtailment of [the] habitat or range" of fish or wildlife, but the Senate deleted that language from the bill before enacting it. Second, respondents argued that Congress intended the Act's express authorization for the Federal Government to buy private land in order to prevent habitat degradation in § 5 to be the exclusive check against habitat modification on private property. Third, because the Senate added the term "harm" to the definition of "take" in a floor amendment without debate, respondents argued that the court should not interpret the term so expansively as to include habitat modification.

The District Court considered and rejected each of respondents' arguments, finding "that Congress intended an expansive interpretation

22. Respondents also argued in the District Court that the Secretary's definition of "harm" is unconstitutionally void for vagueness, but they do not press that argument here. [Court's fn. 3]

23. The woodpecker was listed as an endangered species in 1970 pursuant to the statutory predecessor of the ESA. See 50 CFR § 17.11(h) (1974), issued pursuant to the Endangered Species Conservation Act of 1969, 83 Stat. 275. [Court's fn.4]

24. See 55 Fed. Reg. 26114 (1990). Another regulation promulgated by the Secre-

tary extends to threatened species, defined in the ESA as "any species which is likely to become an endangered species within the foreseeable future throughout all or a significant portion of its range," 16 U.S.C. § 1532(20), some but not all of the protections endangered species enjoy. See 50 CFR 17.31(a) (1994). In the District Court respondents unsuccessfully challenged that regulation's extension of § 9 to threatened species, but they do not press the challenge here. [Court's fn. 5]

of the word 'take', an interpretation that encompasses habitat modification." The court noted that in 1982, when Congress was aware of a judicial decision that had applied the Secretary's regulation, it amended the Act without using the opportunity to change the definition of "take". The court stated that, even had it found the ESA "silent or ambiguous" as to the authority for the Secretary's definition of "harm," it would nevertheless have upheld the regulation as a reasonable interpretation of the statute (quoting Chevron U.S.A. Inc. v. Natural Resources Defense Council, Inc.). The District Court therefore entered summary judgment for petitioners and dismissed respondents' complaint.

A divided panel of the Court of Appeals initially affirmed the judgment of the District Court. After granting a petition for rehearing, however, the panel reversed. Although acknowledging that "[t]he potential breadth of the word 'harm' is indisputable," the majority concluded that the immediate statutory context in which "harm" appeared counseled against a broad reading; like the other words in the definition of "take," the word "harm" should be read as applying only to "the perpetrator's direct application of force against the animal taken . . . The forbidden acts fit, in ordinary language, the basic model 'A hit B.' " The majority based its reasoning on a canon of statutory construction called *noscitur a sociis*, which holds that a word is known by the company it keeps.

* * *

Chief Judge Mikva, who had announced the panel's original decision, dissented. In his view, a proper application of *Chevron* indicated that the Secretary had reasonably defined "harm," because respondents had failed to show that Congress unambiguously manifested its intent to exclude habitat modification from the ambit of "take." Chief Judge Mikva found the majority's reliance on *noscitur a sociis* inappropriate in light of the statutory language and unnecessary in light of the strong support in the legislative history for the Secretary's interpretation. He did not find the 1982 "incidental take permit" amendment alone sufficient to vindicate the Secretary's definition of "harm," but he believed the amendment provided additional support for that definition because it reflected Congress' view in 1982 that the definition was reasonable.

The Court of Appeals' decision created a square conflict with a 1988 decision of the Ninth Circuit that had upheld the Secretary's definition of "harm." See Palila v. Hawaii Dept. of Land and Natural Resources, 852 F.2d 1106 (1988) (Palila II). The Court of Appeals neither cited nor distinguished *Palila II*, despite the stark contrast between the Ninth Circuit's holding and its own. We granted certiorari to resolve the conflict. * * * Our consideration of the text and structure of the Act, its legislative history, and the significance of the 1982 amendment persuades us that the Court of Appeals' judgment should be reversed.

II

Because this case was decided on motions for summary judgment, we may appropriately make certain factual assumptions in order to frame the legal issue. First, we assume respondents have no desire to harm either the red-cockaded woodpecker or the spotted owl; they merely wish to continue logging activities that would be entirely proper if not prohibited by the ESA. On the other hand, we must assume *arguendo* that those activities will have the effect, even though unintended, of detrimentally changing the natural habitat of both listed species and that, as a consequence, members of those species will be killed or injured. Under respondents' view of the law, the Secretary's only means of forestalling that grave result—even when the actor knows it is certain to occur—to use his § 5 authority to purchase the lands on which the survival of the species depends. The Secretary, on the other hand, submits that the § 9 prohibition on takings, which Congress defined to include "harm," places on respondents a duty to avoid harm that habitat alteration will cause the birds unless respondents first obtain a permit pursuant to § 10.

The text of the Act provides three reasons for concluding that the Secretary's interpretation is reasonable. First, an ordinary understanding of the word "harm" supports it. The dictionary definition of the verb form of "harm" is "to cause hurt or damage to: injure." Webster's Third New International Dictionary 1034 (1966). In the context of the ESA, that definition naturally encompasses habitat modification that results in actual injury or death to members of an endangered or threatened species.

Respondents argue that the Secretary should have limited the purview of "harm" to direct applications of force against protected species, but the dictionary definition does not include the word "directly" or suggest in any way that only direct or willful action that leads to injury constitutes "harm." Moreover, unless the statutory term "harm" encompasses indirect as well as direct injuries, the word has no meaning that does not duplicate the meaning of other words that § 3 uses to define "take." A reluctance to treat statutory terms as surplusage supports the reasonableness of the Secretary's interpretation. * * *

Second, the broad purpose of the ESA supports the Secretary's decision to extend protection against activities that cause the precise harms Congress enacted the statute to avoid. In TVA v. Hill, 437 U.S. 153, 98 S.Ct. 2279, 57 L.Ed.2d 117 (1978), we described the Act as "the most comprehensive legislation for the preservation of endangered species ever enacted by any nation." Whereas predecessor statutes enacted in 1966 and 1969 had not contained any sweeping prohibition against the taking of endangered species except on federal lands, the 1973 Act applied to all land in the United States and to the Nation's territorial seas. As stated in § 2 of the Act, among its central purposes is "to provide a means whereby the ecosystems upon which endangered species and threatened species depend may be conserved ..." 16 U.S.C. § 1531(b).

In *Hill*, we construed § 7 as precluding the completion of the Tellico Dam because of its predicted impact on the survival of the snail darter.

Both our holding and the language in our opinion stressed the importance of the statutory policy. "The plain intent of Congress in enacting this statute," we recognized, "was to halt and reverse the trend toward species extinction, whatever the cost. This is reflected not only in the stated policies of the Act, but in literally every section of the statute." Although the § 9 "take" prohibition was not at issue in *Hill*, we took note of that prohibition, placing particular emphasis on the Secretary's inclusion of habitat modification in his definition of "harm." In light of that provision for habitat protection, we could "not understand how TVA intends to operate Tellico Dam without 'harming' the snail darter." Congress' intent to provide comprehensive protection for endangered and threatened species supports the permissibility of the Secretary's "harm" regulation.

Respondents advance strong arguments that activities that cause minimal or unforeseeable harm will not violate the Act as construed in the "harm" regulation. Respondents, however, present a facial challenge to the regulation. Thus, they ask us to invalidate the Secretary's understanding of "harm" in every circumstance, even when an actor knows that an activity, such as draining a pond, would actually result in the extinction of a listed species by destroying its habitat. Given Congress' clear expression of the ESA's broad purpose to protect endangered and threatened wildlife, the Secretary's definition of "harm" is reasonable.[25]

* * *

We need not decide whether the statutory definition of "take" compels the Secretary's interpretation of "harm," because our conclusions that Congress did not unambiguously manifest its intent to adopt respondents' view and that the Secretary's interpretation is reasonable suffice to decide this case. See generally, Chevron, U.S.A. Inc. v. Natural Resources Defense Council, Inc. The latitude the ESA gives the Secretary in enforcing the statute, together with the degree of regulatory expertise necessary to its enforcement, establishes that we owe some degree of deference to the Secretary's reasonable interpretation. See Breyer, Judicial Review of Questions of Law and Policy, 38 Admin.L.Rev. 363, 373 (1986).

* * *

25. The dissent incorrectly asserts that the Secretary's regulation (1) "dispenses with the foreseeability of harm" and (2) "fail[s] to require injury to particular animals." As to the first assertion, the regulation merely implements the statute, and it is therefore subject to the statute's "knowingly violates" language, see 16 U.S.C. §§ 1540(a)(1), (b)(1), and ordinary requirements of proximate causation and foreseeability. Nothing in the regulation purports to weaken those requirements. To the contrary, the word "actually" in the regulation should be construed to limit the liability about which the dissent appears most concerned, liability under the statute's "otherwise violates" provision. The Secretary did not need to include "actually" to connote "but for" causation, which the other words in the definition obviously require. As to the dissent's second assertion, every term in the regulation's definition of "harm" is subservient to the phrase "an act which actually kills or injures wildlife." [Court's fn. 13]

IV

When it enacted the ESA, Congress delegated broad administrative and interpretive power to the Secretary. See 16 U.S.C. §§ 1533, 1540(f). The task of defining and listing endangered and threatened species requires an expertise and attention to detail that exceeds the normal province of Congress. Fashioning appropriate standards for issuing permits under § 10 for takings that would otherwise violate § 9 necessarily requires the exercise of broad discretion. The proper interpretation of a term such as "harm" involves a complex policy choice. When Congress has entrusted the Secretary with broad discretion, we are especially reluctant to substitute our views of wise policy for his. See *Chevron*. In this case, that reluctance accords with our conclusion, based on the text, structure, and legislative history of the ESA, that the Secretary reasonable construed the intent of Congress when he defined "harm" to include "significant habitat modification or degradation that actually kills or injures wildlife."

In the elaboration and enforcement of the ESA, the Secretary and all persons who must comply with the law will confront difficult questions of proximity and degree; for, as all recognize, the Act encompasses a vast range of economic and social enterprises and endeavors. These questions must be addressed in the usual course of the law, through case-by-case resolution and adjudication.

The judgment of the Court of Appeals is reversed.

Justice O'Connor, concurring.

My agreement with the Court is founded on two understandings. First, the challenged regulation is limited to significant habitat modification that causes actual, as opposed to hypothetical or speculative, death or injury to identifiable protected animals. Second, even setting aside difficult questions of scienter, the regulation's application is limited by ordinary principles of proximate causation, which introduce notions of foreseeability. These limitations, in my view, call into question Palila v. Hawaii Dept. of Land and Natural Resources, and with it, many of the applications derided by the dissent. Because there is no need to strike a regulation on a facial challenge out of concern that it is susceptible of erroneous application, however, and because there are many habitat related circumstances in which the regulation might validly apply, I join the opinion of the Court.

* * *

Justice Scalia, with whom The Chief Justice and Justice Thomas join, dissenting.

I think it unmistakably clear that the legislation at issue here (1) forbade the hunting and killing of endangered animals, and (2) provided federal lands and federal funds *for the acquisition of private lands*, to preserve the habitat of endangered animals. The Court's holding that the hunting and killing prohibition incidentally preserves habitat on private lands imposes unfairness to the point of financial ruin—not just upon the rich, but upon the simplest farmer who finds his land conscripted to national zoological use. I respectfully dissent.

I

The Endangered Species Act of 1973, 16 U.S.C. § 1531 *et. seq.* (1988 ed. and Supp. V) (Act), provides that "it is unlawful for any person subject to the jurisdiction of the United States to take any [protected] species within the United States." § 1538(a)(1)(B). The term "take" is defined as "to harass, *harm*, pursue, hunt, shoot, wound, kill, trap, capture, or collect, or to attempt to engage in any such conduct." § 1532(19) (emphasis added). The challenged regulation defines "harm" thus:

> " 'Harm' in the definition of 'take' in the Act means an act which actually kills or injures wildlife. Such act may include significant habitat modification or degradation where it actually kills or injures wildlife by significantly impairing essential behavioral patterns, including breeding, feeding or sheltering." 50 CFR § 17.3 (1994).

In my view petitioners must lose—the regulation must fall—even under the test of Chevron USA Inc. v. Natural Resources Defense Council, Inc., so I shall assume that the Court is correct to apply *Chevron*.

The regulation has three features which, for reasons I shall discuss at length below, do not comport with the statute. First, it interprets the statute to prohibit habitat modification that is no more than the cause-in-fact of death or injury to wildlife. Any "significant habitat modification" that in fact produces that result by "impairing essential behavioral patterns" is made unlawful, regardless of whether that result is intended or even foreseeable, and no matter how long the chain of causality between modification and injury. See, e.g., Palila v. Hawaii Dept. Of Land and Natural Resources (Palila II) (sheep grazing constituted "taking" of palila birds, since although sheep do not destroy full-grown mamane trees, they do destroy mamane seedlings, which will not grow to full-grown trees, on which the palila feeds and nests). See also Davison, Alteration of Wildlife Habitat as a Prohibited Taking under the Endangered Species Act, 10 J. Land Use & Envtl. L. 155, 190 (1995) (regulation requires only causation-in-fact).

Second, the regulation does not require an "act": the Secretary's officially stated position is that an omission will do. The previous version of the regulation made this explicit. See 40 Fed. Reg. 44412, 44416 (1975) (" 'Harm' in the definition of 'take' in the Act means an act or omission which actually kills or injures wildlife ..."). When the regulation was modified in 1981 the phrase "or omission" was taken out, but only because (as the final publication of the rule advised) "the [Fish and Wildlife] service feels that 'act' is inclusive of either commissions or omissions which would be prohibited by section [1538(a)(1)(B)]." 46 Fed. Reg. 54748, 54750 (1981). In its brief here the Government agrees that the regulation covers omissions (although it argues that "[a]n 'omission' constitutes an 'act' ... only if there is a legal duty to act").

The third and most important unlawful feature of the regulation is that it encompasses injury inflicted, not only upon individual animals, but upon populations of the protected species. "Injury" in the regulation includes "significantly impairing essential behavior patterns, including *breeding*," 50 CFR § 17.3 (1994) (emphasis added). Impairment of breeding does not "injure" living creatures; it prevents them from propagating, thus "injuring" *a population* of animals which would otherwise have maintained or increased its numbers. What the face of the regulation shows, the Secretary's official pronouncements confirm. The Final Redefinition of "Harm" accompanying publication of the regulation said that "harm" is not limited to "direct physical injury to an individual member of the wildlife species," 46 Fed.Reg. 54748 (1981), and refers to *"injury to a population," id.*, at 54749 (emphasis added). See also *Palila II*, 852 F.2d, at 1108; Davison, *supra*, at 190, and n. 177, 195; M. Bean, The Evolution of National Wildlife Law 344 (1983).

None of these three features of the regulation can be found in the statutory provisions supposed to authorize it. The term "harm" in § 1532(19) has no legal force of its own. An indictment or civil complaint that charged the defendant with "harming" an animal protected under the Act would be dismissed as defective, for the only operative term in the statute is to "take". If "take" were not elsewhere defined in the Act, none could dispute what it means, for the term is as old as the law itself. To "take," when applied to wild animals, means to reduce those animals by killing or capturing, to human control. See, *e.g.*, 11 Oxford English Dictionary (1933) ("Take . . . To catch, capture (a wild beast, bird, fish, etc.)"); Webster's New International Dictionary of the English Language (2d ed. 1949) (take defined as "to catch or capture by trapping, snaring, etc., or as prey"); Geer v. Connecticut, 161 U.S. 519, 523, 16 S.Ct. 600, 602, 40 L.Ed. 793 (1896) ("[A]ll the animals which can be taken upon the earth, in the sea, or in the air, that is to say, wild animals, belong to those who take them") (quoting the Digest of Justinian); 2 W. Blackstone, Commentaries 411 (1766) ("Every man . . . has an equal right of pursuing and taking to his own use all such creatures as are (*"ferae naturae"*) This is just the sense in which "take" is used elsewhere in federal legislation and treaty. See, e.g., Migratory Bird Treaty Act, 16 U.S.C. § 704 3 (1988) ed., Supp. V) (no person may "pursue, hunt, take, capture, kill, [or] attempt to take, capture, or kill" any migratory bird); Agreement on the Conservation of Polar Bears, Nov. 14, 1973, Art. I, T.I.A.S. No. 8409 (defining "taking" as "hunting, killing and capturing"). And that meaning fits neatly with the rest of § 1538(a)(1), which makes it unlawful not only to take protected species, but also to import or export them; to possess, sell, deliver, carry, transport, or ship any taken species; and to transport, sell, or offer to sell them in interstate or foreign commerce. The taking prohibition, in other words, is only part of the regulatory plan of § 1538(a)(1), which covers all the stages of the process by which protected wildlife is reduced to man's dominion and made the object of profit. It is obvious that "take" in this sense—a term of art deeply embedded in the statutory and common law concerning wildlife-describes a class of acts (not omissions) done directly and intentionally (not indirectly and by accident) to particular animals (not population of animals).

      * * *

As I understand the regulation that the Court has created and held consistent with the statute that it has also created, habitat modification can constitute a "taking", but only if it results in the killing or harming of individual animals and only if that consequence is the direct result of the modification. This means that the destruction of privately owned habitat that is essential, not for the feeding or nesting, but for the breeding, of butterflies, would not violate the Act, since it would not harm or kill any living butterfly. I, too, think it would not violate the Act—not for the utterly unsupported reason that habitat modifications fall outside the regulation if they happen not to kill or injure a living animal, but for the textual reason that only action directed at living animals constitutes a "take."

The Endangered Species Act is a carefully considered piece of legislation that forbids all persons to hunt or harm endangered animals, but places upon the public at large, rather than upon fortuitously accountable individual landowners, the cost of preserving the habitat of endangered species. There is neither textual support for, nor even evidence of congressional consideration of, the radically different disposition contained in the regulation that the court sustains. For these reasons, I respectfully dissent.

Notes and Questions

1. The Endangered Species Act is not a balancing statute where costs and benefits of species protection can be weighed. At the same time the dissent and majority are at extreme ends of the debate over the scope of coverage of the Act. Does the majority simply defer to the Interior Department's interpretation because of the *Chevron* doctrine, or is it in effect drawing its own conclusions on the statutory requirements stated in the Act? Which view do you find more persuasive?

2. The Endangered Species Act had earlier been tested in the celebrated case of TVA v. Hill, 437 U.S. 153, 98 S.Ct. 2279, 57 L.Ed.2d 117 (1978), which involved the fate of the "snail darter" an endangered species whose sole habitat was threatened by the operation of the Tellico Dam. Chief Justice Burger writing for the Court affirmed the injunction granted by the court below over pleas that the Court reach some reasonable accommodation between the Act and the operation of the dam:

> We agree with the Court of Appeals that in our constitutional system the commitment to separation of powers is too fundamental for us to pre-empt congressional action by judicially decreeing what accords with "common sense and the public weals." Our constitution vests such responsibilities in the political branches.

3. Subsequent to *Hill*, the Endangered Species Act was amended. One of the most important amendments provides for an exemption when "(i)

there are no reasonable and prudent alternatives to the agency action; (ii) the benefits of such action clearly outweigh the benefits of alternative courses of action consistent with conserving the species or its critical habitat, and such action is in the public interest; and (iii) the action is of regional or national significance * * * " 16 U.S.C.A. § 1536(h) (1976 & Supp. II 1978).

In 1978, the supporters of the Tellico Dam project applied for an exemption under a slightly modified version of the three part test. The application was denied based on the findings that prudent alternatives were available and that the benefits of completion did not clearly outweigh the benefits of alternative action. Their persistence continued, however, and, in 1979, a special legislative exemption was enacted as an amendment to the Energy and Water Development Appropriations Act of 1980, Pub. L. No. 97–99, 93 Stat. 437 (1979). See Rosenberg, Federal Protection of Unique Environmental Interests: Endangered and Threatened Species, 58 N.C. L. Rev. 491, 520–524 (1980). Ironically, since 1978, the snail darter has been discovered in locations other than the Little Tennessee River.

4. *Sweet Home Chapter* and *Hill* raise the issues associated with whether all values can be monetized, the problem of accounting for the interests of future generations, and whether species have rights (moral if not legal) independent of the utility derived from their existence by humans. Do you think a species has some right to exist independent of human pleasure? Suppose the species could only be preserved at a cost of several billion dollars and that this amount could be used to discover a cure for AIDS? Can you think of a way to rationally rank these conflicting values?

5. As noted above, one argument for protecting endangered species beyond the level of protection that would evolve in the free market is that future generations are unable to express themselves in today's markets. Similarly, current generations were unable to express themselves in the past when we know that other species became extinct. Do you feel that you were not sufficiently protected by past generations? Can you think of any species you wish still existed? How much would you be willing to pay for the existence of that species? Would you pay different amounts for some now-extinct furry pygmy bear than you would for a now-extinct species of wood worm? If so, what principle, if any, would you be applying? Should you apply this principle to animals that are now on the verge of extinction?

6. While the ESA is a non-balancing statute, inevitably cost-benefit considerations creep in and the agency has to deal with them. Two situations where this happens are (1) methods for determining which species moves up the waiting line for consideration; and, (2) how the habitats for endangered species are determined.

a. As to the queue, consider that as of December 15, 2003 there were 117 species of animals and 139 species of plants awaiting a listing decision.[26] In addition, every five years the Fish and Wildlife Service (FWS) must reconsider all species already designated as threatened or endangered. Since agency resources are limited, how the FWS ranks these species becomes a matter of prioritizing that incorporates several choices.[27] While these factors

26. *http://ecos.fws.gov/tess_public/TessStatReport.*

27. The FWS ranking process addresses the magnitude of the threat the species

do not explicitly involve economic considerations, the ranking of species for five year review is based on their "management impact," which involves the costs they impose on habitats.

b.   The "critical habitat designation" expressly involves economic considerations. The FWS is required to base a critical habitat determination on "the basis of the best scientific data available and after taking into consideration the economic impact, and any other relevant impact, of specifying any particular area as critical habitat. See 16 U.S.C. § 1533(6)(b)(2) (2003).

Do these determinations undermine the non-economic values behind the ESA? How else would you make these calls? For that matter, should the ESA itself be amended to provide for CBA?

VANDE ZANDE v. STATE OF WISCONSIN DEPARTMENT OF ADMINISTRATION

United States Court of Appeals, Seventh Circuit, 1995.
44 F.3d 538.

Before POSNER, CHIEF JUDGE, and ENGEL and EASTERBROOK, CIRCUIT JUDGES.

POSNER, CHIEF JUDGE.

In 1990, Congress passed the Americans with Disabilities Act, 42 U.S.C. §§ 12101 et seq. The stated purpose is "to provide a clear and comprehensive national mandate for the elimination of discrimination against individuals with disabilities," said by Congress to be 43 million in number and growing. §§ 12101(a), (b)(1). "Disability" is broadly defined. It includes not only "a physical or mental impairment that substantially limits one or more of the major life activities of [the disabled] individual," but also the state of "being regarded as having such an impairment." §§ 12102(2)(A), (C). The latter definition, although at first glance peculiar, actually makes a better fit with the elaborate preamble to the Act, in which people who have physical or mental impairments are compared to victims of racial and other invidious discrimination. Many such impairments are not in fact disabling but are believed to be so, and the people having them may be denied employment or otherwise shunned as a consequence. Such people, objectively capable of performing as well as the unimpaired, are analogous to capable workers discriminated against because of their skin color or some other vocationally irrelevant characteristic. * * *

The more problematic case is that of an individual who has a vocationally relevant disability—an impairment such as blindness or paralysis that limits a major human capability, such as seeing or walking. In the common case in which such an impairment interferes with the individual's ability to perform up to the standards of the workplace, or increases the cost of employing him, hiring and firing decisions based

faces; the immediacy of the threat; and the   43098.
taxonomy of the species. See 48 Fed. Reg.

on the impairment are not "discriminatory" in a sense closely analogous to employment discrimination on racial grounds. The draftsmen of the Act knew this. But they were unwilling to confine the concept of disability discrimination to cases in which the disability is irrelevant to the performance of the disabled person's job. Instead, they defined "discrimination" to include an employer's "not making reasonable accommodations to the known physical or mental limitations of an otherwise qualified individual with a disability who is an applicant or employee, unless ... [the employer] can demonstrate that the accommodation would impose an undue hardship on the operation of the ... [employer's] business." § 12112(b)(5)(A).

The term "reasonable accommodations" is not a legal novelty, even if we ignore its use (arguably with a different meaning, however), in the provision of Title VII forbidding religious discrimination in employment. It is one of a number of provisions in the employment subchapter that were borrowed from regulations issued by the Equal Employment Opportunity Commission in implementation of the Rehabilitation Act of 1973, 29 U.S.C. §§ 701 et seq. Indeed, to a great extent the employment provisions of the new Act merely generalize to the economy as a whole the duties, including that of reasonable accommodation, that the regulations under the Rehabilitation Act imposed on federal agencies and federal contractors. We can therefore look to the decisions interpreting those regulations for clues to the meaning of the same terms in the new law.

It is plain enough what "accommodation" means. The employer must be willing to consider making changes in its ordinary work rules, facilities, terms, and conditions in order to enable a disabled individual to work. The difficult term is "reasonable." The plaintiff in our case, a paraplegic, argues in effect that the term just means apt or efficacious. An accommodation is reasonable, she believes, when it is tailored to the particular individual's disability. A ramp or lift is thus a reasonable accommodation for a person who like this plaintiff is confined to a wheelchair. Considerations of cost do not enter into the term as the plaintiff would have us construe it. Cost is, she argues, the domain of "undue hardship" (another term borrowed from the regulations under the Rehabilitation Act)—safe harbor for an employer that can show that it would go broke or suffer other excruciating financial distress were it compelled to make a reasonable accommodation in the sense of one effective in enabling the disabled person to overcome the vocational effects of the disability.

These are questionable interpretations both of "reasonable" and of "undue hardship." To "accommodate" a disability is to make some change that will enable the disabled person to work. An unrelated, inefficacious change would not be an accommodation of the disability at all. So "reasonable" may be intended to qualify (in the sense of weaken) "accommodation," in just the same way that if one requires a "reasonable effort" of someone this means less than the maximum possible effort, or in law that the duty of "reasonable care," the cornerstone of the law of negligence, requires something less than the maximum possible care. It is understood in that law that in deciding what care is reasonable the court considers the cost of increased care. (This is explicit in Judge Learned Hand's famous formula for negligence. United States v. Carroll Towing Co., 159 F.2d 169, 173 (2d Cir.1947).) Similar reasoning could be used to flesh out the meaning of the word "reasonable" in the term "reasonable accommodations." It would not follow that the costs and benefits of altering a workplace to enable a disabled person to work would always have to be quantified, or even that an accommodation would have to be deemed unreasonable if the cost exceeded the benefit however slightly. But, at the very least, the cost could not be disproportionate to the benefit. Even if an employer is so large or wealthy—or, like the principal defendant in this case, is a state, which can raise taxes in order to finance any accommodations that it must make to disabled employees—that it may not be able to plead "undue hardship," it would not be required to expend enormous sums in order to bring about a trivial improvement in the life of a disabled employee. If the nation's employers have potentially unlimited financial obligations to 43 million disabled persons, the Americans with Disabilities Act will have imposed an indirect tax potentially greater than the national debt. We do not find an intention to bring about such a radical result in either the language of the Act or its history. The preamble actually "markets" the Act as a cost saver, pointing to "billions of dollars in unnecessary expenses resulting from dependency and nonproductivity." § 12101(a)(9). The savings will be illusory if employers are required to expend many more billions in accommodation than will be saved by enabling disabled people to work.

The concept of reasonable accommodation is at the heart of this case. The plaintiff sought a number of accommodations to her paraplegia that were turned down. The principal defendant as we have said is a state, which does not argue that the plaintiff's proposals were rejected because accepting them would have imposed undue hardship on the state or because they would not have done her any good. The district judge nevertheless granted summary judgment for the defendants on the ground that the evidence obtained in discovery, construed as favorably to the plaintiff as the record permitted, showed that they had gone as far to accommodate the plaintiff's demands as reasonableness, in a sense distinct from either aptness or hardship—a sense based, rather, on considerations of cost and proportionality—required. On this analysis, the function of the "undue hardship" safe harbor, like the "failing company" defense to antitrust liability is to excuse compliance by a firm that is financially distressed, even though the cost of the accommodation to the firm might be less than the benefit to disabled employees.

This interpretation of "undue hardship" is not inevitable—in fact probably is incorrect. It is a defined term in the Americans with Disabilities Act, and the definition is "an action requiring significant difficulty or expense." 42 U.S.C. § 12111(10)(A). The financial condition of the employer is only one consideration in determining whether an accommodation otherwise reasonable would impose an undue hardship. See 42 U.S.C. §§ 12111(10)(B)(ii), (iii). The legislative history equates "undue hardship" to "unduly costly." These are terms of relation. We must ask, "undue" in relation to what? Presumably (given the statutory definition and the legislative history) in relation to the benefits of the accommodation to the disabled worker as well as to the employer's resources.

So it seems that costs enter at two points in the analysis of claims to an accommodation to a disability. The employee must show that the accommodation is reasonable in the sense both of efficacious and of proportional to costs. Even if this prima facie showing is made, the employer has an opportunity to prove that upon more careful consideration the costs are excessive in relation either to the benefits of the accommodation or to the employer's financial survival or health. In a classic negligence case, the idiosyncrasies of the particular employer are irrelevant. Having above-average costs, or being in a precarious financial situation, is not a defense to negligence. One interpretation of "undue hardship" is that it permits an employer to escape liability if he can carry the burden of proving that a disability accommodation reasonable for a normal employer would break him.

Lori Vande Zande, aged 35, is paralyzed from the waist down as a result of a tumor of the spinal cord. Her paralysis makes her prone to develop pressure ulcers, treatment of which often requires that she stay at home for several weeks. The defendants and the amici curiae argue that there is no duty of reasonable accommodation of pressure ulcers because they do not fit the statutory definition of a disability. Intermittent, episodic impairments are not disabilities, the standard example being a broken leg. But an intermittent impairment that is a characteristic manifestation of an admitted disability is, we believe, a part of the underlying disability and hence a condition that the employer must reasonably accommodate. Often the disabling aspect of a disability is, precisely, an intermittent manifestation of the disability, rather than the underlying impairment. The AIDS virus progressively destroys the infected person's immune system. The consequence is a series of opportunistic diseases which (so far as relevant to the disabilities law) often prevent the individual from working. If they are not part of the disability, then people with AIDS do not have a disability, which seems to us a very odd interpretation of the law, and one expressly rejected in the regulations. We hold that Vande Zande's pressure ulcers are a part of her disability, and therefore a part of what the State of Wisconsin had a duty to accommodate—reasonably.

Vande Zande worked for the housing division of the state's department of administration for three years, beginning in January 1990. The housing division supervises the state's public housing programs. Her job was that of a program assistant, and involved preparing public information materials, planning meetings, interpreting regulations, typing, mailing, filing, and copying. In short, her tasks were of a clerical, secretarial, and administrative-assistant character. In order to enable her to do this work, the defendants, as she acknowledges, "made numerous accommodations relating to the plaintiff's disability." As examples, in her words, "they paid the landlord to have bathrooms modified and to have a step ramped; they bought special adjustable furniture for the plaintiff; they ordered and paid for one-half of the cost of a cot that the plaintiff needed for daily personal care at work; they sometimes adjusted the plaintiff's schedule to perform backup telephone duties to accommodate the plaintiff's medical appointments; they made changes to the plans for a locker room in the new state office building; and they agreed to provide some of the specific accommodations the plaintiff requested in her * * * Reasonable Accommodation Request."

But she complains that the defendants did not go far enough in two principal respects. One concerns a period of eight weeks when a bout of pressure ulcers forced her to stay home. She wanted to work full time at home and believed that she would be able to do so if the division would provide her with a desktop computer at home (though she already had a laptop). Her supervisor refused, and told her that he probably would have only 15 to 20 hours of work for her to do at home per week and that she would have to make up the difference between that and a full work week out of her sick leave or vacation leave. In the event, she was able to work all but 16.5 hours in the eight-week period. She took 16.5 hours of sick leave to make up the difference. As a result, she incurred no loss of income, but did lose sick leave that she could have carried forward indefinitely. She now works for another agency of the State of Wisconsin, but any unused sick leave in her employment by the housing division would have accompanied her to her new job. Restoration of the 16.5 hours of lost sick leave is one form of relief that she seeks in this suit.

She argues that a jury might have found that a reasonable accommodation required the housing division either to give her the desktop computer or to excuse her from having to dig into her sick leave to get paid for the hours in which, in the absence of the computer, she was unable to do her work at home. No jury, however, could in our view be permitted to stretch the concept of "reasonable accommodation" so far. Most jobs in organizations public or private involve team work under supervision rather than solitary unsupervised work, and team work under supervision generally cannot be performed at home without a substantial reduction in the quality of the employee's performance. This will no doubt change as communications technology advances, but is the situation today. Generally, therefore, an employer is not required to accommodate a disability by allowing the disabled worker to work, by himself, without supervision, at home. * * * An employer is not required to allow disabled workers to work at home, where their productivity inevitably would be greatly reduced. No doubt to this as to any generalization about so complex and varied an activity as employment there are exceptions, but it would take a very extraordinary case for the employee to be able to create a triable issue of the employer's failure to allow the employee to work at home.

And if the employer, because it is a government agency and therefore is not under intense competitive pressure to minimize its labor costs or maximize the value of its output, or for some other reason, bends over backwards to accommodate a disabled worker—goes further than the law requires—by allowing the worker to work at home, it must not be punished for its generosity by being deemed to have conceded the reasonableness of so far-reaching an accommodation. That would hurt rather than help disabled workers. Wisconsin's housing division was not required by the Americans with Disabilities Act to allow Vande Zande to work at home; even more clearly it was not required to install a computer in her home so that she could avoid using up 16.5 hours of sick leave. It is conjectural that she will ever need those 16.5 hours; the expected cost of the loss must, therefore, surely be slight. An accommodation that allows a disabled worker to work at home, at full pay, subject only to a slight loss of sick leave that may never be needed, hence never missed, is, we hold, reasonable as a matter of law.

* * *

[Vande Zande complains about] * * * the kitchenettes in the housing division's building, which are for the use of employees during lunch and coffee breaks. Both the sink and the counter in each of the kitchenettes were 36 inches high, which is too high for a person in a wheelchair. The building was under construction, and the kitchenettes not yet built, when the plaintiff complained about this feature of the design. But the defendants refused to alter the design to lower the sink and counter to 34 inches, the height convenient for a person in a wheelchair. Construction of the building had begun before the effective date of the Americans with Disabilities Act, and Vande Zande does not argue that the failure to include 34–inch sinks and counters in the design of the building violated the Act. She could not argue that; the Act is not retroactive. But she argues that once she brought the problem to the attention of her supervisors, they were obliged to lower the sink and counter, at least on the floor on which her office was located but possibly on the other floors in the building as well, since she might be moved to another floor. All that the defendants were willing to do was to install a shelf 34 inches high in the kitchenette area on Vande Zande's floor. That took care of the counter problem. As for the sink, the defendants took the position that since the plumbing was already in place it would be too costly to lower the sink and that the plaintiff could use the bathroom sink, which is 34 inches high.

Apparently it would have cost only about $150 to lower the sink on Vande Zande's floor; to lower it on all the floors might have cost as much as $2,000, though possibly less. Given the proximity of the bathroom sink, Vande Zande can hardly complain that the inaccessibility of the kitchenette sink interfered with her ability to work or with her physical comfort. Her argument rather is that forcing her to use the bathroom sink for activities (such as washing out her coffee cup) for which the other employees could use the kitchenette sink stigmatized her as different and inferior; she seeks an award of compensatory damages for the resulting emotional distress. We may assume without having to decide that emotional as well as physical barriers to the integration of disabled persons into the workforce are relevant in determining the reasonableness of an accommodation. But we do not think an employer has a duty to expend even modest amounts of money to bring about an absolute identity in working conditions between disabled and nondisabled workers. The creation of such a duty would be the inevitable consequence of deeming a failure to achieve identical conditions "stigmatizing." That is merely an epithet. We conclude that access to a particular sink, when access to an equivalent sink, conveniently located, is provided, is not a legal duty of an employer. The duty of reasonable accommodation is satisfied when the employer does what is necessary to enable the disabled worker to work in reasonable comfort.

In addition to making these specific complaints of failure of reasonable accommodation, Vande Zande argues that the defendants displayed a "pattern of insensitivity or discrimination." She relies on a number of minor incidents, such as her supervisor's response, "Cut me some slack," to her complaint on the first day on which the housing division moved into the new building that the bathrooms lacked adequate supplies. He meant that it would take a few days to iron out the bugs inevitable in any major move. It was clearly a reasonable request in the circumstances; and given all the accommodations that Vande Zande acknowledges the defendants made to her disability, a "pattern of insensitivity or discrimination" is hard to discern. But the more fundamental point is that there is no separate offense under the Americans with Disabilities Act called engaging in a pattern of insensitivity or discrimination. The word "pattern" does not appear in the employment subchapter, and the Act is not modeled on RICO. As in other cases of discrimination, a plaintiff can ask the trier of fact to draw an inference of discrimination from a pattern of behavior when each individual act making up that pattern might have an innocent explanation. The whole can be greater than the sum of the parts. But in this case all we have in the way of a pattern is that the employer made a number of reasonable and some more than reasonable—unnecessary—accommodations, and turned down only requests for unreasonable accommodations. From such a pattern no inference of unlawful discrimination can be drawn.

AFFIRMED.

Notes and Questions

1. In *Vande Zande*, the plaintiff accepted that the term "undue hardship" would permit an employer not to take steps that would "break him." This view was implicitly rejected by the Second Circuit Court of Appeals in Borkowski v. Valley Central School Dist., 63 F.3d 131 (2d Cir.1995). Writing for the Court, Judge Guido Calabresi reasoned:

   Such a holding would require the Rehabilitation Act to be read, in effect, to subsidize inefficient employers by relieving them of burdens that are imposed on their more efficient competitors. The listing of regulatory factors pertinent to the individual employer does not on its face require such an interpretation. But the issue is not before us, and so we need not resolve it at this time.

The Court went on:

Whether a proposed accommodation is reasonable, however, is another question. "Reasonable" is a relational term: it evaluates the desirability of a particular accommodation according to the consequences that the accommodation will produce. This requires an inquiry not only into the benefits of the accommodation but into its costs as well. See Vande Zande v. Wisconsin Dep't of Admin., 44 F.3d 538, 542 (7th Cir.1995). We would not, for example, require an employer to make a multi-million dollar modification for the benefit of a single individual with a disability, even if the proposed modification would allow that individual to perform the essential functions of a job that she sought. In spite of its effectiveness, the proposed modification would be unreasonable because of its excessive costs. In short, an accommodation is reasonable only if its costs are not clearly disproportionate to the benefits that it will produce.[28]

As to the requirement that an accommodation be reasonable, we have held that the plaintiff bears only a burden of production. This burden, we have said, is not a heavy one. It is enough for the plaintiff to suggest the existence of a plausible accommodation, the costs of which, facially, do not clearly exceed its benefits. Once the plaintiff has done this, she has made out a prima facie showing that a reasonable accommodation is available, and the risk of nonpersuasion falls on the defendant.

At this point the defendant's burden of persuading the fact finder that the plaintiff's proposed accommodation is unreasonable merges, in effect, with its burden of showing, as an affirmative defense, that the proposed accommodation would cause it to suffer an undue hardship. For in practice meeting the burden of nonpersuasion on the reasonableness of the accommodation and demonstrating that the accommodation imposes an undue hardship amount to the same thing. * * *

---

28. In evaluating the costs and benefits of a proposed accommodation, * * * Section 504 does not require that the employer receive a benefit commensurate with the cost of the accommodation. The concept of reasonable accommodation, developed by regulation under Section 504, received the imprimatur of congressional approval with the passage of the Americans With Disabilities Act, 42 U.S.C.A. §§ 12101 et seq. (West Supp.1994); see also 29 U.S.C.A. § 794(d) (West Supp.1994) (stating, in a 1992 amendment, that Section 504 is to be interpreted consistently with the employment-related provisions of the Americans With Disabilities Act). As set forth by statute and regulation, the concept of reasonable accommodation permits the employer to expect the same level of performance from individuals with disabilities as it expects from the rest of its workforce. But the requirement of reasonable accommodation anticipates that it may cost more to obtain that level of performance from an employee with a disability than it would to obtain the same level of performance from a non-disabled employee. And Congress fully expected that the duty of reasonable accommodation would require employers to assume more than a de minimis cost. It follows that an accommodation is not unreasonable simply because it would be more efficient, in the narrow sense of less costly for a given level of performance, to hire a non-disabled employee than a disabled one. [Court's fn. 3]

Undue hardship is not a self-explanatory concept, however. As we have already noted, the regulations implementing Section 504 go some distance in giving substance to the bare phrase. They require consideration of: (1) The overall size of the recipient's program with respect to number of employees, number and type of facilities, and size of budget; (2) The type of the recipient's operation, including the composition and structure of the recipient's workforce; and (3) The nature and cost of the accommodation needed. But even this list of factors says little about how great a hardship an employer must bear before the hardship becomes undue. Does Section 504 require, for example, that employers be driven to the brink of insolvency before a hardship becomes too great? We think not. Cf. Jeffrey O. Cooper, Comment, Overcoming Barriers to Employment: The Meaning of Reasonable Accommodation and Undue Hardship in the Americans with Disabilities Act, 139 U. Pa. L. Rev. 1423, 1448 (1991) (noting that, during the debate over the Americans with Disabilities Act, Congress considered and rejected a provision that would have defined an undue hardship as one that threatened the continued existence of the employer). Similarly, where the employer is a government entity, Congress could not have intended the only limit on the employer's duty to make reasonable accommodation to be the full extent of the tax base on which the government entity could draw.

What, then, does undue hardship mean? We note that "undue" hardship, like "reasonable" accommodation, is a relational term; as such, it looks not merely to the costs that the employer is asked to assume, but also to the benefits to others that will result. The burden on the employer, then, is to perform a cost-benefit analysis. In a sense, of course, that is what the plaintiff also had to do to meet her burden of making out a prima facie case that a reasonable accommodation existed. But while the plaintiff could meet her burden of production by identifying an accommodation that facially achieves a rough proportionality between costs and benefits, an employer seeking to meet its burden of persuasion on reasonable accommodation and undue hardship must undertake a more refined analysis. And it must analyze the hardship sought to be imposed through the lens of the factors listed in the regulations, which include consideration of the industry to which the employer belongs as well as the individual characteristics of the particular defendant-employer. If the employer can carry this burden, it will have shown both that the hardship caused by the proposed accommodation would be undue in light of the enumerated factors, and that the proposed accommodation is unreasonable and need not be made.

Despite the ambiguities of the statutory and regulatory language, we believe that the resulting standards should not prove difficult to apply. First, the plaintiff bears the burden of proving that she is otherwise qualified; if an accommodation is needed, the plaintiff must show, as part of her burden of persuasion, that an effective accommodation exists that would render her otherwise qualified. On the issue of reasonable accommodation, the plaintiff bears only the burden of identifying an accommodation, the costs of which, facially, do not clearly exceed its benefits. These two requirements placed on the plaintiff will permit district courts to grant summary judgments for defendants in cases in which the plaintiff's proposal is either clearly ineffective or outlandishly costly. Second, we do not at all intend to suggest that employers, in attempting to meet their burden of persuasion on the reasonableness of the proposed accommodation and in making out an affirmative defense of undue hardship, must analyze the costs and benefits of proposed accommodations with mathematical precision. District courts will not be required to instruct juries on how to apply complex economic formulae; a common-sense balancing of the costs and benefits in light of the factors listed in the regulations is all that is expected.

2.   Based on the opinions of Judges Posner and Calabresi, do you think you would know what to advise a client who employs a disabled person? Both Judges rule out a "conventional" cost-benefit analysis. Is this necessary? Wouldn't a profit-maximizing employer acting in its own interest make any accommodations that were justified by the benefits in terms of higher worker productivity?

3.   As already noted, one could apply an analysis that required employers to balance costs and benefits to themselves of employing the disabled. Another approach—implied by Judge Posner—would be to require employers to make accommodations as long as total societal gains exceeded the cost of accommodation. A third possibility is that the disabled are to be afforded "rights" that transcend any conventional notion of cost-benefit analysis. Which view do you favor? Which view would you favor if you were making the decision behind the "veil of ignorance," without knowledge of your own abilities or disabilities? Which view would you favor if you were a member of Congress with a disability? Which view is most consistent with the public interest?

4.   If it is true that a profit maximizing employer would accommodate any disabled worker to the extent that the benefits off-set the costs of doing so, can the requirement that employers go further be regarded as a type of subsidy? Who should pay this subsidy (or tax): coworkers, shareholders, customers, taxpayers? Does your decision on this depend on your perspective? For example, which would you choose not knowing if you were going to be an employer, an employee or a politician seeking reelection?

A NOTE ON WHO BEARS THE COSTS OF REGULATION

An important issue to consider when non-cost-justified standards are imposed on employers is whether these costs are passed on to employees and consumers. Figure 9 illustrates a competitive labor market. D1 and S1, are the supply and demand for labor prior to requiring employers to take measures designed to lower accident risks. The equilibrium wage is W1 and the equilibrium level of employment is E1.

Figure 9

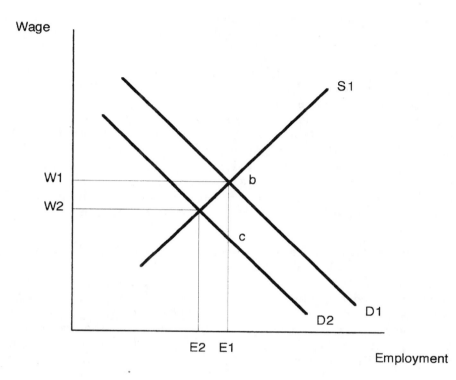

One possible effect of requiring improved working conditions is a decrease in the demand for labor. To understand why, recall from Chapter One that demand is a schedule of prices, or in this case wages, and the amount that would be purchased at each price. Another way of describing demand is that it shows the highest wage employers would be willing to pay for each quantity of labor. When a business is forced to incur expenses associated with the use of labor, the amount it is willing to pay for each quantity of labor will remain the same. Now, however, some of this compensation must be used to make the required improvements in working conditions. What remains is what the firm is willing to offer to workers in the form of wages. D2 illustrates the post-improvement demand as perceived by workers. It has shifted downward and to the left reflecting the fact that employers will not pay as much to workers in the form of direct compensation. In the graph, when demand has moved to D2, the new equilibrium wage is W2 and the equilibrium level of employment is E2. Clearly, part of the costs of improved working conditions has been passed down to workers in the form of lower wages and fewer employment opportunities.

This is not to say that the entire cost is passed through to employees. The cost to management of the improvement, on a per unit of labor basis, is the vertical downward shift in the demand curve. In the graph this is the distance between points b and c. Equilibrium wage has decreased by the distance between W1 and W2, which is less than this amount. The remaining costs of the improvement will be absorbed partly by the owners of the firm and probably partly passed on to consumers in the form of higher prices for the final output.

The division of the cost of improvements between workers, employers and consumers is, in large measure, determined by their relative elasticities of demand and supply. Elasticity is a measure of how responsive demanders or suppliers are to price changes. Generally speaking, the party who absorbs the largest portion of the cost is the one who is least able to respond. In the case of government-mandated improvements, one would expect the costs to be passed on to workers if workers have few employment alternatives and are unable to leave the labor market altogether. If, on the other hand, employers cannot conveniently substitute other inputs for labor, the firm will absorb the cost and attempt to pass it along to consumers.

So far we have examined only the impact on the demand side of the market. It seems likely that more healthful working conditions would attract labor and cause supply to increase. The impact of an increase in supply will tend to be to offset the decrease in employment resulting from the lower demand. The eventual employment level will depend upon whether the increase in supply is larger, smaller or the same as the shift in demand. In Figure 10, D1, D2 and S1, are the same as they were in Figure 9. S2 represents a new, higher supply curve drawn to only partially off-set the effect of the lower demand. A shift all the way to S3 on the other hand, would return us to the original equilibrium level of employment.

Figure 10

Although an increase in supply will offset the employment effects of a decrease in demand, these changes have the same kind of influence on wages. In effect, as supply increases, a larger share of the cost of improvement is borne by labor. These supply induced pass-throughs, however, may not be of great concern. What they indicate is that workers prefer the safer environment even at lower wages. In short, lower wages are "compensated" for by better working conditions. This is best illustrated by the conditions that exist when supply increases to S3. The equilibrium level of employment is at the original level, E1.

The equilibrium wage is only W3 but when the expenses spent on improving working conditions are included—the vertical distance between D1 and D2—the total compensation is equal to the original wage. Workers have, in effect, "consented" to the exchange of some of their wages for compensation in the form of a more healthful environment.

It is important to note that the case involving no involuntary pass-through of the cost of complying with mandated standards only occurs when supply increases at least enough to completely off-set the decline in demand. How likely do you think this is? If the potential for this equal shift existed, do you think the parties would already have negotiated an exchange of lower wages for better working conditions? Why or why not?

Finally, the model presented here is based on the assumption that the labor market is competitive; that is, neither party possesses market power to depart from a competitive price. Although most of the conclusions discussed here would hold even in cases when one party or the other possesses market power, it is far more difficult to predict the outcome when both parties possess significant power. Under these circumstances, called bilateral monopoly, the results may be more a function of bargaining strategy than traditional economic factors.[29]

3. BALANCING COSTS AND BENEFITS

As suggested in the Introductory comments to this chapter, virtually all regulatory decisions come down to a consideration of costs and benefits in one form or another. The previous section illustrates that this may not be a one-to-one comparison with the decision resting solely on whether costs exceed benefits. Even in those decisions and other more rigorous analyses, the process can be highly technical and based on estimates and assumptions. Probably more unsettling to most people, however, is that regulations often deal with the exposure one will experience to harmful substances and that it is economically as well as politically unrealistic to achieve a risk-free environment. Thus, choices are made about the "acceptable" levels of exposure to deadly substances. As the next case illustrates, this can be a complex and uncertain process.

BAN OF LAWN DARTS

Consumer Product Safety Commission, 1988.
16 CFR Parts 1306 and 1500.

* * *

A regulation, issued in 1970 by the Food and Drug Administration under the Federal Hazardous Substances Act ("FHSA") and now administered by the Commission, currently bans lawn darts, except for those intended for adult use that (1) are labeled to warn against use by children, (2) include instructions for safe use, and (3) are not sold by toy stores or by store departments dealing predominantly in toys or other children's articles. Despite these restrictions, which are intended to ensure that lawn darts are sold only for use as a game of skill by adults, children have continued to suffer serious injuries and deaths while playing with lawn darts. Accordingly, the Commission proposed to prohibit the sale of lawn darts that are intended to stick in the ground, on the basis that these darts present a risk of skull punctures.

* * *

Under Section 3(I)(1) of the Federal Hazardous Substances Act ("FHSA") and Section 9(f)(2) of the Consumer Product Safety Act ("CPSA"), the Commission is required to publish with the regulation a

---

29. See Roger Blair and Jeffrey L. Harrison, Monopsony: Economic Theory and   Antitrust Policy (1993).

final regulatory analysis containing: (A) A description of the potential benefits and potential costs of the regulation, including any benefits or costs that cannot be quantified in monetary terms, and an identification of those likely to receive the benefits and bear the costs.

* * *

BENEFITS

The benefits of the rule will accrue through a decrease in the deaths and injuries associated with lawn darts. While the rule was originally intended to address the risk of skull puncture injuries to children, all lawn darts are found to present this risk, and their elimination will also eliminate the punctures of other parts of the body, as well as the lacerations, fractures, and other injuries, that have been associated with lawn darts in the past. This also fulfills the will of Congress expressed in H.R. 5552, which is discussed in Section I of this notice. An analysis by the Commission's Directorate for Epidemiology indicates that about 670 lawn-dart-related injuries have occurred annually over the last ten years. Economic studies indicate that the average cost of these injuries was about $7,500 per occurrence. The estimated total yearly cost of injuries associated with lawn darts is about $5 million.

The Commission is aware of 3 deaths associated with lawn darts over the period 1970–1987. If it is assumed that other variables, such as exposure and use characteristics, have remained constant and that the Commission is aware of all such deaths, the darts may present a 17 percent risk of one death in a given year. If a statistical valuation of $2 million for loss of life were assigned, lawn darts would have additional expected losses of about $300,000 per year.

Therefore, the estimated total yearly costs of death and injury associated with lawn darts are about $5.4 million. A reduction of these injuries and of the risk of death will make up the benefits accruing from the rule. Since the average useful life of a lawn dart is estimated to be ten years, and since it should take about 20 years to phase out the lawn darts that are currently in consumers' hands, a portion of the benefits of the rule will phase in each year, until, after about 20 years, the full benefit of the rule will accrue each year and will continue as long as the rule is in effect.

The benefits derived will be further affected by the choice of substitute activities. For example, if consumers chose a risk-free lawn game as a substitute, the reduction in injury would be completely realized after the existing stocks of elongated-tipped lawn darts in consumers' hands have become worn out, been misplaced, or otherwise passed from use. However, if consumers choose a substitute with a similar or higher risk of death or injury, the expected benefits of this action will be offset.

The benefits will be to purchasing consumers and their families and friends, but will accrue disproportionately to those 15 years old or younger, since over 75 percent of injuries and 100 percent of the deaths have occurred to this age group. Both the costs and benefits associated with a prohibition on the sale of elongated-tipped lawn darts are expected to be relatively small.

Costs

The costs of the rule to marketers of elongated-tipped lawn darts are the loss of future sales of a product with a demonstrated steady demand. Annual sales of these lawn darts are estimated at 1–1.5 million units, holding relatively stable in recent years. The typical retail price of a set of four lawn darts is about $5; thus, the total loss of sales will be about $5–7.5 million annually at the retail level. The intermediate and final markups of these products have been estimated at more than 50 percent of the retail price; thus, industry revenues from the sale of elongated-tipped lawn darts likely exceed $2.5 million annually. These revenues will be eliminated. However, the loss of these revenues could be largely recouped by sales of substitute products that will occupy the display and storage space previously allotted to lawn darts.

The vast majority of lawn darts sold in the U.S. are imported. However, the value of these imports is so small as to be negligible compared to total U.S. imports. There are no known U.S. exports of lawn darts. Thus, the rule is expected to have no effect on U.S. trade.

The one known domestic manufacturer will bear costs associated with the disposal of molds and production processes associated with the manufacture of these lawn darts as well as foregone profit on future sales. The manufacturer could produce lawn darts for export, but this is considered unlikely since the firm does not now export lawn darts and is unlikely to develop overseas markets rapidly. If production machinery is adaptable to the manufacture of another product for which there is a demand, the cost effect may be minimized. If molds and machinery are scrapped, and no available substitute is produced to offset lost sales, the domestic manufacturer may incur significant economic costs. Also, this manufacturer has indicated that it will have raw materials for about 50,000 sets of lawn darts. If other uses for these materials cannot be found, the cost of acquiring these materials will not be recouped.

The impact of lost sales of lawn darts will be the loss of net profit associated with production and marketing of these products, less any profit derived from other products marketed in their stead.

The distributional effect on marketers will depend on their share of the market and on what share they may take of the sale of substitute products. Importers and retailers will similarly be affected by the extent of the relative volumes they sell of these goods.

Costs borne by consumers will take two forms. Consumers will be unable to purchase a game which has a proven popularity and will be induced to purchase alternate games to fill that demand. There are ready substitutes available, at approximately the same price; however, it is not clear whether these substitutes provide a similar level of utility (enjoyment) as the products they would replace. If consumers are compelled to purchase more costly games in order to receive the same utility as that provided by prohibited lawn darts, the rule may result in increased costs to consumers. Further, there may be a loss in consumer surplus associated with the unavailability of lawn darts if consumers were willing to pay more than they now pay at retail for the game in order to acquire it, thus indicating that they value the product in excess of the retail price. The extent of any lost consumer surplus is unknown, but is expected to be small.

The Commission has anecdotal information indicating that elderly persons may play lawn darts more than other typical adults do. The Commission has no information to indicate the extent to which handicapped persons may play lawn darts. Either of these groups, however, should be able to find suitable recreational substitutes for lawn darts.

The domestic manufacturer and certain marketers and retailers may be considered small businesses. The overall effect of the rule on the domestic manufacturer may be substantial, but other small businesses are not expected to experience significant adverse effects associated with the rule. This issue is discussed further in Section G of this notice.

It is likely that the marketing firms (wholesalers and private labelers) will initially bear the costs associated with the rule. The costs, including those of retrieval and disposal of unsaleable inventories and foregone profits, will begin on the effective date * * * and applies to all products in the chain of distribution at that time.

Since the commission is making the rule banning elongated-tipped lawn darts effective 30 days after the publication of the final rule, and since the rule applies to all such lawn darts in the chain of distribution on the effective date, the potential for injuries from darts distributed before the effective date will be minimized. Also, the Commission believes that at this time of year there will be fewer sets of lawn darts at the retail level or elsewhere in the chain of distribution. Furthermore, the industry will have had the opportunity not to enter into contracts for new goods pending a Commission decision, thus further reducing any inventory in the chain of distribution and other economic consequences of the rule. Therefore, the Commission believes that costs caused by inventory being held on the effective date of the rule will not be substantial.

The Commission also does not expect that the cost to retailers due to foregone profits from the sale of lawn darts will be substantial, since other products could be promoted in the retail space vacated by the prohibited products.

COMPARISON OF COSTS AND BENEFITS

As explained above, the quantifiable benefits of the rule are based on an estimated saving of the $5.4 million annual cost of deaths and injuries once lawn darts are no longer in use. This figure could be offset to the extent that consumers choose to engage in activities that involve risk during the time they would otherwise be playing lawn darts.

The quantifiable costs will consist basically of lost industry revenues, which are estimated at somewhat more than $2.5 million per year. However, the loss of these revenues can be largely recouped by the manufacture and sale of substitute items. Unquantifiable costs, discussed above, include consumers' loss of enjoyment of lawn darts.

After considering the costs and benefits of the rule, the Commission concludes that the benefits of the rule will bear a reasonable relationship to its costs.

* * *

Any lawn dart is a banned hazardous product.

Notes and Questions

1. The possible goals of this cost-benefit analysis could be stated in three ways:

    a. To the extent possible eliminate all injuries related to lawn dart use.

    b. Impose a regulation as long as the benefits of the regulation exceed the costs.

    c. Regulate so as to maximize the difference between the costs of the regulation and the benefits. In other words, at each possible level of regulation compare the costs and benefits and choose the level of regulation that maximizes this difference. This distance can be viewed as the net gain from the regulation.

Is there a difference between these standards? Did the Consumer Product Safety Commission seem to adopt any one of these approaches in deciding to ban lawn darts?

2. If the Commission had been able to accurately quantify "consumer surplus" and it had been quite large, do you think it would have reached a different outcome even though the cost of injury would have remained the same? How would you account for the fact that some of the consumer surplus is a direct result of the danger the darts present?

3. In a 1970 regulation, the Food and Drug Administration under the Federal Hazardous Substances Act had banned lawn darts except for those that were labeled to warn against hazards, that included instructions for safe use, and that were not sold primarily in toy stores. Evidently, this did not solve the problem of the dangerous lawn darts. When do you think a regulation should be limited to a warning and when should it be an outright ban?

4. Has the Commission substituted itself for parental supervision? If so, which is less costly to administer: parents supervising children or the Federal government standing in the shoes of the parents? Should adult users of lawn darts and taxpayers be required to subsidize what amounts to parental supervision even if the costs are less than the benefit?

5. The Commission engaged in a cost-benefit analysis as required by the relevant legislation. Now, Executive Order 12,866 further directs agen-

cies to "assess all costs and benefits of available regulatory alternatives and, when regulation is necessary, to select regulatory approaches that maximize net benefits (including potential economic, environmental, public health and safety, and other advantages; distributive impacts; and equity)." 58 Fed. Reg. 51735 (Sept. 30, 1993), as amended by Executive Order 13,258, 67 Fed. Reg. 9385 (Feb. 26, 2002). What does the term "net benefits" mean? Which of the standards in Question 1 above would be consistent with "net benefits?" Is it meaningful to call for a net benefit determination in the context of the other factors that are listed by Executive Order 12,866?

6. The Regulatory Flexibility Act "requires agencies to analyze regulatory options that would minimize any significant impact on small entities." Is this reasonable? Should a small business be held less accountable for externalities it produces than an large company would be? Is the RFA yet another cost-benefit statute that requires a separate balancing process? Might its subsidy-motivated inquiry counterbalance the goals of other legislation like the ADA because small businesses are the primary producers of jobs in America?

A NOTE ON REGULATION OF CIGARETTE ADVERTISING AND SALES TO CHILDREN

Another area in which parental supervision and warning labels appear not to be achieving desired goals is that of reducing deaths caused by use of tobacco. Thus in 1995 the Food and Drug Administration (FDA) under Dr. David Kessler set out to curb the use of cigarettes by young people when they first make the decision to smoke. The plan was to restrict sales of cigarettes to children and direction of promotional efforts toward them. The following is an excerpt from the FDA's cost-benefit analysis of its proposed rules:

> Each year, an estimated 1 million adolescents begin to smoke cigarettes. This analysis calculates that at least 24 percent of these youngsters will ultimately die from causes related to their nicotine habit. (Other epidemiological studies suggest even higher rates of excess mortality. For example, CDC projections indicate that 1 in 3 adolescents who smoke will die of smoking-related disease.) As a result, FDA projects that the achievement of the "Healthy People 2000" goals would prevent well over 60,000 early deaths, gaining over 900,000 future life-years for each year's cohort of teenagers who would otherwise begin to smoke. At a 3 percent discount rate, the monetary value of these benefits are projected to total from about $28 to $43 billion per year and are comprised of about $2.6 billion in medical cost savings, $900 million in productivity gains from reduced morbidity, and $24.6 to $39.7 billion per year in willingness-to-pay values for averting premature fatalities. (Because of the long periods involved, a 7 percent discount rate reduces total benefits to about $9.1 to $10.4 billion per year.) In addition, the proposed rule would prevent numerous serious illnesses associated with the use of smokeless tobacco products.

> The full realization of this goal would require the active support and participation of State and local governments, civic and community organizations, tobacco manufacturers, and retail merchants. Even if

only a fraction of the goal were achieved, the benefits would be substantial. For example, * * * halting the onset of smoking for only ½₀ of the 1 million adolescents who become new smokers each year would provide annual benefits valued at from $2.9 to $4.3 billion a year.

To comply with the initial requirements of the rule, FDA projects that manufacturers and retailers of tobacco products would incur one-time costs ranging from $26 to $39 million and annual operating costs of about $227 million. Manufacturers would be responsible for about $15 to $28 million of the one-time costs and $175 million of the annual costs (mostly for educational programs). In addition, they would face significant advertising restrictions. Retailers would pay $11 million in one-time costs and $52 million in annual costs. On an annualized basis, using a 3 percent discount rate over 15 years, costs for these initial requirements total about $230 million (also about $230 million at a 7 percent discount rate). Achieving the "Healthy People 2000" goals, however, could demand still further efforts by tobacco manufacturers to restrict youth access to tobacco products. Moreover, FDA plans to propose additional requirements that would become effective only if these goals were not met.

Consumers would incur costs to the extent that they lose positive utility received from the imagery embodied in product advertising campaigns. Consumers would also lose the convenience offered by the use of cigarette vending machines. Costs for these compliance activities were based on the agency's best estimate of the resources that would be needed to establish effective programs for decreasing the incidence of lifelong addictions to nicotine-containing cigarettes and smokeless tobacco products.

* * *

In sum, FDA finds that compliance with this proposed rule would impose some economic costs on the tobacco industry and short-term costs on several other industry sectors. With regard to small businesses, most impacts would be small or transitory. For a small retail convenience store not currently complying with this proposal, the additional first year costs could reach $320. For those convenience stores that already check customer identification, these costs fall to $35. Moreover, the proposed rule would not produce significant economic problems at the national level, as the gradual displacement in tobacco-oriented sectors would be largely offset by increased output in other areas. Thus, pursuant to the Unfunded Mandates Act, FDA concludes that the substantial benefits of this regulation would greatly exceed the compliance costs that it would impose on the U.S. economy. In addition, the agency has considered other alternatives and determined that the current proposal is the least burdensome alternative that would meet the "Healthy People 2000" goals.

60 Fed. Reg. 41,314, 41360 (August 11, 1995).

President Clinton personally announced the FDA's Final Rule on tobacco advertising and distribution to children. 61 Fed. Reg. 44396 (Aug. 28, 1996); 21 C.F.R. Parts 801, 803, 804, 807, 820, 897. The FDA program included a proposal for a national media campaign—to be paid for by the tobacco industry—to reduce smoking by young people.

At the core of the Rule were requirements to reduce children's easy access to tobacco products by (a) requiring age verification by photo ID for anyone under age 27 who desires to purchase such products, (b) banning vending machine and self-service displays except in "adult" facilities (e.g., certain nightclubs), and (c) banning free samples and similar promotions.

To reduce the appeal of tobacco products to children, the Rule (a) prohibited billboards within 1,000 feet of schools and playgrounds, (b) permitted black-and-white text-only advertising in publications with significant youth readership, (c) prohibited sale or giveaways of caps or gym bags with cigarette logos or brand names, and (d) prohibited brand-name sponsorship of sporting or entertainment events.

The rule was challenged and set ultimately aside by the Supreme Court. In FDA v. Brown & Williamson Tobacco Corp., 529 U.S. 120, 120 S.Ct. 1291, 146 L.Ed.2d 121 (2000), the Court ruled 5–4 that the FDA did not have the jurisdiction to issue the Tobacco rule discussed above. After analyzing the FDA's change of mind on its regulatory powers and extensively reviewing the 50 year legislative history, Justice O'Connor concluded that Congress did not intend for the FDA to regulate tobacco. The majority saw as a fatal weakness in the FDA's jurisdiction, its unwillingness to ban tobacco (which as a non effacious drug it would have had to do) rather than to regulate the cigarette as a nicotine delivery device. Justice Breyer, in dissent, viewed the FDA's decision not to ban cigarettes as "devices and to focus instead on regulating access to tobacco by minors as a regulatory choice the FDA was entitled to make." 509 U.S. at 172–75.

1. The majority decided the case under Step 1 of *Chevron*. Does the extensive use of legislative history comport with your understanding of the clear statement rules required to stay within Step 1? How do you view the involvement of President Clinton in the preparation, announcement and political use of this Rule? Should that help its acceptance by a reviewing court? Or did it render such approval less likely?

2. You may recall that the CPSC was aware of 3 deaths related to the use of lawn darts for the period 1970–87. If lawn darts are banned, how can you justify the decision not to ban the use of cigarettes? Do you suppose that this difference in treatment is a result of cost-benefit analysis or something else? The tobacco industry can profitably spend billions in opposing regulations that would decrease the use of cigarettes. On the other hand, even if you were inclined to contribute to an anti-smoking lobby, wouldn't you rather someone else did? Does this mean there is free riding in political markets just as there is in conventional markets? How should this be accounted for in predicting legislative action?

3. In the aftermath of *Brown & Williamson*, the federal government sought unsuccessfully to legislate tobacco payments for Medicare expenses (the ill-fated McCain bill sought over $300 billion). Thereafter, the states entered into Master Settlement Agreements with the tobacco companies that provided for over $250 billion in settlements payable annually over a 50 year period. These settlements are to be paid from taxes levied on cigarette sales. As a result, the States have now become unwilling partners with the tobacco

companies in the preservation of tobacco sales, since tobacco taxes increasingly drive state revenues in tight budget times. Indeed most states which originally agreed to use the tobacco revenues to support health care measures against diseases caused by tobacco have, under fiscal stress, used the revenues to balance their budgets. In these circumstances, are states still disinterested regulators?

UNITED STATES v. OTTATI & GOSS, INC.

United States Court of Appeals, First Circuit, 1990.
900 F.2d 429.

Before CAMPBELL, CHIEF JUDGE, and BROWN and BREYER, CIRCUIT JUDGES.

BREYER, CIRCUIT JUDGE.

Nearly ten years ago the Environmental Protection Agency ("EPA") began this lawsuit by asking a court to require several companies to clean up a thirty-four acre hazardous waste site near Kingston, New Hampshire. The suit eventually consisted of two claims that are relevant here, both made under the Comprehensive Environment Response, Compensation and Liability Act of 1980 ("CERCLA"). First, EPA said that "actual or threatened release[s] of hazardous substance[s]" from the site posed "an imminent and substantial endangerment to the public health or welfare or the environment." It therefore asked the district court, in the light of the problem, "to grant such relief as the public interest and the equities of the case may require." 42 U.S.C. § 9606(a) (first sentence). Second, EPA pointed out that it had spent considerable government money beginning to clean up the site. It asked the court to require defendants in the case, various owners, operators, and handlers, to repay the government for "all costs of removal or remedial action incurred by the United States ... not inconsistent with the national contingency plan." 42 U.S.C. § 9607(a).

The suit was complicated. The United States originally brought suit under § 7003 of the Resource Conservation and Recovery Act (RCRA), 42 U.S.C. § 6973, but later amended its complaint to allege causes of action under CERCLA, 42 U.S.C. §§ 9601–9657. By 1983 the State of New Hampshire and the Town of Kingston had joined as plaintiffs, many of the defendants had filed third-party claims and cross claims, and a total of seventeen individuals and firms (present or previous owners, handlers, or operators) had become defendants. The site itself consisted of several different areas, including a one-acre site leased to defendant Ottati & Goss, Inc. (the "O & G site"), and a six-acre site owned by defendant Great Lakes Container Corporation (the "GLCC site"). On or near the site were two brooks, a pond, and a marsh area.

While the litigation proceeded, EPA itself began to clean up part of the site, adding to the costs it intended to recover, and two of the defendants also began to help clean up. In the meantime, the court divided the trial itself into two phases. The first phase would determine which defendants the law required to help clean up and to pay costs. The second phase would determine precisely what further cleanup actions the law (42 U.S.C. § 9606(a) (first sentence)) required, and how much the liable firms should pay EPA (42 U.S.C. § 9607).

The court began the first phase of trial on December 5, 1983, concluded the trial on June 13, 1985 and found that the law required fifteen defendants either to engage in further cleanup or to pay part of the costs, or both. The second phase of trial began on February 2, 1987, concluded on July 16, 1987 and culminated in injunctive orders requiring particular defendants to engage in certain specified additional cleanup, and to pay certain specified costs. Before, during, or just after the trial, all but one of the defendants agreed to settle their dispute with EPA. One of the defendants, International Minerals & Chemical Corporation (IMC), which had owned and operated the GLCC portion of the site for about three years between 1973 and 1976, would not settle. The EPA has appealed the court's final injunctive order insofar as it applies to that single remaining defendant.

* * *

* * * EPA argues that the record does not adequately support the relief determinations that the district court made. It believes that the record required that court to order IMC to clean up the site somewhat more thoroughly. EPA's arguments are highly fact-specific and evidence-related. We have examined those portions of the record (compiled over ten years and amounting to more than 40,000 pages) that the parties have cited in their briefs. Having done so, we conclude that the district court's determinations of fact and of proper relief are adequately supported, with one exception. The exception consists of the cleanup ordered in respect to volatile organic compounds (VOC's).

* * *

We shall now explain how we have reached these legal conclusions.
* * *

II

EPA has raised a host of evidence-related issues. Although the district court adopted most of EPA's suggestions for relief, EPA believes the record required it to order yet more stringent relief in respect to contamination by 1) metals, 2) volatile organic compounds (VOCs), and 3) chemicals called "PCBs." Obviously, reviewing a 40,000 page record to determine whether a specific fact-based finding has adequate support poses difficult practical problems for a busy court of appeals. Recognizing that the parties have had a full opportunity to argue these matters at length in the district court, that the district court is better able than we are to resolve such issues, and that the factual issues before us concern not whether the site will be cleaned up, but rather likely concern who should pay the added cost of making it extremely clean, we have held both EPA and IMC to the specific language of their briefs. * * *

* * *

B. Volatile Organic Compounds (VOCs)

The EPA claims that the district court should have ordered IMC to clean up the soil on the 5.88 acre GLCC site further in order to reduce the concentration of several volatile organic compounds (VOCs). The district court concluded that IMC's 1984 cleanup efforts reduced VOC concentration sufficiently, and that EPA itself should pay for any further VOC reduction efforts. EPA says 1) that the court should have measured IMCs efforts against EPA's "one part per million" VOC soil concentration standard and 2) that, in any event, IMC failed to meet even the more generous "five to ten parts per million" standard that the court approved.

1. *The standard.* After reviewing the briefs and the record pages cited, we cannot say that the district court had to conclude that "the public interest and the equities of the case," 42 U.S.C. 9606(a), required it to adopt a "one" instead of a "five to ten" part per million standard governing VOCs in the soil. On the one hand, EPA points to the remedial conclusions of its own administrative proceedings and the expert evidence that underlay them. That evidence suggests that a "one part per million" standard would reduce the risk of human cancer (from lifetime exposure) to close to one in a million. It would prove fairly easy to monitor compliance with such a standard. And applying so stringent a standard to the soil would also reduce the cancer risk caused by water running through the soil, picking up VOCs, and later entering a drinking water system.

On the other hand, IMC points out that the very report and expert study on which EPA relies says that a VOC level of 7 parts per million in the soil would reduce lifetime exposure cancer risks to one in a hundred thousand, a level that, in various contexts (including EPA's basic studies), EPA asserts to be its "goal". Moreover, EPA monitored IMC's cleanup efforts, EPA was fully aware that IMC's method would reduce VOC soil concentrations to levels of five to ten parts per million, yet, at that time, EPA did not urge further cleanup. IMC meets EPA's argument that lower VOC soil concentrations are now needed to protect against higher water concentrations by noting that the district court separately ordered run-off water cleanup to appropriately low levels. And it also says that the special additional cleanup method (digging up, heating in a special machine, and then replacing about 14,000 cubic yards of soil) will cost an added several million dollars (IMC has already spent about $2.6 million), all for very little purpose (since one part per million is not significantly safer than five or ten).

There is simply no way for us to say, on the basis of this kind of general evidence, or on the basis of other highly general, tangentially related record material to which EPA refers, that the district court was wrong in its choice of standard. EPA must convince us of fact-related error, and it has failed to do so.

2. *Compliance with the "five to ten parts per million" VOC standard.* The district court concluded that "there is evidence in some areas

that ppms total of VOC levels exceeded substantially the norm," but "overall ... the IMC cleanup of the soil contamination substantially cleared up the VOCs." We take as the "norm" the "five to ten parts per million" that IMC says was its "goal". IMC's brief adds that "it is evident that the court accepted the propriety of IMC's target range of 5–10 ppm when it found that 'IMC ... substantially cleaned up the VOCs.'" And we shall hold IMC to its stated arguments, just was we have done with EPA. We therefore understand EPA to argue that the record does not permit the district court to find that IMC reduced VOC levels, overall, to "five to ten parts per million," even allowing for an occasional "hot spot" departure. We agree.

EPA points to two studies in the record, one conducted by an EPA contractor, the other representing an IMC contractor's "check" of the EPA contractor's sampling. After IMC finished cleaning up its site, the EPA contractor tested the results by digging a series of "test pits." It randomly dug 62 test pits, each about eight feet long, three feet wide, and eight feet deep, evenly spaced throughout an area somewhat larger than a football field. The contractor then took soil samples from different levels within each bit. It found that soil in over thirty of the sixty-two pits contained VOCs concentrated at levels higher than ten parts per million. Many samples were much higher than ten parts per million, and the high concentration samples appeared at different levels in many pits.

IMC makes two arguments in its effort to support the district court's conclusion. First, it says that EPA's contractor did not test the soil in a fair way. Rather, the contractor would use a meter to detect just where in the pit concentration was the highest; then, the contractor would take soil from that place. IMC's contractor testified that such a "hot spot" might be the size of "a softball." Since other evidence in the record suggests that a lifetime of exposure to VOC concentration of, say, seventy parts per million would produce a cancer risk of one in ten thousand, one might ask just how a scattering of such "softballs" throughout the area could hurt. No one seems likely to suffer much from occasionally digging up some dirt mixed with a tiny amount of something like gasoline or benzene or turpentine; the court's other remedies should make certain that the ground water flowing through the area stays clean; and, even if someone builds a house in the area and sinks a well, the small size of the "softball" would help assure that no significant amount of gasoline-like liquid mixes with the water.

The difficulty with this argument is that we cannot read the record as showing no more than the occasional "softball". IMC's contractor's own report indicates that thirty-three of the sixty-two wells have VOC concentrations that exceed ten parts per million (and, again, many of them exceed it by ten times or more). Although that report indicates, in respect to a few pits (pit 117, for example) that the "hot" area does not comprise the whole pit, the very fact that the contractor made notes stating, in respect to some pits, that the high concentration is found in only part of the pit, suggests that, where no such note exists, the high concentration area is fairly widespread within the pit. (The contractor testified that he would indicate in his notes whenever the "hot" area was significantly limited within a single pit). The report suggests that high concentrations were limited to very small areas in only a few instances; indeed, nowhere does it indicate "softball-sized" areas; and in some instances (pit 121, for example) the report specifically notes that high concentrations exist throughout the pit (e.g., 350 ppm at two feet deep, 340 ppm also at two feet, 400 ppm at four feet in one part of the pit and 606 ppm at four feet in another part). The contractor also testified that "in other cases [the "hot spot"] . . . could be half a test pit," and he seems to have accepted a characterization of an "average" level of 87 parts per million as reasonable. Having read through both the "IMC" and "EPA" reports, and finding little conflict in this respect between them, we have a firm conviction that one cannot reasonably characterize the "over ten parts per million" VOC concentrations as "few" or "far between". Rather, the studies and related testimony indicate that such "over-standard" concentrations are widespread, and in significant amounts, within the total test area.

IMC also points to testimony suggesting that it would be wasteful to require IMC to dig up the several acre site again to process 14000 or so cubic yards of soil. An IMC expert testified that, even if nothing further is done, by the year 2000 probably more than half of the VOCs in the soil would have diffused into the atmosphere. Moreover, VOCs released into the ground water will be taken care of by the ground water treatment ordered by the court. Since IMC's $2.6 million dollar expenditure has brought us so near absolute safety, why force expenditure of millions of dollars more to buy so little?

The problem with this second argument is that the court expressed no view about its validity or direct relevance. Rather, the court's opinion assumes (as IMC and EPA both read it) that "five to ten parts per million is the appropriate standard," and it goes on to say that IMC has substantially complied. We, too, therefore, express no view about this second kind of argument, except to note that the district court did not adopt it. Thus, we remand this aspect of the case to the district court so that it can devise a further VOC cleanup remedy, which, in light of its findings about danger to the public health, will adequately satisfy "the public interest." 42 U.S.C. § 9606(a).

C.   PCBs

EPA also asked the district court to order a cleanup of soil and sediments at the waste site to reduce to safe levels the concentration of a carcinogenic chemical, PCB. The court applied a standard of 50 parts per million for soil concentration, which it determined IMC's 1984 cleanup had met, and a standard of 20 parts per million for sediment concentration, which it orders IMC to meet. EPA now argues that the standards are too lenient; it says that the court should have selected a soil standard of 20 parts per million and a sediment standard of one part per million, and that, in any event, the soil cleanup did not meet the court's own 50 ppm standard. After examining the record, however, we find adequate legal support for the court's conclusions.

1. *The soil standard.* The evidence that EPA offered to show that the soil PCB cleanup should reduce concentration to *at least* fifty parts per million is strong. EPA pointed to a Toxic Substances Control Act regulation that insists for (TSCA purposes) upon incineration (or storage in special dumps) of soil with PCB concentrations greater than that. 40 C.F.R. 761.60. Of course the TSCA standard does not say that soil with less than 50 PCB parts per million is safe. Nonetheless, the evidence that EPA offered in support of its lower, 20 ppm, standard is weak. The 20 ppm evidence consists almost entirely of a two page calculation prepared by an EPA expert, Dr. Tsai (and Dr. Tsai's explanatory testimony). In her calculation, Dr. Tsai makes clear that her conclusion—that only 20 ppm (or lower) PCB concentrations will achieve EPA's cancer goal (a lifetime cancer risk of less than one in a hundred thousand)—rests upon her assumptions that a) developers will build residential housing on the site, b) small children, playing in the backyard, will eat dirt containing PCBs, and c) the children will eat a little bit of dirt each day for 245 days per year for three and a half years (about six ounces altogether, as we calculate it).

At the same time, IMC produced witnesses that suggested that residential development was unlikely; it noted that Dr. Tsai's calculation also indicated that concentration levels as high as 70 ppm might be safe (if the children ate the dirt on only 70, rather than on 245, days per year); and it obtained testimony from EPA project manager Hohman that, in context, makes it seem as if EPA was uncertain just where to draw the line between a 70 ppm standard and a 20 ppm standard (though TSCA constrained EPA to urge a standard of 50 ppm or less). IMC also noted that EPA was fully aware that IMC's own cleanup plan called for PCB reduction to 50 ppm, that EPA, at one point, called the plan "extremely commendable," that EPA employees, contractors or officials were present throughout IMC's cleanup, and that EPA (while not binding itself to accept IMC's cleanup as sufficient) nonetheless said nothing at the time about reducing PCB levels further. Finally, IMC's brief, and EPA's studies, make clear that IMC's cleanup, reducing PCB and VOC soil levels to 50 ppm and 10 ppm respectively, cost about $2.6 million; to reduce those levels further, to 20 ppm PCBs and 1 ppm VOCs, will cost an additional $9.3 million. One might conclude from the cited portions of the record that this amounts to a very high cost for very little extra safety.

On balance, after reading the cited portions of the record, we have no "firm conviction," that the district court's determination was wrong; its factual conclusions do not seem "clearly erroneous," nor its judgment unreasonable. We cannot say that the "public interest and equities of the case" require a stricter standard than the court applied.

2. *Implementation of the soil standard.* EPA argues that IMC's cleanup did not meet even the 50 ppm PCB standard. Its evidence that

this is so consists of analyses of soil samples taken from soil several feet below the surface in five of the 63 test pits. Three samples exceeded 50 ppm (56, 134, and 143 ppm, respectively). The explanatory testimony to which EPA also points, however, indicates that these samples were not taken randomly. Rather the five samples were taken from areas where the experts found "discolored soils." That being so, one might reasonably conclude that EPA could find evidence in only three of the 62 test pits of PCB concentrations that exceed the standard. (Although EPA's expert also said that there were other areas of "discolored" soils, he did not make clear how many there were, where they were, whether they were outside the five test pits from which the samples were taken, or whether they more likely reflected the "more than 50 ppm" present in the three noncomplying "discolored soil" samples.) In our view, the areas of noncompliance are sufficiently small in number to warrant a conclusion that the likelihood that a child would eat this soil, consistently over a period of many days or years, is virtually nonexistent; and, the very occasional patches of below-surface noncomplying soil would seem sufficiently scattered to warrant a conclusion of no significant risk. We cannot say that the district court was "clearly erroneous" or unreasonable in reaching such a conclusion, and we therefore find no legal error.

3. *PCB "sediment" standard.* The district court required IMC to clean the marsh and the south brook to the point where PCB concentration in the sediments would not exceed 20 parts per million. EPA argues that the standard is too lenient. It says that the court should have imposed a standard of one part per million PCBs.

The EPA supports its argument with citations to only a handful of statements. Its own administrative report simply says in highly general language that there should be a standard of one part per million in order to protect birds, fish, and mammals, as well as human beings. The study upon which the EPA based its report offered several alternative remedies, only one of which recommended that same standard for that same reason. And Dr. Tsai testified that she chose that same standard, again, for the same reason.

IMC correctly points out, however, that the study upon which EPA based its report also, in another alternative remedy, recommended a sediment PCB standard of 50 ppm. It points to a discussion in the record of a federal fish and wildlife study that finds no "significant health risk" at the pond, despite the potential 20 ppm PCB sediment concentrations. And it adds that EPA has nowhere explained how, or why, animal and human protection requires a more stringent standard. Indeed, out of the entire record, EPA mentions only a handful of highly general, conclusory sentences about the PCB sediment standard. (*E.g.,* the EPA's basic study simply says without elaboration, that the "action level of 1 ppm for PCB's in sediments was selected after discussions with State and federal officials because of the potential for bioaccumulation of these PCB's by wetland biota.") The only more concrete explanation given is that of Dr. Tsai, who, after repeating the same general conclusory sentence, added the EPA considered a "two parts per million" standard for concentration in fish. But Dr. Tsai did not explain the relation between PCB concentration in the sediment at the bottom of a pond and concentration within a fish.

In our view, the district court was entitled to hold EPA to somewhat higher standards of detailed proof than those met in the pages we have cited. And, in the absence of that proof, given the other (also skimpy) indications in the record that less stringent "alternatives" would be adequate, we believe the court could reasonably choose a 20 parts per million standard. That is to say, we cannot find that such a standard is "clearly erroneous" or its choice unreasonable.

* * *

Notes and Questions

1.   The rulings on lawn darts (or even tobacco) seem relatively simple when compared to the complexity of the EPA challenges in *Ottati*. What factors account for this difference in complexity? When the scientific and regulatory standards are constantly shifting, how should one seek to improve the enforcement process? Does it come down to an allocation of regulatory resources? For every EPA action, how many other important actions have to be ignored?

2.   After he wrote *Ottati & Goss,* Judge Breyer had occasion to speculate about the problems that case posed in a series of lectures at the Harvard Law School (the Holmes lectures published as Breaking The Vicious Circle: Toward Effective Risk Regulation (1992)). He emphasized that the primary regulatory problem was one of "tunnel vision":

> Tunnel vision, a classic administrative disease, arises when an agency so organizes or subdivides its tasks that each employee's individual conscientious performance effectively carries single-minded pursuit of a single goal too far, to the point where it brings about more harm than good. In the regulation of health risks, a more appropriate label is "the last 10 percent" or "going the last mile." The regulating agency considers a substance that poses serious risks, at least through long exposure to high doses. It then promulgates standards so stringent— insisting, for example, upon rigidly strict site cleanup requirements— that the regulatory action ultimately imposes high costs without achieving significant additional safety benefits. A former EPA administrator put the problem succinctly when he noted that about 95 percent of the toxic material could be removed from waste sites in a few months, but years are spent trying to remove the last little bit. Removing that last little bit can involve limited technological choice, high cost, devotion of considerable agency resources, large legal fees, and endless argument.
>
> Let me provide some examples. The first comes from a case in my own court, *United States v. Ottati & Goss,* arising out of a ten-year effort to force cleanup of a toxic waste dump in southern New Hampshire. The site was mostly cleaned up. All but one of the private parties had settled. The remaining private party litigated the cost of cleaning up the last little bit, a cost of about $9.3 million to remove a small amount

of highly diluted PCBs and "volatile organic compounds" (benzene and gasoline components) by incinerating the dirt. How much extra safety did this $9.3 million buy? The forty-thousand-page record of this ten-year effort indicated (and all the parties seemed to agree) that, without the extra expenditure, the waste dump was clean enough for children playing on the site to eat small amounts of dirt daily for 70 days each year without significant harm. Burning the soil would have made it clean enough for the children to eat small amounts daily for 245 days per year without significant harm. But there were no dirt-eating children playing in the area, for it was a swamp. Nor were dirt-eating children likely to appear there, for future building seemed unlikely. The parties also agreed that at least half of the volatile organic chemicals would likely evaporate by the year 2000. To spend $9.3 million to protect non-existent dirt-eating children is what I mean by the problem of "the last 10 percent." Id. at 11–12. (Footnotes omitted.)[30]

3.   Recall the possible parameters of a cost-benefit standard suggested in Note 1, following the lawn dart ruling. Which of those approaches seems to be used in *Ottati*?

4.   How can federal agencies be required to take account of the "last ten percent" problem? Will doing so require Congress and the courts to play crucial roles in deciding how agency agendas should be interpreted? Suppose, for example, the last ten percent involves an EPA clean up in your congressional district? Or, better still, suppose your congressional district has a super-fund site that has not yet been reached because of EPA's shortage of regulatory resources. How do you move up the queue?

5.   What should an agency do when *both* action and inaction threaten to cause significant harm? The Food and Drug Administration faces that problem in much of what it does. Approval of a new drug without adequate testing could result in injury to thousands of people, but during the time that the testing is being undertaken, thousands more could suffer irreparable harm or even death because the drug was unavailable to them. See, e.g., Schering Corporation v. Food and Drug Administration, 51 F.3d 390 (3d Cir.1995); Rutherford v. United States, 616 F.2d 455 (10th Cir.1980); Mary K. Olson, Regulatory Agency Discretion Among Competing Industries: Inside the FDA, 11 J. Law, Economics & Organization 379 (1995).

NOTE ON THE RELATIONSHIP OF RISK ASSESSMENT, TO COST–BENEFIT ANALYSIS

The cases in this Chapter have illustrated that many regulatory schemes seem to deviate from a strict comparison of the costs and benefits of regulation. In some instances, the decision to do so has been made on the basis that the value of the interest to be protected is incalculable. In other instances, costs and benefits are compared in a

---

30.   This analysis has been criticized for its preference of "scientific" to "political" decisionmaking, on the ground that science can be equally political. See Liza Heinzerling, Political Science, 62 U. Chi. L. Rev. 1 (1995) ("If Breyer gets to keep his politics, why doesn't everyone else?") But the Breyer analysis has also been extolled by a fellow federal judge who believes a consensus can emerge in favor of CBA. See Stephen F. Williams, Squaring the Vicious Circle, 53 Ad. L. Rev. 257 (2001).

general sense but the uncertainties about the external valuations make it hard to view the process as anything but a very rough approximation.

Earlier, Republicans typically embraced cost-benefit analysis and Democrats usually were skeptical. But after about 1995, both Democrats and Republicans seemed to agree on the value of risk assessment to measure the costs and benefits of regulatory decisions. In the 103d Congress, bills introduced in the Senate requiring the EPA to conduct risk analysis of all its regulations drew close to unanimous support.[28]

In looking at cost-benefit analysis and risk/benefit analysis, it is important not to let the labels get in the way of understanding. The terms look similar but they use the word "benefit" in opposite ways. In "cost-benefit" analysis, "costs" are the burden imposed on industry and "benefits" are harm avoided. "Risk-benefit" analysis uses "risk" to describe harms to be avoided, and "benefit" to describe industry savings from not being regulated further.[29] Regardless of the form of expression, the basic analysis should be the same. A complete accounting for the costs of a regulation should include both the actual cost of the regulation in terms of administration and the benefits of the regulated activity that may be foregone when regulation takes place. Similarly the benefits will be the increase in some measure of well-being associated with the regulation.

Although there is not a clear line between cost-benefit analysis and risk-benefit analysis, the former is exhibited by the lawn dart example where actual human experience could be used to determine roughly the external costs of placing lawn darts into the market. Risk/benefit analysis tends to be more technical and the only way of assessing the risk may be by relying on animal or other experimentation and then extrapolating the results to humans.

Risk analysis is typically viewed as involving four steps:

1. Identification of the potential hazard.

2. Determining the relationship between exposure and harm.

3. Determining the actual amount of exposure.

4. Determining the result in terms of the overall magnitude of the risk.[30]

For example, in *Ottati & Goss*, Judge Breyer and the parties involved were concerned with the likelihood that a child eating the contaminated dirt would eventually be harmed. This would involve the determination of a connection between PCBs and illness, the amount

28. See S. 171, 103 Cong., 2d Sess. (1993) (Senate votes 95–3 to require risk assessment by EPA). See also D. Clarke, The Elusive Middle Ground in Environmental Policy, Issues in Science and Technology (Spring 1995) ("Time and again in the last Congress, risk reform proposals won strong bipartisan votes in both the House and Senate.")

29. This explanation is from Robert Percival, Allen S. Miller, Christopher H. Schroder & James P. Leape, Environmental Regulation: Law, Science, and Policy 521 (1992).

30. National Research Council, Risk Assessment in the Federal Government: Managing the Process (1983).

that it would take to cause the illness, the likely exposure of individuals to PCBs in the soil and the impact of this exposure on an overall basis. Obviously, each of these steps can involve disagreements in the scientific community. Steps one and two may rely entirely or largely on animal experimentation without certain knowledge as to how these result translate to the risk for humans. Despite scientific appearance, these complexities leave a great deal of room for discretion and political pressures.[31] Moreover, risk assessment does not result in a single dollar amount as a measurement of the harm of an activity. Instead it is a probability driven estimate that almost certainly is dependent on a number of assumptions.

There are two aspects of this weighing process that are especially troubling to many people. The first is the need to reduce human suffering and life itself to some quantitative measure. Aside from making people uncomfortable, these evaluations may involve racial or class biases.[32] The second is related to the goal of maximizing "net benefits" and also Justice Breyer's notion of the last 10%. If one adopts the view that benefits are the harms avoided by regulation and costs are the burdens attributed to the regulation, the purpose of determining net benefits is to maximize the difference between the two. That may mean stopping well short of saving every life and avoiding every harm.

At a more practical level, some of the difficulties in reaching agreement in the area of risk assessment can be explained by regulatory behavior. Professor McGarity describes two types of decision making that takes place in agencies. He entitles a section of his book: "Rational Analysis and the Two Rulemaking Cultures:"

> Although the goal of rational agency decisionmaking seems unexceptional, its proponents had in mind a very ambitious agenda. They meant to interject a new and very different way of thinking into a firmly entrenched bureaucratic culture. Following the conventional nomenclature, we may label this new kind of thinking "comprehensive analytical rationality." The term "comprehensive" suggests that this kind of thinking ideally explores all possible routes to the solution of a problem. The term "analytical" implies that it attempts to sort out, break down, and analyze (quantitatively, if possible) all of the relevant components of a problem and its possible solutions. The term "rationality" captures the pride that its proponents take in its objectivity and the dispassion with which it debates the pros and cons of alternative solutions without regard to whose ox is being gored. In practice, comprehensive analytical rationality has been dominated by the paradigms of neoclassical micro-economics.

> This kind of rationality contrasts sharply with the thinking that has traditionally dominated the rulemaking process in most

31. See Juniun C. McElveen Jr. & Chris Amantea, Legislating Risk Assessment, 63 U. Cin. L. Rev. 1553 (1995).

32. See Daniel C. Wigley & Kristin S. Shrader–Frechette, Environmental Racism and Biased Methods of Risk Assessment, 7 Risk: Health, Safety & Envirn. 55 (1996).

regulatory agencies, which I shall refer to as "techno-bureaucratic rationality." I use the term techno-bureaucratic to distinguish the thinking that dominates highly technical rulemaking activities from bureaucratic thinking in general. Techno-bureaucratic rationality is a special brand of bureaucratic thinking that arises in the context of regulatory activities that must grapple with highly complex (and often unresolvable) issues of science, engineering, and public policy. Some of the existing models of bureaucratic thinking, such as Lindblom's perceptive "muddling through" model, are relevant to techno-bureaucratic thinking, but do not capture the essence of bureaucratic programs that have highly technical, scientific, and engineering components. I use the word "rationality" because, unlike many students of regulation, I do not believe that this kind of thinking is irrational per se. Techno-bureaucratic rationality is a rationality built on a unique understanding of the regulatory universe that is born out of frustrating hands-on experience with unanswerable questions of extraordinary complexity. It is, in a sense, a "second best" rationality that recognizes the limitations that inadequate data, unquantifiable values, mixed societal goals, and political realities place on the capacity of structured rational thinking, and it does the best that it can with what it has.[33]

Whatever one's possible suspicions about cost-benefit analysis or risk/benefit analysis, it is hard to deny that there is a lack of rationality or at least consistency in our approach to regulation. For example, it is estimated that regulations prohibiting unvented space heaters result in costs of about $100,000 per life saved. Side door impact requirements on automobiles cost roughly $800,000 per life saved. The ban on the use of diethylstilbestrol (DES) in cattlefeed is estimated to cost over $120 million per life saved. Even more extreme is the cost per life saved of limits on exposures to formaldehyde which is $86 billion dollars.[34] One may find these figures unobjectionable because they reflect the value of life that is not easily reduced to dollars, especially if the life is your own. On the other hand, the issue whether resources are allocated in ways that do the most good cannot be ignored.

This disparity in "values" reflects the pressures felt by regulatory officials as they engage in the process of weighing costs and benefits. Take, for example, three different perspectives in the context of cleaning up the contaminated soil around the former site of a factory. As a manager, shareholder or even employee, your interest would support a standard that does not require a massive and expensive cleaning effort. However, if you are a manager, shareholder or employee of a corporation whose business it is to clean up toxic substances, you are likely to favor quite rigid standards.[35] Finally, you may just be a concerned citizen with

33. Thomas O. McGarity, Reinventing Rationality—The Role of Regulatory Analysis in the Federal Bureaucracy 6–7 (1991) (Footnotes omitted.)

34. There figures are from U.S. Office of Management & Budget, Regulatory Pro-gram of the United States Government, April 1, 1991–March 1, 1992.

35. See Stephen F. Williams, Risk Regulation and Its Hazards, 93 Michigan L. Rev. 1498 (1995).

a more general interest in the environment. This may seem to make your decision easy—less pollution is better. Right? Suppose, however, that your efforts to force a manufacturer to clean up toxic substances increases the costs of car seats for children or for automobiles?

The salient point is that the quality of analysis undertaken by administrative agencies matters and that the quality of "agency science" is itself a major policy issue. This has led some to suggest that scientific analysis by agencies should be subject to the same level of scrutiny that science receives in the federal courts (under the *Daubert* principle) before it is admitted into evidence.[36]

Further, consider the increasingly central problem of *risk perception*. As Justice Breyer suggests,[37] risks ranked by objective criteria differ greatly from those ranked by perception. Literature on the psychology of risk perception is extensive and compelling,[38] and government officials will be under great pressure to deal with what citizens perceive to be risks rather than to address only what the scientific data may suggest are more serious problems. Does this make decisionmaking more complex?[39] Does it make it impossible?

CONCLUDING NOTE ON VALUATION OF LIFE

Cost-benefit analysis ultimately must deal with what is called in the regulatory jargon calls the "value of statistical life" (VSL). OMB/OIRA in its 2003 Report to Congress provides the following description:

> Some describe the monetized value of small changes in fatality risk as the "value of statistical life" (VSL) or, less precisely, the "value of a life." The latter phrase can be misleading because it suggests erroneously that the monetization exercise tries to place a "value" on individual lives. You should make clear that these terms

36. See Alan Charles Raul & Julie Zampa Dwyer, "Regulatory *Daubert*": A Proposal to Enhance Judicial Review of Agency Science by Incorporating *Daubert* Principles in Administrative Law, 66 Law & Contemp. Probs. 7 (2003); Compare Thomas O. McGarity, On the Prospect of "Daubertizing" Judicial Review of Risk Assessment, 66 Law & Contemp. Probs. 155 (2003).

37. Stephen F. Breyer, Breaking the Vicious Circle: Toward Effective Risk Regulation 33–39 (1993) (ordering of perceived risks by members of the public versus experts; for example, the threat of nuclear power ranked 1st in a survey of college students and 20th in a similar survey of experts). See also Howard F. Chang, Risk Regulation, Endogenous Public Concerns and the Hormones Dispute: Nothing to Fear but Fear Itself? (Penn Law Working Paper: Dec. 11, 2003) (Discussing the role that fear of hormone treated beef should

play in the World Trade Organization rulings against the European Community's restriction on U.S. treated beef).

38. E.g., W. Kip Viscusi & Wesley A. Magat, Learning About Risk: Consumer and Worker Responses to Hazard Information (1987).

39. Professor Sunstein raises questions about how courts should evaluate an agency's use of cost-benefit analysis on judicial review. Should there be "legal floors and ceilings" that establish parameters of reasonableness around such issues as valuation of life? More broadly, should the Courts employ principles of cost-benefit that are presumptive? See Cass R. Sunstein, Cost–Benefit Default Principles, 99 Mich. L. Rev. 1651, 1709–012 (2002). See also Cass R. Sunstein, Lives, Life–Years and Willingness to Pay, 104 Colum.L.Rev. 205 (2004) (preferring value of a statistical life year over the VSL).

refer to the measurement of willingness to pay for reductions in only small risks of premature death. They have no application to an identifiable individual or to very large reductions in individual risks. They do not suggest that any individual's life can be expressed in monetary terms. Their sole purpose is to help describe better the likely benefits of a regulatory action.

Confusion about the term "statistical life" is also widespread. This term refers to the sum of risk reductions expected in a population. For example, if the annual risk of death is reduced by one in a million for each of two million people, that is said to represent two "statistical lives" extended per year (2 million people x 1/1,000,000 = 2). If the annual risk of death is reduced by one in 10 million for each of 20 million people, that also represents two statistical lives extended.

The adoption of a value for the projected reduction in the risk of premature mortality is the subject of continuing discussion within the economic and public policy analysis community. A considerable body of academic literature is available on this subject. This literature involves either explicit or implicit valuation of fatality risks, and generally involves the use of estimates of VSL from studies on wage compensation of occupational hazards (which generally are in the range of 10^{-4} annually), on consumer product purchase and use decisions, or from an emerging literature using stated preference approaches. A substantial majority of the resulting estimates of VSL vary from roughly $1 million to $10 million per statistical life.[40]

John Graham, head of OIRA, sparked a controversy when he sought to establish a single VSL number, which discounted a life based on age. The AARP took offense to "age discounts," producing colorful posters carried by seniors that said "I'm worth 1/3 less." OIRA ultimately capitulated:

> The age of the affected population has also been identified as an important factor in the theoretical literature. However, the empirical evidence on age and VSL is mixed. In light of the continuing questions over the effect of age on VSL estimates, you should not use an age-adjustment factor in analysis using VSL estimates.[41]

The VSL technique raises several questions:

1.   Can life be valued at all? Are people's lives of different worth? Isn't everyone's life of infinite value? If you believe nothing is of infinite value, then should we treat all lives as equally valuable? If not, what criteria would you use to distinguish among lives?

2.   Should a life be discounted for age or any other factors, sex, minority status, etc.? Don't actuaries engage in these kinds of judg-

40. OMB, Informing Regulatory Decisions: 2003 Report to Congress on the Costs and Benefits of Federal Regulations and Unfunded Mandates on State. Local, and Tribal Entities, at App. D, 9 146–147, available at *http://www.whitehouse.gov/omb/inforeg/regpol-reports_congress.html*.

41. Id. at 147 (footnote omitted).

ments? If you were running a life insurance company, would you let such facts enter into your judgments?

3. The OMB/OIRA report bases VSL calculations on a person's willingness to pay for reductions of small risks in premature death.[42] Is willingness to pay an accurate or fair measure? Is such a measure practical for an agency to use? Why or why not?

4. Would older people be expected to pay less than younger people to reduce the risk of premature death. Is the premise that the remaining years of older people are of lesser value? To test this proposition, consider whether you observe older people tending to engage in riskier behavior than younger people?

B. CREATION OF EXCHANGEABLE PROPERTY RIGHTS AS AN ALTERNATIVE FORM OF REGULATION

When transaction costs are not prohibitive, resources may be expected to flow to their most valued uses as determined by what individuals are willing and able to pay. In the previous sections we have seen efforts by government to force individuals to act. More recently, however, agencies have tried to be less coercive. Our first illustration is of a program that is designed to create a market in public harm. That is, it lets people for whom compliance is less costly "sell" the rights they would otherwise have to impose externalities on others. People for whom compliance is more costly can then buy a "right" to "do wrong" and in that way minimize the total social cost of reaching the desired levels of clean-up.

1. SELLING THE RIGHT TO CREATE ACID RAIN

ACID DEPOSITION CONTROL
42 U.S.C.A. § 7651.

§ 7651. Findings and purposes

(a) Findings

The Congress finds that—

(1) the presence of acidic compounds and their precursors in the atmosphere and in deposition from the atmosphere represents a threat to natural resources, ecosystems, materials, visibility, and public health;

(2) the principal sources of the acidic compounds and their precursors in the atmosphere are emissions of sulfur and nitrogen oxides from the combustion of fossil fuels;

---

42. See W. Kip Viscusi, Fatal Tradeoffs: Public & Private Responsibilities for Risk 17–33 (1992) (describing the methodology, which involves the dollar values a person is willing to pay to avoid a particular risk; these values are then aggregated to establish a VSL).

(3) the problem of acid deposition is of national and international significance;

(4) strategies and technologies for the control of precursors to acid deposition exist now that are economically feasible, and improved methods are expected to become increasingly available over the next decade;

(5) current and future generations of Americans will be adversely affected by delaying measures to remedy the problem;

(6) reduction of total atmospheric loading of sulfur dioxide and nitrogen oxides will enhance protection of the public health and welfare and the environment; and

(7) control measures to reduce precursor emissions from steam-electric generating units should be initiated without delay.

(b) Purposes

The purpose of this subchapter is to reduce the adverse effects of acid deposition through reductions in annual emissions of sulfur dioxide of ten million tons from 1980 emission levels, and, in combination with other provisions of this chapter, of nitrogen oxides emissions of approximately two million tons from 1980 emission levels, in the forty-eight contiguous States and the District of Columbia. It is the intent of this subchapter to effectuate such reductions by requiring compliance by affected sources with prescribed emission limitations by specified deadlines, which limitations may be met through alternative methods of compliance provided by an emission allocation and transfer system. It is also the purpose of this subchapter to encourage energy conservation, use of renewable and clean alternative technologies, and pollution prevention as a long-range strategy, consistent with the provisions of this subchapter, for reducing air pollution and other adverse impacts of energy production and use.

* * *

§ 7651b. Sulfur dioxide allowance program for existing and new units

(a) Allocations of annual allowances for existing and new units

(1) For the emission limitation programs under this subchapter, the Administrator shall allocate annual allowances for the unit, to be held or distributed by the designated representative of the owner or operator of each affected unit at an affected source in accordance with this subchapter. * * *

(b) Allowance transfer system

Allowances allocated under this subchapter may be transferred among designated representatives of the owners or operators of affected sources under this subchapter and any other person who holds such allowances, * * *

* * *

(e) New utility units

After January 1, 2000, it shall be unlawful for a new utility unit to emit an annual tonnage of sulfur dioxide in excess of the number of allowances to emit held for the unit by the unit's owner or operator. * * * New utility units may obtain allowances from any person, in accordance with this subchapter.

Notes and Questions

1.   Sulphur dioxide and the resulting acid rain are obvious externalities that would be difficult to curb through simple market transactions. The sulfur dioxide trading program created by the above legislation treats clean air like an inherently scarce resource and issues "allowances" that permit the owners to emit one ton of sulfur dioxide. The program also calls for the gradual reduction of sulfur dioxide emissions by 10 million tons by 2010. About 70% of sulfur dioxide is produced by electric utilities.[43] These allowances are auctioned off and the owners may "use" them, resell them or just hold them for the future. In fact, the allowances can and have been purchased by environmentalists who want to make sure they are not used at all.

2.   Given that the allowances are generally available, is the market now finally able to allocate clean air between polluters and non-polluters on the basis of who values the air the most? What do you find objectionable about this, if anything? Will there be a danger of free riding by environmentalists?

3.   When the program was initiated, it was predicted that each allocation would be worth $1500. In mid 1995 they were selling for around $125 each. What would explain this lower value? One possibility is that utilities have found less expensive ways to reduce their emissions. One commentator, though, says that utilities are not buying the allocations even when it would be less expensive than reducing the emissions. Some possible theories are that potential buyers are concerned about the speculative nature of investing in pollution "futures," while another is that they are uncertain how regulatory agencies will react to efforts by buyers to pass the costs of allowances on to customers. See Eileen L. Kahaner, GAO's Analysis of Title IV's Sulphur Dioxide Emissions Allowance Trading, 2 Environmental L. 239 (1995); Note, New Strategies for a New Market: The Electric Industry's Response to the Environmental Protection Agency's Sulphur Dioxide Emission Allowance Trading Program, 47 Admin. L. Rev. 469 (1995).

4.   As you saw in Chapter 4, utilities typically are only permitted to pass on some costs to consumers. If you were the manager of a utility and you purchased an emission allowance that was subject to variations in price, would this give you concern about what price could be passed on?

5.   One could take the view that a market solution like that employed in the case of sulfur dioxide side-steps the outcomes that might occur if special interests were constantly involved in the process of determining rights and obligations. This was certainly not the case, at least with the setting up of the program. For example, existing utilities received an initial

43.   See Laurie Morse, Price of Polluting Drops in the U.S., The Financial Times, March 30, 1995.

allocation free, while new entrants were required to pay. See generally, Liza Heinzerling, Selling Pollution, Forcing Democracy, 14 Stan. Envtl. L.J. 300 (1995).

2. GOVERNMENT LIABILITY IN CONTRACT FOR INDUCING RELIANCE

In Chapter 3, we examined some of the financial and regulatory problems faced by the nation's savings and loan industry in the 1980s. As part of the effort to restore the health of that industry with minimum expenditure of taxpayer funds, regulatory agencies sought to interest banks and other investors in acquiring "sick" but potentially salvageable institutions.

As part of the "currency" to induce those purchases, the agencies proposed to change certain accounting conventions theretofore applied to the institutions. Later, Congress concluded that course had been unwise and had made some situations worse instead of better. Thus, Congress mandated a return to accounting conventions that rendered some of the institutions technically insolvent. Our next case considers whether government may change the "rules of the game" without penalty.

UNITED STATES v. WINSTAR CORPORATION

Supreme Court of the United States, 1996.
518 U.S. 839, 116 S.Ct. 2432, 135 L.Ed.2d 964.

JUSTICE SOUTER announced the judgment of the Court * * *.

The issue in this case is the enforceability of contracts between the Government and participants in a regulated industry, to accord them particular regulatory treatment in exchange for their assumption of liabilities that threatened to produce claims against the Government as insurer. Although Congress subsequently changed the relevant law, and thereby barred the Government from specifically honoring its agreements, we hold that the terms assigning the risk of regulatory change to the Government are enforceable, and that the Government is therefore liable in damages for breach.

I

* * *

A

The modern savings and loan industry traces its origins to the Great Depression, which brought default on 40 percent of the Nation's $20 billion in home mortgages and the failure of some 1700 of the nation's approximately 12,000 savings institutions. In the course of the debacle, Congress passed three statutes meant to stabilize the thrift industry. The Federal Home Loan Bank Act created the Federal Home Loan Bank Board (Bank Board), which was authorized to channel funds to thrifts for loans on houses and for preventing foreclosures on them. Next, the Home Owners' Loan Act of 1933 authorized the Bank Board to charter and regulate federal savings and loan associations. Finally, the National Housing Act created the Federal Savings and Loan Insurance Corporation (FSLIC), under the Bank Board's authority, with responsibility to insure thrift deposits and regulate all federally insured thrifts.

The resulting regulatory regime worked reasonably well until the combination of high interest rates and inflation in the late 1970's and early 1980's brought about a second crisis in the thrift industry. Many thrifts found themselves holding long-term, fixed-rate mortgages created when interest rates were low; when market rates rose, those institutions had to raise the rates they paid to depositors in order to attract funds. When the costs of short-term deposits overtook the revenues from long-term mortgages, some 435 thrifts failed between 1981 and 1983.

The first federal response to the rising tide of thrift failures was "extensive deregulation," including "a rapid expansion in the scope of permissible thrift investment powers and a similar expansion in a thrift's ability to compete for funds with other financial services providers." Along with this deregulation came moves to weaken the requirement that thrifts maintain adequate capital reserves as a cushion against losses, a requirement that one commentator described as "the most powerful source of discipline for financial institutions." Breeden, [Thumbs on the Scale: The Role that Accounting Practices Played in the Savings and Loan Crisis, 59 Fordham L.Rev. S71 (1991)], at S75. The result was a drop in capital reserves required by the Bank Board from five to four percent of assets in November 1980, and to three percent in January of 1982; at the same time, the Board developed new "regulatory accounting principles" (RAP) that in many instances replaced generally accepted accounting principles (GAAP) for purposes of determining compliance with its capital requirements. According to the House Banking Committee, "[t]he use of various accounting gimmicks and reduced capital standards masked the worsening financial condition of the industry, and the FSLIC, and enabled many weak institutions to continue operating with an increasingly inadequate cushion to absorb future losses." The reductions in required capital reserves, moreover, allowed thrifts to grow explosively without increasing their capital base, at the same time deregulation let them expand into new (and often riskier) fields of investment.

While the regulators tried to mitigate the squeeze on the thrift industry generally through deregulation, the multitude of already-failed savings and loans confronted FSLIC with deposit insurance liabilities that threatened to exhaust its insurance fund. According to the General Accounting Office, FSLIC's total reserves declined from $6.46 billion in 1980 to $4.55 billion in 1985, when the Bank Board estimated that it would take $15.8 billion to close all institutions deemed insolvent under generally accepted accounting principles. By 1988, the year of the last transaction involved in this case, FSLIC was itself insolvent by over $50 billion. And by early 1989, the GAO estimated that $85 billion would be needed to cover FSLIC's responsibilities and put it back on the road to fiscal health. In the end, we now know, the cost was much more even than that. * * *

Realizing that FSLIC lacked the funds to liquidate all of the failing thrifts, the Bank Board chose to avoid the insurance liability by encouraging healthy thrifts and outside investors to take over ailing institutions in a series of "supervisory mergers." Such transactions, in which the acquiring parties assumed the obligations of thrifts with liabilities that far outstripped their assets, were not intrinsically attractive to healthy institutions; nor did FSLIC have sufficient cash to promote such acquisitions through direct subsidies alone, although cash contributions from FSLIC were often part of a transaction. Instead, the principal inducement for these supervisory mergers was an understanding that the acquisitions would be subject to a particular accounting treatment that would help the acquiring institutions meet their reserve capital requirements imposed by federal regulations.

B

Under Generally Accepted Accounting Principles (GAAP) there are circumstances in which a business combination may be dealt with by the "purchase method" of accounting. The critical aspect of that method for our purposes is that it permits the acquiring entity to designate the excess of the purchase price over the fair value of all identifiable assets acquired as an intangible asset called "goodwill." In the ordinary case, the recognition of goodwill as an asset makes sense: a rational purchaser in a free market, after all, would not pay a price for a business in excess of the value of that business's assets unless there actually were some intangible "going concern" value that made up the difference. For that reason, the purchase method is frequently used to account for acquisitions, and GAAP expressly contemplated its application to at least some transactions involving savings and loans. Goodwill recognized under the purchase method as the result of an FSLIC-sponsored supervisory merger was generally referred to as "supervisory goodwill."

Recognition of goodwill under the purchase method was essential to supervisory merger transactions of the type at issue in this case. Because FSLIC had insufficient funds to make up the difference between a failed thrift's liabilities and assets, the Bank Board had to offer a "cash substitute" to induce a healthy thrift to assume a failed thrift's obligations. * * *

　　　　* * *

Some transactions included yet a further inducement, described as a "capital credit." Such credits arose when FSLIC itself contributed cash to further a supervisory merger and permitted the acquiring institution to count the FSLIC contribution as a permanent credit to regulatory capital. * * *

　　　　* * * [T]he accounting treatment to be accorded supervisory goodwill and capital credits was the subject of express arrangements between the regulators and the acquiring institutions. While the extent to which

these arrangements constituted a departure from prior norms is less clear, an acquiring institution would reasonably have wanted to bargain for such treatment. Although GAAP demonstrably permitted the use of the purchase method in acquiring a thrift suffering no distress, the relevant thrift regulations did not explicitly state that intangible good-will assets created by that method could be counted toward regulatory capital. Indeed, * * * [such treatment] circumvented the whole purpose of the reserve requirements, which was to protect depositors and the deposit insurance fund. * * * To those with the basic foresight to appreciate all this, then, it was not obvious that regulators would accept purchase accounting in determining compliance with regulatory criteria, and it was clearly prudent to get agreement on the matter.

    * * *

C

Although the results of the forbearance policy, including the departures from GAAP, appear to have been mixed, it is relatively clear that the overall regulatory response of the early and mid–1980's was unsuccessful in resolving the crisis in the thrift industry. As a result, Congress enacted the Financial Institutions Reform, Recovery, and Enforcement Act of 1989 (FIRREA), with the objects of preventing the collapse of the industry, attacking the root causes of the crisis, and restoring public confidence.

FIRREA made enormous changes in the structure of federal thrift regulation * * *. [Most] importantly for the present case, FIRREA * * * obligated OTS to "prescribe and maintain uniformly applicable capital standards for savings associations" in accord with strict statutory requirements. * * * [The FIRREA statute expressly altered the accounting treatment that had made acquisition of the failing institutions attractive to purchasers.] According to the House Report, these tougher capital requirements reflected a congressional judgment that "[t]o a considerable extent, the size of the thrift crisis resulted from the utilization of capital gimmicks that masked the inadequate capitalization of thrifts."

The impact of FIRREA's new capital requirements upon institutions that had acquired failed thrifts in exchange for supervisory goodwill was swift and severe. * * * Despite the statute's limited exception intended to moderate transitional pains, many institutions immediately fell out of compliance with regulatory capital requirements, making them subject to seizure by thrift regulators.

D

* * * Respondents Glendale Federal Bank, FSB, Winstar Corporation, and The Statesman Group, Inc. acquired failed thrifts in 1981, 1984, and 1988, respectively. After the passage of FIRREA, federal regulators seized and liquidated the Winstar and Statesman thrifts for failure to meet the new capital requirements. * * * Believing that the Bank Board and FSLIC had promised them [accounting rules that would

have avoided their failure], * * * respondents each filed suit against the United States in the Court of Federal Claims, seeking monetary damages on both contractual and constitutional theories. That court granted respondents' motions * * * finding in each case that the Government had breached contractual obligations to permit respondents to count supervisory goodwill and capital credits toward their regulatory capital requirements. In so holding, the Court of Federal Claims rejected two central defenses asserted by the Government: that the Government could not be held to a promise to refrain from exercising its regulatory authority in the future unless that promise was unmistakably clear in the contract, and that the Government's alteration of the capital reserve requirements in FIRREA was a sovereign act that could not trigger contractual liability. * * *

* * * The Federal Circuit * * * [affirmed]. * * * We granted certiorari, and now affirm.

II

* * *

B

It is important to be clear about what these contracts did and did not require of the Government. Nothing in the documentation or the circumstances of these transactions purported to bar the Government from changing the way in which it regulated the thrift industry. Rather, what the Federal Circuit said of the Glendale transaction is true of the Winstar and Statesman deals as well: "the Bank Board and the FSLIC were contractually bound to recognize the supervisory goodwill and the amortization periods reflected" in the agreements between the parties. We read this promise as the law of contracts has always treated promises to provide something beyond the promisor's absolute control, that is, as a promise to insure the promisee against loss arising from the promised condition's nonoccurrence. Holmes's example is famous: "[i]n the case of a binding promise that it shall rain tomorrow, the immediate legal effect of what the promisor does is, that he takes the risk of the event, within certain defined limits, as between himself and the promisee." Holmes, The Common Law (1881) * * *. Contracts like this are especially appropriate in the world of regulated industries, where the risk that legal change will prevent the bargained-for performance is always lurking in the shadows. * * * The drafters of the Restatement attested to this when they explained that, "[w]ith the trend toward greater governmental regulation parties are increasingly aware of such risks, and a party may undertake a duty that is not discharged by such supervening governmental actions...." Restatement (Second) of Contracts § 264, Comment a. "Such an agreement," according to the Restatement, "is usually interpreted as one to pay damages if performance is prevented rather than one to render a performance in violation of law."[44]

44. See, e.g., Hughes Communications Galaxy, Inc. v. United States, 998 F.2d 953, 957–959 (C.A.Fed.1993) (interpreting contractual incorporation of then-current gov-

When the law as to capital requirements changed in the present instance, the Government was unable to perform its promise and, therefore, became liable for breach. We accept the Federal Circuit's conclusion that the Government breached these contracts when, pursuant to the new regulatory capital requirements imposed by FIRREA, 12 U.S.C. § 1464(t), the federal regulatory agencies limited the use of supervisory goodwill and capital credits in calculating respondents' net worth. In the case of Winstar and Statesman, the Government exacerbated its breach when it seized and liquidated respondents' thrifts for regulatory noncompliance.

* * *

III

The Government argues for reversal, first, on the principle that "contracts that limit the government's future exercises of regulatory authority are strongly disfavored; such contracts will be recognized only rarely, and then only when the limitation on future regulatory authority is expressed in unmistakable terms." Hence, the Government says, the agreements between the Bank Board, FSLIC, and respondents should not be construed to waive Congress's authority to enact a subsequent bar to using supervisory goodwill and capital credits to meet regulatory capital requirements.

The argument mistakes the scope of the unmistakability doctrine. The thrifts do not claim that the Bank Board and FSLIC purported to bind Congress to ossify the law in conformity to the contracts; they seek no injunction against application of FIRREA's new capital requirements to them and no exemption from FIRREA's terms. * * * The question, then, is not whether Congress could be constrained but whether the doctrine of unmistakability is applicable to any contract claim against the Government for breach occasioned by a subsequent act of Congress. The answer to this question is no.

A

The unmistakability doctrine invoked by the Government was stated in Bowen v. Public Agencies Opposed to Social Security Entrapment [477 U.S. 41 (1986)]: " '[S]overeign power ... governs all contracts subject to the sovereign's jurisdiction, and will remain intact unless surrendered in unmistakable terms.' " This doctrine marks the point of intersection between two fundamental constitutional concepts, the one traceable to the theory of parliamentary sovereignty made familiar by Blackstone, the other to the theory that legislative power may be limited, which became familiar to Americans through their experience under the colonial charters, see G. Wood, The Creation of the American Republic 1776–1787, pp. 268–271 (1969).

ernment policy on space shuttle launches not as a promise not to change that policy, but as a promise "to bear the cost of changes in launch priority and scheduling resulting from the revised policy") * * * [Court's fn. 17]

In his Commentaries, Blackstone stated the centuries-old concept that one legislature may not bind the legislative authority of its successors: "Acts of parliament derogatory from the power of subsequent parliaments bind not.... Because the legislature, being in truth the sovereign power, is always of equal, always of absolute authority: it acknowledges no superior upon earth, which the prior legislature must have been, if it's [sic] ordinances could bind the present parliament." 1 W. Blackstone, Commentaries on the Laws of England 90 (1765).

In England, of course, Parliament was historically supreme in the sense that no "higher law" limited the scope of legislative action or provided mechanisms for placing legally enforceable limits upon it in specific instances; the power of American legislative bodies, by contrast, is subject to the overriding dictates of the Constitution and the obligations that it authorizes. Hence, although we have recognized that "a general law ... may be repealed, amended or disregarded by the legislature which enacted it," and "is not binding upon any subsequent legislature," on this side of the Atlantic the principle has always lived in some tension with the constitutionally created potential for a legislature, under certain circumstances, to place effective limits on its successors, or to authorize executive action resulting in such a limitation.

* * *

Merrion, Bowen, and Cherokee Nation [cases reviewed in material omitted here] thus announce no new rule distinct from the canon of construction adopted in *Providence Bank* [4 Pet. 514 (1830)] and *Charles River Bridge* [11 Pet. 420 (1837)]; their collective holding is that a contract with a sovereign government will not be read to include an unstated term exempting the other contracting party from the application of a subsequent sovereign act (including an act of Congress), nor will an ambiguous term of a grant or contract be construed as a conveyance or surrender of sovereign power[45] (e.g., to tax or control navigation), or to a claim that cannot be recognized without creating an exemption from the exercise of such a power (e.g., the equivalent of exemption from social security obligations). The application of the doctrine thus turns on whether enforcement of the contractual obligation alleged would block the exercise of a sovereign power of the Government.

* * *

As construed by each of the courts that considered these contracts before they reached us, the agreements do not purport to bind the Congress from enacting regulatory measures, and respondents do not ask the courts to infer from silence any * * * limit on sovereign power * * *. The contracts have been read as solely risk-shifting agreements and respondents seek nothing more than the benefit of promises by the

---

45. "Sovereign power" as used here must be understood as a power that could otherwise affect the Government's obligation under the contract. The Government could not, for example, abrogate one of its contracts by a statute abrogating the legal enforceability of the contract, government contracts of a class including that one, or simply all government contracts. No such legislation would provide the Government with a defense under the sovereign acts doctrine. [Court's fn. 22]

Government to insure them against any losses arising from future regulatory change. * * *

Nor do the damages respondents seek amount to exemption from the new law, in the manner of the compensation sought in *Bowen*. Once general jurisdiction to make an award against the Government is conceded, a requirement to pay money supposes no surrender of sovereign power by a sovereign with the power to contract. * * *

We recognize, of course, that while agreements to insure private parties against the costs of subsequent regulatory change do not directly impede the exercise of sovereign power, they may indirectly deter needed governmental regulation by raising its costs. But all regulations have their costs, and Congress itself expressed a willingness to bear the costs at issue here when it authorized FSLIC to "guarantee [acquiring thrifts] against loss" that might occur as a result of a supervisory merger. Just as we have long recognized that the Constitution "bar[s] Government from forcing some people alone to bear public burdens which, in all fairness and justice, should be borne by the public as a whole," Dolan v. City of Tigard, so we must reject the suggestion that the Government may simply shift costs of legislation onto its contractual partners who are adversely affected by the change in the law, when the Government has assumed the risk of such change.

The Government's position would not only thus represent a conceptual expansion of the unmistakability doctrine beyond its historical and practical warrant, but would place the doctrine at odds with the Government's own long-run interest as a reliable contracting partner in the myriad workaday transaction of its agencies. Consider the procurement contracts that can be affected by congressional or executive scale-backs in federal regulatory or welfare activity; or contracts to substitute private service-providers for the Government, which could be affected by a change in the official philosophy on privatization; or all the contracts to dispose of federal property, surplus or otherwise. If these contracts are made in reliance on the law of contract and without specific provision for default mechanisms, should all the private contractors be denied a remedy in damages unless they satisfy the unmistakability doctrine? The answer is obviously no because neither constitutional avoidance nor any apparent need to protect the Government from the consequences of standard operations could conceivably justify applying the doctrine. Injecting the opportunity for unmistakability litigation into every common contract action would, however, produce the untoward result of compromising the Government's practical capacity to make contracts, which we have held to be "of the essence of sovereignty" itself. From a practical standpoint, it would make an inroad on this power, by expanding the Government's opportunities for contractual abrogation, with the certain result of undermining the Government's credibility at the bargaining table and increasing the cost of its engagements. As Justice Brandeis recognized, "[p]unctilious fulfillment of contractual obligations is essential to the maintenance of the credit of public as well as private debtors.''

* * *

IV

The Government's final line of defense is the sovereign acts doctrine, to the effect that '' '[w]hatever acts the government may do, be they legislative or executive, so long as they be public and general, cannot be deemed specially to alter, modify, obstruct or violate the particular contracts into which it enters with private persons.' '' Horowitz v. United States, 267 U.S., at 461, 45 S.Ct., at 344–345 (quoting Jones v. United States, 1 Ct.Cl. 383, 384 (1865)). Because FIRREA's alteration of the regulatory capital requirements was a ''public and general act,'' the Government says, that act could not amount to a breach of the Government's contract with respondents.

The Government's position cannot prevail, however, for two independent reasons. The facts of this case do not warrant application of the doctrine, and even if that were otherwise the doctrine would not suffice to excuse liability under this governmental contract allocating risks of regulatory change in a highly regulated industry.

In *Horowitz,* the plaintiff sued to recover damages for breach of a contract to purchase silk from the Ordnance Department. The agreement included a promise by the Department to ship the silk within a certain time, although the manner of shipment does not appear to have been a subject of the contract. Shipment was delayed because the United States Railroad Administration placed an embargo on shipments of silk by freight, and by the time the silk reached Horowitz the price had fallen, rendering the deal unprofitable. This Court barred any damages award for the delay, noting that ''[i]t has long been held by the Court of Claims that the United States when sued as a contractor cannot be held liable for an obstruction to the performance of the particular contract resulting from its public and general acts as a sovereign.'' This statement was not, however, meant to be read as broadly as the Government urges, and the key to its proper scope is found in that portion of our opinion explaining that the essential point was to put the Government in the same position that it would have enjoyed as a private contractor. * * *

* * *

* * * [A]llowing the Government to avoid contractual liability merely by passing any ''regulatory statute,'' would flaunt the general principle that, ''[w]hen the United States enters into contract relations, its rights and duties therein are governed generally by the law applicable to contracts between private individuals.'' Careful attention to the cases shows that the sovereign acts doctrine was meant to serve this principle, not undermine it. * * *

A

If the Government is to be treated like other contractors, some line has to be drawn in situations like the one before us between regulatory legislation that is relatively free of government self-interest and therefore cognizable for the purpose of a legal impossibility defense and, on the other hand, statutes tainted by a governmental object of self-relief. Such an object is not necessarily inconsistent with a public purpose, of course, and when we speak of governmental "self-interest," we simply mean to identify instances in which the Government seeks to shift the costs of meeting its legitimate public responsibilities to private parties. * * *

* * * The greater the Government's self-interest, however, the more suspect becomes the claim that its private contracting partners ought to bear the financial burden of the Government's own improvidence, and where a substantial part of the impact of the Government's action rendering performance impossible falls on its own contractual obligations, the defense will be unavailable.

* * *

B

In the present case, it is impossible to attribute the exculpatory "public and general" character to FIRREA. Although we have not been told the dollar value of the relief the Government would obtain if insulated from liability under contracts such as these, the attention given to the regulatory contracts prior to passage of FIRREA shows that a substantial effect on governmental contracts is certain. * * *

* * * [I]t does not answer the legislative record to insist, as the Government does, that the congressional focus is irrelevant because the broad purpose of FIRREA was to "advance the general welfare." We assume nothing less of all congressional action, with the result that an intent to benefit the public can no more serve as a criterion of a "public and general" sovereign act than its regulatory character can. While our limited enquiry into the background and evolution of the thrift crisis leaves us with the understanding that Congress acted to protect the public in the FIRREA legislation, the extent to which this reform relieved the Government of its own contractual obligations precludes a finding that the statute is a "public and general" act for purposes of the sovereign acts defense.

* * *

We affirm the Federal Circuit's ruling that the United States is liable to respondents for breach of contract. Because the Court of Federal Claims has not yet determined the appropriate measure or amount of damages in this case, we remand for further proceedings consistent with our opinion.

[The concurring opinions or JUSTICES BREYER, SCALIA, KENNEDY & THOMAS, and the dissenting opinion of CHIEF JUSTICE REHNQUIST & JUSTICE GINSBURG, are deleted].

Notes and Questions

1. What do you think of the regulatory strategy chosen by the agencies in this case? Did it make sense to you that they would "buy" firm conduct instead of coerce it? Is there any reason to expect one approach will be more in the public interest than the other?

2. Do you agree with the plurality that, if the Government is going to enter into market transactions, it should have to live with its contracts? Is it really true that any time the government chooses an incentive-based form of regulation, it should not be able to change direction without paying a substantial penalty? If that is the standard to which the Government is held, are we likely to see many more such attempts at non-coercive regulation?

3. Was Congress' problem that it did not permit a sufficient transition period over which the buying institutions could amortize the "good will"? Might one justifiably criticize action that renders apparently healthy institutions immediately insolvent but permit the action if the firms are given time to sell assets, reduce liabilities, or otherwise adjust to the new regulatory realities?

4. Is the problem presented in *Winstar* any different from the general problem of regulatory transition raised in Chapter 1? Locally-regulated industries like taxicabs routinely argue they have acquired a property right in reliance upon existing government regulation. Should taxicab owners be able to bootstrap themselves into a position that government failure to issue new taxi medallions, for example, constitutes a commitment not to issue new ones?

5. Who profited from the change in accounting standards and the adoption of the approach to regulation that Congress later disowned? Was it the Federal Deposit Insurance Fund that avoided the need to acquire some of the institutions purchased under the new accounting conventions? Was it investors shrewd enough to understand that the agencies had made a bad bargain for the government? Must the government be strictly liable for its mistakes or should these "winners" be required to bear a reasonable degree of risk that Congress will ultimately come to its senses?

6. The Chief Justice in dissent expressed a general concern that taxpayers should not be liable for all the actions of government contracting agents. As we go through an era of reinventing and privatizing government, will *Winstar* hamstring government as it seeks to deregulate? Or is the presence of government liability an appropriate concept with which privatized government alternatives should be expected to deal? See Gillian E. Metzger, Privatization as Delegation, 103 Colum. L. Rev. 1367 (2003) (proposing a delegation theory for privatization activities of government that would encompass *Winstar* type liability).

7. Read *Winstar* in conjunction with the Takings Clause cases discussed in Chapter 2. Indeed, the plurality cites Dolan v. City of Tigard to

explain that government may not shift burdens to particular individuals that should be borne by the public as a whole. If the Court increasingly holds governments responsible for economic injury caused by changes in state and federal regulation, more exceptions to the unmistakability and sovereign acts doctrines can be expected. Moreover, if state rather than federal action is involved, the Contracts Clause may also be invoked. If this occurs, the issues raised by *Charles River Bridge* in Chapter 1 will also be replayed.

8.   The case subsequently went to trial and $908 million was awarded to Glendale Savings. See New York Times, April 12, 1999. But this was only the beginning. Estimates were that damages in *Winstar*-type cases could exceed $30 billion. See Note, Winstar Damages: Restitution Where Benefit Conferred on the Defendant is Greater than Plaintiff's Out of Pocket Cost, 94 N.W. L. Rev. 305 (1999) (documenting over 120 cases then pending before the Court of Claims). However, the Government has resisted such awards successfully on appeal. See, e.g., Bluebonnet Savings Bank v. United States, 339 F.3d 1341 (2003); Vanessa Blum, The S&L Payouts That Never Came, Legal Times, Feb. 16, 2004, p. 1.

C. THE ALTERNATIVE OF SELF REGULATION

Current regulatory techniques include some which encourage or even demand that private enterprise police itself. In the early days of the Roosevelt Administration, industry-inspired codes of self regulation were looked upon with disfavor.[46] Today, self regulation is more accepted, in part because private enterprise may be less "suspect" than it may once have been.[47]

"Self regulation" means involving the industry or firm subject to regulation in the setting of goals and enforcement. Some advantages of self regulation stem from possible costs saved due to the fact that industry insiders are likely to have more access to relevant information and a better understanding of the economics of the industry. In short, self regulation may be more efficient than traditional regulation.

Self regulation may also be more flexible in that it can be tailored on a firm-by-firm basis. In addition, one can make the argument that an industry and its customers should pay the cost of the regulatory process. In effect, regulation itself could be viewed as a kind of externality that those who benefit from the industry—shareholders, employees and consumers—should bear.

Of course self regulation can become the ultimate form of capture. In addition, much of what passes for industry self regulation may be highly anticompetitive—a way to impose externalities on the public rather than reduce such externalities.

---

46. During the New Deal period, of course, the Court struck down attempts by the Executive branch and Congress to delegate governmental power to private bodies. See A.L.A. Schechter Poultry Corp. v. United States, 295 U.S. 495, 55 S.Ct. 837, 79 L.Ed. 1570 (1935); Carter v. Carter Coal Co., 298 U.S. 238, 56 S.Ct. 855, 80 L.Ed. 1160 (1936).

47. See Paul R. Verkuil, Reverse Yardstick Competition: A New Deal for the Nineties, 45 Florida L. Rev. 1 (1993).

Self regulation is actually more common than it might initially appear. For example, the practice of law, the production of pharmaceuticals and cosmetics,[48] mining safety, securities markets, motion picture production and television broadcasting[49] are all subject to self regulation in one form or another. Product standardization can also be viewed as a form of industry self regulation.

A proposal for self regulation offered by Professors Ian Ayres and John Braithwaite[50] suggests the concept of "enforced self regulation" and distinguishes it from "coregulation." Coregulation refers to industry-wide standards, while enforced self regulation would, in their model, apply to individual firms. The core of the model is the involvement of the individual firm in setting and enforcing standards. Proposing standards that are too lenient would force the firm to comply with possibly more onerous standards applied by the relevant public officials. Similarly, compliance would be determined through an internal audit with the firm risking legal sanctions if it did not comply. According to Ayres and Braithwaite, under a system of enforced self regulation, standards and goals could be more responsive to the character of particular firms. In addition, self-regulated firms would arguably be more committed to compliance and more interested in regulatory innovation.

Similar to "enforced self regulation" is "sector-based regulation" which has been pioneered in the Netherlands. Under that system, the regulatory agency enters into an enforceable agreement with the firm, the subject of which might be the firm's level of pollution. See Daniel J. Fiorino, Toward a New System of Environmental Regulation: The Case for an Industry Sector Approach, 26 Env. Law Rptr. 457 (1996). The EPA has utilized what it calls "Project XL" to allow individual companies to develop unique environmental strategies for their industries. Under this protocol, according to its proponents, technological innovation is fostered, compliance costs reduced and greater amounts of pollution prevented. This is a form of regulatory reinvention[51] that has its critics as well as supporters. See generally Daniel A. Farber, Triangulating the Future of Reinvention: Three Emerging Models of Environmental Protection, 2000 U. Ill. L. Rev. 61.

Finally, in the past there has been experimentation with what is termed "yardstick competition."[52] This phrase refers to competition between a privately-owned producer and a government-owned producer. In effect, the private firm is left unregulated except it must meet the challenge of the government-operated firm. When there is no direct

---

48. See Jacqueline A, Greff, The Regulation of Cosmetics That Are Also Drugs, 51 Food & Drug L.J. 243 (1996).

49. See Les Brown, Self–Regulation in American Television in Areas Aside From Program Content, 13 Cardozo Arts & Ent. L. J. 705 (1995).

50. Ian Ayres & John Braithwaite, Responsive Regulation (1992).

51. What after all is the EPA's "bubble concept" reviewed by the Court in *Chevron* but a form of regulatory reinvention?

52. See generally, Jeffrey L. Harrison, Yardstick Competition: A Prematurely Discarded Form of Regulatory Relief, 53 Tulane L. Rev. 465 (1979); Paul Verkuil, supra n. 49.

competition, the government firm can be used as a source of data for assessing the performance of the private firm. Yardstick competition was more common in the early part of the 20th Century and, on a large scale, it still exists in the operation of the Tennessee Valley Authority. It is not however, a growing source of enforced self regulation; indeed, the question today is more what the private sector has to teach government than the other way around.[53] Still the fact that Fannie Mae and Freddie Mac provide government subsidized mortgage loans and securitization of mortgages, indicates that a role for government still exists even if it means competing with private sector activities.

Inspired by the work of key scholars[54], Regulatory Negotiation (or "Reg–Neg") became law in 1990. Negotiated Rulemaking Act of 1990, 5 U.S.C. § 561–70 (Supp. 2003). It is, in effect, government supervised self-regulation. Its proponents view rulemaking under the statute as better focused and, therefore, producing higher quality rules that have more legitimacy. But since the participants in Reg–Neg are limited in order to gain these advantages, its use has not been uncontroversial. Its critics cite the potential for outcome manipulation by interested parties and the favoring of powerful interests. See Jody Freeman & Laura I. Langbein, Regulatory Negotiation and the Legitimacy Benefit, 9 N.Y.U. Env. L.J. 60 (2000).

The idea of self regulation contains within it the promise (or hope) that voluntarily arrived at commitments will be more effective in the long run because industry commitment will be greater. Considering what you know about Public Choice Theory (as well as Public Interest Theory), do you share this hope?

Or put differently, assume the reality is that an overworked and understaffed federal regulatory agency cannot do the job adequately through normal enforcement mechanisms. Isn't self-regulation a way to stretch the agency's resources and reach results that are at least semi-effective? In this regard, it should be recalled that OSHA began its life by converting industry workplace standards into regulatory norms rather than creating its own standards anew.

SILVER v. NEW YORK STOCK EXCHANGE

Supreme Court of the United States, 1963.
373 U.S. 341, 83 S.Ct. 1246, 10 L.Ed.2d 389.

Mr. Justice Goldberg delivered the opinion of the Court.

We deal here today with the question, of great importance to the public and the financial community, of whether and to what extent the federal antitrust laws apply to securities exchanges regulated by the Securities Exchange Act of 1934. More particularly, the question is

---

53. See Paul R. Verkuil supra note 46, at 10–11 (quoting Lawton Chiles, Governor of Florida, that "government in America is failing").

54. See Philip J. Harter, Negotiating Regulations: A Cure for Malaise, 71 Geo. L.J. 1 (1982).

whether the New York Stock Exchange is to be held liable to a nonmember broker-dealer under the antitrust laws or regarded as impliedly immune therefrom when, pursuant to rules the Exchange has adopted under the Securities Exchange Act of 1934, it orders a number of its members to remove private direct telephone wire connections previously in operation between their offices and those of the nonmember, without giving the nonmember notice, assigning him any reason for the action, or affording him an opportunity to be heard.

* * *

The fundamental issue confronting us is whether the Securities Exchange Act has created a duty of exchange self-regulation so pervasive as to constitute an implied repealer of our antitrust laws, thereby exempting the Exchange from liability in this and similar cases.

It is plain, to begin with, that removal of the wires by collective action of the Exchange and its members would, had it occurred in a context free from other federal regulation, constitute a per se violation of § 1 of the Sherman Act. The concerted action of the Exchange and its members here was, in simple terms, a group boycott depriving petitioners of a valuable business service which they needed in order to compete effectively as broker-dealers in the over-the-counter securities market. Fashion Originators' Guild of America v. Federal Trade Comm., 312 U.S. 457, 61 S.Ct. 703, 85 L.Ed. 949 [(1941)] * * *. Unlike listed securities, there is no central trading place for securities traded over the counter. The market is established by traders in the numerous firms all over the country through a process of constant communication to one another of the latest offers to buy and sell. The private wire connection, which allows communication to occur with a flip of a switch, is an essential part of this process. Without the instantaneously available market information provided by private wire connections, an over-the-counter dealer is hampered substantially in his crucial endeavor—to buy, whether it be for customers or on his own account, at the lowest quoted price and sell at the highest quoted price. Without membership in the network of simultaneous communication, the over-the-counter dealer loses a significant volume of trading with other members of the network which would come to him as a result of his easy accessibility. These important business advantages were taken away from petitioners by the group action of the Exchange and its members. * * * [A]bsent any justification derived from the policy of another statute or otherwise, the Exchange acted in violation of the Sherman Act. In this case, however, the presence of another statutory scheme, that of the Securities Exchange Act of 1934, means that such a conclusion is only the beginning, not the end, of inquiry.

The difficult problem here arises from the need to reconcile pursuit of the antitrust aim of eliminating restraints on competition with the effective operation of a public policy contemplating that securities exchanges will engage in self-regulation which may well have anti-competitive effects in general and in specific applications.

The need for statutory regulation of securities exchanges and the nature of the duty of self-regulation imposed by the Securities Exchange Act are properly understood in the context of a consideration of both the economic role played by exchanges and the historical setting of the Act. Stock exchanges perform an important function in the economic life of this country. They serve, first of all, as an indispensable mechanism through which corporate securities can be bought and sold. To corporate enterprise such a market mechanism is a fundamental element in facilitating the successful marshaling of large aggregations of funds that would otherwise be extremely difficult of access. To the public the exchanges are an investment channel which promises ready convertibility of stock holdings into cash. * * * Moreover, because trading on the exchanges, in addition to establishing the price level of listed securities, affects securities prices in general, and because such transactions are often regarded as an indicator of our national economic health, the significance of the exchanges in our economy cannot be measured only in terms of the dollar volume of trading. * * *

The exchanges are by their nature bodies with a limited number of members, each of which plays a certain role in the carrying out of an exchange's activities. The limited-entry feature of exchanges led historically to their being treated by the courts as private clubs, and to their being given great latitude by the courts in disciplining errant members. As exchanges became a more and more important element in our Nation's economic and financial system, however, the private-club analogy became increasingly inapposite and the ungoverned self-regulation became more and more obviously inadequate, with acceleratingly grave consequences. This impotency ultimately led to the enactment of the 1934 Act. * * * It was, therefore, the combination of the enormous growth in the power and impact of exchanges in our economy, and their inability and unwillingness to curb abuses which had increasingly grave implications because of this growth, that moved Congress to enact the Securities Exchange Act of 1934. * * *

The pattern of governmental entry, however, was by no means one of total displacement of the exchanges' traditional process of self-regulation. The intention was rather, as Mr. Justice Douglas said, while Chairman of the S.E.C., one of "letting the exchanges take the leadership with Government playing a residual role. Government would keep the shotgun, so to speak, behind the door, loaded, well oiled, cleaned, ready for use but with the hope it would never have to be used." Douglas, Democracy and Finance (Allen ed. 1940), 82. Thus the Senate Committee Report stressed that "the initiative and responsibility for promulgating regulations pertaining to the administration of their ordinary affairs remain with the exchanges themselves. It is only where they fail adequately to provide protection to investors that the Commission is authorized to step in and compel them to do so." S.Rep. No. 792, at 13. * * *

Thus arose the federally mandated duty of self-policing by exchanges. Instead of giving the Commission the power to curb specific instances of abuse, the Act placed in the exchanges a duty to register with the Commission, § 5, 15 U.S.C. § 78e, and decreed that registration could not be granted unless the exchange submitted copies of its rules, § 6(a)(3), 15 U.S.C. § 78f(a)(3), and unless such rules were 'just and adequate to insure fair dealing and to protect investors,' § 6(d), 15 U.S.C. § 78f(d). The general dimensions of the duty of self-regulation are suggested by § 19(b) of the Act, 15 U.S.C. § 78s(b), which gives the Commission power to order changes in exchange rules respecting a number of subjects, which are set forth in the margin.[55]

One aspect of the statutorily imposed duty of self-regulation is the obligation to formulate rules governing the conduct of exchange members. The Act specifically requires that registration cannot be granted "unless the rules of the exchange include provision for the expulsion, suspension, or disciplining of a member for conduct or proceeding inconsistent with just and equitable principles of trade * * *," § 6(b), 15 U.S.C. § 78f(b). In addition, the general requirement of § 6(d) that an exchange's rules be "just and adequate to insure fair dealing and to protect investors" has obvious relevance to the area of rules regulating the conduct of an exchange's members.

The § 6(b) and § 6(d) duties taken together have the broadest implications in relation to the present problem, for members inevitably trade on the over-the-counter market in addition to dealing in listed securities, and such trading inexorably brings contact and dealings with nonmember firms which deal in or specialize in over-the-counter securities. It is no accident that the Exchange's Constitution and rules are permeated with instances of regulation of members' relationships with nonmembers including nonmember broker-dealers. A member's purchase of unlisted securities for itself or on behalf of its customer from a boiler-shop operation creates an obvious danger of loss to the principal in the transaction, and sale of securities to a nonmember insufficiently capitalized to protect customers' rights creates similar risks. In addition to the potential financial injury to the investing public and Exchange members that is inherent in these transactions as well as in dealings with nonmembers who are unreliable for any other reason, all such intercourse carries with it the gravest danger of engendering in the

---

55. 'The Commission is * * * authorized * * * to alter or supplement the rules of * * * (an) exchange * * * in respect of such matters as (1) safeguards in respect of the financial responsibility of members and adequate provision against the evasion of financial responsibility through the use of corporate forms or special partnerships; (2) the limitation or prohibition of the registration or trading in any security within a specified period after the issuance or primary distribution thereof; (3) the listing or striking from listing of any security; (4) hours of trading; (5) the manner, method, and place of soliciting business; (6) fictitious or numbered accounts; (7) the time and method of making settlements, payments, and deliveries and of closing accounts; (8) the reporting of transactions on the exchange and upon tickers maintained by or with the consent of the exchange, including the method of reporting short sales, stopped sales, sales of securities of issuers in default, bankruptcy or receivership, and sales involving other special circumstances; (9) the fixing of reasonable rates of commission, interest, listing, and other charges; (10) minimum units of trading; (11) odd-lot purchases and sales; (12) minimum deposits on margin accounts; and (13) similar matters.' [Court's fn. 7]

public a loss of confidence in the Exchange and its members, a kind of damage which can significantly impair fulfillment of the Exchange's function in our economy. Rules which regulate Exchange members' doing of business with nonmembers in the over-the-counter market are therefore very much pertinent to the aims of self-regulation under the 1934 Act. Transactions with nonmembers under the circumstances mentioned can only be described as "inconsistent with just and equitable principles of trade," and rules regulating such dealing are indeed "just and adequate to insure fair dealing and to protect investors."

The Exchange's constitutional provision and rules relating to private wire connections are unquestionably part of this fulfillment of the § 6(b) and § 6(d) duties, for such wires between members and nonmembers facilitate trading in and exchange of information about unlisted securities, and such contact with an unreliable nonmember not only may further his business undesirably, but may injure the member or the member's customer on whose behalf the contract is made and ultimately imperil the future status of the Exchange by sapping public confidence. In light of the important role of exchanges in our economy and the 1934 Act's design of giving the exchanges a major part in curbing abuses by obligating them to regulate themselves, it appears conclusively—contrary to the District Court's conclusion—that the rules applied in the present case are germane to performance of the duty, implied by § 6(b) and § 6(d), to have rules governing members' transactions and relationships with nonmembers. The Exchange's enforcement of such rules inevitably affects the nonmember involved, often (as here) far more seriously than it affects the members in question. The sweeping of the nonmembers into the currents of the Exchange's process of self-regulation is therefore unavoidable; the case cannot be disposed of by holding as the district judge did that the substantive act of regulation engaged in here was outside the boundaries of the public policy established by the Securities Exchange Act of 1934.

But, it does not follow that the case can be disposed of, as the Court of Appeals did, by holding that since the Exchange has a general power to adopt rules governing its members' relations with nonmembers, particular applications of such rules are therefore outside the purview of the antitrust laws. Contrary to the conclusions reached by the courts below, the proper approach to this case, in our view, is an analysis which reconciles the operation of both statutory schemes with one another rather than holding one completely ousted.

The Securities Exchange Act contains no express exemption from the antitrust laws or, for that matter, from any other statute. This means that any repealer of the antitrust laws must be discerned as a matter of implication, and "(I)t is a cardinal principle of construction that repeals by implication are not favored." United States v. Borden Co., 308 U.S. 188, 198, 60 S.Ct. 182, 188, 84 L.Ed. 181 [(1940)] * * *.

Although the Act gives to the Securities and Exchange Commission the power to request exchanges to make changes in their rules, § 19(b),

15 U.S.C. § 78s(b), and impliedly, therefore, to disapprove any rules adopted by an exchange, see also § 6(a)(4), 15 U.S.C. § 78f(a)(4), it does not give the Commission jurisdiction to review particular instances of enforcement of exchange rules. * * * The issue is only that of the extent to which the character and objectives of the duty of exchange self-regulation contemplated by the Securities Exchange Act are incompatible with the maintenance of an antitrust action.

The absence of Commission jurisdiction, besides defining the limits of the inquiry, contributes to its solution. There is nothing built into the regulatory scheme which performs the antitrust function of insuring that an exchange will not in some cases apply its rules so as to do injury to competition which cannot be justified as furthering legitimate self-regulatory ends. By providing no agency check on exchange behavior in particular cases, Congress left the regulatory scheme subject to "the influences of * * * [improper collective action] over which the Commission has no authority but which if proven to exist can only hinder the Commission in the tasks with which it is confronted," Enforcement of exchange rules, particularly those of the New York Stock Exchange with its immense economic power, may well, in given cases, result in competitive injury to an issuer, a nonmember broker-dealer, or another when the imposition of such injury is not within the scope of the great purposes of the Securities Exchange Act. Such unjustified self-regulatory activity can only diminish public respect for and confidence in the integrity and efficacy of the exchange mechanism. Some form of review of exchange self-policing, whether by administrative agency or by the courts, is therefore not at all incompatible with the fulfillment of the aims of the Securities Exchange Act. * * * Since the antitrust laws serve, among other things, to protect competitive freedom, i.e., the freedom of individual business units to compete unhindered by the group action of others, it follows that the antitrust laws are peculiarly appropriate as a check upon anticompetitive acts of exchanges which conflict with their duty to keep their operations and those of their members honest and viable. Applicability of the antitrust laws, therefore, rests on the need for vindication of their positive aim of insuring competitive freedom. Denial of their applicability would defeat the congressional policy reflected in the antitrust laws without serving the policy of the Securities Exchange Act. Should review of exchange self-regulation be provided through a vehicle other than the antitrust laws, a different case as to antitrust exemption would be presented. * * *

Yet it is only frank to acknowledge that the absence of power in the Commission to review particular exchange exercises of self-regulation does create problems for the Exchange. The entire public policy of self-regulation, beginning with the idea that the Exchange may set up barriers to membership, contemplates that the Exchange will engage in restraints of trade which might well be unreasonable absent sanction by the Securities Exchange Act. Without the oversight of the Commission to elaborate from time to time on the propriety of various acts of self-regulation, the Exchange is left without guidance and without warning as to what regulative action would be viewed as excessive by an antitrust court possessing power to proceed based upon the considerations enumerated in the preceding paragraphs. But, under the aegis of the rule of reason, traditional antitrust concepts are flexible enough to permit the Exchange sufficient breathing space within which to carry out the mandate of the Securities Exchange Act. Although, as we have seen, the statutory scheme of that Act is not sufficiently pervasive to create a total exemption from the antitrust laws, * * * it is also true that particular instances of exchange self-regulation which fall within the scope and purposes of the Securities Exchange Act may be regarded as justified in answer to the assertion of an antitrust claim.

The final question here is, therefore, whether the act of self-regulation in this case was so justified. The answer to that question is that it was not, because the collective refusal to continue the private wires occurred under totally unjustifiable circumstances. Notwithstanding their prompt and repeated requests, petitioners were not informed of the charges underlying the decision to invoke the Exchange rules and were not afforded an appropriate opportunity to explain or refute the charges against them.

Given the principle that exchange self-regulation is to be regarded as justified in response to antitrust charges only to the extent necessary to protect the achievement of the aims of the Securities Exchange Act, it is clear that no justification can be offered for self-regulation conducted without provision for some method of telling a protesting non-member why a rule is being invoked so as to harm him and allowing him to reply in explanation of his position. No policy reflected in the Securities Exchange Act is, to begin with, served by denial of notice and an opportunity for hearing. Indeed, the aims of the statutory scheme of self-policing—to protect investors and promote fair dealing—are defeated when an exchange exercises its tremendous economic power without explaining its basis for acting, for the absence of an obligation to give some form of notice and, if timely requested, a hearing creates a great danger of perpetration of injury that will damage public confidence in the exchanges. The requirement of such a hearing will, by contrast, help in effectuating antitrust policies by discouraging anticompetitive applications of exchange rules which are not justifiable as within the scope of the purposes of the Securities Exchange Act. In addition to the general impetus to refrain from making unsupportable accusations that is present when it is required that the basis of charges be laid bare, the explanation or rebuttal offered by the nonmember will in many instances dissipate the force of the ex parte information upon which an exchange proposes to act. The duty to explain and afford an opportunity to answer will, therefore, be of extremely beneficial effect in keeping exchange action from straying into areas wholly foreign to the purposes of the Securities Exchange Act. And, given the possibility of antitrust liability for anti-competitive acts of self-regulation which fall too far outside the scope of the Exchange Act, the utilization of a notice and hearing procedure with its inherent check upon unauthorized exchange action will diminish rather than enlarge the likelihood that such liability will be incurred and hence will not interfere with the Exchange's ability to engage efficaciously in legitimate substantive self-regulation. Provision of such a hearing will, moreover, contribute to the effective functioning of the antitrust court, which would be severely impeded in providing the review of exchange action which we deem essential if the exchange could obscure rather than illuminate the circumstances under which it has acted. Hence the affording of procedural safeguards not only will substantively encourage the lessening of anticompetitive behavior outlawed by the Sherman Act but will allow the antitrust court to perform its function effectively.

Our decision today recognizes that the action here taken by the Exchange would clearly be in violation of the Sherman Act unless justified by reference to the purposes of the Securities Exchange Act, and holds that that statute affords no justification for anti-competitive collective action taken without according fair procedures. * * *

Judgment reversed and the case is remanded with directions.

MR. JUSTICE CLARK concurs * * *

MR. JUSTICE STEWART, whom MR. JUSTICE HARLAN joins, dissenting.

The purpose of the self-regulation provisions of the Securities Exchange Act was to delegate governmental power to working institution which would undertake, at their own initiative, to enforce compliance with ethical as well as legal standards in a complex and changing industry. This self-initiating process of regulation can work effectively only if the process itself is allowed to operate free from a constant threat of antitrust penalties. To achieve this end, I believe it must be held that the Securities Exchange Act removes antitrust liability for any action taken in good faith to effectuate an exchange's statutory duty of self-regulation. The inquiry in each case should be whether the conduct complained of was for this purpose. If it was, that should be the end of the matter so far as the antitrust laws are concerned—unless, of course, some antitrust violation other than the mere concerted action of an exchange and its members is alleged.

Notes and Questions

1.   According to Justice Douglas (who served as Chair of the SEC), in the case of SEC review of Exchange self regulation, the government should "keep the shotgun . . . ready for use." In the materials you have seen in this book so far, can you spot any instances in which you think self regulation would work? If so, what would constitute the "shotgun"?

2.   What are some factors that would determine whether self regulation will work on an industry-wide basis or a firm-by-firm basis? What might concern you about self regulation?[56]

56.   Tribes of Native Americans are self-regulating on a completely different juris- dictional basis but the interplay of their regulation with that of the jurisdictions

3. Suppose the day care centers in your community agreed not to hire care-givers who had not studied CPR and enacted other standards with respect to the types of toys that would be available and the food to be offered to the children. Would any of the dangers discussed in *Silver* be present in such an arrangement? Should you be concerned that higher standards might price some care out of the reach of low-income persons?

4. The application of the antitrust laws in industries subject to direct federal or state regulation is explored more fully in Chapter Six. *Silver* remains a useful illustration of the intersection between regulation and antitrust, but its view that antitrust liability varies with the degree of procedural protection provided by self-regulatory bodies is not still good law. In Northwest Wholesale Stationers, Inc. v. Pacific Stationery & Printing Co., 472 U.S. 284, 105 S.Ct. 2613, 86 L.Ed.2d 202 (1985), the Court refused to apply *Silver* to an alleged group boycott of a former participant in a group buying program, saying that "the absence of procedural safeguards can in no sense determine the antitrust analysis." Cf., e.g., Paul R. Verkuil, State Action, Due Process and Antitrust, 75 Col. L. Rev. 328, 345–47 (1975).

5. How might self regulation be instituted and enforced with respect to the following:

   a. Observing an honor code when taking law school exams.

   b. Violence on television.

   c. Automobile emissions.

   d. Product labeling.

   e. Occupational safety.

   f. Half-time shows at the Super Bowl.

A NOTE ON PRIVATE ASSOCIATIONS AND PROCEDURAL FAIRNESS

Because associations, such as the New York Stock Exchange, are private entities, they are not bound by the due process requirements of the Fifth or Fourteenth Amendment which are triggered by federal or state "action." The determination of "state action" turns on the connection (or involvement) of government in the work of the association. See NCAA v. Tarkanian, 488 U.S. 179, 109 S.Ct. 454, 102 L.Ed.2d 469 (1988) (holding 5–4 that NCAA is not a state actor). Compare Brentwood Academy v. Tennessee Secondary School Athletic Association, 531 U.S. 288, 121 S.Ct. 924, 148 L.Ed.2d 807 (2001) (holding state athletic board to be a state actor). In Silver v. NYSE, the Court tried to use the threat of antitrust exposure to force procedural protections upon the Exchange.

One way to deal with this problem is to expand the category of "actors" who are connected to the state or federal governments. For example, in the *Tarkanian* case, the NCAA has so many contacts with government (state universities, etc.) as to be a very close call. But we

around them provide some interesting analogies to industry self-regulation. See, e.g., Seminole Tribe of Florida v. Florida, 517 U.S. 44, 116 S.Ct. 1114, 134 L.Ed.2d 252 (1996).

must also remember that the absence of state action does not mean there are no legal constraints on private association conduct. Contract and tort law can impose fairness requirements on associations. See Developments in the Law: Judicial Control of Actions of Private Associations, 76 Harv. L.Rev. 983 (1963). See also Symposium, Private Accreditation in the Regulatory State, 57 Law & Contemporary Problems 1 (1994); Harding v. U.S. Figure Skating Association, 851 F.Supp. 1476 (D.Or.1994) (skater granted injunctive relief to participate in Olympics due to unfairness of limited time to respond to Association's charges).

Naturally, the state action debate takes on added importance as categories of industries controlled by self-regulatory principles grows and as the privatization movement takes hold. The internet is a good example of an activity that stands somewhere between the government and the private sector. Arguments for keeping government interference to a minimum are frequently heard, but issues of state sales tax on products distributed through the internet (not to mention "indecent" products) keep government in the picture. A more traditional "industry" like health care and managed care also has public and private aspects that can produce clashes between the private sector and government. See generally, Gillan E. Metzger, Privatization as Delegation, 103 Colum. L. Rev. 1367 (2003).

Silver reflects a desire to make private regulatory bodies more responsible. In the aftermath of the recent corporate governance scandals, including the level of compensation received by President Dick Grasso of the New York Stock Exchange, self regulatory regimes like the Exchange will likely undergo heightened public scrutiny by oversight agencies (such as the SEC). Will they become "state actors"?

D. PRIVATIZATION AS A REGULATORY ALTERNATIVE

Privatization is the process whereby provision of traditional government services are turned over to the private sector. The Bush Administration favors privatization because it tends to make government appear smaller. But this is not just a Republican concept. In the case of provision of public welfare, for example, the 1996 welfare legislation, signed by President Clinton, authorized implementation of welfare programs "through contracts with charitable, religious, or private organizations."[57] These organizations were expressly drafted into what was previously an exclusively public sector. In a way, privatization can be viewed as a form of "unbundling" where, rather than traditional natural monopolies, parts of government service monopolies are broken up and spun off to private sector participants.

Implicit in any privatization decision, however, is the question whether private firms that replace government in providing comparable

---

57. See Personal Responsibility and Work Opportunity Reconciliation Act of 1996, 42 U.S.C. § 604 a (a) (1) (H) (2000). This has led to states issues private contracts valued at $1.5 billion in 2001. See Gillian E. Metzger, supra, at 1384.

services should be regulated, and if so, how. How close, for example, should government monitor contracts entered into by the private actors, e.g., creating standards used to hire welfare providers? To what extent should government still compete with the private sector in the provision of some of the services, e.g., vouchers for educational services?

Privatization also brings with it calls for more accountability. It has produced a counter movement labeled "publicization," i.e., a desire to assure that private actors commit themselves to traditionally public goals. See Jody Freeman, Extending Public Law Norms Through Privatization, 116 Harv. L. Rev. 1285, 1285 (2003) (mentioning the norms of accountability, due process, equality and rationality).

One important area of privatization at both the state and federal levels is the provision of prison services. The next case explores the issues that arise when public law norms have to be reconciled with the realities of private enterprise.

RICHARDSON v. McKNIGHT

Supreme Court of the United States, 1997.
521 U.S. 399, 117 S.Ct. 2100, 138 L.Ed.2d 540.

JUSTICE BREYER delivered the opinion of the Court.

The issue before us is whether prison guards who are employees of a private prison management firm are entitled to a qualified immunity from suit by prisoners charging a violation of 42 U.S.C. § 1983. We hold that they are not.

I

Ronnie Lee McKnight, a prisoner at Tennessee's South Central Correctional Center (SCCC), brought this federal constitutional tort action against two prison guards, Darryl Richardson and John Walker. He says the guards injured him by placing upon him extremely tight physical restraints, thereby unlawfully "subject[ing]" him "to the deprivation of" a right "secured by the Constitution" of the United States. Richardson and Walker asserted a qualified immunity from § 1983 lawsuits, see Harlow v. Fitzgerald, 457 U.S. 800, 807, 102 S.Ct. 2727, 2732, 73 L.Ed.2d 396 (1982), and moved to dismiss the action. The District Court noted that Tennessee had "privatized" the management of a number of its correctional facilities, and that consequently a private firm, not the state government, employed the guards. See Tenn.Code Ann. § 41–24–101 et seq. (1990 and Supp.1996); see generally Cody & Bennett, The Privatization of Correctional Institutions: The Tennessee Experience, 40 Vand. L.Rev. 829 (1987) (outlining State's history with private correctional services). The court held that, because they worked for a private company rather than the government, the law did not grant the guards immunity from suit. It therefore denied the guards' motion to dismiss. The guards appealed to the Sixth Circuit. That court also ruled against them. The Court of Appeals conceded that other courts had reached varying conclusions about whether, or the extent to which, private sector defendants are entitled to immunities of the sort the law provides governmental defendants. But the court concluded, primarily for reasons of "public policy," that the privately employed prison guards were not entitled to the immunity provided their governmental counterparts. We granted certiorari to review this holding. We now affirm.

II

* * *

B

History does *not* reveal a "firmly rooted" tradition of immunity applicable to privately employed prison guards. Correctional services in the United States have undergone various transformations. See D. Shichor, Punishment for Profit 33, 36 (1995) (Shichor). *Government*-employed prison guards may have enjoyed a kind of immunity defense arising out of their status as public employees at common law. See Procunier v. Navarette, 434 U.S. 555, 561–562, 98 S.Ct. 855, 859–860, 55 L.Ed.2d 24 (1978) (extending qualified immunity to state prison guards). But correctional functions have never been exclusively public. Private individuals operated local jails in the 18th century, G. Bowman, S. Hakim, & P. Seidenstat, Privatizing the United States Justice System 271, n. 1 (1992), and private contractors were heavily involved in prison management during the 19th century.

During that time, some States, including southern States like Tennessee, leased their entire prison systems to private individuals or companies which frequently took complete control over prison management, including inmate labor and discipline. G. Bowman, S. Hakim, & P. Seidenstat, Privatizing Correctional Institutions 42 (1993); see generally B. McKelvey, American Prisons: A Study in American Social History Prior to 1915, pp. 172–180 (1968) (describing 19th-century American prison system); G. de Beaumont & A. de Tocqueville, On the Penitentiary System in the United States and Its Application in France 35 (1833) (describing more limited prison contracting system in Massachusetts and Pennsylvania). Private prison lease agreements (like inmate suits) seem to have been more prevalent after § 1983's enactment, see generally M. Mancini, One Dies, Get Another (1996), but we have found evidence that the common law provided mistreated prisoners in prison leasing States with remedies against mistreatment by those private lessors. See, e.g., Dade Coal Co. v. Haslett, 83 Ga. 549, 550–551, 10 S.E. 435, 435–436 (1889) (convict can recover from contractor for injuries sustained while on lease to private company) * * *. Yet, we have found no evidence that the law gave purely private companies or their employees any special immunity from such suits. * * * The case on which the dissent rests its argument, Williams v. Adams, 85 Mass. 171 (1861) (which could not—without more—prove the existence of such a tradition and does not, moreover, clearly involve a private prison operator) actually supports our point. It suggests that no immunity from suit would exist for the type of intentional conduct at issue in this case. * * *

Correctional functions in England have been more consistently public, see generally 22 Encyclopedia Brittanica, "Prison" 361–368 (11th ed.1911); S. Webb & B. Webb, English Prisons Under Local Government (1922) (Webb), but historical sources indicate that England relied upon private jailers to manage the detention of prisoners from the Middle Ages until well into the 18th century. 1 E. Coke, Institutes 43 (1797). The common law forbade those jailers to subject " 'their prisoners to any pain or torment,' " whether through harsh confinement in leg irons, or otherwise. See In re Birdsong, 39 F. 599, 601 (S.D.Ga.1889) * * *. And it apparently authorized prisoner lawsuits to recover damages. Apparently the law *did* provide a kind of immunity for certain private defendants, such as doctors or lawyers who performed services at the behest of the sovereign. See J. Bishop, Commentaries on Non–Contract Law § § 704, 710 (1889). But we have found no indication of any more general immunity that might have applied to private individuals working for profit.

Our research, including the sources that the parties have cited, reveals that in the 19th century (and earlier) sometimes private contractors and sometimes government itself carried on prison management activities. And we have found no conclusive evidence of a historical tradition of immunity for private parties carrying out these functions. History therefore does not provide significant support for the immunity claim.

C

Whether the immunity doctrine's *purposes* warrant immunity for private prison guards presents a closer question. Wyatt v. Cole 504 U.S. 158[, 112 S.Ct. 1827, 118 L.Ed.2d 504] (1992), consistent with earlier precedent, described the doctrine's purposes as protecting "government's ability to perform its traditional functions" by providing immunity where "necessary to preserve" the ability of government officials "to serve the public good or to ensure that talented candidates were not deterred by the threat of damages suits from entering public service. Earlier precedent described immunity as protecting the public from unwarranted timidity on the part of public officials by, for example, "encouraging the vigorous exercise of official authority," Butz v. Economou, 438 U.S. 478, 506, 98 S.Ct. 2894, 2911, 57 L.Ed.2d 895 (1978), by contributing to "principled and fearless decision-making," Wood v. Strickland, 420 U.S. 308, 319, 95 S.Ct. 992, 999, 43 L.Ed.2d 214 (1975) * * * and by responding to the concern that threatened liability would, in Judge Hand's words, "dampen the ardour of all but the most resolute, or the most irresponsible," public officials, *Harlow* (quoting Gregoire v. Biddle, 177 F.2d 579, 581 (C.A.2 1949) (L.Hand, J.) * * *; see also Mitchell [v. Forsyth, 472 U.S. 511 (1985)], (lawsuits may "distrac[t] officials from their governmental duties").

The guards argue that those purposes support immunity whether their employer is private or public. Since private prison guards perform the same work as state prison guards, they say, they must require immunity to a similar degree. To say this, however, is to misread this Court's precedents. The Court has sometimes applied a functional approach in immunity cases, but only to decide which type of immunity—absolute or qualified—a public officer should receive. And it never has held that the mere performance of a governmental function could make the difference between unlimited § 1983 liability and qualified immunity, especially for a private person who performs a job without government supervision or direction. Indeed a purely functional approach bristles with difficulty, particularly since, in many areas, government and private industry may engage in fundamentally similar activities, ranging from electricity production, to waste disposal, to even mail delivery.

Petitioners' argument also overlook certain important differences that, from an immunity perspective, are critical. First, the most important special government immunity-producing concern—unwarranted timidity—is less likely present, or at least is not special, when a private company subject to competitive market pressures operates a prison. Competitive pressures mean not only that a firm whose guards are too aggressive will face damages that raise costs, thereby threatening its replacement, but also that a firm whose guards are too timid will face threats of replacement by other firms with records that demonstrate their ability to do both a safer and a more effective job.

These ordinary marketplace pressures are present here. The private prison guards before us work for a large, multistate private prison management firm. C. Thomas, D. Bolinger, & J. Badalamenti, Private Adult Correctional Facility Census 1 (10th ed.1997) (listing the Corrections Corporation of America as the largest prison management concern in the United States). The firm is systematically organized to perform a major administrative task for profit. Cf. Tenn.Code Ann. § 41–24–104 (Supp.1996) (requiring that firms contracting with the State demonstrate a history of successful operation of correctional facilities). It performs that task independently, with relatively less ongoing direct state supervision. Compare § 41–4–140(c)(5) (exempting private jails from certain monitoring) with § 41–4–116 (requiring inspectors to examine publicly operated county jails once a month or more) and § 41–4–140(a) (requiring Tennessee Correctional Institute to inspect public correctional facilities on an annual basis and to report findings of such inspections). It must buy insurance sufficient to compensate victims of civil rights torts. § 41–24–107. And, since the firm's first contract expires after three years, § 41–24–105(a), its performance is disciplined, not only by state review, see § § 41–24–105(c)–(f), 41–24–109, but also by pressure from potentially competing firms who can try to take its place. Cf. § 41–24–104(a)(4) (permitting State, upon notice, to cancel contract at any time after first year of operation); see also § § 41–24–105(c) and (d) (describing standards for renewal of contract).

In other words, marketplace pressures provide the private firm with strong incentives to avoid overly timid, insufficiently vigorous, unduly fearful, or "nonarduous" employee job performance. And the contract's provisions—including those that might permit employee indemnification and avoid many civil-service restrictions—grant this private firm freedom to respond to those market pressures through rewards and penalties that operate directly upon its employees. To this extent, the employees before us resemble those of other private firms and differ from government employees.

This is not to say that government employees, in their efforts to act within constitutional limits, will always, or often, sacrifice the otherwise effective performance of their duties. Rather, it is to say that government employees typically act within a *different* system. They work within a system that is responsible through elected officials to voters who, when they vote, rarely consider the performance of individual subdepartments or civil servants specifically and in detail. And that system is often characterized by multidepartment civil service rules that, while providing employee security, may limit the incentives or the ability of individual departments or supervisors flexibly to reward, or to punish, individual employees. Hence a judicial determination that "effectiveness" concerns warrant special immunity-type protection in respect to this latter (governmental) system does not prove its need in respect to the former. Consequently, we can find no *special* immunity-related need to encourage vigorous performance.

Second, "privatization" helps to meet the immunity-related need "to ensure that talented candidates" are "not deterred by the threat of damages suits from entering public service." *Wyatt*. It does so in part because of the comprehensive insurance-coverage requirements just mentioned. The insurance increases the likelihood of employee indemnification and to that extent reduces the employment-discouraging fear of unwarranted liability potential applicants face. Because privatization law also frees the private prison-management firm from many civil service law restraints, it permits the private firm, unlike a government department, to offset any increased employee liability risk with higher pay or extra benefits. In respect to this second government-immunity-related purpose then, it is difficult to find a *special* need for immunity, for the guards' employer can operate like other private firms; it need not operate like a typical government department.

Third, lawsuits may well "distrac[t]" these employees "from their . . . duties," *Mitchell * * ***, but the risk of "distraction" alone cannot be sufficient grounds for an immunity. Our qualified immunity cases do not contemplate the complete elimination of lawsuit-based distractions. * * * And it is significant that, here, Tennessee law reserves certain important discretionary tasks—those related to prison discipline, to parole, and to good time—for state officials. Tenn. Code Ann. § 41–24–110 (1990). Given a continual and conceded need for deterring constitutional violations and our sense that the firm's tasks are not enormously different in respect to their importance from various other publicly

important tasks carried out by private firms, we are not persuaded that
the threat of distracting workers from their duties is enough virtually by
itself to justify providing an immunity. Moreover, Tennessee, which has
itself decided not to extend sovereign immunity to private prison operators (and arguably appreciated that this decision would increase contract
prices to some degree), can be understood to have anticipated a certain
amount of distraction.

D.

Our examination of history and purpose thus reveals nothing special
enough about the job or about its organizational structure that would
warrant providing these private prison guards with a governmental
immunity. The job is one that private industry might, or might not,
perform; and which history shows private firms did sometimes perform
without relevant immunities. The organizational structure is one subject
to the ordinary competitive pressures that normally help private firms
adjust their behavior in response to the incentives that tort suits
provide—pressures not necessarily present in government departments.
Since there are no special reasons significantly favoring an extension of
governmental immunity, and since *Wyatt* makes clear that private actors
are not *automatically* immune (i.e., § 1983 immunity does not automatically follow § 1983 liability), we must conclude that private prison
guards, unlike those who work directly for the government, do not enjoy
immunity from suit in a § 1983 case. Cf. Forrester v. White, 484 U.S., at
224, 108 S.Ct., at 542 (Officers "who seek exemption from personal
liability have the burden of showing that such an exemption is justified").

* * *

For these reasons the judgment of the Court of Appeals is affirmed.

JUSTICE SCALIA, with whom THE CHIEF JUSTICE, JUSTICE KENNEDY, and
JUSTICE THOMAS join, dissenting.

In Procunier v. Navarette, 434 U.S. 555, 98 S.Ct. 855, 55 L.Ed.2d 24
(1978), we held that state prison officials, including both supervisory and
subordinate officers, are entitled to qualified immunity in a suit brought
under 42 U.S.C. § 1983. Today the Court declares that this immunity is
unavailable to employees of private prison management firms, who
perform the same duties as state-employed correctional officials, who
exercise the most palpable form of state police power, and who may be
sued for acting "under color of state law." This holding is supported
neither by common-law tradition nor public policy, and contradicts our
settled practice of determining § 1983 immunity on the basis of the
public function being performed.

I

* * *

Private individuals have regularly been accorded immunity when
they perform a governmental function that qualifies. We have long

recognized the absolute immunity of grand jurors, noting that like prosecutors and judges they must "exercise a discretionary judgment on the basis of evidence presented to them." Imbler [v. Pachtman, 424 U.S. 409,] at 423, n. 20, [96 S.Ct. 984, 47 L.Ed.2d 128 (1976)]. "It is the functional comparability of [grand jurors'] judgments to those of the judge that has resulted in [their] being referred to as 'quasi-judicial' officers, and their immunities being termed 'quasi-judicial' as well." Ibid. Likewise, witnesses who testify in court proceedings have enjoyed immunity, regardless of whether they were government employees. "[T]he common law," we have observed, "provided absolute immunity from subsequent damages liability for all persons—*governmental or otherwise*—who were integral parts of the judicial process." Briscoe [v. LaHue, 460 U.S. 325, 335, 103 S.Ct. 1108, 75 L.Ed.2d 96 (1983)] (emphasis added). I think it highly unlikely that we would deny prosecutorial immunity to those private attorneys increasingly employed by various jurisdictions in this country to conduct high-visibility criminal prosecutions. There is no more reason for treating private prison guards differently.

II

Later in its opinion, the Court seeks to establish that there are policy reasons for denying to private prison guards the immunity accorded to public ones. As I have indicated above, I believe that history and not judicially analyzed policy governs this matter—but even on its own terms the Court's attempted policy distinction is unconvincing. The Court suggests two differences between civil-service prison guards and those employed by private prison firms which preclude any "special" need to give the latter immunity. First, the Court says that "unwarranted timidity" on the part of private guards is less likely to be a concern, since their companies are subject to market pressures that encourage them to be effective in the performance of their duties. If a private firm does not maintain a proper level of order, the Court reasons, it will be replaced by another one—so there is no need for qualified immunity to facilitate the maintenance of order.

This is wrong for several reasons. First of all, it is fanciful to speak of the consequences of "market" pressures in a regime where public officials are the only purchaser, and other people's money the medium of payment. Ultimately, one prison-management firm will be selected to replace another prison-management firm only if a decision is made by some *political* official not to renew the contract. This is a government decision, not a market choice. If state officers turn out to be more strict in reviewing the cost and performance of privately managed prisons than of publicly managed ones, it will only be because they have *chosen* to be so. The process can come to resemble a market choice only to the extent that political actors *will* such resemblance—that is, to the extent that political actors (1) are willing to pay attention to the issue of prison services, among the many issues vying for their attention, and (2) are willing to place considerations of cost and quality of service ahead of such political considerations as personal friendship, political alliances, in-state ownership of the contractor, etc. Secondly and more importantly, however, if one assumes a political regime that *is* bent on emulating the market in its purchase of prison services, it is almost certainly the case that, short of mismanagement so severe as to provoke a prison riot, *price* (not discipline) will be the predominating factor in such a regime's selection of a contractor. A contractor's price must depend upon its costs; lawsuits increase costs;[58] and "fearless" maintenance of discipline increases lawsuits. The incentive to down-play discipline will exist, more-over, even in those States where the politicians' zeal for market emulation and budget cutting has waned, and where prison-management contract renewal is virtually automatic: the more cautious the prison guards, the fewer the lawsuits, the higher the profits. In sum, it seems that "market-competitive" private prison managers have even greater need than civil-service prison managers for immunity as an incentive to discipline.

The Court's second distinction between state and private prisons is that privatization "helps to meet the immunity-related need to ensure that talented candidates are not deterred by the threat of damages suits from entering public service" as prison guards. This is so because privatization brings with it (or at least has brought with it in the case before us) (1) a statutory requirement for insurance coverage against civil-rights claims, which assertedly "increases the likelihood of employee indemnification," and (2) a liberation "from many civil service law restraints" which prevent increased employee risk from being "offset . . . with higher pay or extra benefits." As for the former (civil-rights liability insurance): surely it is the *availability* of that protection, rather than its actual presence in the case at hand, which decreases (if it does decrease, which I doubt) the *need* for immunity protection. (Otherwise, the Court would have to say that a private prison-management firm that is not required to purchase insurance, and does not do so, is more entitled to immunity; and that a government-run prison system that *does* purchase insurance is *less* entitled to immunity.) And of course civil-rights liability insurance is no less *available* to public entities than to private employers. But the second factor—liberation from civil-service limitations—is the more interesting one. First of all, simply as a philosophical matter it is fascinating to learn that one of the prime justifications for § 1983 immunity should be a phenomenon (civil-service laws) that did not even exist when § 1983 was enacted and the immunity created. Also as a philosophical matter, it is poetic justice (or poetic revenge) that the Court should use one of the principal economic benefits of "prison out-sourcing"—namely, the avoidance of civil-service salary and tenure encrustations—as the justification for a legal rule rendering out-sourcing

---

58. This is true even of successfully defended lawsuits, and even of lawsuits that have been insured against. The Court thinks it relevant to the factor I am currently discussing that the private prison-management firm "must buy insurance sufficient to compensate victims of civil rights torts." Belief in the relevance of this factor must be traceable, ultimately, to belief in the existence of a free lunch. Obviously, as civil-rights claims increase, the cost of civil-rights insurance increases. [Court's fn. 3]

more expensive. Of course the savings attributable to out-sourcing will not be wholly lost as a result of today's holding; they will be transferred in part from the public to prisoner-plaintiffs and to lawyers. It is a result that only the American Bar Association and the American Federation of Government Employees could love. But apart from philosophical fascination, this second factor is subject to the same objection as the first: governments *need not* have civil-service salary encrustations (or can exempt prisons from them); and hence governments, no more than private prison employers, have any *need* for § 1983 immunity.

There is one more possible rationale for denying immunity to private prison guards worth discussing, albeit briefly. It is a theory so implausible that the Court avoids mentioning it, even though it was the primary reason given in the Court of Appeals decision that the Court affirms. McKnight v. Rees, 88 F.3d 417, 424–425 (6th Cir.1996). It is that officers of private prisons are more likely than officers of state prisons to violate prisoners' constitutional rights because they work for a profit motive, and hence an added degree of deterrence is needed to keep these officers in line. The Court of Appeals offered no evidence to support its bald assertion that private prison guards operate with different incentives than state prison guards, and gave no hint as to how prison guards might possibly increase their employers' profits by violating constitutional rights. One would think that private prison managers, whose § 1983 damages come out of their own pockets, as compared with public prison managers, whose § 1983 damages come out of the public purse, would, if anything, be more careful in training their employees to avoid constitutional infractions. And in fact, States having experimented with prison privatization commonly report that the overall caliber of the services provided to prisoners has actually improved in scope and quality. Matters Relating To The Federal Bureau Of Prisons: Hearing before the Subcommittee on Crime of the House Committee on the Judiciary, 104th Cong., 1st Sess., 110 (1995).

* * *

In concluding, I must observe that since there is no apparent *reason,* neither in history nor in policy, for making immunity hinge upon the Court's distinction between public and private guards, the precise *nature* of that distinction must also remain obscure. Is it privity of contract that separates the two categories—so that guards paid directly by the State are "public" prison guards and immune, but those paid by a prison-management company "private" prison guards and not immune? Or is it rather "employee" versus "independent contractor" status—so that even guards whose compensation is paid directly by the State are not immune if they are not also supervised by a state official? Or is perhaps state supervision alone (without direct payment) enough to confer immunity? Or is it * * * the formal designation of the guards, or perhaps of the guards' employer, as a "state instrumentality" that makes the difference? Since, as I say, I see no sense in the public-private distinction, neither do I see what precisely it consists of.

Today's decision says that two sets of prison guards who are indistinguishable in the ultimate source of their authority over prisoners, indistinguishable in the powers that they possess over prisoners, and indistinguishable in the duties that they owe toward prisoners, are to be treated quite differently in the matter of their financial liability. The only sure effect of today's decision—and the only purpose, as far as I can tell—is that it will artificially raise the cost of privatizing prisons. Whether this will cause privatization to be prohibitively expensive, or instead simply divert state funds that could have been saved or spent on additional prison services, it is likely that taxpayers and prisoners will suffer as a consequence. Neither our precedent, nor the historical foundations of § 1983, nor the policies underlying § 1983, support this result.

I respectfully dissent.

Notes and Questions

1.   As Justice Breyer shows, privatization of prisons has a long history in English as well as American law. Does this background make you more receptive to the privatizing idea? Should historical factors be part of every analysis of the transfer of government functions to private contractors?

2.   The debate between Justices Breyer and Scalia has an economic dimension. Justice Scalia sees the Court's decision as driving up the costs to private prison companies by denying them immunities available to the public sector. Is this a relevant issue? Do you think the majority takes sides in the privatization debate?

3.   One question Justice Scalia addresses is whether private companies are more likely to deprive prisoners of their constitutional rights than state officials. There is no solid evidence either way, but do you think it more or less likely that private guards would abuse prisoners? Which way does the profit motive cut? Does the fact that New York City, for example, pays millions in judgments annually for unlawful acts of its police officials give you pause? Are public sector "monopolists" likely to be more or less responsible than private competitors? Doesn't the answer depend on how contracts are awarded and monitored?

4.   In Correctional Services Corp. v. Malesko, 534 U.S. 61, 122 S.Ct. 515, 151 L.Ed.2d 456 (2001), the Court refused to extend *Bivens* liability to private companies and guards working in federal prisons. In essence the *Richardson* minority (plus Justice O'Connor) formed the majority. Justices Scalia and Thomas, in a separate concurrence, asserted that the Court's animosity towards implying rights of action *a la Bivens* drove the result. Is there an inconsistency in subjecting federal officials to *Bivens* liability, but not private officials? Does this "make up" for *Richardson's* denial of immunity to private guards?

5.   As *Richardson* and *Malesko* show, there is no question that prison guards are "state actors" and subject to constitutional controls. But, as the note above indicates, private groups delegated public responsibilities are not always subject to constitutional standards. In these cases, "self regulation"

must fill the gap, often in creative ways that the *Silver* case explores. It is hard to argue against the view that the growing trend towards privatization produce a need for more responsible self-regulation. The question then becomes how best to achieve this kind of "regulation." Obviously self regulation in the Ayres and Braithwaite model (see p. 495 infra) balances enforcement with discretion and permits those so "regulated" to shape the nature of their regulation. We believe this approach can best serve both government private needs.

6. Consider also whether the use of the antitrust laws, discussed in the next Chapter, becomes another method of self regulation.

Chapter 6

REGULATION AND THE ANTITRUST ALTERNATIVE

By this point in the course, you know that "deregulation" rarely eliminates regulation of an industry or practice. Regulation takes many forms, and even if an explicit regulatory scheme is abolished, other forms of regulation remain that limit a company's discretion. Most important for this chapter, the antitrust laws remain to impose significant limits on the conduct of individual companies and the coordination of the companies' behavior.

Antitrust law presupposes that competition among producers creates incentives to lower costs and prices, improve product quality, and otherwise promote consumer welfare. Indeed, because competitive processes and effects can be almost instantaneous, competition is seen by many as the ideal way to "regulate."

Antitrust law is concerned whenever two or more firms agree to moderate or eliminate their competition through a "contract, combination or conspiracy in restraint of trade." If the only two companies in an industry, for example, agree that one will only sell east of the Mississippi River and the other will sell only west, that division of markets would eliminate competition between them and violate Section 1 of the Sherman Act.

Section 2 of the Sherman Act prohibits "monopolization" or "attempts to monopolize," i.e., to achieve or preserve a dominant position in the marketplace by means deemed to be improper. Distinguishing improper practices from desirably vigorous competition is often difficult, but the premise that markets should be open to potential competitors remains important.[1]

---

1. These examples only scratch the surface of antitrust law, and ignore important qualifications of the prohibitions where combinations or arguably exclusionary practices serve important pro-competitive functions. For a more detailed discussion of antitrust issues, consult ABA Section of Antitrust Law, Antitrust Law Developments (5th ed. 2002); Herbert Hovenkamp, Federal Antitrust Policy: The Law of Competition and its Practice (2d ed. 1999); E. Thomas Sullivan & Jeffrey L. Harrison, Understanding Antitrust and its Economic Implications (3d ed. 2003).

Of course, as we have seen throughout this book, many regulatory programs explicitly seek to set common prices among firms in an industry and others require that services be provided by one or a limited number of firms. It thus may be tempting to think of direct regulation and antitrust enforcement as polar extremes; under this view, if an industry is appropriate for direct regulation, competition would have no place and the antitrust laws should not apply to the conduct of the regulated firms.

However, the dichotomy is not so sharp. Many kinds of regulation can coexist with substantial amounts of competition. Furthermore, competition can stimulate efficient, low-cost production and thus help cure one of the persistent "illnesses" of a regulated industry. It may be that antitrust principles should be applied—indeed the antitrust laws should be enforced—even with respect to the conduct of firms that are otherwise heavily regulated.[2]

To what extent are the antitrust laws displaced when Congress or the states subject an industry to direct regulation? May agencies intervene in antitrust cases so as to assert agency concerns? Must regulatory agencies factor the values of competition into their own decisions? Is it appropriate for a court in an antitrust case to defer to a federal regulatory agency's findings of fact or conclusions of law? May agencies confer immunity from antitrust liability as part of their regulatory mission? Questions such as these present basic issues of the proper roles of regulation and competition in our society and are the subject of this chapter.

A. ENFORCING THE ANTITRUST LAWS AGAINST FEDERALLY–REGULATED FIRMS

Direct regulation as a method of organizing American society's resources is even older than the federal antitrust laws. The Interstate Commerce Commission was in place three years before the Sherman Act became law in 1890, for example, a fact that may have given the defendants in our first case a false sense of security.

UNITED STATES v. TRANS–MISSOURI FREIGHT ASSOCIATION

Supreme Court of the United States, 1897.
166 U.S. 290, 17 S.Ct. 540, 41 L.Ed. 1007.

[On March 15, 1889, the defendant railroads formed the Trans–Missouri Freight Association and agreed to be governed by its articles of agreement. All competitive traffic between member railroads was to be included if it originated west of a line running from eastern Texas, along

---

2. For example, in his days as a law professor, Justice Breyer argued that regulation should be undertaken in a manner that is least restrictive of the principles of competition. See Stephen Breyer, Regulation and Its Reform (1982).

the Red River, then north to Kansas City, then along the Missouri River to the eastern boundary of Montana, then north to Canada.

[A committee was created to establish rates and regulations affecting this traffic. Proposed rate reductions had to be filed at least five days before a committee meeting. If unanimously approved, changes could be implemented immediately; otherwise, they were subject to arbitration. Any member railroad could give written notice that, despite disapproval of the rate decrease, it would be implemented ten days later. The Association, in turn, reserved the right to match the decreased rates. In addition, any member railroad could, without notice to anyone, make a rate or rule change if necessary to meet the competition of a line that was not a member of the Association. However, if it were later determined that such a rate change were not made in good faith to meet such competition, the offending railroad would have to pay a fine of up to $100. A railroad could withdraw from the Association by giving thirty days notice to the others.

[The Government filed its complaint on January 6, 1892, alleging that the defendants were common carriers that, prior to the agreement, operated separately and in competition. They were alleged to operate in interstate commerce and to have the purpose of "unjustly and oppressively" increasing rates. The complaint asked for an injunction against future coordinated ratemaking by Association members.

[The defendants admitted they were common carriers engaged in the interstate transportation of persons and property. They denied any intent to increase rates unjustly, and denied that the agreement destroyed, prevented or illegally limited or influenced competition; they denied that arbitrary rates were fixed or charged, that rates had been increased, or that the effect of free competition had been counteracted. They alleged that the proper object of the association had been simply to establish and maintain reasonable rates, rules and regulations on all freight traffic. Most important for our purposes, they alleged that they were subject to the Interstate Commerce Act of 1887 and thus not to the new antitrust Act.

[The trial court dismissed the Government's complaint and the Eighth Circuit affirmed. From that dismissal, the Government here appeals.]

MR. JUSTICE PECKHAM, after stating the facts, delivered the opinion of the court.

* * *

The language of the [antitrust] act includes every contract, combination in the form of trust or otherwise, or conspiracy, in restraint of trade or commerce among the several States or with foreign nations. * * * The point urged on the defendants' part is that the statute was not really intended to reach that kind of an agreement relating only to traffic rates entered into by competing common carriers by railroad; that it was intended to reach only those who were engaged in the manufacture or sale of articles of commerce, and who by means of trusts, combinations and conspiracies were engaged in affecting the supply or the price or the place of manufacture of such articles. The terms of the act do not bear out such construction. Railroad companies are instruments of commerce, and their business is commerce itself. An act which prohibits the making of every contract, etc., in restraint of trade or commerce among the several States, would seem to cover by such language a contract between competing railroads * * *.

    * * *

But it is maintained that an agreement like the one in question on the part of the railroad companies is authorized by the Commerce Act, which is a special statute applicable only to railroads, and that a construction of the Trust Act (which is a general act) so as to include within its provisions the case of railroads, carries with it the repeal by implication of so much of the Commerce Act as authorized the agreement. * * * On a line with this reasoning it is said that if Congress had intended to in any manner affect the railroad carrier as governed by the Commerce Act, it would have amended that act directly and in terms, and not have left it as a question of construction to be determined whether so important a change in the commerce statute had been accomplished by the passage of the statute relating to trusts.

The first answer to this argument is that, in our opinion, the Commerce Act does not authorize an agreement of this nature. It may not in terms prohibit, but it is far from conferring either directly or by implication any authority to make it. * * * The provisions of that act look to the prevention of discrimination, to the furnishing of equal facilities for the interchange of traffic, to the rate of compensation for what is termed the long and the short haul, to the attainment of a continuous passage from the point of shipment to the point of destination, at a known and published schedule, * * * to procuring uniformity of rates charged by each company to its patrons, and to other objects of a similar nature. * * * As the Commerce Act does not authorize this agreement, argument against a repeal by implication, of the provisions of the act which it is alleged grant such authority, becomes ineffective. There is no repeal in the case, and both statutes may stand, as neither is inconsistent with the other.

    * * *

It is said that Congress had very different matters in view and very different objects to accomplish in the passage of the [Sherman Act]; that a number of combinations in the form of trusts and conspiracies in restraint of trade were to be found throughout the country, and that it was impossible for the state governments to successfully cope with them because of their commercial character and of their business extension through the different States of the Union. Among these trusts it was said in Congress were the Beef Trust, the Standard Oil Trust, the Steel Trust, the Barbed Fence Wire Trust, the Sugar Trust, the Cordage Trust, the Cotton Seed Oil Trust, the Whiskey Trust and many others, and these trusts it was stated had assumed an importance and had acquired a power which were dangerous to the whole country, and that their existence was directly antagonistic to its peace and prosperity. To combinations and conspiracies of this kind it is contended that the act in question was directed, and not to the combinations of competing railroads to keep up their prices to a reasonable sum for the transportation of persons and property. It is true that many and various trusts were in existence at the time of the passage of the act, and it was probably sought to cover them by the provisions of the act. Many of them had rendered themselves offensive by the manner in which they exercised the great power that combined capital gave them. But a further investigation of "the history of the times" shows also that those trusts were not the only associations controlling a great combination of capital which had caused complaint at the manner in which their business was conducted. There were many and loud complaints from some portions of the public regarding the railroads and the prices they were charging for the service they rendered, and it was alleged that the prices for the transportation of persons and articles of commerce were unduly and improperly enhanced by combinations among the different roads. * * * A reference to this history of the times does not, as we think, furnish us with any strong reason for believing that it was only trusts that were in the minds of the members of Congress, and that railroads and their manner of doing business were wholly excluded therefrom.

     * * *

     * * * Congress has, so far as its jurisdiction extends, prohibited all contracts or combinations in the form of trusts entered into for the purpose of restraining trade and commerce. The results naturally flowing from a contract or combination in restraint of trade or commerce, when entered into by a manufacturing or trading company * * *, while differing somewhat from those which may follow a contract to keep up transportation rates by railroads, are nevertheless of the same nature and kind, and the contracts themselves do not so far differ in their nature that they may not all be treated alike and be condemned in common. * * * We see nothing either in contemporaneous history, in the legal situation at the time of the passage of the statute, in its legislative history, or in any general difference in the nature or kind of these trading or manufacturing companies from railroad companies, which would lead us to the conclusion that it cannot be supposed the legislature in prohibiting the making of contracts in restraint of trade intended to include railroads within the purview of that act.

     * * *

     The general reasons for holding agreements of this nature to be invalid even at common law, on the part of railroad companies are quite strong, if not entirely conclusive.

     * * *

     The Interstate Commerce Commission, from whose reports quotations have been quite freely made by counsel for the purpose of proving the views of its learned members in regard to this subject, has never distinctly stated that agreements among competing railroads to maintain prices are to be commended, or that the general effect is to be regarded as beneficial. They have stated in their fourth annual report that competition may degenerate into rate wars, and that such wars are as unsettling to the business of the country as they are mischievous to the carriers, and that the spirit of existing law is against them. They then add: "Agreements between railroad companies which from time to time they have entered into which a view to prevent such occurrences have never been found effectual, and for the very sufficient reason, that the mental reservations in forming them have been quite as numerous and more influential than the written stipulations." It would seem true, therefore, that there is no guaranty of financial health to be found in entering into agreements for the maintenance of rates, nor is financial ruin or insolvency the necessary result of their absence.

* * *

* * * It may be that the policy evidenced by the passage of the act itself will, if carried out, result in disaster to the roads and in a failure to secure the advantages sought from such legislation. Whether that will be the result or not we do not know and cannot predict. These considerations are, however, not for us. If the act ought to read as contended for by defendants, Congress is the body to amend it and not this court, by a process of judicial legislation wholly unjustifiable. * * *

* * *

For the reasons given, the decrees of the United States Circuit Court of Appeals and of the Circuit Court for the District of Kansas must be reversed, and the case remanded to the Circuit Court for further proceedings in conformity with this opinion.

MR. JUSTICE WHITE, with whom concurred MR. JUSTICE FIELD, MR. JUSTICE GRAY and MR. JUSTICE SHIRAS, dissenting.

* * *

* * * The statute, commonly known as the Interstate Commerce Act, was a special act, and it was intended to regulate inter-state commerce transported by railway carriers. All its provisions directly and expressly related to this subject. The [Sherman] act of 1890, on the contract, is a general law, not referring specifically to carriers of inter-state commerce. The rule is that a general will not be held to repeal a special statute unless there be a clear implication unavoidably resulting from the general law that it was the intention that the provisions of the general law should cover the subject-matter previously, expressly and specifically provided for by particular legislation. * * *

* * *

Now, a consideration of the terms of the [Interstate Commerce] statute, I submit, makes it clear that the contract here sought to be avoided as illegal is either directly sanctioned or impliedly authorized thereby. That the act did not contemplate that the relations of the carrier should be confined to his own line and to business going over such line alone, is conclusively shown by the fact that the act specifically provides for joint and continuous lines; in other words, for agreements between several roads to compose a joint line. That these agreements are to arise from contract is also shown by the fact that the law provides for the filing of such contracts with the commission. And it was also contemplated that the agreements should cover joint rates, since it provides for the making of such joint tariffs and for their publication and filing with the commission. * * * That the interstate commerce rates, all of which are controlled by the provisions as to reasonableness, were not intended to fluctuate hourly and daily as competition might ebb and flow, results from the fact that the published rates could not either be increased or reduced, except after a specified time. It follows, then, that agreements as to reasonable rates and against their secret reduction conform exactly to the terms of the act. * * * [S]uppose three joint lines of railroads between Chicago and New York, each made up of many roads. How could a joint rate be agreed on by the roads composing one of these continuous lines, without an ascertainment of the rate existing on the other continuous line? What contract could be made with safety for transportation over one of the lines without taking into account the rate of all the others? There certainly could be no prevention of unjust discrimination as to the persons and places within a given territory, unless the rates of all competing lines within the territory be considered and the sudden change of the published rates of all such lines be guarded against.

> * * *

It is, I submit, therefore not to be denied that the agreement between the carriers, the validity of which is here drawn in question, seeking to secure uniform classification and to prevent the undercutting of the published rates, even though such agreements be made with competing as well as joint lines, is in accord with the plain text of the Interstate Commerce Act, and is in harmony with the views of the purposes of that law contemporaneously expressed to Congress by the body immediately charged with its administration, and tacitly approved by Congress.

> * * *

* * * To my mind, the judicial declaration that carriers cannot agree among themselves for the purpose of aiding in the enforcement of the provisions of the interstate commerce law, will strike a blow at the beneficial results of that act, and will have a direct tendency to produce the preferences and discriminations which it was one of the main objects of the act to frustrate. The great complexity of the subject, the numerous interests concerned in it, the vast area over which it operates, present difficulties enough without, it seems to me, its being advisable to add to them by holding that a contract which is supported by the text of the law is invalid, because, although it is reasonable and just, it must be considered as in restraint of trade.

Notes and Questions

1. Was the Court correct to reject the defendants' view that the Sherman Act was not intended to apply to railroads?

    a. If the ICC could disapprove any "unreasonable" rates proposed by the railroads, what harm could there be in letting the railroads agree on what rates to submit to the ICC?

    b. Might "reasonableness" cover a range of possible rates? Is the Court's concern that the railroads might propose rates that are at the high end of reasonableness rather than the lower end that they might propose in the absence of coordination?

    c. Is the Court in a position to conduct a mini-ratemaking case to determine what a proper rate should be? Might the Court refer the matter to the ICC for such a determination? Should all price fixing agreements such as this be illegal regardless of whether the Court has a way to determine whether the rates fixed were reasonable?

2. Might railroads have more need than many firms to engage in multi-firm setting of rates and rules?

    a. Was Justice White correct that many shipments must travel over two or more railroads? Remember that, unlike trucks, a train can only go where its tracks go. "Joint rates" for railroads, i.e., rates covering shipments that travel on two or more lines, are absolutely essential. Is there any good way to arrive at joint rates other than by agreement among the affected railroads?

    b. Do you agree with Justice Peckham that such practical problems illuminate only the wisdom or "policy" of the antitrust law and thus should not affect the Court's analysis of whether the antitrust and regulatory statutes are in conflict?

3. Did the Court too quickly discount the argument that railroads would tend to be driven into cut-throat competition that would deny all of them a reasonable rate of return?

    a. Think back to what we saw in Chapter 3. At least in the 1890s, railroads were still the quintessential "natural monopolies". By definition, a natural monopoly is a firm whose marginal cost of production does not increase with an increase in output, at least not over the relevant ranges of production. Thus, there are always further economies of scale, or at least no diseconomies, if such firms increase production. In the case of a railroad, once the track is laid and equipment purchased, for example, it is as cheap or cheaper per mile to go 100,000 miles as 1,000.

    b. A related effect of this phenomenon is that the marginal cost of a natural monopolist is consistently below its average cost. The result is that, if forced to price competitively, a natural monopoly will tend to charge at or above marginal cost but below average cost. Do you see (or remember) why? They will then lose money and ultimately go out of business. Should a recognition of that argument have changed the result here?

4. To say the least, railroads were unhappy with the *Trans–Missouri* decision and in its next term, the Supreme Court was in effect asked to reconsider. This time the defendants were the railroads operating *east* of the Mississippi River and there was also an effort to allocate an "equitable" proportion of the traffic to each participating railroad. In United States v. Joint Traffic Association, 171 U.S. 505, 19 S.Ct. 25, 43 L.Ed. 259 (1898), the Court again reached the same result.

However, the questions suggested by *Trans–Missouri* did not go away. They resurfaced most interestingly when a private plaintiff tried to assert the *Trans–Missouri* rule.

KEOGH v. CHICAGO & NORTHWESTERN RAILWAY CO.

Supreme Court of the United States, 1922.
260 U.S. 156, 43 S.Ct. 47, 67 L.Ed. 183.

Mr. Justice Brandeis delivered the opinion of the court.

This action * * * was brought by Keogh in * * * November, 1914. Eight railroad companies and twelve individuals were made defendants. The case heard upon demurrer to a special plea; the demurrer was overruled and judgment was entered for defendants, plaintiff electing to stand upon its demurrer; and this judgment was affirmed by the Circuit Court of Appeals for the Seventh Circuit. The case is here on writ of error.

The cause of action set forth was this: Keogh is a manufacturer of excelsior and flax tow at St. Paul, Minn. The defendant corporations are interstate carriers engaged in transporting freight from St. Paul to points in other states. Prior to September 1, 1912, these carriers formed an association known as the Western Trunk Line Committee. The individual defendants are officers and agents of the carriers and represent them in that committee. It is a function of the committee to secure agreement in respect to freight rates among the companies, railroad companies, which would otherwise be competing carriers. By means of such agreement, competition as to interstate rates from St. Paul on excelsior and tow was eliminated, uniform rates were established, and interstate commerce was restrained. The uniform established were arbitrary and unreasonable; they were higher than those theretofore charged; and they were higher than the rate would have been, if competition had not been thus eliminated. Through this agreement for uniform rates Keogh was damaged. The declaration contains a schedule of the amounts paid by him in excess of those which would have been paid under rates prevailing before September 1, 1912, and which, but for the conspiracy, would have remained in effect. He claims damages to the extent of this difference in rates. He also alleges as an item of damages that the increase in freight rates lessened the value of his St. Paul factory through loss of profits.

Defendants set up the fact that every rate complained of had been duly filed by the several carriers with the Interstate Commerce Commission; that upon such filing the rates had been suspended for investigation, upon complaint of Keogh, pursuant to the Act to Regulate Commerce of February 4, 1887; that after extensive hearings, in which Keogh participated, the rates were approved by the Commission; and that they were not made effective until after they had been so approved. * * *

The case is presented on these pleadings. Whether there is a cause of action under section 7 of the Anti–Trust Act is the sole question for decision. Keogh contends that his rights are not limited to the protection against unreasonably high or discriminatory rates afforded him by the Act to Regulate Commerce; that under the Anti–Trust Act he was entitled to the benefit of competitive rates; that the elimination of competition caused the increase in his rates; and that, as he has been damaged thereby, he is entitled to recover. The instrument by which Keogh is alleged to have been damaged are rates approved by the Commission. It is, however, conceivable that, but for the action of the Western Trunk Line Committee, one or more of these railroads would have maintained lower rates. Rates somewhat lower might also have been reasonable. Moreover, railroads had often, in the fierce struggle for business, established unremunerative rates. Since the case arose prior to the Transportation Act of February 28, 1920, the carriers were at liberty to establish or maintain even unreasonably low rates, provided they were not discriminatory.

All the rates fixed were reasonable and nondiscriminatory. That was settled by the proceedings before the Commission. But under the Anti–Trust Act a combination of carriers to fix reasonable and nondiscriminatory rates may be illegal; and, if so, the government may have redress by criminal proceedings under section 3, by injunction under section 4 and by forfeiture under section 6. That was settled by United States v. Trans–Missouri Freight Association and United States v. Joint Traffic Association. The fact that these rates had been approved by the Commission would not, it seems, bar proceedings by the government. It does not, however, follow that Keogh, a private shipper, may recover damages under section 7 because he lost the benefit of rates still lower, which, but for the conspiracy, he would have enjoyed. There are several reasons why he cannot.

A rate is not necessarily illegal because it is the result of a conspiracy in restraint of trade in violation of the Anti–Trust Act. What rates are legal is determined by the Act to Regulate Commerce. Under section 8 of the latter act the exaction of any illegal rate makes the carrier liable to the "persons injured thereby for the full amour damages sustained in consequence of any such violation," together with a reasonable attorney's fee. Sections 9 and 16 provide for the recovery of such damages either by complaint before the Commission or by an action in a federal court. If the conspiracy here complained of resulted in rates which the Commission found to be illegal because, unreasonably high or discriminatory, the full amount of the damages sustained, whatever their nature, would have been recoverable in proceedings. Can it be that Congress intended to provide the shipper, from whom illegal rates have been exacted, with an additional remedy under the Anti–Trust Act? And if no remedy under the Anti–Trust is given where the injury results from the fixing of rates which are illegal, because too high or discriminatory, may it be assumed Congress intended to give such a remedy where, as here, the rates complained of have been found by the Commission to be legal and while in force had to be collected by the carrier?

Section 7 of the Anti–Trust Act gives a right of action to one has been "injured in his business or property." Injury implies violation of a legal right. The legal rights of shipper as against carrier in respect to a rate are measured by the published tariff. Unless and until suspended or set aside, this rate is made, for all purposes, the legal rate as between carrier and shipper. The rights as defined by the tariff cannot be varied or enlarged by either contract or tort of the carrier. And they are not affected by the tort of a third party. This stringent rule prevails, because otherwise the paramount purpose of Congress prevention of unjust discrimination—might be defeated. If a shipper could recover under section 7 of the Anti–Trust Act for damages resulting from the exaction of a rate higher than that which would otherwise have prevailed, the amount recovered might, like a rebate operate to give him a preference over his trade competitors. It is no answer to say that each of these might bring a similar action under § 7. Uniform treatment would not result, even if all sued, unless the highly improbable happened, and the several juries and court gave to each the same measure of relief.

The character of the issues involved raises another obstacle to the maintenance of the action. The burden resting upon the plaintiff would not be satisfied by proving that some carrier would, but for the illegal conspiracy, have maintained a rate lower than that published. It would be necessary for the plaintiff to prove, also, that the hypothetical lower rate would have conformed to the requirements of the Act to Regulate Commerce. For unless the lower rate was one which the carrier could have maintained legally, the changing of it could not conceivably give a cause of action. To be legal a rate must be nondiscriminatory. And the proceedings before the Commission in this controversy illustrate how readily claims of unjust discrimination arise. For this reason, it is possible that no lower rate from St. Paul on tow and excelsior could have been legally maintained without reconstituting the whole rate structure for many articles moving in an important section of the country. But it is the Commission which must determine whether a rate is discriminatory; at least, in the first instance. It has been suggested that this requirement does not necessarily bar an action involving that issue; for a court might suspend its proceeding until the question of discrimination had been determined by the Commission. But here the difficulty presented could not be overcome by such a practice. The powers conferred upon the Commission are broad. It may investigate and decide whether a rate has been, whether it is, or whether it would be, discriminatory. But by no conceivable proceeding could the question whether a hypothetical lower rate would under conceivable conditions have been discriminatory, be submitted to the Commission for determination. And that hypothetical question is one with which plaintiff would necessarily be confronted at a trial.

* * *

Affirmed.

Notes and Questions

1. Was the Court departing from *Trans–Missouri* and saying here that the antitrust laws have no place in industries subject to the jurisdiction of the ICC? What examples of antitrust enforcement does the Court expressly suggest? Is that approach consistent with the Court's professed view of the regulatory process? Based on your knowledge of the realities of the regulatory process, does it make sense to preserve some antitrust remedies even in a highly-regulated industry?

2. Is the issue here one of "exemption" from the antitrust laws or an allocation of authority for the fashioning of particular remedies?

a. Do you share the Court's concern that any damages awarded by a court in an antitrust case would constitute a "rebate" which would give one shipper illegally lower rates than its competitors? Under principles of collateral estoppel, could a court's decision as to the appropriate rate be binding on the railroad in subsequent suits by other shippers? Under modern procedural techniques, could a class action or consolidation of several cases by disgruntled shippers help avoid the problem of inconsistent judgments?

b. Is the problem really that the Court lacks "expertise" sufficient to determine what is an appropriate rate for a given route? What is the nature of the necessary expertise? Based on what you have seen in prior chapters, can it seriously be argued that there is an objectively-determinable proper rate which anyone with sufficient time and information should be able to discern? Can you argue to the contrary that deference to the agency's "expertise" is based on something else? Might it be based on a belief that rate-making is a policy-making function, as much or more than a mathematical calculation, and that the policy-making responsibility has been allocated by Congress to the ICC?

c. Should the case have been referred to the ICC solely for a determination of any questions peculiarly within its responsibility? What might such questions have been? Referral of particular questions by a court defers to the "primary jurisdiction" of an agency. Do you agree with the court that in this case the questions would have been "hypothetical"?

3. As this case illustrates, "exclusive jurisdiction" refers to the removal of particular kinds of questions from the scrutiny of courts in antitrust cases and the entrusting of those questions exclusively to administrative agencies.

a. How can you tell a question appropriate for "exclusive" agency resolution from one in which the antitrust courts have a role? Does *Keogh* suggest some elements? Can you propose others?

b. If an agency expressly considers the competitive consequences of its ruling, is its judgment "exclusive"? If an agency is empowered to make rules permitting conduct inconsistent with usual antitrust principles but does not do so, should a court entertain an antitrust suit brought to challenge such a decision? Consider such questions in light of our next case.

GEORGIA v. PENNSYLVANIA RAILROAD CO.

Supreme Court of the United States, 1945.
324 U.S. 439, 65 S.Ct. 716, 89 L.Ed. 1051.

MR. JUSTICE DOUGLAS delivered the opinion of the Court.

The State of Georgia by this motion for leave to file a bill of complaint seeks to invoke the original jurisdiction of this Court under Art. III, § 2 of the Constitution. * * *

The essence of the complaint is a charge of a conspiracy among the defendants in restraint of trade and commerce among the States. It alleges that they have fixed arbitrary and noncompetitive rates and charges for transportation of freight by railroad to and from Georgia so as to prefer the ports of other States over the ports of Georgia. It charges that some sixty rate bureaus, committees, conferences, associations and other private rate-fixing agencies have been utilized by defendants to fix these rates; that no road can change joint through rates without the approval of these private agencies; that this private rate-fixing machinery which is not sanctioned by the Interstate Commerce Act and which is prohibited by the anti-trust Acts has put the effective control of rates to and from Georgia in the hands of the defendants. The complaint alleges that these practices in purpose and effect give manufacturers, sellers and other shippers in the North an advantage over manufacturers, shippers and others in Georgia. It alleges that the rates so fixed are approximately 39 percent higher than the rates and charges for transportation of like commodities for like distances between points in the North. It alleges that the defendants who have lines wholly or principally in the South are generally dominated and coerced by the defendants who have northern roads, and therefore that, even when the southern defendants desire, they cannot publish joint through rates between Georgia and the North when the northern carriers refuse to join in such rates.

* * *

We think it is clear from the *Keogh* case alone that Georgia may not recover damages even if the conspiracy alleged were shown to exist. That was a suit for damages under § 7 of the Sherman Act. * * * The Court recognized that although the rates fixed had been found reasonable and non-discriminatory by the Commission, the United States was not barred from enforcing the remedies of the Sherman Act. * * * It held, however, that for purposes of a suit for damages a rate was not necessarily illegal because it was the result of a conspiracy in restraint of trade. * * * The reasoning and precedent of that case apply with full force here. But it does not dispose of the main prayer of the bill, stressed at the argument, which asks for relief by way of injunction.

* * *

The relief which Georgia seeks is not a matter subject to the jurisdiction of the Commission. Georgia in this proceeding is not seeking an injunction against the continuance of any tariff; nor does she seek to have any tariff provision canceled. She merely asks that the alleged rate-fixing combination and conspiracy among the defendant-carriers be enjoined. As we shall see, that is a matter over which the Commission has no jurisdiction. * * *

These carriers are subject to the anti-trust laws. * * * Conspiracies among carriers to fix rates were included in the broad sweep of the Sherman Act. Congress by § 11 of the Clayton Act entrusted the Commission with authority to enforce compliance with certain of its provisions "where applicable to common carriers" under the Commission's jurisdiction.[3] It has the power to lift the ban of the anti-trust laws in favor of carriers who merge or consolidate * * * and the duty to give weight to the anti-trust policy of the nation before approving mergers and consolidations. McLean Trucking Co. v. United States, 321 U.S. 67 (1944). But Congress has not given the Commission comparable authority to remove rate-fixing combinations from the prohibitions contained in the anti-trust laws. * * * Regulated industries are not per se exempt from the Sherman Act. It is true that the Commission's regulation of carriers has greatly expanded since the Sherman Act. * * * But it is elementary that repeals by implication are not favored. Only a clear repugnancy between the old law and the new results in the former giving way and then only pro tanto to the extent of the repugnancy. None of the powers acquired by the Commission since the enactment of the Sherman Act relates to the regulation of rate-fixing combinations. * * * In view of this history we can only conclude that they have no immunity from the anti-trust laws.

* * * [T]he present bill does not seek to have the Court act in the place of the Commission. It seeks to remove from the field of ratemaking the influences of a combination which exceed the limits of the collaboration authorized for the fixing of joint through rates. It seeks to put an end to discriminatory and coercive practices. The aim is to make it possible for individual carriers to perform their duty under the Act, so that whatever tariffs may be continued in effect or superseded by new ones may be tariffs which are free from the restrictive, discriminatory, and coercive influences of the combination. That is not to undercut or impair the primary jurisdiction of the Commission over rates. It is to free the rate-making function of the influences of a conspiracy over which the Commission has no authority but which if proven to exist can only hinder the Commission in the tasks with which it is confronted.

* * * The fact that the rates which have been fixed may or may not be held unlawful by the Commission is immaterial to the issue before us. The *Keogh* case indicates that even a combination to fix reasonable and non-discriminatory rates may be illegal. The reason is that the Interstate

---

3. Section 11, 15 U.S.C. § 21, grants to the ICC, FCC, CAB, FRB, and FTC the authority to enforce §§ 2, 3, 7, and 8 of the Clayton Act. [Court's fn. 5]

Commerce Act does not provide remedies for the correction of all the abuses of rate-making which might constitute violations of the anti-trust laws. Thus a "zone of reasonableness exists between maxima and minima within which a carrier is ordinarily free to adjust its charges for itself." United States v. Chicago, M., St. P. & P.R. Co., 294 U.S. 499 [(1935)]. Within that zone the Commission lacks power to grant relief even though the rates are raised to the maxima by a conspiracy among carriers who employ unlawful tactics. If the rate-making function is freed from the unlawful restraints of the alleged conspiracy, the rates of the future will then be fixed in the manner envisioned by Congress when it enacted this legislation. Damage must be presumed to flow from a conspiracy to manipulate rates within that zone.

Moreover, the relief sought from this Court is not an uprooting of established rates. We are not asked for a decree which would be an idle gesture. We are not asked to enjoin what the Commission might later approve or condone. We are not asked to trench on the domain of the Commission; nor need any decree which may be ultimately entered in this cause have that effect. * * * Rate-making is a continuous process. Georgia is seeking a decree which will prevent in the future the kind of harmful conduct which has occurred in the past. * * * Dissolution of illegal combinations or a restriction of their conduct to lawful channels is a conventional form of relief accorded in anti-trust suits. No more is envisaged here. If the alleged combination is shown to exist, the decree * * * will restore that degree of competition envisaged by Congress when it enacted the Interstate Commerce Act. It will eliminate from rate-making the collusive practices which the anti-trust laws condemn and which are not sanctioned by the Interstate Commerce Act. * * * The damage alleged is sufficient to satisfy the preliminary requirements of this motion to file. There is no administrative control over the combination. And no adequate or effective remedy other than this suit is suggested which Georgia can employ to eliminate from ratemaking the influences of unlawful conspiracy alleged to exist here.

The motion for leave to file the amended bill of complaint is granted.

[The dissenting opinion of MR. CHIEF JUSTICE STONE, joined in by JUSTICES ROBERTS, FRANKFURTER, and JACKSON, is omitted.]

Notes and Questions

1. The Court concedes that *Keogh* prohibits Georgia from seeking damages for the conspiracy alleged. Is injunctive relief more or less disruptive of the administrative process than the award of monetary relief?

2. The Court concludes that the relief sought "is not a matter subject to the jurisdiction of the Commission." Is the Court correct? If so, would evidence of a combination or conspiracy nonetheless be relevant and admissible in an ICC rate proceeding? To what extent, if any, would the ICC's expertise be of aid in determining whether or not a conspiracy existed or was unlawful if found to exist? Although dissolution of an "illegal combination"

is not relief that "can be obtained from the Commission for it has no supervisory authority over the combination," is the ICC without power to render the combination harmless? As a practical matter, what steps, if any, would you expect the ICC to take? Should such questions be relevant?

3. Georgia's complaint alleges that the contested rates are discriminatory "so as to prefer the ports of other States over the ports of Georgia." Could Georgia prevail on the merits and obtain equitable relief without proving that allegation? If not, which body is better able to determine that issue, the ICC or the Court? Has the ICC already done so? If not, should judicial action be deferred until it has?

4. Assume that, rather than a conspiracy of railroads, Georgia had alleged that one railroad had "monopoly power" strong enough to exert "coercive" influences. Would the Court's decision have been the same? If so, does that suggest that agencies cannot regulate a "monopolist"?

5. The dissent (in an opinion here omitted) advanced the proposition that § 16 cannot be employed to enjoin a conspiracy without inevitably interfering with or prejudging the "lawfulness of matters which Congress has indubitably placed within the jurisdiction of the administrative agency." How does the majority opinion deal with this argument?

6. Reacting to Georgia v. Pennsylvania R.R., Congress provided the Interstate Commerce Commission with the statutory authority over rate association agreements that Justice Douglas found lacking at the time of the case. In June 1948, Congress passed the Reed–Bulwinkle Act, 62 Stat. 472, 49 U.S.C.A. § 5b, that empowered the commission to approve agreements among carriers (establishing and operating rate bureaus, conferences, and associations) that are filed with the commission. Commission approval carries with it relief from the operation of the antitrust laws with respect to conduct of the parties pursuant to the agreement. 49 U.S.C.A. § 5b(9). The Georgia litigation itself was eventually dismissed by stipulation of the parties.

7. The Reed–Bulwinkle Act was substantially amended by the 4R Act of 1976 and is currently codified at 49 U.S.C. § 10706. Rate agreements approved by the Surface Transportation Board are still exempt from the antitrust laws, but the conditions for approval are closely monitored by the Board and the Federal Trade Commission is instructed to prepare periodic assessments of the anticompetitive features of agreements approved under this section.

8. Failure to comply with the provisions of § 5(b) has led to criminal antitrust actions.

a. What, if any, role should the Surface Transportation Board have in determining whether the rate agreement violates the section 5b (now § 10706) exemption? Should the Court acknowledge the Board's "primary jurisdiction" as to such issues?

b. Does the possibility of criminal liability increase or render less necessary the need for Board intercession?

c. If the Board did give its views on the legality of the activity, what weight should they be accorded by the district judge in the criminal antitrust case? Cf. United States v. Bessemer and Lake Erie Railroad, 717 F.2d 593 (D.C.Cir.1983).

The cases we have been reading were only preliminary, however, to the consideration of perhaps the most dramatic example of modern "judicial deregulation"—the breakup of AT & T.

UNITED STATES v. AMERICAN TELEPHONE & TELEGRAPH CO.

United States District Court, District of Columbia, 1978.
461 F.Supp. 1314.

GREENE, J. The motions before the Court address the Court's jurisdiction and they raise fundamental issues concerning the discovery that should govern the future path of this antitrust litigation. * * *

The complaint * * * alleges violations of Section 2 of the Sherman Act by the American Telephone and Telegraph Company (AT & T), Western Electric Company, Inc. (Western Electric)[4] and Bell Telephone Laboratories, Inc. (Bell Labs).[5] In sweeping language the complaint alleges that an unlawful combination and conspiracy exists and has existed for many years among the defendants and certain co-conspirator (primarily the Bell Operating Companies),[6] designed to permit AT & T to maintain control over Western Electric, Bell Labs, and the Bell Operating Companies; to restrict competition from other telecommunications[7] systems and carriers and from other manufacturers and suppliers of telecommunications equipment; and to cause Western Electric to supply substantially all the telecommunications requirements of the Bell System.

The complaint explains that the defendants are violating the antitrust laws by various monopolistic practices including the refusal to sell terminal equipment to subscribers of Bell System telecommunications service, the creation of obstructions to the interconnection of various carriers with the Bell System, and the maintenance of a monopolistic manufacturing and purchasing relationship between Western Electric and the Bell System. It is further alleged that, as a consequence of these practices (1) defendants have achieved and are maintaining a monopoly of telecommunications service and equipment; (2) competition in these

---

4. Western Electric is the 12th largest individual corporation in the United States, with sales of over $7 billion. It owns fifty percent of the stock of Bell Labs, and it has at least one wholly owned subsidiary. It is not regulated by any federal or state regulatory authority. [Court's fn. 2]

5. Bell Labs is owned in equal parts by AT & T and Western Electric. It conducts research and development primarily for AT & T, Western Electric, and Bell Operating Companies. Like Western Electric, it is not regulated by any federal or state regulatory authority. [Court's fn. 3]

6. There are 23 Bell Operating Companies which, along with many other non-Bell companies, provide primarily intrastate, and some interstate service, pursuant to certificates of public convenience and necessity. [Court's fn. 4]

7. Telecommunications is defined as the electronic and electromagnetic transmission of voice, data, and other communications by wire, cable, microwave radio, and communications satellite. [Court's fn. 5]

areas has been restrained; and (3) purchasers of telecommunications service and equipment have been denied the benefits of a free and competitive market. Among other relief, the action seeks the divestiture by AT & T of all Western Electric stock; the separation of some or all of the Long Lines Department of AT & T from the Bell Operating Companies; the divestiture by Western Electric of its manufacturing and other assets sufficient to insure competition in the manufacture and sales of telecommunications equipment; and such relief against Bell Labs as the Court may find appropriate.

Defendants' Answer, and the Court *sua sponte,* raised two threshold defenses: (1) that a decree entered in 1956 * * * (United States v. Western Electric Co. (D.N.J.1956)) is *res judicata,* and (2) that the matters complained of by the government are within the exclusive jurisdiction of the Federal Communications Commission and therefore immune from scrutiny under the antitrust laws. * * * [T]he Court rejected the claim of *res judicata,* and * * * ruled that defendants do not possess blanket immunity from antitrust liability by virtue of the Communications Act of 1934 or their regulation by the Federal Communications Commission. In rejecting the plea that the FCC has exclusive jurisdiction over the subject matter of this litigation, the Court further stated, however, that it might in the future refer particular issues to the Commission under the so-called doctrine of primary jurisdiction. United States v. American Tel. & Tel. Co., 427 F.Supp. 57 (D.D.C.1976) (Waddy, J.), cert. denied, 429 U.S. 1071 (1977). * * *

In all of their submissions to this Court, defendants have vigorously and consistently raised the jurisdictional issue. They insist that an irreconcilable conflict exists between the antitrust laws and the regulatory scheme established by the relevant statutes, that when there is such a conflict the antitrust laws must give way, and that therefore the Court lacks jurisdiction over this action. * * *

Telecommunications carriers clearly do not enjoy an express statutory immunity from antitrust enforcement with respect to the activities here involved. While Congress has not hesitated in so many words to exempt the practices of other industries from the antitrust laws,[8] and while it has statutorily exempted some activities of telephone companies from those laws,[9] it has not done so with respect to the conduct which is the subject matter of this complaint. Likewise, defendants have cited nothing in the legislative history of the statutes regulating the telecommunications industry which would lead to the conclusion that an antitrust immunity was contemplated when those statutes were enacted. Thus, if the Court lacks jurisdiction, it could only be because defendants

---

8. E.g., insurance (McCarran–Ferguson Act, 15 U.S.C. § 1012); air transportation (Federal Aviation Act, 49 U.S.C. § 1384); export trade associations (Webb–Pomerene Act, 15 U.S.C. § 62); surface transportation (Reed–Bulwinkle Act of 1948, 49 U.S.C. § 5b(9)). [Court's fn. 18]

9. 47 U.S.C. §§ 221(a) and 222(c)(1) exempt certain FCC-approved consolidations and mergers of telephone companies. [Court's fn. 19]

enjoy an immunity by implication, resulting from an incompatibility between the antitrust laws and the statutes which regulate the telecommunications industry.

The problem created by the tension between the antitrust laws and economic regulation has been long recognized. See, e.g., United States v. Trans–Missouri Freight Association; 2 A. Kahn, The Economics of Regulation: Principles and Institutions 1, 4–5 (1971). Broadly speaking the antitrust laws are rooted in the proposition that the public interest is best protected by competition, free from artificial restraints such as price-fixing and monopoly. The theory of regulation, on the other hand, presupposes that with respect to certain areas of economic activity the judgment expert agencies may produce results superior to those of the marketplace, and that for this reason competition in a particular industry not necessarily serve the public interest. Because of these diverse objectives, it could be, and has been, argued that whenever the Congress has established a scheme of regulation through an independent commission, it must be deemed to have determined that the antitrust laws should not apply to the industry thus being regulated. That, however, is not the law.

The Supreme Court has repeatedly noted that "repeals of antitrust laws by implication from a regulatory statute are strongly disfavored, and have only been found in cases of plain repugnance between the antitrust and regulatory provisions." Otter Tail Power v. United States, 410 U.S. 366 (1973), quoting United States v. Philadelphia National Bank, 374 U.S. 321 (1963).

Regulated industries "are not *per se* exempt from the Sherman Act" (Georgia v. Pennsylvania R.R. Co.),[10] and they are not necessarily exempt even if the conduct complained of in an antitrust context has been expressly approved by the agency charged with regulating the particular industry.

In United States v. Radio Corporation of America, 358 U.S. 334 (1959), a decision by the Federal Communications Commission specifically approving an exchange of television stations was asserted as a defense to an antitrust divestiture action. The Supreme Court rejected that contention, holding, as Mr. Justice Harlan expressed it in his concurring summary of the Court's decision, "a Commission determination of 'public interest, convenience, and necessity' cannot either constitute a binding adjudication upon any antitrust issues that may be involved in the Commission's proceeding or serve to exempt a licensee pro tanto from the antitrust laws * * *."

* * *

10. The antitrust laws apply notwithstanding regulation in such industries as the production of natural gas (California v. Federal Power Commission 369 U.S. 482, 82 S.Ct. 901, 8 L.Ed.2d 54 (1962)); generation and transmission of electric power (Otter Tail Power Co. v. United States, supra). national banking (United States v. Philadelphia National Bank, supra). securities and commodities exchanges (Silver v. New York Stock Exchange, supra; Ricci v. Chicago Mercantile Exchange, 409 U.S. 289, 93 S.Ct. 573, 34 L.Ed.2d 525 (1973)); and broadcasting (United States v. Radio Corporation of America, 358 U.S. 334, 79 S.Ct. 457, 3 L.Ed.2d 354 (1959)). [Court's fn. 23]

Regulated conduct is, however, deemed to be immune by implication from the antitrust laws in two relatively narrow instances; (1) when a regulatory agency has, with congressional approval, exercised explicit authority over the challenged practice itself (as distinguished from the general subject matter) in such a way that antitrust enforcement would interfere with regulation, and (2) when regulation by an agency over an industry or some of its components or practices is so pervasive that Congress is assumed to have determined competition to be an inadequate means of vindicating the public interest.

* * *

Thus, the inquiry in this case must focus upon (1) whether the activities which are the subject of this complaint were required or approved by the Federal Communications Commission, pursuant to explicit statutory authority, in a way that is incompatible with antitrust enforcement, and (2) whether these activities are being so "pervasively" regulated that an immunity from antitrust action must be assumed. In my judgment, these questions must be answered in the negative.

We do not start with a clean slate, neatly balancing whether there should or should not be antitrust jurisdiction. The complaint alleges serious violations of the Sherman Act, and if the government is able to prove these allegations, it follows that a substantial violation of that fundamental charter of American economic life has occurred. The burden is on defendants to demonstrate that they or their practices were intended to be exempt or immune from the broad mandate of the Act. To carry that burden, defendants rely on the Supreme Court decisions discussed above which found certain companies to be immune from the antitrust laws based upon a degree of regulation by government agencies which, as a practical matter, left them no choice but to follow the regulatory schemes and orders. But such regulation is not present in this case.

At the outset, it must be noted that two of the defendants in the instant action, Western Electric and Bell Labs, are not subject to direct regulation by the Federal Communications Commission at all. * * * Legislative history over the years shows that congressional concern over AT & T's intracorporate structure never matured beyond directing the Federal Communications Commission to conduct a study. Once that study was completed, Congress took no further action, nor was the Commission given authority to take further action.

Consequently, it has been the Federal Communications Commission's consistent position that it has no authority to alter, regulate, or otherwise to interfere with AT & T's internal structure, including its relationships with Western Electric and Bell Labs. Beyond broad general statements, defendants have cited nothing to the contrary. In view of this history, it is difficult to see on what basis Western Electric, Bell Labs, or the relationships involving them, could be considered immune from the antitrust laws on any theory.

AT & T's Long Lines Department and the Bell operating Companies are in a somewhat different posture, for they are subject to FCC regulation in a variety of ways, and the Commission has to a substantial extent exercised this authority. But there is nothing in either the Communications Act or the related statutes to suggest that, with respect to the activities and relationships which are significant to this case, Congress intended to vest in the Federal Communications Commission such pervasive regulatory authority as to override antitrust consider- ations, nor is there anything to indicate that the antitrust laws are incompatible with the operation of these regulatory statutes as intended by the Congress.

The situation here is thus considerably different from that presented in Gordon v. New York Stock Exchange, [422 U.S. 659 (1975)].[11] In *Gordon* the Supreme Court said that the antitrust laws could not be applied where the Congress had given the Securities and Exchange Commission exclusive jurisdiction to supervise the fixing of rates of commission for transactions on the stock exchanges and where the Securities and Exchange Commission had in fact exercised that jurisdic- tion. By contrast, the Federal Communications Commission has not been granted exclusive jurisdiction over what may be called the interconnec- tion areas, but by statute shares that jurisdiction with the courts. 47 U.S.C. § 406.

More importantly, the regulatory charter of the Commission itself, while broad in many respects, is at the same time relatively weak. For example, telephone tariffs—a primary regulatory tool—become effective upon filing by the carrier after 90 days notice without the necessity for Commission scrutiny or approval; a carrier may file a new or revised tariff at any time, and the power of the Commission to suspend a tariff is limited to a five-month maximum. The weakness of the regulatory scheme is reinforced by a volume of tariff filings beyond the capacity of the Commission to handle. During the 12–month period from September 1974 through August 1975, the Commission received 1,371 tariff filings totaling 11,491 pages, and because of this volume, it was able to investigate only a small percentage of the tariffs. Thus, it is not surpris- ing that the Commission has concluded that "rate filings generally proceed from the carrier's independent judgment." * * *

The statutory weaknesses, the general inability of the Commission to scrutinize all the tariffs submitted to it, and perhaps other factors (e.g., the lack of adequate resources effectively to regulate AT & T, a corporate giant), have produced the result of a far less than pervasive or specific regulation of the areas that are critical to this case. In any event, whatever the reasons, it is clear that regulation of defendants' conduct

---

11. The distinction is significant inas- much as *Gordon*, and its companion case United States v. National Association of Securities Dealers, represent the outer lim- its of the Supreme Court's application of the implied immunity doctrine. other Su- preme Court law is even more hospitable to the antitrust laws and less apt to imply an immunity. [Court's fn. 32]

has not been such that this antitrust action would disturb or interfere with it.[12]

The FCC—unlike, for example, the SEC in the stock exchange cases—has consistently taken the position that antitrust enforcement through court action is not precluded in this area. * * *

Among the considerations it cited in support of its position, the Commission stressed, *inter alia,* that, while under section 214 of the Communications Act, 47 U.S.C. § 214, it has exclusive market entry authority, antitrust actions not only do not necessarily conflict with that authority, but might even complement it in appropriate circumstances; the courts and the Commission have concurrent responsibilities, but when there is a conflict, the doctrine of primary jurisdiction is adequate to resolve the matter; the Commission has never considered its authority over equipment interconnection to displace the antitrust laws; and even with respect to tariffs, since, as noted supra, they often become effective without Commission scrutiny or approval, the courts appropriately exercise antitrust jurisdiction.[13]

An examination of the complaint in this proceeding against the implied immunity doctrine and its philosophic underpinnings verifies the Commission's conclusion. The allegations of the complaint describe conduct that quite obviously was not stimulated by regulatory supervision or coercion; it is of a character that reflects defendants' business judgment that its profits might be maximized if potential competitors were discouraged from entering the various markets AT & T controls.

According to the complaint, defendants have chosen to engage in a variety of predatory activities designed to shut out potential competitors from the telecommunications markets, including the denial to competing entities of interconnection privileges with AT & T's monopoly facilities; unlawful rate adjustments in response to competition; refusal to permit telephone customers to provide their own terminal equipment and to interconnect it to AT & T's network; and perpetuation of various production and marketing practices designed to curb competition. There is absolutely nothing to suggest that Congress expected the Commission to require or approve, or that the Commission did require or approve any of these practices. These activities not only violate the antitrust laws but they are also inconsistent with the purpose of the regulation, or at the very least they are not required or encouraged either by regulatory theory or by regulatory action.

* * * The purpose of the implied immunity rule is to eliminate adherence to antitrust standards when there are irreconcilable differ-

---

12. Even when the regulation is "pervasive," and the precise conduct attacked in an antitrust suit is being regulated, an immunity will be found only if the antitrust remedy conflicts with rather than complements the enforcement efforts of the regulatory agency. Mt. Hood Stages, Inc. v. Greyhound Corp., 555 F.2d 687 (9th Cir. 1977), vacated and remanded on other grounds, 437 U.S. 322, 98 S.Ct. 2370, 57 L.Ed.2d 239 (1978). [Court's fn. 36]

13. The Commission considers, however, that when it has prescribed or specifically approved a tariff, its judgment must control (FCC Memorandum of December 30, 1975, p. 20). [Court's fn. 39]

ences between the antitrust laws and federal regulatory statutes.[14] But the antitrust laws cannot be held hostage to a supposed irreconcilability between antitrust and regulatory enforcement when no such irreconcilability exists in fact, nor can the alleged unlawful actions of defendants be deemed protected from the Sherman Act by the cloak of generalized regulation of AT & T by the Commission.

In short, it would be a gross misconception of the realities to equate the instant statutory scheme, the relatively weak regulatory controls which have implemented that scheme, and defendants' alleged activities which offend both the antitrust laws and the regulatory purposes, with the kind of explicit regulation endorsing industry conduct which the Supreme Court has held in relatively few instances to be inconsistent with antitrust enforcement.[15]

* * *

For these reasons, the Court rejects defendants' contention that the Court lacks antitrust jurisdiction over the matters alleged in the complaint. However, in the event that it should subsequently appear after the issues have been crystallized—e.g., after discovery has been completed—that with respect to some of defendants' conduct the Commission has special expertise or there may be a conflict between antitrust enforcement and regulation, the issues relating to such conduct will be referred to the Commission under the doctrine of primary jurisdiction.[16]

14. Immunity will be implied only if necessary to make the regulatory statutes work, "and even then only to the minimum extent necessary." Gordon v. New York Stock Exchange, supra, 422 U.S. at 685, 95 S.Ct. at 2613. [Court's fn. 42]

15. Additionally, it is not insignificant that, even with respect to that portion of defendants' activities which the Commission does regulate, only the courts can grant complete relief. The Commission has little authority to vindicate injury to competitors; there is no statutory provision authorizing it to order divestiture; and it is unable to adopt remedies designed to foreclose future anticompetitive conduct. Congress could hardly be deemed by implication to have conferred immunity on carriers such as these defendants when the effect of its assumed action would be to insulate the alleged antitrust violators from effective sanctions or relief. [Court's fn. 43]

16. While the term "primary jurisdiction" has been widely used, including by the U.S. Supreme Court, it deserves some clarification. A referral under that doctrine does not oust a court of jurisdiction. It merely serves as a means for requesting a regulatory agency to make preliminary factual and legal determinations while reserving to the court the authority to decide the ultimate questions. Judge Waddy's opinion of November 24, 1976, concluded that some of the issues herein might be referred to the FCC under that doctrine. It is clear * * * that such a referral is appropriate particularly where there is a need to resolve possible conflicts between the objectives of the antitrust laws and the regulatory standards, and where an adjudication of such issues by the regulatory body will be of material aid in the ultimate decision of the antitrust issues. It is my intention as it was Judge Waddy's, to make such appropriate references to the FCC. According to the Commission, issues which substantially affect the following matters should be referred to it under the principle of primary jurisdiction: (1) entry into or exit from a communications carrier market. (2) FCC orders requiring interconnection; and (3) tariff provisions which the Commission has approved or precluded. It would be premature at this point to conclude the extent to which these conditions exist with respect to particular issues in this case, or whether there may be other matters appropriate for referral to the Commission. [Court's fn. 45]

Notes and Questions

1. The AT & T litigation provides perhaps the ultimate example of the interaction between antitrust and regulation. It was the largest antitrust action ever commenced against a regulated entity and it resulted in the largest breakup of any business in history.

a. Did it seem odd to you that a regulated firm like AT & T could be charged with violating Sherman Act Section 2 ("monopolization")? Wouldn't one expect and want a natural monopoly to monopolize?

b. Might it be that AT & T was really more complex than a textbook natural monopoly? Did the existence of unregulated subsidiaries like Western Electric and Bell Labs give credence to that view? Does telephone service have natural monopoly characteristics anymore? Think of the competitive alternative provided by cell phones. What does the Telecommunications Act of 1996 assume the characteristics of the industry are?

c. Does this case demonstrate the two quite different meanings of "monopolize" under Section 2? Was AT & T accused here of having the "status" of monopolist (sometimes called the "structural" approach under Section 2), or of denying others the reasonable chance to do business (the "conduct" approach)? Should "structure" be an FCC matter but "conduct" something the courts can consider? Is such a distinction too simple?

2. Are you persuaded that the antitrust issues were not, in fact, ones Congress had entrusted to the FCC?

a. Again, are the unregulated subsidiaries the company's Achilles heel? Is the Court's assertion nearly as persuasive that Congress did not intend FCC jurisdiction to be exclusive as to matters the agency in fact could regulate?

b. How important is the intensity of actual regulation to the question of exclusive jurisdiction? Suppose Congress created a regulatory agency to supervise a company but did not appropriate funds for it? Suppose the FCC said it was not actively regulating AT & T because the company was doing what the agency wanted without being ordered to do so?

c. Is prosecution of this antitrust case inconsistent with some value the regulatory scheme was designed to further? Does it charge AT & T with doing something the FCC had ordered the firm to do? Does that mean that the *Keogh* concerns are not presented here?

d. If the company had been forced to pay treble damages, would it have been permitted to pass the cost on to the ratepayers? Were the "anticompetitive" activities with which AT & T was charged in at least the short-run interest of its ratepayers? If so, should that in itself be enough to find that the antitrust suit was inherently inconsistent with the regulatory scheme?

3. The last footnote of Judge Greene's decision identifies issues that might require referral to the FCC as matters of primary jurisdiction. May this listing be another way of stating the effective limits of FCC jurisdiction over the matters explicitly at issue in this case? Does such an inquiry provide a method for analyzing similar primary jurisdiction problems?[17]

---

17. Judge Greene was relieved of further oversight of AT & T by the Telecommunications Act of 1996. Pub.Law 104–104, 110 Stat. 143 (1996).

4. If a statute or agency order contemplates integrating competition into a regulatory scheme, could a violation of that regulation also constitute a violation of the antitrust laws? That issue was addressed by the Supreme Court in the next case.

VERIZON COMMUNICATIONS INC. v. LAW OFFICES OF CURTIS V. TRINKO, LLP

Supreme Court of the United States, 2004.
___ U.S. ___, 124 S.Ct. 872, 157 L.Ed.2d 823.

JUSTICE SCALIA delivered the opinion of the Court.

The Telecommunications Act of 1996 imposes certain duties upon incumbent local telephone companies in order to facilitate market entry by competitors, and establishes a complex regime for monitoring and enforcement. In this case we consider whether a complaint alleging breach of the incumbent's duty under the 1996 Act to share its network with competitors states a claim under § 2 of the Sherman Act.

I

Petitioner Verizon Communications Inc. is the incumbent local exchange carrier (LEC) serving New York State. Before the 1996 Act, Verizon, like other incumbent LECs, enjoyed an exclusive franchise within its local service area. The 1996 Act sought to "uproot" the incumbent LECs' monopoly and to introduce competition in its place. Verizon Communications Inc. v. FCC, 535 U.S. 467, 488, 152 L.Ed.2d 701, 122 S.Ct. 1646 (2002). Central to the scheme of the Act is the incumbent LEC's obligation under 47 U.S.C. § 251(c) to share its network with competitors, see AT & T Corp. v. Iowa Utilities Bd., 525 U.S. 366, 371, 142 L.Ed.2d 834, 119 S.Ct. 721 (1999), including provision of access to individual elements of the network on an "unbundled" basis. New entrants, so-called competitive LECs, resell these unbundled network elements (UNEs), recombined with each other or with elements belonging to the LECs.

Verizon, like other incumbent LECs, has taken two significant steps within the Act's framework in the direction of increased competition. First, Verizon has signed interconnection agreements with rivals such as AT & T, as it is obliged to do under § 252, detailing the terms on which it will make its network elements available. (Because Verizon and AT & T could not agree upon terms, the open issues were subjected to compulsory arbitration under § § 252(b) and (c).) In 1997, the state regulator, New York's Public Service Commission (PSC), approved Verizon's interconnection agreement with AT & T.

Second, Verizon has taken advantage of the opportunity provided by the 1996 Act for incumbent LECs to enter the long-distance market (from which they had long been excluded). That required Verizon to satisfy, among other things, a 14–item checklist of statutory requirements, which includes compliance with the Act's network-sharing duties.

Checklist item two, for example, includes "nondiscriminatory access to network elements in accordance with the requirements" of § 251(c)(3). Whereas the state regulator approves an interconnection agreement, for long-distance approval the incumbent LEC applies to the Federal Communications Commission (FCC). In December 1999, the FCC approved Verizon's § 271 application for New York.

Part of Verizon's UNE obligation under § 251(c)(3) is the provision of access to operations support systems (OSS), a set of systems used by incumbent LECs to provide services to customers and ensure quality. Verizon's interconnection agreement and long-distance authorization each specified the mechanics by which its OSS obligation would be met. As relevant here, a competitive LEC sends orders for service through an electronic interface with Verizon's ordering system, and as Verizon completes certain steps in filling the order, it sends confirmation back through the same interface. Without OSS access a rival cannot fill its customers' orders.

In late 1999, competitive LECs complained to regulators that many orders were going unfilled, in violation of Verizon's obligation to provide access to OSS functions. The PSC and FCC opened parallel investigations, which led to a series of orders by the PSC and a consent decree with the FCC. Under the FCC consent decree, Verizon undertook to make a "voluntary contribution" to the U.S. Treasury in the amount of $3 million; under the PSC orders, Verizon incurred liability to the competitive LECs in the amount of $10 million. Under the consent decree and orders, Verizon was subjected to new performance measurements and new reporting requirements to the FCC and PSC, with additional penalties for continued noncompliance. In June 2000, the FCC terminated the consent decree. The next month the PSC relieved Verizon of the heightened reporting requirement.

Respondent Law Offices of Curtis V. Trinko, LLP, a New York City law firm, was a local telephone service customer of AT & T. The day after Verizon entered its consent decree with the FCC, respondent filed a complaint in the District Court for the Southern District of New York, on behalf of itself and a class of similarly situated customers. The complaint, as later amended, alleged that Verizon had filled rivals' orders on a discriminatory basis as part of an anticompetitive scheme to discourage customers from becoming or remaining customers of competitive LECs, thus impeding the competitive LECs' ability to enter and compete in the market for local telephone service. According to the complaint, Verizon "has filled orders of [competitive LEC] customers after filling those for its own local phone service, has failed to fill in a timely manner, or not at all, a substantial number of orders for [competitive LEC] customers . . ., and has systematically failed to inform [competitive LECs] of the status of their customers' orders." The complaint set forth a single example of the alleged "failure to provide adequate access to [competitive LECs]," namely the OSS failure that resulted in the FCC consent decree and PSC orders. It asserted that the result of Verizon's improper "behavior with respect to providing access to its local loop" was to "deter potential customers [of rivals] from switching." The complaint sought damages and injunctive relief for violation of § 2 of the Sherman Act, pursuant to the remedy provisions of §§ 4 and 16 of the Clayton Act. The complaint also alleged violations of the 1996 Act, § 202(a) of the Communications Act of 1934, and state law.

The District Court dismissed the complaint in its entirety. As to the antitrust portion, it concluded that respondent's allegations of deficient assistance to rivals failed to satisfy the requirements of § 2. The Court of Appeals for the Second Circuit reinstated the complaint in part, including the antitrust claim. We granted certiorari, limited to the question whether the Court of Appeals erred in reversing the District Court's dismissal of respondent's antitrust claims.

II

To decide this case, we must first determine what effect (if any) the 1996 Act has upon the application of traditional antitrust principles. The Act imposes a large number of duties upon incumbent LECs—above and beyond those basic responsibilities it imposes upon all carriers, such as assuring number portability and providing access to rights-of-way. Under the sharing duties of § 251(c), incumbent LECs are required to offer three kinds of access. Already noted, and perhaps most intrusive, is the duty to offer access to UNEs on "just, reasonable, and nondiscriminatory" terms, a phrase that the FCC has interpreted to mean a price reflecting long-run incremental cost. See Verizon Communications Inc. v. FCC. A rival can interconnect its own facilities with those of the incumbent LEC, or it can simply purchase services at wholesale from the incumbent and resell them to consumers. The Act also imposes upon incumbents the duty to allow physical "collocation"—that is, to permit a competitor to locate and install its equipment on the incumbent's premises—which makes feasible interconnection and access to UNEs.

That Congress created these duties, however, does not automatically lead to the conclusion that they can be enforced by means of an antitrust claim. Indeed, a detailed regulatory scheme such as that created by the 1996 Act ordinarily raises the question whether the regulated entities are not shielded from antitrust scrutiny altogether by the doctrine of implied immunity. See, e.g., United States v. National Ass'n. of Sec. Dealers, Inc., 422 U.S. 694, 45 L.Ed.2d 486, 95 S.Ct. 2427 (1975). In some respects the enforcement scheme set up by the 1996 Act is a good candidate for implication of antitrust immunity, to avoid the real possibility of judgments conflicting with the agency's regulatory scheme "that might be voiced by courts exercising jurisdiction under the antitrust laws."

Congress, however, precluded that interpretation. Section 601(b)(1) of the 1996 Act is an antitrust-specific saving clause providing that "nothing in this Act or the amendments made by this Act shall be construed to modify, impair, or supersede the applicability of any of the antitrust laws." This bars a finding of implied immunity. As the FCC has put the point, the saving clause preserves those "claims that satisfy established antitrust standards."

But just as the 1996 Act preserves claims that satisfy existing antitrust standards, it does not create new claims that go beyond existing antitrust standards; that would be equally inconsistent with the saving clause's mandate that nothing in the Act "modify, impair, or supersede the applicability" of the antitrust laws. We turn, then, to whether the activity of which respondent complains violates preexisting antitrust standards.

III

The complaint alleges that Verizon denied interconnection services to rivals in order to limit entry. If that allegation states an antitrust claim at all, it does so under § 2 of the Sherman Act, which declares that a firm shall not "monopolize" or "attempt to monopolize." It is settled law that this offense requires, in addition to the possession of monopoly power in the relevant market, "the willful acquisition or maintenance of that power as distinguished from growth or development as a consequence of a superior product, business acumen, or historic accident." United States v. Grinnell Corp., 384 U.S. 563, 570–571, 16 L.Ed.2d 778, 86 S.Ct. 1698 (1966). The mere possession of monopoly power, and the concomitant charging of monopoly prices, is not only not unlawful; it is an important element of the free-market system. The opportunity to charge monopoly prices—at least for a short period—is what attracts "business acumen" in the first place; it induces risk taking that produces innovation and economic growth. To safeguard the incentive to innovate, the possession of monopoly power will not be found unlawful unless it is accompanied by an element of anticompetitive *conduct.*

Firms may acquire monopoly power by establishing an infrastructure that renders them uniquely suited to serve their customers. Compelling such firms to share the source of their advantage is in some tension with the underlying purpose of antitrust law, since it may lessen the incentive for the monopolist, the rival, or both to invest in those economically beneficial facilities. Enforced sharing also requires antitrust courts to act as central planners, identifying the proper price, quantity, and other terms of dealing—a role for which they are ill-suited. Moreover, compelling negotiation between competitors may facilitate the supreme evil of antitrust: collusion. Thus, as a general matter, the Sherman Act "does not restrict the long recognized right of [a] trader or manufacturer engaged in an entirely private business, freely to exercise his own independent discretion as to parties with whom he will deal." United States v. Colgate & Co., 250 U.S. 300, 307, 63 L.Ed. 992, 39 S.Ct. 465 (1919).

However, "the high value that we have placed on the right to refuse to deal with other firms does not mean that the right is unqualified." Aspen Skiing Co. v. Aspen Highlands Skiing Corp., 472 U.S. 585, 601, 86 L.Ed. 2d 467, 105 S.Ct. 2847 (1985). Under certain circumstances, a refusal to cooperate with rivals can constitute anticompetitive conduct and violate § 2. We have been very cautious in recognizing such exceptions, because of the uncertain virtue of forced sharing and the difficulty of identifying and remedying anticompetitive conduct by a single firm. The question before us today is whether the allegations of respondent's complaint fit within existing exceptions or provide a basis, under traditional antitrust principles, for recognizing a new one.

The leading case for § 2 liability based on refusal to cooperate with a rival, and the case upon which respondent understandably places greatest reliance, is *Aspen Skiing,* supra. The Aspen ski area consisted of four mountain areas. The defendant, who owned three of those areas, and the plaintiff, who owned the fourth, had cooperated for years in the issuance of a joint, multiple-day, all-area ski ticket. After repeatedly demanding an increased share of the proceeds, the defendant canceled the joint ticket. The plaintiff, concerned that skiers would bypass its mountain without some joint offering, tried a variety of increasingly desperate measures to re-create the joint ticket, even to the point of in effect offering to buy the defendant's tickets at retail price. The defendant refused even that. We upheld a jury verdict for the plaintiff, reasoning that "the jury may well have concluded that [the defendant] elected to forgo these short-run benefits because it was more interested in reducing competition . . . over the long run by harming its smaller competitor."

Aspen Skiing is at or near the outer boundary of § 2 liability. The Court there found significance in the defendant's decision to cease participation in a cooperative venture. The unilateral termination of a voluntary (*and thus presumably profitable*) course of dealing suggested a willingness to forsake short-term profits to achieve an anticompetitive end. Similarly, the defendant's unwillingness to renew the ticket *even if compensated at retail price* revealed a distinctly anticompetitive bent.

The refusal to deal alleged in the present case does not fit within the limited exception recognized in *Aspen Skiing.* The complaint does not allege that Verizon voluntarily engaged in a course of dealing with its rivals, or would ever have done so absent statutory compulsion. Here, therefore, the defendant's prior conduct sheds no light upon the motivation of its refusal to deal—upon whether its regulatory lapses were prompted not by competitive zeal but by anticompetitive malice. The contrast between the cases is heightened by the difference in pricing behavior. In *Aspen Skiing,* the defendant turned down a proposal to sell at its own retail price, suggesting a calculation that its future monopoly retail price would be higher. Verizon's reluctance to interconnect at the cost-based rate of compensation available under § 251(c)(3) tells us nothing about dreams of monopoly.

The specific nature of what the 1996 Act compels makes this case different from *Aspen Skiing* in a more fundamental way. In *Aspen Skiing,* what the defendant refused to provide to its competitor was a product that it already sold at retail—to oversimplify slightly, lift tickets representing a bundle of services to skiers. Similarly, in Otter Tail Power Co. v. United States, 410 U.S. 366, 35 L.Ed.2d 359, 93 S.Ct. 1022 (1973), another case relied upon by respondent, the defendant was already in the business of providing a service to certain customers (power transmission over its network), and refused to provide the same service to certain other customers. In the present case, by contrast, the services allegedly withheld are not otherwise marketed or available to the public. The sharing obligation imposed by the 1996 Act created "something brand new"—"the wholesale market for leasing network elements." Verizon Communications, Inc. v. FCC. The unbundled elements offered pursuant to § 251(c)(3) exist only deep within the bowels of Verizon; they are brought out on compulsion of the 1996 Act and offered not to consumers but to rivals, and at considerable expense and effort. New systems must be designed and implemented simply to make that access possible—indeed, it is the failure of one of those systems that prompted the present complaint.[18]

We conclude that Verizon's alleged insufficient assistance in the provision of service to rivals is not a recognized antitrust claim under this Court's existing refusal-to-deal precedents. This conclusion would be unchanged even if we considered to be established law the "essential facilities" doctrine crafted by some lower courts, under which the Court of Appeals concluded respondent's allegations might state a claim. See generally Areeda, Essential Facilities: An Epithet in Need of Limiting Principles, 58 Antitrust L. J. 841 (1989). We have never recognized such a doctrine, and we find no need either to recognize it or to repudiate it here. It suffices for present purposes to note that the indispensable requirement for invoking the doctrine is the unavailability of access to the "essential facilities"; where access exists, the doctrine serves no purpose. Thus, it is said that "essential facility claims should ... be denied where a state or federal agency has effective power to compel sharing and to regulate its scope and terms." P. Areeda & H. Hovenkamp, Antitrust Law, p. 150, P773e (2003 Supp.). Respondent believes that the existence of sharing duties under the 1996 Act supports its case. We think the opposite: The 1996 Act's extensive provision for access makes it unnecessary to impose a judicial doctrine of forced access. To the extent respondent's "essential facilities" argument is distinct from its general § 2 argument, we reject it.

IV

Finally, we do not believe that traditional antitrust principles justify adding the present case to the few existing exceptions from the proposition that there is no duty to aid competitors. Antitrust analysis must always be attuned to the particular structure and circumstances of the

---

18. Respondent also relies upon United States v. Terminal R. Ass'n, 224 U.S. 383, 56 L.Ed. 810, 32 S.Ct. 507 (1912), and Associated Press v. United States, 326 U.S. 1, 89 L.Ed. 2013, 65 S.Ct. 1416 (1945). These cases involved *concerted* action, which presents greater anticompetitive concerns and is amenable to a remedy that does not require judicial estimation of free-market forces: simply requiring that the outsider be granted nondiscriminatory admission to the club. [Court's fn. 3]

industry at issue. Part of that attention to economic context is an awareness of the significance of regulation. As we have noted, "careful account must be taken of the pervasive federal and state regulation characteristic of the industry." United States v. Citizens & Southern Nat. Bank, 422 U.S. 86, 91, 45 L.Ed. 2d 41, 95 S.Ct. 2099 (1975); see also IA P. Areeda & H. Hovenkamp, Antitrust Law, p. 12, P240c3 (2d ed. 2000). "Antitrust analysis must sensitively recognize and reflect the distinctive economic and legal setting of the regulated industry to which it applies." Concord v. Boston Edison Co., 915 F.2d 17, 22 (1st Cir. 1990) (Breyer, C. J.) (internal quotation marks omitted).

One factor of particular importance is the existence of a regulatory structure designed to deter and remedy anticompetitive harm. Where such a structure exists, the additional benefit to competition provided by antitrust enforcement will tend to be small, and it will be less plausible that the antitrust laws contemplate such additional scrutiny. Where, by contrast, "there is nothing built into the regulatory scheme which performs the antitrust function," Silver v. New York Stock Exchange, 373 U.S. 341, 358, 10 L.Ed.2d 389, 83 S.Ct. 1246 (1963), the benefits of antitrust are worth its sometimes considerable disadvantages. Just as regulatory context may in other cases serve as a basis for implied immunity, it may also be a consideration in deciding whether to recognize an expansion of the contours of § 2.

The regulatory framework that exists in this case demonstrates how, in certain circumstances, "regulation significantly diminishes the likelihood of major antitrust harm." Consider, for example, the statutory restrictions upon Verizon's entry into the potentially lucrative market for long-distance service. To be allowed to enter the long-distance market in the first place, an incumbent LEC must be on good behavior in its local market. Authorization by the FCC requires state-by-state satisfaction of § 271's competitive checklist, which as we have noted includes the nondiscriminatory provision of access to UNEs. Section 271 applications to provide long-distance service have now been approved for incumbent LECs in 47 States and the District of Columbia.

The FCC's § 271 authorization order for Verizon to provide long-distance service in New York discussed at great length Verizon's commitments to provide access to UNEs, including the provision of OSS. Those commitments are enforceable by the FCC through continuing oversight; a failure to meet an authorization condition can result in an order that the deficiency be corrected, in the imposition of penalties, or in the suspension or revocation of long-distance approval. Verizon also subjected itself to oversight by the PSC under a so-called "Performance Assurance Plan" (PAP). See In re New York Telephone Co., 197 P. U. R. 4th 266, 280–281 (N. Y. PSC, 1999). The PAP, which by its terms became binding upon FCC approval, provides specific financial penalties in the event of Verizon's failure to achieve detailed performance requirements. The FCC described Verizon's having entered into a PAP as a significant factor in its § 271 authorization, because that provided "a strong financial incentive for post-entry compliance with the section 271 checklist," and prevented " 'backsliding.' "

The regulatory response to the OSS failure complained of in respondent's suit provides a vivid example of how the regulatory regime operates. When several competitive LECs complained about deficiencies in Verizon's servicing of orders, the FCC and PSC responded. The FCC soon concluded that Verizon was in breach of its sharing duties under § 251(c), imposed a substantial fine, and set up sophisticated measurements to gauge remediation, with weekly reporting requirements and specific penalties for failure. The PSC found Verizon in violation of the PAP even earlier, and imposed additional financial penalties and measurements with *daily* reporting requirements. In short, the regime was an effective steward of the antitrust function.

Against the slight benefits of antitrust intervention here, we must weigh a realistic assessment of its costs. Under the best of circumstances, applying the requirements of § 2 "can be difficult" because "the means of illicit exclusion, like the means of legitimate competition, are myriad." United States v. Microsoft Corp., 253 F.3d 34, 58 (D.C. Cir. 2001) (en banc) (per curiam). Mistaken inferences and the resulting false condemnations "are especially costly, because they chill the very conduct the antitrust laws are designed to protect." Matsushita Elec. Industrial Co. v. Zenith Radio Corp., 475 U.S. 574, 594, 89 L.Ed.2d 538, 106 S.Ct. 1348 (1986). The cost of false positives counsels against an undue expansion of § 2 liability. One false-positive risk is that an incumbent LEC's failure to provide a service with sufficient alacrity might have nothing to do with exclusion. Allegations of violations of § 251(c)(3) duties are difficult for antitrust courts to evaluate, not only because they are highly technical, but also because they are likely to be extremely numerous, given the incessant, complex, and constantly changing interaction of competitive and incumbent LECs implementing the sharing and interconnection obligations. *Amici* States have filed a brief asserting that competitive LECs are threatened with "death by a thousand cuts,"—identification of which would surely be a daunting task for a generalist antitrust court. Judicial oversight under the Sherman Act would seem destined to distort investment and lead to a new layer of interminable litigation, atop the variety of litigation routes already available to and actively pursued by competitive LECs.

Even if the problem of false positives did not exist, conduct consisting of anticompetitive violations of § 251 may be, as we have concluded with respect to above-cost predatory pricing schemes, "beyond the practical ability of a judicial tribunal to control." Effective remediation of violations of regulatory sharing requirements will ordinarily require continuing supervision of a highly detailed decree. We think that Professor Areeda got it exactly right: "No court should impose a duty to deal that it cannot explain or adequately and reasonably supervise. The problem should be deemed irremediable by antitrust law when compulsory access requires the court to assume the day-to-day controls characteristic of a regulatory agency." Areeda, 58 Antitrust L. J., at 853. In this case, respondent has requested an equitable decree to "preliminarily and permanently enjoin [Verizon] from providing access to the local loop market . . . to [rivals] on terms and conditions that are not as favorable" as those that Verizon enjoys. An antitrust court is unlikely to be an effective day-to-day enforcer of these detailed sharing obligations.

The 1996 Act is in an important respect much more ambitious than the antitrust laws. It attempts "*to eliminate the monopolies* enjoyed by the inheritors of AT & T's local franchises." Verizon Communications Inc. v. FCC (emphasis added). Section 2 of the Sherman Act, by contrast, seeks merely to prevent *unlawful monopolization*. It would be a serious mistake to conflate the two goals. The Sherman Act is indeed the "Magna Carta of free enterprise," United States v. Topco Associates, Inc., 405 U.S. 596, 610, 31 L.Ed.2d 515, 92 S.Ct. 1126 (1972), but it does not give judges *carte blanche* to insist that a monopolist alter its way of doing business whenever some other approach might yield greater competition. We conclude that respondent's complaint fails to state a claim under the Sherman Act.

Accordingly, the judgment of the Court of Appeals is reversed, and the case is remanded for further proceedings consistent with this opinion.

[The opinion of JUSTICES STEVENS, SOUTER AND THOMAS, concurring in the judgment, but finding that the plaintiff-respondent lacked standing, is omitted.]

Notes and Questions

1.   Do you agree with the result in this case? If the statutory policy is clearly in favor of open competition, why don't the antitrust laws provide an appropriate reinforcement of standards for determining the terms of that competition?

2.   Are you confident that the regulatory process is sufficient to guarantee that Verizon and other incumbent local carriers will comply with their obligations to allow competitors appropriate access to their facilities? Does the enforcement history the Court recounts suggest that there has been substantial voluntary compliance in the past?

3.   Does the Court give adequate weight to Congress' explicit declaration that the Telecommunications Act did not "modify, impair, or supersede the applicability of any of the antitrust laws?" Do you agree that Congress seemed to be saying that the Telecommunications Act therefore should not be deemed to impose obligations greater than those imposed by the antitrust laws?

4.   Does the Court seem to be concerned that, if it had reached a different result here, plaintiffs would have litigated the future of telecommunications deregulation in the "generalist antitrust courts" rather than before the FCC? Do you agree that generalist courts would not have been capable of assuming that responsibility? Are there any other reasons that reliance on the courts rather than the FCC would have be undesirable?

5. Is the Court's view of the regulatory role of the FCC the same as that of the District Court in United States v. AT & T, supra? Might a court's sense of the scope and nature of that regulatory role change depending on who the plaintiff in the case is?

B. APPLICATION OF ANTITRUST PRINCIPLES BY REGULATORY AGENCIES

In the last section, the courts used both the term "implied immunity" and the term "exclusive jurisdiction" to describe the issues presented. Are the concepts the same? Does the term "immunity" confuse the issue? Must the FCC consider competitive consequences of its decisions? This section of this chapter deals with such questions.

CENTRAL VERMONT RAILWAY INC. v. INTERSTATE COMMERCE COMM'N

United States Court of Appeals, District of Columbia Circuit, 1983.
711 F.2d 331.

Before WILKEY and WALD, CIRCUIT JUDGES, and BONSAL, SENIOR DISTRICT JUDGE for the Southern District of New York.

WALD, CIRCUIT JUDGE:

We review here a decision of the Interstate Commerce Commission approving unconditionally the merger of the Maine Central/Boston & Maine Railroad with the Delaware & Hudson Railroad [hereinafter cited as Delaware & Hudson Merger]. Petitioner Canadian National, a competitor of the Delaware & Hudson, asked the ICC to protect it from competitive harm due to the merger by requiring the merged entity to provide Canadian National with trackage rights over a major north-south route. The ICC declined to impose this protective condition, finding that the condition was not needed to preserve competition because there would still be effective truck competition and that Canadian National had not shown that the condition was needed to prevent harm to "essential services."

Canadian National appeals to this court, claiming that the ICC misanalyzed the effect of the merger on competition among rail carriers and that the ICC's "essential services" test for imposing protective conditions is too strict and does not comply with the statutory directive that the ICC consider the effect of the merger on "adequacy of transportation to the public." 49 U.S.C. § 11,344(b)(1)(A). We affirm the Commission's determination that protective conditions are unnecessary because there exists effective truck competition.

* * *

Canadian National operates joint north-south service (from Montreal to New York and points south) with the Boston & Maine. Canadian Pacific also operates north-south service jointly with the Boston &

Maine. Conrail and the Delaware & Hudson operate competing north-south routes.

* * *

II. THE MERGER'S EFFECT ON NORTH-SOUTH RAIL SERVICE

* * *

* * * [T]he Commission will consider imposing conditions on a merger for two reasons—to prevent significant reduction in competition and to preserve "essential services." The Commission found that neither reason for imposing conditions was present here. We agree.

A.   Anticompetitive Effects

The Commission found that Guilford's participation in three of the four north-south routes would not have serious anticompetitive consequences because there was strong truck competition. The presence of truck competition limited the importance of reduction in rail competition. See Delaware & Hudson Merger, 366 I.C.C. at 407 ("A change in the number of rail competitors is less significant where there is strong motor carrier competition * * *.") Also, truck competition would make it impractical for Guilford to seek to divert traffic to the Delaware & Hudson by downgrading service on Boston & Maine's north-south line:

> The extent to which any rail carrier can exercise control over traffic is greatly diminished in the face of intense motor carrier competition. If rail carriers want to preserve traffic in these circumstances, they cannot afford to favor inefficient routes over efficient ones, even if this means that they will not preserve their longest possible haul.

Canadian National raises several objections to this analysis.

1.   Including Trucks in the Product Market

First, Canadian National argues that the Commission improperly relied on *truck* competition to ameliorate the substantial lessening of *rail* competition caused by the merger. It would have the Commission focus exclusively on rail competition. In antitrust terms, the Commission, in effect, defined the relevant product market as "transportation of freight," while Canadian National argues that "[t]he product [market] is the transportation of goods by *rail only.*" We believe the Commission properly considered truck competition.

The Interstate Commerce Act broadly instructs the ICC to determine if a merger is "consistent with the public interest." 49 U.S.C. § 11,344(c). Canadian National relies on Congress' instruction to the Commission to "consider," in making that public interest determination, "whether the proposed transaction would have an adverse effect among *rail carriers* in the affected region." § 11,344(b)(1)(E) (emphasis added).

Section 11,344(b)(1) also, however, permits the Commission to consider factors other than those specifically listed * * *. The legislative history of § 11,344(b)(1)(E) confirms that the subsection merely codifies prior ICC practice and does not restrict the factors that the ICC may consider. As Congressman Panetta explained in introducing the provision as a floor amendment to the Staggers Rail Act of 1980:

> My amendment is not intended to in any way tie the hands of the ICC on the question of mergers * * *. [C]ompetition plays an important role in the Commission's decisionmaking on railroad mergers. This is as it should be. My amendment would insure that this remains the case.

Thus, the Commission may consider "intermodal" competition between truck and rail, so long as it also considers "intramodal" competition among rail carriers.

The only remaining question is whether the Commission has authority to give dominant weight to rail-truck competition, as it did when it concluded that reduction in competition among rail carriers is of little moment in light of vigorous rail-truck competition. We hold that the Commission has this power.

As a general rule, when a statute requires an agency to "consider" a factor, the agency must reach "an 'express and considered conclusion' about the bearing of [the factor], but need not give 'any specific weight' to th[e] factor."

In this case, the ICC properly considered the relevance of competition among rail carriers, explaining that:

> A change in the number of rail competitors is less significant where there is strong motor carrier competition which prevents carriers from obtaining and exploiting monopoly power.

We think it appropriate to follow that general rule here. A major impetus behind the deregulation of railroads in the Staggers Rail Act of 1980 was Congress' recognition that railroads generally had to compete with other modes of transportation. See, e.g., H.R.Rep. No. 1430 (Conf. Rep.), reprinted in 1980 U.S.Code Cong. & Ad.News 4110:

> [H]istorically the enactment of the Interstate Commerce Act was essential to prevent an abuse of monopoly power by railroads * * *. However, today, most transportation is competitive and many of the Government regulations affecting railroads have become unnecessary and inefficient. Nearly two-thirds of intercity freight is transported by modes of transportation other than railroads.

If Congress can rely on truck-rail competition to obviate the need for regulation, surely the ICC can do so as well. This is especially so in light of the congressional policy "to minimize the need for Federal regulatory control over the rail transportation system." 49 U.S.C. § 10,101a(2).

Moreover, in considering truck-rail competition, the ICC was following the accepted antitrust definition of a "product market": Two products belong in a single product market if they are "regarded by consumers as * * * close substitutes." 2 P. Areeda & D. Turner, Antitrust Law

¶ 52a (1978).[19] If truck and rail transport are good substitutes for each other in the Montreal-to-New York corridor, it makes no sense in terms of antitrust policy to treat them, as Canadian National wants to, as if they were not. We will not lightly impute to Congress an intent to foreclose the ICC from following the antitrust principles incorporated in the antitrust laws.[20]

2. *The Existence of Truck Competition*

Canadian National also disputes whether trucks in fact provide strong competition in the Montreal-to-New York corridor. We think that substantial evidence supports the Commission's finding that they do.

The Commission explained that it relied both on analysis of the principal commodities carried by the Delaware & Hudson and on testimony by shippers:

> The commodities the D & H and B & M carry over these routes are generally commodities for which rail service is not considered market dominant. [Guilford] submitted verified statements from [three] shippers of pulp and paper which it serves. [The shippers] all testify that there is motor carrier competition for this traffic.

Canadian National correctly notes that two of the three shippers cited by the Commission are Maine paper companies who appear to use mostly the Boston & Maine/Delaware & Hudson east-west route. Thus, only one shipper could testify directly to the existence of truck competition for north-south freight movement.

Even Canadian National's witnesses, however, admitted the existence of some truck competition. Moreover, Canadian National apparently concedes that rail service is not "market dominant," i.e., that the commodities now carried by rail are susceptible to truck competition. Finally, the ICC could properly rely, as Congress did in deregulating railroad rates in 1980, on the well-known fact that railroads carry only about one-third of all intercity freight and that "the railroads' decline in market share seems to cut across * * * almost every commodity group." Putting these various pieces together, we find sufficient support for the ICC's finding that there is pervasive truck competition for north-south traffic.

3. *Geographic Market*

19. See also Brown Shoe Co. v. United States, 370 U.S. 294, 325, 82 S.Ct. 1502, 1523, 8 L.Ed.2d 510 (1962) ("The outer boundaries of a product market are determined by the reasonable interchangeability of use ... between the product itself and substitutes for it.") (footnote omitted); Union Pac. Corp.—Control—Missouri Pac. Corp., 366 I.C.C. 459, 503–04 (1982) (applying the *Brown Shoe* definition of product market), [modified sub nom. Southern Pac. Transp. Co. v. ICC, 736 F.2d 708 (D.C.Cir. 1984)]. [Court's fn. 9]

20. We hold only that the ICC may evaluate anticompetitive effects in terms of the "product markets" and "geographic markets" used in antitrust law, not that it must do so. See Seaboard Air Line R.R. v. United States, 382 U.S. 154, 86 S.Ct. 277, 15 L.Ed.2d 223 (1965) (per curiam) (ICC need not directly apply antitrust analysis in reviewing a rail merger). [Court's fn. 10]

Canadian National also contends that the ICC misanalyzed the relevant "geographic market" within which competitive effects must be assessed. It points to the ICC's statement that the Delaware & Hudson line and the Canadian National line "serve different geographic markets and are not perfect substitutes for each other."

Canadian National argues that if the two lines compete for the same traffic, they are necessarily in the same "geographic market" as that term is used in antitrust analysis.[21]

This looks to us to be no more than a semantic quibble. Concededly, the Commission used the term "geographic market" loosely. The two rail lines are in separate geographic markets only for local traffic, and are in the same geographic market for most long-haul traffic. But the ICC unquestionably recognized this. In the same sentence in which the phrase "geographic market" appears, the Commission explained that the two lines were not "perfect" substitutes; it did not say that they were not substitutes at all. Elsewhere in its decision, the ICC stated that the lines "compete for * * * overhead traffic." Indeed, if the two lines really served entirely separate geographic markets, the Commission's whole analysis of anticompetitive effects would have been pointless.

In sum, we find reasonable the Commission's reliance on truck competition to mitigate any reduction in rail competition. * * *

III. CONCLUSION

The ICC reasonably concluded that Canadian National's north-south rail service is neither essential to local shippers nor needed to provide effective competition to Guilford's north-south service. * * * [T]he Commission's decision approving Guilford's acquisition of the Delaware & Hudson and denying Canadian National's request for protective conditions is affirmed.

Notes and Questions

1. In the *Central Vermont* case, the ICC engaged in the type of antitrust analysis that courts have encouraged since McLean Trucking Co. v. United States, 321 U.S. 67, 64 S.Ct. 370, 88 L.Ed. 544 (1944).

a. The ICC, in particular, had been required to include competitive considerations in its determination of the public interest. See, e.g., the "market dominance" standard for railroad maximum rate regulation enacted in the Railroad Revitalization and Regulatory Reform Act of 1976 and the "adverse effect on competition" standard of the 1980 Staggers Act.

b. In addition, Congress amended the Interstate Commerce Act in 1980 to provide standards for consolidations and mergers of railroads and motor carriers. 49 U.S.C.A. §§ 11343–11344. With regard to rail mergers between

---

21. The ultimate test for inclusion of two producers in a market, whether "product" market or "geographic" market is reasonable substitutability of use. See 2 P. Areeda & D. Turner, Antitrust Law ¶ 518 (1978); United States v. Marine Bancorp., 418 U.S. 602, 619, 94 S.Ct. 2856, 2868, 41 L.Ed.2d 978 (1974). [Court's fn. 14]

"Class I railroads" (railroads with operating revenues of $50 million or more, 49 C.F.R. § 1240.l(a)), the ICC (now the Department of Transportation) was required to consider the following factors:

(A) the effect of the proposed transaction on the adequacy of transportation to the public;

(B) the effect on the public interest of including, or failing to include, other rail carriers in the area involved in the proposed transaction;

(C) the total fixed charges that result from the proposed transaction;

(D) the interest of carrier employees affected by the proposed transaction;

(E) whether the proposed transaction would have an adverse effect on competition among rail carriers in the affected region.

2. In fact, the presence of intermodal competition from trucks seems to be a crucial part of the ICC's justification for approving the rail merger in *Central Vermont*.

a. If intermodal competition is a key ingredient in rail merger policy, what does or should that say about truck merger policy?

b. Does the interaction between rail and truck routes make intermodal mergers a good or bad idea? Should these mergers receive more or less antitrust scrutiny than intramodal mergers?

3. The motor carrier merger provisions were not directly amended by the Staggers Act amendments although section 11344(d) does provide for a second standard for review of all but Class I railroad mergers. That provision, which by its terms would include motor carriers, reads as follows:

In a proceeding under this section which does not involve the merger or control of at least two Class I railroads, as defined by the Commission, the Commission shall approve such an application unless it finds that—

(1) as a result of the transaction there is likely to be substantial lessening of competition, creation of a monopoly, or restraint of trade in freight surface transportation in any region of the United States; and

(2) the anticompetitive effects of the transaction outweigh the public interest in meeting significant transportation needs.

a. Is this provision more or less favorable to rail and truck mergers than the provisions of section 11344(b) involved in *Central Vermont?*

b. In light of the intermodal competition conclusions of *Central Vermont,* should motor carrier mergers of any size be treated the same as smaller rail mergers under this subsection? Consider People of State of Illinois v. Interstate Commerce Commission, 687 F.2d l047 (7th Cir.1982).

4. Are there costs associated with competition that the court fails to discuss here? What might such costs be? Are they greater in some situations than others? What was it about this situation that made competition seem particularly possible?

5.   Does this case help illustrate why the Justice Department may have a useful role to play in regulatory proceedings? Is it likely that the pro-competition position will be before the agency and courts without such intervention? Are there other ways to achieve this advocacy objective?

a.   Might a "Consumer Protection Agency" appear instead and articulate all issues of concern to consumers? Would that approach be preferable to the present system?

b.   Might each agency have a "competition bureau" to articulate the issues and submit a staff recommendation in each case? What benefits and costs would be associated with that course?

6.   The Supreme Court has not always looked kindly on agency attempts to take antitrust concerns into account in the form of "leveling the playing field" by giving breaks to new entrants that are not given to the incumbent, former monopoly firm. See, e.g., MCI Telecommunications Corp. v. American Telephone & Telegraph Co., 512 U.S. 218, 114 S.Ct. 2223, 129 L.Ed.2d 182 (1994).

7.   Under the Telecommunications Act of 1996, however, the Federal Communications Commission is required to consult with the Department of Justice before permitting a Bell Operating Company to begin offering interexchange service. The Commission is required to afford the Department's evaluation "substantial weight" but the evaluation is not to have "preclusive effect." Pub.Law 104–104, 110 Stat. 89 (1996).

a.   If the FCC fails to follow the Justice Department recommendation, should the Department have standing on appeal to assert that insufficient weight was given to its evaluation? Would such standing tend to give the Department's view greater weight in the initial FCC decision?

b.   Would that be consistent with what Congress seems to have intended? How would a reviewing court apply the *Chevron* doctrine in this context?

c.   In decisions implementing the Telecommunications Act, courts have required the FCC to factor considerations of the effect on competition into determinations of appropriate rate formulas and application of the general "public interest" standard. E.g., Sprint Communications v. Federal Communications Commission, 274 F.3d 549 (D.C.Cir.2001).

C.   COEXISTENCE OF FEDERAL ANTITRUST POLICY AND STATE REGULATION

Ultimately, issues of the interplay between federal antitrust policy and federal regulatory statutes are matters of statutory construction and congressional intent. Things are not so simple when it is a state regulatory policy that dictates a result that federal antitrust policy would forbid. Clearly, the Supreme Court could invoke the Supremacy Clause and declare the state regulation invalid. As the following cases illustrate, however, that is not the route the Court has chosen.

PARKER v. BROWN

Supreme Court of the United States, 1943.
317 U.S. 341, 63 S.Ct. 307, 87 L.Ed. 315.

MR. CHIEF JUSTICE STONE delivered the opinion of the Court.

The questions for our consideration are whether the marketing program adopted for the 1940 raisin crop under the California Agricultural Prorate Act is rendered invalid (1) by the Sherman Act or (2) by the Agricultural Marketing Agreement Act of 1937, 7 U.S.C. § 601 et seq., or (3) by the Commerce Clause of the Constitution.

Appellee, a producer and packer of raisins in California, brought this suit in the district court to enjoin appellants—the State Director of Agriculture, Raisin Proration Zone No. 1, the members of the State Agricultural Prorate Advisory Commission and of the Program Committee for Zone No. 1, and others charged by the statute with the administration of the Prorate Act—from enforcing, as to appellee, a program for marketing the 1940 crop of raisins produced in "Raisin Proration Zone No. 1". After a trial upon oral testimony, a stipulation of facts and certain exhibits, the district court held that the 1940 raisin marketing program was an illegal interference with and undue burden upon interstate commerce and gave judgment for appellee granting the injunction prayed for. The case was tried by a district court of three judges and comes here on appeal.

As appears from the evidence and from the findings of the district court, almost all the raisins consumed in the United States, and nearly one-half of the world crop, are produced in Raisin Proration Zone No 1. Between 90 and 95 per cent of the raisins grown in California are ultimately shipped in interstate or foreign commerce.

The harvesting and marketing of the crop in California follows a uniform procedure. The grower of raisins picks the bunches of grapes and places them for drying on trays laid between the rows of vines. When the grapes have been sufficiently dried he places them in "sweat boxes" where their moisture content is equalized. At this point the curing process is complete. The growers sell the raisins and deliver them in the "sweat boxes" to handlers or packers whose plants are all located within the Zone. The packers process them at their plants and then ship them in interstate commerce. * * *

The packers sell their raisins through agents, brokers, jobbers and other middlemen, principally located in other states or foreign countries. Until he is ready to ship the raisins the packer stores them in the form in which they have been received from producers. The length of time that the raisins remain at the packing plants before processing and shipping varies from a few days up to two years, depending upon the packer's current supply of raisins and the market demand. The packers frequently place orders with producers for fall delivery, before the crop is harvested, and at the same time enter into contracts for the sale of raisins to their customers. In recent years most packers have had a substantial "carry over" of stored raisins at the end of each crop season, which are usually marketed before the raisins of the next year's crop are marketed.

The California Agricultural Prorate Act authorizes the establishment, through action of state officials, of programs for the marketing of agricultural commodities produced in the state, so as to restrict competition among the growers and maintain prices in the distribution of their commodities to packers. The declared purpose of the Act is to "conserve the agricultural wealth of the State" and to "prevent economic waste in the marketing of agricultural crops" of the state. It authorizes the creation of an Agricultural Prorate Advisory Commission of nine members, of which a state official, the Director of Agriculture, is ex-officio a member. The other eight members are appointed for terms of four years by the Governor and confirmed by the Senate * * *.

Upon the petition of ten producers for the establishment of a prorate marketing plan for any commodity within a defined production zone, and after a public hearing, and after making prescribed economic findings showing that the institution of a program for the proposed zone will prevent agricultural waste and conserve agricultural wealth of the state without permitting unreasonable profits to producers, the Commission is authorized to grant the petition.

> * * *

The seasonal proration marketing program for raisins, with which we are now concerned, became effective on September 7, 1940. This provided that the program committee should classify raisins as "standard", "substandard", and "inferior"; "inferior" raisins are those which are unfit for human consumption, as defined in the Federal Food, Drug and Cosmetic Act, 21 U.S.C. § 301 et seq. The committee is required to establish receiving stations within the zone to which every producer must deliver all raisins which he desires to market. The raisins are graded at these stations. All inferior raisins are to be placed in the "inferior raisin pool", to be disposed of by the committee "only for assured by-product and other diversion purposes". All substandard raisins, and at least 20 per cent of the total standard and substandard raisins produced, must be placed in a "surplus pool". Raisins in this pool may also be disposed of only for "assured by-product and other diversion purposes", except that under certain circumstances the program committee may transfer standard raisins from the surplus pool to the stabilization pool. Fifty per cent of the crop must be placed in a "stabilization pool".

Under the program the producer is permitted to sell the remaining 30 per cent of his standard raisins, denominated "free tonnage", through ordinary commercial channels, subject to the requirement that he obtain a "secondary certificate" authorizing such marketing and pay a certificate fee of $2.50 for each ton covered by the certificate. Certification is stated to be a device for controlling "the time and volume of movement" of free tonnage into such ordinary commercial channels. Raisins in the stabilization pool are to be disposed of by the committee "in such manner as to obtain stability in the market and to dispose of such raisins", but no raisins, (other than those subject to special lending or pooling arrangements of the Federal Government) can be sold by the committee at less than the prevailing market price for raisins of the same variety and grade on the date of sale. Under the program the committee is to make advances to producers of from $25 to $27.50 a ton, depending upon the variety of raisins, for deliveries into the surplus pool, and from $50 to $55 a ton for deliveries into the stabilization pool. The committee is authorized to pledge the raisins held in those pools in order to secure funds to finance pool operations and make advances to growers.

* * *

Appellee's allegations of irreparable injury are in general terms, but it appears from the evidence that he had produced 200 tons of 1940 crop raisins; that he had contracted to sell 762 1/2 tons of the 1940 crop; that he had dealt in 2,000 tons of raisins of the 1939 crop, and expected to sell, if the challenged program were not in force, 3,000 tons of the 1940 crop at $60 a ton; that the pre-season price to growers of raisins of the 1940 crop, before the program became effective, was $45 per ton, and that immediately afterward it rose to $55 per ton or higher. It also appears that the district court having awarded the final injunction prayed, appellee has proceeded with the marketing of his 1940 crop and has disposed of all except twelve tons, which remain on hand. * * *

Validity of the Prorate Program Under the Sherman Act

Section 1 of the Sherman Act makes unlawful "every contract, combination * * * or conspiracy, in restraint of trade or commerce among the several States". And § 2 makes it unlawful to "monopolize, or attempt to monopolize, or combine or conspire with any other person or persons, to monopolize any part of the trade or commerce among the several States". We may assume for present purposes that the California prorate program would violate the Sherman Act if it were organized and made effective solely by virtue of a contract, combination or conspiracy of private persons, individual or corporate. We may assume also, without deciding, that Congress could, in the exercise of its commerce power, prohibit a state from maintaining a stabilization program like the present because of its effect on interstate commerce. occupation of a legislative "field" by Congress in the exercise of a granted power is a familiar example of its constitutional power to suspend state laws.

But it is plain that the prorate program here was never intended to operate by force of individual agreement or combination. It derived its authority and its efficacy from the legislative command of the state and was not intended to operate or become effective without that command. We find nothing in the language of the Sherman Act or in its history which suggests that its purpose was to restrain a state or its officers or agents from activities directed by its legislature. In a dual system of government in which, under the Constitution, the states are sovereign, save only as Congress may constitutionally subtract from their authority, an unexpressed purpose to nullify a state's control over its officers and agents is not lightly to be attributed to Congress.

The Sherman Act makes no mention of the state as such, and gives no hint that it was intended to restrain state action or official action directed by a state. * * *

There is no suggestion of a purpose to restrain state action in the Act's legislative history. The sponsor of the bill which was ultimately enacted as the Sherman Act declared that it prevented only "business combinations." That its purpose was to suppress combinations to restrain competition and attempts to monopolize by individuals and corporations, abundantly appears from its legislative history.

True, a state does not give immunity to those who violate the Sherman Act by authorizing them to violate it, or by declaring that their action is lawful, Northern Securities Co. v. United States, 193 U.S. 197 [(1904)]; and we have no question of the state or its municipality becoming a participant in a private agreement or combination by others for restraint of trade, cf. Union Pacific R. Co. v. United States, 313 U.S. 450 [(1941)]. Here the state command to the Commission and to the program committee of the California Prorate Act is not rendered unlawful by the Sherman Act since, in view of the latter's words and history, it must be taken to be a prohibition of individual and not state action. It is the state which has created the machinery for establishing the prorate program. Although the organization of a prorate zone is proposed by producers, and a prorate program, approved by the Commission, must also be approved by referendum of producers, it is the state, acting through the Commission, which adopts the program and which enforces it with penal sanctions, in the execution of a governmental policy. The prerequisite approval of the program upon referendum by a prescribed number of producers is not the imposition by them of their will upon the minority by force of agreement or combination which the Sherman Act prohibits. The state itself exercises its legislative authority in making the regulation and in prescribing the conditions of its application. The required vote on the referendum is one of these conditions.

The state in adopting and enforcing the prorate program made no contract or agreement and entered into no conspiracy in restraint of trade or to establish monopoly but, as sovereign, imposed the restraint as an act of government which the Sherman Act did not undertake to prohibit.

* * *

VALIDITY OF THE PROGRAM UNDER THE COMMERCE CLAUSE

The court below found that approximately 95 per cent of the California raisin crop finds its way into interstate or foreign commerce. It is not denied that the proration program is so devised as to compel the delivery by each producer, including appellee, of over two-thirds of his 1940 raisin crop to the program committee, and to subject it to the marketing control of the committee. The program, adopted through the exercise of the legislative power delegated to state officials, has the force of law. It clothes the committee with power and imposes on it the duty to control marketing of the crop so as to enhance the price or at least to maintain prices by restraints on competition of producers in the sale of their crop. The program operates to *eliminate competition* of the producers in the terms of sale of the crop, including price. And since 95 per cent of the crop is marketed in interstate commerce the program may be taken to have a substantial effect on the commerce, in placing restrictions on the sale and marketing of a product to buyers who eventually sell and ship it in interstate commerce.

The question is thus presented whether in the absence of congressional legislation prohibiting or regulating the transactions affected by the state program, the restrictions which it imposes upon the sale within the state of a commodity by its producer to a processor who contemplates doing, and in fact does work upon the commodity before packing and shipping it in interstate commerce, violate the Commerce Clause.

The governments of the states are sovereign within their territory save only as they are subject to the prohibitions of the Constitution or as their action in some measure conflicts with powers delegated to the National Government, or with Congressional legislation enacted in the exercise of those powers. This Court has repeatedly held that the grant of power to Congress by the Commerce Clause did not wholly withdraw from the states the authority to regulate the commerce with respect to matters of local concern, on which Congress has not spoken.

* * *

Examination of the evidence in this case and of available data of the raisin industry in California, of which we may take judicial notice, leaves no doubt that the evils attending the production and marketing of raisins in that state present a problem local in character and urgently demanding state action for the economic protection of those engaged in one of its important industries. Between 1914 and 1920 there was a spectacular rise in price of all types of California grapes, including raisin grapes. The price of raisins reached its peak, $235 per ton, in 1921, and was followed by large increase in acreage with accompanying reduction in price. The price of raisins in most years since 1922 has ranged from $40 to $60 per ton but acreage continued to increase until 1926 and production reached its peak, 1,433,000 tons of raisin grapes and 290,000 tons of raisins, in 1938. Since 1920 there has been a substantial carry over of 30 to 50% of each year's crop. The result has been that at least since 1934 the industry, with a large increase in acreage and the attendant fall in price, has been unable to get its product and has been compelled to sell at less than fair market prices and in some years at prices regarded by students of the industry as less than the cost of production.

The history of the industry at least since 1929 is a record of a continuous search for expedients which would stabilize the marketing of the raisin crop and maintain a price standard which would bring fair return to the producers. It is significant of the relation of the local interest in maintaining this program to the national interest in interstate commerce, that throughout the period from 1929 until the adoption of the prorate program for the 1940 raisin crop, the national government has contributed to these efforts either by its establishment of marketing programs pursuant to Act of Congress or by aiding programs sponsored by the state.

It thus appears that whatever effect the operation of the California program may have on interstate commerce, it is one which it has been the policy of Congress to aid and encourage through federal agencies in conformity to the Agricultural Marketing Agreement Act, and § 302 of the Agricultural Adjustment Act. Nor is the effect on the commerce greater than or substantially different in kind from that contemplated by the stabilization programs authorized by federal statutes. As we have seen, the Agricultural Marketing Agreement Act is applicable to raisins only on the direction of the Secretary of Agriculture who, instead of establishing a federal program has, as the statute authorizes, cooperated in promoting the state program and aided it by substantial federal loans. Hence we cannot say that the effect of the state program on interstate commerce is one which conflicts with Congressional policy or is such as to preclude the state from this exercise of its reserved power to regulate domestic agricultural production.

We conclude that the California prorate program for the 1940 raisin crop is a regulation of state industry of local concern which, in all the circumstances of this case which we have detailed, does not impair national control over the commerce in a manner or to a degree forbidden by the Constitution.

Reversed.

Notes and Questions

1. What is the source of the exemption of state-regulated activity from antitrust scrutiny?

a. Is it to be found in the language of the Sherman Act itself? What language might seem to grant such an exemption?

b. Is it premised on a view that regulation is usually imposed involuntarily upon unwilling firms? Based on what you have seen throughout this course, is that premise sound?

2. Can an argument be made that exempting activity regulated under state law does no harm? Can it be presumed that regulation provides all necessary "protection" of the consumer against the natural excesses of a monopolist or cartel?

3. Do you agree that the economic problems faced by raisin growers were primarily local in character? Is it relevant that virtually all the nation's

raisins are grown in one state? Will the effects of the California program be felt only in California? Does *Parker* allow the legislature of one state to benefit business firms resident there at the expense of citizens of other states?

4.   The Commerce Clause arguments rejected by the Court in *Parker* were later successfully used to preempt state health regulations used to bar out of state milk. See, e.g., The Great Atlantic & Pacific Tea Co. v. Cottrell, 424 U.S. 366, 96 S.Ct. 923, 47 L.Ed.2d 55 (1976) (Mississippi health regulation forbade Louisiana milk unless Louisiana permitted Mississippi milk; public health defense labeled "frivolous"). Remember also West Lynn Creamery v. Healy, in Chapter 2. Do these decisions undermine the *Parker* rationale? How might you reconcile the lines of cases?

5.   *Parker* was decided at the end of the Supreme Court's controversial substantive due process era. What is the relationship between the principles announced in *Parker* and the judicial restraint inherent in the demise of substantive due process? See Paul R. Verkuil, State Action, Due Process and Antitrust: Reflections on Parker v. Brown, 75 Columbia L. Rev. 328 (1975).

6.   What is the "rule" of Parker v. Brown? Which facts were decisive?

a.   Was it critical that the suit was brought to enjoin state officials, e.g., the state director of agriculture, instead of against private parties?

b.   Suppose there had been no reinforcing federal agricultural legislation to support the *Parker* decision; would or should the Court have reached the same result? Compare Phillip Areeda, Antitrust Analysis 12–30 (1981).

c.   Was it that the program represented a clearly articulated state policy and not merely a ratification of the wishes of private firms?

d.   Was the decision based on the compulsory character of the program, i.e., the idea that a private firm could not be said to "conspire" to obey state law?

e.   Was it that the regulatory program had been adopted by a state instead of a city or other lesser governmental unit?

7.   Were all of the above factors necessary to the decision? The absence of one or more of them has been the basis for most of the subsequent litigation in this area. After *Parker* was decided, it took the Supreme Court over 30 years to address the problem again.[22]

a.   When it did so, in Goldfarb v. Virginia State Bar, 421 U.S. 773, 95 S.Ct. 2004, 44 L.Ed.2d 572 (1975), it began a line of inquiry that has produced a number of important cases. *Goldfarb* itself involved minimum fees set by the Fairfax County Bar Association upon suggestion of the Virginia State Bar. The Court held that the State had not, through its Supreme Court Rules, *required* such conduct and, therefore, the *Parker* doctrine did not apply.

b.   The need for a specific regulatory *requirement* was later relaxed, however, and the two standards became those articulated in California Retail

---

22.   The one exception during that period was Schwegmann Brothers v. Calvert Distillers, 341 U.S. 384, 71 S.Ct. 745, 95 L.Ed. 1035 (1951) which held that a state statute permitting retail price maintenance was outside the protection of the *Parker* doctrine.

Liquor Dealers Ass'n v. Midcal Aluminum, Inc., 445 U.S. 97, 100 S.Ct. 937, 63 L.Ed.2d 233 (1980):

> "First, the challenged restraint must be 'one clearly articulated and affirmatively expressed as state policy'; second, the policy must be 'actively supervised' by the state itself."

The *Midcal* test was itself not self-defining, however, and remained to be developed and transformed in cases such as the following.

SOUTHERN MOTOR CARRIERS RATE CONFERENCE v. UNITED STATES

Supreme Court of the United States, 1985.
471 U.S. 48, 105 S.Ct. 1721, 85 L.Ed.2d 36.

JUSTICE POWELL delivered the opinion of the Court.

Southern Motor Carriers Rate Conference, Inc. (SMCRC) and North Carolina Motor Carriers Association, Inc. (NCMCA), petitioners, are "rate bureaus" composed of motor common carriers operating in four Southeastern States. The rate bureaus, on behalf of their members, submit joint rate proposals to the Public Service Commissions in each State for approval or rejection. This collective rate-making is authorized, but not compelled, by the States in which the rate bureaus operate. The United States, contending that collective rate-making violates the federal antitrust laws, filed this action to enjoin the rate bureaus' alleged anticompetitive practices. * * *

I

A

In North Carolina, Georgia, Mississippi, and Tennessee, Public Service Commissions set motor common carriers' rates for the intrastate transportation of general commodities.[23] Common carriers are required to submit proposed rates to the relevant Commission for approval. A proposed rate becomes effective if the state agency takes no action within a specified period of time. If a hearing is scheduled, however, a rate will become effective only after affirmative agency approval. The State Public Service Commissions thus have and exercise ultimate authority and control over all intrastate rates.

In all four States, common carriers are allowed to agree on rate proposals prior to their joint submission to the regulatory agency. By reducing the number of proposals, collective rate-making permits the agency to consider more carefully each submission. In fact, some public service commissions have stated that without collective rate-making they

23. * * * The Interstate Commerce Commission has the power to fix common carriers' rates for the interstate transportation of general commodities. The Interstate Commerce Act, however, expressly reserves to the States the regulation of common carriers' intrastate rates, even if these rates affect interstate commerce. 49 U.S.C. § 10521(b). [Court's fn. 1]

would be unable to function effectively as rate-setting bodies.[24] Nevertheless, collective rate-making is not compelled by any of the States; every common carrier remains free to submit individual rate proposals to the Public Service Commissions.

As indicated above, SMCRC and NCMCA are private associations composed of motor common carriers operating in North Carolina, Georgia, Mississippi, and Tennessee. Both organizations have committees that consider possible rate changes. If a rate committee concludes that an intrastate rate should be changed, a collective proposal for the changed rate is submitted to the State Public Service Commission. Members of the Bureau, however, are not bound by the joint proposal. Any disapproving member may submit an independent rate proposal to the state regulatory commission.

B

* * * [T]he United States instituted this action against SMCRC and NCMCA in the United States District Court for the Northern District of Georgia. The United States charged that the two rate bureaus had violated § 1 of the Sherman Act by conspiring with their members to fix rates for the intrastate transportation of general commodities. The rate bureaus responded that their conduct was exempt from the federal antitrust laws by virtue of the state action doctrine. See Parker v. Brown. They further asserted that their collective rate-making activities did not violate the Sherman Act because the rates ultimately were determined by the appropriate state agencies. The District Court found the rate bureaus' arguments meritless, and entered a summary judgment in favor of the Government. * * *

The Court of Appeals for the Fifth Circuit, sitting en banc, affirmed the judgment of the District Court. * * *

* * *

We granted certiorari to decide whether petitioners' collective rate-making activities, though not compelled by the States in which they operate, are entitled to *Parker* immunity.

II

In Parker v. Brown, this Court held that the Sherman Act was not intended to prohibit States from imposing restraints on competition. There, a raisin producer filed an action against the California director of agriculture to enjoin the enforcement of the State's Agricultural Prorate Act. * * *

* * *

The circumstances in which *Parker* immunity is available to private parties, and to state agencies or officials regulating the conduct of

---

24. * * * Moreover, the uniformity in prices that collective rate-making tends to produce is considered desirable by the legislature of at least one State [North Carolina] and the Public Service Commission of another [Mississippi]. [Court's fn. 5]

private parties, are defined most specifically by our decision in California Retail Liquor Dealers Assn. v. Midcal Aluminum, Inc. In *Midcal*, we affirmed a state-court injunction prohibiting officials from enforcing a statute requiring wine producers to establish resale price schedules. We set forth a two-pronged test for determining whether state regulation of private parties is shielded from the federal antitrust laws. First, the challenged restraint must be "one clearly articulated and affirmatively expressed as state policy." Second, the State must supervise actively any private anticompetitive conduct. This supervision requirement prevents the state from frustrating the national policy in favor of competition by casting a "gauzy cloak of state involvement" over what is essentially private anticompetitive conduct.[25]

III

The *Midcal* test does not expressly provide that the actions of a private party must be compelled by a State in order to be protected from the federal antitrust laws. * * *

   * * *

B

The Court of Appeals held that even if *Midcal* were applicable here, the rate bureaus would not be immune from federal antitrust liability. According to that court, the actions of a private party cannot be attributed to a clearly articulated state policy, within the meaning of the *Midcal* test's first prong, "when it is left to the private party to carry out that policy or not as he sees fit." In the four States in which petitioners operate, all common carriers are free to submit proposals individually. The court therefore reasoned that the States' policies are neutral with respect to collective ratemaking, and that these policies will not be frustrated if the federal antitrust laws are construed to require individual submissions.

In reaching its conclusion, the Court of Appeals assumed that if anticompetitive activity is not compelled, the State can have no interest in whether private parties engage in that conduct. This type of analysis ignores the manner in which the States in this case clearly have intended their permissive policies to work. Most common carriers probably will engage in collective rate-making, as that will allow them to share

---

25. The dissent argues that a state regulatory program is entitled to *Parker* immunity only if an antitrust exemption is "necessary to make the ... [program] work...." This argument overlooks the fact that, with the exception of a questionable dictum in Cantor [v. Detroit Edison, Co., 428 U.S. 579 (1976)], the dissent's proposed test has been used only in deciding whether Congress intended to immunize a federal regulatory program from the Sherman Act's proscriptions. See, e.g., Silver v. New York Stock Exchange. In this context, if the federal courts wrongly conclude that an antitrust exemption is "unnecessary," Congress can correct the error. As the dissent recognizes, however, the Supremacy Clause would prevent state legislatures taking similar remedial action. Moreover, the proposed test would prompt the "kind of interference with state sovereignty ... that ... *Parker* was intended to prevent." Therefore, we hold that state action immunity is not dependent on a finding that an exemption from the federal antitrust laws is "necessary." [Court's fn. 21]

the cost of preparing rate proposals. If the joint rates are viewed as too high, however, carriers individually may submit lower proposed rates to the commission in order to obtain a larger share of the market. Thus, through the self-interested actions of private common carriers, the States may achieve the desired balance between the efficiency of collective rate-making and the competition fostered by individual submissions. Construing the Sherman Act to prohibit collective rate proposals eliminates the free choice necessary to ensure that these policies function in the manner intended by the States. The federal antitrust laws do not forbid the States to adopt policies that permit, but do not compel, anticompetitive conduct by regulated private parties. As long as the State clearly articulates its intent to adopt a permissive policy, the first prong of the *Midcal* test is satisfied.[26]

* * *

IV

A

Our holding that there is no inflexible "compulsion requirement" does not suggest necessarily that petitioners' collective ratemaking activities are shielded from the federal antitrust laws. A private party may claim state action immunity only if both prongs of the *Midcal* test are satisfied. Here the Court of Appeals found, and the Government concedes, that the State Public Service Commissions actively supervise the collective ratemaking activities of the rate bureaus. Therefore, the only issue left to resolve is whether the petitioners' challenged conduct was taken pursuant to a clearly articulated state policy.

The Public Service Commissions in North Carolina, Georgia, Mississippi, and Tennessee permit collective ratemaking. Acting alone, however, these agencies could not immunize private anticompetitive conduct. * * * *Parker* immunity is available only when the challenged activity is undertaken pursuant to a clearly articulated policy of the State itself, such as a policy approved by a state legislature or a state supreme court.

In this case, therefore, the petitioners are entitled to *Parker* immunity only if collective ratemaking is clearly sanctioned by the legislatures of the four States in which the rate bureaus operate. North Carolina, Georgia, and Tennessee have statutes that explicitly permit collective ratemaking by common carriers. The rate bureaus' challenged actions, at least in these States, are taken pursuant to an express and clearly articulated state policy. Mississippi's legislature, however, has not specifically addressed collective ratemaking. We therefore must consider whether, in the absence of a statute expressly permitting the challenged conduct, the first prong of the *Midcal* test can be satisfied.

---

26. Under the Interstate Commerce Act, motor common carriers are permitted, but not compelled, to engage in collective interstate rate-making. It is clear, therefore, that Congress has recognized the advantages of a permissive policy. We think it unlikely that Congress intended to prevent the States from adopting virtually identical policies at the intrastate level. [Court's fn. 22]

B

The Mississippi Motor Carrier Regulatory Law of 1938 gives the State Public Service Commission authority to regulate common carriers. The statute provides that the commission is to prescribe "just and reasonable" rates for the intrastate transportation of general commodities. The legislature thus made clear its intent that intrastate rates would be determined by a regulatory agency, rather than by the market. The details of the inherently anticompetitive rate-setting process, however, are left to the agency's discretion. The state commission has exercised its discretion by actively encouraging collective ratemaking among common carriers. We do not believe that the actions petitioners took pursuant to this regulatory program should be deprived of *Parker* immunity.

A private party acting pursuant to a anticompetitive regulatory program need not "point to a specific, detailed legislative authorization" for its challenged conduct. City of Lafayette v. Louisiana Power & Light Co. [435 U.S. 389 (1978)] (opinion of BRENNAN, J.). As long as the State as sovereign clearly intends to displace competition in a particular field with a regulatory structure, the first prong of the *Midcal* test is satisfied. In *Goldfarb* the Court held that *Parker* immunity was unavailable only because the State as sovereign did not intend to do away with competition among lawyers. * * *

If more detail than a clear intent to displace competition were required of the legislature, States would find it difficult to implement through regulatory agencies their anticompetitive policies. Agencies are created because they are able to deal with problems unforeseeable to, or outside the competence of, the legislature. Requiring express authorization for every action that an agency might find necessary to effectuate state policy would diminish, if not destroy, its usefulness. Therefore, we hold that if the State's intent to establish an anticompetitive regulatory program is clear, as it is in Mississippi, the State's failure to describe the implementation of its policy in detail will not subject the program to the restraints of the federal antitrust laws.

* * *

V

We conclude that the petitioners' collective rate-making activities, although not compelled by the States, are immune from antitrust liability under the doctrine of Parker v. Brown. Accordingly, the judgment of the Court of Appeals is reversed.

JUSTICE STEVENS, with whom JUSTICE WHITE joins, dissenting.

* * * In this case, * * * four southern States have established programs for evaluating the reasonableness of rates that motor carriers propose to charge for intrastate transport, but the States do not require price fixing by motor carriers. They merely tolerate it.

Reasoning deductively from a dictum in California Retail Liquor Dealers Assn. v. Midcal Aluminum, Inc., the Court holds that Congress did not intend to prohibit price fixing by motor carrier rate bureaus—at least when such conduct is prompted, but not required, by a state public service commission. The result is inconsistent with the language and policies of the Sherman Act, and this Court's precedent. The Sherman Act only would interfere with the regulatory process if the States compelled price fixing that is unlawful under federal law. In that situation, the regulated carriers would face conflicting obligations under state and federal law, and the success of the States' regulatory programs would be threatened. Except under those circumstances, immunity from the antitrust laws under the state-action doctrine is not available for private persons.

I

* * *

* * * [T]his Court has repeatedly held that collusive price fixing by railroads is unlawful even though the end result is a reasonable charge approved by a public rate commission. Georgia v. Pennsylvania R. Co. [324 U.S. 439 (1945)]; United States v. Trans–Missouri Freight Assn. [166 U.S. 290 (1897)]. In the *Pennsylvania Railroad* case, the Court explained why this is so:

> " * * * [E]ven a combination to fix reasonable and non-discriminatory rates may be illegal. [Keogh v. Chicago & Northwestern R. Co.]. The reason is that the Interstate Commerce Act does not provide remedies for the correction of all the abuses of rate-making which might constitute violations of the anti-trust laws. Thus a 'zone of reasonableness exists between maxima and minima within which a carrier is ordinarily free to adjust its charges for itself.' Within that zone the Commission lacks power to grant relief even though the rates are raised to the maxima by a conspiracy among carriers who employ unlawful tactics.... Damage must be presumed to flow from a conspiracy to manipulate rates within that zone."

* * *

The defendants have stipulated that their price fixing arrangements are identical to those followed by the Carrier Rate Committees in the *Pennsylvania Railroad* case which were declared unlawful under the Sherman Act. They also acknowledge that neither the Reed–Bulwinkle Act, nor any other federal statute expressly exempts their price fixing from the antitrust laws. * * *

* * *

III

* * *

The Court's reliance today on vague "principles of federalism" obscures our traditional disfavor for implied exemptions to the Sherman Act. We have only authorized exemptions from the Sherman Act for businesses regulated by federal law when "that exemption was necessary in order to make the regulatory Act work 'and even then only to the minimum extent necessary.' " No lesser showing of repugnancy should be sufficient to justify an implied exemption based on a state regulatory program.

Any other view separates the state-action exemption from the reason for its existence. The program involved in the *Parker* case was designed to enhance the market price of raisins by regulating both output and price. In other words, the state policy was one that replaced price competition with economic regulation. Price support programs like the one involved in *Parker* can not possibly succeed if every individual producer is free to participate or not participate in the program at his option. In *Parker*, the challenged price fixing was the heart of California's support program for agriculture; without immunity from the Sherman Act, the State would have had to abandon the project.

* * * When, as here, state regulatory policies are permissive rather than mandatory, there is no necessary conflict between the antitrust laws and the regulatory systems; the regulated entity may comply with the edicts of each sovereign. Indeed, it is almost meaningless to contemplate a "regulatory" policy that gives every regulated entity carte blanche to excuse itself from the consequences of the regulation. Even a policy against speeding could not be enforced if every motorist could drive as fast as he chose. When a State declares that a regulated entity need not follow a regulatory procedure, it as much as admits that this element is inconsequential to the ultimate success of the regulatory program.

* * *

Active supervision of the rate bureau process—like that provided in the Motor Carrier Act of 1980—might minimize the anticompetitive effects of collective ratemaking. To the extent that the state regulatory commissions are structured like the ICC in the *Pennsylvania Railroad* case, however, they only have the power to reject the rates proposed by the carriers if those rates fall outside the "zone of reasonableness." Unless the commissions "actively supervise" the price-fixing process itself, they cannot eliminate the upward pressure on rates caused by collusive rate-making. Unfortunately, the nature of the "active supervision" of those carriers who take part in collective rate-making is not fully disclosed by the record.

IV

Whether it is wise or unwise policy for the Federal Government to seek to enforce the Sherman Act in this case is not a question that this Court is authorized to consider. The District Court and the Court of Appeals correctly applied established precedent in holding that the Government is entitled to an injunction against the defendant's price fixing. * * *

Notes and Questions

1. Does all this sound familiar? Remember that the western railroads made an argument almost a century ago in *Trans–Missouri* that sounded a lot like that of the truckers here? How did the argument fare then? How did it fare in *Keogh* and in Georgia v. Pennsylvania Railroad? Why should it fare better today?

2. Is motor carrier price setting something that requires collective action?

a. Are you convinced by the dissenters that even if the rates are later approved by the state, this collective process will have an upward effect on the rates? If not, why are the truck lines engaged in this activity?

b. Are trucks "natural monopolies" like railroads have been thought to be? Do truck lines have high fixed costs relative to their variable costs? Do they need the same protection against "cut-throat competition" that the railroads asserted in *Trans–Missouri* and about which we expressed some sympathy in discussing that case?

3. Notice the seemingly substantial shift in the Court's approach to whether the state had "clearly articulated and affirmatively expressed" a state regulatory policy in the decade between *Goldfarb* and *Southern Motor Carriers*.

a. What has happened to the idea that private action must be compelled by the state in order not to be conspiratorial and thus violate the Sherman Act?

b. Should it be enough to say that the state had a clearly articulated policy to set trucking rates? Should the requirement instead be that the state articulate a policy that truck lines may collectively formulate the rates?

c. Can you see reasons why the Court has abandoned its narrower position? Does the approach taken here make the test easier to apply? Is the new standard principled?

d. Cases involving conflicts between antitrust policy and the behavior of partially-regulated firms promise to keep the courts occupied in the coming years.

In Praxair, Inc. v. Florida Power & Light Co., 64 F.3d 609 (11th Cir.1995), the charge was that utilities situated so as to be capable of competing for the plaintiff's business had engaged in an illegal division of markets and refused to so compete. The Court, per Judge Roney, found that the market division was consistent with an Order of the Florida Public Service Commission and granted summary judgment for the utility.

Lancaster Community Hospital v. Antelope Valley Hospital District, 940 F.2d 397 (9th Cir.1991), on the other hand, found that a requirement of advance authority to open a hospital did not constitute a policy of abandoning the possibility of competition among hospitals.

4. What has happened to the *Midcal* requirement that the states actively supervise the regulatory process? Given the difficulty of determining

how clearly articulated a state policy is in certain cases, might the courts give greater weight to this element of the *Midcal* tests?

a.   Should supervision be deemed inherently adequate if a state agency can disapprove the rates collectively proposed by the truck lines? Should the courts require that state officials be part of the collective rate setting process?

b.   In Patrick v. Burget, 486 U.S. 94, 108 S.Ct. 1658, 100 L.Ed.2d 83 (1988), the state had followed federal policy and adopted a requirement that hospitals have peer review committees to assure the competence of doctors practicing there. When a doctor was terminated by such a body, he sued under the antitrust laws, alleging a group boycott. The Court found that while the policy of having peer review had been clearly articulated, the process had not been actively supervised by independent state officials and thus was not immune from antitrust scrutiny.[27]

c.   Similarly, in Federal Trade Commission v. Ticor Title Insurance Company, 504 U.S. 621, 112 S.Ct. 2169, 119 L.Ed.2d 410 (1992), the Court held that two states' "negative option" system under which company-proposed rates went into effect unless the state objected constituted inadequately independent review to protect the rate-making system from antitrust scrutiny.

A NOTE ON THE ANTITRUST LIABILITY OF MUNICIPALITIES

If action by a state to regulate an industry does not violate the antitrust laws—and protects the regulated parties from violation—does it follow that similar action by a city has comparable effects? The arguments against liability would be the same; cities routinely grant monopoly franchises for garbage collection, cable television service, golf course operation, and the like. Sometimes they even provide the services directly, and in either case, the city's citizens should not be liable for treble damages. To the surprise of many, however, the Supreme Court has not found the analysis to be that simple.

1.   In City of Lafayette v. Louisiana Power & Light Co., 435 U.S. 389, 98 S.Ct. 1123, 55 L.Ed.2d 364 (1978), for example, the defendants were city-owned and operated power companies who were accused of refusing to "wheel" wholesale power, engaging in other illegal boycotts, and filing "sham" litigation. Defendants alleged that as city entities, they were immune from antitrust liability. The Supreme Court (5–4) disagreed. Cities are "persons" within the meaning of the antitrust laws and "petitioners are in error in arguing that all governmental entities, whether state agencies or subdivisions of a state, are, simply by reason of their status as such, exempt from the antitrust laws." The Court went on:

27.   Congress has stepped in and granted such peer review bodies immunity from liability if their action is taken "in the reasonable belief that [it] was in the furtherance of quality health care." Health Care Quality Improvement Act of 1986, 42 U.S.C. § 11101.

In 1972, there were 62,437 different units of local government in this country. Of this number 23,885 are special districts which have a defined goal or goals for the provision of one or several services, while the remaining 38,552 represent the number of counties, municipalities, and townships, most of which have broad authority for general governance subject to limitations in one way or another imposed by the State. These units may, and do, participate in and affect the economic life of this Nation in a great number and variety of ways. When these bodies act as owners and providers of services, they are fully capable of aggrandizing other economic units with which they interrelate, with the potential of serious distortion of the rational and efficient allocation of resources, and the efficiency of free markets which the regime of competition embodied in the antitrust laws is thought to engender. If municipalities were free to make economic choices counseled solely by their own parochial interests and without regard to their anticompetitive effects, a serious chink in the armor of antitrust protection would be introduced at odds with the comprehensive national policy Congress established.

Chief Justice Burger found decisive that here "the plaintiff cities are engaging in what is clearly a business activity" as opposed to regulating others. In addition to the plurality's basic test, he would ask "whether the implied exemption from the federal law was necessary in order to make the [state] regulatory Act work, and even then only [create an exemption] to the extent necessary."

2. Community Communications Co. v. City of Boulder, 455 U.S. 40, 102 S.Ct. 835, 70 L.Ed.2d 810 (1982), involved a "home rule" city, i.e., one that had "the full right of self-government" with the power to adopt ordinances that superseded even state law. Boulder had awarded the plaintiff a cable television franchise to serve a small area of the city. As technology improved, the firm wanted to serve more citizens with a wider range of services. A competing company also proposed service, however, and the city adopted an ordinance prohibiting the plaintiff's expansion until the city could explore letting more cable companies provide service. Plaintiff's response was to charge the city with a violation of § 1 of the Sherman Act. The city cited *Parker*.

The Supreme Court held that home rule status did not make a city the functional equivalent of a state and did not meet the *City of Lafayette* requirement of specific state authorization of anticompetitive activity. Thus the *Parker* defense was unavailable, although as Justice Stevens noted, this was not the same as saying that opening up the market to competition was substantively a violation of the Sherman Act.[28]

---

28. In response to pressure from the potentially affected cities, Congress has now reversed the municipal liability cases legislatively. While cities can be enjoined under the antitrust laws, they may not be held liable for damages, costs or attorney's fees. Local Government Antitrust Act of 1984, 98 Stat. 2750, 15 U.S.C. §§ 34–36.

3. Town of Hallie v. City of Eau Claire, 471 U.S. 34, 105 S.Ct. 1713, 85 L.Ed.2d 24 (1985), decided the same day as *Southern Motor Carriers*, involved a battle among municipalities. The City of Eau Claire had a sewage treatment system; neighboring towns did not. Eau Claire said the towns could use its sewage treatment facility only if they also let Eau Claire pick up their garbage. The nearby towns said this was both an attempt to monopolize and a tying arrangement.

In a unanimous opinion, the Court found Eau Claire entitled to *Parker* protection. The state of Wisconsin had expressly granted its cities authority to refuse to collect garbage in unincorporated areas, the Court said, and would be presumed to have thought about the anticompetitive consequences that such a refusal might have. Further, the Court may presume a municipality will act in the public interest. Thus, while there is a requirement of active state supervision of regulation of *private* parties, there is no similar requirement that a state actively supervise a municipality's regulatory program.[29]

D. ANTITRUST LIABILITY FOR SEEKING REGULATORY PROTECTION

Related to the question whether the *effect* of a regulatory requirement may be an antitrust violation is whether *seeking* a requirement that may benefit one firm or industry vis-a-vis another should violate the antitrust laws. That question was addressed in the period between *Parker* and *Goldfarb* and remains of interest today.

EASTERN R.R. PRESIDENTS CONF. v. NOERR MOTOR FREIGHT, INC.

Supreme Court of the United States, 1961.
365 U.S. 127, 81 S.Ct. 523, 5 L.Ed.2d 464.

MR. JUSTICE BLACK delivered the opinion of the Court.

American railroads have always largely depended upon income from the long-distance transportation of heavy freight for economic survival. During the early years of their existence, they had virtually no competition in this aspect of their business, but, as early as the 1920's, the growth of the trucking industry in this country began to bring about changes in this situation. For the truckers found, just as the railroads had learned earlier, that a very profitable part of the transportation business was the long hauling of heavy freight. As the trucking industry became more and more powerful, the competition between it and the railroads for this business became increasingly intense until, during the period following the conclusion of World War II, at least the railroads, if

---

29. Among articles critically analyzing these cases, see John E. Lopatka, State Action and Municipal Antitrust Liability: An Economic Approach, 53 Fordham L. Rev. 23 (1984); Daniel J. Gifford, The Anti- trust State Action Doctrine After Fisher v. Berkeley, 39 Vanderbilt L. Rev. 1257 (1986); John F. Hart, "Sovereign" State Policy and State Action Antitrust Immuni- ty, 56 Fordham L.Rev. 535 (1988).

not both of the competing groups, came to view the struggle as one of economic life or death for their method of transportation. The present litigation is an outgrowth of one part of that struggle.

The case was commenced by a complaint filed in the United States District Court in Pennsylvania on behalf of 41 Pennsylvania truck operators and their trade association, the Pennsylvania Motor Truck Association. This complaint, which named as defendants 24 Eastern railroads, an association of the presidents of those railroads known as the Eastern Railroad Presidents Conference, and a public relations firm, Carl Byoir & Associates, Inc., charged that the defendants had conspired to restrain trade in and monopolize the long-distance freight business in violation of §§ 1 and 2 of the Sherman Act. The gist of the conspiracy alleged was that the railroads had engaged Byoir to conduct a publicity campaign against the truckers designed to foster the adoption and retention of laws and law enforcement practices destructive of the trucking business, to create an atmosphere of distaste for the truckers among the general public, and to impair the relationships existing between the truckers and their customers. The campaign so conducted was described in the complaint as "vicious, corrupt, and fraudulent," first, in that the sole motivation behind it was the desire on the part of the railroads to injure the truckers and eventually to destroy them as competitors in the long-distance freight business, and, secondly, in that the defendants utilized the so-called third-party technique, that is, the publicity matter circulated in the campaign was made to appear as spontaneously expressed views of independent persons and civic groups when, in fact, it was largely prepared and produced by Byoir and paid for by the railroads. The complaint then went on to supplement these more or less general allegations with specific charges as to particular instances in which the railroads had attempted to influence legislation by means of their publicity campaign. One of several such charges was that the defendants had succeeded in persuading the Governor of Pennsylvania to veto a measure known as the "Fair Truck Bill," which would have permitted truckers to carry heavier loads over Pennsylvania roads.

The prayer of the complaint was for treble damages * * * and an injunction restraining the defendants from further acts in pursuance of the conspiracy. Insofar as the prayer for damages was concerned, a stipulation was entered that the only damages suffered by the individual truck operators was the loss of business that resulted from the veto of the "Fair Truck Bill" by the Governor of Pennsylvania * * *. The prayer for injunctive relief was much broader, however, asking that the defendants be restrained from disseminating any disparaging information about the truckers without disclosing railroad participation, from attempting to exert any pressure upon the legislature or Governor of Pennsylvania through the medium of front organizations, from paying any private or public organizations to propagate the arguments of the railroads against the truckers or their business, and from doing "any other act or thing to further ... the objects and purposes" of the conspiracy.

In their answer to this complaint, the railroads * * * denied that their campaign was motivated either by a desire to destroy the trucking business as a competitor or to interfere with the relationships between the truckers and their customers. Rather, they insisted, the campaign was conducted in furtherance of their rights "to inform the public and the legislatures of the several states of the truth with regard to the enormous damage done to the roads by the operators of heavy and especially of overweight trucks, with regard to their repeated and deliberate violations of the law limiting the weight and speed of big trucks, with regard to their failure to pay their fair share of the cost of constructing, maintaining and repairing the roads, and with regard to the driving hazards they create...." Such a campaign, the defendants maintained, did not constitute a violation of the Sherman Act, presumably because that Act could not properly be interpreted to apply either to restraints of trade or monopolizations that result from the passage or enforcement of laws or to efforts of individuals to bring about the passage or enforcement of laws.

Subsequently, defendants broadened the scope of the litigation by filing a counterclaim in which they charged that the truckers had themselves violated §§ 1 and 2 of the Sherman Act by conspiring to destroy the railroads' competition in the long-distance freight business and to monopolize that business for heavy trucks. * * *

In this posture, the case went to trial. After hearings, the trial court entered a judgment, based upon extensive findings of fact and conclusions of law, that the railroads' publicity campaign had violated the Sherman Act while that of the truckers had not. In reaching this conclusion, the trial court expressly disclaimed any purpose to condemn as illegal mere efforts on the part of the railroads to influence the passage of new legislation or the enforcement of existing law. Instead, it rested its judgment upon findings, first, that the railroads' publicity campaign * * * was malicious and fraudulent—malicious in that its only purpose was to destroy the truckers as competitors, and fraudulent in that it was predicated upon the deceiving of those authorities through the use of the third-party technique; and, secondly, that the railroads' campaign also had as an important, if not overriding, purpose the destruction of the truckers' goodwill, among both the general public and the truckers' existing customers, and thus injured the truckers in ways unrelated to the passage or enforcement of law. * * *

　　　* * *

* * * Because the case presents a new and unusual application of the Sherman Act and involves severe restrictions upon the rights of these railroads and others to seek the passage or defeat of legislation when deemed desirable, we granted * * * [the petition for certiorari].

We accept, as the starting point for our consideration of the case, the same basic construction of the Sherman Act adopted by the courts below—that no violation of the Act can be predicated upon mere attempts to influence the passage or enforcement of laws. It has been recognized * * * that the Sherman Act forbids only those trade restraints and monopolizations that are created, or attempted, by the acts of "individuals or combinations of individuals or corporations." Accordingly, it has been held that where a restraint upon trade or monopolization is the result of valid governmental action, as opposed to private action, no violation of the Act can be made out. * * *

We think it equally clear that the Sherman Act does not prohibit two or more persons from associating together in an attempt to persuade the legislature or the executive to take particular action with respect to a law that would produce a restraint or a monopoly. Although such associations could perhaps, through a process of expansive construction, be brought within the general proscription of "combination[s] ... in restraint of trade," they bear very little if any resemblance to the combinations normally held violative of the Sherman Act, combinations ordinarily characterized by an express or implied agreement or understanding that the participants will jointly give up their trade freedom, or help one another to take away the trade freedom of others through the use of such devices as price-fixing agreements, boycotts, market-division agreements, and other similar arrangements. * * * [We] think that the question is conclusively settled, against the application of the Act, when this factor of essential dissimilarity is considered along with the other difficulties that would be presented by a holding that the Sherman Act forbids associations for the purpose of influencing the passage or enforcement of laws.

In the first place, such a holding would substantially impair the power of government to take actions through its legislature and executive that operate to restrain trade. In a representative democracy such as this, these branches of government act on behalf of the people and, to a very large extent, the whole concept of representation depends upon the ability of the people to make their wishes known to their representatives. To hold that the government retains the power to act in this representative capacity and yet hold, at the same time, that the people cannot freely inform the government of their wishes would impute to the Sherman Act a purpose to regulate, not business activity, but political activity, a purpose which would have no basis whatever in the legislative history of that Act. Secondly, and of at least equal significance, such a construction of the Sherman Act would raise important constitutional questions. The right of petition is one of the freedoms protected by the Bill of Rights, and we cannot, of course, lightly impute to Congress an intent to invade these freedoms. Indeed, such an imputation would be particularly unjustified in this case in view of all the countervailing considerations enumerated above. For these reasons, we think it clear that the Sherman Act does not apply to the activities of the railroads at least insofar as those activities comprised mere solicitation of governmental action with respect to the passage and enforcement of laws. We are thus called upon to consider whether the courts below were correct in holding that, notwithstanding this principle, the Act was violated here because of the presence in the railroads' publicity campaign of additional factors sufficient to take the case out of the area in which the principle is controlling.

The first such factor relied upon was the fact, established by the finding of the District Court, that the railroads' sole purpose in seeking to influence the passage and enforcement of laws was to destroy the truckers as competitors for the long-distance freight business. But we do not see how this fact, even if adequately supported in the record, could transform conduct otherwise lawful into a violation of the Sherman Act. All of the considerations that have led us to the conclusion that the Act does not apply to mere group solicitation of governmental action are equally applicable in spite of the addition of this factor. The right of the people to inform their representatives in government of their desires with respect to the passage or enforcement of laws cannot properly be made to depend upon their intent in doing so. It is neither unusual nor illegal for people to seek action on laws in the hope that they may bring about an advantage to themselves and a disadvantage to their competitors. * * * Indeed, it is quite probably people with just such a hope of personal advantage who provide much of the information upon which governments must act. * * * We reject such a construction of the Act and hold that, at least insofar as the railroads' campaign was directed toward obtaining governmental action, its legality was not at all affected by any anticompetitive purpose it may have had.

The second factor relied upon by the courts below to justify the application of the Sherman Act to the railroads' publicity campaign was the use in the campaign of the so-called third-party technique. The theory under which this factor was related to the proscriptions of the Sherman Act, though not entirely clear from any of the opinions below, was apparently that it involved unethical business conduct on the part of the railroads. * * * We can certainly agree with the courts below that this technique, though in widespread use among practitioners of the art of public relations, is one which falls far short of the ethical standards generally approved in this country. It does not follow, however, that the use of the technique in a publicity campaign designed to influence governmental action constitutes a violation of the Sherman Act. Insofar as that Act sets up a code of ethics at all, it is a code that condemns trade restraints, not political activity, and, as we have already pointed out, a publicity campaign to influence governmental action falls clearly into the category of political activity. The proscriptions of the Act, tailored as they are for the business world, are not at all appropriate for application in the political arena. Congress has traditionally exercised extreme caution in legislating with respect to problems relating to the conduct of political activities, a caution which has been reflected in the decisions of this Court interpreting such legislation. All of this caution would go for naught if we permitted an extension of the Sherman Act to regulate activities of that nature simply because those activities have a commercial impact and involve conduct that can be termed unethical.

* * *

In addition to the foregoing factors * * * the courts below rested their holding that the Sherman Act had been violated upon a finding that the purpose of the railroads was "more than merely an attempt to obtain legislation. It was the purpose and intent . . . to hurt the truckers in every way possible even though they secured no legislation." Specifically, the District Court found that the purpose of the railroads was to destroy the goodwill of the truckers among the public generally and among the truckers' customers particularly, in the hope that by doing so the over-all competitive position of the truckers would be weakened, and that the railroads were successful in these efforts to the extent that such injury was actually inflicted. * * * It is inevitable, whenever an attempt is made to influence legislation by a campaign of publicity, that an incidental effect of that campaign may be the infliction of some direct injury upon the interests of the party against whom the campaign is directed. And it seems equally inevitable that those conducting the campaign would be aware of, and possibly even pleased by, the prospect of such injury. To hold that the knowing infliction of such injury renders the campaign itself illegal would thus be tantamount to outlawing all such campaigns. We have already discussed the reasons which have led us to the conclusion that this has not been done by anything in the Sherman Act.

There may be situations in which a publicity campaign, ostensibly directed toward influencing governmental action, is a mere sham to cover what is actually nothing more than an attempt to interfere directly with the business relationships of a competitor and the application of the Sherman Act would be justified. But this certainly is not the case here. No one denies that the railroads were making a genuine effort to influence legislation and law enforcement practices. Indeed, * * * that effort was not only genuine but also highly successful. Under these circumstances, we conclude that no attempt to interfere with business relationships in a manner proscribed by the Sherman Act is involved in this case.

In rejecting each of the grounds relied upon by the courts below to justify application of the Sherman Act to the campaign of the railroads, * * * we have restored what appears to be the true nature of the case—a "no-holds-barred fight" between two industries both of which are seeking control of a profitable source of income. Inherent in such fights, which are commonplace in the halls of legislative bodies, is the possibility, and in many instances even the probability, that one group or the other will get hurt by the arguments that are made. In this particular instance, each group appears to have utilized all the political powers it could muster in an attempt to bring about the passage of laws that would help it or injure the other. But the contest itself appears to have been conducted along lines normally accepted in our political system, except to the extent that each group has deliberately deceived the public and public officials. And that deception, reprehensible as it is, can be of no consequence so far as the Sherman Act is concerned. * * *

Reversed.

Notes and Questions

1. *Noerr* was followed four years later by United Mine Workers v. Pennington, 381 U.S. 657, 85 S.Ct. 1585, 14 L.Ed.2d 626 (1965). The mine workers union and leading coal companies had gotten together (1) to lobby the Secretary of Labor to establish minimum wages for coal miners, and (2) to lobby the TVA not to make spot purchases of coal that weren't subject to Walsh–Healy prevailing wage requirements. The Supreme Court held: "Joint efforts to influence public officials do not violate the antitrust laws even though intended to eliminate competition. Such conduct is not illegal, either standing alone or as part of a broader scheme itself violative of the Sherman Act." You will see references to the results in these two cases cited as the *"Noerr–Pennington"* doctrine.

2. If regulatory protection itself does not violate the antitrust laws, does it inevitably follow that seeking such regulation must also be protected activity?

a. Will such a conclusion stimulate the production of regulation? The antitrust laws make it very costly to engage in collective private conduct tending to reduce industry output or raise price. Get a state to "require" the firms to do the same thing, however, and there is no such liability.

b. Was the real problem in *Noerr* that the Court could not fashion an appropriate remedy for the activity? Was there any doubt that a broad injunction against seeking legislation could not survive constitutional scrutiny?[30]

3. Remember that at the end of *Noerr,* the Court added a caveat: "There may be situations in which a publicity campaign, ostensibly directed toward influencing governmental action, is a mere sham to cover what is actually nothing more than an attempt to interfere directly with the business relationships of a competitor and the application of the Sherman Act would be justified."

a. Do you agree that such a situation, if documented, *should* justify antitrust liability? Would there be any First Amendment reason not to permit a tort action for "intentional interference with contractual relations"?

b. Is the argument against antitrust liability any stronger? Remember that *Parker* and *Noerr* were both at least partly based on a statutory argument limiting the reach of the Sherman Act. Should any such limit be found here?

4. The "mere sham" exception in *Noerr* was largely undefined until the Court's decision in California Motor Transport v. Trucking Unlimited,

---

30. For a brief time, the Court seemed to say that firms may seek any regulation they wish but a regulation sought by the industry itself would not protect firms against antitrust liability. Cantor v. Detroit Edison Co., 428 U.S. 579, 96 S.Ct. 3110, 49 L.Ed.2d 1141 (1976) (electric utility found to "monopolize" distribution of light bulbs as a result of provision in its tariff that public utility commission had "required" the utility to adopt at the utility's request). However, the Court wisely backed away from this approach the next term, in Bates v. State Bar of Arizona, 433 U.S. 350, 97 S.Ct. 2691, 53 L.Ed.2d 810 (1977).

404 U.S. 508, 92 S.Ct. 609, 30 L.Ed.2d 642 (1972). Defendants were national truckers who operated in California. They were sued by truckers who operated *only* in California. Defendants allegedly intervened in administrative proceedings trying to keep plaintiffs from getting new operating rights. If they lost the first time, they would seek rehearing, appeal, and otherwise make life hard for the intrastate truckers.

The defendants said their conduct was clearly protected under *Noerr–Pennington*, but the Court answered that there was a difference between acts done in seeking legislation and unethical conduct in an adjudicative proceeding. There have long been rules against abuse of civil process and courts have long sanctioned misbehavior before them, Justice Douglas wrote. Any carrier may petition a court or agency, using proper procedures, to defeat a route application. Intent is irrelevant to that right, i.e., the purpose may be to improve one's own wealth or even to create a monopoly. But a combination to harass competitors and deny them "free and unlimited access" to agencies and courts can be prohibited consistent with the First Amendment and was held prohibited by the Sherman Act.

a.   Does this distinction make sense to you? Is the line real? Even in adjudication, are general industry policies often tested and evaluated in individual adjudicated cases?

b.   Is "denial of access" to the process a test that one is likely ever to be able to apply literally? What short of "denial" should be actionable?[31] How about the conduct in our next case?

COLUMBIA v. OMNI OUTDOOR ADVERTISING, INC.

Supreme Court of the United States, 1991.
499 U.S. 365, 111 S.Ct. 1344, 113 L.Ed.2d 382.

SCALIA, J., delivered the opinion of the Court.

This case requires us to clarify the application of the Sherman Act to municipal governments and to the citizens who seek action from them.

I

Petitioner Columbia Outdoor Advertising, Inc. (COA), a South Carolina corporation, entered the billboard business in the city of Columbia, South Carolina (also a petitioner here), in the 1940's. By 1981 it controlled more than 95% of what has been conceded to be the relevant market. COA was a local business owned by a family with deep roots in the community, and enjoyed close relations with the city's political leaders. The mayor and other members of the city council were personal friends of COA's majority owner, and the company and its officers occasionally contributed funds and free billboard space to their cam-

---

31. An interesting set of cases address when economic boycotts will be seen as lobbying or even constitutionally protected protest activity and when they will be seen as per se illegal antitrust violations. Compare, e.g., State of Missouri v. National Organization for Women, 620 F.2d 1301 (8th Cir.1980), cert. denied, 449 U.S. 842, 101 S.Ct. 122, 66 L.Ed.2d 49 (1980), with FTC v. Superior Court Trial Lawyers Assn., 493 U.S. 411, 110 S.Ct. 768, 107 L.Ed.2d 851 (1990). See also, Thomas D. Morgan, Modern Antitrust Law and Its Origins 587–90 (2nd ed. 2001).

paigns. According to respondent Omni Outdoor Advertising, Inc., these beneficences were part of a "longstanding" "secret anticompetitive agreement" whereby "the City and COA would each use their [sic] respective power and resources to protect . . . COA's monopoly position," in return for which "City Council members received advantages made possible by COA's monopoly."

In 1981, Omni, a Georgia corporation, began erecting billboards in and around the city. COA responded to this competition in several ways. First, it redoubled its own billboard construction efforts and modernized its existing stock. Second—according to Omni—it took a number of anticompetitive private actions, such as offering artificially low rates, spreading untrue and malicious rumors about Omni, and attempting to induce Omni's customers to break their contracts. Finally (and this is what gives rise to the issue we address today), COA executives met with city officials to seek the enactment of zoning ordinances that would restrict billboard construction. COA was not alone in urging this course; concerned about the city's recent explosion of billboards, a number of citizens, including writers of articles and editorials in local newspapers, advocated restrictions.

* * * In September 1982, after a series of public hearings and numerous meetings involving city officials, Omni, and COA (in all of which, according to Omni, positions contrary to COA's were not genuinely considered), the city council passed a new ordinance restricting the size, location, and spacing of billboards. These restrictions, particularly those on spacing, obviously benefitted COA, which already had its billboards in place; they severely hindered Omni's ability to compete.

In November 1982, Omni filed suit against COA and the city in Federal District Court, charging that they had violated §§ 1 and 2 of the Sherman Act, as well as South Carolina's Unfair Trade Practices Act. Omni contended, in particular, that the city's billboard ordinances were the result of an anticompetitive conspiracy between city officials and COA that stripped both parties of any immunity they might otherwise enjoy from the federal antitrust laws. In January 1986, after more than two weeks of trial, a jury returned general verdicts against the city and COA on both the federal and state claims. It awarded damages, before trebling, of $600,000 on the § 1 Sherman Act claim, and $400,000 on the § 2 claim. * * * Petitioners moved for judgment notwithstanding the verdict, contending among other things that their activities were outside the scope of the federal antitrust laws. In November 1988, the District Court granted the motion.

A divided panel of the United States Court of Appeals for the Fourth Circuit reversed the judgment of the District Court and reinstated the jury verdict on all counts. We granted certiorari.

II

In the landmark case of Parker v. Brown, we rejected the contention that a program restricting the marketing of privately produced raisins, adopted pursuant to California's Agricultural Prorate Act, violated the Sherman Act. Relying on principles of federalism and state sovereignty, we held that the Sherman Act did not apply to anticompetitive restraints imposed by the States "as an act of government."

Since *Parker* emphasized the role of sovereign States in a federal system, it was initially unclear whether the governmental actions of political subdivisions enjoyed similar protection. In recent years, we have held that *Parker* immunity does not apply directly to local governments. We have recognized, however, that a municipality's restriction of competition may sometimes be an authorized implementation of state policy, and have accorded *Parker* immunity where that is the case.

The South Carolina statutes under which the city acted in the present case authorize municipalities to regulate the use of land and the construction of buildings and other structures within their boundaries. It is undisputed that, as a matter of state law, these statutes authorize the city to regulate the size, location, and spacing of billboards. It could be argued, however, that a municipality acts beyond its delegated authority, for *Parker* purposes, whenever the nature of its regulation is substantively or even procedurally defective. On such an analysis it could be contended, for example, that the city's regulation in the present case was not "authorized" by S.C. Code Ann. § 5–23–10 (1976), if it was not, as that statute requires, adopted "for the purpose of promoting health, safety, morals or the general welfare of the community." * * *

We * * * believe that in order to prevent *Parker* from undermining the very interests of federalism it is designed to protect, it is necessary to adopt a concept of authority broader than what is applied to determine the legality of the municipality's action under state law. * * * It suffices for the present to conclude that here no more is needed to establish, for *Parker* purposes, the city's authority to regulate than its unquestioned zoning power over the size, location, and spacing of billboards.

Besides authority to regulate, however, the *Parker* defense also requires authority to suppress competition—more specifically, "clear articulation of a state policy to authorize anticompetitive conduct" by the municipality in connection with its regulation. We have rejected the contention that this requirement can be met only if the delegating statute explicitly permits the displacement of competition. It is enough, we have held, if suppression of competition is the "foreseeable result" of what the statute authorizes. That condition is amply met here. The very purpose of zoning regulation is to displace unfettered business freedom in a manner that regularly has the effect of preventing normal acts of competition, particularly on the part of new entrants. A municipal ordinance restricting the size, location, and spacing of billboards (surely a common form of zoning) necessarily protects existing billboards against some competition from newcomers.[32]

32. The dissent contends that, in order successfully to delegate its *Parker* immunity to a municipality, a State must expressly authorize the municipality to engage (1) in specifically "economic regulation," (2) of a specific industry. These dual specificities

The Court of Appeals was therefore correct in its conclusion that the city's restriction of billboard construction was prima facie entitled to *Parker* immunity. The Court of Appeals upheld the jury verdict, however, by invoking a "conspiracy" exception to Parker that has been recognized by several Courts of Appeals. That exception is thought to be supported by two of our statements in *Parker*: "We have no question of the state or its municipality becoming a participant in a private agreement or combination by others for restraint of trade." "The state in adopting and enforcing the prorate program made no contract or agreement and entered into no conspiracy in restraint of trade or to establish monopoly but, as sovereign, imposed the restraint as an act of government which the Sherman Act did not undertake to prohibit." *Parker* does not apply, according to the Fourth Circuit, "where politicians or political entities are involved as conspirators" with private actors in the restraint of trade.

There is no such conspiracy exception. The rationale of *Parker* was that, in light of our national commitment to federalism, the general language of the Sherman Act should not be interpreted to prohibit anticompetitive actions by the States in their governmental capacities as sovereign regulators. The sentences from the opinion quoted above simply clarify that this immunity does not necessarily obtain where the State acts not in a regulatory capacity but as a commercial participant in a given market. * * * Since it is both inevitable and desirable that public officials often agree to do what one or another group of private citizens urges upon them, such an exception would virtually swallow up the *Parker* rule: All anticompetitive regulation would be vulnerable to a "conspiracy" charge.[33]

are without support in our precedents, for the good reason that they defy rational implementation.

If, by authority to engage in specifically "economic" regulation, the dissent means authority specifically to regulate competition, we squarely rejected that in Hallie v. Eau Claire, 471 U.S. 34 (1985). * * * Seemingly, however, the dissent means only that the State authorization must specify that sort of regulation whereunder "decisions about prices and output are made not by individual firms, but rather by a public body." But why is not the restriction of billboards in a city a restriction on the "output" of the local billboard industry? It assuredly is—and that is indeed the very gravamen of Omni's complaint. It seems to us that the dissent's concession that "it is often difficult to differentiate economic regulation from municipal regulation of health, safety, and welfare," is a gross understatement. Loose talk about a "regulated industry" may suffice for what the dissent calls "antitrust parlance," but it is not a definition upon which the criminal liability of public officials ought to depend.

Under the dissent's second requirement for a valid delegation of *Parker* immunity—that the authorization to regulate pertain to a specific industry—the problem with the South Carolina statute is that it used the generic term "structures," instead of conferring its regulatory authority industry-by-industry (presumably "billboards," "movie houses," "mobile homes," "TV antennas," and every other conceivable object of zoning regulation that can be the subject of a relevant "market" for purposes of antitrust analysis). To describe this is to refute it. Our precedents not only fail to suggest, but positively reject, such an approach. "The municipality need not 'be able to point to a specific, detailed legislative authorization' in order to assert a successful Parker defense to an antitrust suit." *Hallie* (quoting Lafayette v. Louisiana Power & Light Co., 435 U.S. 389 (1978)). [Court's fn. 4]

33. The dissent is confident that a jury composed of citizens of the vicinage will be able to tell the difference between "independent municipal action and action taken for the sole purpose of carrying out an

Omni suggests, however, that "conspiracy" might be limited to instances of governmental "corruption," defined variously as "abandonment of public responsibilities to private interests," "corrupt or bad faith decisions," and "selfish or corrupt motives." * * *

A conspiracy exception narrowed along such vague lines is similarly impractical. Few governmental actions are immune from the charge that they are "not in the public interest" or in some sense "corrupt." The California marketing scheme at issue in *Parker* itself, for example, can readily be viewed as the result of a "conspiracy" to put the "private" interest of the State's raisin growers above the "public" interest of the State's consumers. The fact is that virtually all regulation benefits some segments of the society and harms others; and that it is not universally considered contrary to the public good if the net economic loss to the losers exceeds the net economic gain to the winners. *Parker* was not written in ignorance of the reality that determination of "the public interest" in the manifold areas of government regulation entails not merely economic and mathematical analysis but value judgment, and it was not meant to shift that judgment from elected officials to judges and juries. If the city of Columbia's decision to regulate what one local newspaper called "billboard jungles" is made subject to ex post facto judicial assessment of "the public interest," with personal liability of city officials a possible consequence, we will have gone far to "compromise the States' ability to regulate their domestic commerce," Southern Motor Carriers Rate Conference, Inc. v. United States [471 U.S. 48 (1985)]. The situation would not be better, but arguably even worse, if the courts were to apply a subjective test: not whether the action was in the public interest, but whether the officials involved thought it to be so. This would require the sort of deconstruction of the governmental process and probing of the official "intent" that we have consistently sought to avoid. * * *

The foregoing approach to establishing a "conspiracy" exception at least seeks (however impractically) to draw the line of impermissible action in a manner relevant to the purposes of the Sherman Act and of *Parker*: prohibiting the restriction of competition for private gain but permitting the restriction of competition in the public interest. Another approach is possible, which has the virtue of practicality but the vice of being unrelated to those purposes. That is the approach which would

anticompetitive agreement for the private party." No doubt. But those are merely the polar extremes, which like the geographic poles will rarely be seen by jurors of the vicinage. Ordinarily the allegation will merely be (and the dissent says this is enough) that the municipal action was not prompted "exclusively by a concern for the general public interest," (emphasis added). Thus, the real question is whether a jury can tell the difference—whether Solomon can tell the difference—between municipal-action-not-entirely-independent-because-based-partly-on-agreement-with-private-parties that is lawful and municipal-action-not-entirely-independent-because-based-partly-on-agreement-with-private-parties that is unlawful. The dissent does not tell us how to put this question coherently, much less how to answer it intelligently. "Independent municipal action" is unobjectionable, "action taken for the sole purpose of carrying out an anticompetitive agreement for the private party" is unlawful, and everything else (that is, the known world between the two poles) is un-addressed. * * * [Court's fn. 5]

consider *Parker* inapplicable only if, in connection with the governmental action in question, bribery or some other violation of state or federal law has been established. Such unlawful activity has no necessary relationship to whether the governmental action is in the public interest. A mayor is guilty of accepting a bribe even if he would and should have taken, in the public interest, the same action for which the bribe was paid. * * * When, moreover, the regulatory body is not a single individual but a state legislature or city council, there is even less reason to believe that violation of the law (by bribing a minority of the decision-makers) establishes that the regulation has no valid public purpose. Cf. Fletcher v. Peck, 6 Cranch 87, 130 (1810). To use unlawful political influence as the test of legality of state regulation undoubtedly vindicates (in a rather blunt way) principles of good government. But the statute we are construing is not directed to that end. * * *

For these reasons, we reaffirm our rejection of any interpretation of the Sherman Act that would allow plaintiffs to look behind the actions of state sovereigns to base their claims on "perceived conspiracies to restrain trade" * * *.

III

* * * [B]eginning with Eastern Railroad Presidents Conference v. Noerr Motor Freight, Inc. [365 U.S. 127 (1961)], we have developed a corollary to *Parker*: The federal antitrust laws also do not regulate the conduct of private individuals in seeking anticompetitive action from the government. * * *

Noerr recognized, however, what has come to be known as the "sham" exception to its rule * * *. The Court of Appeals concluded that the jury in this case could have found that COA's activities on behalf of the restrictive billboard ordinances fell within this exception. In our view that was error.

The "sham" exception to *Noerr* encompasses situations in which persons use the governmental process—as opposed to the outcome of that process—as an anticompetitive weapon. A classic example is the filing of frivolous objections to the license application of a competitor, with no expectation of achieving denial of the license but simply in order to impose expense and delay. See California Motor Transport Co. v. Trucking Unlimited [404 U.S. 508 (1972)]. A "sham" situation involves a defendant whose activities are "not genuinely aimed at procuring favorable government action" at all, Allied Tube & Conduit Corp. v. Indian Head, Inc., 486 U.S. 492 (1988), not one "who 'genuinely seeks to achieve his governmental result, but does so through improper means.' "

Neither of the Court of Appeals' theories for application of the "sham" exception to the facts of the present case is sound. The court reasoned, first, that the jury could have concluded that COA's interaction with city officials " 'was actually nothing more than an attempt to interfere directly with the business relations [sic] of a competitor.' " This analysis relies upon language from *Noerr*, but ignores the import of the critical word "directly." Although COA indisputably set out to disrupt Omni's business relationships, it sought to do so not through the very process of lobbying, or of causing the city council to consider zoning measures, but rather through the ultimate product of that lobbying and consideration, viz., the zoning ordinances. The Court of Appeals' second theory was that the jury could have found "that COA's purposes were to delay Omni's entry into the market and even to deny it a meaningful access to the appropriate city administrative and legislative fora." But the purpose of delaying a competitor's entry into the market does not render lobbying activity a "sham," unless (as no evidence suggested was true here) the delay is sought to be achieved only by the lobbying process itself, and not by the governmental action that the lobbying seeks. "If *Noerr* teaches anything it is that an intent to restrain trade as a result of the government action sought ... does not foreclose protection." Sullivan, Developments in the *Noerr* Doctrine, 56 Antitrust L. J. 361, 362 (1987). As for "denying ... meaningful access to the appropriate city administrative and legislative fora," that may render the manner of lobbying improper or even unlawful, but does not necessarily render it a "sham." We did hold in *California Motor Transport* that a conspiracy among private parties to monopolize trade by excluding a competitor from participation in the regulatory process did not enjoy *Noerr* protection. But *California Motor Transport* involved a context in which the conspirators' participation in the governmental process was itself claimed to be a "sham," employed as a means of imposing cost and delay. ("It is alleged that petitioners 'instituted the proceedings and actions ... with or without probable cause, and regardless of the merits of the cases.' ") The holding of the case is limited to that situation. To extend it to a context in which the regulatory process is being invoked genuinely, and not in a "sham" fashion, would produce precisely that conversion of antitrust law into regulation of the political process that we have sought to avoid. Any lobbyist or applicant, in addition to getting himself heard, seeks by procedural and other means to get his opponent ignored. Policing the legitimate boundaries of such defensive strategies, when they are conducted in the context of a genuine attempt to influence governmental action, is not the role of the Sherman Act. * * *

Omni urges that if, as we have concluded, the "sham" exception is inapplicable, we should use this case to recognize another exception to *Noerr* immunity—a "conspiracy" exception, which would apply when government officials conspire with a private party to employ government action as a means of stifling competition. We have left open the possibility of such an exception, as have a number of Courts of Appeals. * * *

Giving full consideration to this matter for the first time, we conclude that a "conspiracy" exception to *Noerr* must be rejected. We need not describe our reasons at length, since they are largely the same as those * * * for rejecting a "conspiracy" exception to *Parker*. As we have described, *Parker* and *Noerr* are complementary expressions of the principle that the antitrust laws regulate business, not politics; the former decision protects the States' acts of governing, and the latter the citizens' participation in government. Insofar as the identification of an immunity-destroying "conspiracy" is concerned, *Parker* and *Noerr* generally present two faces of the same coin. The *Noerr*-invalidating conspiracy alleged here is just the *Parker*-invalidating conspiracy viewed from the standpoint of the private-sector participants rather than the governmental participants. * * *

IV

Under *Parker* and *Noerr*, therefore, both the city and COA are entitled to immunity from the federal antitrust laws for their activities relating to enactment of the ordinances. * * *

* * *

* * * The judgment of the Court of Appeals is reversed, and the case is remanded for further proceedings consistent with this opinion.

JUSTICE STEVENS, with whom JUSTICE WHITE and JUSTICE MARSHALL join, dissenting.

* * * History, tradition, and the facts of this case all demonstrate that the Court's attempt to create a "better" and less inclusive Sherman Act is ill advised.

* * *

II

There is a distinction between economic regulation, on the one hand, and regulation designed to protect the public health, safety, and environment. In antitrust parlance a "regulated industry" is one in which decisions about prices and output are made not by individual firms, but rather by a public body or a collective process subject to governmental approval. Economic regulation of the motor carrier and airline industries was imposed by the Federal Government in the 1930's; the "deregulation" of those industries did not eliminate all the other types of regulation that continue to protect our safety and environmental concerns.

The antitrust laws reflect a basic national policy favoring free markets over regulated markets. In essence, the Sherman Act prohibits private unsupervised regulation of the prices and output of goods in the marketplace. That prohibition is inapplicable to specific industries which Congress has exempted from the antitrust laws and subjected to regulatory supervision over price and output decisions. Moreover, the so-called "state-action" exemption from the Sherman Act reflects the Court's understanding that Congress did not intend the statute to pre-empt a State's economic regulation of commerce within its own borders.

* * *

Unlike States, municipalities do not constitute bedrocks within our system of federalism. And also unlike States, municipalities are more apt to promote their narrow parochial interests "without regard to extraterritorial impact and regional efficiency." Lafayette v. Louisiana Power &

Light Co. [435 U.S. 389 (1978)]; see also The Federalist No. 10 (J. Madison) (describing the greater tendency of smaller societies to promote oppressive and narrow interests above the common good). * * *

* * * [T]he mere fact that a municipality acts within its delegated authority is not sufficient to exclude its anticompetitive behavior from the reach of the Sherman Act. "Acceptance of such a proposition—that the general grant of power to enact ordinances necessarily implies state authorization to enact specific anticompetitive ordinances—would wholly eviscerate the concepts of 'clear articulation and affirmative expression' that our precedents require." Community Communications Co. v. Boulder [455 U.S. 40 (1982)].

Accordingly, we have held that the critical decision to substitute economic regulation for competition is one that must be made by the State. That decision must be articulated with sufficient clarity to identify the industry in which the State intends that economic regulation shall replace competition. * * *

III

Today the Court adopts a significant enlargement of the state-action exemption. The South Carolina statutes that confer zoning authority on municipalities in the State do not articulate any state policy to displace competition with economic regulation in any line of commerce or in any specific industry. As the Court notes, the state statutes were expressly adopted to promote the " 'health, safety, morals or the general welfare of the community.' " Like Colorado's grant of "home rule" powers to the city of Boulder, they are simply neutral on the question whether the municipality should displace competition with economic regulation in any industry. * * *

* * *

In this case, the jury found that the city's ordinance—ostensibly one promoting health, safety, and welfare—was in fact enacted pursuant to an agreement between city officials and a private party to restrict competition. In my opinion such a finding necessarily leads to the conclusion that the city's ordinance was fundamentally a form of economic regulation of the billboard market rather than a general welfare regulation having incidental anticompetitive effects. Because I believe our cases have wisely held that the decision to embark upon economic regulation is a nondelegable one that must expressly be made by the State in the context of a specific industry in order to qualify for state-action immunity, I would hold that the city of Columbia's economic regulation of the billboard market pursuant to a general state grant of zoning power is not exempt from antitrust scrutiny.

* * *

The Court's assumption that an agreement between private parties and public officials is an "inevitable" precondition for official action * * * is simply wrong. Indeed, I am persuaded that such agreements are the exception rather than the rule, and that they are, and should be, disfavored. The mere fact that an official body adopts a position that is advocated by a private lobbyist is plainly not sufficient to establish an agreement to do so. Nevertheless, in many circumstances, it would seem reasonable to infer—as the jury did in this case—that the official action is the product of an agreement intended to elevate particular private interests over the general good.

* * *

The difficulty of proving whether an agreement motivated a course of conduct should not in itself intimidate this Court into exempting those illegal agreements that are proved by convincing evidence. Rather, the Court should, if it must, attempt to deal with these problems of proof as it has in the past—through heightened evidentiary standards rather than through judicial expansion of exemptions from the Sherman Act. * * *

Unfortunately, the Court's decision today converts what should be nothing more than an anticompetitive agreement undertaken by a municipality that enjoys no special status in our federalist system into a lawful exercise of public decisionmaking. * * *

IV

* * * Although I agree that the "sham" exception to the *Noerr–Pennington* rule exempting lobbying activities from the antitrust laws does not apply to the private petitioner's conduct in this case for the reasons stated by the Court in Part III of its opinion, I am satisfied that the evidence in the record is sufficient to support the jury's finding that a conspiracy existed between the private party and the municipal officials in this case so as to remove the private petitioner's conduct from the scope of *Noerr–Pennington* antitrust immunity. Accordingly, I would affirm the judgment of the Court of Appeals * * *.

Notes and Questions

1.   Are you persuaded that the Court should have closed the door to suits alleging a conspiracy between a city and its favored corporate citizens?

a.   Was the plaintiff's story implausible here? Does one have to be a cynic to believe that a city council might try to protect a South Carolina business against a sophisticated operation from Atlanta? Is such discrimination beyond the scope of interests furthered by the antitrust laws?

b.   What would be the likely effect of the city council's action on the price of advertising in Columbia? Is that the sort of effect the antitrust laws were designed to help prevent?

2.   Is the real problem here that it would be too easy to allege a conspiracy and thus get a case to the jury?

a.   How do you think juries would react to stories of conspiracies by municipal officials? Would cynicism about government decision makers tend to lead to finding conspiracy behind a great many decisions? Would jurors' liability as taxpayers for paying at least part of some antitrust judgments help overcome such a tendency?

b. Is this a problem of federalism? Is the majority right that decisions of state officials should not be reviewable in the federal courts? Do we adhere to that principle consistently in most other areas of the law?

3. Both the majority and dissenters agreed that lobbying for the billboard limitations did not constitute a "mere sham" within the meaning of *Noerr* and *California Motor Transport*, but the question remained whether litigation designed primarily to put economic pressure on a competitor might constitute such a sham. In Professional Real Estate Investors v. Columbia Pictures, 508 U.S. 49, 113 S.Ct. 1920, 123 L.Ed.2d 611 (1993), the Court made clear that rarely if ever would that be the case. Writing for the Court, Justice Thomas outlined "a two-part definition of 'sham' litigation":

> First, the lawsuit must be objectively baseless in the sense that no reasonable litigant could realistically expect success on the merits. If an objective litigant could conclude that the suit is reasonably calculated to elicit a favorable outcome, the suit is immunized under *Noerr*, and an antitrust claim premised on the sham exception must fail.[34] Only if challenged litigation is objectively meritless may a court examine the litigant's subjective motivation. Under this second part of our definition of sham, the court should focus on whether the baseless lawsuit conceals "an attempt to interfere directly with the business relationships of a competitor," *Noerr*, through the "use [of] the governmental process—as opposed to the outcome of that process—as an anticompetitive weapon," *Omni*.

Further, the Court explained: "This two-tiered process requires the plaintiff to disprove the challenged lawsuit's legal viability before the court will entertain evidence of the suit's economic viability. Of course, even a plaintiff who defeats the defendant's claim to *Noerr* immunity by demonstrating both the objective and the subjective components of a sham must still prove a substantive antitrust violation." * * *

a. Has the Court now cleared up all confusion about the "mere sham" exception to *Noerr*? Can you think of any litigation that is "objectively baseless?" See also Marina Lao, Reforming the *Noerr-Pennington* Antitrust Immunity Doctrine, 55 Rutgers L. Rev. 965, 1022 (2003)(proposing a "fraud" exception, separate from "sham"). Is this consistent with *Prof. Real Estate*?

b. Justices Stevens and O'Connor suggested that the Court was too quick to reject the idea that repetitive litigation with objective basis but no subjective interest in the result could constitute an antitrust violation. Do you agree? Is there a sound policy reason to immunize such conduct from

---

34. A winning lawsuit is by definition a reasonable effort at petitioning for redress and therefore not a sham. On the other hand, when the antitrust defendant has lost the underlying litigation, a court must "resist the understandable temptation to engage in post hoc reasoning by concluding" that an ultimately unsuccessful "action must have been unreasonable or without foundation." Christiansburg Garment Co. v. EEOC, 434 U.S. 412, 98 S.Ct. 694, 54 L.Ed.2d 648 (1978). The court must remember that "even when the law or the facts appear questionable or unfavorable at the outset, a party may have an entirely reasonable ground for bringing suit." [Court's fn. 5]

antitrust scrutiny? Are there enough other remedies, e.g., Federal Rule 11, that we may doubt the conduct would ever be observed?

c. Is the concern instead one of avoiding turning every Rule 11 motion into a potential antitrust claim? In that light, does the decision make sense?

d. Does the rationale of *Professional Real Estate Investors* also apply where the defendant is accused of making misrepresentations to an administrative agency? Over a vigorous dissent, Armstrong Surgical Center, Inc. v. Armstrong County Memorial Hospital, 185 F.3d 154 (3d Cir.1999), cert.denied 530 U.S. 1261, 120 S.Ct. 2716, 147 L.Ed.2d 982 (2000), relying heavily on *Omni Outdoor Advertising*, says that it does.

4. By this point in the course, you have looked at the processes of regulation and deregulation from a variety of perspectives. Was the Court too cynical in *Omni* when it said that regulation always involves persons seeking to benefit themselves at others' expense? Has the Court bought into the Public Choice view of regulation?

Was Justice Scalia instead saying that to the extent Public Interest and Public Administration perspectives prevail, it will have to be through citizen action in the political and administrative process? Seen in that light, is the message of the Court—far from being cynical—a call for the kind of work by informed citizens that characterizes the best in a democracy?

E. FOREIGN REGULATION AND THE ANTITRUST LAWS

Finally, we close by looking at regulation in the international context that has become increasingly important today. How is Sherman Act liability affected by the regulatory scheme, not of a U.S. state, but a State in the European Union or any other national sovereign? Our next case gives the most authoritative current answer.

HARTFORD FIRE INSURANCE CO. v. CALIFORNIA

Supreme Court of the United States, 1993.
509 U.S. 764, 113 S.Ct. 2891, 125 L.Ed.2d 612.

JUSTICE SOUTER * * * delivered the opinion of the Court * * *.

* * * These consolidated cases present questions about the application of [the Sherman] Act to the insurance industry, both here and abroad. The plaintiffs (respondents here) allege that both domestic and foreign defendants (petitioners here) violated the Sherman Act by engaging in various conspiracies to affect the American insurance market. * * * We hold that * * * the principle of international comity does not preclude District Court jurisdiction over the foreign conduct alleged.

I

The two petitions before us stem from consolidated litigation comprising the complaints of 19 States and many private plaintiffs alleging that the defendants, members of the insurance industry, conspired in violation of § 1 of the Sherman Act to restrict the terms of coverage of commercial general liability (CGL) insurance available in the United States. Because the cases come to us on motions to dismiss, we take the allegations of the complaints as true.

A

According to the complaints, the object of the conspiracies was to force certain primary insurers (insurers who sell insurance directly to consumers) to change the terms of their standard CGL insurance policies to conform with the policies the defendant insurers wanted to sell. The defendants wanted four changes.

First, CGL insurance has traditionally been sold in the United States on an "occurrence" basis, through a policy obligating the insurer "to pay or defend claims, whenever made, resulting from an * * * [event] that occurred during the * * * period the policy was in effect." In place of this traditional "occurrence" trigger of coverage, the defendants wanted a "claims-made" trigger, obligating the insurer to pay or defend only those claims made during the policy period. Such a policy has the distinct advantage for the insurer that when the policy period ends without a claim having been made, the insurer can be certain that the policy will not expose it to any further liability. Second, the defendants wanted the "claims-made" policy to have a "retroactive date" provision, which would further restrict coverage to claims based on incidents that occurred after a certain date. Such a provision eliminates the risk that an insurer, by issuing a claims-made policy, would assume liability arising from incidents that occurred before the policy's effective date, but remained undiscovered or caused no immediate harm. Third, CGL insurance has traditionally covered "sudden and accidental" pollution; the defendants wanted to eliminate that coverage. Finally, CGL insurance has traditionally provided that the insurer would bear the legal costs of defending covered claims against the insured without regard to the policy's stated limits of coverage; the defendants wanted legal defense costs to be counted against the stated limits (providing a "legal defense cost cap").

To understand how the defendants are alleged to have pressured the targeted primary insurers to make these changes, one must be aware [that] * * * primary insurers * * * usually purchase insurance to cover a portion of the risk they assume from the consumer. This so-called "reinsurance" may serve at least two purposes, protecting the primary insurer from catastrophic loss, and allowing the primary insurer to sell more insurance than its own financial capacity might otherwise permit. Thus, "the availability of reinsurance affects the ability and willingness of primary insurers to provide insurance to their customers." * * * Many of the defendants here are reinsurers or * * * play some other specialized role in the reinsurance business * * *.

B

The prehistory of events claimed to give rise to liability starts in 1977, when ISO began the process of revising its 1973 CGL form. * * *

* * * [The complaints charge that in] March 1984, primary insurer Hartford persuaded General Reinsurance Corporation (General Re), the largest American reinsurer, to take steps either to procure desired changes in the ISO CGL forms, or "failing that, [to] 'derail' the entire ISO CGL forms program." General Re took up the matter with its trade association, RAA, which created a special committee that met and agreed to "boycott" the 1984 ISO CGL forms unless a retroactive-date provision was added to the claims-made form, and a pollution exclusion and defense cost cap were added to both forms. * * *

The four primary insurer defendants (Hartford, Aetna, CIGNA, and Allstate) also encouraged key actors in the London reinsurance market, an important provider of reinsurance for North American risks, to withhold reinsurance for coverages written on the 1984 ISO CGL forms. As a consequence, many London-based underwriters, syndicates, brokers, and reinsurance companies informed ISO of their intention to withhold reinsurance on the 1984 forms, and at least some of them told ISO that they would withhold reinsurance until ISO incorporated all four desired changes into the ISO CGL forms.

For the first time ever, ISO invited representatives of the domestic and foreign reinsurance markets to speak at an ISO Executive Committee meeting. At that meeting, the reinsurers "presented their agreed upon positions that there would be changes in the CGL forms or no reinsurance." The ISO Executive Committee then voted to include a retroactive-date provision in the claims-made form, and to exclude all pollution coverage from both new forms. (But it neither eliminated the occurrence form, nor added a legal defense cost cap.) * * * After ISO got regulatory approval of the 1986 forms in most States where approval was needed, it eliminated its support services for the 1973 CGL form, thus rendering it impossible for most ISO members to continue to use the form.

The [complaints also] * * * charge a conspiracy among a group of London reinsurers and brokers to coerce primary insurers in the United States to offer CGL coverage only on a claims-made basis. The reinsurers collectively refused to write new reinsurance contracts for, or to renew long-standing contracts with, "primary * * * insurers unless they were prepared to switch from the occurrence to the claims-made form;" they also amended their reinsurance contracts to cover only claims made before a " 'sunset date,' " thus eliminating reinsurance for claims made on occurrence policies after that date.

[Further, the complaints] charge another conspiracy among a somewhat different group of London reinsurers to withhold reinsurance for pollution coverage. * * * In accordance with this agreement, the parties have in fact excluded pollution liability coverage from CGL reinsurance contracts since at least late 1985.

* * *

C

Nineteen States and a number of private plaintiffs filed 36 complaints against the insurers involved in this course of events, charging that the conspiracies described above violated § 1 of the Sherman Act. [T]he defendants moved to dismiss for failure to state a cause of action * * *. The District Court granted the motions to dismiss. It held that the conduct alleged fell within the grant of antitrust immunity contained in § 2(b) of the McCarran–Ferguson Act, because it amounted to "the business of insurance" and was "regulated by State law" within the meaning of that section; none of the conduct, in the District Court's view, amounted to a "boycott" within the meaning of the § 3(b) exception to that grant of immunity. The District Court also dismissed the three claims that named only certain London-based defendants, invoking international comity * * *.

The Court of Appeals reversed. Although it held the conduct involved to be "the business of insurance" within the meaning of § 2(b), it concluded that the defendants could not claim McCarran–Ferguson Act antitrust immunity * * *. * * * [A]s to the three claims brought solely against foreign defendants, the court * * * concluded that the principle of international comity was no bar to exercising Sherman Act jurisdiction.

* * * We now affirm in part, reverse in part, and remand.

II

[All members of the Court agreed that there were sufficient allegations of "boycott" that the McCarran–Ferguson Act did not grant antitrust immunity, although they differed about what conduct the term "boycott" includes.]

* * *

III

Finally, we take up the question * * * whether certain claims against the London reinsurers should have been dismissed as improper applications of the Sherman Act to foreign conduct. * * *

At the outset, we note that the District Court undoubtedly had jurisdiction of these Sherman Act claims, as the London reinsurers apparently concede. * * * Although the proposition was perhaps not always free from doubt, it is well established by now that the Sherman Act applies to foreign conduct that was meant to produce and did in fact produce some substantial effect in the United States. Such is the conduct alleged here: that the London reinsurers engaged in unlawful conspiracies to affect the market for insurance in the United States and that their conduct in fact produced substantial effect.

According to the London reinsurers, the District Court should have declined to exercise such jurisdiction under the principle of international comity. The Court of Appeals agreed * * *. This availed the London reinsurers nothing, however. To be sure, the Court of Appeals believed that "application of [American] antitrust laws to the London reinsurance market 'would lead to significant conflict with English law and policy,'" and that "such a conflict, unless outweighed by other factors, would by itself be reason to decline exercise of jurisdiction." But other factors, in the court's view, including the London reinsurers' express purpose to affect United States commerce and the substantial nature of the effect produced, outweighed the supposed conflict and required the exercise of jurisdiction in this case.

When it enacted the Foreign Trade Antitrust Improvements Act of 1982 (FTAIA), Congress expressed no view on the question whether a court with Sherman Act jurisdiction should ever decline to exercise such jurisdiction on grounds of international comity. We need not decide that question here, however, for even assuming that in a proper case a court may decline to exercise Sherman Act jurisdiction over foreign conduct * * *, international comity would not counsel against exercising jurisdiction in the circumstances alleged here.

The only substantial question in this case is whether "there is in fact a true conflict between domestic and foreign law." The London reinsurers contend that applying the Act to their conduct would conflict significantly with British law, and the British Government, appearing before us as amicus curiae, concurs. They assert that Parliament has established a comprehensive regulatory regime over the London reinsurance market and that the conduct alleged here was perfectly consistent with British law and policy. But this is not to state a conflict. "The fact that conduct is lawful in the state in which it took place will not, of itself, bar application of the United States antitrust laws," even where the foreign state has a strong policy to permit or encourage such conduct. Restatement (Third) Foreign Relations Law § 415, Comment j. No conflict exists, for these purposes, "where a person subject to regulation by two states can comply with the laws of both." Restatement (Third) Foreign Relations Law § 403, Comment e. Since the London reinsurers do not argue that British law requires them to act in some fashion prohibited by the law of the United States, or claim that their compliance with the laws of both countries is otherwise impossible, we see no conflict with British law. We have no need in this case to address other considerations that might inform a decision to refrain from the exercise of jurisdiction on grounds of international comity.

IV

The judgment of the Court of Appeals is affirmed in part and reversed in part, and the case is remanded for further proceedings consistent with this opinion.

Justice Scalia delivered * * * a dissenting opinion * * * in which Justice O'Connor, Justice Kennedy, and Justice Thomas have joined.

* * *

II

The petitioners [who are] * * * British corporations and other British subjects argue that certain of the claims against them constitute an inappropriate extraterritorial application of the Sherman Act. It is important to distinguish two distinct questions raised by this petition: whether the District Court had jurisdiction, and whether the Sherman Act reaches the extraterritorial conduct alleged here. On the first question, I believe that the District Court had subject-matter jurisdiction over the Sherman Act claims against all the defendants (personal jurisdiction is not contested). The respondents asserted nonfrivolous claims under the Sherman Act, and 28 U.S.C. § 1331 vests district courts with subject-matter jurisdiction over cases "arising under" federal statutes. * * * [T]hat is sufficient to establish the District Court's jurisdiction over these claims. * * *

The second question—the extraterritorial reach of the Sherman Act—has nothing to do with the jurisdiction of the courts. It is a question of substantive law turning on whether, in enacting the Sherman Act, Congress asserted regulatory power over the challenged conduct. If a plaintiff fails to prevail on this issue, the court does not dismiss the claim for want of subject-matter jurisdiction—want of power to adjudicate; rather, it decides the claim, ruling on the merits that the plaintiff has failed to state a cause of action under the relevant statute.

There is, however, a type of "jurisdiction" relevant to determining the extraterritorial reach of a statute; it is known as "legislative jurisdiction," Restatement (First) Conflict of Laws § 60 (1934), or "jurisdiction to prescribe," 1 Restatement (Third) of Foreign Relations Law of the United States 235 (1987). This refers to "the authority of a state to make its law applicable to persons or activities," and is quite a separate matter from "jurisdiction to adjudicate." There is no doubt, of course, that Congress possesses legislative jurisdiction over the acts alleged in this complaint: Congress has broad power under Article I, § 8, cl. 3 "to regulate Commerce with foreign Nations," and this Court has repeatedly upheld its power to make laws applicable to persons or activities beyond our territorial boundaries where United States interests are affected. But the question in this case is whether, and to what extent, Congress has exercised that undoubted legislative jurisdiction in enacting the Sherman Act.

Two canons of statutory construction are relevant in this inquiry. The first is the "long-standing principle of American law 'that legislation of Congress, unless a contrary intent appears, is meant to apply only within the territorial jurisdiction of the United States.' " *Aramco.* [EEOC v. Arabian American Oil Co., 499 U.S. 244 (1991).] Applying that canon in *Aramco*, we held that the version of Title VII of the Civil Rights Act of 1964 then in force did not extend outside the territory of the United States even though the statute contained broad provisions extending its prohibitions to, for example, " 'any activity, business, or industry in commerce.' " We held such "boilerplate language" to be an insufficient indication to override the presumption against extraterritoriality. The Sherman Act contains similar "boilerplate language," and if the question were not governed by precedent, it would be worth considering whether that presumption controls the outcome here. We have, however, found the presumption to be overcome with respect to our antitrust laws; it is now well established that the Sherman Act applies extraterritorially. See Matsushita Elec. Industrial Co. v. Zenith Radio Corp. [475 U.S. 574 (1986)].

But if the presumption against extraterritoriality has been overcome or is otherwise inapplicable, a second canon of statutory construction becomes relevant: "An act of congress ought never to be construed to violate the law of nations if any other possible construction remains." Murray v. The Charming Betsy, 2 Cranch 64, 118 (1804) (Marshall, C.J.). This canon is "wholly independent" of the presumption against extraterritoriality. It is relevant to determining the substantive reach of a statute because "the law of nations," or customary international law, includes limitations on a nation's exercise of its jurisdiction to prescribe. Though it clearly has constitutional authority to do so, Congress is generally presumed not to have exceeded those customary international-law limits on jurisdiction to prescribe.

Consistent with that presumption, this and other courts have frequently recognized that, even where the presumption against extraterritoriality does not apply, statutes should not be interpreted to regulate foreign persons or conduct if that regulation would conflict with principles of international law. * * *

* * *

* * * More specifically, the principle was expressed in United States v. Aluminum Co. of America [148 F.2d 416 (2d Cir. 1945)] * * *. In his opinion for the court, Judge Learned Hand cautioned "we are not to read general words, such as those in [the Sherman] Act, without regard to the limitations customarily observed by nations upon the exercise of their powers; limitations which generally correspond to those fixed by the 'Conflict of Laws.' "

More recent lower court precedent has also tempered the extraterritorial application of the Sherman Act with considerations of "international comity." See Timberlane Lumber Co. v. Bank of America, N.T & S.A., 549 F.2d 597 (9th Cir.1976). The "comity" they refer to is not the comity of courts, whereby judges decline to exercise jurisdiction over matters more appropriately adjudged elsewhere, but rather what might be termed "prescriptive comity": the respect sovereign nations afford each other by limiting the reach of their laws. * * *[35]

* * *

35. Some antitrust courts, including the Court of Appeals in the present case, have mistaken the comity at issue for the "comity of courts," which has led them to characterize the question presented as one of "abstention," that is, whether they should "exercise or decline jurisdiction." * * * [T]hat seems to be the error the Court has

Under the Restatement [(Third) of Foreign Relations Law], a nation having some "basis" for jurisdiction to prescribe law should nonetheless refrain from exercising that jurisdiction "with respect to a person or activity having connections with another state when the exercise of such jurisdiction is unreasonable." Restatement (Third) § 403(1). The "reasonableness" inquiry turns on a number of factors including, but not limited to: "the extent to which the activity takes place within the territory [of the regulating state]," § 403(2)(a); "the connections, such as nationality, residence, or economic activity, between the regulating state and the person principally responsible for the activity to be regulated," § 403(2)(b); "the character of the activity to be regulated, the importance of regulation to the regulating state, the extent to which other states regulate such activities, and the degree to which the desirability of such regulation is generally accepted," § 403(2)(c); "the extent to which another state may have an interest in regulating the activity," § 403(2)(g); and "the likelihood of conflict with regulation by another state," § 403(2)(h). Rarely would these factors point more clearly against application of United States law. The activity relevant to the counts at issue here took place primarily in the United Kingdom, and the defendants in these counts are British corporations and British subjects having their principal place of business or residence outside the United States. Great Britain has established a comprehensive regulatory scheme governing the London reinsurance markets, and clearly has a heavy "interest in regulating the activity." Finally, § 2(b) of the McCarran–Ferguson Act allows state regulatory statutes to override the Sherman Act in the insurance field, subject only to the narrow "boycott" exception set forth in § 3(b)—suggesting that "the importance of regulation to the [United States]," is slight. Considering these factors, I think it unimaginable that an assertion of legislative jurisdiction by the United States would be considered reasonable, and therefore it is inappropriate to assume, in the absence of statutory indication to the contrary, that Congress has made such an assertion.

It is evident from what I have said that the Court's comity analysis, which proceeds as though the issue is whether the courts should "decline to exercise * * * jurisdiction," rather than whether the Sherman Act covers this conduct, is simply misdirected. * * * [The Court] concludes that no "true conflict" counseling nonapplication of United States law (or rather, as it thinks, United States judicial jurisdiction) exists unless compliance with United States law would constitute a violation of another country's law. That breathtakingly broad proposition, which contradicts the many cases discussed earlier, will bring the Sherman Act and other laws into sharp and unnecessary conflict with the legitimate interests of other countries—particularly our closest trading partners.

* * *

fallen into today. Because courts are generally reluctant to refuse the exercise of conferred jurisdiction, confusion on this seemingly theoretical point can have the very practical consequence of greatly expanding the extraterritorial reach of the Sherman Act. [Dissent fn. 9]

Literally the only support that the Court adduces for its position is § 403 of the Restatement (Third) of Foreign Relations Law—or more precisely Comment e * * *. The Court has completely misinterpreted this provision. Subsection (3) of § 403 (requiring one State to defer to another in the limited circumstances just described) comes into play only after subsection (1) of § 403 has been complied with—i.e., after it has been determined that the exercise of jurisdiction by both of the two states is not "unreasonable." That prior question is answered by applying the factors (inter alia) set forth in subsection (2) of § 403, that is, precisely the factors that I have discussed in text and that the Court rejects.

I would reverse the judgment of the Court of Appeals on this issue, and remand to the District Court with instructions to dismiss for failure to state a claim on the three counts at issue * * *.

Notes and Questions

1.   Were you convinced by the Court that jurisdiction over the London reinsurers was clear? Should the only question be whether the antitrust laws will require the foreign firms to violate their own law?

a.   Put the matter in a domestic setting. When we ask whether state regulation creates antitrust immunity under Parker v. Brown, do we ask only whether compliance with the Sherman Act would require violation of the state law? Think of *Southern Motor Carriers*; were the trucking firms *required* to act through the rate bureau?

b.   Why have the cases accommodating state and federal regulation developed in this way? Is it because of Constitutional requirements or an express exception written into the antitrust laws? Is it because the courts have been trying to accommodate parallel and often-inconsistent systems of regulation? Does the variety of regulatory systems around the world present a similar set of issues?

2.   Do you agree with Justice Scalia that each case should require a balancing of factors such as those set forth in the Restatement (Third) of Foreign Relations Law?

a.   Might such an approach give too little guidance to business persons trying to know what they may and may not do?

b.   On the other hand, is Justice Scalia right that we are so inextricably involved in the global economy that the majority's analysis is likely to offend foreign governments who regulate through different institutions, e.g., industry groups or professional culture, than those employed by Congress and American states?[36]

c.   In recognition of the complexity of these issues, the Department of Justice and Federal Trade Commission have issued the Enforcement Guidelines for International Operations (1995). Among other provisions, the

---

36. For a highly critical assessment of *Hartford*, for example, see Eleanor M. Fox, National Law, Global Markets, and *Hart-* *ford*: Eyes Wide Shut, 68 Antitrust L.J. 73 (2000).

agencies acknowledge that the *Noerr–Pennington* doctrine permits firms to lobby foreign governments as well as our own. The agencies also promise to exercise discretion not to charge an antitrust violation where such a charge would injure relations between the United States and a foreign government.

3. Issues of American jurisdiction over the conduct of foreign firms continue to expand and be limited.

a. In Empagran S.A. v. F. Hoffman–LaRoche, Ltd., 315 F.3d 338 (D.C.Cir.2003), cert. granted ___ U.S. ___, 124 S.Ct. 966, 157 L.Ed.2d 793 (2003), for example, the D.C. Circuit upheld a claim for treble damages filed under U.S. antitrust law by foreign purchasers of vitamins whose prices had been set by a worldwide cartel. The Supreme Court has agreed to decide whether the Foreign Trade Antitrust Improvements Act, 15 U.S.C.A. § 6a, indeed does make the United States an available forum for suits by foreign plaintiffs against foreign defendants where the plaintiffs' only injury is suffered abroad.

b. The Foreign Sovereign Immunities Act, 28 U.S.C.A. §§ 1602–1611, in turn, limits United States courts' jurisdiction to hear claims filed against foreign governments for regulatory conduct abroad. See, e.g., Corzo v. Banco Central de Reserva del Peru, 243 F.3d 519 (9th Cir.2001) (suit barred seeking compensation from Peruvian monetary authority for commercial losses caused when value of Peruvian currency declined).

4. Such issues, of course, seem to take us far beyond the question whether a regulator should permit construction of the Charles River Bridge with which this book began. But are today's issues fundamentally different from those Massachusetts faced in 1758? Perhaps not. Perhaps you might conclude that questions of when to regulate entry and rates, when to compensate for the impact of regulatory change, and when one or more forms of deregulation can make markets work better are fundamentally relevant across time, jurisdictions and even across many cultures. The questions, in short, remain the same; only the answers keep changing!

*

Index

References are to Pages

603